A MONG THE FLOOD TIDE of emigrants who left the British isles for the 'Southern world' of South Africa, Australia and New Zealand in the later 19th century were many thousands of young men who relied on their muscle and native wit to make a living. Not a few were from criminal backgrounds in the warrens of industrial Britain, or had left after a brush with the law at home. Here Charles van Onselen brilliantly evokes this darker underside of the great emigration, the restless, transient, unsettled lives of young men without homes or attachments, wandering from continent to continent in new and ill-policed societies. Drawing on a mass of archival and other contemporary sources, he traces the ordinary/extraordinary life of Jack McLoughlin, from his family's origins in famine-stricken Donegal, to the industrial slums of Victorian Manchester (and its prisons), and the casual employments and criminal opportunities of gold-rush South Africa and Australia. McLoughlin's criminal career, and its unhappy end, make a gripping story, but in van Onselen's hands they also illuminate the human desperation that accompanied what we sometimes think of as the great age of imperialism. This is a marvellous addition to the social history of empire.

Professor John Darwin, Nuffield College, Oxford University

C HARLES VAN ONSELEN HAS long been acknowledged as among the finest of contemporary social historians. But this book will add to his reputation in a major way. Through the painstaking archival detection that is the hallmark of his work, he has traced the global career of an intriguing late 19th and early 20th century career criminal and murderer. As he leads his reader across the world in pursuit of 'One-armed' Jack, he provides not just a brilliant account of the life and psyche of a tormented individual, but also a deep understanding of the places and institutions that made him. These days many historians promise us 'transnational' history, but few have the ability to pull it off in the way that van Onselen does. This is not just another biography – it is an education in the history of the era in which the world we live in was created.

Professor Jonathan Hyslop, Colgate University and the University of Pretoria

ALSO BY CHARLES VAN ONSELEN

Chibaro: African Mine Labour in Southern Rhodesia 1900-1933,
London 1976

New Babylon, New Nineveh: Studies in the Social and Economic History of the Witwatersrand, 1886–1914,
London and New York 1982, Johannesburg 2001

The Small Matter of a Horse: The Life of 'Nongoloza' Mathebula, 1867–1948,
Johannesburg 1984, Pretoria 2008

The Seed is Mine: The Life of Kas Maine, A South African Sharecropper, 1894–1985,
London, Johannesburg and New York 1996

The Fox and the Flies: The World of Joseph Silver, Racketeer and Psychopath,
London, Johannesburg and New York 2007

Masked Raiders: Irish Banditry in Southern Africa, 1880–1899,
Cape Town 2010

Showdown at the Red Lion

The Life and Times of
Jack McLoughlin

1859–1910

❦

Charles van Onselen

Jonathan Ball Publishers
Johannesburg & Cape Town

Originally published in South Africa in 2015 by
JONATHAN BALL PUBLISHERS
A division of Media24 Limited
PO Box 33977
Jeppestown
2043

ISBN 978-1-86842-622-5
EBOOK ISBN 978-1-86842-623-2

Twitter: www.twitter.com/JonathanBallPub
Facebook: www.facebook.com/JonathanBallPublishers
Blog: http://jonathanball.bookslive.co.za/
Cover design by Michiel Botha
Design and typesetting by Triple M Design, Johannesburg
Printed and bound by CTP Printers, Cape
Set in 11/15pt Bembo Std

MIX
Paper from
responsible sources
FSC
www.fsc.org   FSC™ C017578

For BK Murray and KSO Beavon
Good Friends and Gifted Teachers

Contents

Spring

୧୫୬

Summer

꧁꧂

Autumn

Winter

ᏣᎨᎦ

List of Maps

Dystopia's Militants

— c 1850–1900 —

I look to death in quest of life;
I seek health in infirmity
And freedom in captivity;
I search for rest in bitter strife
And faithfulness in treachery.
But fortune always was unkind:
I know that it was designed
By adverse fate and heaven's decree
That, since I seek what cannot be,
What can be I shall never find.

CERVANTES

Jack Kerouac, who spent more time on the road than most, savoured the company of all the unusual characters he encountered. But his prefer-ence, like the moon on a cloudless night, was there for all to see. 'The only people for me,' he wrote, 'are the mad ones, the ones who are mad to live, mad to talk, mad to be saved, desirous of everything at the same time, the ones who never yawn or say a commonplace thing, but burn, burn, burn, like fabulous roman candles exploding like spiders across the stars.' Every age throws up its own shower of such meteorites and the depth, nature and trajectory of every manifestation of such 'madness' is of enduring interest to historians. Viewed closely, through the microscope rather than the telescope, the glow of these outliers becomes simultaneously more ordinary and more wondrous still.

This is a study of a man who demanded trust from those given to betrayal. It is the story of an individual who sought satisfaction in tension, and who strived to retain his independence after he lost an arm. It is the tale of a man who glimpsed peace in confinement and flirted with – no, found – death in his search for emotional fulfilment. Born in one of the great cities of his time, he adapted to the countryside everywhere and felt most settled whilst on the move. At first by choice and later by circumstance, he pursued his paradoxical quests across half the world. To many casual observers he may indeed have seemed to be just 'mad'.

Admiring of heroes who lived on the outer margins of society, he found the dispensation he was born into so insufferably ordered and restrictive that he slipped away through Suez in search of adventure in the new worlds of Australia, New Zealand and southern Africa. Determined to avoid the enslavement of industry, urban existence and wage labour, he also turned his back on the larger part of humanity – women. He spent most of his life on the road, on the frontiers of empire, amidst fraternal solidarities where affection, conduct and deeds were expressed through, and governed by, the codes of courage, honour and masculinity he admired.

He was an unusual man or, as used to be said, 'quite a character'. A charismatic figure with a passion for frontier life, he was revered by many in the underworld circles he most often frequented, and feared by colonial authorities intent on developing and stabilising the modern socio-economic order he had rejected and intended subverting. At one time he was sought on two continents and it took the imperial machinery 14 years to track him down and bring him to justice. The authorities considered him responsible for a murder; but he refused to see it as a crime because it flowed from a breach of the code of manly conduct that he expected all men to run their lives by. In truth, the personal and professional reasons for committing the deed that shaped the rest of his eventful life had by then become irrevocably intertwined.

Such unconventional men or women are often dismissed as curiosities, as part of historical freak-shows, and relegated to the margins of mainstream studies. We can do this, but if we do, we do so at our peril. These people are, of course, 'extraordinary', 'special' or 'strange', in the same sense that all human beings are distinctive when they manifest strong or unfamiliar qualities. But our interest in those from the outer margins should lie not only with how they differed from the rest of humanity, but in the many ways in which their rarer attributes were accommodated or rejected in the sub-cultures they occupied as well as the main streams of society. When a 'deviant' fits into a rapidly mutating social setting, such as that found on frontiers, it often tells us as much about the roots that the new settlements have sprung from and the nature of the coming order as it does about the newly arrived stranger. With the passage of time and benefit of hindsight we can see that societies, too, can at various moments be 'mad'.

Indeed, it is precisely because marginal figures are, by definition, 'unusual' that they constitute a litmus test for societal norms. Sometimes their actions tell us more about the direction, nature and pace of change of society than they do about their behaviour. We can, if we insist, see McLoughlin, too, as being 'extraordinary' or 'weird'. But if we focus *only* on his exceptionality and the deeds that came to cost him his life, we will forfeit the fuller understanding that comes from the realisation that there were thousands of other men who, in most respects, were more like him than they were not. If we stand back and view him as a member of an awkward, disgruntled male cohort born in industrial Lancashire between 1850 and 1870 that came to engage the British colonies of the southern hemisphere in distinctive social, economic and political ways, his behaviour becomes easier to understand and significantly less unusual. The microscope is essential, but we abandon the telescope at our peril.

Every generation, only partially free to engage destiny on its own terms, stands between the one that went before it and the one that follows. Each cohort looks back to where it came from, assesses its prospects and considers where it, or its successor, will find itself over time. The answer it arrives at will in part be shaped, if not wholly determined, by the circumstances in which it finds itself. The more dire the present, the greater the propensity to look back on the past with a measure of nostalgia or to seek out new horizons; or both. Life for working men and women in industrial England in the mid-nineteenth century was grim even though, in a few of the great cities, including Manchester, the tide of urban reform was already becoming noticeable. For most of the working-class Irish, however, life in industrial Lancashire was bleak beyond reason.

For many but not all Irish peasants and rural labourers, the short journey into the furnaces of the Industrial Revolution and their emergence as incompletely moulded factory workers was brief and painful. The Great Famine of 1847–52, occasioned by the potato blight, led to a million Irish men and women starving to death. Subsequent attempts to introduce more balanced forms of agricultural production sparked the Land Wars of 1879–82, which saw another million demoralised Irish abandoning the country. With their motherland under British rule and devastated by economic disaster, small-scale Irish farmers and labourers had to endure the trauma of mass emigration to places where they were perceived as foreign and their Catholicism viewed with suspicion. The poorest, who settled on the closest shore, in Lancashire, had to endure the added shocks of industrialisation and urbanisation.[1]

The demands and travails occasioned by structural readjustments on so massive a scale left their mark on many ordinary Irish men and women in generational terms and exacerbated new and existing social pathologies associated with drunkenness, homelessness and unemployment. After the famine, a church-led, guilt-driven 'Devotional Revolution' called on young men to consider chastity and the priesthood as a way of life, and the plea may have resonated with many others for different reasons. But, whatever the causes, many in a generation of badly shaken males – acutely vulnerable in social and economic terms – chose to lead single lives: as late as 1911, over a quarter of all Irish-born men were unmarried, while many others delayed marriage until after the age of thirty.[2]

It was not only the Irish factory workers and small-scale traders who found the increasingly ordered life of the new industrialising society difficult or impossible to adjust to before abandoning Britain and setting out for the frontiers of the southern colonies. McLoughlin had worked briefly as a child labourer in Manchester's notorious cotton mills in the late 1860s,

4

but, amongst his closest Irish friends who followed him out to southern Africa were the sons of a fishmonger, a grain trader, and a pharmacist. As 'JJ', another of his contemporaries, who found himself in prison at Barberton, in the South African Republic, observed in 1891:

> I was, at a suitable age apprenticed to a shoe-maker, but the daily routine
> of my life became after a time so distasteful to me, that I determined to
> emancipate myself from irksome drudgery and to follow a path more in
> accordance with my own foolish inclinations.[3]

There were hundreds of thousands of other men drawn from the same cohort in industrialising society, and many from less ordinary walks of life, who abandoned the northern hemisphere for the southern colonies during the Long Depression that lasted from 1873 into the mid-1890s.

But it was not just hard times, the chafing caused by industrial discipline and serious social dislocation that drove southwards the young men who came of age around 1880. As the beneficiaries of reforms which, by 1870, were nudging their way towards compulsory education, most of the lads in McLoughlin's cohort were fully or partially literate. They not only *heard* what their fathers told them about earlier – possibly better – times, but *read* 'sensational novels' in which heroes were often 'highwaymen, pirates or brigands' who 'openly defied authority' and 'revelled in bloodshed'.[4] In the small Ancoats library, only blocks away from where McLoughlin grew up, GA Sala's *Strange Adventures of Captain Dangerous* and Walter Scott's *Rob Roy* – the Scottish Robin Hood – were among the most frequently borrowed books in the 1860s. 'If a Man's tastes lead him toward the Open, the Bold and the Free,' suggested Captain Dangerous in the 'old-fashioned English' in which he rendered his story, then 'let him ship himself off to a far climate, the hotter the better, where Prizes are rich, and the King's writ in Assault and Battery runneth not...'[5] It was a credo that appealed to many a lad.

In the hotter climates themselves, new myths and legends were later laid down atop older Celtic and English encrustations – tales and truth born directly out of the colonial experience and then transported across the southern colonies. Thus, Jack McKeone, the Krugersdorp bank robber of Irish descent, was deeply influenced by the doings of the quintessential colonial anti-hero, Ned Kelly, whose own favourite novel, *Lorna Doone*, was replete with tales of brigands in south-west England.

The actions of fictional heroes in far-away, imaginary, worlds and the factual basis to cunning forms of Irish resistance to British rule as lived out in their grandfathers' time, fed into the minds of boys mired in industrial slums. They also conflated the past and the present in ways that fantasy permits. Some of the residual influences could be traced in 'scuttling' – a naval term rooted in the era of sail – which, used as a verb, described the violent confrontations between adolescent street gangs in Manchester.[6] But many disillusioned young men needed a larger stage on which to express post-Napoleonic notions of bravery and heroism, and where better to do so than on the distant frontiers of empire? In that respect the cohort of 1850–70 was perhaps uniquely privileged.

Never in the history of the world had there been a better moment in north-western Europe for ordinary people to align their desire to travel with the means to do so at affordable prices. The Age of the Great Migrations in the latter half of the nineteenth century was predicated on the extraordinary advances made in the development and intercontinental spread of the railway networks, steamship passages and telegraphic networks.[7] New economic opportunities and significant mineral discoveries in Australia (gold, 1850s), New Zealand (gold, 1860s) and southern Africa (diamonds, 1860s and gold, 1880s) lured millions of adventurous and entrepreneurial men – and then women and their children – to the new southern colonies.

Australia emerged as a federation in 1901. New Zealand became a dominion in 1907 and a fully empowered self-standing legal entity the following year. In South Africa, where the most deeply rooted section of whites went to war against the empire, union came belatedly, in 1910. But well before Henry Parkes and Alfred Deakin, or John Seddon and Joseph Ward, or Louis Botha, John Merriman and Jan Smuts piloted the constitutional advances that gave rise to modern Australia, New Zealand and South Africa (and helped elevate them to the status of 'imperial statesmen'), the names of Jack Donohue and Ned Kelly, or James McKenzie and Ned Slattery, or

Jack McKeone and Scotty Smith, were on the lips of many ordinary men and women as anti-heroes.

Significantly, many of these early folk heroes were of Irish or Scottish ancestry, elements hostile to the imperial project and opposed to the law-enforcement agencies of colonial states trying to curtail their new freedom and emerging economic opportunities. Britain's first colony – Ireland – provided much of the political yeast that raised the consciousness of settlers in the southern colonies. The measured political incorporation and dominance of certain Celtic ethnic elements in parts of Britain was liable to greater challenge on the remote outer margins of the realm.

Although hardly of legendary outlaw status because he was often more at home in the town than the countryside, 'One-armed Jack' McLoughlin – born Manchester, 1859, died Pretoria, 1910 – slotted firmly into a tradition that had some popular resonance across the colonies. McLoughlin's career fell squarely within the period when frontier societies were giving way to the formation of states – but, unlike Kelly and Slattery or to a lesser extent Smith, his criminal activities were spread over several countries. His career overlapped with the dramatic shrinking of the world that came with the expansion of railway systems (c 1860–80), the improvement of the steamship engine (c 1870–90) and the extension of the international telegraph system (c 1860–90). The emerging states and imperial authorities, aware that the advent of a new global age increased the chances of trans-national crime, responded accordingly. The Fugitive Offenders Act of 1881 made possible the extradition of those wanted to answer criminal charges in the colonies and remained on the statute book right until 1966. It was the chosen instrument for delivering scores of fraudulent insolvents between the southern colonies in the late nineteenth century. As with Jack McLoughlin, however, it was occasionally also employed to deliver men for the administration of justice in cases that could lead to the gallows.

For the poorest Lancastrian-Irishmen, the sons of Manchester, those whose parents were not trying to defy economic gravity as small-scale hawkers, shopkeepers or traders but labouring in the bowels of the factories and warehouses, even the cheapest ways of reaching the promise of the south were beyond reach. For the destitute, those beyond even the cheapest steamship fares, only state-aided passages could enable them to cross the ocean of frustration that separated hope and imagination from the distant realities of promise in the southern colonies. Fortunately, in the shape of the armed services, the empire and the state presided over precisely such schemes for subsidised global travel.[8]

Conquest and limited economic opportunities at home meant that the Irish had been well represented in the British army and navy throughout the Napoleonic and revolutionary wars. In the case of the army, they were disproportionately well represented. In 1831, 42 per cent of all men in the army were Irish, and as late as 1871, one in four were still Irish. For many in the cohort of 1850–70, the army remained not only the primary refuge for many of the unemployed through the latter stages of the Industrial Revolution, but also the transport provider of choice for dreamers in search of opportunity in the colonies.

For those already of an antisocial bent or unambiguously criminal in their intent, the army could be a home from home. As 'JJ' – who, like McLoughlin, had taken the Queen's Shilling and been sent to southern Africa – put it:

> The hard cases in my regiment, finding out by a sort of old established freemasonry that I gave fair promise of being a creditable disciple, took me in hand. In an incredibly short space of time I was acquainted with most of the dodges for circumventing those in authority. I could use my belt as a weapon, offensive or defensive as well as most of my comrades; in short, I considered myself as smart a soldier as ever was court-martialled.[9]

Indeed, in some cases frontier forts and garrison towns inadvertently acted as colleges of banditry, helping to arm, organise and train brigands-in-the-making who on occasion unintentionally helped 'soften up' new territories for subsequent incorporation into the empire. In Kruger's South African Republic, the challenge of McLoughlin and his 'Irish Brigade' to the police and prisons authorities exposed the vulnerability and weakness of the state in ways that encouraged imperial hubris. But even in the colonies criminal activity was never the predominant feature.

Primary and, to a lesser extent, secondary industries in the south saw the development of a new 'imperial working class' characterised not only by cultural and political links between Britain and the individual colonies, but also by a significant degree of inter-colonial movement of labour and trade-union solidarity.[10] Beneath and beyond this more easily identifiable, 'respectable' and urban-based hemisphere-wide working class, however, were hundreds of thousands of casual, less-skilled, itinerant outdoor male labourers with many different callings.

Bagmen, builders, brick-makers, camel-drivers, dam-builders, drovers, farriers, fencers, fruit-pickers, harvesters, loggers, navvies, painters, rabbiters, road workers, shearers, shepherds, stumpers, swagmen, wool-washers and well-sinkers of European descent were to be found in most of the southern colonies throughout the latter part of the nineteenth century. Together with men drawn from scores of other long-lost occupations, they helped build up small rural towns, construct the rail and road networks that linked them, or laboured in the extensive but remote agricultural districts that brought economic life to most places beyond the cities, mines and ports of the colonies. Although they were more likely to be encountered on their regional than on inter-continental travels, the number and velocity of movement of peripatetic labourers, many of whom worked seasonally in teams, could reach surprising proportions.[11]

Drifting in and out among these itinerant workers were tens of thousands of others who constituted the dangerous classes, or *éléments déclassés,* those whom Marx categorised as forming a 'lumpen' or sub-proletariat, made up largely of:

> Vagabonds, discharged soldiers, mountebanks, *lazzaroni,* pickpockets, *literati,* organ-grinders, rag-pickers, knife grinders, tinkers, beggars – in short, the whole indefinite disintegrated mass thrown hither and thither... The scum, offal, refuse of all classes.[12]

And, arguably, beneath even those in the dangerous classes were the pathologically dislocated, those who, from choice or trauma, had taken permanently to mere wandering as a way of life in and of itself; thousands of men of the road – the bums, hoboes, tramps and vagrants.

In the latter half of the nineteenth century the Anglophone world witnessed huge structural dislocations in the industrialising north and an extraordinary exodus of males to the developing colonies in the south. Codes of masculinity and highly physical contact sports were successfully – and lastingly – transplanted into the southern hemisphere not only because they were 'manly', but because they were inserted into frontier, gender-skewed, social settings where family life was less widespread.

After 1850, more than 200 000 migrants left Britain each year and while many were skilled men with wives and children, not all were.[13] Even highly skilled miners such as the Cornish 'hard rock' men often remained long-distance migrants, intent on making the cash savings that would, in time, facilitate a return to their families in Britain. Many itinerant labourers, however, aspired to finding a wife and settling down in the colonies as age inevitably sapped their energies and the ability to chase after the opportunities in far-off, casual, labour markets.

The much-sought-after 'respectable' working men of the age, those who aspired to, and settled into, a conventional family life in communities that formed the backbone of settler societies, had few reservations about the social menace – real or imagined – that most women posed to their behaviour and their life-styles, beyond those routinely recited by younger bachelors. But for those free spirits intent only on following a career in crime along the frontiers of the colonies, those in the dangerous classes given to itinerant life-styles or those down-and-outs whose very existence was tied to ceaseless mobility, women, children, family life, homes and fixed property threatened all that was meaningful.

For such restless souls, already bound by the prevailing Victorian codes of masculinity and given to male bonding that sometimes culminated in homosexual relationships of greater or lesser meaning, women were prone to being fixed in place and, because they were sessile, had either to be avoided completely or limited to providing casual sexual couplings or part-time domestic help. The roots of McLoughlin's great life-crisis lay precisely in those emotional complexities and lures of domesticity that come from the fork in the road confronting most men in their mid-thirties.

As a boy, WH Davies – the 'Super-Tramp' later befriended by George

Bernard Shaw – was warned 'against reposing confidence in the other sex'. Arthur Roskell, who tramped through southern Africa in the late 1870s and early 1880s, was of the opinion that: '... if ever I have been refused a crust of bread or a night's lodgings, it had been directly through the instrumentality of a woman. It seems hard to make this statement but it is only too true.' And, that quintessential Lancastrian, Aloysius Smith, a veritable 'tramp royal' who lost a wife and made his way across several continents, including a lengthy sojourn in southern Africa, cautioned the unwary: 'Aye, women... They surely anchor you to the inferior life.'[14]

These attitudes, prevalent among older wanderers, were frequently found – often in even starker form – among the younger dangerous classes, including bandits, burglars, bushrangers, brigands, coach-robbers and highwaymen. Given to global movement and a peripatetic existence, these men were free from the need to produce passports or other forms of identification, including photographs. As mobile agents of doubtful purpose in an era that lacked meaningful forensic capacity, the state depended on them being identified personally in order to obtain successful prosecutions. Most men in the dangerous classes were at liberty to invent careers and assume new names and nationalities, with or without the use of disguises.[15] McLoughlin himself, despite bearing the mark of Cain in his truncated arm, switched between 'English' and 'Irish' identities. Predictably, such men often put the fear of God into the very citizens they preyed on.

Men without established antecedents – with assumed names, no fixed abode, uncertain occupation, and a propensity towards movement between continents – posed a growing risk to the southern colonies in the latter half of the nineteenth century. Some states, such as New South Wales, had vagrancy laws dating back to the first part of the century, but it is noteworthy how in the southern colonies most of the catch-all vagrancy laws, building on age-old British precedents, were passed after significant mineral discoveries primed immigration and subsequent social dislocation.[16] Robber economies – centred largely on short- to medium-term mineral extraction – are prone to extruding marginal men.

In Australia, the 1835 Vagrancy Act in New South Wales was followed, 'with minor amendments', by those in Queensland (1859), South Australia (1863) and Victoria (1865). In New Zealand, where settled life was largely confined to two islands and transient males seemed to pose a special terror in cities and country towns, the Vagrancy Act (1866) was responsible for almost a third of all prosecutions for petty crime over the two decades that followed. In southern Africa, the discovery of diamonds prompted so much movement by 'undesirable' elements in the neighbouring territory that the Orange Free State passed a Vagrancy Act (1878) a year before the Cape Colony itself (1879). In the South African Republic, where the modest goldfields in the Zoutpansberg prompted Boer agitation to control the flow of itinerants as early as 1875, debate instantly gave way to action in the form of a Vagrancy Act (1881) when gold was discovered in the Barberton district of the De Kaap Valley.

Most newly invented 'vagrants' were netted in the hold-all clauses of acts that were deliberately vague so as to empower the police of emerging states and placate settler opinion in colonies undergoing rapid change. But, that said, the number and the velocity of international movement by dislocated members of the underclasses within the Indian Ocean Basin and all across the southern colonies of settlement after the first mineral discoveries of the 1860s should not be underestimated. When nervous authorities in India amended the Vagrancy Act of 1871 to cope with only modest numbers, in 1874, the changes 'brought Americans, Australians, Continental Europeans and white South Africans under its purview'.[17]

Ordinary citizens, settler-farmers and states alike were clearly alarmed by and reacted to the global movement of members of the dangerous classes in and around the nodes of economic development across the southern hemisphere during the latter part of the nineteenth century. The menace of so many young males of unknown character who prided themselves on their manliness and who moved about town and countryside in significant numbers was evident to many, including those in the underclasses themselves. WH Davies, the self-styled Super-Tramp, noted that among itinerant labourers 'the more timid workmen waited for one another until they were sufficiently strong in number to discharge themselves and travel without fear'. George Bernard Shaw spelt out the hazard even more clearly, suggesting that Davies 'makes it clear that only by being too destitute to be worth robbing and murdering can a tramp insure himself against being robbed and murdered by his comrade of the road'.[18] Uncertainty reinforced the need for mutual trust.

For men engaged in crime in town or countryside, such as Ned Kelly or Jack McLoughlin, the fear of police informers capable of identifying gang members and providing evidence of specific crimes was pervasive. If ordinary citizens in settler societies were alarmed by *outsiders* who appeared as 'folk devils' to them, then those involved in organised crime were fearful of informers who, like witches, came from *within* their ranks.

On colonial frontiers, where trust was at a premium amidst incoming streams of new immigrants and itinerant strangers, it was not only the army, the police or the Catholic Church that called on their officers to take oaths of loyalty. The Friendly Societies, such as the Freemasons, the Oddfellows and True Templars, did so too.[19] Male bonding and oath-taking, a feature of small communities within relatively settled societies in the nineteenth century, took on an added significance on the frontiers of the unknown. All-male associations, including criminal quasi-'families' such as the Mafia, built trust from within largely by excluding exotic elements.

The unwritten codes of manliness – the need to display courage, fairness and fraternal solidarity – were often sealed with oaths of loyalty that formed the underpinnings of many Victorian working-class institutions, including some trade unions. When such codes and oaths extended to criminal organisations they posed a menace to the state only when they transcended their customary apolitical opportunism and threatened to take root as 'social bandits' operating in environments of disillusion on the margins of society.

In southern Africa that sense of menace was palpable between 1886 and 1896. As early as 1887, the same year that Jack McLoughlin and other deserters formed the criminal 'Irish Brigade' that was later to challenge the police and prison services of the Kruger state and then provide a partial template for the Jameson Raid, Arthur H Roskell, alarmed by the number of tramps he saw, wrote, in prophetic terms:

> Were I to credit other people's accounts of the number of men passing
> here and there on foot, the number would reach a fabulous figure. But
> in this I need only assert what I have actually witnessed with my own

eyes, for even then I think it will be quite sufficient to convince the majority of people that, unless some means be provided for suppressing this little 'army of tramps' crime *must* increase to an alarming extent, and the day may not be far distant when the peaceful inhabitants of the [Cape] Colony will awake to find a 'Kelly Gang' in full swing in South Africa.[20]

Only months later Jack McKeone, a man with close links to the Irish Brigade and deeply influenced by tales of Ned Kelly, robbed a bank in Krugersdorp, while his brother and yet another Irishman became highway robbers who crossed the length and breadth of the southern Highveld.[21]

Jack McKeone escaped arrest and justice alike by fleeing to Australia, and his success must have emboldened others, including 'One-Armed Jack' himself when he fled Johannesburg and disappeared onto the Indian Ocean Rim, in 1895. Unlike with Jack McKeone, however, the Kruger government and successive British and Boer administrations in the Transvaal never fully abandoned their interest in pursuing McLoughlin to the empire's furthest southern corners.

'One-Armed Jack' McLoughlin's life was in many respects 'exceptional' and 'unusual'. Few in his cohort travelled as extensively with so few resources or, more pertinently, were sentenced to death for living out their lives by a fading code of manly conduct. But, set within its appropriate, wider, context, in a world where the global was becoming increasingly local and the local increasingly global, it is evident that his life was simultaneously unique and quite ordinary. And, in that, perhaps, lies the real appeal of trying to understand his paradoxical quests.

SPRING

CHAPTER ONE

Deep Code

OLD ERIN
— *c* 1800–1850 —

So listen carefully, and you'll hear a true story that could never,
perhaps, be equalled by any of those fictional ones
that people compose with such care and skill.

CERVANTES

Viewed from the heavens – perhaps from heaven itself – Ireland, already listing at an angle in northern waters, seems barely to cohere. Claws of fire, ice and water, acting when millennia rather than men marked out units of time, left enormous rents in much of its shoreline. In the south, around counties Cork and Kerry, huge fjords slice inland along either side of sandstone mountains. So deep and sharp are these rasps of salt water that, to the casual observer poring over a map, it would seem that all that lies between Killarney and Mizen Head is at risk of breaking off and drifting away across the chilled Atlantic. On the west coast proper, massive elongated indentations filled by deep lakes outline a tell-tale scar running through the counties Galway and Mayo and remind one how a powerful force once attempted to wrench everything between Clare and Kilala from the mainland. But it is in the very far north, north even of the most northern point of what became Northern Ireland – where Donegal turns its back on Derry – that the gods appear to have come closest to achieving their objective.

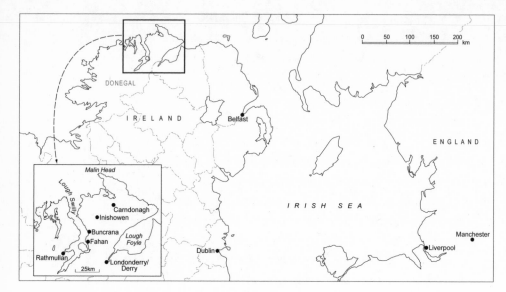

Inishowen Peninsula, Ireland

Malin Head, nearer to Iceland than is Belfast to Berlin, marks the north-ernmost extremity of what, at first glance, seems like an island bracketed by formidable mountains running down its eastern and western shores. Yet, despite the Gaelic prefix, *inis* ('island'), Inishowen is in fact a peninsula, albeit one of unusual upside-down triangular shape with the apex pointing perversely south. Attached to the mainland and nestling wholly within the confines of Donegal, Inishowen, about 25 miles long and broad at its widest point, lies between the two most idyllic inlets in the Atlantic world. But, for all the difference they make, Lough Foyle, which describes the eastern boundary of the peninsula, and Lough Swilly, which marks its western ex-tremity, might as well contain an island. Inishowen was, in many ways, a world apart.

On summer days, beneath clear skies and with mouths agape in the un-familiar heat, the loughs easily take in the sparkling blue and foaming white of the ocean along with huge shoals of fish in search of placid waters in which to feed. But in midwinter, with jaws clenched against driving rain and wind coming in off the open Atlantic, even the sheltered lower reaches of the loughs seem encased in great sheets of impenetrable grey steel. From the heart of the peninsula, short but surprisingly strong rivers tumble down steep mountain-sides and then strike out across small fertile coastal flats until they reach the shores of the nearby loughs. Behind them for many centuries bogs, caves, fountains, glens, lakes, nooks, ravines, springs and valleys lay hidden in forested thickets of beech and oak; indeed most are there still, changed.

Yet, for all that they hold in common, the loughs resent being known only for locking the peninsula into position. In fairness, they do offer much more. Swilly, in particular, known to the ancients as the 'Lake of Shadows', has as many mysteries as it has surprises. About half-way down its course from the ocean, on the eastern shoreline, near Buncrana, where the returning salmon glide into the river to spawn, it throws up what looks like an enormous hill blocking the passage south. But daunting as Inch Island and the surrounds may seem at first glance, they herald the appearance of what is, arguably, Inishowen's loveliest and best-kept secret. Opposite the island, back on the mainland, looms an elongated mountain often shrouded in mist with a dome of black rock that is forever glistening with moisture. On its seaward side, the Scalp overlooks the fertile fields of Lower Fahan ('Fawn' or 'Fahn') and, beyond that, a scimitar-shaped beach of inviting white sand which, when the sun is out, can be seen stretching lazily for many a mile. And beyond all of that, behind the Scalp, hides yet another delight, Upper Fahan, which tumbles down onto the greenest of undulating folds.

It was in these seductive environs, in the sprawling parish of Shandrim of Lower Fahan, on the thinner soils immediately below that scowling fastness of the Scalp, that Jack's father, William McLoughlin, was born into a poor Catholic farming family in early 1823.[1] Like most other venerable families in and around Buncrana, including the once-mighty Dohertys and the Hegertys, the McLoughlin clan (or sept) traced its roots back to the earliest rulers of the peninsula and, with much greater precision, to the times of Patrick himself. Indeed, it was shortly after the fifth-century conversion of Owen ('Eoghan of the O'Neills') by the Saint himself that the 300 square miles of greenery wedged between Foyle and Swilly took on the misleading moniker of Inishowen.

The McLoughlins, like most of the established inhabitants of Inishowen

an offshoot of the founding Owens, formed an important part of the entrenched, intermarried yet frequently warring factions that had competed
ceaselessly for control of the peninsula for hundreds of years.[2] But they, no less
than any other notables, were never fully isolated from distant external influences. Inishowen's strategic location guarding the northernmost approaches
to Ireland ensured frequent collisions with inward-bound foreigners. Some
of the newcomers, like the friendly Scots whose homeland just across the
water was visible from Malin Head on a clear day, were largely welcome.
Others, like the fearsome Viking invaders of the ninth century who swept
into the lochs from afar in their long boats, were not. Both groupings, it is
now claimed, contributed to the genetic makeup of the McLoughlins and,
perhaps, helped shape some of the clan's own, often ferocious, soldier-sailors.
Between the mid-eleventh and thirteenth centuries the McLoughlins were
the undisputed rulers of all that lay between Loughs Foyle and Swilly.[3]

In retrospect, however, Ireland and Inishowen's most formidable tormen-
tors came not from the north or even from the south as did the Normans,
but once again from just across the sea, from the east. From the moment
that Henry VIII broke with Rome and established himself as head of the
newly founded Church of England, in 1534, strained relations between
Catholic Ireland and Protestant England were almost inevitable. The resulting tensions, transmitted into Catholic France and Spain, which had political objectives of their own, fed inter-state conflicts that sometimes played
themselves out on Irish shores.

From the fifth to the seventeenth centuries much of Gaelic power, built
around the O'Connell and O'Neill clans, was concentrated in the north
and west of Ireland. Tyrconnell, to all intents and purposes an independent
medieval state, embraced parts of contemporary Connaught and Ulster and
its capital, *Din na NGall,* was to lend its name to County Donegal. By the
late 1500s, clan chieftains were actively resisting English encroachment and,
by the turn of the century, looking to Catholic allies abroad to assist them
in their struggles. The turning point came in 1601, when a combined Irish-
Spanish force under Rory O'Donnell and Hugh O'Neill was defeated by
the English in the far south of the country at the Battle of Kinsale. After
further, unsuccessful, attempts at resistance the remnants of the indigenous

Gaelic aristocracy decided to go into exile from where new attempts at liberation would be launched. In 1607, the 'Flight of the Earls' saw the O'Donnells and O'Neills and scores of their Gaelic-Ulster allies board a French ship at Rathmullen on the Swilly.[4]

While the rest of Ireland survived Tudor times reasonably well, problems deepened under the Stuarts, who used settler plantations in Ulster to boost the Protestant presence in the province closest to England. But the seeds of truly enduring hatred were scattered more widely after the English civil wars and the execution of Charles I, in 1649. Cromwell's invasion of Ireland and the bloody clockwise coastal sweep of English troops, all the way from Drogheda to Limerick, heralded widespread dispossession of Catholic land-owners and set the stage for full-scale Protestant domination under the Anglican Church of Ireland's sibling, the Church of England. The subjuga-tion of old Gaelic Ireland came to full fruition in 1691, when the forces of Catholic James II of England were defeated by the Protestant Prince William of Orange.[5]

For the next 30 years, and for the better part of a century thereafter, Irish Catholics were subjected to acute economic, political, religious and so-cial discrimination. In practice, severe restrictions on public worship eased after 1720, but Catholics had to wait until 1793 before they could vote and well into the nineteenth century before they were legally entitled to operate schools. Along with all those of other religious persuasions, they were forced to pay tithes to the established but deeply resented Church of Ireland. Those loyal to Pope and Rome rather than King and country also had to forego the opportunity of becoming officers in the army or the navy, or of becoming lawyers. Legalised discrimination of that sort became increasingly difficult to sustain both ideologically and in practice during the latter half of the eighteenth century. The American War of Independence and French Revolution rekindled Irish discontent and, to differing degrees, and in various quarters, fanned the desire for an independent united Ireland. The 1790s saw the formation of the 'United Irishmen' and, with the active help of the French, two failed attempts at rebellion. Britain responded, in 1801, with the hated Act of Union, enforcing a marriage between Ireland and the United Kingdom.

Seen from across the plains of time-past, the vicissitudes of churches, monarchs and states often have limited bearing on the everyday lives or well-being of the faithful, of citizens or subjects. This was perhaps even more true in a place where most of the adults, long deprived of proper education, remained mired in their own myths about fairies, powerful legends, religious mysticism and rank superstition. Ireland, however, was always too close to England and too small in scale for it not to be affected by such changes. For Ulster, Donegal, Inishowen and their inhabitants these developments were proximate and profound in equal measure, and for none more so than Jack's grandparents. Born around the advent of the nineteenth century, at about the time of the binding Act of Union, George and Hester McLoughlin were raised amidst fears of domestic or imported revolution, social trauma occasioned by the Napoleonic Wars and the hand of a state that had dispensed with the need for a velvet glove.

History as well as the hour helped shape Irish men and women for whom the issues of politics and religion were inextricably interwoven into protective veils of confidentiality and silence. Bitter experience gave succour to males who, denied the franchise, legal standing and personal dignity that often underpinned patriarchal domestic regimes elsewhere, actively encouraged visible acts of bravado, a cult of masculinity and the excessive consumption of alcohol in public or private.[6] Dispossessed of what they considered to be their natural birthright and cowed by foreign landlords who enjoyed privileged access to the state and its law-enforcement agencies, vulnerable tenant farmers and agricultural labourers employed quasi-religious oaths to bind themselves into secret societies capable of perpetrating 'agrarian outrages' that could be as cruel as they were cunning.[7] Jack's father, William, filled with tales of old Erin, had not only heard of many such things from *his* father, George, but witnessed a fair number of them for himself whilst still at Lower Fahan.[8]

The McLoughlin family were no strangers to clandestine organised Catholicism. At Upper Fahan, William and his brothers, James and Peter, often played in the ruins of the Abbey of St Mura, which dated back to the sixth century. Their sept had also produced several priests who, like others, had received an excellent education and training in France, Belgium or

Spain. Indeed, one was a noted temperance advocate while another, only 10 miles away, eventually became the Bishop of Derry. But that was later, not many years before the Great Famine of 1845–52.

At the turn of the century, around Shandrim, most still spoke of how at the height of the persecution the faithful would have to sneak off to a sea cave on the Swilly where services were conducted in great secrecy by an O'Hegerty who was betrayed by his brother-in-law and then beheaded by soldiers based at Buncrana.[9] In Inishowen, where youngsters from religious families were still being taught in illegal 'hedge schools' in the early nineteenth century, Catholics were slow to emerge into the full light of public worship.[10] The community at Lower Fahan was formally reorganised in 1817 but it was not until 1833, when William was 10 years old, that a chapel was built that could accommodate them and the believers of Upper Fahan in a parish where those bearing the names McLoughlin, Doherty and Hegerty still easily outnumbered all others.[11]

But the loughs – while offering convenient conduits for travel around the 'island' and easy access to pathways leading to hundreds of places of concealment inland – also helped ensure that the peninsula never became fully captive to the religious-nationalist ideologies of the priests.[12] Most tenant farmers trying to make a living, pay rent and find solutions to everyday problems, had little time for priestly pontification. Others, sensing that the holy fathers were hostile to secret societies and the questionable ways in which those bound to the land supplemented their meagre incomes, kept them at arm's length. Yet others, who noticed that some men of the cloth were not beyond the temptations of alcohol or over-familiarity with the local women, became manifestly anti-clerical.[13] For those in the ranks of the disillusioned or hesitant, there were often alternative sources of inspiration which, although seldom free of religious undertones, came across as more relevant and secular.

In 1796, the exiled founder of the United Irishmen, a young Protestant lawyer and Ulsterman from Belfast, Wolfe Tone, led the first of two attempts at fomenting revolt in Ireland. The first invasion, in the far south, had to be abandoned when a fleet of 40 French ships ran into bad weather. Just two years later, in 1798, and after a rebellion in the south-east of the country had been quashed, Tone launched yet another initiative when he led a second French fleet north, to the mouth of Lough Swilly. But, fore-warned by spies, a far more formidable British force defeated the would-be invaders and Tone, taken prisoner, was bustled ashore at Buncrana. From there he was escorted to the castle at Dublin where he was found guilty of treason and sentenced to death. He chose, however, to slit his throat before he could be executed, thereby providing Ireland with one of the earliest of its secular saints.[14]

Two decades later some of Inishowen's anger was channelled into Daniel O'Connell's countrywide movement for political emancipation, which, when it triumphed in 1829, gave Catholics access to all military ranks and, as importantly, allowed them to serve in the parliament of Westminster. But for the small number of truly militant nationalists on the peninsula, those keen to see the momentum of O'Connell's success taken forward, the next moment of real significance came only after his campaign to have the Act of Union repealed in the early 1840s had already collapsed. Leaders of the newly founded 'Young Ireland', such as Thomas D'Arcy McGee, extended the concept of resistance to embrace violence where necessary, thereby laying the foundations for the ever more radical nationalists who followed. When McGee was forced to flee the country amidst the failed uprising of 1848, he was given refuge in a farmhouse at Culdaff, on the north-east coast of the 'island', before slipping aboard a ship for a noteworthy exile in Canada.[15]

But, as with many others farming around the Scalp, very few of these developments captured the interest of George or Hester McLoughlin and their sons sufficiently strongly for them to register permanently in family lore. Small-scale farmers often had good reason for eschewing conventional politics. At a time when many tenants were expected to turn out and pro-vide a block of votes for landlord-candidates, elections were frequently of limited appeal. Nor was it much of an inducement that those living at Shandrim were forced to pay the tithes that underwrote the living of the Rector of Upper Fahan. The presence of the garrison at nearby Buncrana offered a permanent reminder of an armed British presence, and the small community's proximity to triumphantly Protestant Londonderry, only a cart-ride away, may also have done something to limit the appeal of formal politics. Along with the rest of Inishowen, however, there may have been other reasons – more deep-seated and less visible – for the relative indifference of the inhabitants.

For all its much-vaunted greenery, most of Ireland lacked the fertile soils capable of underwriting commercial agriculture on a large scale. True, there were parts of Donegal – like the grain-rich Laggan to the south, and, to a much lesser extent, small patches in the Rosses in the far west – that could hold their own with the best in the country, but most of the larger landlords, such as the Duke of Abercorn, tended to make up with quantity what they lacked in quality. In the late eighteenth century, however, animal husbandry slowly made way for the potato and more widespread tillage. Comparatively high-yielding and nutritious, potatoes underwrote both a growing number of subsistence farmers and a notable increase in population. In the small but richer coastal strips of Inishowen a good number of tenant farmers, like the McLoughlins, also had easy access to barley, corn and oats and their diets were sometimes supplemented by fresh cod, haddock, mussels and oysters drawn from the loughs.[16]

In addition to that, small farmers in Ulster benefited by custom, if not by law, from 'rights' denied counterparts elsewhere in the country. Thus, while the vast majority of Irish tenant-farmers remained vulnerable to the predations of large landlords when it came to the 'Three Fs' – fair rent, fixity of tenure and freedom to sell an interest in a holding – that the Tenant League campaigned for in mid-century, those of Donegal remained comparatively secure in their tenure. Nevertheless, even in Inishowen these 'rights' remained in the gift of the landlord, and secret associations and agrarian societies such as the Fenians, Ribbonmen and Whiteboys were hardly unknown on the peninsula. Relative prosperity, some of it a by-product of the Industrial Revolution on both sides of the Irish Sea, partly offset the drop in agricultural prices after the Napoleonic Wars even if it failed to eliminate fully the appeal of clandestine politics.[17]

Conditions below the Scalp offered but a variation on these themes. Thin soils meant that, if Shandrim was to support its 2 000 or so inhabitants, it had to be larger than most other viable farming entities. Whereas most 'townlands' (the smaller units of land that had, since medieval times, collectively comprised a parish) averaged about 600 acres, Shandrim spread over some 1 300 acres. At double the average size of most of the adjacent townlands, it formed by far the largest part of Lower Fahan. A little grain and potato production on the lower slopes was supplemented by the sheep that searched out grazing higher up the hillside. 'Mixed farming', even on a modest scale, limited the excessive dependence on potatoes developing elsewhere in Ireland in the early nineteenth century. A more balanced diet may have contributed its share to Inishowen, Lower Fahan and, ultimately, the McLoughlin family's ability to survive the worst of the devastation of the mid-century famine.[18]

Buncrana, rather surprisingly, was Donegal's second largest town even though its inhabitants, too, only numbered about 2 000 before the Great Famine prompted mass emigration, leaving it with little more than 700 souls. Before that the townsfolk, the constabulary, the coastguard and the garrison all helped make it an important outlet for the produce of tenant farmers up and down the Swilly. By the 1840s, however, even Buncrana was benefiting from the rising tide of industrialisation lapping along the shores of northern Ireland; it was becoming more than a mere market town. Attracted by the quality of locally produced flax, the well-off Richardson family of Belfast erected 'extensive mills and factories for spinning of and weaving fine and coarse linens' that employed a 'great number of hands'.[19] William McLoughlin, like the woman from Belfast who was later to become his wife, may have had his first experience of factory work even before he left Lower Fahan.

★   ★   ★

William also knew – it was impossible for any man, young or old, not to know – of another, informal, side to employment in Inishowen, and a largely hidden social life. For all its public prosperity, based seemingly on agriculture, fishing, flax and the like, the presence of the constabulary and

26

garrison at Buncrana spoke of another, illegal and almost totally invisible part of the peninsula's economy that required the enforcement of the law and, when necessary, its backing by a strong military force. It was this 'hidden economy' that not only underwrote the otherwise inexplicable material well-being of many of the inhabitants who lived in the more remote central and northern parts of the peninsula, but also further deepened an already secretive sub-culture born of persecution.

'The distillation of Inishowen whiskey,' Michael Harkin wrote in his historical survey in 1867, 'has been carried on from time immemorial.' No matter what the season, he noted, 'hordes of adventurous chemists are daily engaged in the preparation of this article in their highland huts and mountain caverns.'[20] The illicit production of spirits from grain or potatoes – *poteen* – may indeed have stretched back into the dank mists of Irish time as Harkin suggested, but it seems reasonable to suggest that it may have received a fillip with the arrival of significant numbers of Scots in Ulster, including Donegal, in the seventeenth century.[21]

In those northern parts, spirits were the long-time drink of choice across the class spectrum. The consumption of relatively expensive beer was left largely to workers in the industrialising cities of the east and south, while wine-drinking was confined almost exclusively to the gentry. The production and consumption of whiskey in Ulster increased throughout the eighteenth century as subsistence farming underwrote a rapidly growing population. The state, keen to benefit from growth in the trade during the revenue-sapping revolutionary and Napoleonic Wars, increased the duty on spirits from 10 to 14 pence a gallon in 1775. But revenue commissioners found that poor equipment and unreliable personnel militated against the full collection of dues; in 1779 they embarked on what they thought would be a minor reform and switched their focus to the taxation of registered stills. The consequences were disastrous.[22]

When the new act came into force the following year, it heralded an explosion in the number of illegal stills and opened the floodgates for the production of *poteen* and its consumption in scores of covert *shebeen* houses. At least some of this spirit was of such good quality that it traded not only up and down the loughs and into the very heart of Londonderry, but also back across the Irish Sea into Scotland itself. Most of it, however, was cheaper and manufactured to undercut the legal but far more expensive 'parliament whiskey'. The resulting trade in illicit spirits, strongest in the north and west of the country between 1780 and 1850, was rooted strongly in Donegal, and especially in the most inaccessible parts of Inishowen. At first, excise men were empowered to call upon the military at Buncrana to help track down the peninsula's illicit producers, but after 1832, their efforts were supplanted by the Revenue Police.

A developing hatred of the excise men was compounded when, in those cases where the precise source of *poteen* could not be properly traced, a collective fine was imposed on the entire townland, thereby further impoverishing already hard-pressed tenant farmers. Many distillers responded by posting scouts who employed elaborate alarm systems to forewarn producers of the approach of the revenue commissioners. In 1810, the Inspector-General of Excise for Donegal and Tyrone estimated that there were 700 illicit distilleries in Inishowen, and in 1814, of the 3 500 fines levied for illicit distillation throughout Ireland, some 13 per cent fell to the patch between the loughs.[23]

It was during this period, from 1815 through to the early 1820s, around the time of William McLoughlin's birth, that the battle between the revenue commissioners and many – if not most – of Inishowen's 50 000 inhabitants was at its most pronounced. Given the isolated, clandestine nature of illicit rural distillation, there were few instances of outright violent confrontation between the opposing forces. But, at the height of the struggle excise men engaged in what sometimes took on the appearance of a civil war. Denied full co-operation by landlords and Magistrates locked into complex struggles of their own with resentful tenant farmers, revenue commissioners were forced to resort to the use of informers and spies to gather the intelligence that informed military raids.

The use of secret agents drawn from within the ranks of the community only deepened mistrust and exacerbated the need for closer-knit or kinship-based conspiracies in what was already a divided society. In Ireland, the preparatory work for the more extensive utilisation of informers was undertaken in the heart of the countryside long before it was employed to cope with Fenians and other radical nationalists in the cities. In 1859, Karl Marx, noting the latter development, wrote that: 'At this very moment, John Bull, while giving vent to his virtuous indignation against Bonaparte's spy system at Paris, is himself introducing it at Dublin.'[24] In Inishowen, a special hatred of excise men and the revenue police and their collaborators saw the murder of at least one informer.[25]

Soon after the passing of the act of 1789, and despite their proximity to the garrison at Buncrana, Upper and Lower Fahan were briefly notorious as small-scale centres for the production and consumption of home-distilled whiskey. It was, however, but a brief interlude. The emerging black economy attracted the attention of a particularly powerful enemy in the form of the son of the Protestant Bishop of Derry. Spenser Knox and his ally, Peter Maxwell, spearheaded a drive against illicit distillers that culminated in the wholesale confiscation of livestock when a communal fine could not be paid in cash. This not only dealt a near-fatal blow to the industry in southern Inishowen but also, no doubt, further fuelled anti-clericalism and hatred of the established church amongst distillers.[26]

While the production, distribution and consumption of illicit whiskey dominated subterranean social life in central and north-eastern Inishowen for the better part of half a century, from about 1780 to 1840, it was never the sole component of the black economy. Other illegalities – like poaching salmon, deer or livestock – clearly pre-dated the excise troubles and were but part of the timeless struggle between landlords and tenants everywhere. In similar vein, a little casual rural prostitution, dating back to at least the mid-eighteenth century, could be traced back to more deeply rooted poverty, but would have been boosted by the appearance of shebeens or the licensed liquor outlets to be found around the mills of Buncrana and the shirt factories at Carndonagh.[27]

In general, however, the excise acts – both before and most certainly after 1780 – encouraged inward- and outward-bound smuggling of alcohol in a peninsula blessed with an extensive and ragged coastline. French brandy and good quality wine found ready outlets in the residences of the rural gentry or the homes of those with more regular incomes in places like Londonderry. Illicitly produced 'Inishowen', much-prized by whiskey-loving Scots, was openly traded for barley off the north-east coast of the 'island'.[28] But smugglers, the trade in *poteen*, and the slow spread of the cash economy across Inishowen somehow also managed to draw in small numbers of other anti-social or marginal elements. The supposedly amiable 'Black Thief' – perhaps a 'social bandit' of sorts – was a sufficiently permanent feature for the village of Gaddydaff, 10 miles north of Buncrana, to be named after him. But there were also others operating on the peninsula who were sufficiently menacing for them to be termed 'bandits', 'desperadoes' or 'outlaws'.[29]

Like most of the cohort that came of age just as Inishowen's hidden economy approached its pre-famine peak, William McLoughlin and his siblings were raised in an environment that abounded with real and romanticised tales about the virtues of cunning, manliness and violence. Later in life, in a different setting, he consciously or unconsciously imparted similar values to his male offspring. But while all young men were expected to be able to look after themselves when necessary, not all such aggression could be laid at the door of the ubiquitous *poteen* economy; its roots lay much deeper in Irish society.

As in many rural societies, brute strength, stamina and the ability to wield fists, hands, tools or weapons to good effect were qualities widely admired in the Irish countryside. The celebration or consolation that came with the drinking of 'parliament whiskey' or *poteen* in public houses and shebeens after market day successes or failures often made for bloody brawls and vicious street fights. But while drunken clashes were remarkable for their ferocity and spontaneity, what was more striking still was the propensity of the Irish for large-scale, pre-planned, organised confrontations when questions of courage, honour or pride were at stake. Authorities and participants alike often approved and even encouraged the settling of scores between clans, family members or the inhabitants of neighbouring villages – scores that centred on perceived political, religious or social differences. Ritualised conflict saw massed ranks – not excluding women in supporting roles – engaging in faction- and/or stick-fights that formed a prominent feature of life in a precarious agricultural economy.[30]

As with the secret societies, some of the most dramatic and widespread instances of such collective, organised rural violence took place during periods of marked economic recession in the latter half of the nineteenth century.[31] And, while probably more prominent in the south and west of the country, where they could be seen as distant spasms of rural poverty attributable in part to accelerating industrialisation across the Irish Sea, such occurrences were not entirely unknown in Donegal or the neighbouring counties.[32] Nor, for that matter, was there a dearth of examples of ritualised interpersonal violence in or around Inishowen itself in the late eighteenth and early nineteenth centuries. 'The popular Sir William Richardson of Augher Castle, County Tyrone, devised a system of trial by combat: sturdy disputants who appealed to him in his magisterial capacity were armed with cudgels and dispatched to the back of the backyard of the castle to fight it out.'[33] In similar vein it might be noted that the last formal duel with fatal consequences to be fought in Ireland took place, in 1810, at the old Druminderry Bridge near Buncrana.[34]

★ ★ ★

Uniforms, codes of honour and dangerous intruders were not always the 'island' community's most troubling enemies. Given the number of visible challenges that confronted men and women on the land in Donegal and elsewhere in Ireland by the mid-nineteenth century, it was perhaps ironic that the nemesis of most should – sometimes quite literally – have floated in unseen on summer breezes. Microscopic spores, released upon the wind from the contaminated holds of ships, drifted inland to spread the potato blight, or were unwittingly carried into markets in the form of already infected tubers. In the fields the leaves of the plant turned brown before the tubers upon which nearly a third of the population directly depended inevitably succumbed to rot and crumbled into nothing.

What precisely happened in Lower Fahan, or even within the extended McLoughlin family, was never considered worthy of separate public, or private, recording. For one, the failure of the potato crop in Donegal was not without precedent – it had happened to lesser degrees in 1816–19, 1821–22 and then again in 1830–31. A slight shift away from potato farming to livestock even before the Great Famine may have protected some of the county's inhabitants. It so happened that the coastal resorts of Inishowen, including those around Inch Island, attracted growing numbers of summer visitors throughout the period 1840–50. The price of grain, dairy and poultry all held up well in the local markets and, even at the height of the famine, farmers were still sending produce to Derry. And perhaps crucially, access to fish and other seafoods via the jagged coastline and loughs meant that Donegal never experienced the catastrophic hunger experienced in the poorest western counties.[35]

Amidst the mild and moist conditions in which the blight thrived, the harvest of 1845–46 slumped by 50 per cent. But it was 'Black 47' and the equally bad year that followed, in 1848, that sealed the fate of many Irish men and women, if not those clinging to the fringe of the Scalp. By 1852, a million people had succumbed to hunger and, by the time that the complex readjustments to the rural economy that gave rise to the Land Wars of 1879–1882 were done, Ireland had lost 20 per cent of its population to death or emigration to Atlantic or Pacific destinations – America, Canada and England, or distant Australia and New Zealand.[36]

When the Griffiths land valuations were conducted in the 1850s, it was recorded that George, and perhaps Hester, McLoughlin were still to be found at Shandrim. Rural economies recognised and valued men and property rights more readily than women and family members. By then, however, 'Black 47' had long since prised their 20-something-year-old son William and two of his brothers off the thin soil of Lower Fahan.

At some point in the late 1840s, William McLoughlin joined the exodus to the coast where ships from Inishowen had for several decades been loading the butter, fish, fowl and other livestock that made its way to Glasgow or Liverpool where it fed the gathering mass of urbanised men and women labouring just across the Irish Sea.[37] There had been a time, not long past, when the Industrial Revolution had been content only to consume Ireland's agricultural products and the labour of young migrant agricultural workers at the peak of their physical powers – the *spalpeen*. But the factory-beast across the water now wanted more; much more. The mills and their congested surroundings were devouring the bodies, minds and labour of men, women and small children alike.

Like thousands of others forced to set sail amidst the gales of poverty, William McLoughlin left Ireland with nothing, or very little, to show by way of cash or material goods. But as empty as were his pockets, so full was his mind with attitudes, concepts and half-formed ideas derived from time spent on the Scalp and in Inishowen. A world view nurtured in the countryside and shaped to fit the pace and needs of a venerable rural economy was about to be transplanted to a modern city and an industrialising society that was without historical precedent.

The ghosts of parental culture and socialisation chase after each successive generation of humanity. Their ability to induce courage or fear, to inspire or defeat, may wax and wane with the time and place, but traces − sometimes the faintest of hints − remain; they are always there, they help make us who we are. Grandfathers shape fathers just as surely as fathers shape sons as the cycle endlessly repeats itself. Like the genetic markers of diet and disease, however, the imprimatur of male influence need not always play itself out directly or proportionately among immediate successors. Habits, traits and values can lie dormant for a generation or two and then, long forgotten, re-manifest themselves where and when they are least expected. But it is also true that sometimes the heavy hand of the phantom grandfather or father can readily be detected on the shoulder of the most recent of the offspring.

CHAPTER TWO

ᏪᎨᎲᎦᏋᎧ

The Codes Adapted: Field to Factory

MANCHESTER
— 1850 —

From this filthy sewer [Manchester] pure gold flows. Here humanity attains
its most complete development and its most brutish; here civilisation works its miracle,
and civilised man is turned back into a savage.

ALEXIS DE TOCQUEVILLE

The Manchester that confronted the McLoughlin brothers fleeing Ireland's great hunger was both older and considerably younger than they or most in their cohort appreciated. Originally a Roman frontier fort dating to AD 77–78, the surrounding settlement had sprouted naturally between the River Irwell and two small, adjacent streams, the Irk and Medlock. Benefiting from a favourable position in south-east Lancashire that provided easy access to nearby ports and towns including Liverpool, Preston, Salford and Wigan on the one hand, and trans-Pennine traffic on the other, the town made steady progress and was already of some significance in late medieval times. By the middle of the seventeenth century it was set to become one of the region's more important centres for the production, distribution and trade in linen and woollen cloth.[1]

Manchester's pre-eminence as a capital of global significance for the cotton trade, however, was of comparatively recent vintage, dating back only to the mid-eighteenth century. There had been a shift from a reliance on local

34

materials that could be obtained from within the British Isles – such as flax from Ireland or wool from Yorkshire – first to linen and cotton mixtures and later to the mass importation of raw cotton used in the production of finished goods. Indirectly, that shift could be traced back to the voyages of discovery, a steady growth in intercontinental trade and the development of Liverpool as a port. By 1750, cotton was already displacing linen and wool in the manufacture of cloth. The original importance of the town as a centre for the retail and wholesale trade in textiles, however, provided it with an underlying economic logic that persisted into and beyond the age of machine production. As the most perspicacious historian of the emerging city puts it: 'Industrial Manchester was not a factory town which became a commercial centre; from the beginnings of industrialisation it had been a warehouse town with factories.'[2]

The transformation in the popular imagination of Manchester from a 'warehouse town with factories' to something that was understandably, but erroneously, equated to cotton mills, factories and slums was a by-product of the early Victorian era. It was a perception which, building on the advances that had come with inventions such as the cotton gin, the flying shuttle and the spinning jenny, harked back to the 1780s when, for the first time in history, the large-scale utilisation of steam-power in purpose-built brick factories eclipsed older cottage-based industries and ushered in mass production techniques on an unprecedented scale. It was a view propounded by public servants, travellers from abroad, novelists and political activists who, confronted for the first time by the full social impact of an Industrial Revolution, were shocked by the sudden eruption of huge, festering, rapidly urbanising carbuncles.[3]

Despite this growing importance as a multi-faceted local, national and international market, there was no denying the underlying centrality of cotton mills to first the town's and, after 1853, the city's still expanding factory system. It was largely Manchester that underpinned the increased British appetite for raw cotton, which rose from around 5 million pounds in 1781 to an annual average of about 82 million in the early 1820s, and then 94 million pounds by 1860. Twelve months after the defeat of Napoleon, in 1816, there were 86 steam-powered spinning factories in Manchester and neighbouring Salford; by 1830, there were already well over 500. Britain's mastery of the seas facilitated not only the importing of raw cotton but also allowed it to export finished cloth to expanding imperial markets spread across the world. In 1785 Britain exported cotton yarns and goods worth about £1 million; by 1816, that figure had reached £16 million and, by 1851, it stood at over £30 million. The quasi-magical process of transforming raw cotton into textiles for foreign exchange was a Mancunian triumph.[4]

The insertion of Manchester, 30 miles inland, as a value-adding centre astride expanding import and export shipping routes was made possible by the supplementary economic arteries. New conduits facilitated the movement of coal, finished goods, cotton and various other raw materials into, and out of, its open-mouthed factories. Besides a developing national road network that pointed to the town on the Irwell as England's second city – and one growing more rapidly than London for much of the nineteenth century – transport in Manchester was ever better served by a set of subsystems that formed part of an integrating whole. A modest, early navigable link to Liverpool was supplemented by an extensive system of larger canals leading to and from the coast. Yet others, including the Bridgewater and Rochdale Canal (1804), enabled the movement of coal from areas further inland.[5] Goods and passenger transport received a fillip when, in 1830, Manchester was linked to Liverpool by rail. The city's integration into an emerging global economic intelligence network was complete by 1871, when the trans-oceanic telegraphic system provided for the previously inconceivable world-wide transmission and receipt of trade data.[6]

Many of these developments, primed by the demand for textiles, fed into a self-sustaining logic of growth that facilitated further diversification of the local economy. A growing demand for semi-skilled manual labour fuelled rapid demographic expansion. Larger factories and mills – dependent on continuous machine production served by a rotating shift system staffed by men, women and children working long hours under extreme conditions – stimulated the secondary demand for capital goods ranging from carpentry shops, engineering and metal works to iron foundries. Printed cloth depended on chemicals and dyes, which spawned a need for yet more chemicals, giving rise to related activities including the production of glass.[7]

But it was not only factories and machines that required feeding and re-newal. With an insatiable lust for cheap labour, the city's new, predomi-nantly working-class population grew from about 75 000 in 1801 to over 350 000 by 1861. This in turn underwrote the development of a range of burgeoning food markets – including Smithfield, on Shudehill, and the nearby wholesale potato market on Oldham Road, as well as countless other small retail outlets.[8]

Viewed in the round, Manchester always offered a labour market that was more diverse and segmented than outsiders assumed. In the early 1840s, only 18 per cent – about one in five – of the town's labour force was di-rectly engaged in the mills, while the comparable figures for nearby towns such as Ashton and Oldham was closer to 40 per cent.[9] These proportions could also vary with changes in the trade cycle. Thus the buoyant 1850s gave way to 'cotton famine' and large-scale lay-offs between 1861 and 1865 when the Union blockaded the Confederate south during the American Civil War. The subsequent recovery was halted by downturns in 1877–79 and 1884. Despite the sluggish trade that characterised the Long Depression, dragging on into the 1890s, the number of cotton operatives in Lancashire doubled between 1850 and 1914; but there again, Manchester proved to be an exception, with the number of its mill workers declining.[10]

Despite the economic 'ups and downs', for many males, some women and even a few children, semi-skilled work in the mills constituted the apex of the Manchester labour market during much of the nineteenth century. Cotton spinners, in particular, constituted what later analysts characterised as a 'labour aristocracy'. The weekly wages of spinners, piecers and card-room workers all rose for most of the period between 1850 and 1875. The average earnings of spinners, for example, increased from about 21 to 35 shillings per week over the same 25-year period. It was barely above subsist-ence level, but there were often other benefits – and hidden perils.

One of the advantages for a hard-working and reliable cotton spinner was that, if fortunate enough, he could secure waged employment in the same mill for his wife and children, albeit under unpleasant and humid con-ditions that imperilled the health and education of the younger members of the family. This maximisation of income through closely supervised and collectivised labour remained a hallmark of the industry for several decades, even after slow-in-arriving 'progressive' factory legislation in the 1830s and 1840s sought to regulate the conditions under which labour, including child labour, could be employed. Age-diverse, mixed-gender labour units in the mills – sometimes built around nuclear families or looser family-like structures, or drawing on other elements of social solidarity such as ethnicity and regionalism – became a notable feature of the mid-nineteenth-century Industrial Revolution.[11]

The ramifications of employing family-based labour units within strictly monitored confines sometimes went beyond the commonly recognised problems of education, gross economic exploitation or poor health. For those newly off the land – agricultural workers or peasants accustomed to working out in the open and having their work rhythms set by crop and season – the mills helped shape the emerging notions of urban discipline and industrial time along with patriarchal power and personal freedom.[12] The formative context for these attitudes and values did not escape the notice of observers at the time, even if the behavioural sequels were not always fully understood. The closer interpersonal and more intimate social dynamics of small workshops found in nearby Birmingham were contrasted unfavourably with those to be found in the mighty mills of Manchester.[13] Hippolyte Taine, the French historian who visited the city in 1859, the year of Jack McLoughlin's birth, noted:

> The factories extend their flanks of fouled brick one after another. They are, with shutterless windows, like economical and colossal prisons. The place [Manchester] is a great jerry-built barracks, a 'work house' for four hundred thousand people, a hard-labour penal establishment: such are the ideas it suggests to the mind. One of the factory blocks is a rectangle six storeys high, each storey having forty windows, and inside, lit by gas-jets and deafened by the uproar of their own labour, toil thousands of workmen, penned in, regimented, hands active, feet motionless, all day and every day, mechanically serving their machines. Could there be any kind of life more outraged, more opposed to man's natural instincts?[14]

For fathers intent on commanding the lives of wives and children fully, the confined setting of the mill extended the reach of patriarchal power. It allowed them to control their families at work as well as at home. For those inclined towards benevolence by belief or personal disposition, it helped to maximise family income and strengthened kinship in circumstances that might otherwise have been even more alienating and fragmenting than they already were. But for those of a more authoritarian temperament, or those who revelled in domestic tyranny, it allowed for near total surveillance of the family and enabled a degree of intrusion into the lives of the vulnerable or the weak that could limit personal and sexual development.[15] Patriarchal control in mill-based families helped shape the personalities and behaviour of wives and children at either end of a spectrum ranging from the accommodating, cowed, and disciplined through to the antisocial, ill-disciplined, rebellious and violent. More often than not, it accentuated elements of both patterns in ways that were not always predictable.

Since work-seekers in Manchester were less restricted to the cotton mills for choice than were their counterparts in other Lancashire towns, most contrived to avoid labour in the textile industry in its direct form. There were hundreds of other factories and industries in which semi-skilled males could find work of various sorts.

Shops, stores and warehouses were in need of assistants, messengers and porters when the economy was expanding, while young men with agility and physical strength – such as the navvies who built the infrastructure of the Industrial Revolution – found work on building sites or helped construct bridges, canals, railways and roads. Older women sometimes eked out a living dressmaking at home while many young girls tried to find positions as live-in domestic servants for a growing and increasingly well-off middle class. Many other men, women and children in search of relatively independent, less-regulated work environments gravitated towards the city's markets where they earned their living as barrow-boys, costermongers, hawkers, porters or street-sellers dealing in the basics – food or second-hand clothing.[16]

But even those not wishing to be directly employed in the manufacture of cotton goods could not escape the new mills rising along the Rochdale

Canal, along with the warehouses further west; not least of all because it was around them that the new residential enclaves arose. Industrial slums characterised by indescribable filth and poverty only gave way to more recognisable dimensions as working-class 'suburbs' after 1850, once urban improvements had gathered momentum.[17] The old congested haunts of Angel Meadow and Little Ireland were gradually eclipsed by a new mill-and-wharf heartland comprising Ancoats, Chorlton-on-Medlock, New Cross and Holt Town, and, beyond them, Ardwick, Collyhurst and Hulme.

Viewed from the top of a multi-storeyed mill in Ancoats, where farmland started to give way to more planned development in the early 1770s, most of the canals and the grid of narrow roads below could be seen as part of a logic determined by the need to build around what had once been clear-running rivers and streams. Closer investigation of the residential cluster, however, revealed another logic at work. Amongst the houses, the street grid gave way to any number of twisting alleys, 'back' streets, courts, cul-de-sacs and lanes.[18] On either side of these barely human rat-runs, constructed without sewers or proper toilets, were scores of cottages or houses that spoke of grossly inadequate accommodation hastily erected by contractor-speculators seeking to extract maximum income from minimal investment. Two-storey cottages and houses, built back-to-back so as to obviate the need for additional walls, squatted over unventilated cellars which, given the predominance of low-lying ground, were damp and easily flooded.[19]

A single door along with a pair of modest windows allowing in some light provided row upon row of bricked cubes with the faintest of street-front smiles. Inside, 'one up one down' rooms were sub-let to families comprising anything from seven to ten people. Below ground-level, huddled in cellars, could be found yet more families leading an even more marginal existence.[20] In the 1830s, better-off mule-spinners, earning between 15 and 25 shillings a week, rented stand-alone cottages for five or six shillings a week. Other workers, those renting rooms or cellars, paid two to three shillings a week so as to put a roof over the heads of a few poverty-stricken souls.[21]

Several official reports in the 1830s and 1840s, along with those of other analysts – including Friedrich Engels, whose research was partially shaped by his Irish working-class partner, Mary Burns – drew attention to the conditions prevailing in Manchester and adjacent Salford. These initiatives helped lay the foundations for the progressive, albeit slow, improvements that gathered momentum after mid-century.[22] In the interim, however, poor conditions in the factories, addressed by yet more reforming legislation, and squalid residential quarters continued to seriously undermine the health of labouring men, women and children between 1830 and 1880.[23]

In the mills, lint and dust suspended in pervasive humidity facilitated the spread of asthma, bronchitis and tuberculosis, diseases that thrived in the cold and damp of poorly ventilated rooms or cellars heated by coal fires. The absence of clean drinking water, adequate toilets and an extensive water-borne sewerage system meant that for many decades respiratory infections – at their worst in winter – were supplemented by other diseases such as cholera, diarrhoea and typhoid that favoured summer. Death and the seasons, a pair of hunters that had stalked humanity ever since people could remember, now invaded newly industrialising centres, felling infants at will in vulnerable areas such as Ancoats and picking off working men before they could complete two full decades of employment in the town's factories, mills or warehouses.[24]

★ ★ ★

The arrival of Irish immigrants in Lancashire pre- and post-dated the most disease-ridden years of the Industrial Revolution. It was, however, a cruel irony that it was almost exactly in mid-century, when the worst of the old urban conditions in Manchester were yet to disappear and the best of the new yet to manifest themselves, that the Great Famine of 1847–52 drove unprecedented numbers of Irish country folk off the land. Barely surviving on grossly inadequate diets in squalid urban quarters, they were preyed upon anew by other bacteria and viruses that thrived amidst poverty. Drawn from a colonised and despised people overcome only after centuries of stubborn resistance, who retained a liking for alcohol, fairytales and myths, and who remained loyal to a church long since abandoned by their imperial overlords, the Irish were quintessential 'outsiders'. Derided as 'deckers' who had 'come across with the cattle' destined for the local livestock markets, or as 'micks' and 'paddies' just 'off the bogs', refugees poured into Manchester and anti-Irish prejudice peaked in the 1860s.[25]

Carrying within them an uneven mixture of Catholic fatalism and secular hope, many post-famine immigrants moved into the long-established Hibernian haunts of the town. They clustered around the poles of an axis that ran roughly from Angel Meadow on the Irk, in the north, down to Little Ireland on the Medlock further south and west.[26] There, they had access to a handful of priests – vectors of an on-going and mutating Irish identity-in-exile – attached to two of the older and smaller churches of the inner city, St Chad's and St Mary's. Many others, however, gravitated towards expanding residential areas that enjoyed relatively easy access to markets and the mills, such as Ardwick, Collyhurst, Hulme and New Cross. The latter refugees benefited from newer, larger, churches consecrated in the late 1840s, such as St Anne's and St Wilfrid's. But perhaps the most noteworthy and popular destination of all was hard by the Rochdale Canal, close to the Smithfield Market. Although, like most of the other suburbs, it was never a classic 'ghetto' housing people drawn exclusively from a single, easily identifiable group, Ancoats in the 1850s – and increasingly so as the century wore on – was the single most heavily ethnicised Irish neighbourhood in all of Manchester.[27]

In 1841, there were approximately 30 000 Irish-born inhabitants in Manchester, constituting roughly 12 per cent of the inhabitants. In 1851, with the famine in full swing, the number had risen to over 45 000, accounting for about 15 per cent of the town's population. The latter percentage was never eclipsed and thereafter the number of native-born Irish citizens in Manchester continued to decline right up to the twentieth century. Rural identities, many forged in the impoverished western parts of Ireland such as Leitrim, Mayo and Roscommon, appear to have been supplemented by smaller numbers drawn from neighbouring counties such as Sligo and a few even further north-west. John Doherty, one of the first Irish organisers of cotton mill workers, almost certainly hailed from Donegal, perhaps from Inishowen itself. Like William McLoughlin, Doherty, too, may have had his first taste of mill-work in Buncrana, by the Swilly.[28]

42

The positive features of Irish rural culture transported into a modern English industrial town were there for all to see. Much of it centred on religion. By the mid-nineteenth century the Catholic Church was almost synonymous with things Irish, not excluding a changing repertoire of nationalist politics.[29] Whereas in 1846 Manchester was served by 13 priests in five parishes, by 1870 the number had risen to 30 spread over 13 parishes. The ability of some of the priests to speak Gaelic – still frequently heard in city streets in the mid-1840s – provided them with easy access to the traditionalists in their flock. It also allowed them to mobilise and organise the members of their communities at moments of crisis, such as during epidemics, and for everyday activities ranging from running denominational schools through to temperance societies and voluntary structures that provided support for mothers and wives.[30] These undoubted virtues had, however, to be offset against what many saw as other, more problematic, elements in 'Irish' culture.

Charles Rickards, mid-century Manchester's Stipendiary Magistrate, thought that many if not most of the Irish in the city were 'belligerent' and 'undisciplined' and involved in cases of 'aggravated assault' far more frequently than those drawn from other ethnic groupings.[31] It was a view shared by many citizens and may have had some basis in fact. Although the Irish accounted for only 15 per cent of the local population between 1845 and 1854, they figured disproportionately in the numbers arrested and prosecuted for attacks on police constables (34 per cent), in cases of common assault (28 per cent), or for breaches of the peace (47 per cent).[32]

If accurate, these numbers are hardly surprising. It is well known that those recently off the land, those least educated and semi-literate, are most prone to getting into trouble with the law in urban areas.[33] There may also have been an element of a self-fulfilling prophecy in the figures insofar as policemen, taken in by the stereotype of the 'micks', may have been predisposed to arresting Irishmen even before encountering them on the streets. Moreover, if the Irish *did* resort to fisticuffs to settle real or imagined grievances in the new settings they found themselves in, they were hardly on their own. The English ruling and working classes, although increasingly taken with notions of honour and self-restraint as duelling gave way first to prize-fighting and then to boxing, had themselves long been famous for hand-to-hand combat and a willingness to settle differences through 'fair fights'. Interpersonal violence, with or without restraint, was an important part of popular culture in Manchester and it was rooted in the behaviour of English 'hosts' and immigrants alike.[34]

More difficult for observers to comprehend were collective intra- and inter-communal clashes in which fists, stick-fighting or stone throwing were resorted to. 'Faction fights', familiar enough in the open fields of agricultural Ireland, were adapted to industrial neighbourhoods in Lancashire.[35] Some of these bloody, occasionally fatal, clashes arose on the spur of the moment, spontaneous eruptions propelled by excesses of testosterone and whiskey. Many more, however, including some that were well-organised, could be traced to ancient clan antipathies or county and village rivalries that had their origin in the economics of the countryside but whose underlying causes now fed into the competition for accommodation, jobs or the sexual favours of females in new urban settings. Faction fights were not, and are not, peculiar to the Irish. They play an important role in the ways that peasants becoming workers adjust to huge socio-economic changes.[36]

It is possible that in post-famine working-class Manchester, where collective violence took place against the backdrop of an incomplete, but profound, cultural shift that accompanied the move from field to factory, there may also have been some 'Irish' inspiration for the adolescent gang-violence as expressed in the developing urban cult of 'scuttling'. Like faction fighting, scuttling was informed by intense territoriality centred on the neighbourhood and the need to manifest masculinity.[37]

Speculation aside, what is clear is that alcohol was the trigger for much if not most of the collective, interpersonal or inter-spousal violence in the city. Like most manufacturing and mining towns on the frontiers of industrialisation, Manchester boasted enough alcohol to float a ship. The sea of beer and spirits was mostly legal in origin. It was produced, distributed and consumed under licence, in beer shops sanctioned to operate from homes occupied by ratepayers or in public houses selling malt and spirits. Liquor consumption was policed as a part of the great adjustment necessary for the emergence and entrenchment of industrial time and discipline.

But the number of licensed outlets situated in poor working-class districts continued to exceed the growth of population even as, in other respects, Manchester assumed more ordered and settled proportions. In 1863, there was one licensed liquor outlet in the city for every 154 inhabitants, by 1871 it had grown to one for every 147 residents and, by 1873, it was one for every 139.[38]

With beer and spirits often more accessible than fish and chips, the Irish, recently off the land, once again occupied a difficult, perhaps distinctive, position. Drawn from a culture that tolerated drinking among young males, if it did not actively encourage it, some may already have had a genetic predisposition to alcohol dependence. This further complicated their adaptation to urban society and many had to be treated for 'behavioural and mental problems'.[39] Given their preference for spirits, most Irish men confined serious drinking to the weekends so as to fit in with the rhythm of the working week. But, given that those Irishmen who did not work in mills often earned less, on average, than their English counterparts, they had to find cheaper, illegally manufactured potato spirits – *poteen*. Thus, while accounting for only 15 per cent of the city's population, close on 43 per cent of those arrested for 'Illicit Distillation and Offences against the Excise' between 1845 and 1854 were Irish.[40] The ancient illicit stills of the caves and cottages back in Inishowen were linked, via the threads in Irish male culture, to the modern *poteen* cellars of Lancashire.

It was this same nexus of alcohol, imperialism and masculinity that underpinned much of the 'belligerence' Magistrate Rickards thought of as being quintessentially Irish. Drawn from an island forcibly occupied, where some English landlords lorded it over peasants who were humbled and powerless, from a colony where men and women had to pursue their religion in secret and were denied the vote, many Irish men and women saw the law itself as alien, as something foreign, an imposition. These realities helped shape a culture of contrariness that consistently reasserted the values of masculinity in settings where more conventional indicators of patriarchal power and manliness – such as property and wealth – had been severely eroded. 'Irish' bloody-mindedness increased when those struggling to make a living off the land supplemented their incomes through the production of *poteen* and were then informed on and subjected to raids by the British army, excise men or the police.

Seen from this perspective, the experience of many immigrant Irish did not change markedly when they moved from rural County Mayo to modern metropolitan Manchester. The continuities of conquest and the expectation of an attitude of acceptance or deference, if not outright gratitude, on the part of their all-powerful hosts, reinforced the antipathies of Irish fathers and their Lancashire-born sons to informers and what they saw as repressive 'English' courts, laws, police and prisons.

★   ★   ★

The use of informers was widely frowned upon in progressive political circles during much of the nineteenth century. Covert operations undertaken by police agents, characteristic of more repressive regimes such as those in France and Tsarist Russia, were seen as being at odds with 'English' notions of 'fairness' and the rights of individuals in liberalising democracies. In Ireland, the hatred of informers was born in the countryside but spread to the cities in mid-century as the Royal Ulster Constabulary sought to infiltrate the emerging nationalist opposition. In Lancashire the use of informers extended into criminal operations. The use of covert agents earned the condemnation not only of those engaged in nationalist politics, but of those English and Irish in the working classes who were involved in more conventional crimes against property. In Manchester, 'giving information to the police was taboo' and likely to be counteracted by ostracism or serious physical reprisals.[41]

With police intelligence and testimony alike considered suspect and the law an imposition from distant Westminster – an instrument lacking in popular sanction – it fell to a self-respecting man to challenge any attempt at apprehension. 'Among the Irish resisting arrest was a matter of honour.'[42] Indeed, not only *should* an Irishman resist arrest, but he was almost duty-bound to go to the rescue of any acquaintance or friend similarly threatened. The attempted arrest of Irishmen frequently resulted in brawls, in free-for-alls reminiscent of events at country fairs back in the Old Country. Rescue attempts became so commonplace in Manchester that they warranted separate reporting, and between 1845 and 1854 nearly half of those arrested for obstructing the constables in this way were Irish. In Ancoats, the most heavily populated Irish neighbourhood, an attempt to arrest a man at an illicit *poteen* still, in 1832, degenerated into extensive collective resistance and near riot.[43]

Once arraigned, Irishmen were notorious for manifesting their contempt of court and presiding officer alike either by hurling abuse at the Magistrate, or by making pointedly sarcastic interventions when sentenced. It was yet another sub-cultural trait of opposition that many Irish fathers passed down to their Lancashire-born 'scuttling' sons. By the same token, many former 'scuttlers', Irish emigrants who subsequently made their way out to the colonies and other far-flung outposts of empire, considered it their duty to attempt to escape from 'English' prisons.[44]

Most of this cult of masculinity played itself out in public; indeed, much of it was designed for popular consumption, sometimes assuming the proportions of street-theatre. There was, however, another and darker side to it. Drunk or sober, working men were poorly disposed to domestic dissent and questioning from their wives and children. If working-class patriarchs sensed that their dignity, roles within the family or social worth were being undermined during the early years of the Industrial Revolution, then women and children were left vulnerable in other ways. Domestic violence was sufficiently widespread to prompt an 1853 Act for the 'Better Prevention of Aggravated Assaults on Women and Children'.[45] And if this was true for the 'English', how much more threatening must this have been for women born in Ireland who were isolated from their kin, exposed to social deprivation and, if not wholly vulnerable economically, then dependent on a spouse living out his life in accord with the prescripts of masculinity in an unfamiliar environment?

An undercurrent of misogyny permeated most of Manchester's dank cellars and dismal rooms. It was evident, not only from the beatings that men inflicted on their wives, but also in the adolescent male sub-culture of 'scuttling' which, despite the occasional presence of young women in supportive roles, was poorly disposed to females of all ages.[46] Trapped behind the walls of a male-supremacist ideology, many Irish women looked around for any authority that could trump that of their husbands and sons. Some looked heavenwards, sneaking out of the back door to find solace in the church.[47] It was a move that was not always cost-free. While Irish patriarchs were content to underwrite clerically endorsed nationalism that challenged English hegemony and fed into a broader culture of contrariness, they were less comfortable with priestly advice that sought to temper any excesses of masculinity in their own homes. The advice of frocked men of the cloth, some of whom were suspected of having an inappropriate liking for alcohol, small children and women, could therefore feed into longer-standing anticlerical sentiments of fathers who may have passed them on to their sons.[48]

Irish women could not survive on a diet of hope and prayer alone. An industrial vortex of alcohol, desperation and poverty drew many into the streets and casual, or full-time, prostitution. Although drawn from only 15 per cent of the city's population, Irish-born women regularly accounted for between 25 and 35 per cent of those arrested for prostitution in mid-Victorian Manchester.[49] Confronted by a cohort of post-famine migrant males averse to marriage, and set against the backdrop of a religion that drew a sharp distinction between the ideal of the Madonna and ordinary mortals, the moral shortcomings of Irish female workers added to misogynistic perceptions and endless cycles of domestic violence.[50]

Seen by men and women who had only recently washed in on the tide from across the Irish Sea, mid-nineteenth-century Lancashire looked more like a rocky shoreline than a safe harbour. For those who adapted most readily to urban ways, those determined and hard-working, it offered a pathway to subsistence. Manchester gave one the chance to sit out a generation and wait on better things – or, if the opportunity arose, the chance of seeing one's children escaping to greener pastures via onward migration. For those less sure-footed, those walking into the winds swirling with prejudice, a wrong step could be fatal. All that was required to fail was an indiscretion or two stemming from an old rural culture imperfectly aligned with the new ways of urban living. And, since most people needed a dream, William McLoughlin averted his eyes from the treacherous shore and saw only the promised land.

CHAPTER THREE

❦

The Family: Seeds and Weeds

ANCOATS
— 1850–1875 —

When the larger culture aggrandizes wife beaters, degrades women or
nods approvingly at child slappers, the family gets a bit more dangerous for everyone,
and so, inevitably, does the larger world.

BARBARA EHRENREICH

In ways impossible to present persuasively, let alone prove, there are moments when, in tracing a history over a number of generations, a chronicler can sense the hand of a grandfather resting on the shoulder of a father, and that of the father on that of his son. Imagine patriarchs aligned in this way, and one can sense how a current of attitudes, beliefs and values is transmitted through the successive recipients, each using the diminished charge received to adapt to changing circumstances. If the McLoughlins could be so ordered, then George McLoughlin of Donegal, patriarchal survivor of the Great Famine back on the Scalp, may be seen to have been a formidable man. He appears to have passed on some of his strengths to his sons, and perhaps the odd weakness as well.

From surviving archival fragments it would seem that, from the moment that he arrived in Manchester as a young man in his early twenties, William McLoughlin succeeded, to a considerable extent, in being a disciplined employee, a conscientious father and a reasonably law-abiding citizen. Amidst

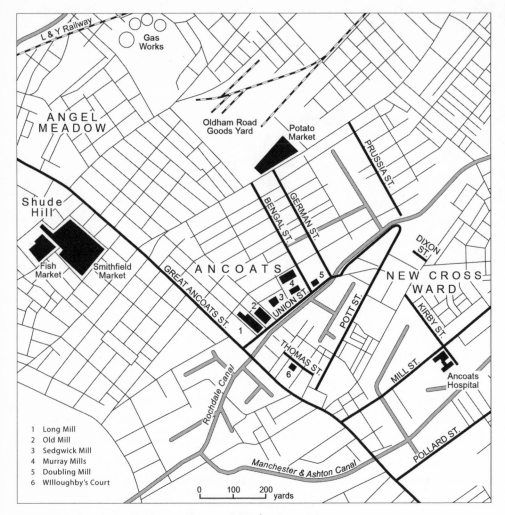

Ancoats, Manchester, c 1860

the limitations of a sub-subsistence existence in an industrialising system, at a time when the average life expectancy of a worker was around 50 years, that was a singular achievement.[1] After serving a formal apprenticeship in the textile industry, he remained in more or less continuous employment as a 'cotton spinner' or 'weaver' from the late 1840s and into the 1850s, through the Cotton Famine of the 1860s, and then on into the 1870s without ever moving three miles beyond central Ancoats. Taken at face value, the census returns suggest that he was a dedicated, reliable and reasonably well-settled mill employee.

There may, however, have been another, lesser known, side to a man who appears to have taken readily to industrial discipline. In August 1873, when he was 50 years old and the father of seven, William McLoughlin fell foul of the School Board Act. Unable or unwilling to pay a fine of two shillings and sixpence, he spent a week in gaol.[2] This scrape with the law – the only one ever recorded – suggests that he had failed to ensure that one or more of his children were attending school regularly. If so, it is not clear whether, at a time when several of his children were working in the family unit, it was at his insistence that they neglected attending classes, or whether a few of his lively youngsters were already beyond parental reach and truanting of their own accord.

As it happens, the full entry on his short prison record hints at a more turbulent life led beyond the mill. Scars on his neck, arm and legs suggest that he had not always shied away from fights and experienced his fair share of trouble that may or may not have been alcohol-fuelled. More worryingly, he also had a blue dot tattooed above his left eyebrow, at a time when such markings were often associated with gang-related theft.[3]

Some of his problems probably date back to the 1860s, when the young McLoughlin family would have been financially stretched to breaking point and anti-Catholic, anti-Irish, sentiment at a peak in the city. His wife and children had little taste for the rigours of closely supervised factory discipline or for the patriarchal authority that followed them home from work. Long before a recession hit Manchester in 1877–78 and tore apart what was left of the few bonds holding the family together, they had abandoned the idea of eking out an existence in the mill. Instead, like many other Irish immigrant families, they turned their attention to the opportunities for self-employment in and around Smithfield Market, or sought out other positions in the local labour market requiring un- or semi-skilled labour.

During the best of the hard times, in the 1850s and the 1860s, when the condition of the working classes in Manchester was improving slowly in response to national and municipal reforms, the McLoughlin family – like others – was constantly on the move. Seldom further than a walk away from the darkest of Ancoats' industrial veins, the Rochdale Canal, they lived in lodgings of various sizes and types at more than a half-dozen insalubrious addresses. In part, these moves were an attempt to accommodate the changing needs of a growing family. But there was also a deeper logic at work that prevented any one dank cellar or poorly lit set of rooms being occupied long enough for it to be considered a 'home'. As post-famine immigration slowed and the housing stock in Ancoats gradually increased after 1850, so pressure on rents eased, encouraging poor families and tenants to seek out slightly better deals.[4]

★ ★ ★

In March 1851, still a bachelor, William McLoughlin shared a small room with a workmate in lodgings on German Street, presided over by an Irish landlady. The house was hard by the Rochdale Canal and round the corner from one of the best established firms and largest mills in Ancoats. Murray, McConnel & Kennedy was owned by one of the powerful Scottish families whose presence in the city dated back to the late eighteenth century.[5] At the age of 24, William was part of a post-famine cohort of half-a-dozen newly qualified young journeymen, mostly from Ireland – possibly even his native Donegal – who had undergone a formal apprenticeship as cotton spinners.[6]

John Scott, an unskilled labourer, was the older brother of one of the German Street lodgers. Like William, he hailed from the shores of Lough Swilly, albeit from across the water, in Rathmullen, rather than Buncrana. The two had had more in common, however, than having once lifted salmon from streams in Inishowen. Single and of the same age, they were already earning what some married man in Ancoats lived on. They were eligible Catholic bachelors in a city that never wanted for young Irish women, some working in the cotton mills.

Scott had identified 18-year-old Bridget-Ann Sloan, a 'spindler', and the younger of two sisters living with their widowed mother just south of the canal, as the woman he would marry later that year. Originally from Donegore, County Antrim, the Sloan women had been left destitute when the patriarch, a moulder, had expired in the early 1840s, before the famine.[7] Unable to find suitable employment in a Belfast linen industry bending before the competitive winds howling in from Lancashire, the widow, Mary, and her two daughters had boarded the ferry for Liverpool before moving on to Manchester.[8]

John Scott introduced his friend, William McLoughlin, to Bridget-Ann's older sister, Elizabeth, aged 20. A 'pack or frame tender' in the mill, Eliza, as she called herself, appears to have had a tougher start in life than Ann, two years her junior. As the oldest of the Sloan sisters, Eliza's education may have been curtailed when, as one suspects, she was sent out to work after her father died. Later, as a mature woman, she claimed to be able to read, but not write. Without a male breadwinner, the plight of the Sloans had been exacerbated shortly after they arrived in Ancoats. In 1851 Mary was responsible for raising a three-year-old grandson of indeterminate parentage. The boy may have been the offspring of another, deceased Sloan daughter named Margaret. If not, the boy was more likely to have been Eliza's child than the younger Ann's.

Although never destined for the convent, Ann and Eliza were devout Catholics, God-fearing young women who, regardless of any moral short-comings, were in earnest about the church and respectful of the priesthood. As the first full-time factory worker in a female-headed household, Eliza Sloan, perhaps less attractive than her sister, may only have begun to enjoy a fuller social life much later than most of her peers. Ann married before her, and even Eliza's most ardent suitor appears to have thought long and hard before agreeing to marry her. But since Eliza proved to be a spirited woman in later life, and more than willing to make up for time lost, it may, of course, have been *she* rather than her husband who thought twice about marriage.

By late 1851, William McLoughlin, now rooming in Bengal Street near his newly married friends the Scotts, and Eliza, still living with her mother in Back Pott Street, were closely involved and she was pregnant. For reasons unknown, the couple, who were no worse-off economically than many of their peers, chose not to marry. Again, one suspects that the stalling may have come from William rather than the mother-to-be. Eliza, however, was not without views of her own. When the baby was born, illegitimately, in 1852, he was named after her late father, James, rather than anyone on his father's side. 'James' was a name that obviously meant a great deal to her, since, over the next eight years, Eliza chose the same name for at least three of her male offspring. Not one of the boys so baptised survived. James, like his two namesakes, died in his infancy.

Drawn together by the loss of the child, the couple remained close even though they continued to reside apart. Eliza was soon pregnant again. Nothing in the interim, however, had changed sufficiently for the couple to reconsider their views on marriage. When the babe was born, in March 1853, Eliza again complied with the law by ensuring that the birth was registered, but, as before, was content to leave the name of the child's father unrecorded. This time, however, the infant survived. A month later, she took the baby off to St Anne's where the priests, willing to forgive a mother's moral dilemmas in an exchange for the promise of a child raised in the grace of the church, baptised her Ellen Sloan.[9]

Sloan in name for the first years of her life, Ellen also became a Sloan in nature, in that, unlike most of her siblings, she assumed many of the positive qualities her mother displayed as a younger woman. Nominally without a father and the oldest child in a family blighted by poverty, Ellen was sent out to work at an early age. In an epoch scarred by child labour, she was soon at work in the mill. Although she attended school for a short time, she, like her mother, remained virtually illiterate and at the time of her own marriage, at age 22, was still incapable of writing her name.[10] Being female in a household that eventually boasted seven children, she, the first child, would also have taken on a disproportionate share of domestic chores and helped raise the younger siblings. From the evidence surviving it would appear that she was very good with the children. At age 17, her aunt – Ann Scott – asked her to become godmother to baby Joseph, her cousin and one of several Scott boys.[11]

Being the firstborn was a position not entirely bereft of benefit. As the oldest child, Ellen for some years enjoyed an elevated status among the siblings, benefiting from the attention and energy of her parents while they were relatively young and not yet at full stretch emotionally or financially. In later life she ignored her legal status as a bastard, accepted William as her father, and used the name McLoughlin. Older children in poor families sometimes also got a marginally better start in life by having access to food in greater quantities, if not quality, than those who followed. Healthy and raised as a good Catholic at a time when her mother was still shouldering a full domestic load, by her early twenties Ellen was skilled and smart enough to take the few chances that came her way. Unlike most of her siblings, she steered clear of trouble with the law and left the family shortly before it imploded. Born amidst the most unpromising of circumstances and married in 1876, Ellen became part of Victorian England's 'respectable' working classes.[12]

The relatively propitious circumstances in which William and Eliza found themselves during the early 1850s persisted for nearly a decade. They remained in near full employment in the mills and were assured of a steady, albeit paltry, income. A weak financial sun filtered light into their otherwise bleak residential dens and the couple's older pups avoided some of the abuse and neglect that came in later, stormier, times. The birth of a second daughter, in 1855, did nothing to change the couple's pattern of child-rearing or legal obligations. Sarah Ann's birth, too, was registered, and like her older sister before her, she was baptised a Sloan without formal noting of her father's name. What, if anything, was William – capable of decisive action when the occasion demanded it – waiting for before he would marry Eliza? It may have been a son.

Sarah Ann, too, appears to have benefited from relatively fair economic and social winds. While she could hardly have sailed through abject poverty entirely unharmed, she emerged sufficiently intact to become a reliable young worker in the cotton mills and, later, a responsible young adult. She, too, avoided problems with the law, and sister Ellen thought well enough of her to make her the godmother of one of her own children. For several years a strong thread of female independence and religion ran through the affairs of the small McLoughlin family.[13]

In the bleak economic springtime of 1857, Eliza lost another child named James. The loss of a second boy bearing her father's name may or may not have been an omen of sorts, but Eliza hesitated before using it again. For William, the loss of the second boy meant that for the better part of a decade – from 1852 to 1859 – he presided over a family without a son, one dominated by the presence of a wife and two small girls, and thereafter, over one in which older females always outnumbered the ranking males by a considerable margin. In an era in which notions of masculinity became ever more prominent in English and Irish working-class cultures, a preponderance of females in his household may not always have sat easily with the patriarch.[14] Most couples, including working-class parents, sought a balance when shaping family profiles.

It is possible, too, that William might have been of the view that, while it did not matter particularly that a man and his common-law wife chose to overlook the legal status of their daughters, the appearance of a male child necessitated a different response. How else is one to account for the fact that by the time that William and Eliza's next child – another boy – was born and baptised, the couple claimed to be married, and that there was no thought of having another 'James' or, more pertinently perhaps, a 'Sloan'? The older girls might technically have been called bastards, but no McLoughlin boy was going to start life with such a disadvantage.

Accustomed to pregnancy, Eliza hauled the latest foetus successfully through the Lancashire summer and then trundled the gathering load into the winter months of 1858. By the time New Year came around she was moving with difficulty. Then, on Sunday, 23 January 1859, at season's ebb, with her health and that of her child compromised by cold, hunger and squalor, she went into labour. It was the fiction of Dickens and the facts of Engels writ large. A midwife – well over 70 – was sent for and the mother cajoled and coaxed into presenting her bundle. The wrinkled baby that emerged was so manifestly in distress that his mother thought he might die even before he could be placed in God's grace. Eliza was hurriedly patched up and the baby wrapped for a hasty excursion down to St Anne's in the hope of finding a priest.

They were relieved to find Peter Liptrott, not yet permanently attached to a new parish barely 10 years old, still at the church.[15] Father Peter had been supportive and understanding when she had taken the girls to him, and he was equally willing to help her with the sickly infant. In the absence of her sister Ann, the midwife, Mrs Crilley, assumed the role of godmother and the boy was at once baptised. But it had been a long day and the priest, struggling to pay attention to a distraught mother he knew better as 'Elizabeth Sloan', incorrectly recorded the names of the child's parents as Edward and Eliza McLoughlin.[16] Thus did John (Jack) McLoughlin – half-dead, half-English and half-Irish – enter the old world.

The infant shook off a first-day challenge from death and survived to draw succour from the same thin gruel that sustained his sisters. Born in the closing days of the 'good times', when there were fewer mouths to feed, the boy may have got more attention from his parents, and more especially his father, than did either Ellen or Sarah. He certainly got a good deal more to eat than did the runts that followed once the economic muscle of the household became strained and then eventually collapsed. His presence and posture as an adult – strong and stout in an age that admired both – never spoke of a man badly malnourished as child.

Ironically, part of the boy's sound early physical development could be attributed to the misfortune of his mother, who continued to hanker after a son she could name after her father. Ellen was seven but Jack still only one when Eliza was again expectant. As before, the boy, born in 1860 and christened James, died almost at once. Thus Jack, the sole surviving male child, was bracketed between brothers named James, both of whom had died almost at birth. The latest death simply prolonged the period in the greater life-cycle of the family during which he was the only male child. It was not until two years later, with the birth of yet another baby boy, that Jack had to share his parents' affection and meagre provisions with a potential male rival.

The newborn, William junior, arrived in 1862 and was named after his father so as to avoid the curse of the Sloans. By then the McLoughlins had moved to 72 Union Street, on the Rochdale Canal, in the shadow of the Murray Mills where William Snr and Eliza, both in their mid-thirties, worked as a 'cotton spinner' and 'frame tender' respectively. But the American Civil War and the Cotton Famine meant that the family was under increasing financial strain and the parents found it difficult to provide their offspring with basic necessities. For a while, Ellen (8) and Sarah (6) avoided being drawn into the maelstrom of mill work and attended school intermittently, but were forced to devote most of their time to a range of domestic chores, including taking care of the two younger male siblings.[17]

In Union Street the McLoughlin parents were less than five minutes away from their place of work, close to the children and within easy reach of Smithfield Market, which provided the poor with access to some of the cheapest food and clothing in the city. But the virtues of a central location were dwarfed by the vices that came with squeezing profit out of the working class – alcohol, crime, filth, overcrowding, prostitution and poverty. Manchester, Ancoats and especially Union Street lay about as close to the heart of human putrefaction as one could get. As Eliza would have known, one in four children died in their first year, and only one in three reached the age of five.[18] Progress barely hobbled along while death pranced about openly.

Back in 1849, when William McLoughlin, newly arrived from Ireland, was lodging in German Street, a reporter on a local newspaper recorded his impressions of Union Street:

> A more perfectly ugly spot you shall not find between sunrise and sunset. Fancy a street one side of which is all mills … the grimiest, sootiest, filthiest lumps of masonry in all Manchester and on the other side lies a canal – a ditch of muddy water, very much like rotten pea soup.[19]

Not much had changed in Union Street. There were three brothels and a half-dozen beer and public houses within a five-minute walk of the McLoughlins' rooms. Another 20 or more pubs were only 10 minutes away. Between them, these outlets ensured a never-ending supply of after-dark drunks, criminals and riotous weekends filled with constables and general street-mayhem.[20] It may have been while living close by the Rochdale Canal that Eliza started losing her way.

Amidst these unsavoury conditions, the McLoughlin parents protected and nurtured their four children as best possible. In physical and psychological terms, however, the price exacted from them – and more particularly from Eliza – continued to rise. Between their sojourn in Union Street during the early 1860s, and their arrival in the early 1870s at nearby Willoughby's Court, on Thomas Street, four blocks away, the McLoughlins lived briefly at two other addresses, also not too far away.

In the interim Eliza had given birth to three more children – a son and two daughters. Thomas (1864) and Mary-Ellen (1866) maintained Eliza's two-yearly birth-rate.[21] The latter's hyphenated name may yet again have been an informal tribute to the child-minding prowess of the oldest sibling. The couple's last child, however, was born in 1870, when Eliza was 39 years old and still working in the mill.[22] Eliza had had a 20-year-long shift and, perhaps not surprisingly after 10 children, was at the outer limit of her capabilities. The pubs were now closer than they had ever been. Although the baby – Elizabeth – seems to have become something of a favourite of her father, then near 50 years old, some in the latter part of the brood – William, Tommy and Mary – appear to have been seriously neglected.

★ ★ ★

Seen through the icy lens of income, the McLoughlin family probably reached its economic – possibly even its social – apogee in 1871, while based at Willoughby's Court, south of the canal, just off Great Ancoats Street, at the point where the street lifted itself for the incline leading up to Shudehill and the Smithfield Market. In that year, with the textile industry back in reasonably robust health, both parents were still employed in the mills, as were 18-year-old Ellen and 16-year-old Sarah – the latter as 'cotton spinners' still living with their parents. The weekly wages generated by four adults were supplemented by the part-time work of Jack (12) and William (9). In line with the reforming legislation that eventually got the patriarch into trouble, the older boys supposedly spent no more than half their time in the mills and half at school. The stragglers in the family – Thomas, Mary and Elizabeth – were too young for either mill or school.[23] Tommy ran wild.

Despite its prissy name, Willoughby's Court, dank and dismal, must for some time have seemed like a relatively secure base for a family that was used to more difficult times and tougher terrain. The problem was, however, that, while in the foothills of longer-term hardship, relative success could pose only briefly as a destination. In truth, Willoughby's was simply a high point on a mountain scaled with great difficulty; from there on, the road suddenly wound down at an alarming angle.

At some point in the mid-seventies, before a full-blown economic crisis hit the family in 1878, the spousal glue that had held the McLoughlins together for more than two decades started giving way. Who knows how, or where, the parting first manifested itself? Maybe Eliza felt that the young children and imminent departure of the older girls demanded a greater presence at home and that William's wages, along with those of the two older boys, who by then were in a position to contribute more financially, would sustain the household. She gave up her position at the mill – or perhaps lost it – and never again occupied a waged position. A little later, when young Tommy, Mary and Elizabeth were of school-going age and could better fend for themselves, she set herself up as a hawker, probably of second-hand clothing, near the Smithfield Market.[24]

It was somewhere between 1871 and 1877 – the same crucial period building up to outright disaster – that Eliza began drinking more heavily. It came at a time when she was no longer being policed at home by her husband, or supervised at work by her spouse or employers. It was also the first time that she had access to limited funds that she could call her own. Independent-minded from an early age, she appears to have spun out of the emotional, physical and financial gravitational field of her husband. Her liking for alcohol and perceived neglect of the youngest children may, in turn, have contributed to another problem. At a time when wife-beating was thought to have assumed epidemic proportions in working-class Manchester, she came to sport two prominent scars – one on the upper lip, the other above her left eye.[25]

Assaults on Eliza at the hands of her husband, or unknown others when she was drunk or giving lip, did little for her dignity in the eyes of her sons. When they were small, Jack, William and Tommy had not been beyond Ellen and Sarah's attempts to control them, but now they were adolescent and operating in a culture brimming with contempt for females when it was not explicitly misogynistic.[26]

While the McLoughlins operated as a unit and were rooted in the mills, living cheek-by-jowl for 18 hours a day, it was the patriarch, William, who had done most to set the tone and tempo of life and work in the family. But once the discipline and surveillance at the mill became uncoupled from that at home, the boys slipped beyond the reach of their parents. Jack, tough, independent and with mill work behind him, had long since put down roots in local gang culture, living much of his life out on the streets; by the mid-1870s his two younger brothers were both in his thrall.

The brothers spent hours moving around cellars, stables, yards and workshops, constantly searching for anything of value to purloin. They looked on as small proprietors used the last of their craft-nous to try to stave off the rising tide of progress. As apprentice criminals they admired skills and tools for reasons of their own. Like the besieged artisans, they wanted craft skills, semi-secret insider knowledge and specialist tools that allowed men to follow an independent calling. Ancoats was simply a large, informal, industrial school or workshop that lads could drift in and out of at will. It was more of a factory than a home. William and Tommy, lacking the cunning and seniority-on-the-street of their hero, became increasingly feral. They were embroiled in mischief of the sort that mutated into juvenile crime. Much of their time was spent clambering about on canal barges and railway trucks moving raw materials around the factories, foundries and workshops of Ancoats. The rest was spent lurking in the unwholesome backwaters of the slums.

It was not long before Tommy, deeply under Jack's spell, was in trouble with the law for several minor felonies. But, in June 1875, aged 11, he was found guilty of larceny. The presiding officer, sensing that the boy was out of control and without effective supervision, sentenced him to a month's imprisonment and, on his release, to an additional five years in a local 'reformatory school'.[27] There was nothing unusual about it; it was 'standard procedure to commit virtually all second offenders to reformatory'. Between 1870 and 1891, over 5 000 children 'without positive parental influence' were sent to such institutions – industrial schools – in Manchester or neighbouring Salford.[28]

Just 18 months later, in December 1876, the family ship lost one of its heavy anchors. Ellen moved out and up. She married John Saxon, a spinner living off the Oldham Road whose family included an established Lancashire mill-owner. At about the same time, with William and Eliza still responsible for two minors under the age of 12 and the household income contracting, the parents finally separated. The youngest girls – Mary and Elizabeth – left with their mother. Thereafter, although the parents remained in loose contact, the family continued to drift apart at a rate determined by the life-cycle, labour market and social conditions in Ancoats. In June 1877, Eliza and several friends were arrested for drunken and riotous behaviour. Unable to stump up a five shilling fine, less than half a week's wages in the cotton mills, she was forced to spend a week in prison when nobody in the family was willing to come to her rescue financially.[29]

Her former husband's unwillingness to help was probably predictable; he was living on his own by then, back in Bengal Street. More telling, perhaps, was the refusal of Ellen or Sarah to help. The senior members of the disintegrating family, but more especially her socially established older daughters, had lost respect for their mother. So, too, had her sister, Ann, who for many years had held down a job in the mill while her own husband, John Scott, earned a pittance by 'scavenging' human waste.[30]

In 1878, penniless in a deepening recession and bitterly cold winter, Eliza, without visible means of support, moved in with Sarah in a small room on Factory Street.[31] At this low point her oldest boys, locked into the criminal sub-culture of Ancoats, drew her into a family-based scheme that relied on contacts at Smithfield Market to dispose of stolen goods. She ended up spending a six-month sentence in the Belle Vue Prison.[32]

Rooted in Catholic beliefs, Eliza continued to see herself as 'married' when she was released from prison in the summer of 1879. But husband William had abandoned all hope of her ever again being a wife or mother. The older girls wanted little to do with her, while the older boys and Tommy, set on paths from which there was seldom a return, also steered clear of her as far as was possible. Total rejection by those supposedly closest to her spoke of a woman enslaved to the public house; a person so far gone that there was little point in attempting to pursue a day-to-day relationship.

It may be that she, like others in a battered Irish cohort, had long been addicted to alcohol. If so, she may have genetically transmitted her predisposition to two of the children – Jack, who drank heavily for the larger part of his life, and Mary, who was set on her own course of drunkenness, criminality and prostitution.[33]

The end could have come from Mrs Gaskell's pen or that of any other Victorian novelist who had witnessed the advent of industrialisation and the birth of mass society. On a wintry morning, in February 1880, Eliza was admitted to the institution the urban poor dreaded above all others – the workhouse. At Chorlton-upon-Medlock, she made little sense and was said to be suffering from dementia – perhaps aggravated by alcohol and neglect. There, although closer to fifty than the 'fifty-five' years recorded against her name, she expired late the following year. Nobody came forward to claim the body and in all of Manchester's by-ways, markets, mills and pubs not a soul stirred to attend the funeral when she was laid to rest in the Union Cemetery on 22 August 1881.[34]

Viewed from across the Irish Sea and the desolation of the potato famine, far-off Ancoats offered a glimmer of hope, beckoning refugees towards the chance for a new life. It drew them in, promising the bare necessities of food, clothing and shelter. But once spread beneath its blackened mantle, it eliminated light, spreading darkness, leaving most flailing about in poverty and squalor. Eliza would not be the only one in her family to die a forsaken, lonely, death unattended by friend or family.

CHAPTER FOUR

The Makings of the Man

AN ANCOATS YOUTH

— 1850–1880 —

All civilisation has from time to time becomes a thin crust over a volcano of revolution.

HAVELOCK ELLIS

Like most mill workers, William McLoughlin spent much of his 'free time' – after work, on weekends, and especially in the winter months – in the warmth of public houses.[1] With every fifth person in the neighbourhood Irish, the pubs were prime sites for immigrants to explore their origins and ideas about the Old Country, contemplate their current circumstances or wonder where they were all bound for. Back at home, in cellars and rooms, fathers built on pub talk, fostering ethnic camaraderie or stoking old clan rivalries, to convey their own childhood experiences to any visitors or their wide-eyed offspring.

Given a willingness to present himself as Irish later in life, young Jack McLoughlin must have been reasonably acquainted with the family history as relayed through anecdote, folk myth or personal experience. It would have been unusual for the son of a first-generation immigrant *not* to have been briefed about perfidious Albion, or why it was that so many Irish laymen and priests had been forced into exile in Catholic Belgium, France and Spain, or sought economic refuge in America or elsewhere. The good life, it seemed, always had to be sought abroad, far away from England on remote frontiers. Irish history, as absorbed by a boy born 'English' by circumstance, raised doubts about the role of Britain and empire and divided his primary political loyalties.[2]

Unless William McLoughlin had led an unimaginably sheltered life back in Inishowen, his reservations about Britain's role in the wider world, and celebration of republican America's support for radical Irish nationalism, would have been illustrated with personalised and localised accounts of 'English' oppression in Donegal. So, too, would stories about customs and excise men and police in search of agrarian secret societies, smugglers, pirates and *poteen* distillers. Dark tales about informers and spies would have retained a certain relevance even when transposed into the context of contemporary Manchester.[3]

In an era when it was assumed, sometimes incorrectly, that to be Irish was to be Catholic, Jack was moulded into both. The boy was packed off to the denominational school, at St Anne's, at an early age. There, under the guidance of Father Peter Liptrott, nuns and priests, quick to resort to physical punishment, ensured that their charges attended mass and mastered the three Rs that formed the basis of a rudimentary education. The lad's earliest school experiences may have contributed to his insistence later in life on maintaining a distinction between messengers and messages. An almost visceral dislike of priests and an unusual sensitivity in the presence of nuns was offset by an underlying acceptance of Catholicism. His readiness to accept formal instruction while entertaining misgivings about the teachers was reinforced by the times. Most of his primary education took place during the decade in which post-famine, anti-Catholic and anti-Irish prejudices peaked in Lancashire.[4] Any positive shaping of a composite Catholic and Irish identity at school would have been reinforced negatively by external forces out on the local streets before he was 10 years old.

In late 1867 – when he was eight years old – three members of the radical Irish Republican Brotherhood, recently returned from the American Civil War and suspected of furthering the nationalist cause, were arrested in Manchester. The following day the police van in which they were being transported was attacked by enraged Irishmen, an officer killed, and a couple of the detainees set free. Three of those responsible for the rescue of the Fenians were arrested, convicted and publicly hanged. The Irish community was in uproar and, each year thereafter, the 'Manchester Martyrs' were honoured with a street parade. If these events did not register in the young McLoughlin's mind at the time, he would have been reminded of them as an adult by an anti-clerical friend, John O'Brien, who claimed to have been the brother of one of the martyrs.[5]

Anger about the martyrs was compounded by developments pre-dating the hangings. In 1850, outraged Protestants cast England as a victim of 'papal aggression' when the Church of Rome restored its religious hierarchy in a realm cleansed of Catholics by Henry VIII. Resentment about an initiative from the Vatican festered among religious fanatics. Within months of the 'martyrs' being hanged, a 'no popery' Protestant demagogue, William Murphy, passed through Manchester and neighbouring centres, giving rise to violent street protests.[6] These and other, similar, events could not have failed to imprint themselves on the minds of youngsters in and around Ancoats. In later life McLoughlin often cast himself as Catholic even when it may not have benefited him directly.

In 1871, at age 12, when the family was living in Willoughby's Court and beginning to unravel, the lad was still dividing his day between school and work in the mills. Despite his father's laxness in ensuring school attendance, Jack seems to have been a reasonably conscientious pupil and enjoyed reading if not writing.[7] Indeed, some of his later anti-imperialist bravado, rebelliousness and cussedness may have been pollinated via self-directed reading during early adolescence.

Much of the schoolboy literature of the time centred on heroic tales of eighteenth-century brigands, highwaymen and pirates.[8] Even in deprived Ancoats the youthful imagination could be fired by weighty historical and fictional figures. In 1864, the most frequently borrowed books in the local library included Sir Walter Scott's tale of the 'Scottish Robin Hood', *Rob Roy,* and GA Sala's *Strange Adventures of Captain Dangerous.* The latter, an English super-hero of his time, was 'a soldier, a sailor, a merchant, a spy, a slave among the Moors, and a Bashaw in the service of the Grand Turk' whose life – like those of the emigrating Irish – played itself out on a global stage.[9] Like Jack Dangerous, whose first name he shared albeit for a different reason, Jack McLoughlin was raised to take matters of honour seriously, travelled extensively and lived in a world boasting many real-life brigands, poachers and highwaymen.

Romanticised accounts of deeds of derring-do in far-off places may have offset the grim reality of shuffling between a rudimentary schooling and the awfulness of labour in the mills. Only rarely is a child incapable of forging a connection between an exciting, imaginary, world and the harshness of the 'here and now'. Even grimy Ancoats, locked into the ever-expanding empire, could raise questions about what was happening at the far ends of the earth. The very fluff that littered the mill floor – cotton – was imported from Egypt, India and the United States. Warehouses filled with finished goods were linked by canal to Liverpool and every ocean across the globe. Even Lancashire lads could dream.

But for boys living on the streets, waiting to be admitted to the murky interior of the public house, coupling the imagination to slum realities was not always easy or socially desirable. In July 1870, when Jack was 11, France declared war on Prussia following a disputed claim as to who should occupy the Spanish throne. Great continental battles fought by rival armies, ended in the defeat of France and the collapse of the Second Empire. But, during the 10 months the conflict endured, the war inflamed religious tensions in the city's working-class neighbourhoods. In Angel Meadow, Ancoats and New Cross, where the McLoughlins lived in Willoughby's Court, street battles erupted between Protestant schoolboys – self-styled 'Germans' – and Catholic rivals presenting themselves as 'Frenchmen'. The resulting 'Rochdale Road War' raged for months with boys between 10 and 18 using boots, fists, knives, pistols, swords, sticks and stones to procure what they thought of as lasting victories.[10]

This displaced religious rivalry was a precursor to the more serious, longer-lived and largely secular street battles that raged in Ancoats and elsewhere between 1870 and the mid-1880s. Antisocial 'scuttlers' composed largely, but not exclusively, of adolescent males formed part of a city-wide, pan-tribal youth cult centred on a so-called 'Kingdom of the Rough'. Elements of old rural English and Celtic cultures including faction-fighting, notions of honour, oath-taking and secret societies blended seamlessly into features of new urban life. Flashy attire, distinctive hairstyles, sexual preco-ciousness and the use of knives or buckles at the end of leather belts were the hallmarks of groupings enforcing territorial integrity. Many of the most feared gangs took their names from streets they lived on – Alum, Bengal, Pollard and Prussia.

The local constabulary struggled to deal with assaults arising from spontaneous clashes, or to prevent pre-arranged battles replete with set pieces that gave rise to horrendous wounds and, sometimes, fatal injuries. In court 'scuttlers' convicted of felonies ranging from assault and murder through to robbery and theft underscored their disdain for officialdom by hurling invective at Magistrates. It was as if entire sections of the city were caught up in a generation-bound, testosterone-fuelled, civil war without end in which the marginal and the poor battled one another to a standstill in order to discover an elusive collective, usually masculine, dignity.[11]

Joining a gang of scuttlers was not optional; in Ancoats it ensured every-day survival on the streets. Only by becoming gang members could young males, with or without escorted females, be guaranteed safe passage through the pathways of an urban jungle. Like wary animals, they had to display dis-tinctive apparel, pace, posture and menace when moving about and, when challenged, had to respond in the dialect manifesting appropriate attitude and accent. Scuttling was, in part, a generational, militaristic adaptation to alienated industrial life in the age of imperialism. And, as with Captain Dangerous, it helped to reconcile the squalid here-and-now with the far-off kingdoms of the imagination. Male camaraderie forged in street battles prepared young men for life in the armed forces and contemporary ob-servers noted how scuttlers who joined the army often became excellent soldiers. What they failed to notice, because it was not immediately visible, was how scuttling could also prepare boys for a far-off life of brigandage, highway robbery or piracy.[12]

Scuttling drew out the identities-in-the-making and sexual preferences of young adults; most of it unequivocally heterosexual in nature. Flashily dressed 'roughs' formed an integral part of 'monkey parades' along the

Oldham Road where it was hoped that sexual partners could be procured through 'clicking' during chance encounters. Although largely good-natured, such promenading occasionally gave rise to vulgar behaviour characterised by lewd and obscene exchanges.[13] Unbridled aggression of this sort led one feminist critic of the day to speculate how scuttling could be linked back to a culture of male domination and wife-beating in working-class homes, if not outright misogyny.[14]

There may have been a further, hidden dimension to scuttling and sexuality that could not be explored publicly at a time when the trial of the most notorious Irishman of the epoch, Oscar Wilde, had not yet rendered such speculation unavoidable.[15] At the height of empire and its attendant militarism, Victorian society sought simultaneously to prescribe intense male bonding and proscribe homosexuality.[16] Ferociously masculine in their public displays of bonding and sexuality, it is possible that some scuttlers may have seen excessive celebrations of manliness give way to affections that culminated in the ultimate horror of Victorian society – homosexuality of the sort associated with the navy.[17]

Far-fetched enough to appear ridiculous at first glance, this possibility nevertheless deserves closer examination. The word 'scuttle' – to sink one's own ship by deliberately holing it, or opening the seacocks to let in salt water – was unambiguously naval in origin. The term, used literally, had obviously positive connotations for bands of young men who went about 'sinking' opponents so close in social terms that they could have been 'one's own'. Indeed, that was precisely the point, to draw a sharp distinction between social elements that poverty otherwise rendered indistinguishable. But admiration for the men of the fleet went further.

Young scuttlers adopted bell-bottom trousers as part of their uniforms and the standard greeting or challenge put to male rivals about to be engaged in street battle was: 'Are you a sailor?' Being asked whether or not you were a 'sailor' was perhaps not as unproblematic as it seems. The salutation 'Hello Sailor!' may already have been acquiring the first tinge of ambiguity that saw it more clearly linked to camp or homosexual behaviour in the twentieth century.[18] Joseph Hillyard, perhaps the most notorious scuttler of the day, sang out 'Hello sailor!' before plunging his knife between the shoulder blades of an already retreating adversary. It is difficult to reconcile this greeting or his subsequent action – clearly fuelled by pure rage – with a 'respectful' greeting for a 'naval' rival.[19]

Jack McLoughlin, who could no more have avoided Ancoats' scuttling sub-culture than he could breathing, retained a preference for male company, and especially that of younger men, throughout his life. There is no record of his ever having had a noteworthy, loving, female relationship either as an adolescent, as a young adult during his time in the armed forces, or in any of the many other male-only settings he sought out.

The hyper-masculinity of scuttling was of a piece with blood-letting in other elements of Mancunian working-class culture. Fighting in public among adult men outside pubs and in the streets may have differed in scale from that of the scuttlers – being, besides, linked to alcohol consumption. But it, too, was often bound up in real or imaginary notions of 'honour' and 'manliness'.[20] The English and Irish both had a liking for hand-to-hand combat which had served them well in faction fights and the Napoleonic Wars. In urban industrial Lancashire, where to fight with bared knuckles was to 'mill', fisticuffs was the poor man's version of duelling.[21]

The informal grinding of opponents into submission fed into and off other, more carefully staged, formal contests. The latter emerged when bare-knuckle 'prize fighting' under the London Rules of 1839 and 1853 eventually gave way to 'boxing', but it took a long time. The Marquess of Queensberry's Rules, devised in the 1860s, were only widely employed in the final decade of the nineteenth century. In Manchester, where 'hard men' were much admired, there was an upsurge in prize fighting in the 1860s, at a time when young Jack was most impressionable. To add to the excitement, many of these illegal contests were staged in secret, behind closed doors in Deansgate, or beyond the city limits.[22] As an adult, Jack McLoughlin retained his interest in a sport which, besides having a powerful Irish component to its history, frequently appealed to more charismatic underworld elements who were involved in organised crime.

McLoughlin's adult interest went beyond betting on the outcome of fights. Like many others, he was fascinated by the social grammar of manly conduct when questions of honour and reputation were at stake. The notion of competing forces being equally balanced, of the need for a fight to be 'fair', was ingrained in him from an early age. Some of the groundwork for this may have derived from scuttling. Street battles throughout Manchester had their own rituals and unwritten rules, among them the idea that – other than the ubiquitous belts and buckles – weapons, including blades and pistols, did not make for 'fair' contests.

In practice, rivals seldom hesitated to take unfair advantage of an opponent. 'Time and again, coroners, magistrates, judges complained that the use of knives in fights was "cowardly" and simply not English.'[23] Thus, at the high tide of British imperialism, when firearms were freely employed in mowing down 'the natives' in huge numbers at a safe distance, the use of the blade at close quarters was associated with supposedly backward 'Mediterranean' cultures. In Athens and in Naples, peasants newly off the land and excluded from an aristocratic duelling culture that employed expensive rapiers to settle questions of honour used knives to settle personal disputes or reputational issues.[24] McLoughlin, who was briefly exposed to urban life around Mediterranean ports as a young sailor, eschewed the use of a knife in personal conflict.

In the Ancoats of his youth the use of firearms was also frowned upon by those entrusted with governing the unruly underclasses. But here, too, everyday realities were already overtaking values handed down from the age of duelling, when settling matters of honour through personal confrontation was *de rigueur* among members of the upper classes. Locally, pistols had already been used during the Rochdale Road War between the 'French' and the 'Germans' in 1870.[25] In an age marked by imperial expansion and techniques of mass production, it was difficult to keep revolvers and, to a lesser extent, rifles from militant nationalists, including the Irish, or any violently inclined working-class criminals.

★ ★ ★

In 1867, when McLoughlin was eight years old, Irish men and women with nationalist sympathies were excited to hear about a series of bold Fenian initiatives taking place across the country. At Chester Castle, 20 miles south of Liverpool, the army had to be called out to prevent Irish radicals from seizing an arsenal of 30 000 rifles while, in London, 12 residents were killed by an explosion triggered at Clerkenwell Prison.[26] Guns and dynamite figured prominently in the dreams and imagination of the Irish community as well as in the mind of McLoughlin, who, as an adult, was always fascinated by the destructive power of both. In Ancoats, at the time, a five or 10-minute walk was all that separated the heart of the slum he lived in from any number of 'rifle-ranges' and 'shooting galleries' around the Smithfield Market on Shude Hill.[27] Captain Dangerous, man of fiction, could be linked to real, live weapons.

For those recently off the land, or those so inclined by personality – and there were many of both – there was also plenty of animal blood on show in the backrooms of pubs or at other, nearby, secret locations. Despite disapproval from on high, badger-baiting, cock- and dog-fighting were standard offerings at venues disclosed only by word of mouth and at the last moment so as to avoid police attention. Wily publicans sought to attract the drinking and betting populace through carefully staged 'ratting' contests. Set against a stopwatch, dogs, matched by weight, were released into pits swarming with rodents and encouraged to kill as many rats as possible in the time nominated.[28] A taste for these working-class pastimes proved enduring for many men in McLoughlin's cohort.

But beneath the aggression and horror of industrialising Lancashire, one or two of the comparatively gentle streams that would eventually flow freely into Edwardian culture were already becoming evident. By the 1860s, athletics and foot racing were beginning to attract a limited following among some of the genteel youth, while some elderly workers engaged in even more innocuous pastimes such as pigeon racing.[29]

The large-scale shift in working-class culture, from following 'blood sports' to participating in or watching organised team sport, only manifested itself much later. The rules for rugby and football were codified in the 1860s and 1870s, laying the foundations for the mass followings that

emerged with the launching of organised professional sport in the 1880s
and 1890s. It was also only around then that working lads' clubs, led by
community activists, helped deflect street aggression and scuttling into socially acceptable channels.[30] For Jack McLoughlin's cohort, however, it was
too little, too late. They were part of a lost generation doomed to experience the worst brutalities of the older order and few of the benefits of the
coming dispensation. They had to dream of getting out of crushing poverty
via other distractions.

Saturday night in the music halls, including in Ancoats, offered a half-way
house between the realities of everyday life and a romanticised idea of what
a better life might be. 'Exotic' dances provided glimpses of attractive women
who, by prevailing standards, were scantily dressed and capable of attracting scuttlers and working men who dreamt of closing the gap between the
fantasy world on stage and the street outside. Twilight visions, conjured up
for the young, the single or the intoxicated, competed with more numerous acts of humour, resignation and self-mockery. Miming, music and lyrics
held a mirror to everyday life, deflecting the inescapable cruelties of the
here-and-now.[31]

Like most slum-dwellers, the men and women of Ancoats were not easily
deluded. They knew only too well that it was money, rather than the mean-
derings of the mind, that offered them their best chance of shaking off the
monster of poverty that was dogging them. More than almost anything else,
it was cash that they yearned for. The working classes invaded and occupied
every space where chance intersected with human design in an attempt to
bend fortune to their will. Despite their own historical misfortunes the Irish,
peasants-turned-workers, were among the greatest believers in luck – 'the
ever-present, glittering possibility of unearned or undeserved benefit'. It was,
they thought, 'the natural coefficient of social and economic limitations'.[32]

The luck of the Irish was proverbial precisely because they had had so
little of it. For them the surest way of short-circuiting luck and money
was through gambling. For the Irish immigrants coming from a tradition
of country fairs and outdoor sport, the Industrial Revolution and urban
Lancashire became bound together in ways that shaped the broader-based,
emerging 'English' working-class culture for decades to come.

Irish workers – mostly Catholic and largely free of the strictures deriving from the Protestant ethic – would willingly bet on just about anything, including the outcomes of blood sports held in secret settings. But it was the outdoor relief that came with attendance at horse-races that appealed most to those who spent their days trapped in factories and mills.[33] Liverpool, Manchester and nearby Salford, where meetings at Kersal Moor pre-dated the industrial age, saw an upsurge in commercial betting and horse-racing in the late 1840s. A new course laid out at Castle Irwell in 1847 lasted only two decades, until 1867, when racing moved to Weaste.[34] But the growing popularity of horse-racing troubled Britain's reforming middle classes who sought to regulate it through new legislation. The Betting Houses Act of 1853 aimed to prevent proprietors from taking wagers in public houses and from bookmakers and runners operating within the mills. In 1879, a new challenge arose with the transmission of race results via the telegraph.[35]

Liverpool and Aintree, famously, became home to the Grand National and steeplechasing. But it was Manchester, overseen by a 'racecourse company' and an even larger number of race-goers, that dominated flat racing. The high point in the year, the 'Manchester Races', coincided with the old English pagan celebration of Summer's Day, which was extended to incorporate 'Whitsun Week'. For three days each year, seven weeks after Easter, Manchester emptied as a 'canvas city' arose on a loop in the River Irwell two miles north of the city and unrestrained celebration supplanted industrial routine. By the late 1860s, horse-racing was replacing blood sports and prize fighting as a focal point in working-class culture. In the 1870s there were constant complaints about the throngs of people hanging about bookmakers' premises, and by 1883 a Manchester daily, *The Sporting Chronicle*, boasted 30 000 readers.[36]

Whitsun week presented the police with problems that went beyond illicit gambling centred on the Smithfield Market.[37] As at most other places and occasions where the privileged found themselves within arm's length of the poor, alcohol and cash contributed to a more relaxed carnival-like atmosphere at the races. Mildly mocking behaviour by elements of the so-called 'respectable' working class hinted at a brief inversion of the social order, but out on the margins could give way to outright criminality and immorality. Flashily dressed bookmakers and their flaunting wives were a subject of wonderment for those with modest winnings and of outright derision among losing punters. Pickpockets, petty thieves and prostitutes often engaged in predatory behaviour of an amateurish sort and, by the turn of the century, racecourses were being frequented by gangs of professional criminals.[38]

At some point in his mid-teens, and cash-strapped, the oldest McLoughlin son developed a passion for gambling, horses and racecourses that lasted a lifetime. Unlike many of his peers, however, he was never under the illusion that luck alone would provide him with a windfall. A hard-headed pragmatist, he visited betting shops only after he had raised cash through other means and never saw bookmakers – whom he viewed as parasites and legitimate targets – as a way of making money.

The racecourse may have provided him with his first glimpse of the industrial age's new brand of urban desperadoes, some of whom might now be classified as psychopaths. In this respect, the Habitual Criminals Act of 1869, which allowed the police to take photographs and keep detailed descriptions of those who had been found guilty of more than one serious offence, formed something of a landmark.[39] Around 1876, when McLoughlin was 17 and the likes of 'Captain Dangerous' had already been relegated to deeper memory, two criminals in particular seem to have imprinted themselves on his mind and those of many in his cohort.

Charlie Peace, son of a lion-tamer, a picaresque burglar and flawed folk hero, was born in nearby Sheffield. After an industrial accident in which a shard of metal shattered his kneecap, Peace took a year off to teach himself to walk in a manner that disguised his disability. But then he somehow also lost a finger. Damaged or lost limbs intrigued him and his injuries evoked sympathy among his many female conquests. He fashioned himself a false arm, with a hole running down the middle, that allowed him to perform various tricks, including manipulating a fork.

In 1876, Peace murdered a policeman during a botched burglary in Manchester and then returned to his home town where he murdered a lover's husband. Suitably disguised, he moved to London, where in 1878 he was put on trial for burglary and the attempted murder of yet another policeman. Betrayed by a female consort, he was sent to Sheffield to stand trial for the earlier murder but, as the train neared Worksop, he persuaded the warders to open a carriage window and leapt from the moving train. Injured and quickly recaptured, he was made to stand trial, convicted and then executed in February 1879.[40]

Born on the Rochdale Road, Bob Horridge was as at home in Ancoats as the next man. In 1876, as an ambitious young burglar, he stripped the contents of shops belonging to a furrier, silk merchant and jeweller. Two years later he was ready for more ambitious projects and fixed on the weekly payroll stored in the safe of an office attached to a textile mill in nearby Bradford. At 4.30 am one Saturday, two associates staged a diversionary fight outside the factory gates when the caretaker did his rounds to stoke a boiler. During the caretaker's absence the safe was hoisted onto a waiting cart and driven away. When the police eventually recovered it from a mill reservoir, they discovered that the back had been removed and the £600 it contained was missing.[41]

Bob Horridge and Charlie Peace both bore the imprimatur of the Industrial Revolution. An apprenticeship as a blacksmith helped Horridge in his safe-cracking exploits and Peace, initially trained in a rolling mill, remained fascinated by anything mechanical. Moreover, both moved through the Midlands at a time when special machine-made tools manufactured in Birmingham were used by professional burglars. Few of these lessons were lost on deprived slum-dwellers. But, as a young man with a romantic twist, McLoughlin was perhaps most taken with Peace's train-jumping exploits and Horridge's safe-lifting template. Like old Captain Dangerous, they embodied audacity.

There was no element of a childhood and adolescence spent in mid-Victorian Ancoats that led ineluctably to a life of crime. Indeed, a large number of youngsters appear, miraculously, to have avoided full-scale collisions with laws set on producing a new and disciplined working class fit to serve the empire. But there was also almost nothing in slum life that did not predispose a young man born into a poverty-stricken immigrant family to explore other, irregular, ways of supplementing family or personal income.

In retrospect, it is hardly surprising that several in the McLoughlin family turned to crime. What does surprise is how long it took to manifest itself. It was the economic downturn of 1877–79 that destroyed the mould of a working family.

᥿᥿᥿

CHAPTER FIVE

Criminal Cousins:
Economic Survival and Social Capital

ANCOATS
— 1875–1880 —

Blood is thicker than water, and when one's in trouble
best to seek out a relative's open arms.
EURIPIDES

On 18 February 1878, Jack McLoughlin, going on 20, made his criminal debut in the Magistrate's Court. It was unlikely to have been
his first encounter with the law even if it was the first recorded. He was
found guilty of having stolen a pair of boots belonging to 16-year-old James
Jarrett, a stoker, and sentenced to three months' imprisonment.[1] It was a
harsh sentence for the midwinter theft of a pair of boots by a first offender.
But McLoughlin's friends probably knew that he had long been a gang
member and took a more sanguine view of proceedings. Three months in
Belle Vue may have given him the chance to reflect on the company he
was keeping because the excursions that followed relied far more heavily,
though never exclusively, on extended family members.

The Ancoats underworld McLoughlin operated in centred on what,
at first glance, appeared to be an unlikely socio-economic stratum. It was
not one that contemporary observers, interested in understanding the

emergence of mid-Victorian rookeries, would have focused on. For the most part its members were not drawn from the chronically unemployed, the hopelessly alienated, or the poorest of the poor. Most were nominally 'Irish' and Catholic, born between 1855 and 1865. They formed part of a co-hort raised just as the first round of educational, sanitary and social reforms in Manchester were starting to have a discernable impact on the quality of working-class life. Some came from families in which the parents had sepa-rated, or a spouse had died. Most were in their late teens or early twenties when first convicted of serious offences. Many were sons of craftsmen or small shopkeepers – the offspring of members of the 'labour aristocracy' or the so-called 'petit bourgeoisie'.

As small children they received a rudimentary education in church schools, but that did not allow religion to influence their later choice of criminal gangs, which were overwhelmingly secular. Literate almost with-out exception, they seem to have retained a passing interest in books and reading even after leaving school, one or two going so far as to work for printers. Most, however, had their first real taste of work at a tender age in the closely supervised surroundings of factory or mill. Judging from their later choice of occupations they almost all left industry with a strong dislike of routine, machine-paced and manual labour, preferring instead to find positions as clerks, hawkers, porters or warehousemen, positions that were physically demanding in other ways.

Strong enough to have fought their corner as 'scuttlers' in their mid-teens, they later chose, for the most part, to avoid unnecessary physical violence and the use of guns or knives. Their primary interest lay in acquir-ing property, equipment, goods or materials, which relied on good intel-ligence systems and stealth rather than raw muscle-power. Most of their targets were decided on with the help of disaffected insiders, employees willing to steal from their masters or the proprietors of shops. In many cases the quantity of goods stolen pointed to a distinct entrepreneurial streak in thieves who enjoyed easy access to illegal distribution networks that included pawnbrokers, professional fences, rival shopkeepers or the many hawkers around Smithfield Market.

Unwilling to be consumed as so much working-class fodder, McLoughlin's cohort bent skills lifted from the factories and mills to shape for themselves a lifestyle and sub-culture reminiscent of other pre-industrial criminal fraternities, and, much later, exported them to the frontiers of an expanding world.[2] Dressing with care, they maintained their identity as individuals, but because of their need to sell-on stolen goods, they were forced to shy away from unnecessary exposure and therefore also placed considerable store on security, privacy and trust. Like scuttlers who lurked in the social waters beneath them, or the craftsmen in Friendly Societies who floated above, they maintained their own codes of honour with oaths and other secret practices.[3] The underlying problem they faced was how best to maintain their individual identities without revealing fully their collective enterprise.

Antisocial scuttlers were all too visible on the streets – indeed, their *raison d'être* was to be a public rather than a private menace. Manchester's Masons and Oddfellows, quintessentially convivial, respectable social groupings, held street parades or wore insignia displayed on jacket lapels. Criminal fraternities, by contrast, could not parade their members publicly. What was needed was a sign that could simultaneously indicate their exclusion from mainstream society, yet mark their inclusion in part of the underworld. The solution lay in a system of partially concealed tattoos; markings plain enough to be without obvious meaning to outsiders, yet visible and distinctive enough to be recognised by insiders within the wider criminal fraternity.

The use of tattoos harked back to the dawn of humanity but received an enormous fillip in the British Isles after the eighteenth-century voyages of exploration. On his return, Captain Cook reported on the exotic body-markings that he and his crew had encountered in the societies of the South Seas. After that tattoos became a 'travelling sign' on 'homeless bodies'. They were favoured by those who had voluntarily undertaken long journeys – including pilgrims, soldiers and sailors – or by those who had been moved involuntarily, such as slaves or transported convicts.[4]

Tattoos were acceptable in many circles of Victorian society. Sailors often had markings on their arms, and given the appeal that the senior service held for scuttlers, it was perhaps predictable that they, too, would sport prominent body-markings. Many teenagers used tattoos to proclaim personalised declarations of love. Others chose objects with wider meanings to be recognised by – such as anchors, which had biblical roots and symbolised hope. The members of McLoughlin's gang, however, took a small blue dot as their imprimatur. It will be recalled that Jack's father, William, sported a similar mark above his right eyebrow.

Seemingly meaningless, the blue dot was said to refer to Ali Baba's 'Forty Thieves' and had first been noted in London's Millbank Penitentiary by Henry Mayhew, in the late 1850s.[5] In Ancoats, 20 years later, less prominent marks included a dot on the forearm, concealed by shirtsleeves, or on the webbing between the thumb and the index fingers, and in one case on the eyelid, where it was briefly visible only when the eye was closed.[6] Remarkably, such tattooed blue dots continued to be displayed by male members of the English underclass well into the late twentieth century.[7]

The name – if it had one – of the brotherhood McLoughlin belonged to remained a secret and was never recorded. Its core, consisting of between six and a dozen members spread across Ancoats, all bore the mark of Ali Baba – Jack's was a blue dot on his left forearm – an exotic touch Captain Dangerous would have approved of. Blue Dots operated in pairs, but when necessary were willing to draw in selected outsiders without markings. In two instances that we know of their numbers were bolstered by drawing in members of the extended McLoughlin family. Likewise, the name of the leader of the gang was never revealed – but it was almost certainly Jack McLoughlin. The leading members of the original Blue Dot gang remained closely associated long after their Ancoats exploits were done, and, over a decade later, continued to work together abroad. Manchester, like other northern cities, exported not only finished goods but criminal networks too.

★ ★ ★

Jack's friend John William (JW) Brown, born in 1858, was the youngest of three sons bearing the first name of their father.[8] The patriarch, John James Brown, born in London, came from a Catholic family in King's Lynn, Norfolk, but in 1850 married Ann Cooney, an Irish lass from Castlebar,

County Mayo. A self-made as well as a self-centred man, Brown senior started out as a confectioner on Union Street, but his ambition led him elsewhere. At some point during the small window of opportunity that presented itself between 1852, when the state compiled its first register of chemists, and 1868, by which time entry into the profession was governed by examination, Brown set himself up as a pharmacist. After 1861 his chemist's shop at 187 Mill Street, where it stood for over 30 years conveniently close by the hospital, became an institution in Ancoats.[9]

But if Brown's chemist's business was steady, then the lives of his nearest were anything but. When his first wife, Ann, died unexpectedly – seemingly during childbirth, in 1862 – three boys and a baby daughter were left without a mother.[10] Within weeks of the bereavement he married Margaret Cooney, Ann's older sister. This meant that by the time that JW was five years old, he had lost his mother only to discover that his aunt had become his stepmother. This may have affected John William more than it did his older brothers, both of whom went on to hold down steady jobs in the mill. The little fellow, however, was sent to a Catholic school where he learnt to read and write, but at home his space was cluttered by two younger sisters; one, a step-sister, the daughter of Margaret Cooney. The Brown household, once dominated by a narcissistic patriarch, suddenly became more female-orientated.

Precisely how the new Mrs Brown ran her home, or how it may have shaped JW, is unknown, but a few things stand out from his adult life. First, like his friend Jack McLoughlin, he never had a long-term relationship with a woman and was still unmarried in his mid-thirties. Secondly, if JW had reservations about women in general, then his attitude to prostitutes – as expressed at the time of the infamous Whitechapel slayings, in 1888 – spoke of misogyny.[11] His views may not have been helped by the fact that, at about the same time, his father, who by then was close to 80 and had outlived Margaret, got married for a third time, this time to a woman about 25 years his junior.[12]

In keeping with his father's own ambitions, JW never laboured in the cotton mills or signed up for a workshop-based trade. In 1871, aged 14, he was an unskilled assistant – a 'helper' – in the Percival Vickers British and

Foreign Flint Glass Works on Union Street, hard by the Rochdale Canal. At the same time his close friend Jack McLoughlin, two years his junior, was working in the nearby cotton mills.

At about that time JW embarked on a criminal apprenticeship, binding himself to a Blue Dot a year older than himself, Charles Beswick. In autumn 1872, amidst a buoyant local economy, there was a rash of attacks on errand boys delivering cash, messages and small articles between businesses and warehouses. One of the pair's victims, Robert Seddon, was relieved of sixpence and items worth a few shillings. The Magistrate, responding to a 'moral panic' about assaults on errand boys, or detecting unusual menace in lads who could do with immediate checking, took a very dim view of the crime. Despite having taken the precaution of lying about their ages so as to avoid the full wrath of the law, the adolescents were sentenced to four days' hard labour each and, thereafter, 10 strokes each to be inflicted, 'in private', with a birch rod.[13]

The experience may have discouraged the chemist's son for a time, but proved ineffectual in the long run. JW spent most of his free time with the Mackey boys, who, like their immigrant Irish father, worked in the nearby mills. In June 1876, 18-year-old JW and Joseph Mackey were sentenced to a month's hard labour each for theft. Months later, in spring 1877, John William and John Mackey stole two books from one JH Wells. Mackey was acquitted but JW was sent down for two months, with hard labour.

When autumn set in that year, JW got himself a position as a stoker with the Sheffield & Lincolnshire Railway Company. It put him in the ideal position to perform the classic Blue Dot manoeuvre of stealing from an employer. In January 1878, he and a new partner, Francis Howell, were convicted for stealing two hundredweight of coal destined for onward selling to a third party and sentenced to two months' imprisonment each with hard labour. Just four months later, in June 1878, JW was put away for another month's hard labour for stealing eight shillings and eight pence from yet another employer.[14] Ancoats and Manchester were becoming too small to easily accommodate JW.

In the interim, Charles Beswick, who had got a reasonably good Church of England school education before going on to work half-days in the mills, had not been idle. The son of a self-employed carter, he aspired to better things in life and had found himself a position as a clerk in a small local business. The proprietor either did not see, or did not understand, the significance of the blue dot tucked into the webbing between the thumb and first finger of the left hand of the new employee. In mid-1877, Beswick was sentenced to two months' hard labour in Strangeways Prison for having stolen £10 from 'his master'.[15]

In terms of age and fighting prowess, if not in underworld status, the most senior member of the Blue Dots was Joseph Wild. Wild, whose surname evokes the image of Jonathan Wild, the gang leader and highwayman in Fielding's eponymous satire, did come from Ancoats' lowest socio-economic stratum, but, perhaps significantly, was not a local. Born in Oldham, in 1850, from a broken home and possibly illegitimate, Wild, too, had acquired basic literacy in a Church of England school. In Manchester his career as a scut-tler, like that of many in his cohort, was not recorded, but a legacy of street-fighting was there for all to see – two missing front teeth, scars between the fingers of the right hand and scars on the lower back consonant with belt-and-buckle attacks. His primary training may have been as a pickpocket, and for many years he eluded the law. But, in 1876, at the ripe old age of 26, he and a partner were sentenced to three months in Strangeways for the theft of three handkerchiefs. It may have been meetings with fences dealing in second-hand clothing – possibly even with Eliza McLoughlin – that first brought him to the attention of JW Brown and Jack McLoughlin. Twelve months later, in 1877, he was locked up again – for a week, for drunken and riotous behaviour.[16]

By the late 1870s and approaching age 20, McLoughlin's world was be-coming more centred on the Blue Dots, many of whom, like him, were still struggling to master their criminal craft. He did not, however, want for other friends who, although not identifiable as Blue Dots, later went on to become successful professional criminals. Among those whom he knew and trusted while still in Ancoats, and who later worked closely with him abroad, three in particular are worthy of note.

Charles Harding was the son of a tailor and may have been yet another of the hidden threads that linked the Blue Dots and junior associates to the wider clothing trade around the Smithfield Market. Like the others, Harding avoided heavy manual labour and, by his late teens and early twenties, was working as a clerk in an office. His paperwork, however, was surpassed by an interest in burglary, office and store-breaking, and years later, half-way across the world, he went on to become one of Jack McLoughlin's most loyal and trusted lieutenants.[17]

McLoughlin may have met Tommy Whelan, a man who in later years brought raw muscle-power to his safe-lifting operations on the frontier, via his young brother. Whelan, like Tommy McLoughlin, had been sentenced to a month's imprisonment for larceny in 1872 and gone on to serve a full five-year stint in industrial school. In 1877, Whelan and his father celebrated his release by assaulting a police constable, for which they received four and three months' imprisonment respectively.[18]

The third man, a specialist of sorts – George Fisher – was never as close to McLoughlin as were Harding and Whelan. Born in 1858, George was the son of a foundry worker who died young. As a boy he was sent out to work in an Ancoats baking powder manufactory, where he went on to become a semi-skilled worker with an interest in chemical reactions. In later years he was more interested in illegal gold-refining.[19]

Looking back it is difficult to arrive at an accurate assessment of the successes and failures of these Blue Dots and their associates. The archival record – comprising police and prison registers – is stacked against them. The files list only criminal failures, leaving no clue as to hidden successes. Even so the failures – low points, where a lack of professionalism intersected with reasonably competent policing – may have left the gang feeling slightly insecure at a time when the authorities had their hands full. In the late 1860s Manchester had a crime rate of 1.86 – nearly two crimes for every citizen – 'around six times the rate in Birmingham, Leeds and Sheffield and over four times the rate in London'.[20] But, even with statistics that seem to have been rather inadequate for the task in hand, the police, who made widespread use of informers, seem to have made a fairly reasonable fist of fighting crime.[21]

It is from the latter perspective that one needs to understand certain gang practices in Ancoats. Codes, oaths and tattoos were designed not only to bind members into antisocial organisations, but also to keep out informers at a time when forensic evidence was at a premium. Just as inexplicable instances of misfortune in traditional societies are sometimes attributed to witchcraft, so the real fear in many criminal organisations stemmed from the hidden enemy within. For 'Irish' adolescents, raised by parents drawn directly from a peasant society where chants and charms were used to ward off the evil eye, 'bad luck' was an omnipresent danger. So, too, was the threat posed by informers. The Royal Ulster Constabulary had never hesitated to use informers. Fear of betrayal rendered the search for trustworthy allies never-ending.

It is within that context too – the need to guard against potentially malign outsiders – that one needs to understand why it was that the Blue Dots sought to bolster their numbers for criminal projects by turning inwards, to their kith and kin. But, while recruiting from within the family might have limited the need for oaths and tattoos, it did not necessarily guarantee success. The problem with using family members in criminal operations was that, while the levels of trust usually went up, they were not necessarily matched by increases in levels of competence or skill.

The McLoughlin boys never wanted for cousins or more distant relatives drawn from their father's side of the family. The Burns, Lyons, Ogden and Scott lads were all locally based and sufficiently closely related to be considered part of an extended family. Some, like the Scotts, were even less economically and socially secure than the McLoughlins and appear to have been in awe of their formidable cousins. Tommy McLoughlin's exploits with the Burns boys illustrate some of the advantages and several of the problems of doing criminal business with young kinsmen.

After an early release from the industrial school, possibly because of a heart condition, Tommy, in the thrall of his oldest race-going brother, began working with horses. It became a passion that later led him to taking on a position as a groom and, again like brother Jack, developing a liking for the great outdoors. However, shortly after his release, at age 14, Tommy linked up with his cousin, James Burns. In February 1878, he laid into Burns with a poker, beating him about the head so severely that his cousin lay 'in a somewhat dangerous condition' in the infirmary for several days. When the pair appeared in court, Jimmy Burns declined to prosecute because, or so he claimed, he was intoxicated at the time and 'knew very little about the affair'.[22] It was probably a wise choice.

A year later Tommy linked up with another of the Burns boys, John, who was working for Edward Cockshoot, a coach proprietor on Blossom Street, in New Cross. With cousin John acting as the insider enjoying privileged access to the premises, they stole eight bags of horse provender valued at £4 for onward sale. The Magistrate, taking the view that the crime had been instigated by Tommy, sentenced him to six months with hard labour and Burns, the lesser party, to four months' hard labour.[23]

By the late 1870s all three McLoughlin brothers – Jack, William and Tommy – were semi-professional criminals operating within and beyond the Blue Dot gang and disposing of stolen goods on the black market. In better times, discretionary criminal activities supplemented small incomes earned from part-time employment. But when the textile industry went into full recession, in autumn 1878, and lingered in a depressed state for more than a year, waged employment became harder to find and the tables turned.[24] A steady income from crime became central to economic survival and casual employment a mere occasional bonus.

The Blue Dots avoided any brushes with the law during late 1878 and over the sluggish summer months of 1879 when there was an uptick in seasonal work. If they did enjoy unrecorded criminal successes it could have been because the police were more stretched than usual, or because the members of the gang were becoming more professional, or both.

But by autumn 1879 casual employment was again at a premium. With cash for clothing, food and fuel almost impossible to come by, most working-class families were in distress and those that were economically dysfunctional even more so. It was at this juncture that Jack McLoughlin and JW Brown set about planning their most ambitious project yet, a series of break-ins on a scale that, if successful, would meet their needs and those of their dependants for weeks to come. They set their eyes on the 'Uncles' to be found throughout working-class Manchester.

★ ★ ★

Pawnshops – marked by three golden balls suspended from an iron bar outside the premises – developed as an offshoot of commercial banking in medieval Italy, but spread to industrialising England where they were first licensed in the eighteenth century. By the mid-nineteenth century, counties with large working-class populations, such as Lancashire and Warwickshire, saw a rapid growth in numbers of pawnshops. Workers in search of money for anything from food, clothing and rent, through to quick cash for alcohol or gambling, pledged items of personal property up to the value of £10 – ranging from clothing to jewellery – as collateral in return for interest-bearing loans. If the goods were not redeemed, the 'Uncle', effectively insured against serious loss, sold the items by public auction.

By 1870, Manchester had 248 licensed pawnshop operators. Many of them were shady practitioners with contacts in the underworld looking for outlets for stolen goods that included heavy-duty winter clothing. For most of the century pawnbrokers had been entitled to charge 20 per cent interest on sums under two guineas, but in 1872, a new act had effectively increased the rate to a punishing 25 per cent. The new provision meant that 'the smaller the loan the higher the interest', and that the heaviest rate fell on people who were least able to bear it.[25]

As bankers to the poor, many pawnshop owners occupied morally ambiguous positions and seldom endeared themselves to ordinary working men and women. Richard Roberts, raised in a 'classic slum' in neighbouring Salford, saw their 'Uncle' as a cold-eyed, tight-lipped man with a 'heart of stone'. In Manchester, pawnbrokers and second-hand dealers, including those specialising in cheap clothing, were closely watched by the police precisely because so many of them dealt in stolen goods. Unscrupulous pawnbrokers often knowingly provided criminals with the chance of converting purloined articles into cash.[26]

But professional thieves, too, had a love-hate relationship with profiteering or unreliable Uncles who, put under pressure, might talk to the police. In the absence of detailed evidence, it is impossible to know why the Blue Dots singled out pawnbrokers as targets. It may have been that, over the years, the experiences of poverty and pledging had fostered a dislike of extortionate lenders-of-the-last-resort. As likely, the gang may have been the victim of professional sharp practice as its members attempted to unload stolen goods in return for cash. Either way, pawnbrokers – objects of derision at the best of times – would have been seen as legitimate targets in the deepening recession of 1878–79.

McLoughlin and JW Brown had no difficulty in finding an insider for their first job. The Pughs, who for many years had run an eating house, lived on Great Ancoats, where the street crossed the Rochdale Canal. The Pugh boys did reasonably well at school but were sent out to work when the family business collapsed in the mid-1870s.[27] The oldest boy got a job as a manual labourer at the market and the younger, William, was taken on as a clerical assistant by Joseph Oldham, the pawnbroker, just a few houses away. William Pugh was soon in trouble. In summer 1877, he had his first brush with the law when he was hauled in as a witness after Brown and Mackey stole some books from an employer.[28]

A good deal younger than his new Blue Dot friends, Pugh may have been keen to impress, but he was out of his depth. He told Jack McLoughlin about the seasonal increase in coats and handkerchiefs being pledged and how, where and when to get into the premises. The idea was that the gang would remove the articles, split the goods and place the stolen items with other brokers to raise cash, or pass the remainder of the apparel on to second-hand dealers to dispose of as best they saw fit.

McLoughlin recruited his 17-year-old cousin, Dennis Scott, to help with the burglary and his mother, Eliza, to hold the bulk of the stolen clothing until such time as it could be split up. The pawnshop was broken into on Sunday night, 15 November 1878, and 13 coats and nine handkerchiefs removed. In the week that followed the items were distributed among a half-dozen insiders, including another cousin, William Ogden, and two young associates, Patrick Denash and Henry Johnson. William Pugh was relieved the burglary went smoothly, but funds raised effortlessly only whetted the Blue Dots' appetite for more.

They now planned a second, more ambitious raid on a pawnbroker, one on a scale that was wholesale rather than retail. The new job, which must once again have drawn on some insider's knowledge of the trade, required more professional assistance; also, given the projected volume of clothing to be removed and placed with brokers or dealers in second-hand clothing, a much longer chain of potential primary distributors.

The new endeavour – thought through over a few days if not hours by McLoughlin and JW Brown – included Dennis Scott and 16-year-old William McLoughlin, as break-and-entry men. Tommy, in prison for the poker attack, was unavailable. Charles Beswick and Joseph Wild, experienced Blue Dots, were brought into a distribution network which, although extended from six to nine in number, was still overseen by Eliza McLoughlin. Also in the know were Pugh, Denash and Johnson, the youngsters who had done well on the job at Oldham's, which was still under investigation. This time the target was William Chorlton's pawnshop – which, like Aladdin's cave, promised unimaginable treasures.

Chorlton's business on Portland Street, Newtown, was so large and successful that its proprietor could afford to live in more desirable residential premises some distance away.[29] The intruders chose the following Sunday, 22 November, for their operations and soon found themselves in a city-centre second-hand paradise. Even then, away from densely populated Ancoats, the job required considerable cunning, muscle-power and organisation. Without being caught either in the act itself or discovered on the streets outside, they removed:

> Ten vests, six pairs of trousers, four dresses, three skirts, four shawls, two pairs of boots, one other boot, twenty shirts, one piece of sheeting, one piece of shirting, one concertina, one jacket, twenty handkerchiefs, two quilts and five pounds in money.[30]

Two pawnshops broken into over successive weekends were impossible to ignore even for a hard-pressed city police force. Jerome Caminada, the city's legendary chief detective, prided himself on a network of informants that he looked after 'long after their usefulness and into his retirement'.[31] But managing a network of professional informers was never easy. In mid-Victorian Britain, a reliance on face-to-face interactions sometimes made it difficult to tell where the police ended and underworld elements began.

There were also connections between informers, those receiving stolen goods and the second-hand trade.[32]

Constables cultivated criminals, but criminals also groomed constables, with the result that justice sometimes not only seemed arbitrary and open to bargaining and negotiation but also highly personalised. McLoughlin and JW Brown, graduates of this street-law academy, had mastered these lessons and later applied them, with considerable success, in southern Africa. Back in Ancoats, however, it was not long before Detective Caminada had the lead he needed. He pressed hard on the least-experienced gang members, Denash and Johnson, and persuaded them to give evidence for the Crown. Officers went out and arrested the McLoughlins, their mother Eliza, cousin Dennis Scott, and JW Brown.

The accused were tried at the City's Quarter Sessions on 12 December 1878, and for the second time that year the doings of one or more members of the McLoughlin clan were drawn to the attention of the readers of the *Manchester Evening News*.[33] For the burglary at Oldham's, Jack, Eliza and Scott were charged on two counts – breaking and entering the premises and/or receiving stolen goods. It was a potentially messy business, with William Pugh, the insider-employee, listed only as a witness. Pugh, however, survived the ordeal and, magically, kept his job at Oldham's.

For the second burglary – at Chorlton's – the McLoughlin brothers and Scott, along with JW Brown, were charged with breaking and entering and/or receiving stolen property. Making allowances for the boys' obviously decrepit mother, Eliza was charged separately and only with receiving stolen goods. The Magistrate found the three oldest males guilty of breaking and entering and sentenced each to six months' imprisonment with hard labour; William, in consideration of his youth, received three months with hard labour. Eliza was found guilty of receiving and despite being in poor health got six months with hard labour.[34]

As noted earlier, the imprisonment of three McLoughlins marked the collapse of a family that had more-or-less cohered for nearly three decades under the most adverse urban conditions. The collateral damage, however, extended beyond the nuclear family. The Scotts, angered by their son Dennis's involvement in the burglaries, shunned the McLoughlins after the pawnshop break-ins. When Eliza McLoughlin entered the women's section of Belle Vue prison in December 1878, her sister, Bridget Ann, refused to take her two youngest daughters into care, leaving Mary (12) and Elizabeth (8) more vulnerable than ever. Six months after Eliza was released from prison, in the summer of 1879, she was committed to the workhouse at Chorlton. By the time of her lonely death, the girls had been placed with other kin.[35]

The McLoughlin brothers were better placed to survive the rigours of a prison in which, at night, they could hear the sound of fireworks and music drifting in from the festivities of nearby Belle Vue Gardens, which they had invaded as children. A hard winter may have prompted them to rethink the wisdom of Blue Dot organised crime, since for some time thereafter they appear to have kept largely to themselves. The recession was still being felt in Ancoats when they were released in June 1879 and a little seasonal work helped see them through the summer.

That autumn Tommy, too, was out of prison and back on the streets. Jack continued to keep a close eye on his youngest brother; that winter, they and a few cousins drank heavily – much of it in the Seven Stars, a popular beerhouse with stables on Dixon Street, not far from the mill on Union Street and the Rochdale Canal where they had grown up.[36]

On Christmas Eve 1879, Jack and a few friends found themselves on the streets of nearby working-class Ardwick without funds, contemplating the prospect of more seasonal misery. Judging from the ensuing violence, Tommy, by then a Blue Dot in his own right, may have been party to a small family-based initiative.[37] A combination of alcohol, desperation and the need to find a well-stuffed wallet forced open the door of recklessness. The footpads spotted a mark in a side-street – Humphrey Moore, a grocer's apprentice. Three or four years older than Jack McLoughlin, Moore was reasonably well-heeled and unlikely to offer too much resistance. They tailed him to a suitable spot and grabbed hold of him. But the fellow was surprisingly strong and it took 'considerable personal violence' to wrestle him to the ground and remove his watch as well as seven shillings and sixpence.

The noise attracted the attention of passers-by and one of the assailants was arrested; the others had bolted. Fresh from six months in prison as a result of information supplied by youngsters who were so keen to save their own skins that they were willing to give evidence for the Crown, Jack was not about to break the underworld code of honour himself. The police probed for signs of weakness but he refused to reveal the names of two accomplices and so faced prosecution on his own.[38] It was a straw in the wind – the first recorded indication, age 20, of just how seriously he disapproved of informing or co-operating with the police.

The holding cells were crammed with seasonal offenders – drunks, pickpockets, prostitutes and wife-beaters – in addition to a few professional criminals. Justice, which moved slowly at the best of times, almost ground to a halt over Christmas. It was New Year before he was told that his trial, for 'robbery with violence', was scheduled for 24 January. Sensing a stiff sentence, it may have been his accomplices who raised the money to retain counsel for the defence. The usual reporters were in attendance at Assizes Crown Court on the appointed day to record that the judge was not impressed by Mr Nash's representations for the defence. He found the accused guilty and, taking McLoughlin's previous record into account, sentenced him to a year's imprisonment with hard labour at a prison in the far-off home counties.[39]

★   ★   ★

By the time Jack was released, in November 1880, he had abandoned all thought of returning to Lancashire in the near future. Even though he still yearned to trace the Mersey all the way from Stockport to Liverpool, he never again set foot in Ancoats. It was where the foundations of his personality had been laid by his Irish refugee parents, the church and his slum cohort, but he had no wish to revisit it. Dystopian Manchester and its fiendish machinery spoke only of industrial discipline, compartmentalised time and gross urban poverty. It was a world devoid of excitement, of challenges, imagination and new frontiers. The 'dark Satanic mills' churned out only boredom, predictability and wage slavery.

For any man trapped on an island, the obvious way out is via the sea. The Merchant Navy was a possibility. London was the gateway to the empire and the rest of the world. But the agents of commercial shipping preferred their raw enthusiasm and strength to be balanced with dollops of experience and skill before they were willing to take on younger men.

The Royal Navy was different. With less money at its disposal than it would have liked, it always had less refined tastes. For hundreds of years men without hope or resources had either been impressed into it, or joined it voluntarily. The senior service embraced antisocial attitudes and strong muscles in the belief that, within the confines of an all-male environment, it could convert almost anything into loyalty and skill. In truth, a prison and a ship had much in common, even though some compared them unfavourably. Samuel Johnson argued that: 'No man will be a sailor who has contrivance enough to get himself into a jail; for being in a ship is being in a jail, with the chance of being drowned.'[40]

Cash was the mother of choice, but he had none. So he joined the navy, in London, and was sent to Plymouth where, after a short search, he was pointed in the direction of a three-masted sloop. It was mid-November and already growing chilly, but the vessel was bound for Gibraltar and warm waters, which was cheering. He was directed below, but with nothing of value to stow, returned to the deck. His pockets were empty but, aged 22, his mind was stuffed with ideas about opportunities for adventure in far-off corners of the world. It was a start of the sort that Captain Dangerous himself might have approved.

CHAPTER SIX

ᘓᘓᕉᘃᕉ

Escape into Empire

THE VOYAGE OF THE *ALBATROSS*
— 1880–1881 —

Ship me somewhere east of Suez, where the best is like the worst,
Where there aren't no Ten Commandments, and a man can raise a thirst.

RUDYARD KIPLING

The Europeans' fifteenth- to seventeenth-century voyages of discovery
not only conquered the southern Atlantic, beating a new pathway to
India, but also helped western powers of the day chart the emerging outline
of the globe. Britain's interest in the ocean off its western shores, however,
was not secured until Nelson defeated the French and Spanish navies off
Trafalgar in 1805. That victory gave the fleet control of most of the world's
oceans, but it was the defeat of Napoleon on land, at Waterloo in 1815,
that consolidated Britain's claim to be the world's pre-eminent nineteenth-
century power. Backed by an industrial revolution gaining in momentum
after 1830, the peoples of the island spread out into an expanding world at
an increasing rate. By 1870, 200 000 British subjects a year emigrated into
a formal empire of conquest and settlement, as well as to other territories
where its influence held sway.[1]

Huge fortresses at Gibraltar and Malta safeguarded British trade around
the Mediterranean littoral and helped check Russian ambitions in south-
eastern Europe. Beyond the Horn of Africa, Britain used its foothold in

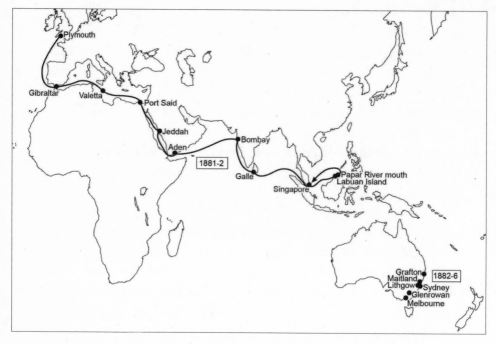

The Voyage of HMS Albatross, 1881–1882

India – then still approachable only via the Cape of Good Hope – to extend its reach into surrounding regions and the Far East. The end of the Opium Wars, marked by the Treaty of Nanking in 1842, opened China to foreign commercial interests; by the late 1860s, Hong Kong and the free port of Singapore in the Straits Settlement were firmly under British control. This eastward shift in the empire's centre of economic gravity was further facilitated by the opening of the Suez Canal in 1869.[2]

The Mediterranean and seaborne approaches to India – which, after the Great Rebellion of 1857, housed most of Britain's limited land forces – grew in importance. Not only did the Union Jack come to flutter over Egypt after 1882, but Aden and various ports down the East African coast assumed greater strategic significance. The British effectively controlled the Indian Ocean Basin, having earlier expelled most of its potential European rivals. Markets throughout the Atlantic, Indian and Pacific Oceans, first prised open through British insistence on 'free trade', were, after 1870, increasingly developed through the enforcement of policies that readily embraced tariffs and other forms of protectionism.[3]

Although in growing need of imported foodstuffs to feed its expanding urban population, Britain's exports soared through most of the late nineteenth century as trade, backed by the gold standard, reinforced a rapidly integrating global economy. Awash with funds, British foreign investments grew dramatically after 1880, doubling by 1900, and then quadrupling by 1913.[4] Even distant colonies, including Australia and New Zealand, benefited from robust economic health at the centre of the empire. Refrigeration and other scientific advances enabled them to expand agricultural production and add value to their exports by partially preparing meat and other edible products. The only notable faltering in the pace of economic growth came during the largely depressed 1890s.[5]

The economic consolidation of empire owed much to three further interconnected technological advances. Two of them traced their pedigree back to harnessing of steam-power during the earliest stage of the Industrial Revolution, while the third was electrically driven. The introduction of huge steel-hulled steamships in the 1880s reduced the tyranny of distance when it came to bulk transport and passenger travel.[6] Voyages that had once taken weeks or months were dramatically reduced in cost and time. By 1885, poor emigrants travelling steerage on cutthroat Atlantic routes could purchase tickets between Hamburg and New York City for as little as seven American dollars. Passenger liners completed the journey from Liverpool to New York in just six days.

Port cities, in turn, were linked into gigantic trans-continental railway systems dating back to the 1870s. By the outbreak of World War I, the world's most industrialised economies were served by tracks covering three-quarters of a million miles. Individually significant, the co-ordinated collective steamship and railway systems proved to be utterly transformative. Reductions in cost not only helped underwrite the export of raw materials and the bulk importation of manufactured goods, but facilitated the mass human migrations that characterised the age.[7]

On land the telegraph – supported by a network of undersea cables transmitting electrical impulses that by the late 1890s circled the globe – formed the economic nervous system of a globalising economy. It helped co-or-dinate industrial muscle, enhancing productivity and lifting profit margins. About 8 000 miles of telegraph wires, in 1872, were extended to cover more than a quarter of a million miles by World War I, with 40 per cent of the lines owned by just one company, the London-based Eastern Telegraph Company. Government subsidies to selected shipping companies ensured the swift and reliable movement of commercial mail between continents. Domestically, huge quantities of handwritten and printed material were shunted to inland destinations by rail.[8]

There was an explosion in the volumes of economic intelligence and information available to, and needed by, a host of interested insiders. Agents, consuls, financial journalists and governments were in constant need of commercial data about the cost of raw materials, shipping rates, trading conditions, or the prices that processed commodities were likely to fetch in far-off markets. By the turn of the twentieth century London had an 'impe-rial press system' that was buying and selling news of all sorts in a way that was said by some to constitute a near 'perfect feedback loop'.[9]

Of course, not all data was accessible through conventional channels, or freely available to anybody who might have an interest in it. As a global power Britain developed and maintained instruments of surveillance that linked London with its distant periphery in ways capable of guaranteeing the security of the empire. Westminster and Whitehall relied on an uninter-rupted supply of confidential or top-secret military and naval intelligence. Law-enforcement agencies, too, used the telegraph and police gazettes to collate and distribute intelligence about criminals who were becoming more mobile.

Most official despatches, including those relating to law enforcement, only surfaced in the press in modified format and prosaic language – in-forming the public about the latest diplomatic, judicial or legal develop-ments. While many of these flows of information were tailored to be audience-specific, moving along pathways linking imperial London to its outposts, they could, on occasion, go beyond their intended destinations. When forwarded directly between colonies, communiqués sometimes gave rise to unforeseen consequences. Newspaper reports of civil or criminal proceedings in Australasia might, for example, be forwarded to southern Africa and vice versa. This sometimes left businessmen or members of the public marginally better-informed about the inter-colonial movement of criminals and other shady characters in the commercial world than the local police.[10] Informal cross-flows of information, together with routine official exchanges between the centre and periphery, meant that, by the late nineteenth century, inhabitants of the wider Anglophone world, law-abiding and law-evading alike, were being subjected to surveillance by what we might term an Imperial Eye.[11]

The Eye may have gathered and interpreted the data that prompted ground-based actions throughout the empire, but the ultimate enforcer in the 'British World System' during the Victorian era was the Royal Navy. Post-Napoleonic governments seeking to entrench British hegemony expanded the navy. But, by the mid-nineteenth century, as the switch from wooden to iron-clad ships gathered momentum, Conservative and Liberal administrations alike vied to limit naval expenditure.[12] For most of the 1870s, naval estimates were restricted to around £11 million per annum and, at one point, construction was reduced to the production of just five armoured ships in five years. Notwithstanding, the navy remained formidable and in 1877, comprised over 550 vessels with a combined tonnage of over 675 000 manned by 25 000 officers and men, 6 000 marines and close on 3 000 boys. The navy policed imperial waters and divided the world's oceans into just eight overseas stations.[13]

★   ★   ★

When McLoughlin boarded HMS *Albatross* in Plymouth, in November 1880, the navy's overall brief remained broadly unchanged. It had to safeguard incoming food supplies and the physical integrity of the British Isles, protect the nation's expanding trade by 'flying the flag' and assist in combating piracy. Yet, for all that, something was different. The most important drivers of foreign policy had recently changed quite dramatically.

In 1876 a section of British public opinion that extended beyond the true

99

believers in the ruling Conservative Party had become perturbed about foreign policy. Disraeli's principal ally against Russian expansionism in the Mediterranean – the Ottoman Turks – had been party to a series of atrocities in Bulgaria. Concerns about this were exacerbated by the manifest decline in Ottoman power and by the Turks' inability to enforce their political will in a near-bankrupt Egypt that stood astride the decade-old Suez Canal and the shortened sea-route to India.[14] Gladstone, in the first electoral campaign in the era of the extended franchise, made foreign policy the focus of his famous Midlothian campaign of 1880. The Liberal Party displaced Disraeli's Conservatives at the polls and Gladstone became Prime Minister of Britain for a second time.

The trans-hemispheric voyage of the *Albatross* in 1880–81 began at a moment of heightened uncertainty in the Middle East. Deep-seated economic problems and growing political instability there not only threatened Britain's trading interests in the Mediterranean but potentially barred easy access to the Suez Canal, the 'Highway to India' and all that lay east and south of it. The timing and trajectory of the patrol laid out for the vessel by the admiralty was routine insofar as it traced established pathways of importance to the empire, but also 'special' given that the warship was to linger in the Mediterranean.[15] The *Albatross* and Jack McLoughlin were bound for Suez and beyond.

The ship was one of six cost-cutting sloops built by the navy over just 24 months in 1873–74. But, caught amidst the tempests of rapid technological change, the sloops were hard to maintain and obsolete almost from the moment they were completed. All six ships were sold before they had seen out two decades of service.[16] Built around iron frames, the 'composites' were sheathed in copper and teak and driven by two-cylinder steam engines fed by three boilers fired from 100-tonne supplies of coal. Looking back on the golden age of sail as well as peering forward into a mechanised future, the sloops were equipped with three masts and rigged out in the manner of barques. Armed with two 7-inch and two 64-pounder guns mounted on pivots, the ship was manned with 13 officers, 19 petty officers, 62 seamen, 19 marines and 12 boys. Having undergone extensive shipyard repairs only the previous year, the ship was recorded as being in 'good condition' when McLoughlin joined it.[17]

Bound for Gibraltar, the *Albatross* left Plymouth in late November 1880 under the command of Commodore AJ Errington, an Irishman who had long since overcome a troubled past in the West Indies.[18] The fortress at the Rock, befitting an outpost at the gateway to the Mediterranean, was a site of unceasing military and naval activity, provisioned by English merchant houses and Jewish traders, and supplied with fresh produce by several hundred Italians who hailed from Genoa. Focused and functional, the port was less exotic and socially turbulent than others in the inland sea, yet, perhaps significantly, had been the first such British outpost to establish an independent police force modelled along the lines of London's Metropolitan Police. After a day or two the ship sailed for Malta, much closer to the heart of the new political storms.[19]

Malta, where the sloop was anchored for a week or more, was closer to the mariner's dream of 'Fiddlers Green' – and McLoughlin's taste – than was Gibraltar. First occupied by the British in 1800, the island had served as a secondary centre during the Crimean War. Since then it had been transformed by a never-ending flow of soldiers and sailors and tourists arriving by steamship. By 1880, Valetta boasted 20 hotels, scores of lodging houses and two theatres. A music hall was being built for artists seeking to avoid the English winter by offering programmes of classic Victorian entertainment. As in most places where they commanded a presence, the army and navy had done little to uphold the moral tone of a town that housed several churches and convents. The presence of unruly soldiers and sailors, it was said, had been complemented by the arrival of many Italian and Spanish artisans and a few Sicilian women of doubtful virtue. By the time the *Albatross* called, the town was experiencing significant problems with drunkenness, gambling and prostitution. Modern methods of detection and policing were being introduced, extending the vision of the Eye.[20]

With the Grand Harbour behind her the *Albatross* steamed east from Valetta, bound for Egypt, where, only a decade earlier, De Lesseps's globe-shrinking construction, authorised by the Khedive Ismail Pasha, had been seen as the guarantor of Egypt's economic progress. In the 1860s, the American Civil War and Cotton Famine had prompted a significant increase in the price of Egyptian cotton. Flush with funds and pleased with the French, 'Ismail the Magnificent' had commissioned a gigantic 'statue of progress', in keeping with the majesty of ancient Egyptian art, to stand at Port Said, at the western entrance of the canal. The work, by a Frenchman, Frédéric-Auguste Bartholdi, was inspired by the Roman ideal of liberty and built on a scale that would allow all to see the light that Egypt was destined to cast over Asia. But by the time the *Albatross* made port, Ismail Pasha was no longer in control, the country was bankrupt and so politically unstable that just months later, in 1882, it was 'temporarily' occupied by British forces. The Statue of Liberty was by then destined for the harbour at New York City and the 'temporary' British presence in Egypt set to last for another 66 years, until 1954.[21]

Mirroring the growth in world trade, the number of ships passing through the canal annually had increased from about 500 in 1870, to more than 2 000 by 1880. But with fewer than 10 ships a day capable of making the passage in each direction, the *Albatross,* along with dozens of other vessels reliant on sail, was forced to lie at anchor in Port Said for several days waiting for its turn. The small desert town, already acquiring a reputation for fraud, immorality and sleaze that was to grow exponentially during the twentieth century, had little to recommend it. The sloop passed through the canal on 15 December 1880 and, upon entering the Red Sea, hugged the northern shore and made Jeddah three days later.[22]

For devout Muslims, Jeddah was but one of many ancient portals on the road to Mecca, which lay panting in the desert sun 40 miles inland. For the faithful, the *Hajj* was the principal marker in a rounded religious life, but the journey was eclipsed by the experience of entering the *Masjid al Harma* mosque. A sense of spiritual renewal came with the ritual circling of the *Kaaba* on the site where Abraham had been called upon to make his sacrifice. The practice of the *Hajj* extended back for many hundreds of years; indeed, for businessmen and the inhabitants of Jeddah one year was much like another. But 1880 was different. When the *Albatross* docked, harbourside labourers and outraged traders in the market were still poring over the details of one of the greatest maritime scandals of the age. For the faithful, it proved again that one's 'fate', or what some called 'destiny', lay only in the hands of an all-merciful *Allah*.

In mid-July, the SS *Jeddah*, Union Jack aloft, had left Singapore and called in at Penang, up the Malay peninsula. By the time the ship set course for Jeddah, it was carrying over 1 000 men, women and children from the Malay states. But after experiencing heavy weather in the Arabian Sea, the *Jeddah* took in water and started listing badly. The captain, his wife, first mate and others, fearing the worst, lowered a boat and abandoned ship, leaving the faithful to an uncertain fate. The captain and his party were picked up by a passing vessel and ferried to Aden. There they told a tale about storms, a foundering ship, and frightened passengers − some of whom, they said, had become violent.

But the *Jeddah* had not sunk. Days after being abandoned, the drifting hulk and its helpless passengers were taken in tow by a French vessel. When the pilgrims disembarked at Aden, their story gave rise to a storm of harbour-side accusations and questions about integrity, morality and professionalism. For McLoughlin, raised on stories about the choices men made between courage and cowardice, the plight of the *Jeddah* would have offered another salutary tale. In naval circles reports about the shortcomings of the captain and his crew had an enduring relevance and refused to die. In 1883, a young Polish seaman passing through Singapore picked up on it and later, as Joseph Conrad, turned it into *Lord Jim,* one of the greatest seafaring novels in the English language.[23]

The crew of the *Albatross*, like sailors everywhere, were for the most part more interested in their shore leave than the religious significance of the port they happened to find themselves in. Christmas was celebrated in Jeddah in the way that came naturally to Jack Tars. There was more drunken carousing on New Year's Day 1881, after the sloop had slipped down through the Straits of Bab al Mandab and berthed in Aden.

The 10-day stay there testified to the importance of a port that had first attracted imperial interest half a century earlier, in the late 1830s. The British had occupied the town when they became exasperated by pirates menacing ships of the East India Company plying the Arabian Sea. Thereafter, the coastal stronghold was administered from Bombay. Bombay was the financial and commercial hub of a region that included not only the Middle East, but also much of the African coastline stretching down to Zanzibar and, albeit more tentatively, as far south as Lourenço Marques.[24] Those economic strands were strengthened when the submarine cable linking Bombay to London, via Aden, Suez and the Mediterranean, was completed in 1870. Aden served as a major coaling station, supplier of boiler water, and communication hub for the region.

From Aden they set out across the Arabian Sea, and in mid-January arrived in Bombay, where they spent close on two weeks. Benefiting from the favourable trade winds throughout mid-century, Bombay was in full flight economically. Construction of a local railway line, in 1853, had been followed by a huge spurt in the development of a trans-national system in the 1860s which, in turn, served regular steamship connections up and down the west coast, leading to the establishment of a Port Trust in 1870. By 1860, Bombay, already the largest cotton market in India, boasted hundreds of mills. As in Egypt, disruptions occasioned by the American Civil War and the Cotton Famine spurred growth. The opening of Suez helped; by 1881, Bombay had three-quarters of a million people.[25]

Like many larger English cities, Bombay was undergoing something of a municipal revolution. Like Birmingham and Manchester, the city was benefiting from a new drainage system and piped water. There was also talk of experimenting with electric lighting in the Crawford Market. New public buildings, including a museum, post office, railway station and university, testified to growing civic pride. Numerous trading houses and a thriving stock exchange underscored the city's economic vibrancy. In the Falklands Road, low-life haunts functioned reasonably openly despite a recent clampdown by the Commissioner of Police. But more importantly, Jack's ears would have pricked up at rumours about the possibility of acquiring wealth in ways that lay beyond the law. Bombay offered a convenient entry point into the Indian interior and the Kolar goldfields, 500 miles south, in Mysore.

Until it reached India, the *Albatross* had had little to do other than fly the flag and help keep clear one of the most sensitive economic and strategic arteries in the imperial system. But the admiralty needed the warship for more important assignments and pressed the captain to proceed to the South China Sea. Errington, however, had reservations about the ship's condition. The sloop was proving difficult and expensive to maintain because of the composite materials used in its construction. A compromise was reached and the *Albatross* instead set course for Galle in Ceylon for the necessary maintenance work.[26]

They left Bombay on 25 January 1881, headed south, rounded Cape Comorin and then, ignoring Colombo, pushed on to the fine natural harbour at the south-western tip of Ceylon. Galle, best seen as the southern-most point of central Asia, commanded a magnificent aspect. Its strategic position allowed one to scan the surrounding ocean through 300 degrees, taking in most of the southern world and good deal of the near northern. It had been a predictable port of call for the earliest navigators, including the Chinese admiral, Zheng He, who had visited it twice in the early fif-teenth century – long before Atlantic explorers had found their way round the Cape to India. Once the Europeans found it, the island was occupied first by the Portuguese, then the Dutch and then, in the early nineteenth century, by the British. Galle was an obvious port of call and point of trans-shipment for modern mail ships, but less suited to inland commerce, which was increasingly focused on Colombo.

A turnstile to the hemispheres – east and west, north and south – Galle was as good a point as any in the world to jump ship and it must have tempted McLoughlin to think through his future anew. Like most war-ships, the *Albatross* was constantly bleeding disillusioned or unhappy sailors and taking in new recruits. It had already drawn in several men of different nationalities in Gibraltar and Malta. The fact that he chose not to desert in Ceylon may have been a sign that he already had another, more promising, destination in mind. He was aboard when, a week later, the sloop set course for Phuket on the Malay peninsula but then swung round, south-east, push-ing through the narrow Straits of Malacca, and on towards that most strate-gically situated city, Singapore.

Little wonder that the navy fell out of love with sloops almost as soon as they were launched. It took more than two months to get the *Albatross* ship-shape. The vessel was in the harbour between 22 February and 27 April and, during that time, was cleaned, re-painted and re-provisioned for cruising in the unsettled South China Sea. The Imperial Eye duly noted McLoughlin's presence when the census was taken on 3 April 1881.[27] Eight weeks in Singapore left him with more than enough time to familiarise himself with those aspects of urban south-east Asian society that appealed to sailors. But it also gave him the opportunity to find out more about the frontiers and gold mines that had sprung up in many of the older British colonies spread across the southern Pacific.[28]

The Malay Peninsula, which enjoyed a reputation of its own for gold deposits, had for aeons attracted enterprising Chinese immigrants. Later, it became the focus of intense competition by rival European powers for trading rights. The English, Dutch, Portuguese and Spanish had all staked out interests in the region, but after the Napoleonic Wars it was the British East India Company, already based at Penang, that had started taking a more active interest in the southern tip of a peninsula that was rightly said to hold the 'Key to the East'. In 1819, the legendary Stamford Raffles, amidst protests from the Dutch that lasted until the matter was formally settled five years later, picked out Singapore as the site for a 'free trade' port that would soon come to dominate the region.

Seven years later, in 1826, Singapore, Malacca and Penang were drawn into a single administrative entity – the Straits Settlement. That arrangement lasted until the Company was effectively nationalised by the British government after the 'Indian Mutiny' of 1857. But, because coastal trading remained predominant, relatively little was known about the interior, and even after 15 years there were still no reliable handbooks or maps of the peninsula – let alone the myriad islands that dotted the South China, Celebes and Sulu Seas, in which pirates had reigned supreme for decades. This situation was only corrected when it became better known that, in addition to gold mines at Raub, there were enormous deposits of tin that had long been mined by the Chinese, with the help of 40 000 labourers. Once the Cornish tin mines started petering out, in the 1870s, the British moved in to control the supply of a metal that was light, durable, well-suited to food packaging and easily transportable.[29]

The prosperous peninsular economy was served by a complex multi-racial population that remained notoriously segregated. Numerically pre-ponderant native Malays were favoured by the British for posts in the lower reaches of government and the police, but the natives were out-muscled in the wider economy by Indian merchants who, in turn, bent the knee before Chinese interests in the growing palm-oil trade. The Chinese, besides dominating many sectors of the formal economy, were sometimes also involved in illegal operations controlled by gangsters belonging to secret societies whose origins lay back in southern China.[30]

In a way, Singapore provided 22-year-old Jack McLoughlin with his first exposure to a pioneering settlement, one replete with an ethnically diverse underworld with distinctive interests in gambling and prostitution. There was something about the economic pulse of the place and the opportunities it presented that excited him, even if he knew that as a European outsider he could never penetrate it successfully. It was the frontier situation that appealed to him – and it only whetted his appetite to find one where he was more at home in terms of language and culture.

These impressions were still settling in his mind when the *Albatross* weighed anchor on 27 April and put Singapore behind her. The sloop slipped into the forbidding South China Sea, and then set a north-east course. For the next five weeks they were well beyond urban frontiers, out on patrol in one of the most unhealthy extremities of empire. The small island of Labuan, off the north-western coast of Borneo, was an outpost used to confront pirates and protect the Hong Kong trade. It had been ceded to Britain by the Sultan of Brunei in 1846 and become a Crown Colony. A fluttering sense of optimism seemed vindicated when, not long thereafter, an abundant supply of coal was discovered. The famous 'White Rajah', James Brooke, Governor of Sarawak, under whom the tiny colony fell, then sought to encourage itinerant Chinese traders to settle on what previously was an uninhabited island.

A promising start faltered and, by the 1870s, the British were looking to divest themselves of the tiny, malaria-infested colony. But they suddenly had second thoughts when it appeared that some of their regional rivals were set to exploit timber resources and trading opportunities in the neighbouring territory of what today is Sabah. An increasingly unsettled political environment prompted Westminster to rethink its strategy and, in 1881, the government granted a Royal Charter to the British North Borneo Company. Diplomatic niceties, the lingering presence of pirates and economic uncertainty all demanded the presence of the *Albatross*.

After exciting stays in Bombay, Malta and Singapore, a month-long patrol of remote outposts plagued by malaria and other tropical diseases proved singularly unpleasant. The sloop sailed north from Labuan to the Papar River mouth and then on to Abai Bay before returning to its island base. The precise circuit they followed – from Labuan out to the Saracen Bank poised at the edge of deep waters – seemed pointless since there were no encounters with pirates worth reporting. They merely rounded the reefs and then, turning south-west, retraced their course down the Sarawak coast before re-entering Singapore in the first week of June.[31]

The crew was pleased to be back in port but, within hours of their return, there was disturbing talk among the officers about the ship having to return to Sarawak to take up a new assignment. The navy was assembling a squadron that would undertake several additional patrols in the South China Sea before heading for Hong Kong, where it would be based for several weeks. Like many an Irish emigrant before him, McLoughlin, bent on going south and east, found the prospect of more-of-the-same singularly unappealing. When HMS *Albatross* set sail from Singapore, on 8 June 1881, he was no longer part of the ship's company.

It was a criminal offence to break contract with the armed services. Most deserters, many of whom continued to move about the oceanic world as seamen in the Merchant Navy after they had abandoned their ships, adopted aliases when they found themselves in ports where the British authorities had an official presence. McLoughlin, feeling his way around the fringes of the empire for the first time, almost certainly did so. Always laconic and loath to divulge unnecessary information, he remained understandably reluctant to talk about his desertion from first, the navy and then, later in life, the army. But, even allowing for that, there may have been other reasons for his profound silence about the six months spent in the navy and the voyage of the *Albatross*. It was, after all, at a time in his life when he was probably both more anonymous and more sexually active than any other. He may have left the navy, but the navy had not left him, in any event. For close observers, he manifested several enduring tell-tale signs of time spent at sea.

After Singapore, he walked with a distinctive gait that the navy and later the army contributed to.[32] The senior service left him with a lasting appreciation of naval office and rank in matters of discipline.[33] In the 1890s, while on the run from the police and already a man of significant stature in his own right, he served as a mercenary, reporting to another deserter from the navy known only as 'the Admiral'. Two decades after that, when he became violent on an ocean liner, the intervention of the ship's captain was sufficient to haul him back into line.[34] The armed forces may also have imbued him with an enhanced sense of racial superiority. The authority exercised over Arabs, Chinese and Indians and routine arrogance displayed towards them in countless day-to-day situations had deep cultural roots in western societies. But, for ordinary soldiers and sailors, that power was often reinforced through the exercise of brutal, direct physical force in social encounters that were far from the field of battle.

For the Manchester-born son of Irish immigrants imperial arrogance could be problematic. One of the tattoos McLoughlin left the navy with bore the coat of arms of the land of his birth, England. It was a prudent display of patriotism for an English sailor on a British warship. But, he also sported the coat of arms of the United States of America – an erstwhile British colony that had gained its independence through force of arms. America was also famous for the generous reception that it had accorded Irish refugees and for political sympathies that were pro-Irish.

But there were other puzzling ambiguities to McLoughlin's bodily displays. In keeping with the image favoured by sailors, his upper arms were festooned with tattoos of a 'ballet girl'. It would certainly be surprising if he and other sailors on the *Albatross* had *not* visited the usual harbour-side dives pushing alcohol, encouraging gambling or selling sex during their voyage across half the world. Yet, if there was one thing that characterised almost his entire life, then it was a consistent lack of interest in women. His preference was always for male company – in army barracks, in bush camps, out drinking, on the roads, on board ship or in prison.[35] The 'ballet girls' may have helped mask more complex attitudes, choices and behaviours.

Finally, if the navy did nothing else, it gave him an idea of the scale of empire and a slightly better understanding of the strengths and limitations of the Imperial Eye. The capacity and reach of law-enforcement agencies across the colonies varied greatly. A man on the run stood a better chance of avoiding the authorities in Bombay than he did in Singapore. And, during the four years that followed – from 1882 to 1885 – he learnt that Australia was perhaps the best country of all in which to hide. Almost nothing is known about him during that period. It was a good time in his life, but the Imperial Eye was becoming sharper with the passing of every year.

CHAPTER SEVEN

༼ະ*ະ༽

Among Legends and Myths of the Bush

AUSTRALIA
— 1882–1886 —

The dominant thought of youth is the bigness of the world, of age its smallness.
JOHN BUCHAN

O f all the McLoughlin children it was Thomas, the youngest boy, who
was cause for greatest concern. Released early from the reformatory
on grounds of ill health, Tommy never settled and was in constant trouble
with the law during a decade noteworthy for 'scuttling' excesses. In April
1882, he and a friend used belts and buckles to tackle two other youngsters
but, not content with their victory, went on to stab one of the victims. He
was sentenced to two months' hard labour but his accomplice was sent
down for a full year. The warning signs were there early on: Tommy was a
potential killer.

An older brother was as close to a father as Tommy ever got as a teenager.
Despite problems of his own and a difference in age of six years, Jack tried
to keep an eye on the lad and be as supportive as possible. Tommy, in turn,
was in awe of his brother and twice followed him to the far ends of the
earth – first, 'down under' to the antipodes in the 1880s and then, a decade
later, to southern Africa. In an otherwise largely dysfunctional family, theirs
was the only male relationship of notable meaning.

After leaving Manchester in 1880, and for some years thereafter, Jack

McLoughlin kept contact with his brother and at least one other member of the old Blue Dot gang by letter. The globalising postal service may have extended the surveillance capacity of the Imperial Eye, but it also enabled antisocial elements to remain in contact via counter-flows of criminal intelligence across the hemispheres. Intercontinental postal exchanges increased rapidly after it was agreed by the Universal Postal Union, in 1878, to levy a flat rate on letters sent anywhere in the world. Within Anglophone territories this was supplemented by the introduction of the Imperial Penny Post, in 1898.[1] Although not a regular correspondent, Jack used the postal services to stay in touch with Tommy after he deserted in Singapore, and, a decade later, with JW Brown when they were reunited in South Africa, in the 1890s.

In mid-1882, 12 months after deserting from the *Albatross,* he wrote to tell Tommy that he was in Australia. Where he was based and how he was earning a living were, like most things about him in this period of a secretive life, unknown. But the economy was growing fast and drawing in thousands of immigrants each year: casual urban or seasonal rural work was easy to find.[2] From Tommy's subsequent movements, it seems that the brothers entered Australia via the country's pre-eminent gateway, 'Marvellous Melbourne'.

★　★　★

The roots of European settlement in Australia lay in the penal colony established at Botany Bay, in New South Wales, in the late eighteenth century. While the transportation of convicts from Britain and Ireland continued for decades thereafter, by the mid-nineteenth century the practice was falling into abeyance and formally ended in 1867. By then, the emerging colonies, including Victoria and its principal city, Melbourne, were set on a different path. Much of east-coast Australia could trace its escape from modest regional agricultural economies into a long cycle of increasingly balanced and vigorous growth back to the transformative effect of gold discoveries of the 1850s and, more especially, the 1860s. For most of the 30 years that followed on the mineral discoveries, Australia experienced an economic boom and increased urbanisation.[3]

The ability of gold to draw in immigrants and strengthen economic development started to wane in the New South Wales and Victorian hinterlands in the late 1870s. But then, new discoveries – in Queensland in the 1880s and Western Australia in the 1890s – proved that the yellow metal could still light the way to frontiers on a continent where size beggared belief. Queensland and Western Australia, partly because of their remoteness from the south-eastern hub of the country, later appealed to the McLoughlin brothers, who for many years shared a preference for the anonymity of frontier life and zones of economic turbulence.

In the 1880s, it was the more densely settled south-east that attracted the brothers. Twenty-three-year-old Jack, in particular, found the colonies much to his liking. Here was a male-dominated society, one where bush legends embodied the attitudes, beliefs and values that appealed to a criminal romantic who had fled the industrial world.[4] Back in Manchester, the heroes of the distant past, such as Captain Dangerous or Rob Roy, had to be conjured up through books or the imagination but, in Australia, bushrangers and their exploits fell well within living memory. Even though the heyday of the bushrangers dated back 30 or 40 years, to the 1850s and the first gold discoveries, one could still sense the awe that men like Ben Hall, Dan Morgan, Harry Power and Jack Donahue – 'The Wild Colonial Boy' – evoked among ordinary folk. Part of the longevity of such tales and myths, the feeling that they might have some on-going pertinence, could be attributed to the way that the sprawling outback continued to dominate the lives of many Australians. In ideological, manly terms the bush and its associated lore often eclipsed city life.

Under ordinary circumstances, time itself might have taken some of the gloss off bush-ranging tales. But then, out of the Victorian bush emerged an extraordinary anachronism, a larger-than-life man who was to achieve iconic status in the country's folklore – Ned Kelly.[5] For those so inclined, like Jack McLoughlin, the distance between legend, myth, place and time was miraculously foreshortened. When Jack arrived in Australia, 24 months after Kelly's execution, in November 1880, the country was alive with tales, real and imagined, of the exploits of the Kelly gang. In their travels through rural New South Wales and Victoria between 1882 and 1886, the brothers from Ancoats moved in the footsteps of the last of Australia's great 'outlaw heroes'.

Like many young men, the McLoughlin brothers had more than an ideological diet of folklore to live on. Although tales about bank robbers and highwaymen-cum-bushrangers contributed centrally to the 'Australian legend', they were never as important as those strands that derived directly from the realities of everyday life in the nineteenth-century outback. The experiences of single working men, as perceived through gendered lenses in the most remote parts of what was eventually to become one of the most highly urbanised countries on earth, became pre-eminent in shaping an emerging national culture.[6]

An admiration for 'bush-craft' and the capacity to survive in the driest and most daunting of physical environments formed an important if not central strand of the developing legend. So, too, did the ability to divert modest economic opportunities into more promising entrepreneurial creeks that fed into far-off coastal markets. A suspicion of 'authority and the established order', in some cases attributable to the attitudes and experiences of Irish men and women who had been forced to bend the knee before an English aristocracy and the monarchy, contributed to an insistent egalitarianism with undertones of anti-clericalism and republicanism. In day-to-day interactions social solidarity in the face of harsh odds was expressed through a male camaraderie or 'mateship' that often included a measure of hard drinking and in its strongest form was rumoured not to preclude homosexual relationships.[7]

The Celtic underpinning of an emerging Australian 'national character' included a Scottish component, but was for the most part determined by an Irish input. Almost a quarter of the convicts sent south from the northern hemisphere between 1791 and 1850 were Irish. Most were drawn from the rural south-midland counties in Ireland itself or from Irish communities in industrial England. Many such involuntary emigrants, with experience of what they saw as political oppression and religious persecution at the hands of the English, were predisposed to challenge and dissent and were said to have a greater propensity to violence.

The move to Australia may have dampened but did not eradicate a streak of rebelliousness among most of the Irish. 'Much Irish crime,' one analyst suggests, 'involved disorganised offences arising from drunkenness, homelessness and unemployment' ... 'The Irish-born offenders were invariably more conspicuous in categories such as vagrancy, breach of the peace and drunken and disorderly behaviour.' In 1889, one in four of those arrested in New South Wales was Irish. Nor were Irish-Australian attitudes palliated by the fact that many of the policemen in the new colonies were Irish too, some having gained their basic training and initial experience in the roundly detested Royal Ulster Constabulary.[8]

There were several traits in this emerging composite national character as manifested in antisocial activities that appealed to the half-English, half-Irish McLoughlins. Schooled in urban lawlessness, the brothers never became fully fledged bushrangers. They nevertheless went on to show signs of partial adaptation to Australia's criminal sub-culture in town and countryside alike. Tommy, with his love of horses, took readily to working livestock in the outback and years later spent months on the run in Queensland. Jack acquired a 'flashness' associated with city dwellers and went on to absorb other, recognisably 'national' characteristics. Ten years later, in southern Africa, underworld informants described him as an 'Australian desperado' and 'a ruffian of the larrikin type' even though he was always more comfortable shifting between his formative 'English' and 'Irish' identities.[9]

When the brothers met in Melbourne, in the early 1880s, Victoria was set on an economic course that was the envy of the western world. The economic tempo and transformative powers of business had long since pushed beyond Melbourne and its satellite towns on the nearby goldfields. Capital had sharpened poverty and emerging class distinctions in the rural hinterland, creating the preconditions for Ned Kelly's banditry in the late 1870s.[10] The International Exhibition of 1880 had underscored the importance of a port housing a quarter of a million inhabitants with thousands of factories and workshops. The city also served as the financial centre for the continent as well as for investors around the globe.[11] By 1890, the state was as populous and rich as California.

There was no shortage of entry points for young men interested in

SHOWDOWN AT THE RED LION

penetrating the local underworld. The city offered the usual array of brothels, drinking dens, gambling outlets and, with a well-entrenched tradition of
horse-breeding, a racecourse already famous for hosting the annual competition for the Melbourne Cup. Victoria, albeit less so than New South Wales,
was also a major exporter of horses. 'Walers' were much sought after by the
armed forces in India because they coped better with the climate on the
subcontinent than did horses shipped in from elsewhere. Jack McLoughlin,
who got to know the city well enough to pretend to have been born there,
later persuaded the authorities in India to deport him to Melbourne and
they did so, placing him aboard a ship that had delivered just such a con-
signment of Walers.

By late 1882, Tommy, still only 18, was working as a groom in nearby
Ballarat. He may have been accompanied there by his older brother who,
for reasons of his own, was becoming more interested in mining towns. A
few months later, in February 1883, Tommy was found guilty of having broken into a local shop and sentenced to 12 months in Pentridge Prison. The
prison, close by Melbourne, made visiting easy and Tommy appears to have
settled into prison life and routine with relative ease. He worked his way up
and through the four categories that separated prisoners and was released
early, in January 1884.[12]

Pentridge, however, was a prison with a pedigree stretching back to the
era of the great bushrangers, steeped in tales about them that neither Tommy,
as inmate, nor Jack, as a visitor, could have failed to hear about. Indeed,
barely 24 months had elapsed since Ned Kelly himself had been executed
in the prison, leaving behind a grisly reminder. The outlaw's body had been
interred in the prison yard but only after the head had been removed for
purposes of scientific study. There were, however, other – older – tales about
Pentridge that might have appealed to a young Irishman with a dreamy
interest in highwaymen. Of those, Harry Power's might have resonated.

Born as Henry Johnstone, in Waterford, in 1819, Power was raised across
the Irish Sea, in Ashton-under-Lyne. As a lad he had worked in cotton mills
within easy walking distance of Ancoats. In 1840, Power was found guilty at
the Salford Assizes of stealing a pair of shoes and sentenced to seven years'
transportation. Thirty-eight years later, when Jack himself had stolen a pair

of boots, in 1878, he was given 'just' three months' imprisonment with hard labour. On his release from Tasmania, Power made his way to Sydney and continued his career in crime. In 1869, aged 50, he escaped from Pentridge and made his way into the badlands of the increasingly unsettled north-eastern Victoria, where he took on 14-year-old Ned Kelly as an apprentice highwayman.[13]

Stories about Power's exploits as highwayman, or those about other bushrangers, failed to encourage the brothers to strike up a partnership and follow suit. The tales may, however, have further softened up Jack's thinking about the need to develop a more broadly based repertoire, because 48 months later he was involved in several highway robberies, albeit half a world away. At the time, however, he harboured serious reservations about becoming directly involved with Tommy, whose impetuosity continued to compromise his growing professionalism. Unerringly accurate with dates when it suited him, Jack later recalled that it was in 1884 – after Pentridge – that he took his leave of Tommy. He also remembered that just 12 months later the Australian police were searching for him personally.[14]

On leaving prison, Tommy, manifesting an ever-more-pronounced liking for life on the frontier, abandoned Victoria and struck out north, across the Murray River and on past Sydney. His brother, too, may by then have been in the north-eastern parts of coastal New South Wales earning a living as an itinerant labourer between criminal escapades under an unknown name. Rural New South Wales was booming, with new railway lines being built to connect previously isolated farming centres.[15] Here, the brothers would have encountered yet more anecdotes about legendary bushrangers and there is indirect evidence to suggest that there was one, in particular, that Jack may have been struck by – the story of another recent Pentridge graduate, executed in Darlinghurst Prison, Sydney, in 1880.

Andrew Scott, son of an Anglican clergyman, was born in County Down, Ireland, in 1845. By the early 1860s, following the frontiers of empire, the family were on the Otago goldfields in New Zealand, when young Scott got drawn into the Maori land wars. Wounded and disillusioned, he then crossed the Tasman Sea to Victoria. In Melbourne, intent on following in his father's footsteps, he became a lay preacher but, in 1869, sent to the small gold mining town of Mount Egerton, he embarked on a more interesting calling. Still in his early twenties and living in the Ned Kelly hinterland, Scott set about indulging his interest in younger males. He adopted the sobriquet 'Captain Moonlite' – a name not unlike those adopted by the leaders of agrarian secret societies back in Ireland – and recruited a gang of bushrangers that included a male lover and several adolescent boys. After several not especially noteworthy exploits and a spell in Pentridge, Scott and his boy-gang undertook a futile last stand against the New South Wales police near Wagga Wagga in 1879.[16]

The story of 'Captain Moonlite' centred on his devotion to his lover, Nesbitt, and formed an integral part of the lore and scandal of the day. Amazingly, the tale only ended 100 or more years later, in 1995, when the bones of the two men, in deference to Andrew Scott's last wish, were interred in the same grave.

In the late 1880s, less than five years after his first passage through rural New South Wales, Jack McLoughlin and several other 'wild colonial boys' on the run from the police fled South Africa and crossed the border into neighbouring Mozambique. There, under the leadership of one John Hutchings, they worked as navvies for several months helping to construct a railway line.

John Hutchings, like many of his recruits, was a deserter from the British Army with some criminal proclivities and, on more than one occasion, literally signed off on his adventures as 'Captain Moonlite'. If Hutchings did not know what other connotations his *nom de guerre* carried then there were several more mobile Irishmen in his gang, including Jack McLoughlin, who could have told him. And, if Hutchings and McLoughlin *knew* about Captain Moonlite's sexual preferences, what does it tell us about the hidden lives of the Irish Brigade that McLoughlin had joined?[17]

Back in New South Wales, in mid-1884, however, Tommy and a friend were on the move. In the Hunter Valley, about 80 miles north of Sydney, huge tracts of trees and untamed bush cleared by ring-barking and scrubbing were making way for a more domesticated landscape that was developing a reputation for horse-breeding and wine-making. In early July, he and John O'Brian, who had been making a nuisance of themselves around

Maitland, were 'arrested on suspicion of being of unsound mind and re-manded for medical treatment'. It may, however, have been an alcohol-fuelled misadventure that prompted their arrest. After a few days, and having been examined by the district surgeon, they were declared to be 'in a fit state to be at large' and released.[18]

Without resources to fall back on, Tommy and O'Brian were forced to turn their attention to stealing what they could. Professional livestock thieves – cattle duffers – rustled animals, changed the brands and then marketed them at a distance from where they had been stolen. But the pair lacked experience and time was not on their side. The police were on to them within a matter of days, but before he could be arrested, Tommy effected an escape that Ned Kelly would have been proud of. 'He mounted a "half-broken mare", without saddle or bridle, and having cleared a fence, dashed through the bush…'. He disappeared and in the months that followed worked his way north towards the point where the Clarence River flowed into the Pacific Ocean near Grafton. There, in December 1884, he was either recognised from a description in the *Police Gazette* or arrested for some new misdemeanour before being sent to Lithgow, in the foothills of the Blue Mountains, to stand trial.[19]

With Tommy back in prison, Jack, operating under aliases that might never be uncovered, may have lingered in small town and rural New South Wales or just across the Queensland border for a considerable time. It was a part of the country – the core of it stretching from Bourke in the west to Tamworth in the east – that he felt comfortable in. Ten years later, in 1902, under radically changed personal circumstances, he traversed much of the same terrain while out on a safe-blasting circuit that followed the recently laid rail tracks.[20] Not all of his exploits between 1882 and 1885 went unpunished, however. Much later, underworld informants in Johannesburg reported that he 'graduated at the prisons of most of the colonies' long before Australia ever became a federation.[21]

The same informants, however, hinted at the fact that caution and cunning may have enabled him to record successes that went unpunished, noting that 'he is well known to the police authorities in Australia, where many a desperate act has been put down to his credit to this day'. Likewise, it was conceded that he only left Australia, in 1886, when he realised that he was 'cultivating what seemed likely to become a too close intimacy with the police'.[22] Whatever name he was operating under, McLoughlin was in danger of receiving a lengthy sentence.

★ ★ ★

Even without knowing the exact details of Jack McLoughlin's career as it unfolded in his mid-twenties, two things seem reasonably clear. First, given his subsequent sojourn in southern Africa, it would appear that it was his experiences in the antipodes that extended his repertoire to include a developing taste for frontier crime. Somewhere along the line between Ancoats and Australia, a few of his more romantic criminal notions were first actualised. Second, it is possible that the dominant legend of the time – that of Ned Kelly – lit up a part of his imagination.

The Kelly gang embodied a mutated form of 'Irishness', manifesting the sort of antisocial actions and political rebelliousness that was to be found in several British colonies. Kelly and three companions set the tone for much of the rural crime and dissent that characterised the contest between established land-owning 'squatters' and struggling, property-acquiring, 'selectors' in rural north-eastern Victoria between 1878 and 1880.[23] Through their individual actions and collective efforts, members of the gang displayed the full repertoire of manly qualities approved of in Victorian societies. Brave, charismatic, loyal and young – just four years older than McLoughlin – Ned Kelly was an excellent bushman, a superb shot and an outstanding horseman. He repeatedly demonstrated extraordinary flexibility and sure-footedness while eluding the state police. A 'bush larrikin' raised in the backyard of the goldfields, with a preference for male company that precluded a premature slide into domesticity, Kelly was a horse-thief turned bushranger, blessed with the ability to think laterally. At home in the hills and valleys around Wangaratta, he and the gang lived off the bush for lengthy periods. When necessary, they invaded nearby hamlets or small towns, taking hostages and robbing banks that controlled hard-pressed farmers' debt.

The Kelly gang's mobility between centres along the newly laid rail-way and out in the open country was impressive. So, too, was its ability to pull a poorly led police force far and wide. Its almost military precision would have appealed to someone already partly trained in, and admiring of, the arts of war. Operating in bandit-like mode, Kelly depended on a broad-based network of sympathisers whose loyalty was carefully cultivated through everyday displays of considered action, generosity and support. This highly personalised network, in turn, rested on an underlying founda-tion of class, ethnicity and kin. A 'bush-telegraph' supplied the gang with a flow of counter-intelligence that did much to offset the usual effects of an extensive network of police informers and spies.

The widespread support of ordinary folk for Kelly over much of north-eastern Victoria was tested after he and three friends were involved in a series of shoot-outs with the police. The bushrangers were declared out-laws and huge rewards posted for their successful apprehension. During the early stages of the 'outbreak' – a term usually associated with contagion and disease – the outlaws were often successful in keeping one step ahead of the police. Aaron Sherritt – a close friend of Joe Byrne, one of the gang members – inveigled himself into a position as double agent, for a time supplying the gang with useful information and the police with unhelpful facts and false rumours.

Growing tensions and mounting uncertainty took its toll on the gang members. A plan to derail a train and capture much-needed police arms and equipment tested the network's solidarity to breaking point. Byrne began to doubt Sherritt's fealty and a decision was taken to execute him. Even then, Sherritt was given a warning, via his mother, that he was about to be shot. From that moment on, the double-agent had the choice of either arming and defending himself when the dreaded moment arrived, or taking the less honourable route and fleeing the community.[24]

In the end, it was not only the murder of the informer that was memo-rable for those who were deadly serious about loyalty, but the manner in which it was to be undertaken. It was Byrne – the man smarting most from a sense of betrayal – who was deputed to execute his former close friend. Byrne would approach the cabin where the newly married Sherritt, having sacrificed his bachelor status, was living under police protection, knock on the door and when he appeared – armed or unarmed – shoot him at point blank range. It was a plan which, with minor improvisations, was put into action. Answering to the voice of an acquaintance who was supposedly lost, Sherritt appeared at the door unarmed and was dispatched while the police cowered behind a partition in the cabin for some hours before leaving.[25]

For anyone with a long-standing interest in codes of loyalty and manly conduct the Kelly gang's determination to avenge Sherritt's alleged betrayal was as salutary as it was brutal. But there were other lessons to be taken from the 'outbreak', among them the hazards of being formally outlawed. In functioning democratic states criminals operated within a framework provided by the rule of law – assaulting, robbing, stealing or murdering within the parameters of established systems. The system itself guaranteed certain fundamental rights and delivered broadly predictable outcomes. There were legal limits to what the police could do while investigating crimes. Suspects had a right to know what charges were being preferred against them and writs of *habeas corpus* ensured timely appearances before properly constituted courts that handed down only penalties specified by the law.

But for those whom the state placed beyond the system and who were declared to be outside the protection of the law, things were very different. Outlaws could, like wild animals, be tracked down by any and all means at the disposal of the authorities or concerned citizens. With a price on their heads, outlaws could be brought in 'alive or dead', often with an unstated preference for the latter. The events at Glenrowan, site of the Kelly gang's last stand, provided awful testimony as to the consequences for those deemed to be beyond the protection of the law.

The police, present in large numbers, directed fusillade upon fusillade of shots into the insubstantially built country inn in which the bandits and their hostages had taken refuge. Kelly – despite having donned armour fashioned from ploughshares – was seriously wounded in a skirmish in the grounds of the inn. A passing Catholic priest, Father Mathew Gibney, drawn to the site by the sound of gunfire, administered the last rites in the mistaken belief that Kelly was fatally wounded. Of the four outlaws, Kelly alone survived to be tried later and executed, in November 1880.[26]

McLoughlin, by his own account, came to understand only too well what it meant to be declared an outlaw. Dick Turpin and other eighteenth-century outlaws who had sallied out of books in the Ancoats library were one thing; those encountered in tales of bushrangers and the living legend of Ned Kelly were quite another. Australia had whetted his appetite for life on the edge but, unable to shake off the attentions of the police and unwilling to spend years locked away in some provincial prison, he looked around for other, more promising settings.

He wanted to be where the law functioned imperfectly and a man worth his salt stood a chance of making his fortune. He sensed that the economic centre of gravity in the southern hemisphere was undergoing one of its periodic shifts. Nobody knew how long the reported boom would last, but adventurers, clerks, prospectors and storekeepers were once again preparing to spread their wings. The shipping lines were standing by, ever ready to facilitate the mass migration of men, money and machines. The Aberdeen Line, which had once linked England to Australia by sail-driven clippers, had set up a new trans-Indian Ocean run. A regular schedule now linked Melbourne to Durban and Cape Town. In late 1886, he left Melbourne for Durban in the colony of Natal.

It was hardly a novel move. Indeed, South Africa owed its latest and greatest promise of prosperity and the gathering boom to George Harrison, an Australian prospector. In an era of accelerating economic development and cheaper international travel the distance separating Australia from South Africa was shrinking rapidly and the mind-maps of professional criminals, too, were being re-adjusted. Some claimed that members of the Kelly gang themselves had contemplated fleeing to South Africa. Many years later, two other members of the gang, Dan Kelly and Steve Hart, were rumoured to have been seen in South Africa, where they had supposedly enlisted with Boer forces challenging a British Army intent on expanding the empire.[27] When Jack McLoughlin left, however, it may well have been the image of Joe Byrne shooting the informer, Aaron Sherritt, in his doorway that lingered longest in his mind. Sherritt had sacrificed gang loyalty for the love of a woman.

SUMMER

CHAPTER EIGHT

❦

The Southern African Mineral Revolution
and the College of Banditry

— *c* 1886 —

'Tis Ireland gives England her soldiers, her generals too.

GEORGE MEREDITH

L ike many others who had turned their backs on the industrialising north and headed south to try their luck in British colonies that commanded huge swathes of the Atlantic, Indian and Pacific Oceans, Jack McLoughlin knew little about his chosen new field of operations.

By the mid-nineteenth century most of land-gorged, rain-scarce southern Africa had languished in an agricultural torpor induced by weak domestic and modest international demand for its products for more than 200 years. Then, in an unguarded moment in the late 1860s, at the centre of an unpromising inland area, nature left one of its most sought-after treasures lying around after a bout of careless play. The discovery of the world's greatest diamond fields aroused the subcontinent from its slumber. It transformed a previously thinly populated plateau exploited only seasonally by many black and a few white nomadic tribesmen of European origin, into a burgeoning market centred on Kimberley. The city harvested excellent gemstones for which there was infinite demand.

But fate, not content with an initial round of mischief-making, went on to ensure that the remote interior was doubly blessed, or twice cursed.

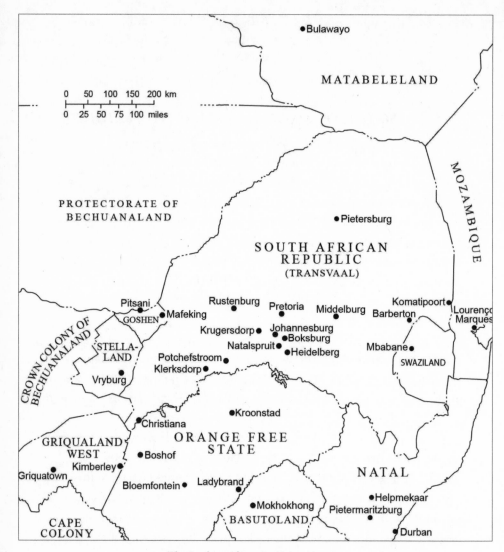

The Southern African Interior c 1880–1895

Barely two decades later, in the early 1880s, it became known that within a
few hundred miles of the new diamond city, gold – in significant quantities –
was to be found in the eastern parts of the sprawling region beyond the Vaal
River. The new discovery lay in the modestly endowed Zuid-Afrikaansche
Republiek (ZAR), whose origins dated back to the last of the deep sleep of

the 1830s, when thousands of Boers, frustrated by the abolition of slavery in the Cape, had trekked north to escape their overbearing British rulers. But the eastern Transvaal goldfields had barely had time to draw the attention of adventurers and the investing public north, when, in 1886, the biggest goldfields ever were discovered along the Witwatersrand.

With industrial Britain approaching the apex of its geopolitical powers, the hitherto neglected southern African interior and its coastal hinterland became the site of armed eruptions between blacks, Boers and Brits and combinations thereof. These would take 50 years to subside to manageable proportions and a century to reach anything approaching a sustainable solution. Imperialism, predicated on expanding trade backed by significant reserves of gold, may not have been driven solely by economics but Britain was never averse to employing its military might. The armed forces secured the island kingdom's incoming supplies of food and raw materials and guaranteed that increasing quantities of finished goods reached distant markets where they enforced 'free trade'.

In southern Africa sustained conflict marked huge expanses of territory underpinned by mineral wealth said to be of staggering proportions. Estimates of reserves were adjusted upwards constantly in places where boundaries had always been semi-permeable and poorly defined. Scores of chieftainships and kingdoms, along with established colonial states and independent republics, new and old, emerged and were incorporated, or mutated and fell, with bewildering rapidity. Borders, frontiers and property, already the subject of deep-seated disputes between indigenous inhabitants of colour and the growing stream of incoming whites, acquired a new and often unenforceable importance.

Boers, long-established or recently-arrived colonists, shopkeepers and white labourers activated by the prospect of profit spread out over the plateau to become commercial farmers, diggers, mine owners, prospectors or traders. By virtue of the colour of their skin, whites competed on privileged or wholly unfair terms with Africans and other cattle owners, hunter-gatherers or subsistence farmers of a darker hue. Indigenous peoples ever more confined to 'locations' or 'reserves' were transformed into peasants, migrant labourers or workers increasingly dependent on wages earned in the new mines or at other places of employment in the mushrooming small towns and cities of the far-off interior.

In the twinkling of an historical eye, over enormous tracts of land stretching tens of thousands of square miles, emerged a would-be country sitting on a cornucopia of mineral wealth. It was a sprawling place that had no convincing natural boundaries to separate it from the rest of the continent. It lacked any over-arching political authority enjoying widespread legitimacy. And it could only aspire to developing the few cultural bonds that came from shared ethnicities, language or religion that hinted at a larger, integrated society. The gods, having left their valuables lying about amidst great natural beauty, condemned the finders to the labour of Sisyphus. They were doomed to perpetual 'nation-building', to a never-ending search for social harmony. It was to be a country without a distinctive name, a place best found by following a direction; it was the southern part of something else, something bigger.

The tremors of imperial expansion set loose the corrosive forces that herald the coming of industrial capitalism everywhere. There were frantic attempts to acquire new territory, to defend the *status quo ante*, secure independence, or seal the best deal in a world turning upside down. Predictably, the area of greatest turbulence lay within the semi-circle that defined the northern limits of the recently discovered diamond and goldfields. Like a rainbow, the appearance of this new multi-textured arc promised that no more disasters were to follow, but the unsettling man-made military and political realities that preceded the outbreak of the South African War of 1899–1902 were all ominous in their own right.

The demise of 'Griqualand West' (1873–1880) and emergence of the Bechuanaland Protectorate (1885) prevented further unwanted squalls from howling in through the back door of the diamond industry. In 1881, conservative and deeply religious Boers living beyond the Vaal River had to defeat the British in the First War of Independence so as to regain, and then attempt to seal off, their slow-rooting republic from the harshest forces of modernisation. But the sealant applied from within, let alone beyond, left much to be desired.

To the south-west of their country, half-way between the Witwatersrand goldfields and diamond mines controlled by an imperialistic Cecil Rhodes, the monopolistic De Beers Company and British colonial authorities, a new and wholly unexpected problem emerged. In 1882, Boer freebooter-mercenaries recruited by chiefly African principals who rewarded them with land-grants carved out the Republic of Stellaland and, almost immediately thereafter, the Republic of Goshen. Then in a potentially menacing move which to British ears briefly offered faint echoes of the American War of Independence, the upstart Boer-bandit republics joined forces to form the short-lived 'United States of Stellaland and Goshen' (1882–1885). Elsewhere, within its own expansive northern and eastern regions, an over-stretched ZAR administration faced constant challenges from powerful African chieftains. In 1890, Rhodes, in an attempt designed to outflank and seal off yet more of the ZAR, recruited a 'pioneer column' to occupy and settle land north of the Limpopo in what was to become Rhodesia.

Yet, despite all the geopolitical positioning and land-grabbing by the dominant British and Boer forces, there was one intractable 'foreign' anomaly that lay to the east. In the neighbouring Portuguese territory of Mozambique, a fine natural harbour at Lourenço Marques occupied a site of considerable strategic importance. Fever-ridden Delagoa Bay soon became the object of envious British and Boer eyes. The proximity of the port to the eastern Transvaal goldfields, the Witwatersrand and the diamond mines of the south pointed to the need for a rail link to steamships that serviced the new oceanic pathways to globalising trade.

Well before the man-made corridor between Delagoa Bay and the Witwatersrand had the railroad imprinted on it in the early 1890s, Lourenço Marques serviced far more than the orthodox, legal import-export trade of the region. As part of a remote colony governed by an opaque legal system, it was without formal extradition treaties binding it to the British colonies to the south or the independent Boer states of the interior. Delagoa Bay occupied an unusual liminal status amidst all the armed conflicts and indus-trialisation of the continent's troubled interior.[1]

Under the nominal control of notoriously corrupt bureaucrats and port officials, Lourenço Marques boasted the usual array of seedy waterside es-tablishments. It was the entry point of choice for smuggled arms as well as illegal immigrants, pimps, prostitutes and spies – and for the trans-shipment of huge supplies of cheap alcohol destined for black and white consumption in the new mining towns.[2]

In return for an unwritten contract that allowed for the taxable import of questionable substances used in the social control of workers on the Highveld, Lourenço Marques took in, and housed, antisocial elements and white fugitives fleeing law-enforcement agencies throughout southern Africa. Throughout the 1880s and 1890s it was the favoured exit point of bandits, bank robbers, confidence tricksters, fraudsters, diamond and gold smugglers, highwaymen, murderers, rapists, thieves and white slave traffickers waiting to escape into the expanding world.[3]

Thus, long before the destruction and slaughter of the notorious turn-of-the-century conflict between Boer and Briton that further promoted the name of a country-in-the-making, many peoples in the northern reaches of southern Africa were either preparing for war, in the throes of one, or recovering from one barely past. Profoundly unsettled political and socio-economic conditions on either side of the borders of states and smaller polities that appeared or disappeared within a matter of months, were an essential part of the preconditions necessary for the emergence of the organised brigandage and other crimes manifesting themselves among the thousands of adventurers, deserters, navvies or otherwise alienated and rootless whites destined for the Highveld. And attached to this feverish body, always feeding into as well as off the pathologies of industrialisation, was the emerging port on Delagoa Bay.

Important as these developments were, however, there were other factors at work in the South African Republic and the neighbouring Orange Free State that contributed to the emerging patterns of European criminality in the northern region. Principal among these was the remoteness of the new industries. The diamond and gold mines lay hundreds of miles inland, on an extended plateau, without rail connections to the cities and ports of the coastal colonies. Capitalists and governments hoping for an import-export bonanza were, for a decade and more, locked into a transport system that depended on horse- or ox-drawn coaches and wagons traversing makeshift roads.

This primitive 'horse-economy' – without a meaningful parallel any-where in the developing world at the time – lingered until the mid-1890s when the last major link in an integrated railway system reached Johannesburg. It added some meaning to the words 'South Africa', which gained full political purchase in 1910. But, until 1895, the mineral industries in the developing north remained locked into a startling contradiction as the largest supplies of diamonds and gold the world had ever known had to be transported over huge distances, leaving them vulnerable to the preda-tions of gangs of coach robbers or highwaymen.

The distance separating the mines from the more densely settled areas of African labour along the coastal areas and at the far north-eastern reaches of the South African Republic further complicated the situation. The absence of secure rail transport provided Boer farmers and cash-strapped newly arrived white criminals and workers drawn from the wider Anglophone world with the opportunity to engage in organised theft and robbery. Black workers making their way across the interior to find work on the mines, so as to meet escalating tax demands, were left at risk. In the north and the east, armed Boers intercepted and diverted Africans into ultra-cheap or unpaid seasonal work on farms that were increasingly market-orientated. On the way back black migrants were no less vulnerable. African workers carrying illegally acquired gemstones from Kimberley or wages in cash or gold specie earned on the Witwatersrand, were stripped of their possessions by bogus white policemen demanding 'passes' or by armed and mounted highwaymen.

★ ★ ★

These, then, were the regional economic dynamics that Jack McLoughlin encountered upon his arrival on the east coast of 'South Africa' at the be-ginning of 1886. The country, but more especially the diamond and gold mining hinterland of the Highveld, was ready to receive him and thousands like him. Many of them were young men in their twenties with chang-ing class and ethnic identities, raised in the mid-Victorian slums of the

Industrial Revolution and exposed to a cult of hyper-masculinity born of an earlier era. Subsidised passages provided by the British Army and the Merchant or Royal Navies enabled them to reach the outer fringes of the empire, where they entered the socio-economic circuits of the English-speaking world, wary of settling into domesticity or paid labour, and furthered careers in organised crime.

But, as McLoughlin soon realised, Durban was not Melbourne. Nor did coastal Natal provide him with the network of Irish or Mancunian contacts that he hoped would get him to the new mining frontiers. Without any real alternative, he decided to do as he had done when he abandoned London and get the taxpayer to support him until such time as he was ready to move inland. The British Army, based in the nearby garrison town of Pietermaritzburg, was unlikely to usher him directly into the emerging centres of Johannesburg or Kimberley, but it would give him the chance to work out the lie of the land and meet a few kindred spirits. The Australian police, too, were unlikely to look for him in the ranks of the army.

Fort Napier already housed a fair number of native-born Irishmen or Anglo-Irish males raised in industrial Glasgow, Liverpool or Manchester. It was easy to understand why that should be so. Ireland was England's first colony. Without significant mineral deposits of the type most in demand by the factories of the nineteenth century and an agricultural potential that was as misunderstood as it was overestimated, much of Catholic Ireland was doomed to live in the shadows of the Industrial Revolution. As with the 'native reserves' of southern Africa, population pressure and restricted access to farming land of good quality combined with natural disasters, such as the Great Famine of 1847–52, to ensure that Ireland's greatest export remained men, women and children.[4]

Economically marginalised and educationally underprivileged, first in rural Ireland and then to a lesser extent in the ethnic neighbourhoods of cities in north-western England and Scotland, young Irishmen flocked to the banner of the employer of the last resort – the army. The alluring tales of the regimental sergeant-major, recounted over beer in the public house and backed by the promise of the King or Queen's shilling a day, ensured that the Irish were disproportionately well represented in the armed forces throughout the nineteenth century. In 1831, without the Napoleonic Wars to stimulate industrial output, an extraordinary 42 per cent of all the men in the British Army were Irish-born. By 1861, before the impact of the American Cotton Famine was fully felt in Lancashire, this figure still stood at 28 per cent. As late as 1871, with gradual assimilation and fuller employment in England being partially offset by the radicalisation of Irish politics at home and abroad, fully 25 per cent, or one in four, of all those serving in the British Army were still Irish.[5]

Fort Napier commanded southern Africa's north-east. It was located just below the arc of turbulence that stretched from the recently belligerent and victorious South African Republic in the west, to the seemingly dormant Zulu kingdom, recently crushed in the Anglo-Zulu War of 1879, in the east. It left the army well situated to respond to regional conflicts stemming from imperial consolidation or expansion. The army was in reasonable shape.

The Cardwell Reforms of 1870 had effectively halved the periods of enlistment in the artillery, cavalry, engineers and infantry to six years, to be followed by six years in the reserves. The reforms did much to shore up the declining appeal of a career in the army for unemployable males and had been followed by further radical re-organisation. Among the regiments affected by the resulting rationalisation, there were two with a significant Irish presence that were destined to be based at Pietermaritzburg – the 2nd South Lancashire Regiment (1884–87) and the Royal Inniskillings (1886–88). In 1887, these 'Irish' regiments were joined by the 'English' 64th Regiment – the North Staffordshires.[6]

Both the Inniskillings, based in north-western Ireland, and the South Lancashires, from Werrington, in Cheshire, had Irishmen of different political persuasions within their ranks. Some, Catholic-Green, were nationalist sympathisers; others, Orange-Protestant, were loyal to the Crown. Private misgivings about serving in the empire's armed forces heightened tensions amongst troops drawn from different backgrounds.[7] Moreover, both 'Irish' regiments had, as part of the post-Cardwell innovations, been forced to amalgamate with older Regiments of Foot. All of this meant that, by the time that the 'Irish' contingents reached Pietermaritzburg, their commanding officers had to work especially hard to develop new regimental loyalties and maintain *esprit de corps.* Most of this was done within Fort Napier itself through familiar, repetitive, means – endless drills, inspections, armed manoeuvres and parades.

This psycho-physical drive to shape a collective identity had, however, to be offset against other countervailing pressures that could promote fissiparous tendencies and divide loyalties. The army was consistently troubled by the prospect of the Zulus remobilising to mount a new challenge to regain their recently lost kingdom. This meant that parts of the regiments were deployed at strategic sites in the Natal countryside.

McLoughlin, who had probably enlisted under his own name in the South Lancashire Regiment and undergone basic training at Fort Napier, was just one of many hundreds despatched to serve in an outlying rural area. For several months he was based at Helpmekaar – a remote outpost less than 20 miles from Rorke's Drift, where, in 1879, a small British garrison had held out against the Zulu army in an epic battle.[8] From Helpmekaar he and others undertook highly unpopular bush patrols to investigate and report on any 'threatening' developments among the nearby Zulu.

Soldiers working in small units under demanding conditions encouraged close, occasionally even intimate friendships. Patrolling the forests, fields and scrubby wastes of Zululand also provided them with excellent supplementary training. It allowed them to develop as bush fighters and enhanced survival skills. As McLoughlin and others were quick to appreciate, however, the same skills could easily be turned to other ends. For antisocial elements intent on furthering their careers as bandits, coach-robbers or highwaymen, Fort Napier was not only a formidable frontier military stronghold but a virtual College of Banditry.

Bush patrols exposed the urban 'Irish' to guns and horses as they learnt how to mount attacks or secure defensive positions. Camping taught them how to 'read' the local topography, find fresh water or hunt for game. For those with a facility for languages, circuit-work enabled them to acquire a smattering of the vernacular that helped grease social relations when dealing with friendly locals or giving instructions to those less inclined to assist the redcoats. As importantly, bush patrols provided an opportunity to learn how the local mounted police moved through remote rural areas by day or by night while tracking gun-runners, cattle-rustlers or horse thieves.[9]

Far from the city and women, bush patrols allowed for the more fulsome expression of the cult of masculinity that dominated nineteenth-century Britain. But the cult sometimes encouraged ambiguities and contradictions that were difficult to control or eliminate. The army viewed most females, other than prostitutes, with suspicion precisely because they threatened to dissolve part of the social glue that held the lower ranks together. The army, or so it claimed, provided troops with an extended 'male family'.

Any formal caring on the part of the army, however, was supplemented through more ambiguous informal roles when soldiers were called upon to undertake chores such as cleaning, cooking, ironing or washing; Victorian work that was quintessentially 'female'. The army, and even more so the navy, allowed men to develop various identities and to express a range of sexual preferences in private. Camaraderie and relationships cultivated on bush patrol could make their way back into the barracks where, left un-checked or engaged in indiscreetly, manifested themselves in the 'problems' of masturbation or homosexuality. Officers also had to deal with complaints about soldiers raping young African males while out on patrol in isolated locations.[10]

After a spell in the navy and a criminal apprenticeship served in the shad-ows of Ned Kelly, entry into the ranks of the South Lancashire Regiment came at a good time for 27-year-old McLoughlin. The army provided him with the opportunity to acquire the skills necessary to further his long-term frontier ambitions. As importantly, the two 'Irish' and other regiments – in-cluding the 6th Dragoons and the Argyll and Sutherland Highlanders – con-tained a significant number of bold malcontents with criminal records who, like him, envisaged their futures elsewhere. All that was needed to trigger their desertion was one or two promising new mineral discoveries in the more remote interior.

But the first half of 1886 was perhaps not the moment to turn one's back on the barracks, the mess, or the Queen's shilling. The diamond-field fron-tiers were closing rapidly. Kimberley was set to become a tightly controlled mining town run by Rhodes and De Beers with the support of police provided by the Cape government. The eastern Transvaal fields along the De Kaap Valley were only slightly more promising. In 1885, a discovery had been made at the 'Golden Quarry' near Barberton that promised much. But, even there, where the ramshackle South African Republican Police were thin on the ground, the most recent figures suggested that production at the older workings may already have peaked. For some months the bold and restless hesitated until it seemed that they might have missed their moment altogether.

★   ★   ★

The leader of the hard-drinking, rebellious set that emerged in the mess at Fort Napier and congregated around the low-class watering-holes in Pietermaritzburg during early 1886 was John Hutchings. Charismatic, Irish-born and an admirer of the agrarian secret societies that challenged the English establishment, Hutchings with his family had emigrated to Lancashire when he was a child. His background as a mill-town lad was presumably not very different from that of Jack McLoughlin and others in the South Lancashire Regiment. Recruited in Devonport, in 1883, Hutchings found army discipline difficult, if not impossible, to cope with. In addition to being made to forfeit his pay and being placed on special rations for weeks on end, he once spent a week in military prison.[11] In South Africa, he became proficient in Isizulu and Siswati and, at various moments later in his career – like McLoughlin – was frequently comfortable in African company. Indeed, Hutchings eventually married a black woman and his descendants are still to be found in Swaziland.[12]

John O'Brien, another recruited in Devonport, was a close friend of Hutchings and the two had been shipmates on the voyage out to Natal in the mid-1880s. A Lancastrian, O'Brien hailed from Manchester, if not from Ancoats itself. A criminal-dreamer with a pronounced anti-clerical streak, O'Brien had strong Irish nationalist sympathies. He often claimed – falsely – that his brother had been one of the Manchester Martyrs. O'Brien was as adept at changing his name or assuming a false identity as were many others in a growing group of malcontents.[13]

James Williams was another fugitive from the hard school of poverty in

Liverpool or Manchester and an early entrant into the criminal dream-world that tempted the first generation of Anglo-Irish. He and his older brother, a habitual offender with a lengthy criminal record, were already in Australia in the late 1870s; in 1884 both were active as thieves in the Melbourne suburb of Fitzroy. It may well have been there that he and Jack McLoughlin first met; in fact, it is possible that they travelled to Natal together.

Williams may have enlisted in the South Lancashires under an assumed name, and later preferred to call himself 'William James Kelly'. Like Ned Kelly, albeit for different reasons, he developed an interest in banks and any form of portable wealth. There was also something of the confidence-trickster about Williams, who had an eye for the ladies, with whom he enjoyed considerable success. Along with other graduates from the College of Banditry, WJ Kelly became an extraordinarily mobile criminal and moved about southern Africa – as well as in and out of Lourenço Marques – with ease during the early 1890s.[14]

It could have been shared Australian experiences that cemented the friendship between WJ Kelly and McLoughlin during the earliest days of their underworld collaboration in southern Africa. The bond was further strengthened when the two of them and John O'Brien shared a life-changing moment five years later, long after they had all turned their backs on army life. But WJ was not McLoughlin's closest friend; that distinction fell to John McCann.

Better known as Jack – to rhyme with 'Mac', as with his friend, McCann was Irish-born, from Dungannon in County Tyrone. As an illiterate 19-year-old labourer, McCann had joined the Inniskillings in 1881, shortly before the regiment set sail for the Straits Settlements. Like Kelly, he may have met McLoughlin when they were much younger and more likely to form lasting friendships. The paths of the Inniskillings and the *Albatross* crossed in Singapore, where the Irishmen could have shared the *demi-monde* delights of Malay Street. McCann contracted syphilis while in the Straits. Then poorly understood, the disease undermined his health and may have helped shape his personality as something of a loner.[15]

A short fellow of restless temperament, McCann was happiest on horseback, crossing borders and covering the huge distances of southern Africa as if they were mere parish boundaries back in rural Ulster. Like most of his Fort Napier cohort, McCann never hesitated to take an alias but, lacking a basic education, was frequently less successful in avoiding the police than many of his underworld associates. His inability to read and write may also have made him more reliant on McLoughlin than he might otherwise have been. Whatever the reason, the two Jacks knew they could rely on each other. [16]

Hutchings, McLoughlin, McCann, Kelly and O'Brien became leaders of those Anglo-Irish and Irish malcontents in the garrison who had difficulty in adjusting to army life. Quintessentially 'hard men' of the type so admired in certain circles of Victorian society, the five renegades soon had a sizeable following in the South Lancashire Regiment. Their followers were drawn largely from the cities at the core of northern, industrialising society. If the events of late 1886 are anything to go by – and they seem to be – the five could 'command' 50 or more disgruntled men. The anger, disillusionment and frustrations of those scarred by the Industrial Revolution were coming to the boil, far away, in the southern hemisphere.

If the primary concern of many in the South Lancashire Regiment could be traced back to the material, as opposed to political, circumstances in which they found themselves, there were others – in the Inniskillings – drawn from rural Ireland, whose grievances were more political than economic. Indeed, just 12 months later, in 1887, tensions between Orange and Green elements within the Inniskillings contributed to a drunken brawl that ended in a mutiny. This low point in regimental discipline culminated in the execution of a soldier, Joseph McCrea. [17]

In 1886–87, Fort Napier was the site of much grumbling by scores of Irishmen of various stripes waiting on the coming of some unknown but better dispensation. In the South Lancashires many of the Anglo-Irish, once removed from Ireland and raised in an acquisitive society, waited for a new economic star to appear in the night sky. For them, it would light the way through the South African bush to the adventurous life and wealth they longed for. Others, accustomed to rural life and contemplating a longer march to happiness, placed their trust in Westminster and dreamt that

Charles Parnell and the new Irish National League would produce the change in political fortunes they longed for back in their motherland.

Locally, things were – on the face of it – becoming more promising. Rumours circulated about yet further mineral discoveries in the South African Republic. Few were believable and they needed verification – a time-consuming business not easily effected within the garrison. In the eastern Transvaal, enticing quantities of gold had been uncovered in the De Kaap Valley as far back as the 1870s, but it took more than a decade for sustainable payloads to be uncovered at Barberton. Likewise, talk of economically viable gold deposits along the Witwatersrand had been around since the 1870s but since then nothing substantial had emerged.

The 'Irish' malcontents were unwilling to wait another 10 years. Kelly and McCann were the first to break ranks. In April 1886, tired of watching for the sign of an economic miracle to appear, Kelly deserted and made his way to Barberton, on the escarpment, 300 miles away.[18] Jack McCann undertook the even longer haul to the badlands around the diamond fields. There, George Lennox, a serial deserter from the armed forces, was forging his reputation as South Africa's 'Robin Hood' under the alias 'Scotty Smith'.

Of Scottish descent, as his moniker proclaimed, Lennox had, as a young man, undergone some training as a veterinary surgeon. He had then made his way to Australia where Ned Kelly and his gang had mastered the dark arts of horse-theft. In South Africa, Smith became the prince of horse-thieves in a horse economy – and, it was said, a good friend to many a lonely widow.[19] While several of McLoughlin's companions were later rumoured to have honed their skills in Smith's company, McCann was certainly not one of them. After deserting, he spent nearly two years working as a winding-engine driver on various Kimberley mines when not engaged in criminal activities.[20]

McCann and Kelly may, however, have bolted in the wrong directions at the wrong time. If they had waited a few weeks, they could have been among the starters for the long-awaited Big Rush. In mid-1886, George Harrison discovered a substantial gold reef on the farm Langlaagte on the Witwatersrand. Harrison's claim was registered in October and, by early December, the township of Johannesburg had been proclaimed and the first plots were being sold to the first of the invading hopefuls. By the end of the year there were 3 000 diggers on what were, after many twists and turns, to become the world's greatest deep-level gold mines.

The explosion of good news about the Rand rocked the barracks in Fort Napier 400 miles away – and the impact was felt most intensely in the rank and file of the South Lancashire Regiment. Men from all the regiments in the garrison deserted their posts to join in the rush, but it was the first-generation Anglo-Irish – those raised in the mills and slums of Manchester – who were most taken with the idea of finding gold, literally or metaphorically. Between September and December 1886, close on 50 men deserted the South Lancashires. Among the roughest of these former 'scuttlers' were P Carroll (1 December), J Dwyer (14 September), John Hutchings (6 November), J McLoughlin (exact date unknown, but likely to have left at round about the same time as Hutchings), John O'Brien (16 October) and J Wiggins (28 October).[21]

The emergence of Johannesburg as *the* centre of opportunity in the interior – a development without parallel since the discovery of diamonds two decades earlier – breathed new life into the entire region. With Barberton reviving briefly as the Golden Quarry metamorphosed into the booming Sheba Mine, Kimberley the well-established centre of the world diamond industry and Johannesburg mushrooming, new coach routes were introduced linking the three outer points of an enormous triangle demarcating the presence of fabulous wealth. Within a matter of months the amounts of cash, diamonds or gold bullion moving overland, between the centres and the coastal ports, increased dramatically.[22]

Neither the table-top-smooth diamond fields nor the modest rocky ridges of the Witwatersrand offered would-be coach-robbers or highwaymen the classic densely forested or mountainous redoubts preferred by bandits. With the old tracks from Pietermaritzburg to Pretoria having acquired new significance as they looped through Johannesburg, the 'road' – busier than ever – came under closer scrutiny from the authorities.[23] The core of the Irish deserters, thinking better of it, decided to ignore the obvious and, instead of making their way directly to the Witwatersrand, worked their way along the hilly escarpment until they reached the hills around

Barberton and the floor of the De Kaap Valley – places that had the added virtue of having a back door that led directly to Mozambique, Delagoa Bay and Lourenço Marques. By December 1886, the Manchester-Irish and others were digging in for a bonanza.

❦

CHAPTER NINE

The Frontiers of Gold and Beyond

EUREKA CITY AND DELAGOA BAY
— 1861–1887 —

Men have a touchstone whereby to try gold,
but gold is the touchstone whereby to try men.
THOMAS FULLER

By 1886, Barberton was briefly resurgent, lifted by income derived from properties owned by the Sheba Reef Gold Mining Company. A reef mine, as opposed to the older alluvial workings in the northern and eastern parts of the South African Republic, offered some hope of permanency. Just 12 months later, however, the town's fortunes started taking a turn for the worse and some journalists were already looking back on the good old days with nostalgia. Back then, one scribbler noted, the hills around the town:

> … were alive with noise and industry. Sunday was no day of rest, the nights were simply a period of darkness, not a season for repose. Day and night there was one continuous volley of blasting. If a man wanted employment there it was at hand and he could fix his own remuneration.[1]

In 1886, the town still had 1 000 white residents, mostly miners, while twice that number of blacks laboured in its sole industry. Pioneering entrepreneurs destined to leave their mark on South African history, including

Abe Bailey, Percy Fitzpatrick and Sammy Marks, took a close interest in the town's small stock exchange and possibly big future.

Not all newcomers had an interest in securing long-term employment, however. John O'Brien, who had arrived early, had talked his way into the police. During his off-duty hours, he took up positions along the surrounding migrant labour routes, intercepting black workers making their way back to Mozambique or Swaziland. He demanded to see their passes before relieving them of their savings. McLoughlin later claimed that this shoddy trick earned O'Brien as much as £30 a day.[2]

WJ Kelly, John Wiggins and McLoughlin were soon employed on the mines. There they served the informal apprenticeships that later provided them with plausible cover as 'miners' during criminal careers on the Highveld. More importantly, they learned how to handle, store and use dynamite. McLoughlin posed as a 'riveter'; Wiggins eventually moved to Kimberley where he worked briefly on the diamond fields, and WJ Kelly for a time even managed a small gold mine on the Witwatersrand.[3]

Barberton, for all its bars and a few famous prostitutes such as 'Cockney Liz', was of interest to the deserters only over the weekend, or when they had acquired money through other means.[4] Most of their day-to-day activities were focused around the Sheba Mine, 10 miles beyond Barberton, which could only be reached by passing through the thickly wooded Elephant's Kloof. There, at the top of a hill, away from the fevers that raged in the valley below, and in true 'Wild West' fashion, a classic frontier settlement had sprung up from nothing late in 1885.[5]

Eureka City reached its peak in 1886, the same year that the wild men from Fort Napier materialised out of the bush. By then it boasted three shops, a bakery, a chemist, a dairy, and a European population of more than 500.[6] For a moment, it looked as if it might come to rival state-favoured Barberton in importance. More importantly for those who had been raised in working-class cities back in England, Eureka also housed three hotels, several bars, a music hall and a racecourse serving a new community intent, in large part, on denying that it was in, or of, Africa. On Saturday nights, once the miners had poured out of the surrounding hills, there were often 1 000 men and a few women out on the streets of Eureka.[7]

Frontier justice and racial segregation were easier to enforce in small 'mining camps' dominated by English-speakers such as those at Eureka City or in nearby Steynsdorp, in the Komati Valley, than in established centres such as Johannesburg or Kimberley. Thomas Neale, a prominent storekeeper and Justice of the Peace in Eureka, sentenced a black labourer found guilty of desertion from a mining company to 25 lashes. The whipping was to be administered by a 'kafir servant' using a 'substantial *sjambok*', the victim 'laid upon a barrel for the purpose'. 'This sort of justice,' a correspondent for the *Gold Fields Times* opined, 'is the very thing required in such a place.'[8] Eureka City's residents, however, were not always content to wait on the Justice of the Peace.

Over a few months, in 1887, African miners started congregating at a few makeshift huts in the bushes half-way down the hill from Eureka to enjoy home-brewed beer and the sexual services of a half-dozen black women. The resulting debauchery, mirroring in part what was occurring on the ridge above, outraged sufficient whites to raise a party of vigilantes that burnt down the offending huts and 'gave those occupants they could catch a good basting'.[9] When two black domestic workers murdered their employers in Steynsdorp, in 1888, the underlying logic was taken to a classic, albeit unusual, conclusion. A party of English-speakers worked itself up into a full-frontier lather, invaded the jail and then lynched the alleged offenders even before they could be tried.[10]

The Fort Napier Irish, deserters-turned-miners, both informed and reflected the lawless and murderous behaviour of a frontier setting where there was often very little to distinguish law enforcers from law breakers.[11] For several weeks they dominated the less salubrious drinking dens during their off-duty hours. For those with a passion for fighting, gambling and the horses – which was most of them – race days held an irresistible attraction. The Victoria Hotel, half-way along the three-furlong racecourse, became an obvious meeting place for the Irish.

It was also in Eureka City, where the ex-Fort Napier men constituted an ethnically distinct, highly disruptive and very visible element, that the deserters were first characterised as being members of an 'Irish Brigade'. Whether the designation was partly self-generated, in tribute to the 64th

Lancashire Rifle Volunteers, a regiment which back home was notorious for its Fenian sympathies, is unknown. It was more likely that the name was pinned on them by resentful Englishmen smarting from political barbs emanating from Irishmen with republican sympathies.[12]

What is clearer in retrospect, however, is that the Irish Brigade was almost always viewed as being antisocial and criminal while it was based in the countryside, in smaller communities, where the class structure was 'flat' and no great distance separated the richest from the poorest. It was only later, once the Brigade relocated to the Witwatersrand, where collective action was circumscribed and its membership exposed to the alienation associated with urbanisation, that the behaviour of its leaders became more difficult to characterise. In Johannesburg, where an economic abyss separated a few dozen 'Randlords' from thousands of ordinary white miners, it was much easier for McLoughlin and one two others to emerge as men with more complex identities – including characteristics that are now associated with 'social bandits'.[13]

There was a shallow crossing at Fever Creek that flowed through the lowest reaches of Elephant's Kloof, marking the start of the road climbing its way up to Eureka City and the Queen of Sheba Hotel above. It offered highwaymen an ideal point at which to mount ambushes. In late 1886 through to early 1887 several men – black and white – were held up at gunpoint and robbed of their possessions.[14] The men of the Irish Brigade were probably not the first or the last to sense that, on the frontier, the worlds of fiction and fact could be brought into closer alignment. 'Masculinities,' it has rightly been suggested, 'are lived out in the flesh, but fashioned in the imagination.'[15] Ned Kelly himself said that his favourite book was Blackmoore's *Lorna Doone,* a novel set in seventeenth-century Exmoor, replete with tales of deep family rivalries and outlaws.[16]

A fertile imagination and ability to link theory to practice distinguished the leader of the Irish Brigade from lesser mortals. Hutchings, preferring the name Hutchinson, already had ambitions beyond the roadside lottery of casual hold-ups. Two smoothly executed coach robberies in the De Kaap Valley were attributed to him and armed accomplices. On each occasion £1 000 in cash and bullion belonging to the bank and mining companies was removed from horse-drawn coaches operated by Gibson Brothers. Here, too, the tales were perhaps re-fashioned so as to fit more readily with the romanticised images of Dick Turpin executing eighteenth-century highway robberies. The De Kaap Valley robbers, it was later claimed, displayed the utmost courtesy while fleecing the passengers and were particularly respectful of the ladies.[17]

This sentimentalised view of the Fort Napier highwaymen probably tells us more about Anglophone cultures, the coding of historical memory and story-telling than it does about the Irish Brigade. It is at variance with what we know about their behaviour as recorded elsewhere, which was almost always boorish, drunken and destructive. Indeed, it was their propensity to behave badly in a small industrial community – unlike 'social bandits' who retreated back into the countryside to find refuge among the peasants they were drawn from – that proved their undoing.

In late February 1887, some of the more restless elements in the Brigade, chafing beneath the weak bonds of the calendar and industrial discipline, abandoned what was threatening to become a humdrum existence. After the usual weekend drinking at Sherwood's 'Queen of Sheba' and neighbouring public houses they were too bored, drunk, or exhausted by Sunday night to crawl back to the surrounding mines. To the dismay of the inhabitants, they stayed on in un-policed Eureka City and a week's mayhem ensued.

Thomas Neale, the only man with the power to recruit and swear in special constables, was unable or unwilling to enforce order in or around the hotels and shops worst affected by the drunken rioting. Seen from one angle, the Brigade members were just like redcoats who, on their return from bush patrol, had collected their back-pay and gone on the spree in Pietermaritzburg. Seen from another, they were an occupying force of Irish renegades who, although lacking the discipline and purpose of Ned Kelly and his gang, had seized control of a hamlet which in their drunken imaginations may have equated to Euroa, Jerilderie or Glenrowan. But in truth, they were more like bandit-raiders in the old Wild West who had suddenly taken occupation of a small frontier town. There were assaults, bar-room brawls, damage to property, thefts and threats made to vulnerable retailers who refused to provide the brigands with the credit or goods they demanded. All three wood-and-iron hotels were wrecked.[18]

The fact that several of the businesses were Jewish-owned may not have helped. Although their status as 'Irishmen', 'Catholics' or 'Nationalists' may all have been open to question, members of the Brigade, like others on the goldfields, were unlikely to have resisted an undercurrent of anti-Semitism flowing through the new mining centres.

Neale watched and waited. Only towards the week's end, on Sunday morning, when he discovered that the shutters to his own shop had been removed in an interrupted attempt at store-breaking, did he act. He saddled his horse and rode across to Barberton to summon the help of the ZAR mounted police. McLoughlin and the raiders saw him depart and realised that he would be returning to the one-horse town with the republican police. The Irish then did as most bandits do when given the opportunity of avoiding a direct engagement with the law.[19]

The Brigade withdrew, making its way down the hill through dense bush and invading the first encampment it encountered. It was a classic military retreat. There, they forced their company on reluctant white miners for the night. But, even before they settled down for some sleep, a gold watch went missing, further alienating the Irish from their reluctant hosts.

An uncomfortable night on the ground, without beds, after an alcohol-ravaged week, left Brigade members disgruntled and resentful. The following morning, unable to return to their own camps for fear of betrayal and arrest, the full extent of a self-created predicament slowly dawned on them. They were on their own, marooned among the English, without friends or social cover. They were also broke, tired and exceptionally hungry. There was nothing to lose. It was a situation that a well-trained British officer recognised all too readily. Leading from the front, Hutchings rallied his troops, preparing them for a frontal attack.

They forced their way into the kitchen, seized the breakfast prepared for miners going on shift and scoffed it. When challenged by some brave soul intent on resisting, the deserters reverted to the feral behaviour of 'scuttlers' and 'almost smashed his head in'. 'Not satisfied with hammering him with their fists,' they 'threw him down and jumped on his head, and other parts of his body.' It was a murderous assault. Mission accomplished and hunger satisfied, the Brigade then withdrew.[20]

Outrage in the mining camp spurred on Neale and the mounted Zarps, who redoubled their efforts to capture the elusive renegades. Looking back, the situation was replete with the type of insanity characteristic of a frontier zone in the Age of Empire. Neale, an unlovable English Justice of the Peace presiding over a one-street village grandiosely named 'Eureka City' was in command of the Afrikaner troops of a Boer Republic. Together, they were pursuing a band of second-generation, low-life, would-be 'Irish' nationalists who had been raised in the far-off industrial world and deserted from the British Army. And the entire episode played itself out in part of what was a former African domain. The world was being turned upside down.

Showing the stubbornness success is born of, Neale's posse pursued the deserters who, adopting guerrilla-like tactics, retreated ever further into the surrounding hills and bush. Neale never stopped tracking them, but by the time he caught up with them Hutchings and most of his fellow deserters had, like men born to brigandage, slipped across the border. The South African Republic's back door to Delagoa Bay was, as ever, wide open. The lesson was not lost on Jack McLoughlin and the three other stragglers that Neale did manage to arrest – John Carroll (under the alias 'John Berry'), Dwyer ('John Jones') and one 'William Smith' (probably William Hankins or Henkins).[21]

The four appeared before the Landdrost in Barberton a few days later. They were charged with contravening Article 69 of the Constitution of the Republic – rather than more prosaic criminal charges that would have required considerable prosecutorial resources if they were to be pursued in the presence of witnesses likely to be suborned. McLoughlin and Dwyer, the supposed ringleaders in the absence of Hutchings, were found guilty and each sentenced to six months' imprisonment with hard labour. But the Magistrate, aware that he was dealing with cross-border bandits and a potential menace to the country, added a rider to the sentence to the effect that: 'upon expiry of their sentence [the convicts were] to be sent back to their respective corps, from which they are believed to have deserted'. This provision, perhaps unenforceable, was never implemented. It was an omission that the ZAR was later to rue. Dwyer, unable to resist a parting shot drawn from an Irish, scuttling, Manchester working-class repertoire, 'directed an insulting expression' at the Magistrate 'for which he was brought back and sentenced to some days' spare diet and solitary confinement'.[22]

Once the Irish horses had bolted for Delagoa Bay the ZAR government acted to ensure that the stable door remained shut. Neale, who had pleaded unsuccessfully for additional police protection over several months, was the moving force behind the formation of the new 'Eureka Mounted Rifles'.[23] It was to be the first, but not the last time in southern Africa that the arrival of the Irish Brigade in town necessitated an augmented police force or heralded a radical reorganisation of the old.

The Barberton jail, constructed on frugal lines as specified by a government that believed the future of the republic lay on the land rather than beneath it, was a ramshackle affair. It already housed one or two other Fort Napier graduates and was unlikely to have won the respect of McLoughlin, who had experience of one of the most modern prisons in the world.[24] He and Dwyer, high-risk convicts, would have been kept under lock and key, unlike petty offenders who were allowed out during the day and often slept on the veranda at night. At a time when Brigade members considered attempting to escape to be *de rigueur,* the two paid the authorities the unintended compliment of serving out their full sentences. In McLoughlin's case, however, this may have come at a price, because he set his mind against further incarceration. When he and Dwyer were eventually set free, in September 1887, they made their way out through the back door and headed for Delagoa Bay, where Hutchings – styling himself 'Muldoon' – was transforming the South Lancashire deserters into railway navvies.

★ ★ ★

Contrary to those propagandists of empire who by the mid-1890s were encouraging Britain to appropriate southern Africa's mineral-rich plateau, governments in Pretoria had never set their minds against industrialisation. Indeed, as the same *ante bellum* critics never tired of pointing out, members of the Boer elite were never averse to the acquisition of personal wealth. Pretoria's Protestants had never rejected capitalism – what they did reject was the development of a form of capitalism in which an unregulated primary industry became paramount. What the Kruger government feared was that the state, rooted in the land, would be overwhelmed by a foreign-owned mining industry served by a numerically preponderant semi-skilled, immigrant European labour force backed by tens of thousands of urban black workers. What the Boer elite wished for was a *balanced* economy, one in which commercial agriculture profited directly from new, urban, industrial markets in ways that did not unnecessarily jeopardise their own historically privileged access to the unlimited supplies of cheap, black, rurally based labour.[25]

The basis of this economic policy was laid in the 1860s; that is, after the discovery of diamonds and the initial development of inland markets, but before the unearthing of the major gold deposits beyond the Vaal in the 1880s. An early indication of Boer enterprise and the elite's fear of imperial encroachment came in the 1870s when President Burgers set about trying to construct a railway line linking Pretoria to Delagoa Bay. But the project, lacking the catalytic input of mineral wealth, had floundered and the imported rails were left to rust in far-off places as the ZAR slouched toward *de facto,* if not *de jure* bankruptcy in the 1870s.

The discovery of gold on the Witwatersrand in 1886 changed all that. Gold was to become the Bank of England's guarantor of the last resort for Britain's growing international trade. Westminster realised that southern Africa would never be the same after the emergence of Johannesburg, but it was the City that acted on the promise. In 1887, Colonel Edward McMurdo, an American who had acquired a concession to operate a railway between Lourenço Marques and Komatipoort on the eastern border of the ZAR, sold his rights to the London-based, grandiosely named Delagoa Bay and East African Railway Company.[26]

The company, working in the tightly networked City, awarded the contract to construct the line to Pauling Brothers, who appointed Sir Thomas Tancred as their chief engineer. It was a pleasantly English arrangement, but out in Africa, Sir Thomas discovered that he had to make do with such raw talent as could be recruited locally. Among those appointed to look after the administrative and clerical staff that serviced the projects was a curious ex-Dubliner, journalist and soldier, Barry Roonan, who took a close interest in the lives of the navvies and black workers.

The aim of the subcontractor was to get the unskilled work done as cheaply as possible using locally recruited African labour. But black workers, for the most part, lacked experience of industrial labour. When called upon to undertake demanding manual labour in a notoriously unhealthy environment at low wages, Africans proved to be 'unreliable' or of 'limited use'. Pauling Brothers knew that much of the infrastructure for the Industrial Revolution – bridges, canals and railways – had been laid down by Irishmen with strong bodies and a poor education.[27] Irish navvies enjoyed an unsurpassed reputation when it came to rail construction and Tancred must have longed for their services. Then, not long after the fracas at Eureka City, in walked between 20 and 50 deserters from the South Lancashire and other regiments. They were soon followed by more white flotsam and jetsam drawn from the mines up-country.[28] A more cost-effective plan was quickly formulated and the ratio of white to black labour employed on the project suddenly changed.

Most of the Irish Brigade, still under the unofficial command of Hutchings (who was by now calling himself 'Muldoon') was absorbed into a labour force presided over by an unnamed revolver-toting 'brute'. McLoughlin, stronger in mind and muscle after labour on public works at Barberton, joined his comrades in September, just as the white workers were being re-organised. In a move designed to minimise conflict but that may unintentionally have strengthened old 'tribal' animosities, Muldoon was put in charge of the 'Irish' navvies. A Christian innocent by the name of Buck Williams headed up a small contingent of American workers, while another murderous brute, remembered only as 'Kentish Jack', took charge of the English, who, on the day, could be as savage as the next.[29]

The importance of harnessing ethnic solidarities to working parties as the line of rail crept across the lowlands of Delagoa Bay and then inland towards the hills of Komatipoort impressed itself on McLoughlin's mind. It was later claimed that a workman who had died of malaria or some other cause lay buried beneath every sleeper along the line. The querulous Irish appear to have retained their social cohesiveness during the coastal sojourn. They may have fought with others, but among them, a truce reigned. At a practical level, McLoughlin extended his skills as a metal worker and 'riveter'; thereafter it became his chosen profession whenever asked by police in southern Africa to state his 'occupation'.

Two further skills acquired during four months of railway construction may have been even more important for his subsequent career. First, mastering lifting techniques that allowed for the moving of exceptionally heavy objects, such as rails, proved most useful. Second, he became even more accustomed to handling explosives.

This familiarity with dynamite came at a time when Irish nationalists in England were exploiting the destructive power of explosives to deadly effect. In Salford, in 1881, and in London, in 1885, the Irish Republican Army had used dynamite as their weapon of choice in a campaign of terror. In southern Africa, a mining-dynamite heaven, members of the Brigade were equally excited about the destructive power of explosives. But alienation and lower levels of consciousness meant that they were more interested in harnessing its potential to criminal than to political projects. All that was necessary for them to close the gap between criminal and political activities, however, and be seen as 'social bandits', was 'English' targets. Only a few months later, the Witwatersrand would provide them with the ideal setting to effect precisely such a transition.

In Delagoa Bay, informal on-the-job training for those with criminal inclinations was supplemented by off-the-job experiences that shored up developing attitudes and behaviour. Free transport up and down the line on working days, and back into Lourenço Marques on paydays at the end of the working week, facilitated unexpected outcomes. Brigade members became increasingly familiar with trains and later demonstrated a robust contempt for any officials tasked with charging for or examining tickets.

Paydays saw a marked increase in social tension in the port. Navvies returned to town, celebrating the end of the working week, and spent, if not all, then most of their wages. As already noted, Lourenço Marques offered an emergency exit for criminals from across the region trying to make their way to Europe or, when all was lost, to Australia, India or the Far East. WJ Kelly, who went on to become a bank robber on the Witwatersrand, was just one of those who learnt which shady dealers were willing to exchange or export illegally acquired cash or gemstones.

★ ★ ★

In Lourenço Marques, nothing was as it seemed. The town was a mess of ambiguities, contradictions and paradoxes that fed into a climate of un-certainty. Quotidian realities were compounded and re-shaped by politi-cal undercurrents sweeping the shoreline. Although the Portuguese were officially in control of the bay and harbour facilities, everyone knew that the most powerful influence at work in the port was the British Consul. Britain was taking an increasing interest in the southern African interior and Delagoa Bay. The Portuguese authorities began to fear that if Lourenço Marques was not to be sold outright, it might be annexed by imperial force despite the fact that Portugal was Britain's oldest ally.[30]

Portugal responded by maintaining a naval presence in the Bay. It also bolstered the police force in an attempt to exercise more control over 200 unruly navvies whose sympathies could be guessed at. Additional, un-trained, African police were brought in from West African outposts and commanded by a few junior officers sent from Lisbon. With international tension mounting, a few Irish nationalists in the Brigade saw the chance to embarrass the English and humiliate the Portuguese.

The arrival of a Portuguese gunboat in the bay presented Hutchings, the most politically conscious member of the Brigade, with the opportunity he was looking for. Despite its still metamorphosing half-Australian, half-Irish provenance, Hutchings took on the name 'Captain Moonlight' as his *nom de guerre*. Setting aside the sexual undertones of a name that McLoughlin, WJ Kelly and others would have been familiar with, Hutchings laid down his challenge to the Portuguese authorities. 'In eccentric English on beer-stained paper,' he crafted a hand-written challenge to the Governor. 'The Hirish savages up the Line,' he wrote, will bust your fort and your tin-pot gunboat tomorrer Nite. Lock up your greasy reis [milreis being the local currency] and keep away from our headquarters at Berg's Hotell. Capt. Moonlight.'[31] The Governor and the military, sensing payday mayhem in the making, took it in, hook, line and sinker.

Every policeman, soldier and sailor in Lourenço Marques – including most of those on the gunboat – was placed on alert. Specially designated platoons were instructed to stake out the Hotel Allemande. The authorities believed that, in the face of overwhelming numbers, the Irish would be intercepted and arrested long before they could undertake any drunken midnight mission in town, or worse, out in the bay. But the Governor had done precisely what the opposing Captain by Moonlight had warned him *not* to do and deployed all his forces around the hotel.

As night fell, Hutchings' troops entered the Hotel Allemande through the front door. But inside, all but three, who were left to stage a drunken diversion in the pub, clambered out of a rear window, split up, made their way back down to the harbour and regrouped. They commandeered a few boats and rowed out to the under-manned Portuguese gunboat where they easily overpowered a few hapless guards. They then systematically worked their way through the ship's wine locker. Back at Hotel Hollow, the Portuguese waited for the navvies, suitably fortified, to emerge. Out in the bay, the wine locker had done its work. By the time the Irish abandoned the gunboat, it 'wore an unkempt look, the flag of Portugal was reversed from the bowsprit to the stays, and diverse articles were protruding from the muzzles of the guns, from which the tompions had been removed'.[32] The mortifying rout was completed when the Governor's armed forced belatedly entered the hotel only to discover that they had been decoyed by just three drunken Irishmen.

A torrent of diplomatic notes between Lisbon and London ensued. But in a word-war where neither of the principal parties could exercise control over wild Irish nationalists working on a project that had been sanctioned in the City, it eventually blew over. 'Captain Moonlight', however, emerged with his reputation enhanced and boasted that, on the night in question, he could have taken the entire city if he chose to.[33]

The failure of the port authorities to discipline or prosecute the Irish only encouraged Moonlight and his troops to look around for other ways of inflicting damage on the hated English and ineffectual Portuguese. The time was ripe for a new outrage because members of the Brigade were preparing for demobilisation as their contracts ended, and getting ready to leave Mozambique and move back up-county. They got their chance in early December 1887, when the ever-alert Hutchings overheard a conversation in which the catering arrangements for the handing-over ceremony of the line at the border town of Komatipoort were discussed.

On 13 December, a day set aside for a three-way international celebration that included officials from the ZAR, the train carrying Sir Thomas Tancred up to Komatipoort was unexpectedly flagged down. It was boarded by an Irish Brigade contingent and a hogshead of beer commandeered. By the time that the next train came through – the one carrying the bulk of the food and drink destined for the official opening – the beer was gone. The second train, too, was looted and limped into Komatipoort without sustenance for the waiting guests. Tancred, livid, sent a telegram to Lourenço Marques demanding the arrest of the banditti.[34] But the port authorities, who suspected that the same Brigade members were responsible for the murder of two West African policemen only weeks earlier, thought better of it. The navvies were allowed to leave as and when they chose. It took them a month – and their departure from Mozambique, while welcome, was not pretty.

Roonan, who entertained the lowest opinion of the Irish-Lancastrians, portrayed them as irredeemably antisocial. They were men, he wrote, who were capable of 'anything from robbing a church to manslaughter without provocation'.[35] These were telling examples. On their way to the Witwatersrand – armed and mounted as befitted brigands on the move – the Irish held up travellers and storekeepers at will.

On 23 January 1888, Jack McLoughlin celebrated his twenty-ninth birthday on the road to Johannesburg. Barring bouts of heavy drinking, he was a man at the peak of his mental and physical powers. Short and stout, the quintessential hard man, his sexual preference was difficult to determine but he steered clear of white working-class women, preferring the company of prostitutes. He was more assertive and confident than he had been as a younger man and had developed an even greater contempt for cowards and informers. Freed from the influence of Hutchings, who had peeled-off from the Brigade to resume life in Barberton, McLoughlin was left with more room to demonstrate his own abilities as a possible Irish Brigade leader.

The army, mines and railways had not only trained him how to use guns and dynamite more intelligently, but also how to work heavy metal – and, from experience gained first in Ancoats and then in Australia, he already knew how to mount modest criminal operations. He had served his apprenticeship and was ready to assume his position as a gang leader in a frontier town overcome with gold fever. It seemed clear that he was more than ready for Johannesburg. Question was, was it ready for him?

CHAPTER TEN

❧✣☙

Organised Crime in a Frontier Town

JOHANNESBURG, THE KRUGER STATE
AND THE DEPRESSION
— 1889–1892 —

Come all my hearties, we'll range the mountainside
Together we will plunder, together we will ride
We'll scour along the valleys and gallop o'er the plains
We'll scorn to live in slavery, bowed down in chains.
'THE WILD COLONIAL BOY'

T he prospectors who emerged from the bush when the Witwatersrand
open diggings were proclaimed barely had time enough to pull up
their camp breeches before the street outlines of Johannesburg were laid
out over the closing three months of 1886. Angled sheets of off-white canvas, the undergarments of Ferreira's Camp, were discarded for more substantial wood and iron structures. For the next year thousands of diggers,
prospectors and speculators rushed to the fields to discover what treasure
nature may have buried at even greater depth.

When McLoughlin and the Irish Brigade got there on horseback around
noon on Friday, 10 February 1888, Johannesburg was barely 12 months old.[1]
It was, strictly speaking, no longer a 'camp' although it was still being described as such three years later. But, lacking basic amenities, it was hardly a
town and would have to wait two decades before it became a 'city'.

About 8 000 white male immigrants and a few women were clustered around the Market Square, while some way off, as intended by the alienated term 'location', three times that number of African men and women, hundreds of 'coloureds' of both sexes and several scores of Asians clung to the outskirts of the white settlement. Johannesburg was still recognisably of the genus Eureka City. To whites, the surrounding ridges and marshes promised 'civilised' life and order of a familiar colonial type in a republic where there was no equality between black and white in matters of church or state, but, unlike at Barberton, Haenertsburg or Steynsdorp, they also cradled the hope of permanence.

Hundreds of mud-brick houses with corrugated-iron roofs provided the few pioneering families with homes. The more robust wood-and-iron structures, owned by entrepreneurial men or hard-up widows, provided 'board and lodging' to anyone ranging from adventurers and criminals through to miners and shopkeepers, or priests and printers.[2] Small stores abounded and there were already more bars along what was to become Commissioner Street than there were Christians in 'the camp'.

Height's was one of a dozen establishments laying claim to the status of 'hotel'. It was a low-slung structure, like most farmhouses to be found across the Vaal. It accommodated two score or more guests while, out on the porch, the foolish and thirsty put away drink and dust in equal measures. Inside, a 120-foot-long 'American Bar' hinted at rough republican equality, with hooch and hormones the favoured cocktail. Through a hallway, 100 diners and residents sat down to dinner each night. And for the British or those with class pretensions and a need for social distance, there was the Rand Club, with 150 members.[3]

Like parched navvies coming down the line at week's end, McLoughlin and his companions knew what they wanted to do, but without back-pay to draw on, found themselves unable to do so. A humid day promising an afternoon thunderstorm was under way when the reconnaissance parties were despatched. 'Loafers entered private boarding-houses and other similar establishments, and on the plea of asking for help, were no doubt "spying out the land" for burglarious operations.' As dusk settled that afternoon – and on the Saturday evening that followed – bands of footpads and highwaymen, three to four strong, took up positions along the approaches to the town. Travellers braving the gloom and drizzle were held up, realising a few small but helpful hauls for bands of thirsty bandits.[4]

With sufficient coins to start the Saturday evening, the Irish made for the bars and beer halls while darkness overcame the settlement and sounds became muted beneath squalls of wind and rain. Inside, their pockets emptied faster than beer mugs could be re-filled. The disequilibrium forced the brigands – less disciplined than they had been the previous night – out, back into the settlement. Fifteen pounds in cash, several gold watches and other valuables disappeared from the Central Hotel in a matter of minutes as a second crime wave surged through the streets. Trading metal for ale, the pubs were then re-occupied until closing time.[5]

At first light on Sunday it became clear that the late-night invasion had gone well beyond armed robbery and burglary. Under cover of a thunderstorm all the demons of race and class had been unleashed and a madman, or two, had indulged his whims to the full. Terrifying strikes of lightning and deafening thunder had provided the brigands with all the cover they needed. Beneath Satan's blanket, in an unlit and under-policed settlement, just about anything could be done with impunity. It was a lesson that was not lost on the new young leader of the Brigade.

There were three corpses. Graham was a one-armed Englishman who had worked as a billiard-marker at the Kimberley Bar. The other two were men of colour whom nobody cared to put names to – a 'Baster-Hottentot' and a 'Zulu'. All three had 'ghastly wounds to the head and the face' – signs of gratuitous violence. The pockets of all three had been turned inside-out in the frantic hunt for coins. Given the widespread nineteenth-century Anglophone belief that no Englishman – or even an Irish-Lancastrian – would stoop to knife a man to death, one reporter suggested that the murders had to have been the work of just 'one man, probably an Italian, or Spaniard, or some or other European scoundrel'.[6]

That red herring failed to draw in so much as a stray cat. Other journalists with bar-room informants laid the blame squarely at the door of 'the Irish', even though they agreed that it did seem to have been the work of just one deranged drunk. Outraged and vulnerable, most of the town's males reverted to frontier mode, using stick-and-carrot tactics to try and flush out the culprit. In public, they claimed that they only wanted to see the offender brought to justice – but in the pubs and huddles out on the Market Square, they were quick to cast the Irish Brigade as 'outlaws', as men beyond the protection of the law who should be found and hanged.

Fearing an outbreak of violence, the government offered a reward of £100 for an arrest leading to a successful prosecution. For a few hours it seemed that the state might succeed in keeping the dogs at bay; but not for long. 'The wildest talk was indulged in everywhere, as the massacre of the loafer-class, who were regarded as the culprits was openly advocated.'[7] Tales of American-style frontier justice, of the sort understood by a public well-versed in the writings of Bret Harte, segued into the praise poetry of Judge Lynch, and a 'Vigilance Committee' was set up. But the cur of direct action was brought to heel when the existing reward was upped to £500 by locals including traders who, fearing the long-term consequences of mob rule, regained control of the situation.[8]

Amidst howls of outrage about inadequate policing, the widely disliked state police – the Zarps – arrested and prosecuted a few suspects for crimes against property and then, very briefly, came up with a murder suspect. Initially described as 'Italian', in alignment with English prejudice, James Butler turned out to be one of the Irish Brigade. But Butler claimed to work on the diggings and soon convinced the police of his innocence.[9] Without a resident detective or any forensic capacity, the Zarps could do little to contain the predations of the Irish invaders.

When the seriousness of the situation was eventually grasped in Pretoria, the Kruger government agreed to the establishment of a detective force on the goldfields. Lacking the services of a qualified burgher who com-manded English, the state found a naturalised Irishman who spoke suf-ficient Afrikaans-Dutch to head up the new division.[10] Robert Ferguson, like most detectives at the time, relied on informers for most of his criminal intelligence and had a liking for low company – including that of the new Irish-Lancastrians. It was the third time in just 18 months that the Brigade had forced states in southern Africa to either adapt, or significantly expand, their police forces in urban areas.

The arrival of Ferguson, who later came to develop a corrupt relationship with some of McLoughlin's friends, was not responsible for the gradual
dissolution of the Brigade over the next few months. An unusual segment
of the 'labour market' did more to erode the cohesion of the brigands than
did the Zarps. In a state where the police were clearly incapable of pro-
tecting property rights, agents working for the emerging capitalists – the
Randlords – recruited some of the insurgents for their own purposes.

Hans Sauer, acting on behalf of Cecil Rhodes, hired several ruffians to
protect the great man's claims when the officers of the High Court proved
incapable of enforcing judgments. Sauer armed the thugs with shillelaghs and
then sent out what he cheerfully termed 'Sauer's Irish Brigade' to ensure that
none of his or Rhodes's claims were 'jumped' by rival diggers. It was classic
frontier stuff. Might was right and brigands became bobbies. Sauer went on
to note, with satisfaction, that when it came to safeguarding property claims,
his Irish were far more effective than the local Diggers' Committee.[11] In
frontier Johannesburg, there were always mining capitalists who placed more
trust in gun-toting opportunists than in the government. Indeed, it was part
of the same template that deep-level mine owners resorted to when they
mounted the abortive Jameson Raid to challenge the Kruger state in 1895.
Capitalism shaped crime and crime helped shape capitalism.[12]

In this turbulent setting, where money was easier to come by than in the
south-east of the subcontinent, the Fort Napier graduates drifted slowly
apart. The Irish Brigade never again quite mustered the numbers for a take-
over of Eureka City, Lourenço Marques or even a large slice of Johannesburg,
but McLoughlin was not unduly concerned. The world-wide postal service
and fortnightly arrival of the mail boat in Cape Town had kept him in contact with several elements in the Manchester underworld. Some of the very
same young criminal-romantics he had grown up with back in Ancoats
were set fair for the newest frontier.

The first to arrive was the chemist's son. JW Brown reached the Cape
in 1887, shortly after McLoughlin had breezed into Natal and headed up
country. In Kimberley, Brown and two companions transformed themselves
into masked highwayman, robbing black migrants of their wages, savings
and any illicit gemstones acquired on the diamond fields. In March 1888,

with a handkerchief covering his face and brandishing a revolver in Wild West fashion, Brown's luck eventually ran out. The robbers were arrested and prosecuted for holding up African workers near the border town of Boshof in the neighbouring Orange Free State.

In prison, Brown read about a madman who had slain and butchered five prostitutes in Whitechapel. It was something he felt he could relate to, perhaps even approve of. Born into a dysfunctional household ruled by a narcissistic patriarch and raised in an adolescent cult of masculinity, Brown – like several others in his cohort – was never far from outright misogyny. By the time that he reached Johannesburg, a place never wanting for prostitutes, a few months later, he had taken to calling himself 'Jack the Ripper' whenever he was arrested by semi-literate Zarps. If the sobriquet was but part of an attempt at black humour, it was unusually long-lived, because he was still using it four years later.[13]

The next to appear was the fishmonger's son. Having successfully put the Rochdale Canal behind him, Mike Hart was a professional gambler with a special interest in hunting, racing and ratting dogs. But there was another side to him. Gregarious and well-dressed, Hart disapproved of firearms and, like Adam Worth, saw himself as more of a gentleman-thief with a liking for gemstones and jewellery. Hart was also on intimate terms with Robert Ferguson and, when necessary, McLoughlin used him as a conduit to Johannesburg's newly appointed Chief Detective.[14]

Three other Ancoats lads, George Fisher, Charlie Harding and Tommy Whelan, were among the early arrivals.[15] In addition to old neighbourhood stalwarts, McLoughlin relied on the help of a few Fort Napier diehards, including WJ Kelly, John O'Brien and, especially, Jack McCann. Together these half-dozen or so men – with the exception of Fisher, who gave up after an early misadventure – constituted the core of what might be seen as the first McLoughlin gang, an abbreviated version of the original 'Irish Brigade'. For larger, more specialised jobs, the gang recruited additional manpower from among other Mancunian criminals.

Unlike the relatively sparsely populated eastern Transvaal or Mozambique, Johannesburg allowed the Ancoats-Manchester 'hard men' to draw on the support of, or conceal themselves among, hundreds of other Lancastrian refugees from the Industrial Revolution. The new frontier settlement was full of under-capitalised diggers having to sell their properties to emerging mine owners, or one-time skilled artisans being turned into semi-skilled white mine workers. A small army of angry and resentful single men, far from home in an uncertain economic climate presided over by a 'foreign' government and aggressive capitalists, was hardly hostile to those intent on preying on rich mine owners. Ethnicity, class and culture all ensured that on the Witwatersrand, as in the northern industrialising world, there was never an absolute divide between the criminal and working classes.

In frontier Johannesburg, the resulting two-way influence between the underclasses was perhaps most easily detected in the functioning of the Friendly Societies and voluntary associations. For reasons that are easy to understand, these working-class institutions were particularly important before the formation of the Mine Employees and Mechanics' Union, in 1892, and continued to serve white miners right up the outbreak of the South African War, in 1899. When the cotton industry 'back home' was going through one of its recurrent depressions, in 1893, 'Lancashire Lads' on the Rand were urged to band together and send on donations to help relieve urban poverty in north-western England.[16] Working men's clubs and lodges offered an immigrant criminal cohort an unlikely model for the power of ethnic friendship, conviviality and social support.

Likewise, by 1893, the Oddfellows – a Friendly Society with the deepest possible Lancastrian roots – had more than 100 members in Johannesburg and had organised itself into a branch that proclaimed 'Manchester Unity'. Not to be outdone, the smaller Order of Rechabites, promoting temperance, boasted 'Salford Unity'. The high-water mark of the Industrial Revolution was thus easily visible along the shorelines of working-class culture on the Witwatersrand. When not actually negotiating the criminal shallows, McLoughlin and his friends would have little difficulty in presenting themselves to ordinary workers as being English, Irish, Lancashire-Irish or more accurately, 'Manchester-Irish'.

The geographical distribution of these working-class ethnic clusters on Witwatersrand mines was not a product of chance. It partly reflected the moment at which the immigrants first entered the local labour market. The

'Cousin Jacks', hard rock men from the tin mines of Cornwall, centred around the Glencairn, Heriot and Jumpers mines, all east of Johannesburg. The Irish – not famed for their mining prowess – gravitated to the west of the town, to around Langlaagte, further west at the Champ D'Or and, beyond that, around Luipaardsvlei.[17] Here, too, there were a few underlying factors at work that require passing examination.

Drawn from the heart of the industrialising world, Lancastrians in general and Mancunians in particular were in demand as skilled workers on the better-paying mines of the west Rand. Like the 'Cousin Jacks' whose reputations went before them, the Lancastrians provided yet another link between the northern and southern labour markets of a globalising world. Even the limited previous industrial experience of those in the trimmed-back Irish Brigade, including JW Brown, McCann, McLoughlin and Whelan, allowed members of the gang to present themselves plausibly as would-be workers. Once employed – only for as long as it took to gather information for possible criminal operations – the gang members were usually to be found on the western fringes of Johannesburg, and further out towards Florida, Witpoortjie and, more especially, Krugersdorp.[18]

McLoughlin's favoured sites for safe-lifting and blasting were, in large measure, determined by the social geography of ethnicity along the Rand. Almost all of the Brigade's earliest out-of-town exploits were west of Johannesburg and it is significant that, with one exception, there is nothing to suggest that the Irish were ever active on the east Rand. Brigade members relied on friends and disgruntled white miners to provide them with information about an accumulation of gold amalgam on the property, or to tip them off about any build-up in cash in the mine offices before payday. This intelligence, transmitted along ethnic circuits, was, however, itself a pale reflection of other, far more deeply seated realities. Crudely put, the fortunes of safe-lifters and blasters during the frontier era, between 1886 and 1892, were closely linked to the geology of the Witwatersrand, the nature of ore reduction works at the time and the various chemical processes involved in the act of gold recovery.

★　★　★

The curved Witwatersrand outcrop, the northern shoreline of what had once been an enormous inland sea, stretched for over 40 miles from Springs in the east to Krugersdorp in the west. While the Main Reef Leader that held most of the gold had the virtue of being virtually continuous, it was also almost all of a low grade. Marginally higher-than-average grades lay to the west and the lower grades to the east. These realities meant that, in the long run, the industry was destined to be both capital and labour intensive. The earliest pick-and-shovel trenches of 1886–89 followed the curve of the outcrop, but, because the reef also dipped steeply to the south, open diggings soon had to make way for adits, shafts and tunnels. For 24 months and more, not even having to work at greater depths curbed the recovery of gold. Specks of gold locked into a coarse conglomerate termed banket were retrieved with relative ease from large volumes of ore-bearing rock that had been partially weathered and readily lent itself to crushing.

From mid-1889, however, a potentially disastrous problem manifested itself as the reef was pursued at depths in excess of 120–150 feet. Gold locked into un-weathered pyritic ores proved increasingly resistant to amalgamation during a recovery process that was reliant on the use of mercury. Deeper mine shafts required additional working capital at a time when mine owners were waiting on a scientific breakthrough to revitalise the faltering gold recovery process. Everything pointed to the need for financial consolidation and reorganisation of the industry.[19]

The resulting crisis lasted from mid-1889 through 1890 and most of 1891. Only the newly developed MacArthur-Forrest process, using cyanide rather than quicksilver as an amalgamating agent in the recovery process, saved the infant industry from disaster. Market re-adjustments and the growing need for capital meant that the Rand only recovered some of its former momentum in mid-1892. Even then most of the upswing was predicated on speculation rather than demonstrable results. The MacArthur-Forrest process, the completion of the rail link to the Cape in September 1892 and the consolidation of the largest mining companies marked the end of the 'frontier era'. For close on three years, however, the mining industry was in crisis and, while it underwent painful corporate and technological changes, Johannesburg and the satellite mining towns on the Reef were mired in depression.[20]

Diggers, prospectors and black labourers who had led a relatively free and mobile social existence centred on trench-mining were among the first casualties of the crisis. By the time the depression lifted, most black workers were living in mine compounds – massed, tightly policed, segregated accommodation. Early entrepreneurs, many of whom had had to make way for the resurgent mining companies, found themselves reduced to the status of white workers and living in boarding houses or married quarters on mining properties close to the mine shafts. By 1893, workers were living in more controlled and segregated social universes.

Lacking the capital to mine at deeper levels, diggers and prospectors had begun to sell their holdings to emerging syndicates as early as 1888 – months before the full impact of the crisis.[21] In 1889, diggers paid the state £137 000 in licence fees; by 1890, the figure had fallen to £96 000 and thereafter it continued to shrink each year.[22] When a few economic survivors attempted to launch a 'diggers club' in 1891, the venture – which would probably have had to serve as a Friendly Society or voluntary association – was swiftly abandoned for want of support.[23]

This wasting-away of small-scale independent miners all along the line of reef over just 36 months was in sharp contrast to the rapidly developing muscle-power of the new corporations. Huge joint-stock companies fed into the formation of a Stock Exchange in 1887. Just 12 months later the old broadly based democratically elected Diggers' Committee was supplanted by the Chamber of Mines. Tightly networked, wealthy mine owners saw to it that the new body dominated all official communication with the Boer government at a time when the industry was undergoing rapid and radical restructuring.[24] This centralisation of economic power was matched by enhanced profits achieved through economies of scale. In 1891, the newly formed Chamber successfully negotiated a 10 per cent reduction in the cost of shipping gold amalgam to the United Kingdom.[25] Further economies were achieved when, 12 months later, the Rand Central Ore Reduction Company was launched. By 1892, 53 companies backed by a handful of finance houses employed 3 400 white and over 300 000 black workers.[26]

Forced out of their trenches, formerly independent small-scale miners and skilled white workers, such as blacksmiths and carpenters, risked being totally dominated by the emerging companies. The formation of the Chamber of Mines, in particular, demanded a matching response from organised labour and, in August 1892, the Witwatersrand Mine Employees' and Mechanics' Union was formed – with, it might be noted, significant help from prominent Lancastrian workers.[27] The mine owners, keen to counter the voice of white labour in Pretoria, responded almost immediately by launching the 'National Union', a political organisation which, among other things, demanded the franchise for all immigrants.[28]

These depression-born developments, a veritable tectonic shift in the development of the mining industry, had a profound influence on the patterns of black and white crime on the Witwatersrand in general, not excluding McLoughlin's reconstructed gang. Two developments are noteworthy.

First, the Irish Brigade was not the only underworld army in or around frontier Johannesburg. Within a year or two of the diggings being proclaimed, a charismatic young Isizulu-speaker, Nongoloza Mathebula, angered and frustrated by colonial injustice, founded a band of African migrants bent on achieving social justice in an otherwise lawless setting. Forced out of the mining settlement proper by passes and racial segregation, *Umkhosi we Zintaba* – the 'Regiment of the Hills' – was based in the abandoned mine shafts, caves and hollows of the surrounding Klipriviersberg. The initial purpose of the Regiment – which, like the Irish, had an eclectic quasi-military structure – was to identify and take direct action, revenge if you will, against those footpads, highwaymen or white employers who had either defrauded or robbed black workers of their earnings without easy recourse to alien laws.[29]

If those in the Regiment of the Hills started out as 'social bandits' of the type first identified by Hobsbawm, it was not long before they abandoned the idea of pursuing justice in a world loaded against them and turned instead to overwhelmingly *anti*social activities. For all the usual reasons then, black men, too, became footpads, highwaymen, rapists or murderers. It was not long, for example, before Africans, too, were impersonating state or municipal policemen and relieving black migrants of their wages.[30] Crime follows the contours of power abused.

Second, during the depression McLoughlin and his gang shifted their focus from burglary and highway robbery to safe-lifting and blasting. Back in Manchester he and the Blue Dots of Ancoats relied on house or store-breaking to raise cash for their weekly needs. On the Witwatersrand, as in Lancashire, stolen goods were frequently disposed of through shady jewellers and pawnshop owners. It was claimed that there were several 'low-class' Jewish jewellers around the Market Square who bought gold amalgam or stolen gold jewellery which they re-fashioned into new items for sale in their stores.[31] In addition, a half-dozen unlicensed pawnshops advanced cash against items of clothing which they knew would never be reclaimed.[32] Such stolen apparel would be sold on to Chinese, Indian and Jewish hawkers or shop owners, undercutting many of the town's resentful English storekeepers.

So-called 'foreign' traders became the object of increasing anger and resentment as the depression deepened. These included several seasonal traders from India's Malabar Coast still using the monsoon winds and ancient trade routes across the Indian Ocean to explore opportunities on the newest frontier economy.[33] Persistent attempts were made to expel non-European traders from Jeppe, at the east end of the settlement, and force them into ghettos. In a disgraceful game of racial snakes-and-ladders, Chinese and Indian traders got poor Jews and others to 'front' as the proprietors of their businesses only to find that they were then pursued by licensing officers empowered to inspect their accounts.[34] English-speaking storekeepers created new 'crimes' they could feed off.

As the depression tightened its grip on the settlement, burglary and store-breaking became increasingly risky. The town's white population shrank and the police took a more active interest in those 'Uncles' who ran pawnshops known to deal in stolen goods.[35] Moreover, with fewer black migrants out on the roads, highway robbery, too, yielded lower returns. For those in the business of crime, like the Irish Brigade, the new market realities of the depression demanded innovative responses.

As we will see, once the economy went into free-fall in 1890, members of the McLoughlin gang joined many other professional criminals and left town to seek out new 'markets'. But they had only been gone for a matter of months when the reconstruction of the mining industry began to revitalise business and create exciting new 'business' opportunities.

After 1892, increasing quantities of semi-processed gold amalgam were stored on mine properties before being transported to the central refinery or coastal ports. From the latter, the amalgam was shipped to England for final refining before it was sold on the open market in London.[36] But it was while it was still on the mines, on the Witwatersrand, that gold amalgam was most vulnerable to theft. Even the latest high-quality free-standing steel safes made in Birmingham could not double as bank vaults and were vulnerable to night-time raids by armed and mounted marauders. The MacArthur-Forrest process did not only come to the rescue of the mining industry; it helped extend the repertoire of professional criminals. A rising tide lifts all the ships in port. The power of the incoming surge was incalculable. In order to appreciate the sea-change of science, it is necessary to revisit the low tide.

★ ★ ★

In January 1890, it was estimated that Johannesburg's population had shrunk by a quarter in a matter of months. By September, it was said to have been reduced by a third.[37] The exodus of artisans, clerks, diggers, prospectors and mechanics unnerved most of the underworld. Scores of burglars, footpads, highwaymen and safe-crackers took to horse-drawn carts and fled south, towards the diamond fields. With the ticks tracking the dogs, mining-town criminals invaded the countryside, changing the pattern of crime in farming centres over two broad circuits that connected Johannesburg to Kimberley. The first ran directly from Potchefstroom to Klerksdorp, Bloemhof and on to Christiana, while the second, less direct route linked Rustenburg to Vryburg and Mafeking.[38]

With Johannesburg and the satellite mining towns emptying steadily and the mines locked into a process of reconstruction that put paid to low-cost re-entry into the industry, the mood among the populace sank to an unprecedented low. White miners spoke about the need to organise a union to safeguard their future while small shopkeepers experiencing a downturn in trade turned their wrath on even smaller competitive outsiders. Ordinary folk railed against the banks, the Chamber of Mines, mine owners and the state, which, they said, were all against the 'small man'. In the midst of an undeclared class war, sullen whites without the franchise saw the new captains of industry and large institutions as the legitimate targets for corrective action. A mood of populist resentment set in, preparing the way for the emergence of some transient anti-hero.

He appeared soon enough in the shape of an unemployed digger-turned-prospector. Jack McKeone was the 24-year-old son of Irish-South African parents, raised in the foothills of the Drakensberg and Malutis where he perfected his horsemanship and use of a revolver. With his head filled with notions of the importance of showing 'manliness' and strongly influenced by the deeds and style of Ned Kelly, McKeone linked up with another young romantic, Joseph Stevens, who had assumed the alias 'Dick Turpin' as his working name. Posing as 'Americans', the two robbed the Standard Bank branch at Krugersdorp of several thousands of pounds in notes and coins, some of which was passed to Irish Brigade accomplices even before they were pursued.[39]

The ensuing chase culminated in a shoot-out with the police, before the two men surrendered and were arrested. At his trial, in a speech reminiscent of Kelly's own address to Sir Redmond Barry, in Melbourne, McKeone, learning that he had been sentenced to 25 years' imprisonment with hard labour, said to Judge Ameshoff: 'Thank you my Lord, may you be judged by your judge on your day and may your sentence be less than mine.'[40] Presenting himself as a champion of the underdog and his family as victims of police persecution, McKeone, like Ned Kelly, won a great deal of sympathy from the disillusioned public. A serial escapee, he eventually managed to elude the police and made his way to Australia, leaving in his wake a press asking: 'Why is McKeone set up as a hero, as a second Dick Turpin or Robin Hood?'[41]

For those locked into a cult of masculinity, including members of the Irish Brigade, there was much to be admired in such audacious behaviour. Jack McKeone set the standard for manly conduct on the frontier and reinforced popular notions about honour. For many ordinary folk, however, it was not so much the virtues of the bank robber that shaped their sympathies, but the vices of the police and prisons officers.

As in most nationalist regimes where race and ethnicity rather than ability or merit constitute the backbone of the state's apparatuses of control, the Zarps were recruited exclusively from the ranks of the politically empowered. The police were, most commentators agreed, deficient in numbers and wanting in skills and training. Badly paid, semi-literate burghers, sons of citizen-farmers, found themselves pitted against hardened foreign – *uitlander* – offenders speaking unfamiliar languages. Many of the English-speaking professional criminals had had their own organisational and police-evading skills burnished in the College of Banditry. Others had graduated from the grimy alleys of the great industrial cities of Lancashire, Yorkshire and Warwickshire.

The two parties were, in short, completely mismatched. In 1894, the disillusioned Commandant of Police, DE Schutte, wrote an open letter to the press stating: 'I acknowledge the *rottenness* of the entire police force, but decline to accept the disgrace attached thereto, having striven to reorganise the same, but failed through lack of support.' A year later, the same police in Johannesburg had to go on strike to get paid.[42] A Boer state rooted in the countryside was not up to urban challenges.

The Volksraad was forced to pass legislation acknowledging, albeit indirectly, that armed robbery was assuming alarming proportions. But, in coming to terms with the footpads and highwaymen, the Boer government was trapped in a dilemma that went to the heart of state power. Unlike in the United States, where an amendment to the constitution in 1791 entrenched the right of citizens to bear arms, the burghers of the South African Republic, locked into a commando system in racially contested terrain, had always accepted that *all* whites had the right to be armed.

Right from the day of its founding, a large number, perhaps most, of the white men in Johannesburg carried Colt or Smith & Wesson revolvers.[43] Side-arms were brandished at the slightest provocation and occasionally used to deadly effect. In September 1893 – by which time the frontier had already moved north – *The Star* still complained that there was 'scarcely a row that occurs on the Rand which does not immediately entail the production of a revolver'.[44] If white miners had the right to brandish unlicensed firearms, how were footpads and highwaymen to be denied weapons?

Unwilling to deprive Europeans of weapons in an emerging state which, in the north and east, was being contested by Africans who refused to pay taxes, the government chose instead to deny various white criminals the accoutrements of their trades. The Gilbert & Sullivan debate that followed captured some of the madness of the frontier. Clause one of Law No 2 of 1891, 'Masks and Disguises', stipulated that: 'The wearing or use of masks, false beards or other means whereby disguises are effected, in public roads or other public places is forbidden.'[45] Public processions and theatrical performances were exempted from the law.

But there were other things troubling the God-fearing members of the Volksraad during the debate that May, including the sexual identities assumed by some of those on goldfields. After a discussion that was unfortunately not recorded, the Raad members voted – by a narrow margin – not to accept an amendment prohibiting men from wearing women's clothing, and vice versa.[46] There is no way of knowing, but it may not have been only the theatre that benefited from such tolerance. Cross-dressing remained unchecked, but highwaymen – including the first few young Afrikaner males unable to wrest a living from the soil during the depression – joined those that preyed on black and white miners until after an integrated railway network offering safer transport was completed in 1895.[47]

Members of the Volksraad were always more comfortable dealing with issues of colour than of class. Most struggled to come to terms with the complexities of urban life on the Rand, let alone aggressive criminal subcultures whose origins lay in northern hemisphere cities. In a state constitutionally bound to uphold racial distinctions, painful lessons awaited. The depression forced the Volksraad to wrestle with new, seemingly wholly insoluble conundrums. How in a state dependent on the labour-power of tens of thousands of indigenous peoples on farms and thousands of semi-skilled white immigrants in industry, were crime, punishment and justice to be reconciled in ways that did not place blacks and whites on an equal footing?

When gold was discovered in the Transvaal countryside in 1886, the

Republic's ramshackle gaols and prisons were geared only to contain and correct the human failings of a limited number of miscreants drawn from a pre-industrial order. No gaol was designed to cope with a new brand of worldly wise foreign criminals, let alone with the spike in numbers occasioned by the depression that quickly followed. The state separated black prisoners – short- and long-term – from whites as effectively as it could.[48] While black prisoners dressed as best possible during periods of incarceration, white males were, when circumstances allowed, provided with distinctive shirts bearing easily recognisable prison markings.[49]

For those in the Irish Brigade and other criminals drawn from modern British penal institutions, the earliest Boer prisons held few terrors. Bound by the codes of masculinity and demands of Irish sub-culture to resist arrest and incarceration, it became almost *de rigueur* for the Irish and English 'hard men' on the Rand to attempt to escape from prison.[50]

The Kruger government was embarrassed by its prison administration. Repeated attempts at escape on the goldfields, including those by Jack McKeone, heightened a smouldering contempt for Afrikaner-Dutch authority. As the depression deepened the authorities responded by attempting to separate out and isolate members of the Irish Brigade and those in other groupings. The government also reinforced and strengthened the Visagie Street prison in Pretoria, which was protected by the only thing approximating to a standing army – the State Artillery.[51]

Those recalcitrant English or Irish elements on the Rand who were not moved to Visagie Street were sent to more remote rural centres such as Barberton or Potchefstroom, where, it was believed, they would find it difficult to get support from within and without when attempting to escape.[52] It was only towards the end of the depression and in the booming mid-1890s that the state got around to constructing more substantial prisons capable of holding dangerous inmates.[53] One, at Potchefstroom, aspired to Panopticon modernity. At about the same time, in the mid-1890s, the main prison in Johannesburg was placed in the charge of Thomas Menton, an Irishman who had deserted from the 59th Infantry Regiment during the First War of Independence in 1881.[54]

The most visible of the stark clashes between the state and its white prisoners took place in prisons on the Rand. Prison staff – like the police, at first recruited almost exclusively from the ranks of the burghers – were often as inexperienced as they were untrained. Poorly paid, a fair number soon gave way to the temptations of corruption. By late 1890, the situation at the Pretoria prison itself was so serious that the Governor and several white warders were relieved of their posts.[55]

At the high point of the depression, administrators were confronted on an almost daily basis by aggressive, contemptuous prisoners set on escaping from shoddily constructed cells. And, in Johannesburg, where dynamite was easily come by and sometimes used by white workers to settle labour disputes, it was not only the integrity of the staff that was tested. In August 1893, amidst great tension, two white inmates used detonators in an attempt to blow up a wall.[56] The flouting of prison regulations necessitated frequent interventions by the Chief Magistrate – either in the Landdrost's Court or at the prison itself.[57] It was a crisis precipitated by three-score Manchester-Irish and a few Englishmen who forced the reluctant government to consider the possibility that, when it came to prison punishment, considerations of class might trump colour.

It was not as if the cupboard was bare to begin with. As befitted a state born of a reluctance to come to terms with the abolition of slavery in the Cape and devoted to agriculture, some of the existing forms of punishment harked back to medieval times and village justice in Europe. In 1889, Jack McKeone was placed in stocks when he threatened to escape.[58] He was not the first or the last to be confined in that way; in the mid-1890s, recalcitrant white prisoners were still routinely subjected to what was already seen by progressives as an outdated form of punishment.

For the incorrigible – including McLoughlin and some of the Manchester-Irish – the blacksmith was sent for. In scenes reminiscent of the slave-states of the American south, they were chained together and set to public works around town.[59] This, too, placed white inmates on the same footing as blacks in a highly visible setting, and, in a society committed to preserving racial distinctions, rendered them vulnerable to public ridicule.[60] But when uniforms, stocks, darkened cells, solitary confinement and the chain gang all failed to discourage crime-hardened whites from attempting to escape, the Kruger government, after careful consideration, agreed to sanction the use of a far more brutal corrective.

In May 1892, after much debate, the Volksraad decided that whites who had fallen foul of the law and prison regulations could be flogged.[61] This startling development, a decade after inflicting stripes had been abandoned by the British navy, was deeply resented by not only those Manchester-Irish already in prison, but also a section of the English-medium press and those in the white underclasses frightened of ending up on the wrong side of the law. The usually progressive *Standard & Diggers' News,* strongly opposed to the flogging of whites, editorialised that: 'The distinction between conqueror and conquered must be maintained even in this matter, and in order also to keep up consistency with this Republic's native policy in other respects.'[62] But neither the government nor its Old Testament-loving supporters were deterred. The emerging Boer elite, it seemed, was as ready to embrace modern notions of class when it suited it, as were English 'liberals' to cling to the old colonial privileges of colour when the situation suited them.

In 1891, from the hilly country around Heidelberg, where the flow of black labour to farms was frequently disrupted by white highwaymen, the Boers submitted a memorial supporting the flogging of whites because, 'on the goldfields white persons committed more robberies than natives'.[63] Although at first rejected, the idea received legislative backing only months later. When, in 1893, Alexander Robb, a footpad with a previous conviction, lured a farmer from Nylstroom into a secluded spot and robbed him, he was sentenced to five years' hard labour and 15 lashes.[64] Criminal upheavals associated with industrialisation were beginning to disrupt the older society founded on racial ordering.

In the prisons, where flogging of whites was a last resort, members of the Irish Brigade were in the forefront of those most frequently punished. Offenders were tied to a wooden triangle and, with arms and legs akimbo, thrashed under the watchful eye of the District Surgeon, Hans Sauer. In one instance, as in the navy, a black inmate poured brine into the wounds of the white prisoner who had been flogged. In keeping with the times, the place, and the prevailing notions of racial ordering, the offended and flogged white man then assaulted the black brine-pourer.[65]

William Kelly – not to be confused with WJ Kelly, who had accompanied Jack McLoughlin to Fort Napier in 1886 – was a disturbed inmate bent on escaping. Over 24 months, between August 1892 and August 1894, Kelly received 55 lashes.[66] Most white offenders, however, were keen to avoid repeated lashings, with one or two being so terrified at the prospect that they were willing to forego any hard-earned reputation as 'hard men' by publicly begging Landdrost van den Bergh for forgiveness – which, not surprisingly, was occasionally forthcoming.[67]

Viewed in retrospect, those intent on controlling early Johannesburg were trying to build on socio-economic foundations that were constantly shifting. A rough frontier settlement opened up around diggings in 1886 took close on a decade to give way to a mining town – the transition consciously slowed down by a republican government intent on seeing agriculture and a 'horse economy' benefiting for as long as possible before an integrated railway system irrevocably opened the republic to outside influences. Even then, the Rand was only slightly less dominated by white men who foregrounded the values of a masculine culture that could be traced back to mid-nineteenth-century industrial Britain. Some of the more acceptable ways of thinking and doing on the frontier came through formally established English institutions, including the churches and Friendly Societies. But others, as we will note in due course, came to the Witwatersrand via far less formalised or institutionalised patterns of male recreation and sport.

These changing profiles of Johannesburg and towns along the Reef had in turn to fit into a state in which political power derived from a poorly educated rural elite locked into a sluggish agricultural economy. The government aspired to maintaining a racially ordered society amidst a rapidly developing mining sector that had the misfortune of falling within the ambit of British imperial ambitions. Seen from this perspective, the emergence of gold mining on the Witwatersrand presented those who governed the South African Republic with a series of inter-related structural problems – problems that invited revolutionary thinking from the mine owners and British imperialists. The depression of 1889–92 and an upsurge in organised crime driven by the Irish Brigade, who many disgruntled white workers saw as 'social bandits', confronted Kruger and his government with

serious challenges. They also hinted darkly at challenges of a far more serious nature. The attempted coup of 1895 – the Jameson Raid – was, in part,
a bandit-like cross-frontier incursion by the self-appointed custodians of
industrial capital's long-term interests. It was the forerunner of what was to
become the most bitterly divisive conflict in the long history of the British
Empire, the South African War of 1899–1902.[68]

Marx suggested that men make their own history, albeit not under circumstances of their choosing. If his adage held true for labouring men and
women, it was probably at least as applicable to those who found themselves
marginalised and left only clinging to the hems of the working classes. The
circumstances that Jack McLoughlin and his Mancunian associates chose to
enter, in 1887 and 1888, might have been consciously sought out by them,
but the impact of those conditions on their lives could hardly have been
foreseen. The depression of 1889–92 recast McLoughlin's own mind and
body in ways that determined not only the remainder of his extraordinary
criminal career, but the rest of his life.

CHAPTER ELEVEN

❦

Metamorphosis

TO POTCHEFSTROOM AND BACK
— 1890 —

He, too, has been changed in his turn,
Transformed utterly:
A terrible beauty is born.

WB YEATS

As to the thief, male or female, cut off his hands:
a retribution for their deeds, and exemplary punishment from Allah,
and Allah is exalted in Power, Full of Wisdom.

SURA 5:38, *THE QUR'AN*

Prior to the Ancoats pawnshop break-ins in 1878, at age 19, Jack McLoughlin had only a minor criminal record. Then he served a year in prison, in London, for a street robbery that went wrong. But, after that, he avoided arrest for deserting from the navy and led a charmed life on the run in Australia before fleeing to Natal. There is no surviving record of his having been in trouble with the law while at the College of Banditry, or in Mozambique. His only setback in southern Africa came at Barberton, where he served six months for the Eureka City invasions. It all pointed to a certain amount of professionalism on his part and the limitations of stretched colonial police forces on the other.

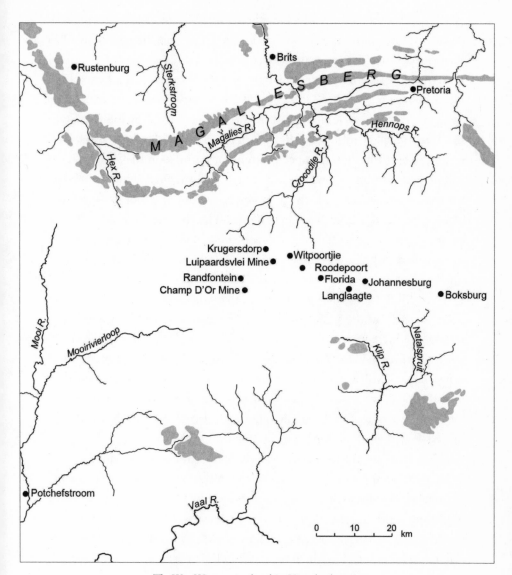

The West Witwatersrand and its Hinterland, c 1895

The same serendipitous combination of cunning and official ineptitude characterised the first 24 months of his stay in Johannesburg, between 1888 and 1890. In the absence of any archival evidence, perhaps the best way of reconstructing what he may have been up to during those two years is to take a peek at the underworld activities of a few of his closest accomplices. Jack McCann – whom he first met in Singapore and then befriended in Pietermaritzburg – is easiest to trace.

In March 1888, a month after the Irish Brigade descended on Johannesburg like a biblical plague, McCann became a part-time barman at Connolly's Sportsman's Arms. A few weeks later he was convicted of the theft of a revolver and spent some time in prison. By the time that he was released, in July, one of the most advanced mining operations on the Rand, which had progressed well beyond open-cast diggings, was already in trouble. The Croesus was part of a group of mines belonging to George Goch and battling to recover gold from pyritic ores. The manager, confronted by a chemical impasse, was forced into crisis mode. His entire stock of quicksilver, stored in huge 70-pound canisters – each containing £10-worth of unrecovered gold – was locked-down in an abandoned battery house.[1]

In August, Harry Fisher, a part-time miner and gang confidant who had been 'working' at the Croesus during the shut-down, told McCann about the store of mercury-amalgam. McCann decided to steal a few of the canisters, and with the help of Fisher, another 'miner', Charles Hartley, and a cab driver named Miller, set up a scheme to sell the canisters to an unnamed Jewish contact who would recover the gold. The battery house was broken into on the night of 11 September and eight casks of quicksilver-gold removed. But, thereafter, things quickly turned sour.

Fisher failed to make the rendezvous at the mine on the night of the break-in, leaving McCann and Miller to lug the heavy canisters to a waiting two-wheeled scotch-cart. The following morning, McCann, who had linked up with Hartley, learned that their Jewish collaborator had backed out of the deal. It necessitated a change of plan. The canisters were moved into rooms at the back of the Brighton Hotel. The Brighton was a dive, replete with 'actresses' doubling as 'barmaids' and other friendly females. But the proprietor was the most successful illicit gold dealer on the Rand in the early to late 1890s, George Mignonette.[2]

Mignonette's real name was George Ackland. Despite being at the centre of amalgam theft in Johannesburg for a decade or more, he was never successfully prosecuted, even when – in 1898 – he was the subject of a sophisticated secret-service type operation mounted by Kruger's reforming State Attorney, JC Smuts.[3] Mignonette may have been a Catholic and had once been based in France but, other than that, little is known about him. Prior to his arrival on the Witwatersrand, he may have been on the Kimberley diamond fields where he may have met McCann, who, after deserting the army, had worked there briefly as a winding-engine driver. Part of Mignonette's mid-career success was attributable to the fact that, by 1893, he was in league with Johannesburg's corrupt Chief Detective, Robert Ferguson. Ferguson, too, was picked up in an undercover operation against gold dealers launched by Smuts in 1898.

But, at the time of the Croesus break-in, the Chief Detective was in the earliest stages of constructing his own network of illicit gold dealers and poorly disposed towards potential underworld rivals. Ferguson spent most of his time in public houses and relied on informants to provide him with a reasonable flow of arrests and convictions. Despite this public persona, Ferguson was understandably secretive about his private life and managed to conceal his corruption well into the 1890s. He may also have been assisted in his own undercover operations by his wife, who – as one of Smuts's secret agents claimed – was an 'off coloured woman'.[4]

Ferguson had more reason than most to know that the use of informers, or guaranteeing underworld associates freedom from prosecution in exchange for giving evidence, were practices deeply abhorrent to most Irishmen. If he did not know, then anyone in Johannesburg could have told him about James Carey. Carey was one of the 'Invincibles', a radical offshoot of the Fenians who had assassinated the Chief Secretary for Ireland, Lord Frederick Cavendish, and his Permanent Undersecretary, Thomas Burke, in Phoenix Park, Dublin, in 1882. In return for turning Queen's evidence, the British had provided Carey with an assumed name and put him aboard the *Melrose Castle* to take on a new life in Natal. But, just off Port Elizabeth, Carey was recognised by a Donegal man, Patrick O'Donnell, and shot as a traitor to the Irish cause.[5]

It is not known who provided Ferguson with his initial lead in the Croesus Mine case, but, acting on information received, he visited the mine and got the manager to check that his store of mercury-amalgam was intact.[6] It was not. Eight canisters were missing and Ferguson arrested McCann, Fisher, Hartley and Mignonette on a charge of 'receiving and dealing in stolen amalgam and quicksilver'. It was one of very few successes the Chief Detective enjoyed during a long term of office that coincided with a remarkable increase in gold recovery as a result of the MacArthur-Forrest process. By 1893, losses of amalgam were becoming so serious that the Chamber of Mines pressed the government to introduce draconian legislation to deal with the mounting problem.

By the time the preliminary examination for the Croesus case took place, on 11 September, the Chief Detective was encouraging Hartley to turn informer.[7] Hartley co-operated and Ferguson, for reasons known only to him, worked up the case in a way that left the Public Prosecutor inclined to pursue only McCann. Fisher and Mignonette were suddenly released and given the time and space in which to reorganise themselves in ways that seem to have kept their earlier relationship with McCann intact. For unknown reasons neither McCann nor his close friend, Jack McLoughlin, were inclined to deal with Hartley in ways the Irish often reserved for police informers.

In October, whilst awaiting trial, McCann escaped by digging his way through a prison wall and teaming up with Jack Burns, another shadowy underworld figure from Ancoats. The two then set course for Delagoa Bay and the freedom of the Indian Ocean world. In Steynsdorp, the pair stole some horses and crossed into Mozambique where, given the absence of an extradition treaty, the policemen tailing them were unable to effect an arrest. Marooned in Lourenço Marques without the funds to get to Australia, McCann changed his name to 'John Boswell' and boarded a steamer for Natal. In Durban, he was recognised while watching a cricket match and arrested as a fugitive from justice. After a few exchanges between Pretoria and Pietermaritzburg he was escorted to Johannesburg and made to stand trial for the theft of mercury. Neither his escape from prison, nor the theft of a horse, attracted further attention.[8]

McCann's trial, in the Johannesburg Circuit Court in mid-July 1889, was marked by shenanigans of the sort that became common as matters pertaining to gold theft, the detective department and the Public Prosecutor's office combined to yield what approximated to 'justice'. Somebody, probably

George Mignonette, retained an advocate to defend McCann in a way that avoided any hint of police corruption and failed to disclose the major network profiting from amalgam theft. When McCann realised that he was being prevented from calling witnesses for his defence, he insisted on the advocate withdrawing. But by then, even though Hartley had not risked giving evidence in court, the damage had been done. Judge Esselen found McCann guilty and sentenced him to two years' imprisonment with hard labour, notwithstanding a later petition for a reduction in sentence based on the fact that his left arm was said to be somewhat shorter than his right.[9]

As a serious offender likely to attempt to escape, McCann was sent to Barberton to serve out his sentence under the sympathetic eye of the chief gaoler and fellow Irishman, Thomas Menton. Menton ensured that McCann was restricted to light duties only and, a little more than a year later, supported his plea for remission of sentence. But Kruger's Executive Committee – the cabinet – denied the request and McCann was eventually only released in February 1891.[10] In effect, his incarceration denied McLoughlin access to his closest and most trusted lieutenant during the worst of the depression.

McCann was not the only loss. William Kelly, ex-Fort Napier and ex-Barberton, had talked his way into the position of manager of the small Royal Gold Mining Company shortly after the Irish Brigade entered Johannesburg. He was soon friends with the influential Victor 'Chinaman' Wolff, a speculator and confidant of Ferguson's, who, a few years later, was found guilty of perjury in a famous libel case which the magnate JB Robinson brought against the author Louis Cohen.[11] Kelly lost his position when the gold-recovery crisis set in, but then returned to the mine and stole six cases of dynamite. He may have been the principal dynamite supplier for the McLoughlin gang's earliest safe-blasting exploits in central Johannesburg. Caught and charged, however, in January 1892 Kelly was sentenced to four years' hard labour for the theft of the dynamite.[12]

The prolonged absence of McCann and Kelly did nothing to restrict the safe-cracking exploits of the McLoughlin gang before, or after, the 1889–92 depression. Prison-time was an occupational hazard and the composition of the gang mutated constantly to accommodate a need for specialist skills and raw muscle-power, and the nature and value of any potential loot. There was also a steady inflow of Manchester-Irish from which to recruit – or, if all else failed, even more English underworld elements hailing from the industrial cities of the north-east or north-west.

The gang's *modus operandi*, although varying in detail, was developed during those earliest months of the frontier era. Its pioneering operations came at a time when smaller open-cast diggings did not make for a significant build-up of gold amalgam on site. So, instead of concentrating on the emerging mines, the gang focused on the premises of successful retailers and wholesalers in the unlit streets around the Market Square. The template they developed there was later adapted, extended and used at isolated mine offices once the deeper-level mines got the MacArthur-Forrest process to yield larger quantities of gold. At deep-level mines, the gold amalgam stored in free-standing safes and cheaply constructed offices before being transported to the banks or moved to a central refining facility proved to be a relatively easy target.

Once a promising retailer or wholesaler's premises had been identified, between three and a dozen men determined when the week's cash-holdings were likely to be at a peak and then waited for the right weather conditions to set in. Moonless, heavily overcast summer or cold and wet winter nights that muted sound and kept people indoors were best suited to the removal and blasting of large safes. Sounds emanating from the nearby mines, as battery-stamps gnashed their way through mountains of rock, helped mask the sound of any explosion but, as already noted, it was the summer thunderstorms that were the safe-crackers' best friend of all. Arcs of lightning and heaven-rending thunder combined to provide optimal conditions of light and sound.

The operation was run on quasi-military lines, in ways a British Army officer might approve of. A detail of two to four muscular thugs would be deployed to fan out, occupy strategic corners and act as sentries. The main party's flanks and rear were thus protected from the unwanted attention of passers-by or policemen on the beat. A smaller party of experienced burglars would then use 'false keys' to gain easy and silent entry to the premises – or, failing that, force the latches and locks on doors or windows.

If for some reason a very heavy safe had to be blown on site, the experts would move into position. These were men who knew about metals and metal-working, detonators and dynamite. But because on-site blasting increased risk unnecessarily, safes were often removed. In such cases a much larger group of men would use ropes to manhandle the safe onto mats or blankets. The safe would be lugged out and placed on a barrow, cart or wagon and transported to the outskirts of the town, or a nearby mining property. There, under the cover of the storm, within earshot of other explosions or the rumble of thunder, the door would be blown, the loot shared and the robbers rapidly dispersed.[13]

After July 1889, as the diggings faltered and gold became harder to come by, the largest safe-lifting, robbing and blasting projects all took place in the town centre. Dunton Brothers, the International Wine & Spirit Company, Payne & Trull and the Permanent Mutual Building & Investment Company were among the businesses that had safes removed or blown during this period. With the exception of the botched job at Dunton Brothers, which saw the conviction of two Irishmen – Cahill and Michell – Ferguson was unable to arrest, let alone prosecute any suspects.[14] These were notable police failures because most of the projects during this period were undertaken by a few of the less experienced stragglers from the old Irish Brigade. By then, many of the 'hard men' had abandoned the town in a search for greener pastures.

By February 1890, many diggers, mechanics, prospectors and unskilled whites, sensing another sad Barberton in the making, were clambering aboard mule carts and heading south towards the diamond fields of Griqualand West.[15] A good number of professional criminals, being less pessimistic and not beholden to anyone, lingered on through the late summer. But when winter set in even they had second thoughts and retreated. In early May, readers of the *Diamond Fields Advertiser* in Kimberley were warned that they should brace themselves for a large influx of 'loafers' as well as a smaller number of dangerous characters.[16]

Unlike most unemployed whites, the core of the old Irish Brigade had acquired some experience of rural and small-town life while moving through the eastern parts of southern Africa and were in no hurry to get to Griqualand West. As former highwaymen they were well aware that prosperous Boer farming communities adjacent to the Witwatersrand had provided the diggings with firewood, meat, fruit and vegetables during the good times. Potchefstroom, Rustenburg, Klerksdorp and Bloemhof had all evolved into modest farming centres with their own administrative, clerical, educational, retail and wholesale resources. They all had courts, government buildings, post offices and shops, but, lacking easy access to secure banks, often saw a significant build-up in cash and negotiable instruments during the intervals between the weekly coach services that connected them to the capital. As McLoughlin and friends saw it, the retreat to Kimberley or beyond could be self-financing.

★   ★   ★

During the winter and spring of 1890, a gang of 10 to 12 bandits was active in the Magaliesberg, just west of the Witwatersrand. Working in the hilly terrain favoured by insurgents, they concentrated their efforts in and around Rustenburg – a district represented in the Volksraad by State President Kruger, who owned a farm at Boekenhoutfontein. In June the mail coach between Pretoria and Rustenburg was held up and robbed of £400.[17] Only weeks later, during a dark and stormy night, on 9 August, the Landdrost's office in Rustenburg was plundered. Skeleton keys were used to gain entry and a huge safe, holding £4 000 in cash, was carried away and blown. It was estimated that it would have required a dozen men to remove the safe. The following night, a smaller group, which may have been an offshoot of the brigands, raided the Central Hotel at Roodepoort, removed and blasted the safe, but only got £100 in cash for their efforts.

Embarrassed by a series of robberies in the presidential backyard, Kruger sent two detectives to investigate, and then, in an unprecedented move, six members of the State Artillery were despatched to assist the police. The bandits dispersed, but one, Charles Brown, and two Manchester-Irish – James Sutherland and William Todd – were found carrying large sums of cash. Hermes-like, Todd was doubling-back to the Magaliesberg when he was arrested near Krugersdorp. His possessions, rolled into a blanket and strapped to his back in the style of an Australian 'swagman', contained coins bearing marks that might have come from an explosion.[18] But it was too little, too late, and the state still had little idea of what it was up against. By then most of the brigands had moved further afield.

Among earlier arrivals in the near western Transvaal that winter was John O'Brien, the ex-Fort Napier confidence man, formerly a policeman at Barberton. Another was the 'Australian' James Williams, aka James William Kelly, another College of Banditry man, who by then was calling himself 'William J Reid'.[19] But, in amongst the general migration of bandits, some of whom were soon behind bars, was the new safe-cracker extraordinaire himself.

In mid-May 1890, with the gold mines in crisis, McLoughlin abandoned if not the Magaliesberg, then certainly the Witwatersrand. Happy to carry notoriously unstable dynamite around with him, he embarked on an exploratory foray, together with two accomplices, into the towns lighting the way to the diamond fields.[20] Their first stop was at Rustenburg, where, working with the flow of the commercial week, they waited until late Friday afternoon, 16 May, before checking into Brink's Hotel.

The next morning they went to the leading retailers in town, Somers & Co, to establish the lie of the land. Then, chancing their arms, they attempted to cash a cheque but a smart assistant, unconvinced by an indistinct signature, refused to help them. Undeterred, they moved through the lanes and yards behind the shops and found a sturdy, unsecured barrow. They then mapped the safest and easiest route from Somers' store to the outskirts of the town. That done, they returned to the hotel where, in low key, they enjoyed a few Saturday evening drinks.

They arose late the next morning, having slept through the sound of early-morning worshippers making their way to church. Towards midday, as the Sunday silence descended upon the town, they made for the residents' bar. Still on their best behaviour, they spent the afternoon talking and drinking before entering the dining room for the evening meal. Around 8.00 pm, they left the hotel and whiled away a few uncomfortable hours out in the chill, waiting for the residents to drift off into a warm winter's sleep before going to collect the purloined barrow.[21]

The main door at Somers' was forced somewhere between 11.00 pm and 2.00 am. Blankets were placed on the floor and the safe was tipped into a makeshift cradle before being hoisted into position on the barrow. Covered by blankets, it was hauled three miles out of town, where, with the sound muffled by mere distance, it was laid on its side and blasted open. Rustenburg was still snoring when the loot was divided. The three men then split up – the tracks of one or two seemingly heading east, in the general direction of the goldfields, but the others – more worryingly for the police – heading west, in the direction of the Bechuanaland border.

Monday morning saw great excitement as news of the heist spread and the extent of the loss became known. It was, even by international standards at the time, an impressive haul: £300 in cash, close on £300 of bearer scrip, promissory notes, life policies and title deeds as well as several gold and diamond rings were missing. The fact that the gang was happy to take negotiable instruments that would have to be traded through shady brokers hinted at the presence of the Irish-Australian, Williams. McLoughlin's own preference was usually for cash, gold, jewellery and gold-chain watches.

The police made good progress tracking the suspects on their way to the Witwatersrand to within an hour of the small hills and ravines around Krugersdorp. This chimed with the idea that McLoughlin was involved because the west Rand town was known to be a favourite haunt of his. Suspicions were confirmed when they obtained descriptions of their suspects. The two were, the police admitted to journalists, 'well known desperate characters'. 'The one is below medium height, being about five feet four inches, dark complexioned, with a black moustache; he is stout and well built.' It was the next best thing to a photograph – a fine word-portrait of Jack McLoughlin at the peak of his physical powers.[22]

But instead of facilitating enquiries that might lead to an arrest, this description – which appeared in a leading Johannesburg newspaper – merely became part of a mystery that surrounded McLoughlin for five more years. Here was a 'desperado', 'well known' to police and press alike, whom no one was willing to put a name to! Neither Ferguson nor Emmanuel Mendelssohn, Editor of the *Standard & Diggers' News,* referred to him by name. Nor, for that matter, did they even mention the Irish Brigade, even though many of its members continued to frequent the town's pubs. It all suggests that long before 1895, when McLoughlin became so notorious that *not* putting a name to his deeds was no longer an option, he was already considered so dangerous and so widely feared that even his most powerful adversaries were cowed into silence.

The police *knew* who they wished to interrogate about the Somers safe-blasting but failed to find their main man. They suddenly lost their appetite for the chase. Several days were wasted obtaining warrants for suspects who, despite the fact that the trail of two of them led to Krugersdorp, were suddenly thought to have been across the border, in Mafeking.[23] Even at the time that must have seemed a touch improbable – but given what followed, it was just absurd.

McLoughlin was no shrinking violet. He exuded confidence and, when flush, spent money freely in public places. He was known for his love of gambling, and when not at the race track spent an inordinate amount of time drinking and dining with scores of admiring 'Irish' and other miners in predictable locations. He may, of course, have kept so low a profile that it was thought that he had 'disappeared' or 'left the country'. But even that excuse must soon have worn thin. Just three weeks after the Somers job, already penniless after a bout of urban carousing and back on the country trails leading to the diamond fields, McLoughlin was arrested on an unrelated charge, operating under his own name, in a nearby town.

★ ★ ★

The Potchefstroom gaol, constructed before the Rand gold rush, housed several tough nuts sent there from Johannesburg during the depression. Others had been locked up there after having fallen foul of the law while en route to Kimberley. Among the latter was James Williams, aka WJ Kelly, aka JW Reid, who had probably been with McLoughlin in Rustenburg only a few weeks earlier. He was soon to be joined by John O'Brien of Manchester, the College of Banditry, Barberton and the Irish Brigade.

For the thousands of white tramps and vagrants negotiating southern Africa in the late nineteenth century, the local parson or priest was the first port of call when searching for a meal or money.[24] But O'Brien was more of a confidence trickster than a 24-hour tramp. He set his sights higher than most tramps, using any hard luck tale that came to mind about God or the Old Country to obtain work and accommodation. In Potchefstroom he found Father Trabaud, an Oblate in the Order of Mary Immaculate, whom he must have thought of as a relatively easy touch.

Trabaud had 'taken his obedience' and moved to Potchefstroom in late 1889 to oversee the erection of a convent for the Sisters of the Sacred Heart. Shortly after building operations commenced, O'Brien drifted into town after a month-long binge in Johannesburg where he, JW Reid and some other unnamed Irishmen had been out on a blinder. The wily Oblate insisted that O'Brien 'take the pledge' to give up drinking before agreeing to take him on as a 'servant' and general odd-job man.

Their arrangement worked reasonably well as O'Brien settled in to ride out the depression. For six months there was no outward sign of discord between the priest and his new manservant. Then, about a month after the Rustenburg robbery, around mid-June 1890, JW Reid suddenly appeared out of nowhere. He and O'Brien resumed a friendship born of shared thirst and were soon in and out of several disreputable pubs in town. Before long, in an incident that reeked of cheap liquor, Reid was jailed for the very 'Irish' offence of obstructing the police in their duties.[25]

Reid's removal and incarceration was God's final concession to O'Brien; a much sterner test lay ahead. Within days McLoughlin materialised, without funds, the worse for wear and hoping to link up with Reid for the journey south. O'Brien, already struggling to stay on the straight-and-narrow, found McLoughlin impossible to deny. He asked Trabaud to help a fellow Catholic, an Irish friend who was passing through Potchefstroom and who had fallen on hard times. The Oblate, softened by hard times, relented and was soon being assisted by two 'servants'.[26]

For some days all seemed well. A feeble winter sun and seasonal cold saw the town's pulse drop to levels that threatened both the physical well-being and sanity of its inhabitants. The correspondent for the *Standard & Diggers' News* was one of those driven to distraction and his judgement faltered. In the closing days of June, he reported to the Editor, in Johannesburg, that there had been a 'robbery at the convent', but that 'everything here remains extremely dull'.[27] If he had shaken off his lethargy and traced 'the story behind the story' it would not only have led him back to the safe robbery at Rustenburg but prepared him for the extraordinary sequel that played itself out over the next four weeks.

On Wednesday afternoon, 25 June 1890, without cash and facing the prospect of another cold, uncomfortable night, McLoughlin and O'Brien decided to rob the priest. As Trabaud returned to his room at dusk and unlocked his front door, he was carefully watched. When he left a minute later, for what they hoped would be a lengthy absence, McLoughlin and O'Brien slipped into his room unseen. Foregoing the role of sentry, McLoughlin sat on the bed as O'Brien rummaged through the Oblate's possessions until he found three small boxes. One contained a few personal belongings, the second the priest's meagre savings and the third about £20 that Trabaud had raised for a library through public subscription. McLoughlin was still sitting and O'Brien moving towards the door with the boxes when the priest walked in.

Realising what was happening, Trabaud played for time. An argument ensued and, after a brief tussle, the Oblate got back two of the boxes, but O'Brien simply refused to let go of the third. At that point, McLoughlin, who had remained seated, joined in the noisy exchange and O'Brien suddenly demanded that the priest provide them with beer. Trabaud, looking for a way out, hauled out a few bottles which they opened and then began to drink. The argument moderated as all three took stock of the position. O'Brien, still clutching the third box, knew that he was in trouble, but McLoughlin's own position was less clear. The two were still thinking through their next move when the priest made a run for it.[28]

By the time that the constables got there, the birds had flown. Trabaud, however, knew where to find O'Brien. He led the police to a 'canteen of questionable repute' run by a Mrs van der Kemp who lived in a corrugated-iron cottage adjoining the bar. Sure enough, O'Brien was at the bar, but of McLoughlin there was no sign. At that point the constables had second thoughts and, deciding that O'Brien could not be arrested without a warrant, set off to find the Magistrate. When they returned, Mrs van der Kemp refused them entry and the canteen doors had to be forced. There was no sign of O'Brien, but the police, warming to the task, went to the cottage and when refused entry for a second time, broke down the door. Inside, oblivious to all the noise, lay McLoughlin, who, on being identified by the Oblate, was arrested and led away.

O'Brien had fled with the cash but the constables knew that it was only a matter of time before he surfaced in one or other pub. And, sure enough, just three days later, they arrested him at Simmonds' Bar. On 20 June, he and McLoughlin appeared before the Magistrate. O'Brien, charged with robbery, was found guilty and held for sentencing. But it was a busy Monday morning, and McLoughlin's case, in which he was charged with complicity, was postponed. The pair were escorted to the gaol, where they found Reid along with various other long-term prisoners from Johannesburg.[29]

The gaol was a ramshackle affair, consisting of a single block divided into four cells that were partly interleading and all unequal in size. The recession on the Rand had, it was said, turned the gaol into a 'convict station' overseen by an acting commanding officer with 10 men who took turns, in shifts each five-strong, to guard the prison by day and night. Two-score criminals, some graduates of the Empire's finest prisons, had been herded into the largest cell. The situation there was so volatile that only two armed warders were allowed into the cell at a time. Forty other prisoners were held in two other cells while the smallest cell of all was reserved to hold a modest number of local civil debtors.

McLoughlin, awaiting trial, and O'Brien, yet to be sentenced, did not qualify as convicts and were placed in the debtors' cell. One of the walls in the cell separated it from the adjacent dispensary, which had a small window overlooking the street and a door leading out into the prison yard, which was without a gate. It was not a serious challenge. McLoughlin and O'Brien told Reid, a short-term prisoner, that they were set on escaping and he persuaded the gaolers to let him move into the debtors' cell with them. The authorities had, unwittingly, assembled a Fort Napier Irish trio.

The three inmates found a short piece of iron for excavating while out in the exercise yard, as well as an old condensed-milk tin. The lid of the tin was removed and a hole gouged out of the side. A candle end was put inside the tin and the makeshift bull's-eye lantern yielded a small beam of light to work with by night. Saturday morning, 26 July, at a low tide in circadian rhythms, was agreed upon as the best moment for the escape.

Excavations began at around 2.00 am and after an hour's digging, the hole through the wall and into the dispensary was large enough to crawl through. But, at about the same time, one of the Boer guards thought that he heard a scraping sound coming from the cells closest to the street and sent a black warder to confirm his suspicions before rousing the gaoler. The gaoler sent for a policeman living close by and told him take up a position that allowed him an unobstructed view of the yard outside the dispensary and the unmanned prison gate beyond. Two other duty-warders took positions beside the main block overlooking a low prison wall that gave them a clear line of fire into the street beyond.

Unaware of what was happening outside, the Irishmen eased aside a wooden table blocking their access to the dispensary and, once inside, silently dismantled the lock on the wooden door leading out into the yard. Inside, the trio were at the point of no return, but outside the gaoler was still uncertain as to where exactly the cell-block wall was about to be breached. The stalemate was broken when the dispensary door burst open and the trio charged into the yard, towards the gate and the street.

In the passageway overlooking the yard, the policeman raised his revolver, shouted four warnings that were ignored and then fired two shots. One of the men, already in the street, stumbled and fell directly opposite the gate. The other two accelerated away down the street. But the guards overlooking the prison wall had heard the gunshots in the yard and were waiting for them. They shouted out three more warnings and then fired several shots in the direction of the fugitives. There was more stumbling and then, total silence. Reid, found lying opposite the gate, had taken two bullets from the policeman. The first had penetrated a lung and the second had splintered a bone in his hip. McLoughlin was found trying to staunch blood streaming from the wrist of his right hand. O'Brien, however, was lying perfectly still: O'Brien was dead.[30]

The attempted escape and its sequel caused a sensation. By Monday everybody in town had heard about the shootings. Irate English-speakers, attuned to thinking the worst of the Kruger administration, saw the gaoler's failure to enter and search the cells before deploying his men as part of a sinister Boer plot. The Landdrost, displaying great tact and understanding, co-operated with the local press, who were given access to all the guards and the prison premises in order to establish the facts of the situation. The findings placated the most agitated imperialists and the town's 'race relations' were restored to a reasonable level.[31]

For some days official reports about the wounded men remained totally confusing and misleading. In a telegram to Pretoria, the Landdrost informed the State Secretary that O'Brien was dead and Reid seriously injured but that McLoughlin had received only a 'superficial' wound. But by 6 August, the full extent of the damage was becoming apparent. Reid was operated on successfully, the wounds in his chest and hip cleaned and stitched. Doctors were confident that he would recover fully.

But McLoughlin was in bad shape. The bullet had shattered his wrist and two doctors had excised the joint, leaving his right arm with a dangling appendage. The pain was excruciating, the prognosis awful. He was told that the hand was useless and that it would have to be amputated.[32] Three weeks later he was still languishing in the gaol 'hospital' receiving, it was said, excellent treatment. Reid was released and returned to the Rand, where, as 'Kelly', he joined up with associates from the Australian underworld to resume an active criminal career.[33]

The charge of McLoughlin having been complicit in the fracas at Trabaud's was dropped and never featured in his subsequent criminal record. There was also no further mention of it in press reports and the story failed to surface in the folklore of the Johannesburg underworld. This structured silence may partly have been engineered by McLoughlin himself. For reasons that can only be speculated on, he seems to have been humiliated by the convent robbery, the death of O'Brien and the amputation of his hand. It did not fit the image of the 'hard man' he had cultivated and, nearly 20 years later, he was still denying – while under oath – that the loss of his hand had anything to do with events at Potchefstroom in 1890. A Boer bullet had shattered his wrist, but it had done even greater damage to his self-perception and he never forgot it.[34]

The danger of infection from the initial procedure receded but the Potchefstroom doctors felt unable to perform the amputation. A new and impressive general hospital had only just opened in Johannesburg and the surgeons there were accustomed to dealing with serious trauma arising from mine accidents.[35] In early summer 1890, McLoughlin was subjected to chloroform for a second time in months. The amputation was successfully performed by Dr John van Niekerk, the recently appointed 'Resident Surgeon and Dispenser' and a graduate of the University of Edinburgh.[36] But it was not without additional personal cost.

The hand could not simply be cut away from what was left of the wrist joint: Van Niekerk was forced to remove part of the lower arm in order to ensure that the procedure was a success and, in that moment a 'terrible beauty' was born. McLoughlin, perhaps half-prepared to accept the loss of his preferred hand, now had a much harsher reality to face. Left without a lower forearm, in underworld circles he became known as 'One-armed Jack', although he was never directly addressed as such.

The agony of the amputation was not the only cause of discomfort while he was recovering in the hospital. There were other mysterious aches which, seeming real enough, could not be rationally accounted for and, over the months that followed, only became worse. The nurses, too, unsettled him. Drawn from the Order of the Holy Family, the sisters would have known about the priest-robbing and death of O'Brien via the Catholic grapevine.[37] He cared little about what other men thought, but the nuns left him feeling uncomfortable: he could not easily look them in the eye.[38] McLoughlin's Catholicism ran deeper than he thought.

He left hospital physically and psychologically diminished, filled with self-pity. It had taken just six months for everything in his life to change. Some said that the bad economic times on the Witwatersrand were lifting and that a new scientific discovery would save the mines, but he could see little sign of it. Like the limbless soldiers selling matches outside Victorian railway stations in Liverpool and Manchester, or the Irish tinkers who wandered about Lancashire's country lanes repairing kettles, he had little of real value to offer anybody. There was no chance of his finding work; even re-entry into the local underworld would be daunting.

❧

CHAPTER TWELVE

Humiliation and Rage:
A Mind and Body Imprisoned

JOHANNESBURG AND PRETORIA
— 1891–1892 —

In a real dark night of the soul it is always three o'clock in the morning, day after day.
F SCOTT FITZGERALD

The events at Potchefstroom and the loss of his hand a few months later were a life-changing episode, one so intense that it is impossible to do justice to it.[1] It produced a prolonged crisis – arguably, one without end – that affected every facet of the hidden ideologies and patterns of thinking that had shaped McLoughlin's behaviour up to that point and beyond. It altered the ways in which he saw himself and his newly asymmetrical body and it changed the ways in which he saw others. For months, possibly years, strange aching sensations reminded him that his body and mind were locked into an immutable arrangement: pain, that could only be relieved by the cheapest analgesic of the age. And, when his body and mind eventually arrived at a settlement, they refined the ways in which he was capable of loving someone, or of being loved.

In the absence of a diary, personal correspondence or reliable accounts from anyone close to him there is no easy way of telling what scars the journey to accommodation, rediscovery and reconstruction left him with.

Seemingly trivial things could easily have cut as deeply as serious ones. How could a man raised in a cult of masculinity that prized notions of honour, loyalty and physical prowess still function on the frontiers of empire with only one arm? More prosaically, how were such noble values to be reconciled with the fact that he could not readily button a shirt, cut meat, pull up his breeches or tie his bootlaces? He had never aspired to being a model citizen, but how was he to fund the life he had become accustomed to? How was a man who relied on picking locks and pockets, lifting catches and forcing latches for his living, let alone moving and blowing up safes, to go about his business? Was he still a man – and, if so, what sort of man, and by whose definition?

Pain prised open old fault-lines of character and behaviour, leaving him more impulsive and irascible. Between 60 and 80 per cent of all amputees experience impulses emanating from so-called 'phantom limbs' for periods whose onset or end cannot be predicted. Discomfort arising from aching, burning or tingling sensations is among the relatively minor symptoms experienced by those who have lost limbs. Others – and more especially those who have lost arms rather than legs – often have to live with the feeling that missing parts have been truncated, or placed in awkward or unnatural positions. Although only 'imagined' by the brain via its disrupted nervous system, the victim nevertheless genuinely experiences acute, chronic pain.[2]

In Johannesburg, men without limbs were not an unfamiliar sight in the 1890s. As the diggings gave way to deep-level mining the usual mishaps with industrial machinery and accidents attributed to unstable dynamite meant that the loss of a limb was hardly a novelty.[3] Although always disastrous for the individual concerned, the ways in which amputees were dealt with varied according to the craft-skill and social standing of the victim. Unmarried miners labouring in the ethnic clusters on the mines looked to their countrymen to help see them though periods of recuperation requiring medical support, or to assist them by raising funds for the long journey home. After 1892, these personalised interventions often gave way to funds set up by the growing number of ethnic associations, Friendly Societies and the new mineworkers' union.

But he was no mine worker and his plight was made all the more serious because, by the time that he underwent the operation, most of his under-world friends had been driven out of town by the recession or were them-selves living a hand-to-mouth existence. There was almost nobody around through the early summer months who could offer him a room in which to recover, or help pay for conventional painkillers. The situation worsened once the autumn chill began to stalk the plateau.

He did not stir until mid-morning. Days and nights were spent wan-dering from bar to bar until he was thrown out. Culturally and perhaps even genetically predisposed to a liking for alcohol, mind and body alike now demanded beer as the cheapest and most readily available palliative.[4] He cadged drinks shamelessly from anyone who could sympathise with a down-and-out one-armed man, or from anybody who had any association with Ireland, Manchester or the underworld. Twenty years later, he claimed that there were 'very few bars' that he 'did not know'.[5] It was quite a claim; Johannesburg had hundreds of beer halls, canteens and pubs.[6] He slept in back yards, on the streets, or wherever he could.

He was just another drunk, a tramp, a half-maimed vagrant in the mid-dle of a recession in a mining town with an uncertain future, and there were few institutions offering on-going charitable relief. When sober, he carried himself like a soldier, but instead of provoking the respect expected of a man drawn from the armed forces, all he evoked was pity. Even some underworld associates saw him not so much as a man who had once played a leading role in the Irish Brigade, but as just another broken Lancastrian stranded on the shifting frontiers of Empire. One or two suggested that he go 'home', but he would hear nothing of it. There was nothing there to return to. Manchester and the mills had consumed virtually all of his family. In any case, with the possible exception of young Tommy, in Australia, he had never much cared for any of them.

Three Manchester stalwarts and steadfast drinking partners, boyhood ac-quaintances from the Smithfield Market, came up with a suggestion of the sort put forward by working men's associations. It may have come to them because for the moment they were not involved in burglary, highway rob-bery or safe-cracking but working as miners. Gorman, King and Whelan – all with the first name Tommy – agreed to put up the money for him to buy a barrow that he could hawk vegetables from on a door-to-door basis.[7] It was an idea straight out of their Ancoats past and his spirits were so low that he agreed to it.[8] He bought a cart and found himself a room behind a house in President Street from which he plied his new trade.[9] He was not selling matches off a tray outside a railway station, but it was not far off, and almost any profits ended up in the pub.

Cheap beer and rot-gut spirit with chemical additives to stimulate the palate and offset the watering down process, dulled the worst of the pain. But they were no panacea. Too much, or too little, drink exacerbated pub tensions. There were arguments with landlords trying to keep order or insisting on closing-up, or conflicts with drunks about things which, the next morning, seemed absurd. In low dives, of which there were many, well-lubricated differences of opinion flared up into outright violence. On 31 March 1891, he was arrested in a pub for the destruction of property and sentenced to the usual fine of £2 or seven days.

A sobering week in prison and no relief from his pain reminded him that, without a hand, he was unable to exercise proper authority or defend himself. He sensed that he was being treated with condescension of the sort reserved for war victims, when all he wanted was respect. Within days of his release, he acquired a device that, even when held in a weaker left hand, forced men to take you seriously. He roamed about the abandoned diggings and mine shafts south of the town, on the Robinson Company's property, emptying the chamber of the Colt revolver until he felt entirely comfortable with it. With a revolver, he could do something more ambitious than selling cabbages from a cart.

Despite a name that suggests otherwise, Maurice – 'Morry' – Hollander was a Lancastrian with solid Irish connections. A professional gambler and jewel thief, Hollander played a pioneering role in organised trans-frontier crime on the goldfields. Indeed, he may have been the anonymous character who, in 1895, boasted to the local press that he was the first white man ever convicted of a crime in Johannesburg.[10] What is beyond doubt is that within 18 months of the diggings being proclaimed, he had twice been arrested on charges of theft, once having slipped across the border into the Free State to sell stolen jewellery in Boshof, a favourite meeting place for

Kimberley diamond thieves. By the mid-1890s, he was so disruptive a force at race meetings at the Johannesburg Turf Club that the stewards got the police to warn him off.

Despite having a criminal profile, Hollander frequently avoided conviction and imprisonment. For this he had well-connected Irish associates and professional gamblers to thank, including Mike Hart, fishmonger's son and friend of Chief Detective Ferguson. Hart was another of those whom the Public Prosecutor seldom got beyond a preliminary examination and had been one of Hollander's accomplices at Boshof.[11]

Henry – known to close friends as 'Harry' – Higgins was, despite his unusual antecedents, solidly Manchester-Irish. His grandparents were from southern Ireland. His father, a cabinet-maker, had emigrated to Wales and then moved up the coast and found himself an Old Country wife.[12] McLoughlin may have got to know him when Higgins was a still a printer's assistant back in Manchester, in the 1870s. If not, their paths would have crossed regularly in the betting shops, gambling dens and public houses of Johannesburg or out at the race track. Like Hollander and Hart, Higgins was a professional punter who lived on the margins of the law while evading its clutches.[13]

In early April 1891, McLoughlin, 'homeless and penniless', gave up hawking vegetables. Not knowing where to turn to, he made his way to a set of tawdry rooms on Commissioner Street which Higgins had bought and, in tribute to his father's County Cork origins, re-named the Queenstown Hotel. He asked Higgins for a place to stay until such time as friends could help raise the cash to re-start his business. Not wanting to deny a brother Irishman, Higgins told him to move into the stables.[14]

Over the next three weeks, McLoughlin and a half-dozen friends, including a few 'working' on nearby east Rand mines, planned a job that would help put him back on the road to recovery. All that is known about the operation is that it was set to coincide with the end of the working week and the end of the month; a time when the town was cash-flush.

On Saturday evening, 2 May, the gang, five-strong, including King and Whelan, sauntered back into the bar at the Queenstown Hotel to celebrate a success and divide the loot. They later swore, under oath, that it was only a meeting to give McLoughlin some of their wages so that he could become a hawker – a tale true in part. Higgins and Hollander were hovering about in the background when McLoughlin was handed a sizeable sum in cash. Great carousing followed until closing time and then on well into the night. McLoughlin, clutching £25 – twice a miner's monthly wage – eventually staggered back to the stable to sleep it all off amidst the midwinter comfort and warmth of the horses.

He slept fitfully and awoke to find the money gone. He recalled waking up briefly and finding Higgins's hand in his pocket, but had then slumped back into semi-consciousness. It was outrageous, but knowing that he was dealing with close friends of Ferguson, he tried to compose himself before walking across to the bar. When Higgins and Hollander appeared he asked for a word in private, ushering them into an adjacent lounge.

Finding himself unable to supplicate, he confronted them directly: 'Give me my swag.' But as the words came out he could see that they were not taking him seriously. They mocked him, feigning ignorance, pretending not to know what 'swag' meant. He felt the anger mounting and the exchanges became so loud and heated that one of the hotel residents, a carpenter named Barlow, appeared to investigate. McLoughlin remained calm enough to tell Barlow: 'They have gone through me for my money.'

Barlow's arrival, however, only emboldened Higgins, who was increasingly arrogant and contemptuous. After one more request, which Higgins, yet again, pretended not to understand, McLoughlin lost his temper and pulled out the Colt. Morry Hollander lost his nerve, blurting out that the money had been taken 'in fun', and asked Higgins to return it. Higgins, however, stood firm, and McLoughlin took a step towards him. 'Do you take me for a fool? I am going to blow your bloody brains out!' Higgins, at last realising the seriousness of the situation, bolted from the room and ran out into Commissioner Street, where he stumbled upon two mounted Zarps.

Left only with the cringing Hollander, McLoughlin put the revolver back into his pocket. Hollander later claimed that when Higgins ran out of the room, he had wrestled the gunman to the floor and that McLoughlin was only freed from his grip when Higgins and the Zarps stormed back into the room. McLoughlin claimed that he told the policemen he had been robbed and that Higgins pleaded with the Zarps: 'For God's sake take this man away: he's got a revolver and threatened to shoot me!'

When the Zarps moved in to arrest him, McLoughlin drew the Colt and fired at Higgins, shouting, 'Take that you bastard.' The bullet grazed his forehead, deflecting off the skull and lodging in a wall behind. It was a 'channel wound' that was 'not serious', but it had been a close call. McLoughlin, with two more bullets in the chamber, made no further effort at firing, and was disarmed, arrested and marched off to the police station.[15]

Faced with a charge of attempted murder, he appeared at a Preliminary Examination spread over two days that eventually dragged on into a third, on 11 May 1891, when the witnesses for the accused were summoned. The safe-robbers cum charitable miners intent on sacrificing part of their wages to buy a vegetable barrow for a stricken colleague proved unconvincing. Nor did McLoughlin, with his criminal record and an arm lost during a recent jail-break, make a favourable impression on wary Magistrate NJ van den Bergh, who dismissed all the defence submissions, saying that 'the whole money story [was] concocted'.

The case was serious enough for it to be directed to the Circuit Court. Coming as it did in the wake of his amputation, it prompted a period of self-reflection. For McLoughlin, who took almost as much pride in his ability to control himself as to conduct himself in manly fashion, the incident at the Queenstown Hotel amounted to a serious failure. He saw himself as having been lured into a thoughtless act by Higgins; one that, in retrospect, might be construed as cowardly. The shooting was portrayed as having been controlled and deliberate, as a response that was unfair and unjustified, and he hated Higgins for it. He was forced to tell the Magistrate that he had become 'aggravated', that he had got into 'a passion', 'lost control' and 'reached the point where he was not aware of what he was doing'.[16] It was unmanly, un-soldier-like.[17]

Issues of courage, honour and self-control formed the core of the code of masculinity that preoccupied him. From medieval times, through the Enlightenment and then on into the Victorian era, the emphasis had shifted from spontaneous outbursts of interpersonal violence between men, to the need for self-restraint and the more thoughtful resolution of conflict governed by rules and regulations. Just as duelling by swords and then pistols had given way to unarmed combat to settle differences, so at that very moment on the Witwatersrand bare-knuckle prize-fighting was slowly giving way to 'scientific', gloved boxing under new rules proposed by the Marquess of Queensberry.[18] Higgins had made him look cowardly.

Nor, if McLoughlin's reading at the time was anything to go by, did his self-examination about personal issues end there. While awaiting trial and sharing a cell with a young fraudster named JS Mead, he read a novel based on the life of a nineteenth-century English social reformer, Charles Bradlaugh. *We Two,* by Edna Lyall, was first published in 1884, and covered terrain that any young man raised in Ancoats could relate to.[19]

Bradlaugh, an atheist and advocate of birth control, trade-unionism, republicanism and women's suffrage, was a noted champion of Home Rule for the Irish. More importantly, he was a man of honour who took all oaths and oath-taking extremely seriously. Elected in 1880 to represent the parliamentary constituency of Northampton, Bradlaugh had declined to take the oath of allegiance and insisted on the right to affirm, which earned him the enmity of the Church of England as well as the Catholic Church. After a long dispute and having to be re-elected at by-elections on four occasions, he eventually took his seat in 1886 and, in 1888, successfully piloted a revised Oaths Act through the House of Commons.

Although Lyall's novel contained a twist in the tail, in keeping with her Christian beliefs, the book explored the need for moral steadfastness amidst the torments of conscience, duty and principle. She cited ancient sages and modern activists alike to drive home her point. Just two examples point in the direction that she wished her readers to follow. 'You begin in error,' Plato argued, 'when you suggest that we should regard the opinion of the many about just and unjust, good and evil, honourable and dishonourable.' The individual had to act out of personal conviction. Longfellow knew what was required of an admirable man: 'There's a brave fellow! There's a man of pluck!', he had written, 'A Man who is not afraid to say his say, Though a whole town's against him.'

It is impossible to know what short or longer-term influence the book had had on McLoughlin. Perhaps the best we can do is to note that some of his subsequent behaviour was in line with the sentiments expressed in *We Two*. What is also worth noting, however, is that his reading of the novel came at a moment when his own reputation had dimmed a bit and that of Jack McKeone – said to be in Australia – was as close to that of the quintessential bandit-hero as it ever got among white miners.[20] As pertinently, with over 200 hardened white inmates to look after, the reputation of the Kruger government's prison administration and management was at a new low as it struggled to cope with an embarrassing number of attempts at escape.[21]

Not all prison breaks were doomed to end in failure. Just 12 months earlier George Stevenson, a young deserter from the North Staffordshire Regiment and a College of Banditry graduate, had escaped from the Johannesburg prison. 'Stevo' was known to be leading a risky existence around Commissioner Street under various names, including Davidson.[22] It was against this background that the fictionalised Charles Bradlaugh and Captain Dangerous met and another adventurous idea was born.

The cell that McLoughlin shared with Mead was separated from the prison's perimeter wall by a 12-foot-wide patch of open ground. Beyond that, not unlike at Potchefstroom, lay the street. Starting one Tuesday night, a length of iron and two tins were used to scrape away at the cement floor of the cell. The inmates then tunnelled beneath the open ground, and then on and out, towards the prison perimeter. Loose stones and soil were carefully placed in 'old handkerchiefs, rags, pieces of blanket' and so on. At first light the dirt was stacked in the emerging tunnel and the entrance covered with bedding. After four nights' digging – by Friday 19th – they were at the foundations of the wall overlooking the street. Two more nights would have been sufficient, but sloppy male housekeeping proved their undoing. On the morning after excavations had commenced, an alert warder noticed loose soil on the cell floor and told the Governor, EJ ter Brugge, that he suspected that the inmates were attempting to burrow their way out of the prison.

Ter Brugge, relishing the chance of being seen to thwart a 'daring attempt' at escape at a time of national crisis in the prison system, allowed the excavations to continue unchecked for three more nights. On Saturday morning, 20 June 1891, he had Mead and McLoughlin sent for and then proceeded to mock them:

> Well men, how about your prospecting syndicate? Have you got shares? You must not blame me if I cannot allow prospecting within the precincts of the gaol. I am chief claims inspector here, and since you have not taken out your claims licences nor paid your poll-tax, and nevertheless are hard at work prospecting, I must refer the matter to the very particular attention of the police magistrate.[23]

Landdrost van den Bergh, irked by on-going problems at the prison, took a dim view of the matter when they appeared before him on 24 June. Despite some surprisingly reluctant evidence from the warders, the men's intentions were plain enough, and, unwilling to apportion blame, the Magistrate found them both guilty. Nor was he inclined to draw any distinctions as to their well-being, and sentenced them each to three months with hard labour. It was another straw in the winds of humiliation. A one-armed man could hardly be expected to do chain-gang duty.[24]

Shortly after that setback, McLoughlin played one of his few remaining Ancoats cards. It illustrated how highly regarded he still was among some – and, more importantly, how seriously matters of friendship and loyalty were taken. At his request, or at Charlie Harding's suggestion – it was never clear which – it was agreed that Harding would break into the building housing Van den Bergh and the Public Prosecutor's records and set fire to the documents in an attempt to subvert proceedings in McLoughlin's upcoming trial. But things went wrong almost immediately after Harding entered the Landdrost's office and before he could set the fire properly. He was arrested, found guilty of breaking and entering and attempted arson and sentenced to three years' imprisonment with hard labour.[25]

A few weeks later, on 3 September 1891, McLoughlin appeared in the Circuit Court before Justice de Korte on a charge of attempted murder. He was in better shape than he had been when he was arrested and the court reporter cast him as 'a strongly-built young man'. The prosecutor did his job as best he could, even though Higgins was as nervous as a kitten up a gum pole. Whelan and the 'miners' gave evidence for the defence, standing by McLoughlin, but the effect was nullified when the prosecutor drew attention to their criminal records. McLoughlin made a final appeal to the jury, raising many of the points he had made at the preliminary examination three months earlier. His efforts were hardly in vain. Under instruction from the judge, the jury backed away from the charge of 'attempted murder' and instead found him guilty on the lesser charge of 'assault with intent to do grievous bodily harm'. De Korte sentenced him to nine months with hard labour.[26] It could have been much worse.

★ ★ ★

The depression, Irish gangsters and the spread of armed robbery into the countryside were taking a toll on the public mood and it had all registered in the mind of the republic's politically ambitious, presidentially minded Chief Justice, JG Kotzé. Things took a turn for the worse when two Boers were murdered while out on the road.[27] But the camel's back broke shortly after McLoughlin's trial ended.

In a wild, unsuccessful attempt to escape from custody, two highwaymen, Hugh McKeone – brother of the more famous Jack – and his demented partner, William Cooper, fired several shots at two mounted Zarps. The bandits, ostensibly 'Irish', were charged with attempted murder, but when they appeared before the Chief Justice in Pretoria, on 21 October 1891, Kotzé amazed everyone by sentencing them to death.[28] The imposition of the death penalty on white men was greeted by a public outcry and led to the mass political mobilisation of the State President's many English-speaking opponents. It precipitated a major political stand-off between Kruger and his Executive on the one hand and the calculating Chief Justice on the other.[29] And it focused the attention of the old Irish Brigade, which was being put on the back foot.

With distinctions between class, colour, crime and politics becoming blurred, anger began to mount inside and outside of the republic's larger prisons, and the government sensed that the integrity of the state itself might be challenged. Five days after the McKeone-Cooper sentence was handed down, authorities in Johannesburg, where a new gaol was already under construction, decided to move the most dangerous prisoners – the 'chain gang' – to Pretoria where the State Artillery was better placed to see off any attempts at escape or rescue.

Escorting 10 of the Rand's most menacing inmates over 30 miles of open veld by coach, albeit under armed guard, was fraught with danger. More than half those moved on 26 October 1891, including McLoughlin and Harding, were notoriously 'hard men' – highway robbers and safe-crackers. The move was effected without incident, but it did put McLoughlin and Harding in close contact for much of 1891–92.[30] More importantly, perhaps, it effectively reconstituted a fair part of the original Irish Brigade. It allowed McLoughlin to link up with some of the Rustenburg mail coach brigands who had taken to the Magaliesberg at the start of the depression, including Todd and Sutherland. And all this took place at a moment when the prison was already a powder keg of tension as McKeone and Cooper, on death row, waited on Kruger and a political campaign to determine their fate.[31] The Visagie Street gaol had become a veritable Irish fort.

On the day Kotzé handed down his controversial decision, on 21 October, two detachments from the State Artillery, each eight-strong, were sent to Visagie Street to help guard the prison around the clock. McLoughlin's reputation, too, preceded him. Within hours of his arrival on 26 October, more artillerymen were sent to the gaol.[32] Four days later, on Friday, 30 October, the police learnt that 'McKeone's friends from Johannesburg' – for which read members of the McLoughlin gang – were planning on storming the prison in a military-like operation to release all the inmates. The prison was linked up to the artillery barracks by telephone and the police instructed to monitor all inbound stage coaches.[33]

The attack commenced that same night at about 11.00, from an unexpected quarter. A barrage of stones was directed onto the prison roof from the grounds of the adjacent Loreto Convent, staffed by Irish nuns whose sympathies for 24-year-old McKeone clearly ran deep. The attackers hoped the warders would open the main gates to the gaol and let in the State Artillery men to secure the cells. The would-be invaders would then storm the gaol, overrun the hard-pressed guards, release the inmates, and amidst all the chaos, free the Irish Brigade.

But the plan failed. As the first stones rained down, the warders took up positions on top of the walls, leaving the artillery free to guard the perimeter. The gates were never opened. Instead, the officer in charge of the artillery despatched a small contingent armed with bull's-eye lanterns to find the hidden stone-throwers. But the friends of the Brigade saw them coming and the guards could spot only two stragglers who then ran off into the dark. The size of the main assault party remained unknown.

The authorities must have thought it formidable. On Saturday morning the State Artillery contingent was doubled and placed under direct command of its senior officer. The streets around the prison were barricaded and the Veld Kornet ordered to mobilise 80 armed burghers to be kept on standby.[34] On Monday, 2 November, the first day after the attack, the State President's Executive Committee endorsed the Chief Justice's decision to impose the death sentence. Inside the prison tensions remained at fever pitch and outside the mood among English-speakers was inflamed by uncertainty surrounding the fate of the condemned men. But, by the Friday, 6 November 1891, in the face of mounting pressure, including an appeal from the King of Portugal, Kruger had announced that the death sentence had been commuted.[35] The State President was a past master of the art of political brinkmanship.

Inside the gaol the announcement only added fuel to pent-up Irish anger. Brigade members, pleased about the reprieve, resented the fact that they had been denied the opportunity to escape. Several journalists, including the Lancastrian, FR Statham, began to speculate about the size of the gang of Celtic renegades challenging the state, but many others, those with imperial sympathies, were unwilling to admit that the opposition was Irish-led.[36] On Monday, 9 November, 25 hard-labour prisoners 'mutinied', refusing to work until the quality of their food improved. The strike, characterised by solidarity of the sort that might be associated with oath-taking, resulted in an armed stand-off and, in the end, 17 inmates were lashed in keeping with prison regulations before the situation returned to 'normal'. The 'mutiny', however, fed into the growing belief in official circles about the need for new, far broader legislation that would allow for the flogging of hardened white criminals.[37]

What part Jack McLoughlin himself played in any or all of these events is unclear; the relevant documents cannot be recovered. But what can be inferred is deliciously ironic – that the prison authorities themselves were responsible in large measure for helping to restore his reputation as an underworld leader. When the police picked him up at the Queenstown Hotel, in May 1891, he was little more than a one-armed Irish drunk. But, by sentencing him to hard labour in the 'chain gang' the state helped him claw back some of his self-respect as a 'hard man' at a time of self-doubt. Likewise, sending him to Pretoria with the rest of the chain gang provided external validation of his status and helped him to recover some lost dignity. He may still have entertained doubts about his standing among his peers, but there was no doubting that the state saw him as a formidable man who constituted a serious menace to society. These strange psychological gains were underwritten by an improvement in his health during his incarceration and enforced sobriety.

These first signs of his self-confidence returning came from improved prison discipline. His time in Visagie Street was marked by an uptick in the quality of his relationships with those around him, including the prison guards. There was no attempt at repeating the painful experiences of Johannesburg or Potchefstroom. He also became acquainted with Matthew J de Beer, a partially anglicised member of the State Artillery who had been brought in to help control members of the Irish Brigade after the convent attack. They were never close friends, but as professionals at opposite ends of the great divide they were confident enough to swop stories about some of the characters in the gaol and note how various inmates tried to cope with institutional life.[38]

By summer's end in 1892, McLoughlin had grown used to the routine and had started thinking about a return to Johannesburg. He would give Higgins and the rest of Ferguson's underworld friends as wide a berth as possible. He also gave some thought to the possibility of extending his network beyond the obvious Ancoats-Irish one, to include the growing number of English adventurers in the Witwatersrand underworld. Things were more promising than when he had left the Reef for Kimberley; visitors reported on an upswing in gold production as the new deep-level mines started living up to expectations. The only problem was that the faster things appeared to move outside the prison, the slower they seemed inside. Autumn dragged on and then colder weather set in. It was a good sign; his release was scheduled for midwinter.

In mid-June, he took leave of some of the Irish inmates, promising to see them over drinks in Johannesburg before too long. Others, including McKeone and Cooper, and Sutherland and Todd, were in for such long stretches that he was unlikely ever to see them again. Most of the warders were decent enough, wishing him well, but it was the farewell of one man that haunted him. For two decades thereafter it crowded in on his consciousness again and again, popping up in some of the remotest places on earth and when he least expected it. It was a ghost-like voice.

Matthew de Beer took leave of him with the customary Afrikaans-Dutch farewell of *totsiens*. Like *au revoir*, its literal meaning was 'until I next see you', but in everyday use it simply meant 'goodbye' – for now. It was usually said with a hint of joy at the prospect of renewing the acquaintance sooner rather than later. But De Beer said the word so slowly and deliberately, almost breaking it into its component parts, that it left him feeling that he had removed any element of chance. It came across as a sort of guarantee that they would be meeting again; it was a question of *when*, rather than *if*. It was puzzling, because he had no intention of ever seeing the man again.

CHAPTER THIRTEEN

❧

Regaining Caste

JOHANNESBURG RISING
— 1892–1893 —

> *On no account brood over your wrongdoing.*
> *Rolling in the muck is not the best way of getting clean.*
> ALDOUS HUXLEY

When the prison authorities removed McLoughlin from Johannesburg, in 1891, it was a rapidly emptying frontier settlement with an uncertain future, mired in economic recession. The state had unintentionally helped see him through the worst personal and professional times of his career. By the time that he returned to the Rand, nine months later, at age 33, it was a more established mining town with the potential of becoming the capital city of the world's gold mining industry. The return of buoyant economic times unleashed the uninhibited social spirit of the frontier as never before, while the government and mine owners struggled valiantly to evoke the discipline and order necessary for a civilised urban environment. The result was a profound disjuncture between the quotidian realities of a frontier-like existence on the one hand and the supposed control that characterised an established state on the other. The interstices of that unstable dispensation provided Jack McLoughlin with a milieu that he was very comfortable in, and, in order to understand fully how his life unfolded between 1892 and

1895, the year that was to determine his fate, it needs somehow to be recaptured.

For the privileged few in search of long-term profit, those with capital and insight, even the bad times are good. For the most financially adroit of the Rand's emerging capitalists, the economic downturn of 1889–92 presented precisely such an opportunity. The MacArthur-Forrest process promised huge profits. Poorly performing mining operations were sold and only the best retained to provide a revenue stream for even more ambitious projects. Extensive blocks of mining rights were bought up to the south of the town where richer and more tractable parts of the reef were intercepted at greater depths. The consolidation of mineral-rich properties allowed for economies of scale in ore-crushing and gold-recovery processes at a time when the industry was setting up a central refinery. Other benefits came from pooling human resources and sharing accountants, geologists, engineers and skilled mine managers.[1]

These advances facilitated the emergence of a new type of financial giant. From 1890, a few of the largest corporations, such as Wernher, Beit and Co, not only rationalised their assets but developed large 'finance houses' to back longer-term developments. Highly diversified portfolios allowed former outcrop mines with proven revenue streams to cross-subsidise deep-level mines where extensive preliminary underground workings militated against instant profitability. Rand Mines Limited, launched in 1893, was the prototype of the 'group scheme' and was soon followed by Consolidated Goldfields of South Africa Ltd and a half-dozen others. These financial and technical initiatives helped stabilise the new mining operations, and despite the persistence of a significant element of pure market manipulation, the stage was set for a recovery of the industry in 1892–94 that eventually peaked in the famous 'Kaffir Boom' of 1895.[2]

Early in 1891, a horse-drawn tramway running close on five miles from Jeppe in the east to Fordsburg in the west was opened and, in September 1892, Johannesburg was at last linked to the Cape by rail. In the grid of dusty streets around Market Square, low-slung whitewashed bars, canteens and shops made way for modern businesses housed in buildings two and three storeys high, some sporting iron-hemmed balconies.[3] The horse-dominated economy slowly retreated in the face of coal, steam-power and modern industry. By 1895, the town boasted close on 100 000 residents, but comparatively few citizens.

As a male-dominated town Johannesburg, by definition, lacked women. A census taken in 1896 revealed that within a three-mile radius of Market Square, white males outnumbered white females by two to one, while black males outnumbered black females by 10 to one. With the notable exception of some wealthy and a few middle-class elements, it was a town almost without wives. A nagging uncertainty about the long-term future of the goldfields and a shortage of houses at affordable rents ensured that most white working-class immigrants, including miners, were seen as being 'single' even when they were married. Better-paid workers lived in boarding-houses or rented rooms in a few large houses.

Some independent-minded white women with domestic skills found positions as cooks, housekeepers or servants in the homes of the rich.[4] Most others entered the entertainment or service sectors where their duties revolved around amusing or caring for tens of thousands of working men without wives. A disproportionately large number of music halls and theatres provided a stream of itinerant actresses, dancers and singers with work where they often had to contend with audiences that were drunk, rude or violent. In the early 1890s, 'chorus girls' were so prone to deserting the show for a husband or lover that the impresario, Luscombe Searelle, demanded a deposit of £250 before agreeing to take them on inland tours to mining towns.[5] Barmaids and prostitutes – categories that could and frequently did overlap – were in the front rank of those women expected to cater for the emotional and physical needs of young, white, working-class males.[6]

The town had more than 500 bars and beer halls, many with names reflecting the city, county or country of origin of the proprietor in a town filled with nostalgic Anglophone immigrants. But beyond a certain sameness on the outside, inside, the pubs catered for a score or more overt or covert functionalities and specialisations, legal and illegal. Barmaids served aficionados from all walks of life in search of company that appreciated athletics, billiards, boxing, burglary, cards, cricket, clan loyalties, darts, dice, deserters, dogs, footpads, Friendly Societies, hunting, hometown boys, horses, kinsmen, music, pigeons, pickpockets, rat-killing, safe-cracking, theatres, whores and a dozen other interests.[7]

Most barmaids were locked into settings designed to ease cash out of male pockets by encouraging libidinous thoughts among drunken bachelors and supposedly single men, and trouble swirled in their footsteps. They fought with the proprietors, their wives, other barmaids and clients importuning them for sex. When they did chance to enter into serious relationships, they frequently found themselves at odds with other lovers, absent or present, known or unknown, and, less frequently, with irate spouses. Some barmaids stole cash or alcohol from the bar, while those who engaged in casual prostitution fleeced unwary customers. One enterprising husband-and-wife team set up an elaborate blackmail operation to entrap a visiting British Member of Parliament.[8]

Even as a tent town, in the 1880s, Johannesburg had its fair share of prostitutes. Predictably, early arrivals included impoverished white women from port cities in the south. They were soon followed, albeit in lesser numbers, by black women from the coastal colonies who may have been even more impecunious. But as with the barmaids – indeed, many of them were barmaids by day and prostitutes by night – women of 'mixed race' soon dominated the sector. The largest influx of 'coloured' prostitutes occurred in the early 1890s, when Cape Town and Port Elizabeth were declared 'scheduled towns' in terms of the Contagious Diseases Act.[9] It was only after 1894–95, once most of the southern African rail network had been completed, that the provision of sexual services by coloured women was eclipsed by 'organised vice' on a grand scale. American gangsters and east European prostitutes, along with Belgian, French and German pimps and women, came to dominate large brothels run along business lines as dedicated mass sexual outlets.[10]

Not all coloured women, however, were either full or part-time prostitutes, and there were several other 'respectable' venues where they met and interacted with immigrant white workers from the northern hemisphere. Coloured women were in demand as chars, general servants and cooks in boarding houses, rented houses, or hotels at a time when few black women, but some black men, were employed as domestic workers. Here, in spaces that lent themselves to greater privacy, they caught the eye of men without women. Chief Detective Robert Ferguson, it will be recalled, was one of those married to an 'off-coloured' Cape woman.

Barmaid-prostitutes, however, remained at the centre of much casual or fully commercialised sex. But, even for them, the distinction between domestic work and prostitution could often become blurred. Some, while working in a bar or beer hall, took on client-lovers who lived in the rooms behind the premises, and then provided them with the full range of home comforts including cooking, laundry and sewing services. Others, operating out of hired rooms, ventured out after dark to cheap working-class outfits – such as the Garrick or Nabob bars – notorious for staging 'low dances' over weekends. At the apex of the trade in commercial sex, however, stood several 'houses of ill-fame' – brothels overseen by 'madams' supervising several younger coloured females.[11]

After 1892 the return of regular and better-waged employment for immigrant miners allowed many workers to engage more freely in other aspects of working-class culture, some of them less female-centred. Much of this involved a frenzied chase after money, made all the more urgent because, even after it had been integrated into the subcontinent's railway network, Johannesburg remained a notoriously expensive place in which to live. Moreover, at a time when mine owners and speculators were becoming millionaires, ordinary folk often fell prey to the feeling that they were losing out on the 'good times' that everybody else was secretly benefiting from.[12] It gave rise to a psychological climate in which everyday gambling and frenetic speculation could go beyond the need for cash or the search for recreation.

Gambling and horse-racing appealed to Lancastrians in general and the Manchester-Irish in particular. These pastimes taking root in the frontier settlement earned the instant disapproval of the State President and his God-fearing government.[13] In 1889, legislation outlawing gambling – but not sweepstakes – was passed in Pretoria. But then, just as the infant gold mining industry dipped into a recession, the republic, along with the rest of southern Africa, was swept up in 'a sweepstake craze'.[14] North of the Vaal, the madness refused to lift despite the prevailing bad times and – perhaps because of this – betting and horse-racing on Sundays were prohibited by law in 1891.[15] Games of chance, too, proved remarkably enduring and positively thrived once the good times returned. By January 1893, police were having to stage regular raids on clandestine 'gambling hells', most of which were within easy walking distance of the Market Square.[16] For much of the period leading up to the Jameson Raid, in 1895, the Kruger government found itself pursuing policies that were poorly aligned, if not in open conflict, with elements of male white working-class culture on the Witwatersrand.

At the height of a betting mania, in late 1893, the tenuous links between chance, spectator sport and wagering took on forms that left most supposedly 'backward' Boers bemused or horrified. It was another of history's ironies that, just as the Kruger government set about attempting to control or eliminate those sports it considered to be undesirable because they were driven only by the need for financial gain, reformers in Britain, including Henry Salt – whose *Animals' Rights: Considered in Relation to Social Progress* was published in 1894 – were seeking to eradicate 'blood sports'. It was a rare moment, one to be savoured, when Old Testament precepts and modern views briefly overlapped.

On the Rand, promoters and publicans, such as Tommy Harris or Henry Croon at the Stockwell Arms, who ran a weekly 'ratting sweepstake', constructed large indoor pits that their sport depended on. Much loved in Lancashire and Staffordshire, 'ratting' was a popular working-class pastime and, by 1893, it succeeded in attracting a significant local following. Rodents – of which there were any number in town – were cast into pits where Manchester or Staffordshire terriers, or dogs of various other breeds were set loose on them. Wagers were taken as to which of the dogs could bite most rats to death within a set time, or how many rats could be killed by a single dog in a period agreed upon.[17]

The Pelican Bar, featuring well-organised dog-fighting, attracted many of the meanest characters in town and soon became notorious. 'That such pitiful scenes are allowed to be enacted in civilized Johannesburg,' the evening paper complained, in 1891, 'surpasses one's comprehension.' Moving along the lines being advocated by Henry Salt, a disapproving reporter suggested that: 'there is no sport in an event which is at once so brutal, bloody and degrading'. But progressive views about animal rights struggled to take root on the Witwatersrand. Reports on upcoming dog-fights were routinely carried in the newspapers well into the mid-1890s.[18]

The Kruger government's attention was focused elsewhere. It had long since decided that there were things more degrading than dog-fighting, among them grown men battering each other to a pulp for money in 'prize-fights' or boxing contests. In this, as with gambling, Pretoria's view was out of line with those in Britain and its evolving male sub-cultures.

Organised fights, with backers putting up the funds for a winner-take-all purse, dated back to earliest times on the goldfields. But contests – held under London Prize Ring Rules, which allowed for a bare-knuckled or thin-skin gloved combination of boxing and wrestling – first attracted the attention of the government when the world heavyweight championship was staged in Johannesburg, in July 1889. Barney Barnato, the diamond magnate, promoted a contest between the 'local' JR Couper, the son of a Scottish minister, and Woolf Bendoff, who, like Barnato, hailed from London's East End, for a purse of £4 500. The fight brought the town to a standstill, attracted international attention, and was won by Couper, who triumphed in a contest lasting 26 rounds.[19]

Back in Pretoria, the fight was considered to be demeaning and morally indefensible. Within days the Volksraad legislated against *all* fighting for financial gain. Law No 2 of 1889 was endorsed by Kruger's Executive Committee on 2 December 1889.[20] But, by prohibiting all contests for financial reward, the state set its face against the winds of change blowing through a sport that was set on becoming better regulated and more 'scientific'. By adopting padded gloves and casting off any residual elements of wrestling, old-style 'prize-fighting' was making way for modern 'boxing'.[21] The Revised London Prize Ring Rules of 1853 were already making way for the new Marquess of Queensberry Rules. In the year that Law No 2 was passed the Queensberry Rules were adopted in both Canada and the United States.

In Johannesburg, where unwritten codes of masculinity packed a bigger punch than the Ten Commandments, Law No 2 was greeted with anger and disbelief. Opposition to the new law was muted during the recession but picked up when money started flowing back into the goldfields in 1893. The town's under-educated, under-trained and under-paid police, the Zarps, had to enforce an all-embracing prohibition on a sport undergoing rapid change and that was well embedded in white popular culture.

The sport was forced underground. On the Market Square news of bouts to be held in the back of the Newcastle Bar, or in private rooms, was spread by word of mouth and details of any purse kept secret.[22] Plans and venues for contests in which local fighters took on visiting pugilists from Britain or Australia and which were likely to attract a larger number of gamblers and spectators were adapted so as to better conceal them from the police. Some fights – reported on after the event by newspapers at odds with the government – were staged either on the outskirts of the town itself, or on a farm hired for the occasion from some understanding local Boer with a preference for pounds over patriotism.[23]

The fraught transition from prize-fighting to boxing took place from late 1892 and on through the winter of 1893. After a round of high-profile arrests an unofficial understanding eventually developed between boxing promoters and the state; there would be no further prosecutions under the provisions of Law No 2 provided that all bouts were governed by the Queensberry Rules. As with gambling by cards or dice, or horse-racing and sweepstakes, the upswing in the economy in 1893 marked a high point in the masculine sub-culture of the Witwatersrand. The testosterone frenzy, however, went well beyond professional circles.

Drunken or spontaneous fights inside bars, where they were enjoyed by fellow-carousers, were commonplace. Taken outside, into the streets, they were watched by cheering clients and passers-by who spontaneously formed themselves into the traditional 'square'. Primitive encounters, rough-and-tumble affairs incorporating punching, kicking and wrestling moves, never disappeared from the repertoire of street-fighting in the town, and it was athleticism, fitness or brute strength that determined the outcome of most such bouts. But, after 1892, everyday conflicts and serious questions of honour alike were more likely to be settled by fights that were partly informed by the Queensberry Rules.[24]

Old-world Pretoria itself was not fully immune to the fever of honour and masculinity sweeping across the Highveld. In January 1893, the continentally educated Editor of the *Volksstem*, Dr FV Engelenburg, angered by disparaging remarks made about Kruger in private during the presidential election campaign, repeatedly challenged his adversary, a Mr Lofthouse, to 'a duel'. But duelling, with pistols or swords, harked back to an earlier era and had been prohibited by legislation passed in 1865. Lofthouse laid a charge against the Editor for encouraging him to engage in a criminal act. Engelenburg, however, continued to lay down challenges until he was arrested. The impasse was eventually overcome by way of a discreet intervention by the State President.[25]

Back in Johannesburg, where revolvers were only a little more likely to remain holstered during disputes, fist-fever raged on unabated well into the mid-1890s. Under-educated 'hard men' without family obligations or the funds to go to law, bashed and smashed away at each other, allowing blood and bruises to decide what reasoned argument could not achieve, while the police looked on.[26] While much of this street-scrapping could be attributed to the dominant English working-class elements drawn from Lancashire, Warwickshire and Yorkshire, there was, however, a minor but identifiably Mancunian component to it that could be traced all the way back to nineteenth-century Ireland.[27] This wafer-thin Celtic streak in local popular culture was further bolstered when 'Marvellous Melbourne' and the Victorian economy went into decline in 1891–93; that is, at the same moment that the Rand was hauling itself out of its own recession.[28]

★ ★ ★

From 1891 to 1895, when the first stream of Celts to the Rand had more or less dried up, the Witwatersrand experienced a modest inflow of Australians and Irish-Australians.[29] Among them were a fair number of miners and mechanics seeking work on the new deeper-level mines. Yet again, 1893 formed the high-water mark for such immigrants; by September that year, the possibility of founding an Australian association was being publicly mooted.[30]

The influx was accompanied by a sharp rise in the number of professional sportsmen from urban New South Wales and Victoria. Among the latter were several bookmakers, billiard players and Irish-Australian boxers.[31] And, bringing up the rear of all of this were a few criminals who joined the ranks of the earlier arrivals such as Jack McLoughlin and WJ Kelly.

After 1891, there was a greater likelihood of meeting an Australian in the bars or on the streets of Johannesburg than there had been in the late 1880s. This is worth noting because, once he reached the zenith of his notoriety in the mid-1890s, McLoughlin was, on more than one occasion, described as being an 'Australian' of the 'larrikin-type'.[32] The outline of his ethnic identity, as perceived by the press and reported to members of the public, portrayed more than just his own preferences; it reflected some of the ed-dies in the wider currents of white male immigration. Gangsters actively construct their ethnic identities – but, for such identities to be plausible, they have to be rooted in the social realities of the day.

Who exactly he was, how to reinsert himself into the underworld and make ends meet were questions that required urgent attention once McLoughlin returned to Johannesburg in June 1892. Of his old Singaporean friend, Jack McCann, there was still no sign, but it was not all bad news. JW Brown, son of the Ancoats pharmacist, calling himself 'Jack the Ripper', had at last found his way north after sitting out most of the recession in the Kimberley gaol for his exploits as a highwayman.[33] McLoughlin, Brown and others took in a 14-year-old pickpocket, James Field, known on the street as 'Scotty Newberry', and set up a gang that appears to have special-ised in house, office and shop break-ins. It was the first recorded instance of McLoughlin taking an interest in the criminal careers of, if not teenage boys, then those of much younger men.[34]

The gang was reasonably successful in and around the town centre and left no archival paper trail to indicate that the police were on to it. McLoughlin, whose drinking had moderated after the trauma of Potchefstroom and his recent spell in prison, seems to have settled down reasonably well and then looked around for new targets along the length of the Witwatersrand. These more ambitious projects were in line with his changing personal priorities and the strengthening economy, and showed sufficient political

consciousness for them to gain a measure of popular support. It was noticeable how, during 1892–93, he frequently singled out the assets of the
Boer state that had cost him an arm, or the mine owners who dispossessed
the diggers of their claims, for criminal attention. It was during this same
24-month period in the resurgent 'good times' that his reputation for buying miners drinks and meals or helping cash-strapped workers with financial assistance grew.[35]

In 1892 there were a half-dozen big jobs which, while impossible to link
conclusively to McLoughlin, nevertheless hinted strongly at his gang's involvement. Amongst them were a few under-reported safe robberies at the
Johannesburg Turf Club, which, for reasons that will become clear shortly,
pointed in his direction. In mid-June, in a move reminiscent of Charlie
Harding's earlier arson attack on the Johannesburg Landdrost's offices, an
unsuccessful attempt was made to remove the safe and set fire to the Mining
Commissioner's office in Boksburg. Eight weeks later over £1 000 in cash
was lost to robbers when a large safe in the government offices at Florida,
on the west Rand, was dynamited.[36]

Whatever the new source of funding was, it was around this time that
Jack McLoughlin appears to have taken greater personal care of himself,
dressed more fashionably and, as we noted above, entertained more frequently.[37] He was not alone in his quest for a touch of sartorial elegance.
His friend, JW Brown, was said to dress 'flashily' and William Cooper, the
highwayman, wore a Mexican-style sombrero and a bright, flaring necktie
while holding up migrant workers. McLoughlin's most notable acquisition,
however, was his extraordinary prosthesis.

The huge wounds inflicted by soft bullets fired from Colt- and Springfield-
manufactured weapons during the American Civil War of 1861–65 had induced the greatest number of amputations ever witnessed in modern times.
In the wake of the war, entrepreneurs designed and developed a growing
range of artificial limbs, including some with moving parts.[38] A mining
town like Johannesburg offered American exporters a ready peace-time
market. McLoughlin, still set on reinventing himself, found what he was
looking for at a leading pharmacy on the Market Square – an artificial arm
with a socket that slipped over his stump. But the real appeal of the thing lay

at its extremity. Attached to the lower arm was a hand, replete with movable fingers that could be adjusted so as to clasp a knife, fork or other small instrument. It wasn't cheap: the accessory as a whole cost him £12 10s – fully a month's wages for an unskilled white miner.[39]

He soon mastered the artificial hand, using it when eating or manipulating the small tools necessary for any after-dark work. In underworld circles and sensationalist sections of the Johannesburg press, the prosthesis eventually acquired mythological proportions. McLoughlin's hand, it was rumoured, had concealed within it a dagger that could be activated mechanically and used to deadly effect.[40] This fiction overlapped, in part, with a contemporary English working-class urban legend associated with garrison towns. 'Spring Heeled Jack', it was said, was a robber with 'iron claws' who, as his name suggested, was capable of prodigious jumping and leaping when fleeing from the police or young women he had molested and left in a dishevelled state.[41]

With JW Brown passing himself off as 'Jack the Ripper' and Jack McLoughlin being seen as a sort of 'Spring Heeled Jack' character, the two men reached a high point in careers marked by a propensity to drift in and out of the real and imagined worlds. Both their ghost-like alter-egos conjured up images of misogyny, if not terror.[42] McLoughlin, who already carried a weapon, used the prosthesis in ways calculated to discomfort people. He added to the air of mystery that surrounded him by removing the limb and placing it on a nearby chair or table when engaging in conversation.[43] For the most part, however, he was interested in the prosthesis as a cosmetic aid that helped provide his vulnerable underlying self-image with a veneer of normality. Dismayed by the obvious difference in colour between the prosthesis and his own complexion, he took to slipping a cotton glove over the artificial hand.[44]

Boasting some of his new-found confidence and cash, McLoughlin set about his 1892 end-of-year campaign with gusto. The gang was so active over late November and early December that not even the Zarps could help noticing a spike in the number of burglaries and thefts leading up to the festive season. On Christmas Eve, McLoughlin, Brown, six other men and the boy-apprentice, Scotty Newberry, appeared before Landdrost van den Bergh charged with theft. The prosecutor was not unduly put out when all of the accused, bar the mastermind, were acquitted for want of any corroborating evidence. McLoughlin's case, however, was different.

First, he had been found to be in possession of 'burglarious implements' and skeleton keys. Secondly, flush with cash, he had hired lawyer AB van Os to defend him as soon as it became clear that the state was far more interested in him than in the other gang members. Asked by the prosecutor what a tool designed for inserting into keyholes and disabling locks was used for, McLoughlin claimed, mischievously, that the instrument was used to curl the ends of his moustache! That suggestion was swiftly refuted by a locksmith who stated that it was known to be a tool used by burglars. Nevertheless Van Os did not labour entirely in vain: instead of being sent to prison, his client was sentenced to three months' hard labour or a fine of £25. It was a snip at the price, the fine was paid and then, just to add insult to prosecutorial injury, an appeal was noted.[45]

The unfortunate Christmas Eve court appearance, reminiscent of what had happened back in 1879, did nothing to deter McLoughlin's on-going scheming for a huge end-of-season haul. The omens were good and the planning far advanced. The last day of the year fell on a Saturday and would coincide with a race-day at Turffontein. The meeting was bound to be followed by a great deal of late-night revelry and noise of the sort one might expect of a mining town. He put a great deal of thought into selecting a team that relied on Ancoats men who would be supported by a few Manchester-Irish who had good reasons to be involved in the job.

Drawing Mike Hart, the jewel thief and a close friend of Ferguson's, into the plot was a stroke of genius. The fishmonger's son provided the ringleaders – McLoughlin and Brown – with excellent insurance. If things did go wrong, the Chief Detective could be relied upon to try to bail out his gambling partner, Hart. The two other members of the gang, Bucklow and Jones, were punters who, like many miners, did not often come off best at the races and had no love of bookmakers. If successful, the robbers could rely on a good deal of working-class sympathy.

The object of their attention was a free-standing safe in the ground-floor offices of the Royal Chambers Building in the town's centre. It belonged to the man who operated the totalisator at Turffontein, William Grey Rattray. There was, however, a good deal more to Rattray than caught the eye. The fellow kept one foot in the Kimberley diamond fields and the other in the goldfields at Johannesburg. He was a financial Jack of all Trades, a 'speculator', at a time when the term covered legal as well as illegal trading. Besides having an interest in betting and horses, which may have helped him launder money, Rattray also dealt in jewellery and scrip. On the Rand, where gold amalgam, gemstones or share certificates were never in short supply, it is possible that McLoughlin and the others had all had other business dealings with him.

Late on the sunny afternoon of 31 December, Rattray left the track with the 'day's profit from the machine' as well as the 'totalisator money not paid out on the last race', made his way back to his deserted office in town and stuffed the cash into an already full safe. Next door, the Royal Bar, which catered for the day-trade, closed shortly before 9.00 pm.

Between three and four in the morning, a barrow was wheeled in through the Fox Street entrance to the building and a specialist screwdriver used to gain entry via an office window. The safe was tipped over onto a bed of unused tote tickets to deaden the sound, then lifted onto the barrow and taken into the veld at the Wemmer Mine only a few miles away. The safe door was split 'clean in two' with a well-placed charge of dynamite. Over £2 300 in notes and gold, cheques worth £500 (which were promptly abandoned), a 'handsome parcel of diamonds' and diamond jewellery worth £1 500 as well as some easily negotiable share certificates were removed. All in all, valuables conservatively estimated to have been worth more than £4 000 were stolen. It was a sum that would have taken five miners four years each to earn.[46]

Brown, recently of Kimberley, took most of his share in gemstones; Hart, with experience of cross-border fencing, may have settled for diamond jewellery, while McLoughlin seems to have taken most of his share in cash. There may have been other Lancastrian friends eligible for a cut because it was claimed that it would have taken more than a half-dozen men to move the safe.

It was thought that the thieves would make for the train and flee south and so it was suggested that the station be watched. But this was unnecessary. Somewhere along the line things had gone wrong, and by Sunday night the main suspects were all in custody. The arrest of a close friend of the Chief Detective's was so unexpected that it occasioned press comment.[47] McLoughlin's team was in trouble – but so too, perhaps, were Ferguson and a few of his friends.

The Chief Detective was already the subject of suspicion in official quarters of being involved in the booming trade in illicitly acquired gold amalgam. It had been a bad year for Ferguson. In 1892, there had been only eight successful convictions for gold law contraventions. The Chamber of Mines was so frustrated by amalgam theft that it was already drafting legislation for the Volksraad in Pretoria that eventually proved so invasive of personal liberties that it threatened to bring the Witwatersrand to a standstill.[48] If Hart, Brown or McLoughlin had known about Ferguson's underworld dealings, as they probably did, his career would have been at stake.

Ferguson, 24 months later, feigned knowing so little about McLoughlin that he could not spell his name correctly or issue a description of the one-armed man. But he could not have failed to notice who the principal suspect in the Rattray case was – coming, as it did, in the wake of McLoughlin's appearance in court only days earlier. The latter, already unhappy with Ferguson for having put away Jack McCann, now had the opportunity to study his adversary at closer quarters and quickly concluded that he had the measure of the man.

It took Ferguson and the state more than a week to arraign the prisoners for a preliminary examination. It was a curious business from the outset. The Public Prosecutor, for reasons he chose not to disclose, asked that Hart and Bucklow be released immediately. Bail for the three other suspects was set at a staggering £1 000, and the case set down to be heard in the Police Court a week later. When McLoughlin, Brown and Jones next appeared before the Police Court, they were represented by counsel who asked that the amount set for their bail be reduced. The Magistrate refused and then recused himself on the grounds that he could not hear the case because he had signed the warrants for the arrest of the suspects. Mystery upon mystery followed.

When McLoughlin next appeared, on 19 January 1893, the prosecutor who had previously asked for bail to be set at £1 000 because the case against the accused was so 'strong', asked that he too be released for want of evidence against him, leaving only Brown and 'Deaf Peter' Jones to face trial. But, hours later, Jones, too, was released and after a further three days, it was reported in the press that: 'John Brown, the last of the accused to be discharged, had the diamonds found in his possession returned to Mr Rattray'. It was 'the last that was likely to be heard about the matter'.[49] McLoughlin, six months out of prison, was off the hook for a major safe-cracking job, very confident and well placed to benefit from the growing economic upswing.

CHAPTER FOURTEEN

❧

The Lures of Domesticity:
Marriages of Inconvenience

JOHANNESBURG
— 1893 —

Those who love to be feared fear to be loved.
ST FRANCIS DE SALES

B y 1893, capital was flowing into the Witwatersrand's emerging deep-level mines at an unprecedented rate and the frontier in southern Africa had shifted north, to Rhodesia, which the 'Pioneer Column' had 'opened up' in 1890. The South African Republic, wary of becoming hemmed in by Rhodes and the expansionary British, had eclipsed the short-lived Boer states of Stellaland and Goshen to the south-west but struggled to contain several independent African kingdoms in the north-east. There was significant resistance from Mojaji (1890–94), Malaboch's Hanwana (1893–94), Makgoba (1895) as well as Makhado's Vhavenda (1898). These new zones of turbulence did not escape the notice of a few ageing brigands in the Irish Brigade, but, lacking proven gold resources, failed to draw them in. The Reef and those mines with small on-site refineries remained central to peri-urban banditry.

The agents of the up-and-coming mining capitalists, the Randlords, along with other investors and speculators, dominated the stock exchange 'between the chains' in Simmonds Street. But with the full effect of the Cape rail link yet to be felt, the Market Square and surrounds remained the focal point for most people in a town busily laying the complex social foundation of the steadily dividing working classes along racial lines.

Most casual labourers, unskilled workers and unemployed had gravitated to unoccupied marshy land west of the market. It provided them with easy access to the food, fuel and produce brought into the square from out-lying districts by ox-wagon. It also placed them within walking distance of the mines closest to town, immediately south of the Main Reef Road, including those owned by the Robinson, Worcester, Wemmer, Salisbury and Jubilee companies.

The poor – spread out in half-moon shape at the western end of the town – were being gradually pushed into racially defined zones. Poor white Afrikaners, in the Brickfields, enjoyed the easiest access to the market and the surrounding stores. Behind them, slightly further away, were the Asians and 'Cape Coloureds' of the 'Coolie Location', and beyond them black Africans, in the 'Kaffir Location'.[1]

The emerging geography of race and class was not, however, without one or two anomalies. Reaching out from Ferreira's Town, which lay to the south-west of Market Square, and stretching a few blocks north-east, was a nondescript zone close to the town centre that continued to reflect a few frontier-like features. It was honeycombed with legal and illegal businesses – bars, boarding houses, brothels, cafes, canteens, clothing stores, gambling joints, grocery shops, stables still serving horse-drawn cabs, laundry ser-vices, restaurants and tailor shops.[2] It was a glorious cosmopolitan mess of ethnic clusters filled with 'Cape Malays' (coloured Muslims), Chinese, Indians, Jews and nondescript southern Europeans. Some chose to live in their shops, others in rooms behind their stores, and yet others in a good number of small houses close by.

The quarter had no distinctive name because it spread out on the an-gle from Ferreira's Town towards the town centre. Most of Ferreira's Town proper, site of one of the original 'camps' on the goldfields, had degen-erated into a slum by 1893. By the mid-1890s, the part closest to where President and Rissik Streets met had so many continental prostitutes that it was known as 'Frenchfontein'. The quarter had two landmarks that residents and visitors could use to orientate themselves. One was the Kerk Street mosque, which served those Asian and coloured Muslims of reasonable means living in the inner city rather than those further out at the 'Coolie Location'.[3] The other was the western end of Commissioner Street, which, Jack McLoughlin said, was 'one of the most dangerous places in Johannesburg'; a man needed 'confidence in himself' to walk there.[4]

Cash-flush after the Rattray robbery and a great deal more cautious than he had been before it, 34-year-old McLoughlin managed to steer clear of the police throughout 1893. Increasingly at one with himself and his artificial hand, he spent most of his time between burglaries and robberies drinking with his underworld friends Gorman, Howard and Whelan – the three Tommies who had been his most generous supporters in the months after his amputation. 'Deaf Peter' Stewart (aka Jones) and his boy-partner, 'Scotty Newberry', operating from in and around the Red Lion Beer Hall, also somehow kept out of trouble until September's end, when they were both arrested for pickpocketing.[5]

Tommy Gorman's year turned sour early on, with an unsuccessful attempt at escape from the Johannesburg gaol while awaiting trial on a charge of burglary.[6] But the economy was buoyant and there was more money around than there had been for some time. Some of the 'hard men' were lulled into a more orderly existence, taking on a little wage labour and enjoying a few of the benefits that came from more settled times. Even McLoughlin was briefly sucked into a 'work' later that year while assessing a set of mine offices for a possible robbery. Howard, who never shirked night-shift work for the gang, found himself a daytime position as a butcher in the quarter. Whelan, already married, got employment as an amalgamator on a mine, working at the heart of the new recovery process at a time when the theft of gold amalgam was reaching epidemic proportions.

It was Tommy Howard – 'Fat Tommy' – who, sensing that McLoughlin was perhaps becoming less intense, succeeded in drawing the gang leader into a slightly more rounded social life. One evening, in March 1893, the fat one coaxed McLoughlin into accompanying him and Rosie Petersen, a coloured prostitute living in Kerk Street, to a dance at a hotel just off

Commissioner Street. At the dance McLoughlin ran into Harry Lobb, a mason from the Cape whom he had first met over drinks at a bar. Lobb, too, was accompanied by a young prostitute.

Sarah Fredericks, Cape Town-born, was an attractive, intelligent, 22-year-old coloured woman – part of a wider network of independent-minded older women who had earlier quit the diamond fields when Kimberley was declared a scheduled town under the Contagious Diseases Act. Further than that, however, she hardly conformed to the stereotype of a prostitute, being neither alienated nor socially rootless. She was capable of forming emotional attachments; indeed, she tended to fall in love with some of her admirers. Nor was she without kin. She had family in the 'coolie location' who took an active interest in her well-being. A complex young woman of considerable spirit, she could easily have come out of a Zola novel.

Fredericks's status as a prostitute was intermittent and ill-defined. She was no street-walker; neither she nor any of the women in her circle had need of a pimp – that was something that only became a prominent feature of 'organised vice' in Johannesburg after 1895, when the mass commercial sex trade fell into the hands of former New York City gangsters. When in love and the times were good, as they were in 1893, she was more common-law wife than whore, cooking, washing and ironing for her man in addition to providing sexual services. She also often worked as a char, cleaning and scrubbing the houses of a few older coloured women.

Between live-in lovers she entertained white miners in her rooms or moved into one of the brothels run by the Kimberley veterans. There, problems with clients or policemen were more difficult to manage and required the adoption of a more professional attitude. Like some of the madams in the brothels, she was on good terms with the police, some of whom she had bribed, supplied with information, or slept with, in order to provide her with the protection necessary to pursue her trade. When slipping into the latter role, she could be as tough as any dockside prostitute on a Saturday night.[7]

It was after that dance that McLoughlin took to visiting Howard and Lobb in the rooms on Kerk Street which the two shared with their coloured lovers. He got on well with Howard and Rosie Petersen, and got to know Lobb, who was older than Fredericks, well enough to be comfortable in their company. By that autumn he had got into the habit of taking his evening meal with one or other of the couples.

Lobb and Fredericks had an affectionate relationship but it may not have precluded McLoughlin from paying her for sex from time to time. But when the cold winter nights set in he looked around for a partner of his own who could also cook, launder and sew for him. He found her living next to the Chinaman's shop around the corner from Fredericks's rooms, in Sauer Street, and moved in with her. Her working name was 'Lizzie Hommel', but in the closely knit Cape Malay community she was better known as Ali Ahmed.[8]

All three sets of liaisons in Kerk and Sauer Streets were occasionally fraught in ways that were perhaps predictable. Howard and McLoughlin, older than their respective partners and with more funds at their disposal, seemed less threatened by any additional employment-related couplings than did Harry Lobb, who became possessive when it came to Fredericks, who was in great demand.

But there were other, cross-cutting, tensions. Fredericks was wary of Jack McLoughlin, almost from the moment they met at the dance. Whether her fear arose from a few shared experiences, from information supplied to her by the police, or via underworld rumours is unclear, but she kept her distance. McLoughlin, too, wanted little to do with her. He knew that she was on friendly terms with some of the Zarps and feared that she might be an informer. He wanted her to know as little as possible about his or the gang's night business.

★　★　★

In late April these already complex relationships were subjected to another twist. At a dance attended by one or two of their partners, McLoughlin and Fredericks met and were immediately captivated by a handsome young fellow who would change their lives for ever. He had, he said, just been released from prison but had first arrived in Johannesburg back in 1890, just as the town was sliding into recession. He had reasons of his own for wanting to conceal his past, but they both wanted to see him again. He, in turn, sensed that they were kindred spirits who might help get him back on his feet.

He was English and his name was George Stevenson. He was born at 'a quarter-past eight on 3 July 1868' near the village of Hixon in Staffordshire and was about 10 years younger than McLoughlin. His father was Joseph and his mother Sarah. The couple had only married in their thirties, but, despite their late start in life, George already had two older brothers and a sister when he was born. He seemed to come from the runt-end of his family.[9]

His parents were farm labourers from Rushy Pitts, near Stowe, in Staffordshire – a part of the country that lay at the centre of an imaginary triangle linking Birmingham, Nottingham and Manchester. But the Stevensons were not a happy couple and the baby, who may have been illegitimate, was not very welcome. By the time the census was taken, in 1871, 36 months after his birth, he had been farmed out to relatives in Hanley, at the heart of the old potteries manufacturing trade that centred on Stoke-on-Trent.[10]

George's mother tried to visit him as frequently as possible and never completely lost touch with him. But the relatives, too, were either unable or unwilling to take proper care of the boy, and at school it was not long before he fell into the company of petty thieves of the type to be found in most West Midlands cities. By late 1878, when he was 10 years old, George was so enmeshed in crime and neglect that he was committed to Werrington Industrial School, which the Magistrate had helped establish a few years earlier.

Werrington, an 'approved school', prepared boys for entry into the industrial world. The lads were given a rudimentary education and taught practical skills that appealed to local employers who took the boys in as part-time workers. Surrounded by older boys and men as he approached puberty, George learnt to look after himself from an early age. Despite a temper prone to flaring up when provoked, he negotiated the four years of reform reasonably well and, in 1882, at age 14, was released back into the care of his family.

By then his parents had given up farm labour and moved across to Marsh

Street, Hanley, where Joseph Stevenson had hired five acres of land and a few clay pits that he mined to provide a local pottery with raw material. The industrial school seemed to have done the trick; under the watchful eye of his mother, George steered clear of most adolescent criminal behaviour. In keeping with the terms of his release, he twice returned to Werrington – in 1884 and 1885 – and each time was reported to be 'doing well' and working in the pits. But George then outgrew clay-mining and, with his father's approval, started looking around for a new start in life.[11]

When he turned 18, in 1886, 'Stevo' – as he was known to his friends – joined the 64th Regiment, the North Staffordshire, and 12 months later, in 1887, the Imperial magic carpet whisked him away to Fort Napier, in Pietermaritzburg. By the time that he entered the College of Banditry, the worst of the gold fever had abated and, with it, large-scale desertions. Accustomed to an all-male regimen from his days at Werrington, army life and heavy drinking for a time agreed with him. A strongly built young man, Stevo admired 'Darkey' Parker, the regimental boxing champion, and honed his own skills to the point where he could hold his own when sparring with professionals.[12] But with no new Zulu war in sight he became bored with garrison living and in late 1889 he deserted.

When Stevo, styling himself 'Ferney', got to Johannesburg early in 1890, the town was shedding jobs at an unprecedented rate and he was forced to resort to a few tricks he had picked up as a boy back in Hanley. The police were soon on the lookout for him for the theft of a gold watch and chain – the pawnbroker's delight – but had trouble in tracking him under his assumed name. While the Zarps were searching for him in town, he stole a horse in the hope of moving about the outskirts as a highwayman – the criminal welfare scheme of choice for unemployed whites eager to prey on black migrants.

But the police, men drawn from farming backgrounds, were better at tracking horse-thieves than pickpockets. When he was arrested, Stevo put up a spirited resistance, insisting that he was 'James Davidson', but a few other Zarps recognised him as 'Ferney' when he appeared in court and the Magistrate, unimpressed by what he had heard, sentenced him to six months' hard labour in the 'chain gang'.

The leg-irons were painful and humiliating and, hating every minute of his time in gaol, Stevo escaped on 12 April 1890. So cunning and nimble-footed was he that he was on the run for 24 months before he was re-arrested, in March 1892. Even then, his capture owed more to ill-discipline than to smart police work. He was collared during a public disturbance and assaulted the policeman who attempted to arrest him. The Landdrost sentenced him to 13 months' hard labour for offences old and new, and he was sent back to the chain gang. This time there were no further disciplinary problems and it was shortly after his release, in early 1893, that he met Jack McLoughlin and Sarah Fredericks, at the dance.[13]

Stevo became a regular visitor at the rooms around Kerk and Sauer Streets. McLoughlin and Howard were a generous source of meals, drinks and cash as he tried to find his feet, while Fredericks helped him with his domestic chores. McLoughlin and Fredericks were both very taken with him.

Stevo was English rather than Irish and from Stoke rather than Manchester, but McLoughlin saw in him much that reminded him of his own child-hood. Hardship, poverty and child-labour were just some of the things they had in common and, in Stevo's experiences at Werrington, he saw much of what he understood about his young brother Tommy, who had also done time in an industrial school. Moreover, they were both deserters from the British Army and graduates of the College of Banditry. Was it not Aristotle who said: 'a friend is a second self'?

More pertinently, McLoughlin saw in Stevenson many of the qualities necessary to succeed as a professional criminal. He was a 'hard man', could take his drink, looked after himself in a pub, and had an almost visceral dislike of the Zarps, which ensured that he would always resist arrest. Stevenson's record of resistance while in prison, and of trying to get out of it, was one that anyone in the old Irish Brigade would have been proud of. That, coming from a veteran of Potchefstroom, was a huge compliment. Stevo presented an almost boyishly athletic figure – he was a fine boxer – a man with two hands and able to use them both to good effect. His impressive muscle-power would be an asset when it came to lifting and moving safes. With neither JW Brown nor Jack McCann around, Stevenson would make a fine lieutenant for the maimed Captain Dangerous. Yet, for all that, McLoughlin hesitated before introducing him to a few of his older Ancoats underworld associates.

Sarah Fredericks was less inclined to examine the opportunities the new-comer presented too closely. He was 25 years old to her 22; it was a pleasant change from the older men that she had to service or work for. They would be a couple by cohort as well as by affection. She had no need of a pimp, preferred having a live-in lover to whoring, and it would be nice to have his big presence around her rooms. Stevo had not led a blameless life, but she sensed that he also longed to be more settled. She could understand why he used an alias – it spoke of some embarrassment about his lifestyle – and she had lived among women who almost always hid their true identity. He was not rootless, corresponded with his family and spoke about his mother with genuine affection. There was a soft side to him – he could cook a bit and, at Werrington, had learnt to use the sewing machine. She would gladly take him in – he might even become her husband.

Her ambitions for Stevo were diametrically opposed to McLoughlin's. The brigand-dreamer admired the hard, wild streak he found in Stevo and hoped that through intense grooming he could seduce him into a more ad-venturous – perhaps even peripatetic – life of crime. She, on the other hand, wished to draw out his gentler side by inviting him into a more homely and settled existence. He wanted the feral, she wanted the domestic. What neither of them knew, however, was what the young man's own inclinations were. If they had had a clearer idea of his self-perception, they might both have spent less time in trying to win his affections.

Stevenson was a man with a secret. His experience of all-male institu-tional life had always been unhappy. He had been so determined to get out of Werrington that he was willing to dig clay for a father he did not care for. The army, too, had bored him – but it was the year in gaol that had done most to convince him that he could not cope with either hardship or exclusively male environments. It was not that he lacked courage – his ring exploits testified to that – but that he was unwilling to sacrifice all prospects of indulging in female company and enjoying the fruits of domestic service.

Leg-irons and prison life had crushed his spirit and he was deeply ashamed of his response, which – fortunately for him – remained known only to him, his warder, and one other. After only a few months in the chain gang and of experiencing the humiliation of labouring in public in an arrowed canvas shirt, the physical and psychological burden became so intolerable that he had asked for a private meeting with the Governor. He was, in effect, a broken man.

The Governor had been so convinced by his expression of 'deep remorse' that he ordered the leg-irons to be removed and agreed to support a plea to the State President for a remission of his sentence even though it still had fully six months to run. But the appeal, on 14 November 1892, had failed to impress either the Landdrost, who remembered him as the elusive 'Ferney', or President Kruger and his Executive Committee, who had turned it down on the grounds that it was 'premature'. So manifestly low were his spirits, however, that barely eight weeks later – on 2 January – 1893, the Governor, once again moved by an expression of 'deepest remorse' had supported a second appeal to the State President. It was a move almost without precedent but the second appeal, too, had been turned down and he had been forced to serve out the full sentence. Beneath Stevo's hard outer shell lay far softer, vulnerable tissue.[14]

To what extent this insight informed Stevenson's first weeks out of gaol is impossible to know but it may be significant that it was not long before he succeeded in alienating Fredericks's affections. She did not have the heart to tell Lobb directly that she had lost interest in their relationship, but he, sensing that she was drifting away from him, rightly blamed Stevenson for the problem.

The tension between Lobb and Stevenson mounted steadily throughout autumn and on into a winter which, in hindsight, was without precedent in the town's history. Men of all classes and from all stations in life, already partly submerged beneath a wave of gambling, were suddenly engulfed by the inrushing tide of boxing mania. With the relative merits of the Queensberry and London Prize Ring Rules being debated in every bar and canteen and in the newspapers, the town was filled not only with talk of fighting, but with chat about any number of organised and spontaneous fights both in the streets and at secret venues.[15] Amidst mounting state disapproval, boxing promoters put on several clandestine events including contests pitting English against Irish opponents. But the showdown of the season, staged on a farm across the Vaal River, was between two former soldiers – Darkey Parker of Stevenson's North Staffordshire Regiment and Ingleton from the Royal Artillery.[16]

By mid-May testosterone had corroded the last vestiges of control. Stevenson and Lobb were incapable of exercising further self-restraint. It started in a bar, fuelled by alcohol, but the brawl spilt over to become 'a rough and tumble in the street'. It was brought to a halt before the Zarps appeared but, in the spirit of the times, it was decided to resolve the matter in the square ring within three days.[17]

Public sparring sessions with leading professional bruisers meant that both men were already well known in local boxing circles. The bout was eagerly anticipated not only because the combatants were well-matched semi-professionals, but because everyone knew that the contest was under-lain by competition for a woman's favours. And, if they did not know, it was there for all to read in the press. On the morning of the contest, it was announced, without mentioning any names, that there was 'bad blood' between two men known for their appreciation of the 'manly arts' and that it would be a 'fight to the finish', one not restricted to a pre-arranged number of rounds.[18]

A stake of £20 was put up for what everybody knew was a 'Prize Fight' by un-named promoters who aimed to recoup their expenses via side bets and a modest entrance fee. The rules were to be a combination of the two codes. Skin gloves harking back to the London Prize Ring Rules rather than padded ones were to be used, although the contest would be governed by the Queensberry Rules. Since the fight was illegal, the venue was not disclosed in the press but spread by word of mouth. Stevenson, wary of the law, fought under the name 'Steele', but Lobb was happy to use his own name.

The bout – a duel by another name – took place in the early evening of Wednesday, 24 May, without police interference, but proved to be wholly anti-climactic. Steele was heavier than an opponent who appeared to lack finesse and therefore fought a less 'scientific' fight. In the fourth round Steele landed a glancing blow causing Lobb to slip and fall onto the ropes, injuring his throat so badly that he could not continue. The contest was sufficiently important, however, for it to be reported on fully in the press on the following afternoon.[19]

Not only was the fight illegal; both participants had strong underworld connections. Their seconds were drawn from the lowest ranks of professional fighters in town and, given the long intervals between secret, paid, bouts it was understandable that Lobb's seconds were known to the police for things other than boxing.[20] Just as in London, where many full-time boxers were part-time burglars, so in Johannesburg several fighters were closely involved in crime. Jack McLoughlin, fascinated by the idea of courage and the codes of masculinity, could not resist gambling on his new friend to win the bout. Years later, in a comment as bitter as it was terse, McLoughlin recalled that: 'I was present when they [Stevenson and Lobb] fought and I was the only man who had a bet on that fight.'[21]

Having won the hand of his lady in combat, Stevenson moved into the rooms in Kerk Street and Lobb, vanquished in love and war, moved out. But while this development may have settled matters between Fredericks's suitors, it did little to ease the conflict between her and McLoughlin. In essence, she and he now went head-to-head for the affections of the stylishly dressed young Stevenson. There were continual skirmishes between them, some of which extended to include Ali Ahmed, who McLoughlin 'boarded' with but referred to as 'my girl'. And it was Fat Tommy, the genial butcher, who was most frequently called upon to play the role of peace-maker.

Out of the sight of Ahmed and Fredericks, McLoughlin continued to lead a mysterious, secretive life. It was said that he 'dressed well' throughout that year despite the fact he was only once employed, and then briefly. Several coloured tailors in the quarter got to know him quite well. He moved about a great deal by day and night, often paying, albeit not very generously, for Nasa Dien Burgess and other Cape Malay cab-drivers to cart him around in some style.[22]

He was also out of town quite frequently, using the train to get to destinations farther afield, including Pretoria. But it was on the misleadingly named 'Rand Tram', the railway to Krugersdorp, that he became notorious for slipping on and off coaches without paying. One of the conductors who was later switched to the Johannesburg–Pretoria line and who became the bane of his life was an Irishman, FR Gill, who was forced to try and extract the price of a ticket from him. Their on-going disputes and skirmishes became more acrimonious as time wore on.

Once Harry Lobb was off the premises McLoughlin, Howard and Stevenson became as thick as thieves. There was no obvious shortage of money during the winter of 1893 and the three spent much of their time drinking, no doubt, the remains of the proceeds from the Rattray robbery. With the mineworkers' union having helped to defeat the proposed Gold Thefts Bill by May Day, the disappearance and sale of gold amalgam – real and bogus – proceeded apace, with Ferguson apparently unable to stem the tide for reasons that were widely suspected, but remained unproven. What success McLoughlin enjoyed during that year remains unknown but, between May and September, there were at least three large robberies – at the Champ D'Or, the New Black Reef and May Deep Mines – that conformed to his gang's modus operandi.[23]

McLoughlin lavished more than money on Stevenson that winter. He invested deeply, in emotional terms, in a relationship with a younger man at a time when his psychological equilibrium had not yet been fully restored. Barely 36 months had passed since his lower arm had been surgically removed, and it is now known that, besides causing 'phantom limb' pains, amputation can trigger depression, loss of body image and a sense of diminished physical attractiveness.[24] Stevenson was everything that McLoughlin no longer was or had ever been – attractive, charming, handsome and virile.

He became emotionally dependent on Stevo. The depth of their relationship, evident enough in the rooms on Kerk Street, was soon also publicly visible. Andries Smorenberg, the Foot Patrol Zarp in their quarter, knew both men sufficiently well to talk to them on personal terms. They, like others on the wrong side of the law in smallish towns, sought to remain on good terms with the officer. Smorenberg noticed that, around mid-1893, the pair were 'very often together' and, in his view, they 'were intimate friends'.[25]

Jack McLoughlin's own words, a decade later, point to infatuation.

Captain Dangerous, his frontier-man alter ego, was being replaced by a do-mesticated, urban, spousal rival. How else does one account for McLoughlin saying: 'I could not say I was in love with him after that naturally'; 'if only I would make friends again he [Stevo] would not *care* for anybody else in Johannesburg'; 'there was a row between us' (a classic formulation for a disagreement among Victorian couples), or 'I knew he did not care when … he turned against me'. And when Fredericks later challenged him, why did he suggest: 'I never had a quarrel with Sarah, I do not know why she should tell lies, *except* that she was living with Stevo.' If these were not the sentiments of a spurned, wounded, lover, what were they?[26]

McLoughlin's affections, never easily won and confined almost exclu-sively to younger men, were fully requited in emotional if not physical terms. Indeed, so keen was he to accommodate Stevo's desire to lead a more conventional life that he even agreed – albeit partly for his own criminal reasons – to take on regular employment. For some months around mid-1893 they worked together as 'riveters' at the Langlaagte Block 'B' Mine.[27] McLoughlin's handicap was no deterrent to his getting a job on a mine known to be Irish-friendly, but it no doubt helped that he had a mate so willing to assist him.[28]

With Stevo in regular work on the mines, Fredericks, too, could lead a slightly more conventional working-class life. She cooked and sewed for a few white miners and did the laundry for some nearby coloured broth-els. A steadier income and loving relationship helped the couple fend off McLoughlin's attempts to drive a wedge between them. With spring com-ing and the hours of darkness shrinking rapidly, McLoughlin's burglary and safe-cracking expeditions too began to tail off, leaving Stevenson freer to enjoy a more independent life.[29] Yet, even under the altered circumstances, the three-way relationship between the parties remained fraught.

Then, in mid-August, Sarah's new life began to collapse. The owner of one of the brothels, Wilhelmina Armstrong, an elderly coloured woman, got into trouble with the law when she took in a young white woman under troubling circumstances. The Zarps normally took little interest in such matters, since bordellos were, in essence, *maisons de tolérance*. But, given that the girl claimed to have been abducted, that she seemed to be under age and was white, the Public Prosecutor insisted that the matter go to trial. Fredericks, a part-time char in the house, and two other women whose roles were never made clear, were accused of being complicit in the abduction.

All four of the coloured women were arrested in late August and, given the seriousness of the charge, refused bail. The prosecution's case, which dragged on over four days, was hardly watertight and leaked credibility as AB van Os – the same attorney that had been retained to explain away Jack's 'burglarious implements' – probed away at it. The police, always hesitant to alienate brothel owners who kept them in cash between paydays, proved to be a source of confusion. On 5 September, the accused women were set free for want of 'positive evidence'.[30]

The trial, reasonably well covered in the morning papers, would not have done Fredericks's ambitions for respectability much good. It raised questions about the nature of her work at a time when she and her lover were intent on taking a new direction. The press reports also undermined her moral authority in her on-going battle to keep McLoughlin from drawing 'her man' into serious crime. Then, to add to her problems, Stevo – her common-law husband – lost his job at almost the same moment that her trial drew to a conclusion.

Stevenson did his best to remain supportive. For some weeks he sparred with a few of the professional boxers, which earned him a few useful under-the-counter payments. He even managed to get himself a bout in which all, bar the official publicity, was clearly professional. On Saturday, 7 October, a special train had been laid on from the east Rand to bring in more than 200 white miners going to the Spring Race Meeting at Turffontein. A promoter by the name of Sullivan hired the Amphitheatre and laid on an evening's boxing to draw in the crowd after the races and before the last train left. Stevenson took on a certain Miller, who, after two rounds of furious non-stop attacking was too exhausted to continue and had to retire.[31] But after that there were no more paid encounters to be had and, for the three months leading up to Christmas, Stevo was without work and wholly reliant on young Sarah's willing support.[32]

★   ★   ★

There was nothing festive about December 1893. There was no money to spare in the Stevenson-Fredericks household – and the McLoughlin gang had had an unusually bad quarter, with not a single large safe-robbery being reported in the press. Tommy Howard may have brought home some bacon, but other than that, there was almost nothing to indulge in. And, as often happens over Christmas, or when times are harder, tensions began to bubble up.

January 1894 was worse. It was the longest month of the financial year, and after the festive season everybody was short of cash. The sun, working up to its midsummer high, baked the poorly ventilated corrugated-iron boxes huddled along treeless streets, until their human contents, like worms being expelled from a half-eaten can of beans, slithered out into the open through hinged wooden doors in an attempt to find a vestige of shade or more cooling moisture.

Fredericks sensed that tough times and low morale would weaken Stevo's defences and push him firmly back into McLoughlin's orbit. She launched a pre-emptive attack by swopping a few recycled police yarns about McLoughlin with Ali Ahmed. Fifteen years later, Jack could still not bring himself to forgive her. As he recalled it, 'Sarah Fredericks was never on good terms with me because I had no liking for the woman. She was a terrible woman with her tongue.'[33]

He regaled Ahmed with his version and she went back and gave Fredericks a roasting. When Stevenson got to hear of it he marched across to McLoughlin's and told him to get Ali to 'keep her tongue to herself'.[34] It did not go down well and they had an argument which, were it not for their physical differences, might have ended differently. Instead, like an old married couple, they stopped talking to one another and communicated only via Howard.

With February beckoning and little on offer locally, McLoughlin decided to explore a few new possibilities – sleepy Boer towns were full of poorly guarded government offices with an accumulation of funds at month's end. He bought himself a ticket at Park Station and boarded a train that was Pretoria-bound. At the other end of the line it took almost no effort at all to find what he was looking for. On the journey back, he mulled it all over and decided that the job would need a minimum of four men: himself and perhaps three others.

He talked it over with Howard, who agreed that they needed two more men. Charlie Harding was one of them. Harding had been released from prison that December after completing his sentence for attempting to assist McLoughlin by burning down the Landdrost's office at the time of the Higgins shooting.[35] Harding was always up for anything. But they struggled to come up with the name of another Ancoats stalwart able to travel out of town at short notice. With time running out, the choice narrowed down to one, obvious, candidate. Howard spoke to Stevenson and when he said that he was interested, persuaded McLoughlin to reconcile with him. In McLoughlin's words, he went around and the two then 'made up' – a formulation familiar to intimate Victorian couples. But the men's relationship remained strained and McLoughlin insisted that his involvement in the job be kept from Fredericks, who remained suspicious of him.[36]

He then disappeared and linked up with Harding. The two of them made their way to Pretoria by train. On Tuesday, 30 January, Howard met Stevenson at Fredericks's rooms in Kerk Street. They told her, she later claimed, that they were 'going after some work this side of Pretoria' that afternoon. That same evening, Ali Ahmed, pleased that things were at last settling down, popped in and told Fredericks that she knew that McLoughlin, Stevenson and Howard had all gone to Pretoria. McLoughlin had warned her not to tell anybody about his movements, but, knowing him, she surmised that they had left 'to commit a crime' and feared that they would all be arrested.[37] It was a watershed moment; the feral and the domestic, the personal and the professional had become fatally intertwined.

AUTUMN

CHAPTER FIFTEEN

Retreat to the New Frontiers

MATABELELAND AND VENDALAND
— 1894 —

The Grizzly Bear is huge and wild;
He has devoured the infant child.
The infant child is not aware
He has been eaten by the bear.

AE HOUSMAN

The countryside and small towns of the South African Republic had not been happy hunting grounds for McLoughlin. During the five years he had spent in Johannesburg not once had he been imprisoned for a crime against property. Had it not been for Higgins and an unfortunate lapse in his discipline, he would never have seen the inside of a republican prison. It was the dorps that had been the sites of truly miserable experiences. Each time he bent down to tie his laces he was reminded how he had lost his hand. He hated the Boers as much as any of the Rand jingoes ever did.

In Pretoria he and Harding wiled away Wednesday, 31 January, drinking and reminiscing, waiting for Howard and Stevenson to appear. When they did eventually arrive he was struck anew by how tight he and Harding were – and how skittish Stevo and even Tommy Howard seemed. Certainly, they were all wanting for cash, but, other than that, they seemed well set.

He had the Colt and dynamite with him. As officer in charge, he took them through the plan, reminding them what they had to do and in what order. When darkness settled in they split up into pairs and did a final sweep along their probable lines of attack and retreat.[1]

The building they targeted was never disclosed, but the reconnaissance work was as decisive as it was disappointing. The original objective was abandoned as too secure, or visible to police patrols. Howard and Stevenson may have been secretly relieved, even if it left them puzzling how they were going to get back home. It was Charlie Harding who suggested they get some sleep, meet in the early hours and then agree on a new target that might help 'cover their expenses'.[2]

McLoughlin led them to the deserted concourse at the Pretoria Railway Station, where the door of the ticket office was easily forced. The small safe was carried out by Harding, flanked by the other three so as to conceal it from outside view as best possible. But nobody saw them. Stevenson later claimed that, even then, Harding had second thoughts and wanted to 'back out of the affair'. Truth was that most of them had reservations, but they pressed on until they found a spot where the safe door could be forced noiselessly rather than blown. It was always the most exciting part of the business – seeing whether the gamble had paid off. It was hugely disappointing; £120 in cash. Small winnings did not make for big friendships. The Manchester lions devoured almost all of what was on offer, leaving the Staffordshire pup with only £13 to show for his share of the collective effort.[3]

They were reluctant to return to the station and catch the train that would take them back to Johannesburg via Germiston. Charlie Harding, the only one not living in the rooms on Kerk and Sauer, said that he wanted to stay on and pass a message to a former cell-mate in the Visagie Street gaol.[4] He left and the three then spent time over drinks and a meal before agreeing to hire a horse-drawn cab to take them to Irene, south of the town, where they would get the train back to Park Station. But as they approached Irene they had second thoughts about boarding the train. The police would prob-ably be monitoring passengers and so they asked the cabbie what it would cost to take them to Johannesburg.[5] He wanted £15 – hopelessly too much, given their disappointing takings – so they pushed on to Irene. There, still in money-saving mode, the three agreed to 'jump' the train to Germiston.[6]

Stevenson, the one whose manliness had failed him in prison, became agitated when he noticed that the guards on the incoming train were behaving unusually.[7] McLoughlin noted that one of them was FR Gill, and knew that, if he were spotted, he would probably be recognised as a regular fare-dodger. Sensing that his courage and leadership might be on the line, McLoughlin was in no mood to make concessions. He asserted his authority, insisting that they 'jump' the train and that, if it became necessary, they stare the conductors down inside the coach.[8]

Caught between the demand for another public display of courage when the conductors arrived and the inner fears that only he knew about, Stevenson stared out of the carriage window for a minute or two and then buckled. He told them he would be getting off at the next stop and making his own way back to Kerk Street. The train took forever, but when it eventually did shudder to a halt, he slipped out onto a small platform and shuffled off into the darkness. At the far end of the platform, from beneath his peaked cap, Gill watched, knowing that there were no more scheduled stops before the train got to Germiston. He had McLoughlin where he wanted him – in a cell on wheels, rolling towards the police.[9]

But even as Stevenson's profile faded into the dark, McLoughlin saw his outline ever more clearly – as that of a coward, a man bereft of loyalty, a potential informer. Only then did it dawn on him what he had allowed him to get away with. Stevo had walked off with all his personal baggage. Stevenson knew almost all there was to know about his intimate, private life and his professional secrets. He – McLoughlin – had prided himself on being the 'hard man' among them but it was the coward who, if he were seduced by Ferguson and the state, now held the upper hand. Their roles had been reversed. Stevo was the strong one, and it would now be his own courage and judgement that would be open to question.

The locomotive grumbled its way out of the station and all McLoughlin could see was one stout little butcher unlikely to hold up under pressure from the police who were probably waiting for them at Johannesburg. As expected, Howard, sensing what might happen next, started 'showing the white feather'. 'I will get 10 years for this job,' he moaned. 'I think I will throw my share out of the window.' McLoughlin told Howard not to be a fool and that if he wanted to get rid of the money he should hand it to him.[10]

By now even he was becoming a little perturbed; the real world was closing in on the dreamy one inhabited by imaginary characters such as Captain Dangerous, or real heroes of the remote past like Rob Roy and Robin Hood. No, what he needed was to be able to draw inspiration from 'real men' that he could identify with, characters such as Ned Kelly or Jack McKeone. But, as the train rumbled on towards the lights of the Jumpers Gold Mine, near present day Heriotdale, he realised that they, too, had little to offer him. And then suddenly, just as the last Heroes of the Head were about to desert him, he caught a glimpse of the very man he needed in the situation – a Manchester man of action – Charlie Peace![11]

Howard was horrified at the idea, but, as a man who had braved a hail of bullets in Potchefstroom, McLoughlin was not about to be denied. Even though 'the train was going at a good speed', he later boasted, 'I had confidence in myself and jumped out of the window', crashing into the embankment.[12] A few fingers on the prosthesis were damaged, his revolver lost in the grass, but other than that no harm had been done. Back in the train, however, Gill had noted his disappearance at almost the same moment that he had jumped, and sounded the alarm. Some way down the line the locomotive was slowing. McLoughlin crawled up the steep embankment, flattened himself, and watched carefully as the train pulled up about a mile or two down the track.

Gill and a few others emerged from the rear of the train and then 'I saw them looking around with lanterns'. Tiny bubbles of light, like fire-flies in the veld, exploded around them as the search party probed the track side for any sign of him. But they found nothing and eventually clambered back aboard the rear of the coach. The Iron Horse snorted once or twice and then trotted off, dragging behind it the coach containing Tommy Howard on his way to meet the Zarps down the line.[13]

Once the train was out of sight he moved off towards Jumpers, knowing that he would be safe there.[14] The police seldom ventured out onto the private property of the mines, preferring to find their men in town. The mine

formed part of a chain of inter-linked Anglophone islands off the coastline
of a republican sea. Whatever the owners thought, the single quarters were
working-class redoubts where anyone from Land's End to John O'Groats
could pass through safely and get a meal and a bed for the night.[15] Few
men, let alone one with an arm perhaps lost in a mining accident, would
be turned away. He had only one night to survive before he would be back
amongst the Lancashire-Irish at the Langlaagte or Robinson Deep Mine, or
even further west, at Luipaardsvlei near Krugersdorp.

Harding, picked up in Pretoria a day later, was held in the Visagie Street
gaol where he remained isolated from the rest of the station-robbers.
Howard was arrested at Park Station that same evening. Stevenson, having got the necessary distance between himself, McLoughlin and Howard,
waited for their train to leave and then doubled-back to the station where
he caught the next one for Johannesburg. But the Zarps were waiting for
him and he, too, was arrested at Park Station.[16] The arrests in Johannesburg
ensured that, despite the fact that the robbery had taken place in Pretoria,
Robert Ferguson was soon involved. As the Chief Detective sheepishly acknowledged, years later, 'I had something to do with the investigation of
that [the Pretoria Railway Station] case.'[17]

Indeed he did. But what is so significant, in hindsight, is how little effort
he put into tracking down the main suspect, the missing fourth man. After
the Higgins shooting and the Rattray robbery it was simply inconceivable
that Ferguson did not know who Jack McLoughlin was. Indeed, not only
did he know who McLoughlin was but he must also have known that
McLoughlin probably knew about his – Ferguson's – own involvement in
gold amalgam thefts and gun-running to Africans in the remote north-eastern parts of the republic, via Lourenço Marques. And so instead of trying to
sniff out the mastermind behind the most successful safe-cracking operations on the Rand over the past half-decade, the Chief Detective chose to
focus on the few men already arrested.

Ferguson played Howard off against Stevenson and vice versa, using
plea-bargaining, a tactic despised by most politically informed underworld
elements, and most especially the Irish. He encouraged them to become
informers and, in return for them providing state's evidence, agreed that

they would not be charged or faced with lesser offences. Ferguson had used the same ruse in Jack McCann's case, with limited success, but this time the hidden cost was potentially far greater. This time Jack McLoughlin was directly involved, and if either Howard or Stevenson cracked and implicated him, the consequences could be dire.

They did their best to fend off Ferguson. Stevenson, in particular, realised that he was in a jam. He was as unwilling to face time in prison as he was to confront McLoughlin. He was a runner by nature and by repute; a man who, unable to face himself, assumed aliases. He had deserted Fort Napier, escaped from police custody and remained on the run for months, and then again run from his friends at Irene. He could do it again. When he was paraded in the courtyard of the police station the morning after his arrest, 2 February 1894, he made a dash for it but was recaptured within hours. The escape cost him two months in prison.[18]

By then Ferguson was already focusing on what he thought was the weakest link in the gang. Even so, it took him several days to move the corpulent little butcher. Eventually Howard braced himself, sat down and wrote two notes. In the first, to the Chief Detective, he agreed to turn state's evidence, saying that he could provide details of other crimes that Stevenson had been involved in. The obvious silence in that note – about McLoughlin – suited Ferguson and Howard for different reasons. The second note was to Rosie Petersen. He then paid an off-duty warder to deliver the notes to Ferguson and to Petersen in Kerk Street.[19]

The warder, however, decided to drop off the Kerk Street note first. Looking back, it was a decision that was later to cost two men their lives. He also mistakenly handed *both* notes to Petersen but she, being unable to read, called in her literate friend, Sarah, to help her. Seeing in black and white that Howard was intent on betraying her lover, Fredericks somehow persuaded the warder not only *not* to deliver the second note but first to show it to Stevenson. When Stevenson saw that Howard was going to betray him, he asked to see the Chief Detective and indicated his willingness to give evidence against the three other station robbers.[20]

When Ali Ahmed got to hear about these developments she, loyal to her own boarder-lover, passed the information on to McLoughlin, who was in hiding among friends on the west Rand. It merely confirmed what he had thought all along. Not only was he in trouble, but more importantly so too were Harding and Howard. As leader of the gang, he felt that he bore the responsibility for Stevenson's betrayal of his friends.

Returning to Johannesburg was not an option. It was 1890 all over again – but this time it was not recession-driven, it was intensely personal, and he would be leaving a booming economy. But he felt he had to retreat into the countryside. Back then, in 1890, a few of his friends had slipped into the 'Pioneer Column' and gone north, to the new frontier in Rhodesia; others had gone home, back to Lancashire.[21] Flight, too, was not risk-free. The world was shrinking. In 1891, Ferguson had sent a list of items worth thousands of pounds – pieces stolen from Simpson's Jewellery, in Market Street – to London and that had culminated in several arrests being made by Scotland Yard detectives.[22] On balance he would be safer in Rhodesia, where new gold mines were opening up all the time. And, if that did not work, he could always head back south.

★   ★   ★

Not even in Matabeleland could a one-armed safe-lifter be guaranteed success. So, at age 35, with his leadership ability and underworld status slightly tarnished, Captain Dangerous persuaded two others to accompany him on the journey north. One of them was probably his friend from the Singapore Straits, Jack McCann. The other, who must have died shortly after they crossed the northern border, because McLoughlin made a point of never volunteering the name of a friend to the authorities, was a hard-drinking young man named Wright.[23]

Knowing they would be passing through 'rough country' – 'rough' being his euphemism for dangerously violent – McLoughlin saw to it that they were well equipped. Raising venture capital at short notice, in mid-month, was not easy and bore further testimony to the support he enjoyed among the part-time 'miners' of the west Rand. They acquired three sturdy mounts and a pack-horse loaded with ammunition and essential supplies. Each man had a revolver and Jack took along a shotgun to shoot for the pot.[24]

They left in mid-February and, so as to avoid the malaria and tsetse-fly problems on the eastern route, headed west across the Magaliesberg towards Bechuanaland. At Mafeking they swung north towards 'the great grey-green, greasy Limpopo River, all set about with fever-trees'. Were they bandits, cattle-rustlers, horse-thieves or safe-crackers? In truth, they were probably all those things at various times and places.[25]

Years later McLoughlin confirmed that he had based himself at Bulawayo, at the centre of a score of small mines in the new Matabeleland goldfields. It was no place for the lily-livered. Only a few months earlier Lobengula, the Ndebele king, had been defeated by the forces of Cecil Rhodes's British South Africa Company with the belated backing of Imperial forces.[26] One of the first things McLoughlin did was to get the fingers of his prosthesis repaired. It spoke of his on-going efforts to align his physical appearance with his self-image.[27]

Bulawayo, in 1894, was like Johannesburg in 1886; there was dynamite aplenty. Louis Cohen, not the most reliable frontier-chronicler, later reported that Jack McLoughlin was 'the leader of a gang of crib-crackers who committed many desperate deeds in the Rhodesian towns'.[28] It is an observation that chimes with what is known about the man, but there is no hard evidence to support Cohen's sweeping assertion. That winter, there was only one press report of significance about the presence of highway-men on the outskirts of Bulawayo, but several others about attempted or successful store break-ins in the town.[29] The latter, if true, smack of a new McLoughlin-led gang in his favoured frontier setting.

At about the time that the gang's Bulawayo campaign came to an end, Harding and Howard's trial came on at the Criminal Sessions, in Pretoria. On April Fool's day Stevenson, oozing self-righteousness, provided the state with incontrovertible evidence about the roles of the accused and the leader of the gang, whose whereabouts were never alluded to. Of Robert Ferguson, the man who had 'turned' Stevo, there was simply no sign.[30] Judge de Korte sentenced Howard to five years' imprisonment with hard labour. But it was not all bad news. Harding was acquitted on a technicality and left the court a free man.

Although relieved to hear about Harding's escape, McLoughlin was mortified by Howard's sentence. He again felt that he had failed and that Ferguson and Stevenson were the men responsible for Howard's fate.[31] The Chief Detective, who had chosen not to activate extradition proceedings against the gang leader, had achieved an outcome he could live with – a partially successful prosecution without having had to deal with 'One-armed Jack' himself. But he and Stevenson both realised that putting the butcher behind bars might have come at a potentially lethal cost. Ferguson saw to it that Stevenson was provided with a police-issue revolver for his protection.[32] Stevo, however, had more to think about.

Fredericks, as loyal as she was brave, had stood by him throughout his trial. Stevo could not think of returning to Johannesburg where he would encounter McLoughlin's friends and members of the Irish Brigade in every pub and on every street-corner. She, too, would be recognised instantly. Fredericks would have to forego her friends, family and work. They moved into rooms in central Pretoria and she took in laundry, washing and ironing for a few white families to keep them going. Even then, he could not relax for a second – the capital city, too, had its share of beer halls and visitors from Johannesburg. It took several weeks for him to become accustomed to what, in essence, was once again a life on the run.[33]

But Fredericks was not on the run and, as her confidence grew, so did her desire to return to Johannesburg. He could not afford, nor did he want to lose her and the chances of him finding steady work were dim regardless of where they found themselves. A compromise was reached and she found a small room, one well away from their old haunts around Kerk and Sauer streets, in working-class Fordsburg. They returned to Johannesburg in July, and had no untoward experiences. But the new room was too cramped for her liking and too far from her friends, so she began looking around for new accommodation. By late that November, they were back, living in West Street, not far from where they had started out on Kerk Street.[34] It was near the heart of the old quarter, close by Commissioner Street. There, it was not long before Stevo was spotted and, as McLoughlin would allege, was 'despised by everybody in town'.[35]

Back in Rhodesia and having outstayed its welcome, McLoughlin's gang, less than six in number, had disbanded. McLoughlin headed south-east, back across the Limpopo, and towards the badlands of the remote north-eastern Transvaal. Louis Cohen claimed that it was there, around Crooks Corner – present-day Pafuri – not far from where the borders of Mozambique and the South African Republic meet, that he lived with 'Kaffirs, freebooters and horse-thieves'.[36] Cohen again got the outline correct, but this time other evidence has survived that allows us to plot the brigand-dreamer's far northern excursion with greater accuracy.

The badlands were bad not only because they allowed for cross-border raids for anything from cattle and horses through to elephant tusks, but because they were well shielded from any Boer commandoes by several densely settled African chieftaincies. By 1894, several of these African polities, which had strongly resisted mounting labour and tax demands from the Kruger administration and the expanding mining industry, had either already been defeated or were in the final phases of resistance. There was, however, one important exception. Chief Makhado's Vhavenda were the last black tribal grouping in the Republic to be conquered by the Boers, and then only in 1898, under his son's rule.[37]

Makhado's well-protected kingdom lay east of the Zoutpansberg, between the Limpopo in the north and Levuvhu River to the south. At its core were several lofty redoubts surrounded by a proliferation of boulders and rocks. These natural fortresses were supplied with fuel, fruit, game, grain, livestock and water drawn from the surrounding countryside which was filled with fields, ravines, steady streams and – to the far south – dense forests. Moreover, his kingdom was protected from most white adventurers, missionaries and traders by myriad small, near-invisible defenders. In the heaviest part of the rainy season, starting in mid-December and lasting throughout the long, hot summer, millions of mosquitoes spread malaria right across the lower parts of his country.[38]

Most of the Vhavenda's successful resistance to white encroachment could, however, probably be attributed to the chief himself. Born around 1840, Makhado had spent much of his adolescence in an elephant hunting economy that fed into ancient trade routes to the east coast from where ivory was shipped to India by Arab dhows. Like many others of his age, he had carried guns for white hunters or while out on his own expeditions. These experiences left him and other local chiefs with a liking for and understanding of modern firearms.[39] Once elephant hunting declined, however, Makhado witnessed how the Boers and English traders readily reverted to dealing in 'black ivory'. Officially it was cast as an 'apprenticeship' scheme, but in truth it was little more than a variation on the illegal slave trade. Vulnerable youngsters of indeterminate status and of both sexes were collected in the ungovernable northern part of the republic and then placed with Boer farmers as agricultural workers or domestic servants.[40]

When Makhado acceded to the chieftainship at age 24, in 1864, he had both the personality and the skills that allowed him to resist further outside intervention. The raw muscle-power for his initiatives came from age-regiments that passed through circumcision and initiation rites at schools attached to the chief's capital. Within 12 months of his accession, he closed the elephant-hunting frontier to the Boers; two years later, he oversaw a military success that effectively drove most whites out of the far north-east region for the better part of two decades.

By 1886, however, the Kruger administration was ready to ratchet up the pressure on his chieftainship and laid the groundwork for a counter-offensive by launching a white settlement scheme in the Zoutpansberg.[41] The discovery of gold on the Witwatersrand later that year only added to the pressures for more effective 'civilised' occupation of the north. Notwithstanding, the Boer government found it virtually impossible to extract labour and tax from the Vhavenda. Makhado not only prevented government agents from establishing themselves within his territory, but also any missionaries or traders that he did not personally approve of.[42] By the time McLoughlin eased into Vendaland, in the winter of 1894, the Kruger administration was almost at the end of its tether in trying to deal with an openly defiant chief, while Makhado, realising that serious trouble was brewing, was ready to take in any white gun-runner, military adviser or mercenary to supplement those he already had in his employ. For McLoughlin and Makhado, it was a classic case of 'my enemy's enemy is my friend'.

The Kruger government, however, was not without resources of its own. It already had a rudimentary 'secret service' in place with several

English-speaking agents and spies. These undercover operatives remained loyal to the republican cause amidst mounting African military resistance and the political machinations of certain Rand mine owners and jingoists.[43] It is the memoirs of two of these agents, Blackburn and Caddell, that enable us to reconstruct the aims and ambitions of Makhado and his advisers in 1894. Predictably, the chief's tiny core of strategists and tacticians was drawn from deserters from the British armed forces. These were men who shared McLoughlin's anti-Boer sentiments and therefore unwittingly helped soften up the republic's social and political underbelly for the big imperialist pushes that came later with the Jameson Raid, in 1895, and then, more decisively, the South African War of 1899–1902.

Shortly after McLoughlin's arrival, Chief Makhado intensified his quest to acquire the heavy firepower needed to see off Pretoria. He became increasingly agitated, to the point where one observer saw him as being 'obsessed with an invasion mania'.[44] If so, his 'mania' was grounded in real fears. He had heard how Boer forces had overrun Malaboch in the nearby Blouberg, forcing men, women and children to seek refuge in caves from which they were only expelled when dynamite was lobbed into their underground lairs. What he needed to check the advance of mounted men, Makhado thought, was the new British weapon of choice – the Maxim gun. A few years earlier, at a demonstration in neighbouring Portuguese territory, he had seen how a Gatling gun had mowed down 20 of his goats at a distance of 300 yards. And he knew the man who could get him the machine-gun he needed.[45]

Captain 'Hicks' Hickey was a charming confidence trickster who, seemingly alienated from the Imperial cause, had been based among the Boers in the north-east for several years.[46] Whether Hickey really had been a 'captain' was unknown, as was the name of his regiment, but he had certainly obtained some military expertise in the British Army. Makhado, reputed to hold a substantial collection of diamonds given to him by young men who had worked as migrant labourers in Kimberley, had no difficulty in persuading Hickey to smuggle in a Maxim gun via Delagoa Bay, where it was always possible to buy anything or anybody.

But the plan went wrong when the Boers got to hear about it. Hickey

was arrested and taken off to Pietersburg, where, despite the gravity of
the charges, he led the life of Riley during two months' incarceration. It
was claimed later that Hickey was freed after he had written to the State
Secretary and persuaded him that he had only been involved in a game of
double-bluff in order to acquire Makhado's diamonds. More importantly,
however, Hickey offered to revisit the chief – where a 'white man, wanted
by the police' in the south, had been 'acting as an adviser to Magato and
counselling an attack on the Boers'.[47] Nobody knew who Makhado's adviser was, but the government was not willing to take a chance. Agent
Blackburn, travelling under an assumed name, was sent to investigate and
report on what was happening in the remote north-east.

Chief Makhado, who enjoyed a reputation for being a shrewd judge
of character and a man capable of dealing with most complex problems,
had not placed all his eggs in one basket.[48] Indeed, it was later claimed
that the chief had a 'half-a-dozen' military renegades at his disposal.[49] The
most senior of these, the man most likely to have recruited or vouched for
McLoughlin, was another marginal figure drawn from the British navy.

His real name was said to be Keith, but he was known to all as 'the
Admiral'. The distant heir to a Scottish baronetcy, he had been unhap-
pily married and joined the navy, in which he had risen to the rank of
officer before deserting. He must have been an impressive figure because
McLoughlin – reluctant to bend the knee to anyone, with the possible
exception of naval officers – readily deferred to him. Keith, a 'soldier of
fortune', had been part of Rhodes's failed attempt to annex Beira, in 1890,
before returning to Johannesburg. It may have been there that he first met
McLoughlin. Besides sharing a naval background, both men held views
antipathetic to the Boer government. Indeed, Blackburn later described the
Admiral as 'a violent hater of anything appertaining to Krugerism, in fact, a
monomaniac'; in short, a natural ally for Makhado.[50]

The Admiral, in his customary chamois leather outfit rounded off with
a broad-rim hat and jackboots, made a distinctive figure around a trading store not far from the chief's village. His one-armed roommate that
winter also cut a dash, albeit for different reasons. McLoughlin appears to
have been a reasonably competent weapons-instructor of sorts. When he

eventually left, only a few months later, he was still on sufficiently good terms with the Admiral and Makhado to know that he could return should he wish to do so. He must also have been paid reasonably well – only days after his eventual departure he was seen to be spending money very freely. But that was only half the story.

★   ★   ★

McLoughlin was deeply troubled. Age and a half-dozen years of city life had reminded him that he was a Manchester man and that banditry and the countryside had perhaps never been his preferred metier. Though he could still do it, if necessary, it was organised crime and safe-cracking that now appealed most. But Stevo had drawn him into a profoundly intimate rela-tionship and, as a result, he had lost his way and forfeited access to both his friends and a future on the goldfields. Howard was doing five years; Harding was lucky to be at liberty; and he was on the run. In Johannesburg, his ac-tions, judgement, and above all else, his manliness would be questioned. All that, while his former young partner and a whore, both protected by Robert Ferguson, went about their business in Commissioner Street as if nothing had happened. And still he did nothing. A 'real' man, a Carey or a Ned Kelly, would have found it intolerable.

He slumped into depression and got drunk frequently. He neglected to attend to his usual natty dressing and sound personal hygiene, and got dragged into mindless physical confrontations with the local blacks. It was a defining moment in a strange career. 'Between the idea and the reality, between the motion and the act,' writes Eliot, 'falls the shadow.'[51]

He knew that staying on as a mercenary with Makhado was not a long-term solution to his problems. He had to rethink where he was in terms of the British empire and the wider world and re-assess his chances. This need for urgent refocusing was brought home to him when the Boer spy passed through their village. He had no way of knowing that it was Douglas Blackburn, but he was quick to spot the danger when an unknown man asking questions passed through the trading store, and did his best to throw him off the military scent.[52] More agents would surely follow, but the show-down would only take place the following winter, when the country was fully malaria-free.[53]

The Boer government, however, had seen enough. Blackburn's account persuaded Kruger of the need to up the stakes and bring home the serious-ness of the situation to Makhado directly. With the winter warfare season against the chief's neighbouring tribes having just drawn to a successful close, the Vice President, Commandant-General PJ Joubert, was dispatched to Vendaland to inform Makhado that the government was going to take a census and then limit the territory under his control to a consolidated 'location'. But the chief would have none of it. He told Joubert that he did not negotiate with intermediaries and, that if Kruger wished to parley, he should do so in face-to-face discussions.[54]

Nothing happened. It took the Kruger government until late January 1895 to respond via a written ultimatum from the Vice President. That let-ter, along with other initiatives, was dismissed by Makhado.[55] The Boers' hesitant response to the Blackburn report encouraged the Admiral and his officers, and McLoughlin too drew a comforting lesson from the long in-terlude. The Boer state, it seemed, was as hard-pressed, inefficient and dys-functional as ever – and nowhere more so than in the offices of the State Attorney, the Detective Department and the Zarps.

The state was indeed in disarray. By late 1894, the position of State Attorney, effectively the Minister of Justice, had been filled by three dif-ferent men in a matter of months and a disillusioned Commissioner of Police was about to be replaced.[56] In Johannesburg, where the population had surged to around 40 000 whites, the Detective Department had so lit-tle success in solving major crimes, including the theft of gold amalgam, that officials in Pretoria began to suspect that Robert Ferguson himself was deeply implicated in the huge illicit trade.[57]

In July 1894, the State Attorney appointed one of Ferguson's own men, LB Donovan, to trap the Chief Detective. But when Ferguson got wind of what was happening he sidelined Donovan, and the State Attorney, the very able Ewald Esselen, was forced to appeal to the Cape government to recommend a trustworthy man he could appoint as Chief Detective for the entire country, with a brief to reorganise the department nation-wide. The new man, Andrew Trimble, incorruptible and Irish, took up his post in November 1894, leaving a self-serving Robert Ferguson angry and uncooperative.[58]

The police in Johannesburg had never been more disorganised. This did not go unnoticed in the underworld – or, as importantly in the longer run, among a section of the Randlords on the Witwatersrand who had reasons of their own for wanting to challenge the Kruger state. As one newspaper put it only a few months later: 'Amongst his somewhat varied accomplishments, however, McLoughlin seems to number the art of logical reasoning and his deductions evidently led him to the sound conclusion that he had very little to fear from the Transvaal police.'[59] But at the time, whenever McLoughlin thought of returning to Johannesburg all he saw was the same roadblock to resuming life there – Stevenson.

He remained trapped in a fog of conflicting thoughts until, one morning, a light breeze lifted the confusion, giving him his first glimpse of a possible way out. It started with a letter that had been forwarded to him at the trading store. It was from the only member of his family that he bothered to remain in contact with. Tommy, who had been ill for some time, was on his way home from Australia, and said that he would call in to see him in Johannesburg. It was inconceivable that his brother should go to such expense and trouble and he not be there to meet him.

And yet he hesitated. Then, over several days, the outlines of a plan so daring that he could not believe it slowly took shape in his mind. It was a scheme bold enough for even Captain Dangerous, one everybody in Kelly's gang would have approved of. It was a course of action brave, very 'Irish' and so manly that when his resolve faltered he thought again of Edna Lyall's novel, We Two, and bolstered it by swearing a solemn oath. Yes, when matters were settled it would be just the two of them; him and Stevenson.

In late November, before the rains came and the mosquitoes emerged, McLoughlin took leave of the Admiral, saying only that he might be passing back through that way in a few weeks' time. He went south, to Haenertsburg, linking up with the Zeederberg coach making its way from Leydsdorp to Pietersburg. A few days later, suitably spruced up, he boarded the stage coach for Pretoria. But there was no hiding his mark of Cain and one of the passengers, Mr Johnson, although kind and courteous enough, could not help noticing that he had only one arm.

But Johnson saw nothing in his behaviour, dress or manners to suggest that he was dealing with a man wanted in connection with a safe robbery in the capital. The passengers relaxed and got to know one another as the coach made its way slowly south. Jack McLoughlin liked talking to Johnson, who seemed to know a lot about the civil service, the police and affairs of state. Mr Johnson, Messenger of the Court at Pietersburg, was witnessing the start of an epic journey – one that, depending on how one viewed it, would take eight weeks or 14 years to complete.[60]

CHAPTER SIXTEEN

❦

The Grammar of Justice: Honour and Death

JOHANNESBURG
— 1895 —

*The paradox of courage is that a man must be a little careless of his life
even in order to keep it.*

GK CHESTERTON

Jack McLoughlin had been half-way round the world in search of
adventure, gold and himself when he got to Pretoria in the first week
of December 1894. He settled into a boarding house, avoided trouble in
a town where he was wanted for safe-robbery, and sent for an Ancoats
man.

He told Harding that he wanted to do one last big job before abandoning
the country and that he needed help in identifying a mine and in putting
together a team built around a core of reliable Manchester-Irish. After some
debate it was agreed that the Champ D'Or at Krugersdorp lent itself to a
military-like raid. The secretary's movements around month's end would
have to be carefully monitored so as to establish when the mine payroll was
put together. McCann was an obvious choice as lieutenant and they could
always rely on two of the Tommies – Gorman and Whelan. The rest would
have to be recruited as they went along.[1]

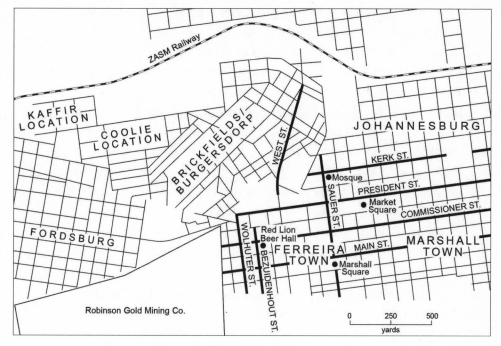

Johannesburg, c 1895

The name of Howard, doing five years in Visagie Street, came up during their discussion, as did those of Robert Ferguson's informers. Harding
knew that Stevenson and Fredericks had left town after the trial and were
living in Johannesburg but little more. McLoughlin did not quiz him about
Stevo's whereabouts but volunteered that, should he come across him, he
would shoot him on sight. Harding left on the first of several round-trips to
the west Rand and McLoughlin stayed on in Pretoria.

The capital city's seedier bars and canteens were as pitted by class, culture
and police corruption as any on the Rand. One of them, an 'Irish' dive, was
replete with a barmaid-informer and the usual coloured prostitutes. The
Australian landlord, a former bookmaker, spoke so freely about his alleged
connection with Ned Kelly that he was later made to answer questions
about it before a commission of enquiry. As in Johannesburg, the city's
Chief Detective was suspected of corruption and the post was being filled

on an interim basis. Neither the police nor the public houses posed much of a threat to a man wanted for a robbery.[2]

Reassured that he was not a subject of unusual interest to the police, McLoughlin ventured out for the start of the summer horse-racing season. His presence at the race track was noted almost at once. Underworld day-trippers from Johannesburg spotted him and noted that he was spending money very freely. The fact that he was back in Pretoria was known on the Rand within 14 days of his move back south. More rumours, includ-ing one that George Stevenson was at risk, began circulating as soon as Harding started recruiting men for a big job on the west Rand.[3] What Robert Ferguson knew, nobody knew.

McLoughlin himself contributed a snippet or two of information when, a few days later, he sent a message to his former Sauer Street 'girl', Ali Ahmed. Ahmed, by then, was living in the Malay Camp – half-way between her old downtown haunts near Kerk Street and Fordsburg. He told her that he was back on the Rand and that he wanted to see her. She, as he prob-ably intended, went straight to West Street and told Sarah Fredericks that he would be coming to Johannesburg. It was an early, albeit very indirect, warning to Ferguson's two informers.[4]

Fredericks was not unduly concerned. She was planning a trip to Cape Town to see family and friends and had no intention of calling it off. She could, she later said, 'have told the police', but didn't.[5] Jack McLoughlin was in Pretoria but did not know where they were living, the detective department was in disarray and Stevo was carrying a police-issue revolv-er. Moreover, while she remained true to 'her man', she was no longer as deeply committed to the relationship as she had once been.

She knew that he was 'disliked' and 'had not any friends' after he gave ev-idence for the state in the Pretoria Station trial. It was guilt more than love that now bound her to Stevo. But not forever. Twelve months later she was married to someone else.[6] In early December, just a day or two after chat-ting to Ahmed, she set out for Cape Town, leaving Stevo on his own for the first time since the station trial. He went off the rails almost at once. A bout of heavy drinking and public fighting culminated in the assault of a police officer. Unable to come up with the cash for a £20 fine, he languished in gaol. It was only when Fredericks got back, around Christmas, managed to raise a loan and pawned a gold watch and chain belonging to him that he was released from prison.[7]

Of McLoughlin, there was no sign that festive season. He failed to put in an appearance at the bars, at Turffontein, or at any of the New Year celebrations, and there were no reported safe-robberies in town. But then, in mid-January, he turned up at Ahmed's, in the Malay Camp.[8] He avoided lower Commissioner Street but did make a few day trips to the west Rand. He also went to the newly opened hospital to visit his younger brother.

He had put off the meeting because he knew that it would be difficult. Tommy was not the problem, it was the Sisters of the Holy Family. It was not just that they would recognise him – there were others who already knew that he was back in town. He 'did not want to be seen by the nurses', because the sisters knew about the convent robbery, about O'Brien's death, and the subsequent amputation of his arm. His underlying Catholicism remained intact. Guilt and shame as much as caution prompted him to send a man up into the wards to tell Tommy to meet him down in the hospital grounds.[9] It was, it seemed, the likeness of the Madonna that he feared more than that of the whore.

It was the first time they had seen each other in a decade. Tommy was suffering from an aneurism, and in Jack's absence had been reduced to doing odd jobs around the hospital in order to earn his keep.[10] The cause of the arterial swelling was not clear – but in the young, it can be associated with the onset of syphilis. If so, it may have accounted for some of Tommy's wilder behaviour. What exactly transpired in the hospital gardens remains unknown, but it seems that the older brother provided his young admirer with funds and persuaded him to return to Australia.

With a few underworld sightings of McLoughlin being reported, Sarah Fredericks became more anxious and persuaded Stevenson that they needed to find different accommodation. They left West Street and, for a time, lived in rooms behind the Newcastle Bar, on Commissioner, where the proprietor had always been well disposed to boxers. But then she had second thoughts. She wanted to be closer to members of her family who could offer additional eyes and ears as they tried to keep abreast of 'One-armed

Jack'. That necessitated another move, south and west, into the alleys, passages and yards off Commissioner Street.

The Red Lion Beer Hall, in Ferreira's Town, stood on the corner of Commissioner and Bezuidenhout Streets. It was not far from the Kerk Street mosque, in a racially mixed quarter dominated by a few Chinese storekeepers, some Jewish immigrants and many coloured Muslims. It was an easygoing, tolerant place, where in addition to the usual bars and canteens there were a large number of small businesses including several bespoke tailors. In between there were one or two stables catering for those coloured cabbies who had not already moved across to neighbouring Fordsburg, where easier access to the market and fodder had already drawn in many of their east European Jewish counterparts.

The streets were filled with the sounds of different languages, anything from Arabic and Afrikaans through to Mandarin and Yiddish. But, for most 'respectable' English-speakers, self-consciously striving to be middle-class, and with segregationist inclinations, Ferreira's Town was part of a liminal zone, a gateway to hell where anything could, and often did, happen. Anyone who frequented it, lived in it, or worked there had questionable credentials or morals, usually both. Like most prejudices, it was not entirely without foundation. On its southern boundary, the quarter suddenly gave way to open veld and myriad disused mine shafts on the Robinson Deep property. These man-made caves, industrial catacombs, were within easy walking distance of the town centre by day or by night and often sheltered criminals of all colours.

But for Sarah Fredericks, the quarter was home. It was close by Kerk Street, where Rosie Petersen and Sarah O'Reilly ran their brothels. Busy women did not have the time to clean and scrub kitchens and toilets and their businesses generated an endless supply of soiled sheets. With Stevo still out of work and bringing in only small sums of cash from things that she would rather not talk about, the Red Lion spoke of renewed economic opportunity. It was also at the centre of a supportive social universe. Her brother had vacated his room in the Red Lion and the proprietor, Morris Said, was pleased to allow her to take it over. She inherited most of her brother's friendly neighbours and was within easy walking distance of him, her sister, and an uncle and aunt. She and Stevo would be better off in the heart of her own community.[11]

The main entrance to the Red Lion looked out on Commissioner Street, but leading out of the rear of the building was a passage connecting the beer hall to a set of nine rooms laid out in an L-shape. Going down the passage, the first two rooms were occupied but the next two were vacant. Theirs was the last room on the left, number five. Beyond that, facing back up the passage was a toilet shared by the bar's patrons and the residents. A waist-level window in their room ensured enough light and air, but beyond that, the facilities bordered on the primitive. Their wooden door had a brass handle and a glass panel that she covered with a strip of material to provide some privacy. But there were things that she could not deal with. An enormous crack in the toilet door meant that not only could one sit and look out up the passage, back towards the beer hall, but that anyone curious enough could peer into the closet when checking to see whether or not it was occupied.

All the residents, bar Stevo, were coloureds and Sarah was on good terms with all of them. Like her, most had more than one name, slipping easily between those they had been given and others they had taken on for reasons of their own. They were mostly folk from the old country, now far from the Cape, in a town that offered a new start to often troubled lives. The Absolums in room one, for example, were working people, but around the Red Lion they were better known as 'Mr and Mrs Dopes'. In much the same vein, Mrs Dopes, who everybody in the community knew as 'Johanna', was 'Jane' in Anglophone Johannesburg.

Every evening Johanna cooked a meal for her husband, a few 'table-boarders' and her 18-year-old nephew Mahomed Arends, who, living up to his name, was so God-fearing and ostentatiously pious that the residents jokingly referred to him as 'Ou Vader' – 'Old Father'. Ernest Jacobs was another of the men that she cooked and did laundry for. Nobody knew what Mrs Turton in number nine did; her occupation, like that of the Dopes, remained a mystery. Sarah and Stevo's room proved to be private, trouble-free and secure, and the hidden pressure on the couple eased as the third week of January slipped by. Fredericks settled into her new rounds and frequently found herself in Kerk Street.[12]

271

But across town, in the Malay Camp, there was a slight increase in tensions as month's end approached. McLoughlin fidgeted a bit, adjusting his prosthesis as if he were uncertain whether to keep it on or take it off. He visited Krugersdorp a bit more frequently and was pleased to be told that his old adversary Gill – as befitted a lackey with Boer sympathies – had left the railways and become a Zarp.[13] But, between a few pub rounds, he just seemed a whole lot more thoughtful.

McLoughlin's problem was all-consuming. He knew why he was in Johannesburg. It was not negotiable. He had taken an oath. He knew when the job had to be done. Early evening, over a weekend, when the Zarps were stretched, dealing with the town's drunk and disorderly. That would also leave him time to savour the moment and recompose himself for the Champ D'Or job. He even had an idea as to where it might happen; the missing details would soon be forthcoming. What he did not know, however, was *how* exactly it would happen. That was crucial. There could be nothing sneaky or unexpected about it. It had to be duel-like, openly done, eyeball-to-eyeball, man-to-man. If there was to be 'no unfair advantage' taken, he would also have to give advance notice of his intentions.[14] And, if it was to be properly done, and it would be, he would have to be sober; there could be no repeat of the Higgins debacle.

That Friday he went to Krugersdorp for the last time, checking on last-minute arrangements. Jack McCann had everything under control; Harding, Gorman and Whelan were all raring to go. A few of the new recruits were a bit too talkative but it was probably to be expected, and one or two appeared to be fairly strong but not so smart. In general, however, he was satisfied that they could go ahead as planned. They had a few drinks and he then took his leave of them. He made his way back to the station, bought a ticket and took the train home, disembarking at Langlaagte, rather than downtown, at the better-policed Park Station.[15]

He awoke to the usual struggle – having to haul on a pair of sunbleached white trousers; up and over first one leg, and then the other. The socks and boots, too, had to be bullied into place before he got into a shirt and donned a dark jacket. He checked to see whether the United States army-issue 'Peacemaker' – the Colt .45 – was loaded with its full complement of six.[16] He tucked its long barrel into the belt beneath his jacket; then, because it was a day as hot as any that summer, put on his felt hat and strolled downtown. For him, and a dozen others, there would never ever be another day quite like it – Saturday, 26 January 1895.

The Kerk Street brothels were an obvious place to begin his enquiries at. He got there in the mid-morning, just as the women were rousing themselves and before the first male interlopers arrived. He knew it was not going to be easy. The madams were accustomed to dealing with the police and would clam up if they sensed that a friend of theirs was under threat. But he felt that he could get it out of them, with liquor, or money, or both.

It turned out to be nearly impossible. Were it not for a chance meeting later that day he might never have found out where the couple were living. He started out at Sarah O'Reilly's, in rooms that formed part of a house she shared with Rosie Petersen. They chatted for a while, making small talk about the old days, but it was hard going. O'Reilly, who had seen Fredericks earlier that day as she set about her charring, was cagey and not about to disclose anything without direct probing. Around midday, he called for a bottle of stout, took off the prosthesis and settled in for the long haul. It was looking hopeless when Fredericks suddenly appeared from one of the rooms to get some instructions from O'Reilly.

He did not know what to do. He wanted nothing to do with her; he was after Stevo, but could not bring himself to say so. So he rounded on her, asking if she had come 'to look for more detective work'. But she hit back, telling him that, had she wanted to, she could have had him put away weeks ago. It only confirmed his suspicions that it was she who had delivered Stevenson into Ferguson's hands. Unable to browbeat her, he instead vented his spleen on the man whose affections she had stolen. Stevo 'was a dirty informer', he told her, 'a low fucking bastard'. Then, speaking not only to Stevenson's failings but of his own innermost fears, he told her that Stevo 'had lost his character', that he had 'lost his pluck' and that he would never again 'earn his keep'. Stevo lacked the virtues a man prized; he was not a man, he was a kept man. But then his nerve failed him and he could not tell her what he wanted to, face-to-face. So he contented himself with muttering that he 'would be even with him some day'.[17] It was not only the Madonna he feared.

It was past noon by the time that he finished sparring with Fredericks and since the chat with O'Reilly had yielded nothing, he went next door to try to pry open Petersen. Rosie was ready for a drink, which suited him. If he got her off the premises, he thought, she might be a bit more forthcoming than O'Reilly, so he suggested that they go across to the Silver King, on the corner of Fraser and Kerk. But loyalty among whores was as good as honour among thieves and Petersen was no more helpful than O'Reilly had been. He had already given up on her when, out of the corner of an eye, he caught sight of the answer to his prayers.[18] If there was one man in the world who would know where Fredericks and Stevenson were living, it had to be Harry Lobb. Lobb had lost Fredericks to Stevenson in the fight, and he had lost Stevenson to Fredericks in a private tussle. They had both lost partners to the couple.

He abandoned Petersen to the last of the beer, telling her that he would be calling in on her later that afternoon, and walked towards Lobb. 'Harry, old boy,' he said in a loud voice, 'how is your old pal Stevo getting on?'[19] After that they were inseparable, two men in a marriage of convenience. It was like old times. They drank, laughed and talked, forgetting about lunch, and eventually Lobb told him where the couple were living. Without further need of Lobb for the moment, he told him that he had to leave and talk to Petersen, but that they should link up for a drink at the popular Wiener Café, on Commissioner Street, at around five o'clock.[20]

Rosie Petersen was leaning in the cottage doorway when he found her and enquired whether Fredericks was around. She was inside, Rosie said, scrubbing the floors, and so she yelled for her. But Fredericks heard nothing. His nerve failed him, again. Instead of going in and speaking directly to her he took the easy way out. 'You need not call her,' he told Rosie. 'Just tell her that I – McLoughlin – say she must go home and tell Stevo that he will be a dead man tonight.'[21] The oath was doing its work; as he strode off, he saw Petersen disappearing into the cottage. Sarah Fredericks was on all fours when she got the message. It electrified her and she bolted – 'she was very excited and jumped up and ran out of the back'. Rosie saw no more of her that day.[22]

He got to the café earlier than expected, around 4.30, and was pleased to see that Lobb was already there. If he had not already told him so over drinks at the Silver King, then it was over tea and snacks at the Weiner that Lobb got to learn that McLoughlin was going to shoot Stevenson before the day was out. Whether Lobb believed him or not, or subtly encouraged him, is impossible to know, but he made no effort to dissuade him. The interaction in the café was emblazoned on Lobb's mind: fully 14 years later, he could still recall it all with ease.

★   ★   ★

Stevo was on the bed reading when Fredericks burst in and blurted out that McLoughlin was nosing around Kerk Street and what he had told Rosie. If he was alarmed, he tried not to show it and did his best to calm her down. Her sister was going to call around but he agreed that, when she left, they should leave too and spend the night across at her aunt's.[23]

Even so, he had to be prepared. So Stevo fossicked about until he found his revolver in one of its customary hiding places. He loaded it and placed it in his trouser pocket. But, as he did so, he realised that the gun lay too deeply in the pocket for him to be able to withdraw it easily. So he cut a makeshift holster out of a tobacco pouch and, using her sewing machine, stitched it up as firmly as possible. He shuffled around for a while, not wanting to attach the holster to his belt while they were still indoors. Eventually he slipped the gun into the pocket of a jacket of his hanging behind the door and they settled down to wait for her sister.[24]

As he left the Weiner, McLoughlin looked up and waited for his eyes to adjust to the light. He paused and realised he had time to spare. A few doubts had crossed his mind. His failure to stare Fredericks down was disappointing, but he had done what was necessary and felt sure that Stevenson knew what to expect. But she remained a worry. He wanted the woman unharmed. Killing her would blur the focus; it would raise potentially awkward questions about his own sexuality and defeat the whole purpose. What if Fredericks got in the way? He needed a drink.

The Oddfellows' Arms was an easy choice. It was a home-from-home, he had held court there often enough. Every gangster in town, every second Irish workman or Lancastrian drank there. If there was one pub in all of Johannesburg suited to announcing his return and his resolve, it was Oddfellows'. And he did so. He ordered a beer and by the time he was done, everybody at the bar counter knew that not only was he intent on killing Stevenson, but that he had 'a list' of names of other men that he was ready to shoot, including Robert Ferguson, newly promoted Sergeant Gill of the Zarps, Henry Higgins of Orange Grove, and 'the man that catches him'.[25] His discipline was threatening to unravel.

The sun was gliding towards the horizon and the shadows already in their sunset positions when he set off down Commissioner Street. Here and there women, sensing that darkness was clambering into their rooms though open windows, drew their curtains and took out candles or lamps to dispel the gloom. In her room behind the Red Lion, Mrs Dopes was preparing her lighting-up ritual. She got the timing just about right, because no sooner was she done than her nephew appeared and she directed him to a washbasin standing in the corner. When one of the table-boarders, Ernest Isaacs materialised, minutes later, she let him stand about in the passage because the room was already crowded. Inside the beer hall one of the cabbies playing dominoes, Nasa Dien Burgess, sensing a call of nature, made his way down the passage and into the closet. He dropped his trousers, got comfortable and sat staring through the crack in the door.

Moving down Commissioner, McLoughlin quickened his pace. The Robinson property was not one that you wanted to negotiate in darkness. Everyone around him seemed to be walking faster, trying to reach their destinations before night caught them. He was not far from Bezuidenhout, but with every step some new anxiety flitted across his mind. He only had one hand; how was he supposed to open a door and then – almost simultaneously – shoot? It had to be a fair contest, but what if Stevenson was in there, just sitting in an armchair, waiting with pistol cocked, ready for him to enter the room? Stevo would use his natural, right, hand – but he would have to make do with his tutored left.

Four blocks to the south-west, Philip Carr and the members of his family were getting ready to go to the mosque for evening prayers. Philip and his brothers, Gamadoela and Mahomed, were hard-working men, well respected in the community. They were shopkeepers and tailors, but the pride of the family was Mustaffa, Philip's 18-year-old son, who had recently returned from Mecca. A qualified tailor, Hadji Carr was known to clients as Joseph, but to his friends and family he remained Mustaffa.

Mustaffa sauntered down to the corner of Main and Wolhuter, waiting for his uncles to join him on the walk to the mosque. A fun-loving fellow who retained some boyish ways, Mustaffa soon attracted other company and was joined by two younger men.[26] His uncles were slow in arriving so the youngsters, all involved in the tailoring trade, passed the time chatting, laughing, pushing and shoving each other in the way that the carefree sometimes do. Mustaffa was in his cohort but the other two looked up to him, subtly acknowledging his newly elevated social status.

A minute or so after seven o'clock Jack McLoughlin entered the Red Lion. He knew the place. He strode in through the beer hall and out into the passage at the back of the main building. Finding the first entrance on the left open, he stuck his head into the doorway and, seeing a woman, said 'Good evening'. Mrs Dopes returned the greeting and he asked her which room Stevenson lived in. 'Ou Vader', looking up from the wash basin, caught a glimpse of a one-armed man. Mrs Dopes went to the door and gestured towards the far end of the passage. The man turned and walked past two unoccupied rooms and then stopped. He retraced his steps to Mrs Dope's, where Isaacs was hovering in the doorway. Looking through the crack in the toilet door, Burgess, recognising McLoughlin, watched as Mrs Dopes accompanied him back down the passage and pointed directly to the door with the glass panel. Burgess stood up, adjusted his shirt, and started 'tying my trousers up'.[27]

With the Colt in his left hand, McLoughlin used his wooden right to knock on the door. Fredericks, expecting her sister, was standing behind a table, Stevenson still in the chair. Each waited for the other to answer the knock. Neither did. McLoughlin knew they were in there, but what if she rather than he came to the door? He banged out a second, more insistent, knock and Fredericks piped up: 'Who's there'? He dared not answer. He could not hold on to the revolver and simultaneously bend down to turn the handle so he gave the door a good kick, hoping that it would swing open. It didn't. Still puzzling as to who it was, Stevenson put down the book, got up, moved forward and lent down for the handle.

The door eased open and, using his foot, McLoughlin forced it wider in order to reveal who was standing behind it. And there he was – 'You fucker, it is *you* I want,' he shouted, and pulled the trigger. Stevenson took it in the chest, lurched backwards and fell onto the bed, scrabbling about for a revolver that was not there. McLoughlin moved into the room, closing the door behind him. Seeing him entering, Stevenson leapt up, calling out: 'Oh God, I am shot,' before jumping out of the window. Fredericks rushed towards the assailant and screamed: 'My God, my man's been shot' and 'Police, help!' He pushed her away, sending her sprawling over a chest. But her continued screaming was unsettling, so he warned her: 'Leave off you bloody cow, or you will have the remains of the content.' He then turned and left, closing the door behind him. But she would not stop screaming so he went back in and yelled: 'You bloody cow,' before firing in her direction as she crawled beneath the bed. The bullet lodged in the wall opposite him. He had made the point. He wrenched the handle off the door so that she could not follow him and walked slowly up the passage, towards the exit.[28]

Mrs Dopes, hearing the shots, ran down the passage towards him, screaming. Peacemaker in hand, he glided past her, ignoring the yelling. At the top of the passage he saw two men standing outside her doorway. He brushed past them, reassuring Isaacs and 'Ou Vader': 'All right boys, I won't harm you.'[29] From down the passage, Mrs Dopes called out to her nephew to follow him. And he did; through the beer hall and out onto Commissioner where he stood screaming: 'Police, Police!' McLoughlin ignored him and turned left, down Bezuidenhout Street.

He walked purposefully, soldier-like, tailed at a respectable distance by 'Ou Vader' and, a quarter-block behind them, a growing number of coloured men who had poured out of the Red Lion and other canteens to track the commotion. His focus was unwavering, his pace unchanged. Slightly ahead of him, half-way down Bezuidenhout, near the Princess Bar, he spotted the owner coming out and taking up a position that was too close for his comfort. He knew Goldberg, and Goldberg knew him only too well. McLoughlin sensed that Goldberg was not a real threat, but he also wanted to discourage all those following him, so he fired a warning shot that went perilously close to the proprietor's head.[30]

But the third shot from the six-shooter did not have the desired effect. Instead of deterring the crowd from closing in, it only fired them up and the cry went up: *'Vang hom! Vang hom!'* – *'Catch him! Catch him!'* It was unsettling; he could not afford to keep glancing sideways or backwards if he was to reach safety before darkness set in. His nerve held and he again increased his pace, 'walking hard' towards Main Street.[31] As he entered it, 'he turned back and warned the people' and barked out: 'If you come near me I will shoot you.'[32] In the distance, at the coming junction with Wolhuter Street, he saw one or two adult men, as well as a youngster and a few young friends, larking about on the corner.

Behind him the shouting from the mob was getting louder but he dared not take his eyes off the youngster and the lads ahead of him; they were much closer than Goldberg had been. Mustaffa, still in playful mood and unaware of what had happened at the Red Lion, misread the situation. As McLoughlin went past him, the Hadji, thinking it might only be a thief, stamped his feet as if to set off and intercept him. He caught a glimpse of it out of the corner of his eye, swung around and shot him straight through the left temple.[33] The Hadji would die within minutes – he now had only two bullets left in the Colt.

The pursuing party, led by 'Ou Vader' and a cab driver he knew, Sah Badein Ben, chased McLoughlin all the way to the end of Main Street, where he scrambled through the fence into the gloom of the mine property. He was about 20 yards in when he glanced round and saw one of the men getting through the barbed wire to follow him. It was Ben. He stopped, raised the Peacemaker, but then thought better of it. There had been enough shooting. He called out: 'Stand back!' It was enough. Ben backed off and the rest, taking their cue, followed suit. They turned round and headed off swiftly, back towards the Red Lion.[34]

He moved into the embrace of total darkness, consoled by the fact that there had not been more deaths. The shooting of the lad on Wolhuter Street was unfortunate – the unavoidable by-product of a fight between two white men. Stevenson was not dead, but he knew that he was badly wounded and hoped that he would die before he could identify his killer. But it really did not matter. He had a sense of being reborn, of having restored his reputation with honour. He could once again look men in the eye. There was more to celebrate than to fret about. And so, as he picked his way past abandoned pits and mine shafts, his thoughts were about returning to Commissioner Street. The night would be his alone.

Back at the Red Lion a mist of silence had eased into the beer hall from the surrounding streets and swirled through the rooms at the back, snuffing out any Saturday night revelry. Outside, dejected coloured men and women stood about in small clusters, whispering the same question again and again – why had fate chosen to arrange a meeting with a young Hadji on Wolhuter Street that evening and a one-armed 36-year-old white man? Inside, Sarah Fredericks's relatives and the curious pressed into the narrow passage to hear news of Stevenson.

It was not good. The wounded man had been helped around the back, into number nine, Mrs Turton's room. Fredericks found him there. Sobbing, she removed his shirt as he lay on the bed bleeding from 'a wound just below his heart'. Stevo tried to calm her, telling her not to cry because he was not badly hurt, but she – and he – knew better.[35] The police and District Surgeon had been sent for but Ferguson, smarting from the fact that Andrew Trimble had been preferred over him as the republic's Chief Detective, was being most uncooperative. Trimble arrived first, followed shortly thereafter by FE Kretzmar, Johannesburg's only Veld Kornet.

Trimble asked Fredericks a few perfunctory questions but then turned his attention to Stevenson, who, although in pain, was conscious. He told Trimble: 'I am dying, I have been shot underneath the heart and I am bleeding internally and I have only a short while to live.'[36] Stevo told him who the gunman was and why he had been shot. Cecil Schultz, the District Surgeon, arrived only to confirm the gravity of the situation. Trimble, sensing that time was of the essence, decided to take a 'dying deposition' before the man was moved. When he was done, Stevenson beckoned to Fredericks and, drawing her closer, asked her to send his ring to his mother if he died. They then removed him to the hospital.

The next morning a more thorough diagnosis was made. The bullet – which was never found – had been on a downward trajectory, passing through the spleen and part of a kidney. Dr van Niekerk, the surgeon who had removed McLoughlin's hand, operated in an attempt to stem the haemorrhaging.[37] The patient survived but then weakened and died that afternoon. Fredericks never left his side; at the last, he beckoned to her once more and, without a word, passed her his ring.[38]

Back on the Robinson property on the night of the shooting, McLoughlin found the small place he had prepared in the catacombs – a 15-minute walk from the town centre – sat down, and took stock of the situation. It could have been the site of his own grave, but it was not. He correctly anticipated that mounted police would be sent to watch all the roads leading out of town. But the Trickster in him had other plans. Just as he had deceived Ferguson by doubling-back from the northern Transvaal to execute his informer, so he would now double-back into town and further humiliate the police. By 8.30 he was walking back along western Commissioner Street – and if the list of names he was said to have compiled in the Oddfellows' Arms was anything to go by, he was on the lookout for Robert Ferguson, FW Gill or Henry Higgins.

CHAPTER SEVENTEEN

The Spectres of Success

JOHANNESBURG TO LOURENÇO MARQUES

— 1895 —

Success has ruined many a man.

BENJAMIN FRANKLIN

After Joe Byrne had walked up to the front door of the cottage of the newly married Aaron Sherritt, waited for the door to open and blasted the police informer to kingdom come, Ned Kelly's gang had neither the desire nor the time to celebrate. But within hours of the Red Lion shootings Jack McLoughlin, brimming with confidence, was back in town ready to link up with McCann for a pre-arranged meeting. The two were swopping notes when, according to Lobb, he happened to chance upon the pair chatting in the street near the Central Hotel. Every busy corner, every pub on Commissioner was by then abuzz with talk not only about the shootings, but also 'the list' of death that had been recited at the Oddfellows' Arms. Lobb was concerned about being seen as an accomplice if the police arrested the wanted man. He rushed up to McLoughlin and, by his own account, said to him: 'There is a rumour in town that you have shot Stevo.' McLoughlin laughed as if he thought it a joke and said: 'Come and have some supper.' The three then set off for a late-night dinner at Rosenthal's Café.[1]

Rosenthal's was a favoured underworld hangout. The celebration there, which went on for hours, exceeded McLoughlin's expectations. Shortly after ten o'clock, Henry Higgins's partner, Morry Hollander, walked into the café – only to flee back down Commissioner Street the moment that he caught sight of McLoughlin. He knew who to run to; his friend Higgins's name was on the list.[2] But the real triumph remained hidden at the time and had to be savoured later. 'Revenge,' they say, 'is a dish best served cold.' And it was.

While the meal was still in progress one of Ferguson's informants spotted the suspect and rushed off to tell the detective that the man the police wanted was out dining, in full view, at Rosenthal's. Ferguson's name, too, was on the list. He claimed later that he received the tip-off long after McLoughlin had left the café, but nobody believed him.[3] Ferguson had any number of reasons for not wanting to tangle with McLoughlin, or to help his new professional rival – Andrew Trimble – apprehend the man. Indeed, within hours it was reliably reported that, on being told about the celebration at Rosenthal's, Ferguson had stated that he 'did not avail himself of the information, not caring to poach on Mr Trimble's preserve, and in view of the treatment he has received from Pretoria, is not particularly anxious to distinguish himself in any way'.[4] Robert Ferguson was in serious trouble.

The meal ended around midnight and the trio dispersed. Lobb and McCann headed off in separate directions and McLoughlin left for his hideout, which was either on the Robinson property, as most believed, or he may already have switched to a house close to the police station in Marshall's Town. It was a frustrating long Sunday with no newspapers. He had to wait until Monday to see how the shootings had played out in the press.[5]

He knew that the best chance of a favourable reception lay in the morning paper. The *Standard & Diggers' News,* occasionally critical of the Kruger government, was usually supportive of white workers. The front page blurted out news about the 'Commissioner Street Murder' but then, uncertain as to what to make of the death of the Hadji, elided otherwise discrete events with another headline about a 'shocking double murder'. But it was the string of sub-headings that followed that lent the most positive interpretation to his motive for the shooting at the Red Lion. 'An Informer's Fate',

'The Chum that Split' and 'The Carey Tragedy Repeated', all pointed in the right direction for him, lending support to what seemed like an Irish assassination of an English police informer – albeit one in a Boer state.[6]

The evening paper, he knew, would offer a sterner test. *The Star,* mouthpiece of the mine owners, was critical of the government and the police force because it always sensed the potential for an anti-capitalist rebellion among revolver-toting white miners whose behaviour often left much to be desired. It would almost certainly be disapproving. Keen to attract investment for the deep-level mines and ensure social stability all along the Witwatersrand, the Editor blew the horn of 'law-and-order' with a regularity matched only by the scorned appeal of church bells on Sundays.

In a market bent on increasing working-class readership, the Stevenson shooting did not even make the front page of *The Star.* Inside, three headings barked out familiar warnings – 'A 'Double Murder', 'A Desperado's Revenge' and, more predictably, 'The Police and the Public'. The execution at the Red Lion Beer Hall was one of two unsolved murders by whites, on whites, that had taken place in the town centre within weeks. The editorial, however, was surprisingly generous and thoughtful – almost satisfying – for a man intent on having his reputation publicly restored. The leader writer likened him to a character from a Bret Harte novel, or Charlie Peace. The writer understood his frustrations at having been forced into exile after the station robbery and was unsparing of the unfortunate Stevenson:

> *De mortuis* etc. is an excellent rule but it is quite impossible to apply it to Stevenson. He was a deserter, a desperado, and an indurated criminal whose crimes were notorious and McLoughlin could hardly help experiencing some annoyance at learning that, while he was technically a fugitive from justice, Stevenson was living in the fat of the land and apparently on the best possible terms with the police.[7]

The same edition lauded young Mustaffa as a 'brave man', noted that he was a member of a respectable family of means and a Hadji only just returned from Mecca. It also provided a respectful, albeit flawed, account of how, earlier that day, the Hadji had been given an Islamic burial. Stevenson was buried the same day, it noted – out of Fredericks's rooms – in a funeral overseen by the Revd JT Darragh of the Church of England.[8]

The press coverage that Monday, offering a shocked but grudging understanding of his motive, was about as good as it got. But information and time are the enemies of first-take explanations: had he scrutinised the later reports a bit more carefully, he would have noted that, just below the veneer of journalistic understanding of the execution at the Red Lion, he was already being re-cast as a one-dimensional urban monster, as a desperado capable of inducing only horror in the minds of those round him.

While the celebrations at Rosenthal's were still afoot, just a few blocks away, a panic-stricken policeman on foot patrol had mistaken an usher at the Empire Theatre as a one-armed man 'drawing a revolver' and clubbed him into a bloodied, unconscious mess. In Pretoria a few days later a one-armed Swede was being shaved when he was yanked from the barber's chair and led off in handcuffs and leg irons. Police throughout southern Africa were on the lookout for a suspect who had assumed Pimpernel-like proportions and he was being seen here, there and everywhere. A local stationer took out a series of advertisements lauding 'Ken Donaldson's Timetable and Diary', as used by 'McLachlan the Murderer'. Six months later, in Rhodesia, yet another innocent was hauled off the streets of Salisbury by worried policemen when it was thought that he might be McLoughlin.[9]

These over-reactions by law-enforcement agencies to a partly disabled suspect who had never assaulted or shot at a police or prison officer, let alone a bank, mine or refinery employee, or any other law-abiding member of the public, could be traced back to the newspapers on the Monday after the shootings. *The Star,* in a separate report foreshadowing events that were to take place only days later, attributed an unconnected Sunday-night robbery on a west Rand mine to the McLoughlin gang. But it was the wildly inaccurate depiction of his prosthesis that did most to underscore the emerging image of him as an ogre. 'This revengeful Corsican-like individual's wooden arm' – the newspaper suggested at a time when knife crimes were viewed as an 'Italian' speciality – 'is so arranged that, when he opens his hand, a mechanical dagger leaps out'. That, too, resonated with the contemporary English urban myth of 'Spring Heeled Jack – the monster endowed with mechanical limbs and a barely suppressed sexual appetite.[10] Similar fabrications were later embroidered into several JM Barrie-like descriptions of McLoughlin as Captain Hook by a cast of amateur historians.[11]

There was no need for fiction, the reality was gripping enough. Early on Tuesday morning, still in hiding and in search of proper attribution if not approval for the Red Lion shooting, he scoured the papers to find out whether his name was being spelt correctly.[12] But, as it became clearer that the man who had dined out in Rosenthal's had not been caught in the police's drag-net, a note of terror was starting to creep into some reports.

A few cranks, revelling in the uncertainty, penned letters to the press purportedly coming from the wanted man. One, affecting working-class prose and mimicking the horror evoked by 'Jack the Ripper' in London a few years earlier, claimed to have been 'written in blood'. The author promised to 'call upon' others named in the Oddfellows' list before leaving town and signed himself 'Jimmy MacLachlan'. A second, attributed to 'JM MacLachlan', conjured up another deeply held English fear and justified Stevenson's execution, stating: 'only an Irishman knows what revenge is'.[13]

This early spasm of irrationality was followed by a full-scale 'moral panic' in that section of the underworld that felt most at risk. Harry Lobb was the first to blink. Shortly after the dinner at Rosenthal's he dashed around to *The Star*'s offices to deny that it was he who had directed McLoughlin to the Red Lion. Morry Hollander, with more reason than many to fear for the continued cleanliness of his underwear, was next to seek help. A trusted confidant had told him that McLoughlin was 'going to blow his head off'. He scurried off to demand police protection – but the Zarps, mired in troubles of their own, told him, in almost so many words, to go to hell.[14]

In the meantime, the Monster of the Deep Shaft, still believed to be hiding out on the Robinson property, was cheered to note that the Detective Department was collapsing. It augured well for the grand exit he had planned for the weekend. On the Tuesday afternoon after the shootings, *The Star,* building on the developing scandal, ran a sub-leader suggesting that, if it were true that Ferguson had refused to answer a call to arrest the suspect at Rosenthal's, he was 'a coward' and that 'the sooner he was drummed out of the force and out of the country the better it will be for all concerned'.[15] The same accusation was repeated in the *Standard & Diggers' News* the following morning.[16] Indeed, Ferguson's fear of the suspect ran so deep that he could not even bring himself to help Andrew Trimble compile a pen picture of McLoughlin.[17] It took the Johannesburg police four full days to produce a brief description of a man known to every cab-driver and pub-owner in town. The mysterious delay only contributed to the tension and news of the scandal spread across all southern Africa.

From under the nose of the police, McLoughlin watched as Ferguson buckled beneath pressure from the press and public. With nowhere to hide, the embattled detective wrote to *The Star*, attempting to explain away his inaction at the time of the Rosenthal dinner. The Editor's response was brutally direct. The 'Chief Detective' was dismissed as being 'ridiculous', advised to seek legal help if the reports of cowardice were false and then go ahead and sue the newspaper.[18] Predictably, there was no comeback.

A week later Robert Ferguson resigned. A single bullet at the Red Lion had taken one man's life and another's soul. Both men had died dishonourable deaths and the frontier code of manliness had been restored. But not fully. It was claimed that Ferguson would henceforth direct 'his attention, on behalf of various gold companies, to the elucidation of gold-theft mysteries'.[19] And, every gangster and Irish nationalist turned refinery worker up and down the length of the Witwatersrand could have been forgiven a wry smile as they saw an old wolf settle down to guard the town's lambs.[20]

For the McLoughlin gang more good news followed. Just as Ferguson took to the letters column of the newspaper to defend himself, a surprising petition began to do the rounds. A few of those who enjoyed the franchise, burghers all, were pressing the government to dismiss Andrew Trimble. The republic's 'Acting Chief Detective', fervent nationalists alleged, spoke no Dutch, was not a naturalised citizen and – sin of sins – had fought for the British during the republicans' First War of Independence back in 1881.[21]

Trimble later had to swear before a commission of enquiry that he had not fought against the Boers and state that: 'I owe nothing to England. I am an Irishman myself. I served my time and purchased my discharge honourably.'[22] Forced to take on the investigation into the Stevenson shooting once Ferguson refused to get involved, Trimble suddenly found himself having to cope with political difficulties as well as several unsolved murder investigations. It was a diversion that he made light of 14 years later, but at the time, it undoubtedly added to his growing list of problems.[23]

With the detectives and Zarps at sixes and sevens, McLoughlin was readying himself to take the next step up in his never-ending quest to demonstrate 'confidence in myself'. On Thursday evening, only slightly disguised, he ventured out from his safe house and took a calculated stroll past the police station. As one reporter remarked, albeit in a slightly different context, 'the man's coolness and daring seem almost incredible'.[24]

His foray to the police station proved salutary for two reasons – one he did not care too much about and the other he could not care enough about. Although he later disputed it for reasons that had nothing to do with an excursion that oozed brigand-like arrogance, he was reported as saying that, as he walked past the station, 'I could hear my girl, Ali Ahmed, inside the charge office, screaming. They detained her for a week because they thought she knew where I had gone to.'[25] He was almost certainly correct. The police, although keen to use 'coloured' females as informants and men as 'spies', were unlikely to have been gentle with the unfortunate Ahmed, whom the press had reported missing from her rooms days earlier.[26]

The awfulness of the screaming may have imprinted itself on his mind, but Ali Ahmed, like Hadji Mustaffa, was treated as just one more person of colour in an unrepentantly racist society. McLoughlin made no effort to go to her assistance directly or indirectly by means of legal or financial aid – a courtesy criminal heroes often extended to close friends. In southern Africa, not even 'social banditry' could fully overcome the barrier of skin colour.

But what really sank in that night was what he allegedly saw in heavy black print on a board outside the police station. If true, then it was a bitter-sweet vision – one that might have nudged Captain Dangerous closer to some of his other boyhood heroes, or to the likes of a Ned Kelly. If the Kruger government had indeed declared him to be an outlaw, then it had bestowed upon him the notoriety that, in many ways, he had always courted. He was a fugitive from justice, a man who could be dealt with by any citizen without having to pay heed to the prescriptions of the law. But, as outlaws across the world knew only too well, it was a status that could evoke the highest price. As he reportedly put it: 'Before I left Johannesburg I saw a notice outside the Charge Office – Jack McLoughlin to be taken alive or dead.'[27]

From surviving archival documents it is impossible to tell whether the Kruger government did in fact issue such a notice. What is more likely is that he saw a copy of an item in the *Government Gazette* offering a reward of £100 for information leading to his apprehension and authorising any officer of the law to call on the assistance of the public while effecting an arrest.[28] Shorn of the vital difference, the notice did evoke elements of life in the 'Wild West' in a town that never wanted for American influences ranging from the names of bars, such as the 'Silver King', through to places like Cleveland, Denver and Selby. As a man known to enjoy a novel, pack a pistol and take oaths, who knows what he had seen?

What is certain, however, is that the government did not want for legislation to declare a man an outlaw. The founding legal documents of the republic, the famed 'Thirty-Three Articles' of 1844–49 and a Volksraad resolution of 1864 both made provision for anyone suspected of treason to be declared an outlaw.[29] Moreover, the state and its agents gave every impression of pursuing him as if he were an outlaw once he was clear of the Witwatersrand. Trimble, who knew how fugitives operated in frontier zones, appointed a specialist tracker, Sergeant-Major Hamilton, formerly of the Bechuanaland Border Police, to follow McLoughlin back into Vendaland.[30] In similar vein, the Magistrate at Pietersburg sent the State Attorney a telegram assuring him that Hamilton would not give up the chase, and that he would bring back the fugitive '*dead or alive*'.[31] Legal niceties aside, McLoughlin was probably right to see himself as an 'outlaw'. Five days after the shootings, he slipped out of town to Krugersdorp.[32]

★ ★ ★

The core of the McLoughlin gang had been active along the greater Witwatersrand since at least 1888. Working in small bands between three and 10 strong, they had been remarkably energetic, focused and disciplined, as might be expected of ex-military men in their late twenties. In their night-time quests for gold amalgam over several years they had not once assaulted or murdered a mine employee or a policeman during their raids on mine offices. But the gang members were ageing and, like their leader, some had put down urban roots and were no longer as willing to see the countryside as a refuge as they had once been. It was a mixed blessing. On the one hand, growing social commitment took off some of the rougher edges of the hardest nuts, but, on the other, some gang members were less inclined to countenance resistance from their victims.

The erosion of a purely bachelor existence – a cornerstone of success-ful brigandage – was evident in the nine or 10 men who met at Mulligan's Hotel in Krugersdorp, late Friday night, 1 February 1895.[33] McLoughlin, McCann and Harding were among a minority who had tried to see off the worst temptations of domesticity, but even they were by then more prone to seek out comfortable accommodation than they had once been. Others had fared less well. John Cranmer, a short-tempered fellow recently involved in stock theft at Nylstroom, still sported many of the scars he had collected as a scuttler in Manchester, but now had interests other than mere fighting. His partner, Lillian Pitt, was a barmaid-prostitute who sold a little pornography on the side to boost her income.[34] Cranmer had become so attached to the woman that he insisted on going back to Johannesburg to spend the night with her at her rented cottage. McLoughlin sent Harding with him to determine whether she could be trusted to hold her tongue should things go wrong.[35]

Tommy Gorman, 40 years old and becoming increasingly trigger-happy, was another on the slippery slope. He was already snared in a classic lov-ers' triangle, with his eye on a young coloured woman who was engaged to someone else.[36] Tommy Whelan was the saddest case of all. It was the full disaster. He had married and fathered a child and turned to drink. Forced into full-time employment, he had worked as a refinery worker at the Champ D'Or and then moved on to the Black Reef. Realising that he was lost to them, McLoughlin relegated him to intelligence-gathering du-ties. But Whelan wanted the best of both worlds – little active part in the robbery so as to avoid risk, but a fair share of the proceeds should it prove to be successful.[37]

The nest-building propensities of men locked into urban living and with a lot to lose did not sit well with an 'outlaw' wanted for murder and ready to skip the country. Nor did it help that, within hours of the Red Lion shootings, the press had speculated that his gang had been involved in a west Rand heist. It meant that Lieutenant Tossel, the Krugersdorp police hero who had brought in Jack McKeone, would be in a state of heightened alert. It added to steadily rising tensions.

The gang planned to limit possible damage. After the job McLoughlin and McCann would head for the northern frontier, via Makhado's stronghold, and then split up. Charlie Harding wanted to go to Pretoria to settle some unfinished business. He would be joined there by Cranmer and Pitt and the three would then take the night train to the Orange Free State and, once safely across the border, would head 'home' to England. Gorman, with his eye on the coloured lass, would stay on the Reef and keep a low profile. Whelan, dragging a domestic ball-and-chain around behind him, would stay at the Black Reef.

The following day, Saturday, gang members remained tightly focused and steered clear of Krugersdorp and the surrounding mines. McLoughlin and McCann went about their own business quietly, laying in supplies for the long ride north. Harding got on well with Cranmer, so he stayed in charge of him and Pitt. And when it became clear that Whelan might lose the plot he, too, was sent off to while away time with Harding and the others at the Johannesburg cottage. Gorman, whose preoccupations remained below rather than above his belt, was granted time off to relax as he best saw fit.

As night fell the gods smiled on them. It started raining, heavily. The damp made things messy but helped to deaden the sound coming from feet that were already clad in 'India rubber' shoes. It was past midnight when they met outside the Champ D'Or Deep property. Armed with a bull's-eye lantern, a heavy stick and other tools of their trade they slipped off into the darkest shadows to take up their positions. The idea was simple. They would take over the bedroom occupied by the mine secretary, L Simpson, and remove his keys. Then, freed from the need to cart off the safe or to use dynamite, McLoughlin and Harding would work the safe door open.

McCann and Whelan secured the perimeter. McLoughlin, Harding, Cranmer and Gorman gained entry to the bedroom using a skeleton key and, as expected, found the safe standing in the corner. Hearing a noise, Simpson sat up, but before he could reach for a weapon he was overpowered, thrown to the floor and his keys taken. Somebody grabbed him around the neck and, holding his head to the floor, nearly strangled him to death as he continued to resist. Then someone, almost certainly Cranmer, used the cudgel to render him unconscious. That blow ended Simpson's working life. Five months later he was still recuperating in a country retreat, unable or unwilling to give evidence for the prosecution in the legal proceedings that followed. In the wake of the Red Lion shootings the brutality of the assault added to the growing perception of McLoughlin as a common murderer.[38]

The bull's-eye was lit, the safe door opened and gold, silver, notes and negotiable scrip worth about £1 200 extracted. It was less than might have been expected, because the mine's wages had been paid out the previous afternoon. Nevertheless, it was in excess of what a miner might earn over a four-year tour of duty. The loot was roughly divided, McLoughlin appropriating half to be shared unequally between himself and McCann. The other half was given to Harding for distribution among the remaining gang members. McLoughlin and McCann set off for open country while Harding and the others retreated to Lillian Pitt's cottage.[39]

The Mine Manager, Charles Hall, and his Assistant Secretary discovered Simpson, in hysterical condition, just a quarter of an hour later. The police were on the trail of the suspects within hours. Hotel owner Mulligan, taken in for questioning on Sunday morning, provided all the clues necessary. Once Tossel knew that McLoughlin was involved, it was not difficult to work out who the one-armed man's assistants might have been. Hall said that he had spotted Harding and Whelan – both of whom he knew – loitering around the mine a few days before the robbery. Tossel was confident of making an arrest; the question was what order the dominoes would fall in.[40]

The bachelor bandits, McLoughlin and McCann, were soon well clear of the Witwatersrand. Gorman, too, could not be found. The others fared less well. Harding, who had taken the lion's share of the half he had been handed, had pocketed £200. By Monday morning he was back at the Prince of Wales Hotel, in Pretoria, where he made no effort to hide the fact that he was in the money and began settling pressing debts. Pretoria's Acting Chief Detective, WH Ueckermann, aware of Ferguson's fate, saw the chance of nabbing Jack McLoughlin and making a name for himself.[41] He went to the Prince of Wales and chatted to the big-spending Harding, who said that he had just returned from a trip to the Free State.

Ueckermann returned to his office to find a telegram from Tossel asking him to arrest Harding – who, by then, was having a drink at the Grand National Hotel and waiting for Cranmer and Lillian Pitt to join him. Ueckermann arrested Harding and found over £30 in gold and £20 in silver on him.[42] Harding, playing the big boy, taunted Ueckermann by claiming that, had he been arrested earlier, a much larger sum could have been recovered. By that Monday night he was behind bars, where he stayed for five months, until mid-June 1895, when he was sentenced to four years in prison with hard labour for 'a crime committed with brutality'.[43]

Ironically, Harding's bungling helped Cranmer and Pitt stage a successful exit from the republic by buying them more time. Not knowing that Harding was in custody, they hung around Pretoria for two days, by which time the police thought that the pair were already safely out of the country. Instead, they took the precaution of calling in on Whelan and telling him that they were Natal-bound. They were not. They boarded a train for the Orange Free State.[44]

But out there, in maize-and-Moses country, far from the gold mining centres, they were soon in trouble when their share of the loot dried up. Cranmer was imprisoned for robbing a church and Pitt was locked up for dealing in pornography. Detectives tracked them to Bloemfontein but, before they could retrieve Cranmer, he escaped from prison and was never again seen. Pitt was extradited and, as feared by McLoughlin, turned state's evidence. She was the leading witness for the prosecution at the trial held in June 1895. Throughout the proceedings she attempted to protect her lover, Cranmer, by heaping responsibility for the violence on Harding and Whelan; to the point where the judge did not believe her. She was just as careful not to mention the role of the state's leading suspect.[45] But she had little cause for concern. McLoughlin and McCann were both missing.

Possibly the biggest loser of all was Tommy Whelan. Without McLoughlin around to oversee the distribution of the loot he was left, like a stray dog behind a butcher shop, to whimper for a share – any share. Thrown a bone so small that he could drink his way through it within hours, he was then betrayed by Lillian Pitt. She portrayed him as the major beneficiary of the robbery, and despite the judge cautioning the jury about her evidence, Whelan was found guilty and sentenced to six months with hard labour. So pathetic a prisoner was he that, barely half way through the sentence, his friendly Irish gaoler, Thomas Menton, felt obliged to support an appeal to the State President for a remission of sentence, which was swiftly denied.[46]

The arrest of Harding and the others left Trimble hopeful that he might yet be able to catch the Big One. But he was fishing in a mirage. Days after the robbery there was no sign of McLoughlin or McCann. This time, shunning the malaria-free western route, the Trickster had risked the rainy season and gone east before eventually turning north, toward Makhado's fortress.[47] He and McCann had a huge start on their tracker. Two weeks later Hamilton picked up the scent at Witklippen, in the eastern Transvaal. Days earlier it had already been reliably reported that McLoughlin was with Makhado, in Vendaland, and despite the crossings on the Limpopo being carefully watched, McCann was soon over the border.[48]

When McCann was eventually tracked, north of the Limpopo, he continued to benefit from the aura of fear that surrounded McLoughlin. Days after the trial in the Circuit Court ended, he was arrested in Rhodesia and extradited south. He then spent week upon week languishing in the Krugersdorp gaol as an awaiting trial prisoner. With the state unable to persuade Simpson or any of the gang members to turn against McCann, he was set free, late in August. Shooting Stevenson did not guarantee honour among thieves, but it clearly concentrated the mind.[49]

★ ★ ★

In Pretoria, Detective Ueckermann, leaning on Harding, broke the news that McLoughlin was bound for Delagoa Bay.[50] He was, but it would not be easy tracking him. As he left Vendaland there was disturbing news from the east coast. Ronga chieftains who had been at loggerheads with one another for some time had turned on the Portuguese colonisers and Lourenço Marques was in a virtual state of siege.[51] As when he had entered Matabeleland 12 months earlier, McLoughlin was going to have to negotiate his way through the countryside at a time when the embers of war were still glowing. As ever, his weary body tagged on behind a mind that was still floating through a dream world without frontiers.

He slipped into Lourenço Marques at the beginning of the third week of February 1895, secure in the knowledge that there was no extradition treaty between Portugal and the South African Republic. He posed a serious problem for any would-be pursuers. Delagoa Bay looked up and down Africa's extensive eastern coastline and stared out across an enormous arc of the Indian Ocean. There was no way of knowing what he would do next. Would he stay in town, head for Australia, the Far East or the United States, or take the northern or southern route back to England?

He knew his way around the port all too well. At a time of heightened racial tension, a smattering of the vernacular acquired during his time as a navvy in the bay helped him find a place to stay. He moved into some rooms behind Crawford's Berea Hotel which he shared with black workers. Trimble knew that race had never been a barrier to his moving about southern Africa. The detective sent out 'coloured spies' to scour the town's backwaters for a one-armed man, but their progress was surprisingly slow.[52]

McLoughlin was in Lourenço Marques for about three weeks. He spent the time reading every English-language newspaper he could lay his hands on so as to catch up on any news about his supposed movements. Now and then he ventured out for a drink at a canteen where he would not attract too much attention. But most of the time was spent thinking about his choice of destination and how to reach it without leaving a paper trail. After dark he slipped down to the water-front, surveying the dhows, sailing ships and steamers in harbour. A former Jack Tar himself, he had no trouble talking to sailors and finding out where they had come from or where they were bound for. He was, or so it seemed, well on course.[53]

There was one minor alarm. A few days before he was due to leave, Robert Ferguson and a sidekick, 'Chinaman' Woolf, suddenly showed up. McLoughlin was briefly worried when they popped up in various bars around town but it did not take long to work out that they were not interested in him. They were there on business of a sort that he understood only too well – arranging for the shipping of gold amalgam stolen on the Witwatersrand.[54]

Trimble, in the meantime, was making a frantic effort to persuade the Governor of Lourenço Marques to make an exception and agree to McLoughlin being extradited on a charge of murder, But it was too late; his spies told him that the fugitive had probably already left town. In the second week of March 1895, it was rumoured in Pretoria that Jack McLoughlin, shunning every modern steamship in the harbour, had slipped out unseen aboard a sailing vessel, bound for an unknown port. It was a fitting departure for a sailor-soldier, a man at home on sea or land.[55]

★　★　★

Back on the Witwatersrand, the one-armed fugitive and his gang had left a remarkable, lingering legacy that was to feed into momentous events later that year and, ultimately, into the coming of the South African War of 1899–1902. No man and no criminal gang had done more than McLoughlin and the Irish Brigade and its criminal off-shoots to influence the establishment, focus and staffing profile of the Johannesburg police force.

It was the invasion of the settlement by the Irish Brigade, in February 1888, that had led to the town's first 'moral panic', the creation of a 'detective department' and the appointment of Robert Ferguson as 'Chief Detective'. And it was Jack McLoughlin who had brought him down, in January 1895. In much the same way, the execution of Stevenson set in train a sequence of events that were without parallel in the history of Johannesburg. Within days of the shooting three other white men were murdered and a nervous public sensed an increase in the number of assaults by black men on white women.[56] Citizens and state alike went into spasm. In mid-February a new Commissioner of Police was appointed and, just two weeks later, it was announced that 60 more Zarps were to be deployed in Johannesburg. And, in May 1895, a commission of enquiry into the Detective Department sat which touched on Ferguson's ineptitude and McLoughlin's career.[57]

The shooting at the Red Lion, the dinner at Rosenthal's, the Champ D'Or Robbery and Jack McLoughlin's escape – which remained officially unconfirmed – all fed into streams of private fear and torrents of public outrage. *The Star* suggested that:

> It is a scandal that, after fourteen years of national life, the extradition laws of the Republic should still be in a condition of hopeless chaos. To this day it is theoretically impossible to arrest a man who, having committed a crime on the north-eastern border of the Transvaal, walks a hundred yards and finds himself in Portuguese territory.[58]

Many believed that McLoughlin was still in hiding in town. It contributed to a run on gun shops, to the point where it became almost impossible to buy the weapons of choice – Colt 45 or Smith & Wesson revolvers.[59] In the first week of March, Jack Casey, a part-time barman at an outlet near the Langlaagte Mine, was found murdered. Casey's friends claimed that he had been collecting information about the Champ D'Or safe robbers in the hope of claiming the reward for its outlaw leader and *The Star* did not hesitate to close the gap in its readers' minds, suggesting that 'some members of the gang, or friends of the desperadoes, hearing of the menace to their liberty, decided, in the expressive language of their kind, to "blot him out".'[60]

Public panic, fanned by ideological winds emanating from the mine owners' mouthpieces, set the stage for the formation of a Vigilance Committee, as it had back in 1888.[61] The meeting, held on 8 March, was chaired by Lionel Phillips, Chairman of the Chamber of Mines. In retrospect, it can be seen how the public mood at the time fed into the perceptions of certain mine owners, including Phillips, that the Kruger state was sufficiently weak for them to contemplate an attempt at a *coup d'état* backed by white miners.

Some of the thinking that lay behind the planning of the Jameson Raid had its origins in gold amalgam thefts perpetrated by the McLoughlin gang and the weakness of the state as exposed by the shootings at the Red Lion.[62]

As he sailed out of Delagoa Bay, Jack McLoughlin had no or little appreciation of the deeper inroads that he had made into southern African society. Instead, he had reason to contemplate some of the personal costs his career had exacted from those around him. It was as if a curse, or at the very least, then serious misfortune, seemed to be following him ever more closely. Three men – O'Brien, Stevenson and Hadji Mustaffa – were dead. Higgins and Simpson had both narrowly escaped death and others including friends like Harding and Whelan were doing time. Perhaps he was grateful that it was all behind him. But was it? Why, in moments of deeper reflection, did the image of the guard from the State Artillery on the day of his release from the Visagie Street prison always come to mind? It was Matthew de Beer who had said that it was not yet farewell, only *tot siens*.

CHAPTER EIGHTEEN

❦

The Reality of Failure

INDIA
— 1895 —

We do not know, in most cases, how far social failure and success are due to heredity, and how far to environment. But environment is the easier of the two to improve.

JBS HALDANE

'Having confidence in myself', as he put it, had become central to McLoughlin after he lost his arm. Like most men, his self-esteem was calibrated, in part, by his standing among his peer group. But the execution of Stevenson had destroyed the conduit linking his self-perception to the opinions of his cohort, giving rise to an insoluble problem. In order to live with himself, he had had to execute a police informer who had placed his own liberty above that of the gang's members, but, by doing so and then fleeing, he had cut himself off from those on whose approval he relied. In a world filled with paradoxes, he had done an honourable thing, but having left, he was condemned to a social death.

With the exception of Tommy – already back in Australia – he was alone in the world. As a fugitive from justice he was an itinerant, a man of no fixed abode, a man forced to conceal his true identity and to deny his past. He was someone who had mortgaged his future to hubris and need-ed to stay on the move. Having chosen the disorientation that came with exile, he was forced to forfeit the social compass that all men need – the one that links time and places past to the present and the foreseeable future.

But by abandoning the Witwatersrand he had also done something far more serious, something potentially fatal. He had turned his back on Johannesburg, a place barely out of its swaddling clothes. It was a rough-and-ready frontier town, one in which ordinary men's notions of right and wrong – especially in cases of murder – spoke to authority about justice and power in male, populist, tones. The mere efflux of time meant that, at some time in the future, any charge of murder would resonate differently in a city where a more settled social order was built around family life. The unwritten code of masculinity that had informed his actions at the Red Lion that night stood a better chance of speaking to 'natural justice' if they were rooted in the appropriate context of time and place. Any explanation as to why it had been necessary to execute Stevenson was more likely to be understood if it were presented beneath a battered corrugated-iron roof of a mining town than if it were to be heard by a middle-class jury in the hallowed halls of justice. For justice to prevail the accused had to be arraigned and tried in his own epoch, by peers who understood the ethos and hidden ideological contours of everyday life. Justice delayed, as the adage has it, is justice denied. By choosing to disappear into the margins of the Indian Ocean world, he was cocking a snook at the logic of history. It was risky. In the short term it might drag out his social death, but, in the longer run, it might ensure a short and nasty demise at the hands of the state executioner.

At one level, he understood that, as a person wanted for the murder of two men, he no longer had a claim to a public persona or a truthful past, let alone one built around crime in several countries. Yet, for all that, it was difficult coming to terms with the new realities. The choice of India as a place of refuge was born of a compromise. On the one hand, he had to avoid the colonies of settlement of the southern oceans – Australia, New Zealand and the Straits – places where the Imperial Eye, in the shape of its governors-general, police, press and the telegraph – swept across horizons with increasing regularity to take in and control a sprawling British world.

On the other, he wished to exploit his talent for safe-blasting in a setting that would sustain him when the Krugersdorp funds were exhausted. He also wanted the opportunity to accumulate the even greater sums he would need once the Eye had tired and his choice of destinations widened. For that to happen he needed access to English-speakers, men with military backgrounds, who had nothing to lose; men who could be moulded into a unit. More importantly, he needed access to gold mines. From the little he had heard when the *Albatross* had called in at Bombay in 1881, and the many positive things that Jack McCann had told him about regimental life on the subcontinent, south-central India had much to offer.

It is uncertain when exactly – let alone whether – he disembarked at Bombay, on the western Malabar Coast, or whether he left the vessel at Madras, on the Coromandel coast, in the east. From the little that *is* known, it would seem that it was in late April, perhaps early May of 1895 that he stepped ashore, probably in Bombay, a port that he was not only familiar with from his earlier visit, but one that was still a natural point of exit from the age-old trans-oceanic monsoon trade routes that linked India to the south-eastern coast of Africa. Gold had once found its way to India from the hand-dug pits of central-southern Africa via Sofala. It added to the irony that it was now a robber from the south who was intent on reliev-ing India of some of the gold from its own ancient workings that had been rejuvenated by recent 'discoveries'. He was a modern thief but some of the gold he hankered after was drawn from sites that were thousands of years old. In the eighteenth century, pirates had roamed the Indian Ocean in search of gold wherever they found it, but by the late nineteenth century it was some of the newly dispossessed from the industrial world who criss-crossed the globe by steamship to secure the precious metal at 'new' points of production.

The Princely State of Mysore, as created by the British in 1799, was a good destination for an amalgam-thief and murderer on the run.[1] Located in the present-day province of Karnataka, in the south of the country, Mysore lay beyond easy diplomatic reach of the South African Republic and, even if the Kruger government somehow did manage to obtain the support of the British, a request for extradition from a quasi-independent Indian state would necessitate considerable political effort. Carved out of the older and once even more extensive Muslim Kingdom of Mysore, the princely state was, after 1881, ruled indirectly by a British surrogate, the Maharaja, and after 1894 by a regent drawn from the prestigious Hindu Wodeyar family.[2]

Situated for the most part along the Deccan Plateau, with its more congenial climate, the princely state's once thriving indigenous textile industries had declined in importance during the late nineteenth century just as surely as Liverpool and Manchester's had grown to dominate the production of cheap cotton fabric for developing international markets. In the south-west the city of Mysore and, to the north-east of it, Bangalore – the administrative centre – remained significant sites of local economic focus. But in the 1870s a new source of revenue for the state's coffers had emerged at the eastern extremity of the plateau, in the slowly reviving Kolar goldfields. The timing of the 'discovery' was hardly fortuitous; it was part of a global search for new sources of the metal as the gold standard emerged as the primary mechanism for underwriting world trade.

In 1871, Michael Lavalle, an Irish soldier who had turned himself into a civil engineer after being bewitched by the yellow metal in New Zealand, was granted the exclusive right to prospect for gold around Kolar. Pre-colonial diggings abandoned because of flooding had, over the past 70 years, been worked intermittently with the help of steam pumps that were becoming increasingly efficient. The first attempt to mine Kolar gold on a fully industrial scale had, however, collapsed in the early 1880s for want of working capital and lack of insight into the nature of the ore-holding body. The discovery of the new 'Champion Lode', in 1885, changed everything.

Within months of finding the new lode the original mining concession was acquired by John Taylor & Son in the City. Under their financial management, several deep-level shafts were sunk, including those belonging to the Balaghat, Champion Reef, Mysore, Nundydroog and Oorgaum Companies. These new ventures, spread over 70 square miles, paid royalties to the princely state and formed part of a state-within-a-state for legal purposes. They proved to be an unparalleled success. Between 1884 and 1907, the output of the mines rose to realise gold worth close on £10 million, allowing over £5 million to be paid in dividends. By 1894, the underground workforce consisted of over 7 000 workers; at its height in 1907 the Kolar goldfields employed close on 30 000 workers. McLoughlin's timing was perfect. When he arrived there, in 1895, the industry was enjoying its most successful year ever and was set on a expansionary trajectory that was to last at least a decade.[3]

He was, it seems, always well informed; when pressed by authorities his knowledge of the world of mining was sufficiently extensive for him to be able to persuade the police, as he had on the Rand, that he was a miner by profession. The fact that he had only one arm added to the plausibility of the story in an era marked by horrific mining accidents and helped account for his otherwise puzzling presence around mine properties. But he was no miner; he was a professional thief.

For the dedicated safe-lifter, safe-blaster and gold thief to succeed required more than a basic understanding of the economics, geography and technology of the mining industry. He needed to have a keen appreciation of the class, ethnic composition and culture of the labour force as a whole, and understand how and where the men were deployed in the mining and refining processes. He also had to have a 'feel' for ways in which the economic problems, personal proclivities and social fracture lines amongst the miners – as manifested in more relaxed off-the-job settings – might enable him to move in and recruit promising individuals for the disciplined teamwork that marked out organised crime. Moreover, he had to be certain that any proceeds from the wholesale theft of gold could be safely disposed of through a secure and reliable chain of retailers made up of goldsmiths, jewellers or money-lenders who were often drawn from an unfamiliar and therefore 'untrustworthy' ethnic stratum. There was more to his business than met the eye. Meeting all these requirements was difficult enough in the Anglophone British colonies such as Australia, New Zealand or southern Africa. In India, where a multiplicity of classes, cultures and ethnic groupings rendered a tiny handful of transient Europeans a subject for demographic mockery, it proved nigh impossible.

Given the climate and undulating nature of the countryside, British residents were occasionally lulled into describing the Kolar goldfields as 'Little England'. It was wishful thinking. Most of the white managerial staff were 'pukka' English but the vast majority of the miners living in bungalows along the more elevated landscaped parts of the mine properties were

Celts, Cornish 'hard-rock' men, and the rest Italians. Immediately below the Europeans, on an aristocratic ladder of colour and social status constructed largely by the industry itself, stood numerous Anglo-Indians – the mixed-race human outcomes of countless cultural collisions between the sexes that were seldom forged from a basis of equality. On the lowest rung stood semi- and unskilled workers drawn from the ranks of the indigenous population from the surrounding provinces of Karnataka, Andhra Pradesh and Tamil Nadu. They occupied huts laid out along ethnically divided 'lines' as determined by the management. As elsewhere in the world it was the locals – the natives of Mysore – who most fiercely resisted the demand for cheap labour to undertake dangerous work.[4]

The pool of indigenous labour, divided unequally between those hired by outside contractors and used for specialised operations underground, and those employed by the companies themselves, was extremely culturally diverse. Many of the least skilled workers were Adi Dravidas – 'untouchables' – some of whom had sought to avoid their caste-fate by converting to Buddhism or Christianity and who had been recruited by unscrupulous touts operating in the drought-prone Arcot region of Tamil Nadu. Skilled work, including blasting and carpentry, was undertaken by 'Maplahs and Malayalees', the latter from Kerala. And, as in other parts of the labour-repressive domains of imperial mining, it was men of militant disposition, those drawn from groups with a warrior tradition – 'Muslims and Punjabis' from the north – who were deputed to oversee the 'ward and watch establishments' of a large security apparatus.[5] McLoughlin would have understood divisions of these types from his experience on the Rand.

The social universe of the Indian labouring poor also manifested one or two other features that any working-class Mancunian would have recognised. *Sowcars*, short-term money-lenders, provided cash-strapped unskilled labourers with credit at rates so exorbitant that many workers were, in effect, locked into a system of debt-slavery that indirectly benefited the mine owners. Underground gang foremen, *maistries,* skilled workers and shopkeepers were alternative sources of credit for the working poor.[6] Yet more money-suckers of a type familiar to the readers of *Germinal* were to be found around mines in the usual guises and numbers. Liquor-sellers worked out of the grog or 'toddy' shops and prostitutes in small brothels.[7]

But the pathologies of extreme poverty generate their own antibodies, most frequently through crimes against property. The systematic theft of mine stores and supplies, especially small items such as candles that could be put to use by the workers or sold to those in even greater need, was an everyday occurrence. McLoughlin, however, was interested only in dynamite and gold; items that might help support his lifestyle. There was no shortage of dynamite. Despite a semi-private police force of nearly 200 men and Magistrates who were inclined to guard the quasi-independent legal status of their courts quite fiercely, mines on the Kolar goldfields lost significant quantities of explosives through theft each year.[8]

By March 1895, sufficient dynamite of murky provenance was being conveyed on public transport systems to warrant the government issuing a notice 'recommending' that explosives not be allowed aboard boats, carriages or trains carrying fee-paying passengers.[9] As in Rhodesia, which he had passed through the previous year, indigenous workers sometimes used dynamite for 'fishing'. It was a practice that he was well aware of: months later, when found in possession of dynamite in New Zealand, he told the Magistrate that he had used the explosive for fishing in India. Indeed, it was entirely probable that the dynamite he was by then lugging around with him had come from half a world away – from the Kolar mines.[10]

If so, it underlined the fact that in India, quite unlike the early Witwatersrand, dynamite was never central to gold theft. In Johannesburg, a few gangs of immigrant whites stole huge quantities of gold from safes, but in India hundreds of indigenous workers purloined minute quantities of the yellow metal from all along the production line. In Kolar, right from the advent of modern mining in the early 1880s, labourers appropriated anything from gold-bearing ore through to amalgam in tiny amounts. They waited until they had accumulated marketable quantities before disposing of them through the scores of indigenous goldsmiths and jewellers to be found throughout the fields. Like African labourers who secreted gems about their person in the diamond mines of southern Africa, Indian workers, too, were ordered to bend over, 'to see if gold was stuffed into the arse'.[11]

It was hardly surprising then that, in Kolar, there was no recorded instance of a gold heist being perpetrated by armed Europeans intent on safe-lifting and safe-blasting to acquire gold or amalgam. The way the precious metal occurred, the nature of the production and refining processes, all militated against it. So, too, did the scale of theft perpetrated by an indigenous working class that enjoyed privileged cultural and linguistic access to retail purchasers of most illicitly acquired gold. Gold theft did gather momentum during the time that McLoughlin was in Mysore, however. In 1897, months after he had left, the companies persuaded the princely authorities to pass the repressive Mysore Mine Regulations, containing provisions designed to curb the 'leakage' of gold.[12] But Bangalore was no frontier settlement and the Kolar goldfield was surrounded by a centuries-old indigenous industry.

★ ★ ★

With little Krugersdorp cash left to draw on after the long haul across the western Indian Ocean and without access to an ethnic or criminal network capable of sustaining him through lean times, McLoughlin was soon locked into a downward spiral. The appeal of cheap liquor stores owned by locals may not have helped.[13] His status as a 'vagrant' or 'mean white' – as rootless English-speaking Europeans in both India and the American South were sometimes referred to – may have been miserable, but not unique. After the Napoleonic Wars each decade saw a significant number of down-and-out adventurers, former sailors or soldiers and unskilled labourers abandoning ships in Indian ports to try their luck on the subcontinent. Most took their chances in Bombay, Calcutta or Madras; others wandered farther afield.[14]

By the mid-nineteenth century, however, this relatively free and easy tolerance of the presence of low-class whites by officialdom began to give way to a more defined attitude and interventionist mode on the part of the emerging state. There were two major reasons for this. First, after the Great Revolt of 1857, the administration not only strengthened its military profile, but also became more sensitive to the need to enhance and protect the image of the thinly spread representatives of the ruling race across a vast

country populated by millions of 'others'. Act 21 of 1869, the European
Vagrancy Act, allowed for the provision of temporary shelter for the many
down-and-out whites who would also be assisted in their attempts to find
employment.

Second, after the opening of the Suez Canal in 1869, and the growing
deployment of steamships over the decades that followed, India's financial
fortunes became more firmly integrated not only into an Indian Ocean
Basin in which time and distance were shrinking, but also into the greater
global economy. Precious metal discoveries in various parts of Australasia
in the 1850s, followed by first diamonds in 1870, and then huge gold
deposits in South Africa, in the 1880s, helped to prime the economies
of the far south and laid down the first flimsy threads of a hemisphere-
wide labour market for skilled and semi-skilled Anglophone workers.[15]
The counter-eddies triggered by these movements brought both more
artisanal skills and more of Europe's poor to India's shores. When the
Vagrancy Act, which already made provision for the voluntary deportation of destitute whites, was amended in 1874, it brought growing numbers of 'Americans, Australians, Continental Europeans as well as white
South Africans under its purview'.[16]

The modest flows of white labour across the southern hemisphere, including a trickle into India, remained largely unregulated by states as yet to
be convinced of the need for passports in an imperial world insistent on 'free
trade'.[17] But it also brought with it some unintended consequences for governments and benefits for the criminal classes – who, as ever, were among
the first to embrace the opportunity of increased mobility via the railways
and steamships. Any increase in the number of transient skilled English-
speaking workers in large cities such as Bombay, Calcutta and Madras
provided antisocial elements, fugitives from justice and 'undesirables' with
some of the social cover needed for criminal activities in an otherwise alien
setting. The fact that India was *not* a colony of European settlement and
therefore not fully integrated into the wider empire in administrative terms
meant that there was no easy way of determining the criminal antecedents
of unwanted whites arriving on the subcontinent.[18] McLoughlin may have
badly misread the potential of the Kolar fields, but it would not have taken

him long to figure out that the best way of recovering his position was by obtaining a state-subsidised passage out of India and back into the realms of the expanding southern Anglophone world.[19]

By the 1890s, many, perhaps most large cities in India had a small but well-established number of charities and state institutions seeking to relieve the everyday plight of rootless white men stranded on the subcontinent. It was in the great urban encrustations of Bombay and Calcutta, however, that 'mean whites' and vagrants stood the best chance of being seen by the authorities as constituting an embarrassment to the ruling class and being voluntarily deported 'home'. For the small minority wishing to reach African shores and the far larger numbers hoping to return to Europe via Suez, the west-facing port of Bombay was the obvious place to make for.[20]

Calcutta, however, had long been an interim destination for that unloved rag-bag of European humanity that saw a future of sorts for itself in India, the Far East or further south and east where the Indian Ocean Basin gave way to the great watery domain of the Pacific. This latter circuit had acquired added importance and a new momentum after the Great Revolt when the revamped Indian army developed a seemingly insatiable appetite for sturdy mounts drawn from the antipodes. After 1857, large numbers of horses known as 'Walers' were imported from New South Wales and New Zealand, attended to on the long sea passage north by adventurous or financially hard-pressed young white grooms who at best were semi-skilled. Once the horses had been delivered to ports in India, however, many of these grooms, believing that it would improve their lot in life, deserted their positions only to find that decent employment and an acceptable lifestyle was just as elusive in India as it had been back in the antipodes, thus giving rise to a new counter-current of deportations home.[21]

For McLoughlin, intent on staging a retreat from the goldfields via Madras in the hope of eventually being deported from Calcutta in order to link up with brother Tommy in Australia, these official policies and practices posed a few formidable challenges. Vagrants in Madras and the southern provinces of India were often either sent to Bombay, or voluntarily made their way there, because it made the cost of deportation to Europe significantly cheaper and more convenient for the administration than from east-coast cities.[22] If McLoughlin, travelling under the assumed name of 'Thomas Kenny', was to avoid being sent to Bombay he had to elude the attention of officials in Madras and Hyderabad while heading north for Calcutta.[23]

Moving about for the first time without so much as even a first name to hint at his true identity, let alone where he hailed from, he used the railway to haul him to West Bengal and got there in short order. Indeed, he may have been on the banks of the Hooghly as early as the first week of July 1895, where, although six months and many thousands of miles away from Johannesburg, he would have felt at home among the many dissolute ex-sailors.[24] A one-armed man, destitute and dishevelled, offered the police a tale plausible enough for them to agree to recommend his deportation.

'Home,' he told the authorities on the basis of information acquired first-hand during his loop through Australia in 1882–85, was Melbourne. As the month of July drew to a close, the Commissioner of Police wrote to the Department of Finance, asking that the latter underwrite the cost of sending Thomas Kenny back to his country of origin. The bureaucrats, easily persuaded, agreed to cover the cost of a passage that would not exceed 150 rupees and additional expenditure amounting to 26 rupees. The latter included the price of a new suit of clothing and – rather alarmingly for 'Mr Kenny' – a photograph for the official record. Although not much interested in the criminal antecedents of those they were called upon to deport, wary clerks were keen to avoid having the exercise or expense repeated down the line.[25]

On Wednesday morning, 31 July 1895, Thomas Kenny, decked out in a smart new outfit notable for a pair of white trousers of the type that he preferred, and clutching a small cloth bag containing a few personal items, was escorted to the dockside by a policeman. From time spent in the navy he had learnt to expect little from the authorities and had steeled himself for a long and potentially uncomfortable voyage on some old tub spluttering south. He had no idea what route the ship would be following to Melbourne and grew ever more resigned when the constable informed him that the ship was on charter and set to return to India carrying a cargo of horses.

As they made their way along the banks of the brown and muddied Hooghly countless dock workers – like a small army of ants around the remains of an earthworm they were intent on ripping apart and devouring – scurried about emptying a line of vessels. The innards were then conveyed to adjacent warehouses amidst much chattering. He enjoyed the stroll and the idea of a man 'wanted for murder' being seen off by the police as he embarked on a voyage paid for by the state to a port of his choice. The mounting sense of pleasure was compounded when they halted beside a modern cargo steamer gleaming so brightly that, for a second or two, he may have imagined the smell of fresh paint rising above the stench of the harbour waters. It was magnificent.

They mounted the gangplank, boarded the *Mount Sirion,* and the constable introduced 'Mr Kenny' to a member of the crew who made the passenger's presence and destination known to the captain. Kenny was not alone. There were a few other passengers, including a woman and child, but the captain was comfortable with a man who, long before the misfortune of losing a limb, had himself been a sailor. The officers were, almost to a man, English; the rest of the crew – as was to be expected – Indian Lascars.

Lifted by the rising tide, the *Mount Sirion* cast off and slid away down the Hooghly, making her way slowly east, towards one of the many sandy mouths of the great Ganges. At 5.00 pm the following afternoon, with the sun showing signs of doubting whether or not it should linger, the vessel cleared the Sundarbans where the river, exhausted by its long journey to the sea, finally collapsed into the Bay of Bengal.[26] On deck, with the failed experience of India and Kolar behind him, 'Mr Kenny' sensed the possibilities of a whole new world opening up as the *Mount Sirion* started shifting and swaying to the rhythm of the open ocean. The wind picked up and he retreated to his cabin below. He eased open the door to the locker, removed the cloth bag, opened it and then rummaged around to find the principal tool of his trade. Satisfied that the dynamite was there, he stowed it away snugly, up against the ship's hull. He remained convinced that they were in for a fine voyage and he was ready to start his new life.

CHAPTER NINETEEN

ᘓᘓᘓ

The Imperial Eye Averted

AUCKLAND, NEW ZEALAND
— 1895–1896 —

The worse the passage the more welcome the port.

THOMAS FULLER

E ven hardened old shipping correspondents, men long past their prime
and reduced to reporting 'arrivals and departures', were impressed by
the new cargo steamer. Perched on bar-stools around the south-western
rim of the Pacific, the hacks were full of praise for a vessel still acquiring its primary layer of salted skin. 'A fine specimen of the modern cargo
steamer,' they opined. The 4 000 ton *Mount Sirion* had been laid down in
the yards of Workman, Clarke & Co in Belfast, for the firm of Smith &
Savage of Glasgow, and launched in March 1895.[1] Fitted with retractable
masts that allowed for easy passage along the Manchester Canal, the vessel
was set to follow an everyday tramping circuit around the margins of the
Irish and North Seas. But then, quite unexpectedly, it was chartered by the
Union Steamship Company which, in turn, was responding to the needs of
Scottish merchants on the banks of the Hooghly.

With warehouses the size of castles – several of which still grace what
is now the Kolkota waterfront – the Scots and Union Company sensed an
opportunity for extending trade between India and the antipodes. Any ship
bringing horses into the country for the army, from ports in Australasia,

could turn under-utilised space on the outward run to profit by hauling south bulk cargoes of castor oil, jute bags and tea. The *Mount Sirion* was bound for Singapore, Auckland and Lyttelton, in New Zealand, and then onward to Melbourne and Sydney to collect Walers for the round voyage back to India when the police eased McLoughlin aboard the vessel in bustling Calcutta.

Under the command of Captain CJ Richardson, the ship set a south-easterly course for its maiden voyage into Indian and Pacific waters. Although it was in no hurry, McLoughlin was impressed by a state-of-the-art steamer that consumed 18 tons of coal a day and was capable of maintaining a speed that, even in heavy going, seldom fell below 10 knots. Enjoying reasonably good but far from outstanding weather, the *Mount Sirion* was made to huff and puff her way across the Bay of Bengal before heading due south to make port in a bit less than a week.

The vessel was unknown in Singapore, on an unfamiliar run, and its imminent arrival failed to raise eyebrows among the city's larger and most successful wholesalers. Alarmed by the lack of interest, the ship's agents had, just days before, rushed to place an advertisement in the newspaper in the hope of drumming up business.[2] The response was disappointing. 'Mr Kenny', wary of getting into trouble in the port where he had jumped a naval ship more than a decade earlier, disembarked for a short tour through the city's *demi-monde* as three more passengers joined the ship. The hoped-for bulk cargo, however, failed to materialise, contributing to a surprisingly short turnaround.[3]

He avoided the devil that had tempted him since his youth and made it back to the quayside with time to spare. It was a relief to be back on board and know that he had evaded police attention. It was probably as well that he did not know it but, on 8 August, the same day that the *Mount Sirion* slipped out of Singapore for Auckland, Jack McCann – arrested in Salisbury, Rhodesia – was moved to the border town of Palaype under armed escort to be handed over to Kruger's police, who wanted him to stand trial for his part in the Champ D'Or robbery.[4] The Imperial Eye might not have caught sight of McLoughlin in the Straits Settlement underworld, but it was out there, always scanning the wider world for him.

He was pleased to be back at sea and beyond the immediate reach of the law; Captain Richardson and his senior officer were less enthused with the return to open waters. Within hours of entering the Java Sea and setting course for Thursday Island, at the northern tip of Australia, the ship encountered more of the same 'strong winds and adverse currents' that had been hampering her progress ever since clearing the Sundarbans. The steamer took a full 11 days to reach the Island and two more to draw abreast of Cooktown on the tropical coast of north-eastern Queensland. 'Kenny' took it all in from the deck, not knowing that, years later, it would become the shoreline that he hated more than any other he had encountered.[5] It truly was a Fatal Shore.

Beyond Cooktown, the *Mount Sirion* veered south south-east, insisting on the direct route to Auckland. But not even the change in course could shake off the conditions hampering the steamer's progress. The ship's wide-open furnace door – like the mouth of a schoolboy in a pantry stuffing his mouth at half-term – gobbled coal in embarrassing quantities as the vessel battled the wind and swell. Richardson hoped that the Pacific would live up to its name as they drew closer to New Zealand's North Island but, instead of abating, the weather grew worse after they rounded Cape Brett on 29 August. The closing stages of the 7 000-mile run south were marked by a strong north-easterly gale with driving rain reducing visibility in notoriously treacherous coastal waters.[6]

The *Mount Sirion* was not the only vessel struggling to find her way to the safety of Auckland through stormy weather. Some way off, to the northeast, making its way down from Portland and San Diego, another steamer, the SS *Rathdown,* began listing when her cargo shifted.[7] It was one of the hazards of life at sea and, back on the *Mount Sirion*, 'Kenny' again made sure that the small canvas bag containing his detonators and five packets of dynamite was properly secured. Even hardened old salts like him found the storms in the Pacific sufficiently menacing and unpleasant to contemplate anew the meaning of life.

After a voyage that had taken him half-way around the world – albeit in two stages separated by several months – he had had enough. The prospect of several more weeks at sea before he could unpack the tools of his trade and resume something like the life he had grown used to was unthinkable.

The closer the ship got to port, the more Auckland appealed to him as a staging post on the longer journey Down Under. A stop-over could do no harm. On the *Rathdown* another sailor of Irish extraction, Butler Norris Wilkinson, was doing the same sum. With some back-pay due to him, Wilkinson resolved to enter Auckland with an open mind and see what happened. Busy ports made for easy onward berths.

In retrospect a few extraordinary things, things that usually rotated around the separate axes of chance and design, were about to happen. They are worth a moment's reflection. Chance, although not a frequent caller, is no stranger at the house of history. When it does call, it often walks through the door unannounced and in disguise. To bend a better-known phrase to our needs, somewhere out in the Pacific, a cormorant flapped its wings and set in motion a sequence of events that culminated in a gale blowing two refugees into the same small corner of the globe.

But precisely because it is uncertain as to how it will be received, chance often spreads its visits over years, if not decades. In Jack McLoughlin's case, however, it visited him on four separate occasions within just 24 months. Three times it brought with it misfortune in the unfamiliar guise of a gale, a blackbird and a newspaper posted to an unlikely recipient in a far-off country. Then, sensing that it may have overplayed its hand, it again intervened, this time to save his life when, amidst a fit of political petulance in Britain, it averted the Imperial Eye.

The *Mount Sirion* docked in Auckland at first light on 30 August and minutes later, 'Thomas Kenny' – the first name of his alias a nod in the direction of his antipodean brother – made his way carefully down the gangway clutching a few worldly possessions in his one natural hand.[8] Dragging the assumed moniker along behind him, he set about rediscovering as much of his identity as possible by orientating himself amidst the harbour-side cluster of bars, boarding houses, chop shops, and missions-to-seamen fishing for the souls of any drunks drifting by.

He reclaimed part of his self by presenting himself as 'John Dell'. It was, like everything in his life now, a messy part of a shrunken universe. It did, however, offer more than psychological balm; it had a few useful applications. If someone from his past suddenly popped up in the local underworld, recognised him and blurted out 'Hello John', he wouldn't have to feign ignorance. 'John' sat easily with him and it would buy him time enough to come up with a suitable response. In his own mind, however, he would always be 'Jack' to the select few he trusted.

Reassuming part of his identity was only one of the challenges confronting him. Concealed snares, things known intuitively by insiders but hidden from the view of casual visitors, immigrants, or outsiders constituted a far more serious hazard. He had come of age in large and complex societies marked by significant differences in class, colour and cultural composition – variations that he learned to read and to shape to his own needs. Countries with diversified economies experiencing rapid growth offered professional thieves their best chances of success. India seemed as if it might meet the economic demands for organised crime but, in the end, had failed to meet some of the social requirements. New Zealand's agricultural economy, with modest commercial and industrial sectors in small towns that were largely culturally homogeneous, fell far short of what was required in almost all respects, including the social.

★   ★   ★

The uncovering of a few gold deposits in the mid-1850s had done little to stimulate New Zealand's pastoral economy, but in the 1860s more substantial finds triggered significant rushes in Otago and on the west coast of South Island. Partially primed, but hardly dependent on mineral discoveries for economic progress, a decade of prosperity had followed.[9] The 1870s saw the development and consolidation of an overwhelmingly Anglophone and youthful immigrant community intent on avoiding most of the pitfalls of the old world and building what it saw as a 'Better Britain'. Amidst the spectacular natural beauty of an earthly paradise, a society characterised by easy friendships, communal cohesion, group solidarity and egalitarian values quickly took shape.[10] But these social virtues came under strain when the economy experienced a downturn in the late 1880s and struggled to recover momentum in the mid-1890s.[11]

The gold rushes unleashed drunkenness and violence on a scale that resonated with most frontier societies. But the far broader contours of an agricultural economy and rural society meant that the overall crime rate in the nineteenth century remained relatively low in a state that was also tightly policed. And yet, as has been argued by one scholar, there was a 'dark side' to this new 'paradise'. The relentless pursuit of communal cohesion and social conformity made for a disproportionately high rate of incarceration for those perceived as being alien or antisocial, those found to be out of place without good reason, or those indulging in petty crimes.[12] Vagrancy accounted for a third of all crime in New Zealand in the 1870s, and although conviction rates fell thereafter, they remained unusually high through most of the 1890s.[13] Drunkenness accounted for a third of 'crime' in the 1880s, and rose after 1893 as the island settlers toyed with the idea of prohibition. By the end of the 1890s, public intoxication accounted for almost half of a very small country's prison population.[14]

When McLoughlin got to the North Island, in 1895, social intolerance was no longer confined to drunkenness and vagrancy as manifested in the behaviour of eccentrics or itinerants of both sexes. More generalised concerns were being expressed about the need to improve 'social hygiene' and to expel that which was 'alien and unwanted'. Christians in New Zealand, like others spread across the English-speaking world, displayed increasing hostility to minority groups, including those few 'heathen' Chinese still to be found working on the older gold diggings.[15]

It was within these thickets of fear and prejudice that 'John Dell' was most likely to encounter the hidden dangers that the society posed for an impecunious one-armed man. It was not that the police were unconcerned about burglars, safe-lifters or fugitives, but that they were even more attuned to looking for drunks, hobos, tramps, itinerant labourers or 'swaggers', and vagrants. It was what was *manifest* about his appearance, prosthesis, dress, demeanour and the fact that he was of no fixed abode that was more likely to get the attention of the constabulary than what was *hidden* – his criminal record, expertise and the tools of his trade.[16] It is chance that nudges the fly towards the spider, but it is the design of the web that snares the prey.

Below 35 degrees south, spring is in no hurry to appear. He spent

September and much of October drifting, cadging drinks, living from hand to mouth and seeing off the last of winter's chill. He waited for the sun's strength to return before exploring inner Auckland for suitable targets and the cover of cold dark nights to stage a few burglaries and thefts capable of keeping body and soul together. It took time but, by early November, he had assembled his kit for everyday work – seven skeleton keys, nine wire picklocks, a 'warding file' for shaping new keys, and several shirts and singlets that matched a pair of dark trousers. But the items he prized most remained stowed away in his canvas bag – a coil fuse, nine dynamite caps and the five packages of dynamite.[17] Burglary barely kept a man alive, safe-blasting allowed him to live.

He had identified a business with a large safe and been monitoring the premises over several weekends, but lacked a handyman partner to offset his physical disadvantage. It was frustrating but no candidate presented himself. Then, on the afternoon of 17 October, the *Rathdown*, in distress for weeks, eventually limped into port. The ship, bound for Liverpool when the cargo had shifted, was bound to have an Irishman aboard, some Lancastrians, possibly even a Mancunian or two.

He met an adventurous but naïve Irishman in a pub close by the Salvation Army Barracks, where he was dossing. It did not take long to discover that Butler Wilkinson could not help with a major job – that would require more time and planning if success was to be guaranteed. The *Rathdown*'s master, Captain Morrissey, was of the opinion that all that was needed was a brief stopover in Auckland. His ship could be reloaded, the cargo properly secured and the voyage resumed. But, wary of losing his crew to the delights of port after a troubled voyage, he took the precaution of making certain that any back-pay due to them was released in dribs and drabs. An unexpected shortage of cash left Wilkinson open to suggestions as to how to raise funds, but any good it did was negated by his belief that the *Rathdown* was about to sail.[18]

But the captain was wrong. To his dismay, Morrissey discovered that the damage was more extensive than initially surmised. Much of his cargo had been ruined by an inrush of seawater when the ship began listing, and the hull needed repairs that would keep the vessel in port for weeks.

McLoughlin watched as the *Rathdown* was dragged into a dry dock and cash-strapped seamen left marooned on the dockside. Each day Wilkinson became more inclined to get involved in a big job. The charismatic 'John Dell', confiding that his 'real name' was 'Tom Kenny', slowly reeled the sailor into his confidence.

Without the revolver that was *de rigueur* on the mining frontier, and keen to avoid unnecessary confrontations, McLoughlin decided that the project was best undertaken over a weekend night. A few days before it he went to Reynold's Cycle Shop and bought a few of the items he would need – a small lamp, a bottle of oil and a chisel for removing unwelcome bolts or locks encountered on any interleading doors. Around sunset on Saturday, 9 November, he left the docks and strolled up to Albert Park, which commanded an elevated view of the city and the harbour below it.

He entered the park on Bowen Street, near the synagogue, and made his way to a small building behind the shrubbery and iron fence that housed the public toilets. In the lavatory stall, he lifted a panel in the wooden floor to reveal a cavity beneath. He placed the skeleton keys and picklocks in the hole, along with the items bought at the bicycle shop, and replaced the panel. On the way out, he hid the canvas bag with the dynamite and its accessories in dense bush. He removed his prosthesis – the hand still covered by a glove – and stuffed it into a sack containing the rest of his paraphernalia along with a rug that could be used to drag a small safe. That bag, too, was stowed in the bushes. Back at the docks, he told Wilkinson what he had done and instructed him to appear at the toilets at half-past nine on the following evening.

Sunday morning saw a bright summer's day across the North Island – any boy's delight. Martin Grace and a few friends ran to the park where they were messing about without purpose when they chanced upon a sluggish-looking blackbird. They chased the bird but it proved to be less vulnerable than they had imagined and it remained out of reach until Grace spotted it taking refuge in an opening beneath the flooring of the public toilets. Flattening himself against the earth, he eased his hand into the mouth of the cavity and, to his surprise, hauled out some keys and wires. Thinking that the keys, if not the wires, might have been lost, and hoping to collect a reward, the lads went to the nearby police barracks where they were directed to the officers on duty. Detectives Bailey and Quirke appeared appreciative and polite but, in truth, were not much interested in the find, and the boys scampered back to the park.

Knowing that he had only explored the mouth of the opening and hoping to find more hidden treasure, perhaps even a few coins, Grace went back to the toilets. Stretching in, at armpit's length, he retrieved a lamp, a bottle of oil and a chisel. These finds, again handed to the police, shook the detectives out of their Sunday torpor. They decided that the collection might belong to a burglar who could return to collect his tools before setting out on a night's work. Around dusk Grace accompanied the policemen to the park and replaced the items, as found. The plain-clothes men hid themselves, waiting to see what would transpire.

At around half-past nine there was the sound of whistling, and a man entered the enclosure surrounding the toilets, disappearing into the surrounding bushes. Watching from their hiding place, the detectives gave him a minute or two to settle and then, abandoning their cover, confronted a one-armed man clutching a rug, with a canvas bag and a sack at his feet. The man, who could have been a vagrant, or any itinerant worker picking up his swag before setting off on an inter-city tramp, was unable to come up with an explanation for his presence other than that he was about to doss down there for the night. The detectives conferred and decided that Detective Bailey would accompany the prisoner – taken in on a charge of vagrancy – to the police barracks and search his possessions. But Quirke, still in disguise, would resume his position and watch to see if the armless loiterer had an accomplice.[19]

Wilkinson was tardy. He eventually materialised out of the gloom at around 10.30 pm, fully an hour late for his rendezvous with McLoughlin. He, too, ventured into the bushes, gave a distinctive whistle and, when the signal was not answered, called out 'Tom' in a low voice. The detective approached him and engaged him in small talk. Wilkinson responded by asking whether Quirke had perhaps seen his one-armed mate hanging around the premises, at which point they were joined by Bailey, who had made his way back to the park. Making use of the hold-all clauses in the Vagrancy

Act, they took Wilkinson, too, into custody and marched him down to the police station to join 'Tom Kenny'.

Asked to account for their movements, Kenny stated that he had entered the country two months earlier. But in order to be able to account for his association with Wilkinson and place as much distance as possible between himself, India and South Africa, he claimed that he had come from America. Wilkinson, realising that his partnership with Kenny was likely to become problematic, immediately said that he was a member of the *Rathdown*'s crew – a fine counter to a charge of vagrancy in a city that never wanted for wandering sailors. It was the contents of Kenny's canvas bag and sack, however, that were most difficult to explain away.

The detectives had little, if any, experience of dealing with safe-blasters. In a country more famous for its care of cattle and sheep than its prowess at excavation or mining, the possession of dynamite was not an offence.[20] Laws, like criminals and those of other persuasions who choose to challenge them, follow the contours of political economy and colour the initial perceptions of both the police and the populace at large.

In New Zealand and India an Irishman carrying around explosives at this time was likely to be perceived as something of a curiosity rather than a serious long-term menace to society. On the lookout for itinerants and petty thieves rather than peripatetic professional criminals with global experience, the police did not know what to make of 'Kenny'.[21] His arrest triggered no detailed questions about his origins, his possible criminal antecedents, or what precisely he was doing in the country. Even the range and sophistication of his equipment left his interrogators bemused rather than puzzled. After his arrest police told an Auckland journalist that his burglar's kit was 'the most complete of the kind they have seen in a considerable time'; perhaps ever, one is inclined to think. The thought that Kenny might be a master blaster, let alone a man wanted for murder, never crossed the official mind. In keeping with time and place, Kenny and Wilkinson were charged with 'vagrancy' and of being 'in possession of burglars' implements'. Both men were remanded for eight days while the police continued looking just straight ahead.[22]

But the Imperial Eye, looking towards Dunedin, had already latched onto an incontrovertible detail that placed McLoughlin's life in jeopardy from the moment he set foot in New Zealand. On 14 November, just four days after 'Kenny's' arrest, the *Otago Witness* – which circulated freely across the South Island – ran an item lifted from the *Auckland Star* entitled 'Arrest of Supposed Burglars'. Relaying the bizarre tale of a blackbird that had pointed the way to a cache of burglars' tools, the report also drew attention to the fact that 'Kenny had his right hand off at the wrist, and in one of the bags was found a dummy hand with a white glove on'.

A gloved prosthesis found in a park in Auckland was probably of only passing interest to readers in Dunedin. But those same readers' networks were becoming rapidly globalised as they benefited from the cheap and expanding imperial postal system.[23] At the far end of the southern hemisphere there were others who had reason to remember that a reward of £100 had been offered for information leading to the arrest and prosecution of a one-armed 'outlaw'. On the South Island, somebody with family or friends in the Cape Colony who had an on-going interest in antipodean affairs, but whose name has been lost to history, was, quite unintentionally, about to activate an extraordinary connection between New Zealand and southern Africa.

A week or so after that edition of the *Otago Witness* had appeared a copy was rolled up, addressed to 'Mr R Grieve, Dutoitspan Road, Kimberley', stamped, and popped into the 'overseas mail'.[24] A trans-oceanic steamer lugged it to Cape Town, 6 000 miles away, from where, three weeks later, it was transported to the diamond fields by the overnight train. Mr Grieve was a careful reader who paid considerable attention to crime stories. He also knew, better than most, how to capture the undivided attention of the Imperial Eye.

Once of Durban, Grieve was a retired policeman. And like other former policemen, he was on the lookout for ways of supplementing a meagre pension. The item on 'Kenny' rang a bell. He thought about it for some time and then wrote a letter to the Commissioner of Police, Kimberley.[25] It was a bit of a lottery, but he had reason to believe that, should he be proved correct, he would be in line for the reward. If 'Tom Kenny' was 'One-armed Jack' McLoughlin, he was also a fugitive, a Lancastrian who had murdered two British subjects in cold blood; one of whom – Mustaffa Hadji – also hailed from the Cape Colony. The Cape government, Secretary of State for the Colonies and the Imperial authorities would all have more than enough reason to pursue enquiries.

Back in Auckland, on 19 November 1895, eight weeks before Grieve approached the Commissioner of Police in Kimberley, 'Kenny' and Wilkinson were arraigned in the Police Court. The Stipendiary Magistrate, in his mid-forties, was HW Northcroft, who hailed from Essex, England, and who had been a ship's captain before turning his attention to law and order. He knew how criminals functioned, and how ships and seamen operated whilst in port – the latter being most fortunate for Wilkinson.

The prosecutor had done his homework and called two locksmiths to provide expert opinion as to the nature of the tools found in 'Kenny's' bags. But given nothing to work on by the detectives, he failed to lead any evidence about the explosives. McLoughlin, sensing a tough legal battle ahead, 'reserved his defence'. Wilkinson, on the other hand, felt that the Magistrate was a man he could reason with. He went to great pains to explain the unusual situation that he had found himself in when the *Rathdown* had been hauled in for repairs, his difficulty in securing any back pay, and stressed how slight his acquaintance with 'Kenny' was.[26]

Northcroft had already formed an opinion about 'Mr Kenny', and was inclined to believe Wilkinson's story. But he wanted more time to work through various depositions before pronouncing on the nature of Wilkinson's relationship with the one-armed man. The hearing was adjourned until the following morning. On 20 November, the Magistrate found that there was insufficient evidence to proceed against Wilkinson and the prisoner was discharged. The case of 'Tom Kenny', however, would be placed on the roll for the next sitting of the Supreme Court.[27]

For all his experience, the Stipendiary Magistrate probably got Wilkinson wrong. Powerfully built, with a scar on his upper lip that spoke of a violent past, and a tattooed crucifix on each of his upper arms, Wilkinson may have been of Irish extraction, but he was born in India and grew up as a 'mean white' before going to sea. Like McLoughlin, he was just another bit of the human flotsam and jetsam of empire floating around the Pacific Rim – a man of the type that Joseph Conrad could conjure up in a few easy sentences. Only three weeks later Wilkinson was again arrested for vagrancy and sentenced to two months' imprisonment. Upon his release, in February 1896, the police remained sufficiently convinced of his potential to do serious harm to society to take the precaution of having him photographed, and when he eventually left the North Island by ship, had him tracked to Melbourne.[28]

During the eight weeks he spent in prison in Auckland, Butler Wilkinson did not want for company. He arrived at the prison, in Lauder Road, to find 'Tom Kenny' already there. Only days after Northcroft had referred his own case, 'Kenny' had appeared before Justice ET Conolly and a jury in the Supreme Court. On 3 December 1895, after conducting his own defence, 'Kenny' was found guilty of possessing 'housebreaking instruments' and sentenced to 'twelve calendar months imprisonment, with hard labour at the common gaol'.[29]

★   ★   ★

McLoughlin looked back on the time spent at Mount Eden as a mere interruption of the sort a gentleman might encounter while travelling abroad. He was, he said many years later – avoiding the words 'imprisoned' or 'jailed' – 'detained' while passing through the country, on his way to Australia.[30] The truth of the matter was that his detour through 'paradise' had turned sour and was set to get worse. At the far end of the Indian Ocean two more, seemingly unrelated, developments were about to unleash forces that would draw the attention of the Imperial Eye and drag his fate in directly opposing directions. In the enforced silence of Mount Eden Prison, part of which was still under construction and coming to fruition along Benthamite lines, it took time for him to learn about struggles that owed their momentum to a report in the *Otago Witness* on the one hand, and a short doctor with overblown imperial ambitions on the other.

On 29 January 1896, the Attorney-General of the Cape Colony, Thomas Upington, acting on the suggestion forwarded to him two weeks earlier by the Commissioner of Police, Kimberley, penned a short note to his counter-part in the South African Republic, HJ Coster. In keeping with the emerg-ing spirit of regional solidarity among southern African states, Upington alerted the State Attorney in Pretoria to the report in the *Witness*, suggest-ing that the one-armed man might be McLoughlin.[31] It took the Kruger government the better part of six months before it was in a position to respond officially to this collegial nudge from the south.[32]

There were good reasons for the delay in getting back to Thomas Upington – not least that between 29 December 1895 and 2 January 1896, the Kruger government had had to see off an armed invasion. Mounted forces led by Dr LS Jameson had attempted to connect with a failed popular uprising in Johannesburg contrived by a 'Reform Committee' controlled by the mine owners.[33] Behind Jameson, however, lay the arch-imperialist and Cape Premier, Cecil Rhodes, and beyond him, the Secretary of State for the Colonies, Joseph Chamberlain. The repercussions of a failed *coup d'état* were felt throughout the region and in Whitehall. Under the circum-stances the Kruger administration did well to respond to Upington at all. When it did do so, it retained its focus on the need for justice in a case that revolved around the murder of two British subjects by a third, and at a time when diplomatic relations between the countries were under severe strain.

As part of an attempt to persuade Upington to use his good offices with the imperial government to get the suspect extradited and tried, the republi-can authorities obtained a new sworn statement from one of the witnesses to the shootings at the Red Lion. They also reissued a warrant for McLoughlin's arrest. The fact that the *prima facie* case they presented focused on the murder of a coloured man, Hadji Mustaffa, rather than that of George Stevenson, may not have been devoid of political purpose. It nevertheless testified to the seriousness of the Boer government's intent. Moreover, in arguments made via the Cape Attorney-General and the British Agent, Kruger's law officers reminded imperial authorities that, despite the absence of a formal extradi-tion treaty between the South African Republic and the United Kingdom, Pretoria had, in the recent past, not only handed over two suspects wanted for ordinary common law offences to the British, but had allowed Jameson to proceed to London so that he might stand trial there.[34]

Persuaded by the pertinence of these arguments, Upington convinced his cabinet colleagues to take up the cudgels on Pretoria's behalf. The Cape government, despite Rhodes's resignation, may still have been sufficiently embarrassed by his involvement in the Jameson Raid to consider it its duty to be as helpful as possible. But, because Kruger went through State Attorneys at the same speed as he did pipe tobacco, Upington warned the Acting State Attorney that while he was supportive, there was no telling what the attitude of the Imperial Government might be.[35]

This promising development, late in May 1895, when McLoughlin had already served half his sentence, triggered a round of petty bureaucratic haggling. At issue was who exactly should bear the cost of sending a telegram to New Zealand. The Imperial Budget, it seemed, had to be sure to balance before the Imperial Eye could be induced to scan the wider world in pursuit of justice for two dead men. Two months later, Kruger's cabinet – steadfast in its unwillingness to be deflected by red tape – agreed to cover any costs that might be incurred as a result of McLoughlin being extradited from the antipodes.[36]

Imperial protocol ensured that it was early August before the High Commissioner in South Africa got around to sending a coded telegram to the Governor of New Zealand, Lord Glasgow. Glasgow was asked to determine whether 'Kenny' was McLoughlin, and to confirm the latter's presence in Auckland. But much to Governor Glasgow's annoyance, the telegram used two words – 'coralfish' and 'hamites' – the former being a reference to the Kruger government, and the latter the South African Republic, that did not appear in his current copy of the code. He nevertheless managed to make sense of the communication reasonably easily and then proceeded to make a few discreet official enquiries.[37]

A few weeks later McLoughlin – by then with only 10 weeks of his sentence left to run – learned that his presence in New Zealand was known in Pretoria. Prison authorities quizzed him about his past and he suddenly realised that there was a possibility that he might be extradited to stand trial for murder. He refused to answer to the name McLoughlin and spun them a tale about his being a miner – his missing hand testifying to an accident – and a 'native of Ireland'. But they were only half taken in. On 16

September, they suddenly re-classified him as 'a dangerous criminal', made a note of tattoos on his upper arms, and had him photographed.[38] All of this impressed upon him the need for sticking to the name 'Dell' or 'Kenny', and making certain that he got out of the country as soon as possible after his scheduled release in December.

But, unbeknownst to him, 'McLoughlin' was about to be let off the hook. Joseph Chamberlain, personally implicated in the Raid, was in no mood to accommodate a Kruger government that had left its British counterpart – and him in particular – embarrassed if not humiliated. When the Governor of New Zealand, having solicited the advice of local legal practitioners as to whether or not 'Kenny alias McLoughlin' (not 'McLoughlin alias Kenny') might be legally extradited, passed on the wisdom of the wigged-ones to the Secretary for the Colonies, Chamberlain, with access to an office budget that did cover the cost of telegraphing, instantly wired the response: 'Her Majesty's Government do not desire the Government of New Zealand to act contrary to the opinion of their legal advisers.'[39]

On 20 November 1896, Glasgow responded to the High Commissioner in Cape Town, informing him of Chamberlain's response, and he, in turn, passed on copies of the correspondence to the long-suffering Kruger administration. The Governor of New Zealand was of the view that, since 'Kenny' was already being held for another offence, 'the law of this Colony would not sanction the arrest or surrender of the criminal McLoughlin or Kenny as requested by His Honour, the President of the Transvaal Republic' (sic).

In his earlier correspondence with Chamberlain, however, Glasgow had gone even further and advised the Secretary for the Colonies that 'Kenny', who at that time was still in prison, 'should now be discharged therefrom as I understand he has earned remission of sentence for which he was convicted at Auckland'. On 26 November, two weeks earlier than the previously scheduled date for his release from Mount Eden Prison, and with his status as a 'dangerous criminal' newly confirmed, a bemused 'Kenny' was suddenly set free.[40]

A fit of political petulance, occasioned by the far-off misadventures of mining capitalists set on extending the indirect control of the British empire in an independent Boer republic, had caused the Imperial Eye to be averted. But it had done so at the cost of pursuing justice – not only for victims supposedly under the protection of Westminster-Whitehall, but also for the one-armed man accused of murdering them. Between the capriciousness of international law and politics on the one hand, and the careers of great men who had gambled on their reputations on the other, was a half-broken man reduced to scurrying around the outer margins of the empire under an assumed identity, uncertain as to whether or not he was wanted on a charge of murder. Chamberlain and Glasgow, adducing high principle while ostensibly serving justice, had taken it upon themselves to inflict an indeterminate sentence of banishment on a fugitive so as to ensure that their imperial enemies, intent only on seeing due process in a case that involved no subjects of their own, were denied the smallest measure of satisfaction in a deadly political contest.

CHAPTER TWENTY

◖❊◗

Courting Solitude

AUCKLAND TO CHRISTCHURCH
— 1896–1900 —

Till you cage in the sky, the sparrows will fly.

CERVANTES

Although McLoughlin's confidence was low, he retained some of his charisma and an ability to lead. On leaving Mount Eden he joined forces with an unknown, recently discharged prisoner and within hours managed to assemble a set of house-breaking implements.[1] He was convinced that his long-term interests were best served by raising the money to get himself to Australia and link up with his brother. But the problem, as before, was how to raise funds for a passage from the east coast of the North Island to Melbourne, more than 1 000 miles away. One thing was certain; he could not afford to linger in Auckland, where he was at risk of being spotted by police who would be quick to monitor the movements of a known felon.

Like betting on horses, something quite irresistible when he was in the money, he never overcame the desire to gamble on safe-blasting when out of pocket. There was nothing quite like the surge of adrenaline a man experienced upon opening a mangled safe door. It was like waiting to see whether a bet on *Safe, Gold* and *Dynamite* had won the trifecta. It was risky stuff, but on the right day it could yield a spectacular return. And, just as race

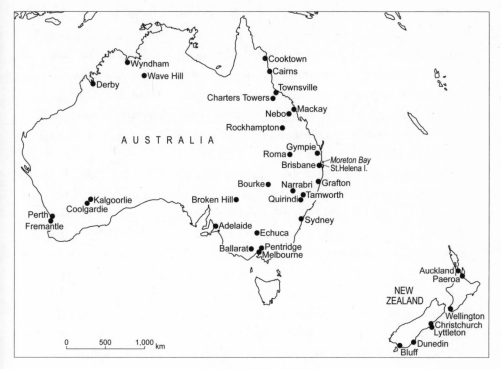

Australia and New Zealand

horses were to be found at turf clubs, so dynamite and gold nestled in mining towns. Only days after his release from Mount Eden, on 8 December 1896, he entered Paeroa, at the foot of the Coromandel Peninsula, 70 miles south-east of Auckland. The village itself had almost nothing to offer a set of needy ex-convicts, but it was only a short walk from the near-exhausted Ohinemuri goldfields.

They travelled separately to Paeroa, having agreed to meet later that night at a paddock on the village outskirts, where they would doss down for the night. In mid-morning he slipped beneath a bridge on the edge of the settlement and hid a leather bag containing the most incriminating tools in thick bush. The bag was discovered there, weeks later, by a miner out on a riverside walk with his dog. McLoughlin ensured that, with the exception of some pieces of loose wire needed for lock-picking, his pockets were completely free of items of interest to nosey policemen.

The condition of his artificial hand, however, was a cause for concern. It was five years old and irreplaceable; he felt incomplete without it and remained at pains to protect the retractable fingers with a glove. He had taken to removing the prosthesis whenever possible so as to minimise the possibility of further damage. Together with the wires, rolled into a blanket, it made the familiar 'swag' that so many antipodean labourers carried, tied across their shoulders, when tramping the countryside in search of casual labour or a place to sleep.

After lunch he wandered about for a while, but it was a Sunday and there was time to kill. By late afternoon he was reduced to 'idling about the township, sitting on doorsteps'. The light was fading when the village's night watchmen, Constables Beattie and Russell, came on duty. They did not recognise him, but he was a man without accommodation, a potential menace to the rural idyll of lower Coromandel. He gave them no cause for alarm and they merely watched him until close on midnight when he suddenly moved out of the village and up towards the paddock. If he slept there, and was a man of no fixed abode, he was a vagrant.

They gave him half an hour to settle in and then made their way to the paddock where they 'found him, and another man lying down together with a blanket over them'. His companion may have been a younger man he was familiar with – something of a pattern in his life. The police either recognised, were not interested in, or were more sympathetically disposed to his partner. They roused the pair, searched McLoughlin but, finding nothing incriminating, asked where his 'swag' was stashed. He told them that he had none, but they soon uncovered the 'dummy hand' and the wires which, he told them, were needed to repair his failing prosthesis. Not per-suaded, they arrested him for 'vagrancy'.[2]

Given his immediate past, he told them he was 'John Dell' but, when pressed, confessed to being 'Thomas Kenny'. The *Police Gazette* revealed a criminal record, a recent release from prison, and his status as 'a dangerous criminal'. The wires suddenly assumed greater importance than any possi-ble charge of vagrancy. Within days he appeared in the Police Court, where he was again charged with being in possession of 'house-breaking imple-ments' and committed for trial.

On the way back to Auckland, where he was due to appear once again before the formidable Justice ET Conolly and a jury, 'Kenny' was escorted by officer Tole. Chatting to Tole, he arrived at the mistaken conclusion that the policeman was sufficiently amiable and pliable for him to be able to ask for assistance. It may have been a mistake predicated on the lenient treatment that his paddock partner had received at the hands of the police. He confided in Tole and told him that the evidence against him did not lie in the wires found on him at the time of his arrest, but in a leather bag hidden below the bridge back in Paeroa. He asked Tole to recover and destroy the bag and its contents. Perhaps predictably – but it is hard to know because it was a question of judgement – Tole proved unwilling to help. In any case the question soon became irrelevant when Garner, the miner from Waitekauri, went out on a stroll and stumbled upon the bag. Within days of his release 'Thomas Kenny' found himself back in prison, at the misleadingly named Mount Eden, awaiting trial.[3]

Given the delays attendant upon the discovery of the bag and yet more police work, it was 9 March 1896 before the case was heard. 'Kenny' chose not to give evidence in his defence but did address the jury directly to tell them that he had used the wires discovered in his swag to repair his artificial hand. The jury retired for 15 minutes and presented Judge Conolly with a 'guilty' verdict. The convict, preparing himself inwardly for the sentencing to come, had reason to believe that he would receive a sentence of around 18 months

During his previous spell in prison, as 'Kenny' alias 'Dell' – the only identities by which he was officially acknowledged in the country – he had earned a remission of sentence for good behaviour. As 'Kenny' he had never been convicted of burglary or safe-blowing in New Zealand; indeed, he had never been found guilty of stealing so much as a cycle lamp, let alone the contents of a house or a safe. He had, it was true, been found with tools that might be used for committing a felony, but the police had been unable to link him to either a target or a victim. Nor had 'Kenny' or 'Dell' ever resisted arrest, or attempted to escape from police custody, or from prison. McLoughlin had found himself in a similar position once before, on the frontiers of Africa but, even there, in wild Johannesburg, such sentences were usually within reasonable limits.

SHOWDOWN AT THE RED LION

As he already knew, but might not have factored into his calculations, since his last appearance in the Supreme Court the Imperial Eye had focused on the North Island, linking his past life – as 'Jack McLoughlin' – to his present one as 'Kenny alias Dell'. Officials in Wellington now bore information about his past but were unable to officially confirm or deny it. Nor were they at liberty to use it for their own ends in open court, or to disclose it to the press. It was true that as 'Kenny' he had once been found to be in possession of explosives, but that in itself was not an offence and there was nothing known about 'Kenny' that warranted his classification as a 'dangerous criminal'. Any information to that effect could only have been transmitted by the Imperial Eye. The question then became, who was in the dock – McLoughlin or 'Kenny alias Dell'?

On the modestly populated North Island, an Eton-educated Judge of the Supreme Court would have been at home in the company of the Governor of New Zealand who had solicited expert opinion as to whether or not McLoughlin might be extradited legally. It was unlikely that talk about a man wanted for murder in Johannesburg did not circulate in the formal or informal legal circles that Conolly, who had been a barrister in England for 13 years, moved in.[4] And, even if Conolly had not heard about it, the *Police Gazette* – easily accessible to any Public Prosecutor – would have recorded clearly that 'Kenny' had suddenly, rather inexplicably, mutated into 'a dangerous criminal'.

Conolly may not have been formally informed that 'Kenny alias Dell' was, in fact, Jack McLoughlin. He may also have remained sufficiently focused and professional not to allow unsolicited incidental information to affect his sentencing. Indeed, the sentence he eventually handed down to 'Kenny' was in line with that handed down by him and other judges in equivalent cases.[5] Nevertheless Conolly too, seemed suddenly to be impressed by the potential menace that 'Kenny' posed to society. How could he possibly have reached that conclusion if he did not have access to the latest information about the Red Lion shootings?

> His Honour [Conolly] in passing sentence said he believed the prisoner
> was one of the very worst characters he had ever dealt with – a most

dangerous character. He was convicted before him a year-and-a-half ago for the very same offence, viz, of having house-breaking implements in his possession, and he was then sentenced to twelve months imprisonment so that he was out of prison but a very short time when he started carrying on the same old game, going to a place where he apparently had nothing to do, and being found with house-breaking implements in his possession. As to the leather bag, he was sure that the jury believed that it was the prisoner's also. He [His Honour] would pass the heaviest sentence upon him that the law would allow, namely three years in prison with hard labour.[6]

It was a harsh sentence for a one-armed repeat offender whose 'dangerous character' appears not to have been demonstrated in the matter at hand. The convicted man obviously felt that he had been done a gross injustice and that the sentence was unreasonably arduous.

The prisoner made an effort to speak, but was removed from the dock by the warders. Before descending the stairs, however, he yelled out: 'I'll do it standing on the top of my … head, you ….' For some minutes after the prisoner went below, a noise as of somebody banging against a door and being very violent was distinctly audible in the Court.[7]

It may have seemed like the ranting of just another oft-convicted man; an audacious and unforgiving criminal who had been willing to take the life of a former friend, someone with an unquenchable thirst for gold and a lust for life, a person who refused to underwrite his needs by doing manual labour in a world dominated by machines and worked for profit by men with capital in a system that many people found difficult to reconcile with notions of social justice. But, if one listened carefully, it was also the anguished plea of an Irish emigrant dispossessed by empire and famine, of a child labourer in the cotton mills of Manchester, of a boy from a broken home, of an adolescent 'scuttler' hurling abuse at a Magistrate, of a man who had the codes of masculinity imprinted indelibly on his mind, and of a lover betrayed.

With the notable exception of the attempted escape at Potchefstroom, he became less inclined to challenge prison discipline as he grew older. Indeed, there are indications that by the time he entered his late thirties, he had grown accustomed to prison regulations in the all-male environment of a 'total institution' – he could, as he said, serve out a sentence, even a lengthy one, standing on his head. He was not in the army or the navy, but prison was not without its stolen comforts and it offered its own securities; he was away from some other temptations, including alcohol.

Captain Dangerous, 'one of the very worst' men Conolly had ever encountered outside Eton, gave the authorities no cause for concern. He was the subject of minor official interest on two occasions in the year that he was taken back in at Mount Eden, 1897, and then once again, in 1898, when a letter confirming his presence in Auckland was sent to the Cape Colony. Other than that, nothing. Indeed, as he worked his way through the days, weeks and months of hard labour in the year of his release, the prison authorities were again sufficiently impressed by his behaviour to grant him a two-month remission of sentence. New Zealand cells had by then claimed four years or 10 per cent of his life up to that point, for merely manifesting the intent to commit a felony.[8]

★ ★ ★

The new century was beckoning when, at the age of 40, 'Kenny aka Dell' was released from Mount Eden for a second time, on 2 September 1899.[9] The newspapers contained cheering news – the Imperial Eye was going to be averted from New Zealand for some time to come. Flushed with imperial loyalty and patriotic fervour, two weeks before a shot was exchanged, the Prime Minister of New Zealand, 'King' Richard Seddon, had offered to send two contingents of men to join British forces in the coming war in southern Africa.

When war was declared, on 11 October 1899, it proved to be immensely popular in the antipodean 'Better Britain', prompting the nation's first contribution of troops to a campaign abroad. Over 6 000 volunteers flocked to the standard and the inhabitants of the North and South Island found that they disliked Afrikaners almost as much as they loved the British. For McLoughlin, once a military adviser to Makhado's regiments, a man with his own reasons for loathing the Boers, it was all ideological manna from heaven. He would have known, better than most, what a war in southern Africa would entail. Dealt with in broad brush strokes so as to avoid unnecessary detail, the topic of the South African War may even have eased 'John Dell's' travels as he made his way around the countryside in search of beer, a chat and a place to spend the night.[10]

But on his release, and determined not to be caught with the tools of his trade for a third time, he had other, personal, things to contemplate. Socially dead since he had fled the Witwatersrand, he felt an increasing need to get to Australia and seek out Tommy. Talking to his brother would help remind him who he was and where they came from – it might even help create a future of sorts. But how was he to avoid spending more time between four walls and behind bars in a country where vagrancy nets had been cast across every city and the countryside? How did one move through social terrain that was so very 'English' without falling prey to laws that might have been designed to snare an impecunious fellow? How was a man to get himself to a port where an old Jack Tar might get a berth aboard a vessel bound for Melbourne?

The response was ingenious. Part of the answer lay in his shifting shape. He needed an identity that English-New Zealanders would not be alarmed by; one that while being 'other', and that of an itinerant, was obviously not that of a 'vagrant' or 'out of place'.[11] Lancashire was full of such men – he had seen them himself, camped in fields, moving up hill and down dale and in the lanes of town and countryside alike.[12] Why had he not thought of it before? True, like their brothers, the gypsies, they were objects of suspicion, but they were not arrested on sight unless something was badly amiss. It would require little effort – indeed he was three-quarters of the way there already. When pressed by the police he had insisted that he was 'a native of Ireland'. Moreover, his interest in gold amalgamation, safe-blowing and plate-laying on the railways of Mozambique all combined to provide him with a working knowledge of metal-working. It was all so obvious! He was a tin-smith – an Irish tinker, no less, working his way across farms in the back-country and, like all the seasonally migrant sheep-shearers, making his way to the port closest to Melbourne, Bluff, at the southern tip of South Island.[13]

The first weeks out of prison, as he battled to get Auckland behind him, were demanding. Without start-up cash, food or clothing it was impossible to avoid the haunts of vagrants and, for a while, he must have relied on the support of a few recently discharged fellow inmates to penetrate much deeper into the countryside. The rural economy was improving slowly after a decade-long recession and casual employment was easier to come by in summer when light and warmth encouraged seasonal, outdoor labour.[14] His needs were modest and he remained sufficiently disciplined to resist the temptation of trying to raise money by engaging in any risky project. It took a month or two, but he assembled most of the tools used by a tin-smith and extended his culinary skills. Cooking was a necessary part of survival for a 'Puck of the Droms', a 'Trickster of the Roads', as the tinkers had it. But it was also a skill that could be marketed on farms where teams of migrant male labourers gathered to do clearing, fencing, harvesting, logging or sheep-shearing. The observation that 'God made the tucker, but the devil made the cooks' was part of folk-wisdom in nineteenth-century New Zealand.[15]

All that summer, from October 1899 through to March 1900, was spent zig-zagging across from Hawke's Bay to Taranaki and working his way down towards Wellington, at the foot of the North Island. Like most of those in his newly chosen profession, he manufactured or repaired the 'buckets, scoops, mugs, milk cans or basins' used in small country stores, on farms or in houses.[16] But, when money was tight, tinkers were famous for being able to live off the countryside by hunting small game or dynamiting rivers for fish – things that 'Dell' knew a fair deal about.[17]

There was a significant overlap between the sub-culture of the many itinerant manual labourers lugging their swag about and that of the handful of tinkers moving steadily along country roads. An Irish tinker would have had little difficulty in segueing into a swagger should circumstances demand it.[18] Both were said to have 'a propensity to play tricks and general deviousness', to be economical with the truth, share a belief in luck, love gambling, horse-racing and, of course, alcohol.[19]

The anti-clericalism of tinkers and a reputation for exploiting priests and nuns, too, would also have sat easily with the newest Puck of the Droms. Known to be unforgiving of his enemies, 'Kenny aka Dell' may also have taken on another element of the wandering tin-smith's culture – the 'withering curse', the infamous 'tinker's cuss'.[20] Bad luck had long dogged his footsteps, affecting not only him, but those friends and associates around him. It had cost the Hadji his life. The tinker's curse, however, was consciously directed outwards, towards those intent on thwarting him. For the superstitious, it may be worth noting how, for those who crossed Jack McLoughlin's path in the closing years of his extraordinary career, the tinker's curse posed a real threat.

Remarkably, 'John Dell', as he now preferred to present himself, managed to avoid a criminal charge throughout that summer. It bore testimony to the fact that there was more money than usual circulating in rural areas. But in late autumn his fortunes took a downward turn. With work falling away faster than the leaves off the trees, it became difficult to meet the everyday need for food, heating and shelter, let alone save for a passage to Australia. Even in the relatively milder climate of the North Island, winter quickly drove the hungry and homeless towards urban areas where the chances of survival were always better than in the countryside. But cities, and especially ports, came with all the familiar sirens. Bars and hotels provided sailors not only with companionship and warmth, but opportunities for drinking, gambling and casual sex. By mid-July he was without funds and firmly stranded in Wellington. For all the difference it made, the short 12-hour journey down the Cook Strait, out of Wellington and then south to Lyttelton, on the Canterbury shore of the South Island, might as well have been as far away, and taken as long, as a journey to Cape Town via Cape Horn.

He may have been acting on his own when he stowed away aboard the SS *Rotomahana,* but what is more likely is that he got some help from a crew member encountered in a bar. The steamer, it was rumoured, had originally been built for a wealthy prince, back in 1879, but the Union Steamship

Company had had it refitted so that it could carry 300 passengers and a limited amount of cargo. Its regular run was between Sydney and eastern ports of the North Island but, that July, the company diverted it from the usual trans-Tasman route. It was bound for Lyttelton where, like the *Mount Sirion* before it, it may have been collecting horses – this time not for India, but for the war in southern Africa, which, by the time it was done two years later, had drawn in more than 8 000 horses from far-off New Zealand.

The Cook Strait posed a serious challenge to navigators at the best of times, let alone in midwinter. But, while the ship's passage was without incident something went sadly wrong for the stowaway. Before he could smuggle himself ashore at Lyttelton, let alone reach nearby Christchurch from where he hoped to work his way to south to Bluff, he was found out. He was unable to pay the third-class fare; a constable was summoned and he was arrested. Back in Calcutta the police had provided a fugitive from justice with a new suit and made sure he left India. In Lyttelton they were waiting to ensure that he did not enter Canterbury a free man.

Lyttelton was in celebratory mood. The first British settlers destined for Canterbury had set foot there exactly 50 years earlier. Their descendants and new arrivals alike deferred to none when it came to Christianity, the bifurcated and racist patriotism of 'country and empire' or hatred for the empire's enemies – the Afrikaner republicans of South Africa.[21] Here then, isolated by Lyttelton's steep cliffs, was Little Britain, the longed-for Better Britain, undiluted by other cultures, ethnic groupings or races; the way God and Queen intended an outpost of empire to be. As they made their way up the hill towards the police station, in a square off Sumner Road, the constable and his prisoner passed the 'British', 'Canterbury' and 'Empire' Hotels. Later that year, as part of the Lyttelton Jubilee celebrations, 'Much amusement was created by a nigger on horseback holding an effigy of that slippery Boer General de Wet, who was being ill-treated in a manner that met with general approval.' And north of Christchurch, in Amuri County, some of the landlords were still referred to as 'Kaffirs' because, a decade earlier, they had threatened to import semi-skilled blacks from the Cape Colony to break a strike by shearers.[22]

'Dell' got the point. Empire transmitted class and colour prejudice almost as readily as it built trans-oceanic notions of ethnic solidarity and political loyalty forged from shared language and skin colour – indeed, it was two sides of the same coin. In the relatively cosmopolitan and more open environment of the North Island, almost one in five inhabitants was of Irish descent, with significantly more Catholics than Protestants.[23] But on South Island things were rather different. So, whereas he had told the Auckland police that he was 'a native of Ireland', born in 1858, in Lyttelton, he informed them he was 'a native of England' and, for good measure, lopped four years off his age, claiming to have been born in 1862. It mattered little, the missing arm spoke a truth all of its own. It never lied and it was all recorded in the *Police Gazette*.[24]

The Justice of the Peace who presided over the Police Court, Captain Marciel, had seen it all before. Deserters, runaway sailors and stowaways were no novelty in Lyttelton. There were only two cases before him that Tuesday morning, 24 July 1900 – a drunk and a stowaway. Remorseful drunks were as common as seagulls' cries, so he convicted the first offender and discharged him with the customary caution. The man had done no harm or damage to property. The stowaway, other than having only one arm, also presented nothing remarkable. If it were up to him, he would send him packing as well. He was reluctant to send a man who was so obviously down on his luck to prison. But Lyttelton lived off the sea and the shipping companies were not to be trifled with, so he sentenced him to a fine of £1, or 14 days, hoping that the poor fellow would somehow come up with 20 shillings. He could not, so he was taken off to jail, two blocks up from the wharf, into Canterbury Street, where, today, two portals are all that remain of a building that once held the Terror of all Johannesburg.[25]

A fortnight's accommodation and food in winter were not the worst thing that could befall a penniless man in a vagrant-obsessed society. He seemed fated to be discharged from prison when spring was in the offing, but the on-going chill made him reluctant to set off for one of the southernmost settlements in the world. Invercargill and Bluff lay some way below 45 degrees south and he felt unable to risk going there. Not only would casual jobs be few and far between, but the cold forced one to seek refuge in places that were likely to be well policed. So, when he was released, on 7 August 1900, he managed to raise the money for the short train ride to Christchurch without raising the ire of the authorities. It is not clear how long he spent in the city, but when it eventually warmed up some weeks later, he gathered up his blanket, tin-smith's tools and a billycan and set off to explore the side roads of Canterbury against the backdrop of some of the most beautiful snow-clad mountains in the world. He did not emerge for nearly three months.

He got to do a good deal of catering for itinerant hired help on out-of-the-way stations where a cook of any sorts often earned about two-thirds of the wages paid to a skilled worker. It brought in a reasonable income and provided steady work in between the irregular flow of cash that came from the piecework that marked out tin-smithying. Cooks were notorious for 'going on the booze' but most remote rural areas had their own externally induced discipline: with fewer bars to pull him towards the beer, he managed to stay out of trouble.[26] There was also a great deal of camaraderie and companionship among the swaggers which made the experience tolerable – at times, positively pleasant.

As September came he noted that many of the more adventurous, trans-Tasman sheep-shearers were, like migratory birds preparing for the change of season, becoming restless.[27] There was much talk about the imminent need to get south and board ships bound for New South Wales and Victoria. This was in order not only to profit from the Australian sheep-shearing season – which, depending on where the stations were, ran from August through to December – but also so as not to miss out on Marvellous Melbourne during the most exciting week of the year. The first Tuesday of November each year, without fail, brought the country to a standstill as the most famous two-mile horse race in the world, the Melbourne Cup, was run amidst a carnival-like atmosphere. Among shearers, 'The one subject that overshadowed all others, was horse-racing. The Christian calendar was abandoned, the years were known by the name of the horse which had won the Melbourne Cup.'[28]

No stranger to Melbourne himself, McLoughlin could relate to this form of popular madness. But a winged bird that had lost its financial fat on a Wellington waterfront the previous year was in no position to undertake the season's migration. He held out for as long as he could, but with the prospect of yet another winter in New Zealand unthinkable, the appeal of the Southland ships, with or without funds, became irresistible. He had long since abandoned the thought of getting to the Cup on time when he put the sheep runs behind him and re-entered Christchurch on 10 November 1900. It was not as though nobody cared. His absence had been noted by the usual police seine-netters, keen to haul in any and all 'vagrants' that might pollute the otherwise pristine environment.

But 'Dell' was sober, in control of himself and had enough cash to cover the cost of a ticket south – perhaps only as far as Dunedin, maybe farther – where he would soon become somebody else's responsibility. The police gazetteers, however, could not resist hauling him in and shaking him down to see what additional information they might tumble out of a 'dangerous criminal'. They got nothing new, or of value, out of him. In the end they were left to note that he was on his way to Southland, where he would probably again be turning his hand to doing some cooking and tin-smithying on a few of the remoter sheep runs.[29]

And so, somewhere out there, in one of the coldest and least densely set-tled parts of the British Empire, between November 1900 and April 1901, the Imperial Eye, as yet without the benefit of passport control in port cities, again lost sight of its quarry. By the time that it next got around to scanning the horizon for him, in August 1901, there was no trace of 'Tom Kenny', 'John Dell' or 'Jack McLoughlin'.[30] The injured bird had somehow got itself to Bluff – and from there, it could have flown off in any direction.

꧁ ❈ ꧂

The Great Walkabout

AUSTRALIA

— 1901–1904 —

Up jumped the swagman, leapt into the billabong,
'You'll never catch me alive,' said he,
And his ghost may be heard as you pass by the billabong,
'Who'll come a-waltzing Matilda with me?'

T he road 'John Dell' took to Bluff on the South Island, in late 1900, was
thronged by labourers, sheep-shearers, 'runaway sailors from Lyttelton
and Dunedin' and its share of common criminals working the great oceanic
circuits of the day. Most of them, like him, were bound for Melbourne, from
where those committed to earning a living would take the train up-country
to Echuca or Albury – on the fringes of Ned Kelly country – to tramp
about in search of seasonal work.[1] The voyage across the Tasman offered
the opportunity of striking up a few shipboard friendships that would help
when he disembarked in Melbourne.

By then, 'Dell' would be out of sight of an Imperial Eye that was focused
on the South African War. It was a lead he held on to for close on a decade.
On 1 June 1900, Lord Roberts's forces occupied Johannesburg, which then
became a centre for British concern. Twelve months later the Eye – freed of
the political grit that had impaired its vision since the Jameson Raid – swept
the South Island, hoping to catch a last glimpse of its old quarry before he

left Bluff. In late 1901, imperial law-enforcement agencies, concerned that the men shot at the Red Lion in January 1895 had both been British subjects, did as the Kruger administration had attempted to do five years earlier, and tried anew to establish the suspect's whereabouts in New Zealand.[2]

By then 'John Dell' was no more. Like 'Thomas Kenny' of India before him, he had evanesced. Instead, 'John Bourke' was born, perhaps re-born, out on the Tasman Sea. It was 'Bourke' who disembarked at Melbourne in mid-1901.[3] For reasons that are unclear, 'Bourke', like 'Dell' before him, insisted on 1862 rather than 1859 as his date of birth, leaving him a few years younger than really he was. A year later, in 1902, he told police in New South Wales that he was a 'Roman Catholic' and, still intent on concealing his southern African past, suggested that he had first set foot in Australia in 1887, arriving on the SS *Mount Sirion* (which was only built in 1895). Not much effort went into constructing 'Bourke's' past because, when all was said and done, he bore the imprimatur of the Boers of Potchefstroom.

Back in the early 1880s, when McLoughlin had first entered Australia, before the police took an interest in him and he had to flee to southern Africa, Melbourne had been good to him. He had visited Tommy, locked up in Pentridge, and developed an underworld network that allowed him to live fairly well and avoid arrest. Back then, the state was in an economic upswing and making a living was relatively easy. But the boom had collapsed in 1891, and now, 10 years later, it was evident that the city and the countryside were still in the wake of a serious depression.[4] Rather worryingly for him, early 1901 had also seen the birth of the 'Commonwealth of Australia'; a development that encouraged police co-operation between the constituent states.

His second stay of a few months in Melbourne, in 1901, was pleasant and trouble-free enough for him to talk about it openly years later.[5] Indeed, if it were not for his own voluntary testimony nobody would have realised that he passed through the city for a second time. He remembered his return visit for two reasons. First, he raised the money for a blacksmith to replace his old prosthesis. It had been bothering him ever since he had damaged it during the jump from the train and it had collapsed almost completely in Auckland. He replaced it with a metal hook that was tolerable in private but an embarrassment when out in public. He liked keeping up appearances and dressing well, and because he did not want to be seen as disabled, got a 'cork hand' attached to the hook which he again covered with a glove.[6] It was functional but nowhere near as menacing as his first prosthesis which had so captured the imagination of Johannesburg journalists.[7]

Secondly, Melbourne was the base from which he re-established contact with Tommy. The inauguration of the Imperial Penny Post, on Christmas Day 1898, helped. It facilitated communication among ordinary men and women across the southern world – which, despite the extension of tele-graph cables, still failed to match the interconnectedness of the northern hemisphere.[8] His brother, having left behind a criminal record in New South Wales, was in the remote north-west of the continent. Also, and equally important, it was in Melbourne that he put together a team for one or other big job that raised the funds necessary for his 1 700 nautical mile ocean voyage to the west coast.[9]

There was much to look forward to, to share. The congestion and squalor of Ancoats had left the McLoughlin brothers with the marks of masculin-ity and poverty – or, seen from a more positive perspective, with a love of adventure, the countryside and frontier society. They had last seen each other in the grounds of the Johannesburg Hospital, in 1894, after Tommy had gone half-way round the world to see his hero. Six years later, Jack was returning the favour by looping around the southern ocean of Australia. Nothing is known about where or when they had their long-anticipated reunion, but the likely venue was Fremantle, around July or August of 1901.

From the moment he entered Australia in the 1880s, Tommy had shown a preference for working with horses, cattle and sheep. After a few mis-adventures out east that included the theft of livestock, he had worked his way up, through New South Wales, and then on into Queensland.[10] Cattle-duffers – stock thieves – stood in relation to butchers as did gold thieves to jewellers, and it may have been through the illegal trade in sheep and cattle that Tommy first met the entrepreneurial Patrick Durack, whose forebears hailed from Ireland.[11]

In the mid-1880s the Duracks were among the state's most successful cat-tle ranchers. They owned a string of properties in south-western Queensland

and a butcher shop in Roma. But uncertain as to the long-term future of the region, Durack's son, Michael, moved to the far north-west where, a decade later, he was joined by his father. The Duracks 'opened-up' a series of cattle stations along the eastern and southern fringes of the Kimberley Plateau and controlled huge properties, some straddling the border between Western Australia and the Northern Territory. They had lost none of their nose for business. In the mid-1890s, the family shipped cattle from the Gulf of Cambridge to Fremantle, profiting from the heightened demand for beef in the burgeoning mining towns of Coolgardie and Kalgoorlie. In 1902, Michael Durack shipped 3 000 live cattle to Durban as new trading patterns slowly spread across the southern Indian Ocean.[12]

By 1901, probably earlier, Tommy McLoughlin was up there in the Kimberleys, working as a stockman on the enormous Texas Downs cattle station around Turkey Creek. He and others guarded livestock belonging to the Duracks and other notables from theft by Aborigines who had been displaced and marginalised by the sudden expansion in commercial livestock farming. Going south to see his brother posed few problems. The Duracks were well disposed to an Irish lad, and there were any number of vessels ferrying cattle south. Moreover, Michael Durack's southern commercial base was in Fremantle, where the new Irish-Australian firm of Connor, Doherty and Durack Ltd supplied hides, skins and beef to the new developing urban markets.[13]

If the trans-hemispheric meeting of the McLoughlin brothers in Fremantle was momentous in terms of expectations, then the outcome was probably disappointing for both. Tommy, whose impulsive and violent behaviour dated back to boyhood, may have been in awe of his brother, but was unwilling to join him in his retreat from the British, who were still very involved in a war with the Boers. He may nevertheless have given Jack some money to help with the great trek back across the width of Australia to the east coast. It is noteworthy that, for more than a year after his arrival in Fremantle with funds raised in Melbourne, and after his meeting with Tommy, 'John Bourke' managed to steer clear of the police and prison. Tommy may also have passed on the names of former east coast associates, because for a time after their meeting, 'Bourke' showed a strong preference for working the border region of northern New South Wales and Queensland.

For his part, Jack saw no point in joining Tommy, still living under the family name, in the north-west. Up there, on tropical stock farms, as down in icy New Zealand, he would be reduced to cooking for swagmen or working as a tin-smith. What he needed was the friends and dynamite necessary for his calling, and to reassert himself. It was not as if a few oath-bound mates, fellows with courage and a little wit, could not survive the depressed economic conditions of the outback.

In America, the great bandits of the post-Civil War period had made their name by milking the banks in small towns or robbing trains.[14] And, when economic disaster struck Johannesburg in 1890, had not some of the best men in the Irish Brigade survived in the western Transvaal countryside by plundering government offices, post offices, or railway stations in out-of-the-way places like Rustenburg? 'John Bourke' was a long way from Krugersdorp, but Coolgardie and Kalgoorlie – indeed all Western Australia – had a familiar feeling.

So, when the reunion in Fremantle was over, the brothers went their separate ways. 'Bourke' went in search of things a travelling man like him could work with and took himself 400 miles east, to the gold frontier towns that he felt most at home in. Tommy, on the other hand, set off on the 2 000-mile journey north, back to the cattle frontier he preferred. They left respecting the differences that separated them but, unbeknown to them, were soon to share the worst pedigree that could befall men. The curse that had followed Jack McLoughlin since he lost his arm drew no distinction between family or foe, land or sea.

Back at Texas Downs, Tommy resumed his duties as a stockman. On 25 September, he and Thomas Durack were out on mounted patrol when, about 35 miles east of the telegraph station at Turkey Creek, they came across a party of Aborigines cutting up the carcass of a cow. It was the classic frontier situation – an expanding pastoral industry controlled by insurgent white settlers laying claim to the traditional preserve of older, indigenous, black hunter-gatherers.

When whites met blacks under those circumstances the ideology of the invaders encouraged – no, demanded – direct action and the meting-out of firm 'lessons'. In contests between rifles and spears, caution and restraint were amongst the first casualties on the side of those enjoying technological superiority. In Tommy's case, his weapon of choice, a Mauser, hinted at southern African experience; it was a rifle favoured by many Boers.[15] Only those of phlegmatic disposition resisted the temptation to impose power and 'justice' in direct form. But out on the frontier, in small-scale confrontations, it was often the mad and the impulsive, rather than the brave and the thoughtful, who advanced the banner of 'civilisation'. History, with its tendency to sanitise the deeds of the conqueror and neglect the vanquished, often privileges the former over the latter.

Abandoning Durack, young McLoughlin charged up to the Aborigines – who recognised him as 'Tommy' – and shouted at them, in the local dialect: 'Stand up all black fellows and I will shoot all black fellows.' For the carcass-cutters the meaning of this seemingly ambiguous exhortation was crystal-clear. Several shots rang out as they ran for cover, leaving two of their number – 'Friday' and 'Jimmy' – behind as dead. As the dust and smoke cleared, so too did the younger McLoughlin's disturbed mind. Even Tommy, who had once cudgelled a cousin to within an inch of his life with a poker, realised that he had murdered two men. He lit a fire and, hoping to eliminate any trace of the slaughter, dragged the corpses into the flames. The bodies of the two Aboriginals were quickly consumed by the blaze, but not the skulls.[16]

Tommy's salvation now lay behind the line of the frontier rather than on it. In the outback it took weeks for the police to be directed to, and find, the charred remains of the two murdered men. A warrant for the suspect's arrest was issued in mid-November, and when Constable JC Thomson attempted to arrest him a few days later, McLoughlin covered him with a rifle and 'scoffed that twenty bastards wouldn't take him', before escaping on horseback.[17] It was a quintessentially 'Irish' response, one that his own Ancoats cohort, Ned Kelly or his one-armed brother would have applauded. It was also a signal to pastoralists to close ranks and protect their notion of frontier justice.[18]

Spearheaded by two generations of Duracks, the ranchers ostracised PC

Thomson for nearly three years for daring to attempt the arrest of a foot-soldier in their war against stock thieves.[19] More pertinently, the cattle mo-guls and their hired hands whipped-around and collected £300 to facilitate Tommy's escape. Along the frontiers of empire, where time slowed and space allowed identities to be renegotiated, there was often little separating fugitives from itinerant labourers. Although far from 'home', the developed world's southern refugees, working on farms and ranches, benefited from the collective brotherly actions born out of the experience of older indus-trial working-class culture in the north.[20] The colonies may have been the distant economic cousins of their northern counterparts but some patterns of male behaviour pointed to their common origins.

For Tommy, frontier sympathies might not have ended there. The ranch-ers may also have given him a set of names on remote Northern Territory and Queensland properties. There, like Ben Bridge, another fugitive from state – as opposed to frontier – justice, a man might hide until the heat had dissipated and he could return to the district.[21]

Tommy took his leave of his Irish-Australian hosts on 25 November 1901, saying: 'You might see me again' – and then disappeared, so Aboriginal folk claimed, to somewhere across the state line, near Wave Hill in the ad-jacent Northern Territory.[22] At some point over the next few months he may again have linked up briefly with his brother. But when he eventually *did* return to the Wyndham district in the Kimberleys, in 1905, and the state attempted to prosecute him for the murder of 'Friday' and 'Jimmy', the case was lost for want of sufficient evidence, including, it seems, corroborating testimony from sympathetic ranchers.[23]

By then 'Bourke' had long since passed through the eastern goldfields of Western Australia. We know that he left no trace of criminal activity in Coolgardie and Kalgoorlie because, months later, when asked about his missing hand, he freely told the police that it was the by-product of a min-ing accident sustained 'out west'.[24] Still intent on avoiding the largest urban centres where the *Police Gazette* was read more avidly, he remained keen on getting an adventurer or two to join in a campaign of safe-robbing up and down a few reasonably prosperous rural towns connected by rail.

But to this end he now had to add a new and unexpected requirement

– staying in touch with Tommy, who, if not in hiding around Wave Hill, was probably sitting it out in south-west Queensland. That meant that the terrain most suited to his needs lay 2 000 miles east – and he had only just traversed the width of the continent. To get to the part of the country he had in mind required crossing the western desert, the desolate Nullarbor Plain and the width of South Australia; all that before he even reached the starting point for his envisaged campaign, the silver-mining town of Broken Hill in New South Wales.

It was the best and the worst of times to be undertaking a trans-continental odyssey. The decade-long effects of the depression of the 1890s lingered, marked by the added handicaps of drought and a plague of rabbits. Employers responded with a push for cheaper, contract-bound labour and increased mechanisation, even of sheep-shearing. The result was a bitter, prolonged labour dispute across the country. The Amalgamated Shearer's Union came out on strike in 1890, 1891–92 and 1899. With the courts, police and pastoralists ranged against the rural workforce and 'sundowners' who arrived at outposts in search of a bed and meal at nightfall, as well as swagmen, there was a marked increase in class-based social tensions through much of the rural economy and in most country towns.[25]

On the largest estates, where there was an increase in the number of absentee and company owners as property values slumped and long-term opportunities beckoned for those with capital, the escalation in socio-economic hostilities saw a decline in traditional bush hospitality. The flip-side of that was a significant extension and deepening of the cult of 'mateship' among working men and casual labourers. Shared hardships and vulnerabilities, or simply being out on the road together, tightened bonds between 'mates' and strangers alike while a scarcity of women in remote regions was said to encourage homosexuality.[26] Jack McLoughlin, soldier, sailor and prison inmate, found himself in a sub-culture that he was familiar, probably even comfortable with.

After a long haul across three-quarters of the continent, 'John Bourke' slipped into Broken Hill in the opening weeks of 1902.[27] After several months on the road the mining town came as a relief, freeing him from the sun and heat of the drought and the prices that sly grog shops charged swagmen for bad beer. Back in the milieu he knew best, he succeeded in recruiting Edward Hogan, 20-year-old William Day, and one James Mulholland, about whom nothing is known. Hogan, a former miner, had little trouble in procuring some dynamite in a mining town, while Day, born in Tamworth, would provide them with local knowledge about possible eastern hideouts as well as raw muscle-power.[28] McLoughlin had once again assembled a group that included at least one young follower old enough to have been his son.

That summer was characterised by fearsome heat and drought. Cyclones and dust storms did enormous damage to property on the farms and in the remote New South Wales outback.[29] His plan was to sit out the season of Satan and then head north, up along the Darling River, towards the town of Bourke.[30] From there they would branch out east, into the upper reaches of the river's tributaries, concentrating on state facilities in small farming centres where country newspapers often complained about police incompetence.[31] Some of the journey would be on foot, swagman-style, but for longer hauls they would, along with the vagrants negotiating the state backwaters, 'jump the rattler' and stow away as best possible.[32] They would take as much cash as they could, but use chisels, picklocks and skeleton keys for the small-scale burglaries that would give them access to food in kitchens or small household items that could be put to use or sold.[33] Even though it was the closest thing to 'a gang' Jack McLoughlin had assembled since fleeing southern Africa, none of them carried revolvers. The real money would come via their safe-blowing exploits.

The four mates, of Irish descent and oath-bound not to betray gang members to the police should things go wrong, set off from Broken Hill for the Darling outback in mid-February. They seemed to have enough in common to be successful and to trust one another in potentially awkward situations. But was it sufficient? Two of them − Hogan and Day − seemed closer to one other than they were to Mulholland, or to 'Bourke', whose antecedents they could not have imagined, let alone believed if revealed to them. The one-armed man was an enigma.

★   ★   ★

350

Like Hermes, 'Bourke' was elusive, multi-faceted and shape-shifting. The ancient patron of gamblers, miners, travellers and thieves could be this worldly – a cairn of stones, a trail-blazer and a guide – but as Greek wisdom cautioned, he either 'led the way or led astray'. As was fitting for the god who escorted the souls of men to Hades, Hermes was also the mythic 'embodiment of ambiguity and ambivalence, doubleness and duplicity, contradiction and paradox'.[34]

There was more to Jack McLoughlin than met the eye. When stealing from those who frequently preyed on the working classes – bookmakers, mine owners, pawn- or stock-brokers – he often worked by night and eschewed violence. But his loyalty to friends had encouraged him to execute an informer. It was easy to see how, as a product of acute deprivation, some saw him as a sort of Robin Hood, a 'social bandit', disturbing the categories of 'truth and property' by exploring the changing boundaries of morality. Hermes, as Lewis Hyde notes, is amoral rather than immoral. The Trickster 'embodies and enacts that large portion of our experience where good and evil are hopelessly inter-twined'.[35] Hogan, Day and Mulholland trusted one another – but could they trust their leader, or was he about to lead them to Hades? And, conversely, could the one-armed fugitive rely on his new chums?

By late February 1902, the four were in the black soils of the Namoi Valley, a prosperous agricultural region focused on the small town of Narrabri. Narrabri had the usual facilities needed by rural folk in search of financial services or wider social connectivity, including banks and a post office, and, by no means unusually, also boasted a racecourse as well as an excellent little local newspaper. Part junction town, Narrabri was well connected by rail to other farming centres, including Moree, 60 miles to the north. It also enjoyed a weekend connection to Sydney, 300 miles south.[36] For burglars there were plenty of small pickings, but it was the railway station and its postal packages that immediately drew the attention of 'John Bourke'.

It took a week to set up the station job and establish what the best lines of approach and exit might be. The intervening days saw a few desultory attempts at burglary. Two attempts had to be aborted when the intruders were disturbed or encountered other problems, but they did manage to get into a room occupied by Mr Loder of the Bank of New South Wales and remove several small items. The police made no arrests, which added to mounting official and public dissatisfaction.[37]

The door to the main office of the station was breached at some time after 10.30 on the night of Wednesday, 5 March. The charge that blew the safe door was so expertly laid and detonated, and the noise of the resulting explosion so well muffled, that not even those people living close behind the 'Refreshment Rooms' heard a sound. It was the work of a master craftsman and a few energetic assistants. The safe yielded cash, cheques and stamps to the value of £34 as well as several other items that might come in handy, including some locks and keys and a pair of handcuffs. The room was ransacked and items to the value of another £20 or so removed from parcels destined for postal delivery. The intruders made off without ever being spotted; it was a perfect night's work.[38]

When the stationmaster got to his office at 6.00 am, he found the place in disarray, with everything covered in a layer of fine dust. The police were summoned and Sergeant Clarke appeared with a 'black tracker' drawn from the local Aboriginal community, the Kamilaroi. They picked up a set of prints leading to the racecourse and the main road that lay beyond it. But that was all; the case was never solved.[39]

Doubling-back, the four retreated 200 miles west, to Bourke, the transport hub par excellence on the upper reaches of the Darling. It was a place from where a man could, if necessary, head off in any direction including into the deepest outback or, as the Australian saying has it, into the 'back of Bourke'. But the hated blue-uniformed constables of the New South Wales police, sometimes still stigmatised as 'Bluebottles', never stirred from Narrabri.

The gang went through money like water. By mid-March the number of petty thefts, including food pilfered from kitchens, reached alarming levels; after dark, those on the streets felt menaced by 'suspicious-looking strangers'.[40] And then, as suddenly as they had appeared, the threatening outsiders disappeared and doors could again be left unlocked. For all that anyone knew, or cared, they could have set off on one of the far interior routes serviced by Afghan camel drivers who hailed from the Hindu Kush mountains of another world. But the gang, which by then saw north-eastern New South Wales as its playground, was again in search of the better-watered black-soil areas where cotton and wheat underwrote sturdy local economies. In the first week of April they crept into tiny Moree, which, much like Narrabri 50 miles further south, was firmly anchored to the main railway line running to distant Sydney.

This time there was no advance warning of an approaching storm. There were no house burglaries or petty thefts. 'Bourke' had enough dynamite to focus four sets of eyes on the main prize – the railway station at the eastern end of the village. Three people lived in a cottage a few hundred yards off, but the stationmaster's residence was a good distance away. The station was abandoned at the end of the day and night-shift constables did not include it in their rounds.[41]

At about 1.30 am on Tuesday, 8 April, the cottage residents heard what might have been the sound of a gunshot but apparently thought no more of it and went back to sleep. The safe had been blasted with minimum effort – a single charge had blown the lock and shattered the door. But the safe contained little more than £20 in cash so the gang, men given to travelling long distances, loaded up on railway tickets instead. It was hardly Narrabri, but would have to do.[42]

Even the police could see that it was the work of professionals, possibly from Sydney. But the robbery bore a striking resemblance to what had happened down the line only a month earlier, so they co-ordinated their efforts with the still-embarrassed Narrabri police.

But the Trickster was well-prepared for any counter-attack. He coached his lieutenants in their lines should they be arrested, emphasising the need for cohesion and group solidarity. In order to confuse the uniformed predators, they would split up. Where the Trickster chose to go to is unknown, but, from what happened subsequently, he may have moved about 250 miles north and spent the winter in the warmth of Queensland with Tommy. The others would separate and move south slowly, across the plains, down towards the Liverpool Ranges around Tamworth, where young Day hailed from. The theft of the railway tickets meant that they had to avoid the trains and rendezvous at Quirindi – 'the nest in the hills'.

'Bourke' disappeared for nearly five months but was never far from a part of rural Australia that he had got to know back in the 1880s. Hogan and Day, too, disappeared; but only for five days. They avoided the trains but then, on passing through Narrabri, were arrested on the basis of information collected by the police at either end of the line. By 14 April, they were back in Moree, where they appeared in the Police Court. The case was remanded for eight days as the constables quizzed them about the whereabouts of the other gang members. Whether out of fear or loyalty they refused to reveal anything about 'Bourke' but may instead have let slip where the fourth man might be found. By 24 April, a uniformed constable had tracked Mulholland for 170 miles across the plains to Quirindi and arrested him before escorting him back to Moree.[43]

But the proof of a police pudding lies not in the arrests made, but in convictions secured – and their case was badly under-egged. James Mulholland was the first to walk, the prosecutor deciding that there was insufficient evidence to warrant even an arraignment in the Police Court. Hogan and Day had a less easy time of it. After appearing in the Police Court, in late April, they were committed for trial. But, when they appeared before the Quarter Sessions, on 12 June, they too were acquitted for want of evidence.[44] The country police, it seemed, were no match for a quartet of well-led professionals. The police had not only failed to make any arrests for a string of burglaries committed in and around Moree and Narrabri that autumn, but had also been unable to obtain convictions for the robberies at two railway stations.

Conspicuous failure fed press and public misgivings and the higher-ups were in an awkward position. They responded as they often do at such times and shuffled their cards. On 1 August, Constable Dunshea of Moree was sent to Tamworth, on the River Peel, half-way between Brisbane and Sydney, and an ambitious young Constable Brodie transferred from Tamworth to Moree to shake things up a bit.[45]

With spring in the offing Trickster Bourke stirred from his hibernation somewhere among the former haunts of the Duracks in south-western Queensland. His off-season survival may have been underwritten by Tommy, still wanted for murder back in the Kimberleys. It had been a year or more since Jack McLoughlin had re-entered Australia and he had twice crossed the continent without colliding with the state police.

It was true that during his great walkabout, the British had been tied up by a Boer guerrilla campaign that had helped disrupt the sweep of the Imperial Eye. But, even then, his experiences in continental Australia contrasted sharply with those in the islands across the Tasman. Predictably, the war had ended in defeat for the Boers; the Treaty of Vereeniging was concluded on 31 May 1902. He would have to be more careful, but it would take time for the British to establish his whereabouts. It was tempting to return to New Zealand just to prove to himself – or perhaps to the police there – that, given a decent start, even those islands could be negotiated successfully by a man on the run. He was a survivor. Had it not been 10 years since he was discharged from prison in Pretoria, and the warder had taken his leave of him by saying 'until we next meet'? But since then the power of the old Boer state had drained away into the sand and veld and it was unlikely that he would see Matthew de Beer again. Southern Africa was a lifetime away and he had to resume his travels 'down under'. Even a journey to nowhere started somewhere.

He was nearly down-and-out when he re-entered Moree, in mid-August. He had no cash or food but knew that a break-in or two would set matters right – the town's police were not the brightest. What he did have was the remnants of a safe-blowing kit, including one last explosive charge. Once he had settled in and done the necessary reconnaissance he would do what the police would least expect of him and return to the main prize, the station. Once the Trickster was fully fed he could head back to Broken Hill for more rest and dynamite.

Only days after his arrival the press, if not the constabulary, picked up on 'a sudden impetus in burglary enterprises'.[46] But he remained so broke that on the Friday night before the envisaged big job – Saturday, 23 August – he had to go out and raise some cash for breakfast the next morning. Night-shift work had its own rhythm and he seldom ate a heavy meal before a big job. Skeleton keys gave him silent, trouble-free entry into the premises of Messrs Barry & Stafford, outfitters. The till, fitted with a mechanical alarm, posed no problems but yielded less than £2 in cash. He slipped out of the

rear of the shop and the whole operation went so smoothly that the proprietors had to be pressed to notice that they had been robbed.[47] He had
many more hours to kill.

Weekends were a favourite time for safe-blowing. It was around 2.00 am
on Sunday when he approached the rear of the deserted railway station,
found the ladder he had stashed away behind the building a few days earlier
and propped it up against the ticket office window. The office housed a safe
so small that even he would be able to manoeuvre it into position. After
their previous job, that April, the inhabitants in the cottage were bound to
investigate the sound if they heard an explosion. In the absence of a blanket,
a section of tarpaulin would have to do as a container in which to drag off
the safe. He found a suitable piece and took it around to the front of the
building, leaving it on the platform, just outside the door to the ticket office.

The window took some encouragement before it popped open and he
clambered into the office. Inside, he opened a holdall and removed a billycan, a knife and the stub of a candle, setting them out on the floor in
preparation for what was to follow. He got out the skeleton keys and went
to the ticket office door, unlocking it so that once he had lifted the safe, he
would have easy access to the tarpaulin on the platform outside. Closing
the door, he checked his pockets for matches, fuse and explosive. He took
a look around to make certain there was nothing that he might trip over.[48]

Constable Brodie, who had come on duty at dusk, had an idea as to why
he had been transferred to Moree at short notice. By then, just about everybody in the rural NSW force knew about Hogan, Day and Mulholland and
the botched police work. There had been a few burglaries in town and he
did not want to get caught flat-footed so he decided to call in at the railway
station when he did his last round for the night. He set out from the police
station, he said, shortly after 2.00 am.

Inside the ticket office it was not all beer and skittles. 'Bourke' was ir-
ritated by a pile of papers that had been carelessly stacked on top of the
safe and he swept them clear, leaving them scattered about the floor. The
safe proved more difficult to move than he had foreseen. It reminded him
why he had become so reliant on help. He hauled the safe away from its
position up against the wall, dragging it to the centre of the room with

some difficulty before tipping it onto its side. But it was hard work even for a strong man, so he decided to sit down and take a breather. Summer was only a few weeks away and the chill of the night discouraged the usual insect noises; all was deadly quiet.

Brodie entered the station grounds and, glancing down the platform, noticed a tarpaulin lying outside the door to the ticket office. Someone would trip over it. It was sloppy, the sort of thing one expected from young railway workers who took little pride in their work. The station master would not be pleased. He strode down the platform, heavy boots banging out the pace, making his way towards the tarpaulin. Outside the ticket office door he stopped and paused for a moment.

Inside, 'Bourke' heard the footsteps and became slightly flustered. He was unarmed and on his own. He did not know what to do. His craft relied more on strength and stealth than it did on tongue and dissembling.

Brodie lent down, turned the handle and, applying a little pressure, was surprised to find the door unlocked. At that instant:

> He heard a slight noise and called out 'Who is there'?, to which he received the reply: 'It's alright, it's the stationmaster'. But the Constable did not think 'it was all right' and, after watching a little, sang out: 'Come out whoever you are'! The man inside then peeped out and tried to close the door. Constable Brodie forced it in and drew his revolver. The suspect then rushed past, but the former called upon him to surrender, caught him and brought him back to the office.[49]

As a member of the fourth estate pointed out, the Constable had 'made a promising beginning in his career of checking crime'. What neither Brodie nor the journalist realised, however, was that a small Australian country town with a modest claim to fame had just witnessed the apprehension of not only the most successful safe-cracker the world's richest goldfields had ever known, but a bandit-outlaw, a coach-robber, highwayman, mercenary and a man who was wanted for murdering a police informer in Johannesburg.[50]

Brodie was no slouch. When he searched the one-armed man and found a £1 commercial banknote on him, in addition to burglary and safe-blow-ing paraphernalia, he concluded that the suspect may have broken into a shop earlier in the week. When he asked about the note and some small change, the man, who suggested that he had lost his hand in a mining ac-cident in Western Australia, said: 'It's mine, no use you asking me any ques-tions, for I'll tell you lies.'[51] 'Bourke' had to rely on his wits.

It was indeed a curious response; one that might well have elicited more official curiosity. But the constable was almost ready to bank his winnings, which, by Moree standards, were already considerable. But then, having thought it through overnight, he went around to Barry & Stafford the fol-lowing day and made more enquiries. After establishing how the till worked, and conducting a few experiments using the skeleton keys found on the suspect, he had enough to charge 'Bourke' with theft as well as the intent to commit a felony on the premises of the NSW railway commissioners.[52]

The accused's appearance in the Police Court three days later, on 26 August, had a predictable sequel. Knowing that the station robbery case was a lost cause, he pleaded guilty to intending to commit a felony but then did his best to sow confusion around the burglary at the outfitters. He had, he said, been found in possession of a stolen bank note and pleaded guilty to that charge but denied breaking into the store or rifling through the till. The argument was unpersuasive; both cases were referred to the Quarter Sessions.[53]

He was not optimistic and spent six weeks brooding in the cells at Moree, awaiting trial. But when he did eventually appear before the Quarter Sessions, in mid-October, things went better than expected – by compari-son with his New Zealand experiences, positively well.[54] Pleading guilty to two out of three charges against him went down reasonably well with a judge who could not have failed to notice that the accused man was with-out a lower right arm.

The prosecution, already frustrated by its failures to obtain a convic-tion in the Hogan and Day case, had to settle for an 18-month sentence, with hard labour, for the 'break-in' at the Moree Station. The state also managed to get a sentence of 12 months, with hard labour, handed down for the theft at Barry & Stafford's , but the judge ruled that the sentences would run concurrently.[55] It could have been worse — a lot worse. Unlike in New Zealand, where stories about his extradition on a charge of murder were doing the rounds in official and unofficial legal circles, the Australians seemed to be wholly unaware of 'Jack McLoughlin'.

Moree had no facilities for long-term prisoners so he had to serve out his sentence at Tamworth. The jail had been built a decade earlier and conditions were tolerable enough to stay out of trouble. But, that said, he was locked up in there for all of 1903, having already spent 1896–1898 and most of 1899 in prison. Since the Red Lion shootings, in 1895, he had spent more time in prison than out of it.

He was released from Tamworth on 16 January 1904, days before his forty-fifth birthday. It may have been a good omen. He shed the moniker which, like 'Kenny' and 'Dell' before it, had outlived its usefulness. But it was not wholly forgotten. The New South Wales *Police Gazette,* like a lover scorned, remembered everything, forgot nothing. An alias was a shadow, not a phantom.

For the next 12 months he and Tommy — who had not bothered to change his name and was starting to think about returning to the Kimberleys — avoided the police and the courts. 1904 was a good year for the McLoughlin brothers and, judging from his movements a year later, much of it may have been spent in the comfort of southern Queensland — well away from Wave Hill and the Northern Territory, still administered from far-away South Australia.

By the time that he left Tommy, he felt confident that the British and the Boers had lost interest in the shooting at the Red Lion and he reverted to his own name. It was a relief not to have to come up with a contrived pedigree. In December 1904, he re-entered Broken Hill, where he had a few mates who had ready access to explosives.

WINTER

CHAPTER TWENTY-TWO

The Fatal Circuit

AUSTRALIA, NEW ZEALAND, AUSTRALIA

— 1904–1909 —

I'm a rambler, I'm a gambler, I'm a long way from home,
And if you don't like me, please leave me alone.
I eat when I'm hungry, I drink when I'm dry,
And if sunshine don't kill me, I'll live 'til I die.
Oh sunshine for dinner, oh sunshine for tea,
Oh sunshine for supper, it's sunshine for me.
I eat when I'm hungry, I drink when I'm dry,
And if sunshine don't kill me, I'll live 'til I die.

OLD IRISH TINKER'S SONG

Almost 10 years had passed since the shootings at the Red Lion and, bar a few desultory queries from officials in New Zealand, nothing of importance had transpired since. The Imperial Eye seemed to have lost interest in him and he felt composed and confident enough to enter Broken Hill under his own name. He sensed that Jack McLoughlin was a more mature and rounded man, and he had become accustomed to the routines of prison life, exclusively male company and life on the road. He knew that he was more at one with himself but realised that he could never settle down. He was, if not a gypsy or a tinker, then a compulsive wanderer, like the *shaughraun,* rooted in the culture of Irish nationalism.[1]

He did not linger in Broken Hill. He had had enough of rural New South Wales and wanted to get out of the state and into a city where he could raise the money for a few drinks, a decent bed, a little gambling and more travel. He left the mining town, with or without dynamite, in late 1904.

Adelaide, free from the usual English sneering, was a town laid out for immigrants rather than convicts. With a population of 150 000, the city offered the full range of possibilities he was in search of. As the only clearing house of substance for South Australia's agricultural economy, it was a commercial and financial hub with well-established links to the eastern cities that dominated the continent. The place that interested him most, however, lay 10 miles farther south. In Port Adelaide a moneyed man commanded all of the southern ocean. He could sail west, to Fremantle and Perth, east to Melbourne or Sydney or, if not those, he could stretch across the world and disappear into Cape Town, Durban, Hobart or even Wellington. He had contacts in all those places.

Adelaide was not Melbourne, where the underworld clung to the city like a drunk to a bar counter, but it was becoming livelier. A burglar or two was always drifting in from up-country and the town, aspiring to better things, already had a few aspirant safe-robbers and even the occasional murderer.[2] He looked around for a convenient place and, as 'Jack McLoughlin', booked into a small rooming house on Cannon Street, managed by Jane Irvin.

If he had the cash to cover the cost of his stay when he arrived, then he certainly did not by the time that he was told to leave a week later. It triggered an outburst of anger which may, in part, have been fuelled by alcohol and contempt for the no-nonsense proprietor. He 'wilfully damaged' four panes of glass and the lock on a door. Irvin could not have cared less. She had no interest in his drinking or his disrespect; all she wanted was what was due to her, and she called for the constables.

It was exactly what he had hoped to avoid; some unnecessary problem with the police. She insisted on his coming up with the rent as well as the cost of the repairs and, when he could not, he was arrested. When he appeared in court, on 12 January 1905, he admitted to having come down from

Broken Hill and to having deliberately damaged property. The Magistrate ordered him to pay the rent of £2, 15 shillings in damages, as well as a fine of £1, or face a month's imprisonment with hard labour.[3] He did not have a mate in town or a penny to his name. The law could not help with cash, but it could direct him to friends.

The Adelaide gaol, like all such places, was a godsend for any visiting merchant of crime. It was a centre for criminal intelligence, a market place of ideas, a place where new projects could be put together. It was a stock exchange of crime, where each day's intake of inmates revealed the ruling price for doing business as calibrated against sentences handed down by the judiciary. It was a great state-funded enterprise, one that had ruined as many men as it had ever rescued. It helped him find his way to a sizeable sum of money within just days of his release.

But the month in gaol also reminded him that, in the longer run, he was still up against the hangman.[4] He was no layabout caught disturbing the peace in a doss house, but a man wanted for murder, and would probably face the death penalty if he were caught. It did not help that the cells in Adelaide were abuzz with a grisly tale, filled with awful detail and morbid vignettes, about the final hours of a youngster who had been executed in the gaol's 'hanging tower' a few days earlier. William Borfield was a club-footed boot-maker with a jealous disposition, who had put three bullets into the breast of an estranged girlfriend whom he had spotted dancing with another man.[5] It was love that was a problem.

It was, he thought, one more reason to take the information he had gleaned in the prison yard and put Adelaide behind him. Even though the authorities gave him no reason to think otherwise – his name had elicited not so much as a casual enquiry – he was infused with a sense of purpose, with the desire to make the best of such time as he might still have. What his immediate objective was, and how, where and when it was executed, all remain unknown. But, by mid-February, he was in the money, in port, and then literally off to the races across the Tasman Sea.

★ ★ ★

What was the fatal attraction that New Zealand held for Jack McLoughlin? The place had bewitched him from the moment he had first glimpsed its shores. It couldn't have been gold, mining towns or wild frontiers, the magnets that never failed; they were long gone. Could it have been a yearning for relief of the sort that the sights, sounds and smells of rural Lancashire offered for a child labourer in Manchester?[26] Perhaps the greenery, mists and rain of the islands offered some respite from the barren circuits of small-town Australia, India and southern Africa? We will never know – he never said – and, as with the mills of Ancoats, New Zealand had never offered him more than incarceration and much hard labour.

His point of entry on the North Island, possibly aboard the same *Rotomahana* that he had once stowed away on, was probably Wellington. But his destination lay elsewhere. This time he was moving around in comparative style. His vagrant-hunting nemeses would have no excuse to intercept him when he could afford hired accommodation. It was the height of the horse racing season and the Auckland Cup and other meetings offered a man the chance not only to make money but to launder it. It was another of Manchester's lessons he had not forgotten.

But the dogs, vigilant as ever, barked even though they could not bite. On 22 February 1905, someone thought they recognised a one-armed man at the Auckland races. The law-enforcement authorities, whose records extended back to the failed attempt at extradition at the time of the Jameson Raid, in 1895, were immediately interested. A month later, they used the *Police Gazette,* which circulated across the Tasman Sea and among police forces throughout the region, to put out a second – special – enquiry about a fugitive with a prosthesis.

> Jack MacLachan, *alias* McLoughlin, *alias* Thomas Kenny *alias* John Dell, is wanted by the Johannesburg police on a charge of having, in 1895, murdered a man there named Stevenson. Offender was seen at a trotting meeting at Auckland on the 22nd ultimo and was then clean-shaved with the exception of a heavy dark moustache, a dark tweed suit, hard black hat, white shirt and collar and black tie with thin white streaks. He was wearing a brown glove on his false hand.[7]

The Imperial Eye, effectively shut since 1901, suddenly had a light shone into it. But the news that he had been spotted was not as bad as it might have been. The New Zealand police knew nothing about 'John Bourke' or the station robberies in New South Wales in 1902. They obviously thought he was still on the islands – why else the local feeler? – but it would take time for them to put it all together. Until then, it was safe enough to return to north-eastern Australia. If he steered clear of 'big jobs' he could get by without the South Africans, Australians and New Zealanders making much sense of his movements.

At face value, the short excursion back to the North Island was a triumph. He was like a nineteenth-century ticket-of-leave man, a prisoner on parole as long as he respected the conditions attached to his 'freedom'. He had re-entered the country under his own name without any difficulty, re-negotiated Auckland and enjoyed time away from the continental prison that was Australia. He had conquered a few personal demons and was ready to move on. Before the winter chill set in fully, probably around April or May 1905, he left the country, again without problem, and re-crossed the Tasman Sea for the third time in five years. But whether he realised it or not, the Imperial Eye had been roused from its long sleep and was, once again, scanning almost the entire region for signs of him.

Personality and profession meant that the principal cities of south-eastern Australia, Melbourne or Sydney, were the places most likely to attract him. But he was aware that urban magnets posed potentially the greatest danger, and so, while he re-entered the country through one of the east-coast ports, he did not tarry there. He had been all too active there two decades earlier and had again helped himself to a slice of financial pie in Melbourne in 1900, on first leaving New Zealand. His best bet was to remain in small places or on the frontier with his brother. It was never a stark choice. It may have been a combination of the two that enabled him to avoid attracting official attention for more than 18 months.

The intervening years, since the brothers had met in Fremantle, in 1901, had been good to Tommy. By 1905, he was back in the Kimberleys after having been on the run in the Queensland outback for some time. He appeared in court at Wyndham that year, but the charge of having murdered the Aboriginals was dropped for want of evidence.[8] Frontier justice saw Tommy take up his old position as a drover-stockman; by 1906, he was sufficiently settled to take out a pastoral lease of his own in partnership with a man named Alfred Gregor.[9] Late 1905 through to mid-1906 would have been an opportune moment for him to host his outlawed brother. Whatever the case, by mid-1906, Jack McLoughlin was back in the state he had long felt most comfortable in – Queensland.

★   ★   ★

From the mid-1840s through to 1900 various points up and down the mountainous coastal strip of Queensland, stretching from Brisbane in the south to Cape York in the north, had witnessed gold rushes. Most of the finds were alluvial and quickly worked out. But here and there, as at Gympie, sluiced diggings pointed to more substantial reefs and the need for mine shafts. The most significant find of all, however, occurred at Charters Towers, about 70 miles south-west of Townsville, in the 1870s. There, a cluster of 10 reefs supported a stock exchange and 30 000 people, making it the second largest town in the state at the time. A few of the Towers' reefs were sufficiently profitable to be mined right up to World War I. But, for the most part, Queensland rushes were half-decade or less propositions that saw their heyday in the 1880s, leaving behind abandoned diggings and hamlets. In some such places, a few Chinese diggers, pioneers from the earliest rushes, such as that at Palmer's in the 1870s, moved in and with customary focus and frugality made a living from working what others had long given up on.[10]

The village of Nebo and the longer-lived mine at Mount Britton in the Connors Range, a third of the way along the road from Rockhampton to Townsville, both fell into the abandoned category. In the early 1880s they had been small but thriving centres, but by the turn of the century they were already lapsing into what they now are – historical curiosities. Who knows what residual appeal they held for Jack McLoughlin, but, like Barberton in the eastern Transvaal and Ohinemuri in New Zealand before them, they drew him in on his way further north. In Charters Towers, another mining town already drained of most of its magic, surely an elderly fellow might be able to lay his hands on a little dynamite and some gold?

He was, he said, English and, less plausibly, a labourer. He had enough equipment to set up a camp that might attract a hard-pressed swagman. His preference for the company of younger men was undiminished, as was his desire to be in charge of some modest project. All he needed was a soulmate on his journey to nowhere. Then, out on the road beyond Mount Britton, on a spring day in August 1906, he met George King. King was a strong, hard-up, 25-year-old without a criminal record, who sported a badly scarred nose, like that of a boxer.[11] Who knows if the fellow reminded him of another George he had known, also a boxer?

Deciding that Mount Britton had nothing left to offer them, the two swagmen set off on a 50-mile hike out of the mountains, down onto the better-watered coastal plain and on to the port beyond it. Subtropical Mackay was surrounded by sugar plantations. The fields, worked by thousands of Kanakas drawn from the Pacific Islands, confirmed that the town's economic backbone, once reliant on mining, now got all its stiffening from agriculture and the docks. But the scars of Queensland's earlier gold sickness were still to be found in the town's business quarter.

When Palmer's Rush, in the far north, played itself out in the mid-1880s, hundreds of Chinese diggers decamped to coastal Cooktown. There, they got them themselves berths to Mackay, hoping to go on and profit from any new discoveries around Mount Britton or Nebo. Most of the newcomers settled into a predictably named 'Chinatown', and while many became shopkeepers, market-gardeners or labourers, a few more daring souls turned their hands to gambling and opium dens or small-scale prostitution to make a living. When the local economy faltered these supposedly 'heathen' vices caused Christian and settler prejudices to boil over and into a full-scale 'anti-Chinese' movement.[12]

But Mackay was not a town without hope for those intent on criminal mischief. Chinese, Kanakas and sailors were lightning conductors of the usual sort for a suspicious settler society, but they also provided enterprising burglars and thieves with possible channels through which to funnel stolen goods. McLoughlin & King set up their new business in a tent on conveniently sited public ground in the first week of September.

The need for an underworld fence, however, never arose because they ran out of money almost before they could plan, let alone execute, a burglary. Desperate times called for desperate measures. It reminded McLoughlin how, when the Irish Brigade entered Johannesburg in 1888, they focused on the boarding houses and hotels for small items that could be easily disposed of on the black market. But, because his partner was a tyro, McLouglin resorted to sneak-thievery of the sort that, in the past, was usually the preserve of youngsters like young 'Stevo'.

On Thursday night, 6 September, Henry Forbes Wiseman, a district sugar manufacturer in town on business, retired to his room in the Prince of Wales Hotel. He left a gold watch and chain worth, he estimated, £17, along with 15s 6d in silver, on the chair besides the bed. Even if his room had been locked, as it probably was, it might not have helped if the post-midnight intruder had a set of skeleton keys. Wiseman woke to find the valuables missing.[13]

Back in camp that Friday morning, McLoughlin, who had pocketed the silver, decided against disposing of the watch immediately. He relied on the police not paying them a visit and, in a fit of vagrant-rousting, discovering the missing timepiece. By the next morning, with the weekend upon them, he was far readier to dispose of the gold chain at a knock-down price. He told King to go and explore backstreet Chinatown to see if he could get rid of the thing for about 30 shillings.

Yuen Sing was not interested in what was probably stolen property. Well, not at 30 shillings. But King was not wholly discouraged and returned to camp to get his partner to persuade Sing to up his offer. He, too, failed to persuade Sing to part with 30 shillings so they gave up, but not before asking for directions to a nearby jewellery store.[14]

With some silver already in his pocket, McLoughlin became as cautious as the Chinaman. He decided that he did not want to be seen in a jewellery store where a visit from a one-armed man may not have been an everyday occurrence. It was King who was in greater need of funds and so he left it up to him to sell the chain. The watch, more conspicuous and valuable than the gold chain, would be held back for sale on a real rainy day. He told King to try his luck in a pub, but warned him to steer clear of the Prince of Wales, which was situated close by the bridge.

King went to the Belmore Arms – a name with an Irish resonance. There he struck up a conversation with Barney McGuire, the proprietor's son, and offered him the chain for 30 shillings. But McGuire was wary, sensing that he was being offered the most clichéd item of stolen property of the Victorian and Edwardian ages. He nevertheless entered the spirit of the bidding contest and attempted to beat the price down by suggesting that he was not certain that it was made of gold. When King, pointing to a stamp, protested that it was, McGuire expressed more doubts and countered with an offer of just 15 shillings. It was an outrageous offer but King, uncertain what to do, yet keen for his share of a sale, said he needed time to consider the offer and would return within the hour. By the time that King left the Belmore Arms McGuire was almost certain that he was dealing with a stolen chain and that beyond it there was probably not only a watch but a second thief.

In the camp, with only King's version to go by, McLoughlin, cash in hand, failed to appreciate fully that hawking the chain could raise questions about the watch. He was in no mood to argue with an apprentice and told King to go back and accept the offer. King scurried back to the hotel and, half an hour later, told McGuire that he would take 15 shillings for the chain. But by then McGuire, relishing the idea of helping to bring two men to book, could not resist baiting the hook further. He told King that he still had some doubts about the authenticity of the chain but that it should be left with him and he would have it assessed. If it turned out to be genuine, King could return and he would then be paid in full.[15]

Taking it all in, King returned to camp with the news. His mentor was either so beguiled, narcissistic or selfish – or all three – that he failed to see that the apprentice's efforts had placed them in danger. It was a mistake. Back at the hotel McGuire, who did not realise that a man's life was at stake but was well pleased with himself, handed the chain, and a man's neck, to the police. The constables did not even have to find the thief. He presented himself to them at the Arms the following morning.[16]

King, hopelessly out of his depth, was persuaded to point out where he had been dossing and accompanied the constables back to the site where they found McLoughlin. Caught unaware, McLoughlin had not had time to conceal the watch. He feigned surprise: 'how the watch got there was a mystery to him'.[17] On the way to the station he whispered to King that, if asked, he should say that he knew nothing about the watch. It was a self-serving instruction that tested the young man's loyalty to breaking point.

On 10 September, McLoughlin was charged with the theft of the watch and chain, and King – who refused to implicate him – on the lesser charge of having received the stolen chain. McLoughlin made no effort to conceal his real name and was confident about the outcome if King did not reveal that he knew that the items had been stolen from a hotel room. The cases were referred to the next sitting of the Supreme Court in Mackay. King, who knew that he would probably have to share a cell with McLoughlin down the line, held out for more than a month. Then, on the day before his trial, on 11 October, he folded. He told the police that he knew that McLoughlin had gone to the Prince of Wales and stolen the watch and chain items because he had told him that he had done so.

The case before Justice Virgil Powers ran a predictable course. McLoughlin attempted some low-order dissembling in a short address directed at the jury. The unfortunate King simply accepted his fate. The jury, equally un-moved by visitations from the spectres of aged deceit and youthful earnestness, took five minutes to find him guilty of theft and King of being an accessory after the fact. Even then, the senior partner must have thought that, without any record of a previous conviction in Australia under the name McLoughlin, he might be entitled to the usual consideration extended to a first offender when it came to sentencing.

But it was not to be. Powers's rooms had already been partially lit up by the gleam of the Imperial Eye. Items of information from police gazettes on both sides of the Tasman were coming together in a way that was potentially life-threatening. Sentencing McLoughlin to three years' imprisonment with hard labour, the judge pointed out that the prisoner had previous convictions in New Zealand for possessing house-breaking tools and one, in New South Wales, under the name 'Bourke', for housebreaking. Powers, correctly,

A spate of robberies at railway stations in rural New South Wales in 1902 culminated in gang leader 'John Bourke' being sentenced to a year's hard labour in Tamworth Gaol. This mugshot is also the only surviving likeness of Jack McLoughlin, who shot George Stevenson, his underworld-intimate turned police informer, in 1895. NEW SOUTH WALES STATE RECORDS

In 1859 the historian Hippolyte Taine, visiting Manchester, noted a factory, a 'rectangle six storeys high' in which thousands of workmen were 'regimented, hands active, feet motionless, all day and every day, mechanically serving their machines'. It could, he wrote, have been a hard labour penal establishment. *Above*, Murray Mill on the corner of Bengal and Union streets, Ancoats. *Below*, the west wing of Belle Vue Prison, a 'factory' for reforming character, saw McLoughlin do three months' hard labour for the theft of a pair of boots in 1878. MANCHESTER LIBRARIES, INFORMATION AND ARCHIVES, MANCHESTER CITY COUNCIL

A roof-top view of Ancoats, 'the world's first industrial suburb', the most densely populated Irish quarter in Manchester – and birthplace of Jack McLoughlin in 1859. He left at age 20 and for three decades thereafter, showing a preference for the countryside, he criss-crossed the British colonies of the Indian Ocean world. MANCHESTER LIBRARIES, INFORMATION AND ARCHIVES, MANCHESTER CITY COUNCIL

RIGHT: Back Mill Street was one of the haunts of John Brown. The son of an Ancoats pharmacist, by 1888 Brown was in Kimberley, working the roads as a highwayman robbing African migrants of their wages. Brown re-joined McLoughlin's gang, in Johannesburg, in the early 1890s. MANCHESTER LIBRARIES, INFORMATION AND ARCHIVES, MANCHESTER CITY COUNCIL

BELOW: Withington Workhouse, where McLoughlin's mother, Eliza, said to be suffering from 'senility', died a pauper at the age of 50. During World War I, the buildings were used to house German prisoners of war, offering a further illustration of how the architecture of certain institutions in early industrial Manchester manifested socially repressive features. MANCHESTER LIBRARIES, INFORMATION AND ARCHIVES, MANCHESTER CITY COUNCIL

Charles Peace, picaresque Midlands burglar, folk-hero and murderer, jumped from a moving train in a failed attempt to elude the police in Worksop, in 1879. It was a feat that McLoughlin emulated successfully on the Witwatersrand 15 years later, in 1894. SHEFFIELD ARCHIVES

A blacksmith's apprentice and contemporary of McLoughlin's, Bob Horridge was an innovative burglar who became an underworld hero when his gang successfully removed a safe holding the payroll from a textile mill in Bradford in 1878.

Up Great Ancoats Street, on Shudehill, the Smithfield Market and its surrounds were central to Jack McLoughlin and his mother, Eliza, who in 1878 was found guilty of receiving stolen goods from her sons.
MANCHESTER LIBRARIES, INFORMATION AND ARCHIVES, MANCHESTER CITY COUNCIL

The Seven Stars was one of two public houses bearing the same name frequented by Jack McLoughlin and his brothers, William and Tommy, in the 1870s. On being sentenced to death McLoughlin expressed his regret at not being able to revisit the pub or the River Mersey. MANCHESTER LIBRARIES, INFORMATION AND ARCHIVES, MANCHESTER CITY COUNCIL

HMS *Albatross.* In 1880–81, a journey across the world aboard this Royal Navy sloop took 21-year-old McLoughlin from Plymouth to Singapore. It marked him as a sailor and placed him within reach of the frontier life and real-life heroes he craved. HAMPSHIRE RECORD OFFICE

Below: Outside Eureka City, on the way to more settled Barberton. The narrowing of the road at Elephant's Creek was a site favoured by Irish Brigade highwaymen in the late 1880s. NATIONAL ARCHIVES OF SOUTH AFRICA

For those with a passion for fighting, gambling and the horses – which was most of them – race days at the Eureka City racecourse held an irresistible attraction. The Victoria Hotel, half-way along the three-furlong racecourse, became an obvious meeting place for the Irish *en route* to yet more mayhem in Delagoa Bay. BARBERTON MUSEUM

The earliest stretches of the Delagoa Bay–Pretoria railway line, completed in 1895, were built by African workers and teams of American, English and Irish navvies. Amongst the latter were the Irishmen who overran a Portuguese gunboat in the harbour at Lourenço Marques in 1887. MUSEUM AFRICA

Commissioner Street, Johannesburg, in 1887, 1889 and 1890. The western end was dominated by gangsters linked to the 'American Club' and 'Irish Brigade'. McLoughlin saw it as 'one of the most dangerous places in Johannesburg' and in 1897 it was the site of a gangland shootout so violent that even the police avoided it. MUSEUM AFRICA

The Goldfields coach deposited McLoughlin outside the Royal Hotel in Potchefstroom in mid-June 1890. After robbing a priest, he organised an Irish Brigade gaol break-out which cost one man his life and left his own wrist so badly shattered by a bullet that the lower part of his arm had to be amputated. MUSEUM AFRICA

Fleeing a depression in Johannesburg, McLoughlin's gang were active in the countryside during the winter of 1890, robbing a mail coach and a store, and removing the Landdrost's safe from this government building in Rustenburg. MUSEUM AFRICA

McLoughlin encountered FR Gill at the Krugersdorp Railway Station in the early 1890s while boarding trains without a valid ticket. It was Gill's attempt to capture him that prompted 'One-armed Jack' to leap from a moving train, in 1894, and that later earned Gill a place on the gangster's 'death list'. NATIONAL ARCHIVES OF SOUTH AFRICA

Edinburgh-trained Dr John van Niekerk was resident surgeon at the Johannesburg Hospital and the doctor who amputated McLoughlin's arm in 1890. He also attended to the dying George Stevenson in 1895. SOUTH AFRICAN MEDICAL JOURNAL

The Hospital Matron, Mother Adele of the Order of the Holy Family, was responsible for nursing McLoughlin back to health after the amputation of his arm. SOUTH AFRICAN MEDICAL JOURNAL

Johannesburg General Hospital, 1893. McLoughlin, ashamed at having robbed a priest and uncomfortable in the presence of nuns, was unwilling to enter the hospital and in 1894 asked his brother, Tommy, to meet him in the grounds. SOUTH AFRICAN MEDICAL JOURNAL

Front entrance, Visagie Street Prison, Pretoria. In 1891, an unsuccessful attempt was made to storm the gaol and free two highwaymen on death row, Jack McLoughlin and several other Irishmen. The breakout was foiled by members of the State Artillery including Constable MJ de Beer. In 1909, De Beer was sent to Australia to identify McLoughlin and escort him back to South Africa. NATIONAL ARCHIVES OF SOUTH AFRICA

Loreto Convent, Pretoria. In 1891, gangsters used a wooded section of its grounds to launch an unsuccessful attack on the adjacent Visagie Street Gaol. NATIONAL ARCHIVES OF SOUTH AFRICA

Left: Thomas Menton, an Irish deserter from the British Army and later jailer at Barberton and in Johannesburg, supported pleas for remissions of sentence by members of the McLoughlin gang. NATIONAL ARCHIVES OF SOUTH AFRICA

Below: The Johannesburg Prison and its ramshackle predecessors saw repeated and sometimes successful attempts at escape by various Irish inmates, including Jack McLoughlin and members of his gang during the early 1890s. MUSEUM AFRICA

The Old Vienna Café, corner of Market and Joubert Streets, where, over tea on a Saturday afternoon in 1895, Jack McLoughlin met Harry Lobb and told him that he intended shooting George Stevenson by sunset. THE STAR, BARNETT COLLECTION

Kerk Street Mosque. Eighteen-year-old Joseph Carr, known within the Muslim community as
Hadji Mustaffa, was on the corner of Main and Wolhuter streets, on his way to prayers, when he
was fatally shot by Jack McLoughlin. MUSEUM AFRICA

A view of Johannesburg from the Robinson Mine, where McLoughlin hid after the shooting. MUSEUM AFRICA

Top: The Champ D'Or Mine job was
McLoughlin's parting shot: the takings
would fund his escape into the vastness of
the Indian Ocean rim. MUSEUM AFRICA

Above: Fred de Wit Tossel, chief of mounted
police, was responsible for arresting the
Krugersdorp bank robbers in 1889 and
investigating the McLoughlin gang's
Champ D'Or Mine heist in 1895. 'Tossel'
was the assumed name of a man who
was himself in some trouble with the
British Army.

Left: At Pentridge Gaol the day before his
execution in 1880, Ned Kelly was a hero
to many Australians and to several men of
Irish extraction on the southern African
highveld, including Jack McLoughlin and,
more especially, Jack McKeone.
UNIVERSITY OF MELBOURNE ARCHIVES

Aaron Sherritt allegedly betrayed members of Ned Kelly's gang to the police. In 1880, newly married and under police protection, he was shot by his closest friend, Joe Byrne.

Joe Byrne, like McLoughlin much later, executed a police informer in the doorway of his residence after sending him advance warning that he was about to be shot.

Andrew Scott, 'Captain Moonlite', was a gay bush ranger whose gang members decorated their horses with pink ribbons. He was captured at Wagga Wagga in 1879. John Hutchings, bandit leader in southern Africa in 1887–88, took 'Captain Moonlite' as his *nom de guerre* some months before Jack McLoughlin assumed leadership of the gang on the Witwatersrand. STATE LIBRARY OF VICTORIA PICTURES COLLECTION

James Nesbitt. Andrew Scott wore a ring made from a lock of Nesbitt's hair and before being executed said, 'My dying wish is to be buried besides my beloved.' Scott's last wish was fulfilled in January 1995 when his bones were exhumed and re-interred with those of Nesbitt.
STATE LIBRARY OF VICTORIA PICTURES COLLECTION

In 1900, while making his way across the Cook Strait, from Wellington to Lyttleton, McLoughlin unsuccessfully stowed away on the SS *Rotomahana*. CLYDE BUILT SHIPS

The muffled sound of an explosion was heard from the small cottage at far right when the McLoughlin gang blasted the safe in the offices of the Moree Railway Station. It was one of three such attacks on small town railway stations in rural New South Wales in 1902.
NEW SOUTH WALES STATE RECORDS

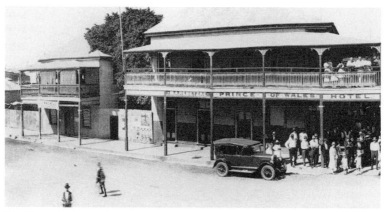

The Prince of Wales Hotel, Mackay, Queensland, site of McLoughlin's last criminal act in Australia in 1906 – the theft of a gold watch and chain. He was sentenced to three years' hard labour in the 'Hell Hole of the Pacific' – the island prison off Brisbane.
NEW SOUTH WALES STATE RECORDS

The SS *Waratah* taking on cargo in Port Adelaide, shortly before it was joined by three men bound for Natal whose names were discreetly left off the official passenger list – Jack McLoughlin and officers De Beer and Mynott. After they had disembarked in Durban, in July 1909, the ship went missing in one of the greatest unsolved mysteries of the Southern Ocean.
STATE LIBRARY OF SOUTH AUSTRALIA

Father Thomas Ryan, OMI, an Irish priest with extensive experience in working-class communities in Australia, England and continental Europe; also a personal friend of General JC Smuts, Acting Minister of Justice. He was called upon to counsel and comfort Jack McLoughlin during his final hours in 1910. OBLATE COLLECTION, MULGRAVE

A *Sunday Times* artist captured Jack McLoughlin, seated at an angle in the dock so as to conceal his missing right arm, at his trial in Johannesburg, in December 1909.
SUNDAY TIMES

George Stevenson, the boxer-gangster and object of McLoughlin's infatuation before he turned police informer. The sketch, from a photograph of Stevenson, was made for the *Sunday Times* at the time of McLoughlin's trial, 14 years after the shooting. SUNDAY TIMES

Sir James Rose Innes, Chief Justice and servant of empire, presided over McLoughlin's trial, which was finalised before the coming of the Union in 1910. NATIONAL ARCHIVES OF SOUTH AFRICA

Jack McLoughlin was hanged at the recently opened Pretoria Central Prison on 10 January 1910. He was among the first 10 white men to be executed at a prison which gained steadily in notoriety in the long twentieth century. NATIONAL ARCHIVES OF SOUTH AFRICA

made no mention of any outstanding charges against McLoughlin and sentenced King to two years' imprisonment with hard labour for knowingly attempting to dispose of the proceeds of a crime.

Powers either did not know that the man he was sentencing was wanted for murder in Johannesburg, or was constrained not to mention the fact because it bore no relevance to the matter before him. The luck of the Irish, in conspicuously short supply across the Tasman, seemed to be holding the line. But, whatever the reason, McLoughlin was grateful. He was in a world where reverse logic ruled. The South African War had provided him with peace of mind, and prison freedom from extradition. Resigned to his fate, he bore King no ill will and made no unfavourable allusions to the loyalty or masculinity of the younger man.[18]

The two got on well enough for neither to object to the other's company. It was as well; they were about to spend two years together in three different prisons. The gaol in Mackay proved that sugar-farming towns could not compete with gold-mining towns when it came to producing hard-nosed criminals. The town's first gaol, deprived of diggers and miners, had closed in the mid-1890s and the newest inmates were kept in a holding cell before being sent up-coast to Stewart's Creek in Townsville.

Stewart's Creek, serving the town, mines around Charters Towers and the outback, was the only prison in Australia with both male and female inmates. It did nothing to soften a forbidding appearance and daunting reputation. Upon their arrival there on 17 October 1906, the pair were processed with customary rigour. A record was made of McLoughlin's appearance along with body markings, hair and eye colour, as well as his height and weight. He was content to have his religion recorded as 'Roman Catholic'. His faith was not negotiable. It was all standard procedure and he thought nothing amiss when his photograph was taken. It was just one more image to match the one taken of him at Tamworth four years earlier. All that it would do was confirm again that he had once used the name 'Bourke'.[19]

But, as with many things in life, the sharpest focus and greatest insight is often achieved at points where chance intersects with rigour. Ever since the Auckland Races the Eye had been scanning prison yards at both ends of the Tasman for a glimpse of him with increased regularity. The South African

War was over and the drive for self-determination across the southern colonies was strengthening the sinews of imperial co-operation and integration. Only a few days after his arrival at Stewart's Creek his photograph and others in the new intake were forwarded to the state capital for more routine processing and systematic record-keeping.

McLoughlin's mugshot circulated through the detective division at Brisbane, where one of the more able – or idle – officers 'was struck with [its] resemblance to a description which had been published some time back in the *New Zealand Police Gazette*. Old numbers of the gazette were hunted up, and the photograph and the description carefully compared.'[20]

They matched! For the first time in more than a decade, there was a real possibility that the law-enforcement machinery in Australia, New Zealand and southern Africa might be aligned without embarrassing British-Boer politics. Indeed, the McLoughlin case fed into the gathering imperial mood perfectly and showed precisely what might be gained from such useful exchanges of information. It predated the meeting of colonial premiers at the Imperial Conference in London, in April–May 1907, by just six months. There, Jameson himself, by then Premier of the Cape Colony, with Alfred Deakin of Australia and Joseph Ward of New Zealand championed closer imperial co-operation before a more sceptical Louis Botha.

Pleased by such a handsome return from a mere paper-hunt, the Brisbane police sent a telegram to British authorities in the Transvaal alerting them to the fortuitous appearance of one of their fugitives in the nets of their own penal system.[21] The Queensland detectives believed they had landed a big fish – one that law-enforcement agencies in southern Africa had made unsuccessful inquiries about in 1895, 1901 and 1905. This time there would be no slip-up, the man would surely be extradited and justice could run its course. The Australian enthusiasm was infectious.

In Johannesburg, Commissioner of the Police EM Showers was all action. In the third week of November 1906, a slew of updated statements were taken from witnesses to the shootings at the Red Lion in 1895. On the basis of these affidavits the Law Department became involved and within days a new warrant for the arrest of Jack McLoughlin was issued. On 21 December the Australian Prime Minister, Alfred Deakin, was informed of an impending extradition.[22] The seasonal slowdown in southern Africa did not halt the gathering momentum. On Christmas Eve cables were still flying between the Governor of the Transvaal Colony, Lord Selborne, and his counterpart in Brisbane, Lord Chelmsford. The Eye was open, functioning perfectly, reading all, scanning every legal process, and the machinery of government on either side of the Indian Ocean was operating at a pace unheard of.[23]

It is impossible to tell from the surviving documents whether trans-oceanic activity at the highest level of government translated itself into more letters and notes within Queensland itself. It may have. On 10 December 1906, the Comptroller-General of Prisons drew up a list of names of 19 hardened prisoners to be moved from Stewart's Creek to the more for-midable St Helena Penal Establishment, on an island in shark-infested Moreton Bay off Brisbane. Among the names of those on the list were 'Jack McLoughlin' – probably already re-classified as 'dangerous' – and his camping mate on the old gold trails, George King.[24]

It had taken one slip, in coastal Queensland, for the imperial system to be brought into alignment in just eight weeks. It was primed and ready to deliver him, body and soul, to judge and jury in Johannesburg. Then, just as Great Britain was poised to strike at one of the sons of the thousands of Irish rebels it had created and helped spread across the world, everything went black. The Eye snapped shut. One of the most intractable powers the British had had to contend with since the loss of their American colonies in the seventeenth century was once again challenging the might of the empire, albeit not through force of arms this time.

★   ★   ★

In late 1905, Britain's Conservative government had been replaced by Campbell-Bannerman's Liberals. The Boers, still smarting from the war, immediately invaded a more sympathetic political landscape, demanding the right of self-government for the Transvaal within a British South Africa. Lord Selborne, better disposed towards Afrikaner nationalists than his predecessor, was in broad agreement. By the time Selborne and Chelmsford swapped notes about McLoughlin's possible extradition, in December 1906, a new constitution for 'responsible government' had already been adopted. By February 1907, a *Het Volk* administration under General Louis Botha was in control of the country's destiny. Botha was more cautious about closer imperial co-operation than were most of his colonial counterparts when they met in London in late 1907. And, somewhere between the adoption of that new constitution and the emergence of the restructured state in Pretoria, another bureaucratic hiatus opened up. Could a threatened change in the political profile of the gold-rich colony come to McLoughlin's rescue for a second time? If it could, he remained blissfully unaware of it for several years.

Established in 1867 and anchored in the heat and damp of the subtropics, St Helena prison was a Janus-faced institution. The island, five miles off the mouth of the Brisbane River, derived its name from an Aboriginal prisoner, one Nugoon, who bore a striking resemblance to Napoleon, who had died in the south Atlantic fortress of the same name in 1821. In its very earliest days the prison had a disproportionate number of staff and inmates of Celtic origin, giving rise to the customary English–Irish hatreds.[25] The full array of Victorian disciplinary devices and procedures – including flogging, the gag, confinement in underground cells and shot-drill – had contributed to the place being seen as 'The Hell Hole of the Pacific' or, more parochially, as 'Queensland's Inferno'.

When Jack McLoughlin was sent there, in 1906, earlier methods of institutionalised brutality had ceased to be used but the level of discipline expected of convicts remained attuned to the highest modern standards.[26] At age 47 it was not crimes committed in Australasia that had got him sent there, but his reputation as a 'dangerous criminal', resting on a frontier shooting half a world away two decades earlier. It was a *Police Gazette* view of him as a murderer, even though he had yet to be tried or convicted; a view that was out of line with the opinions of prison authorities who had repeatedly granted him remissions for good behaviour, and out of keeping with his contemporary criminal career. The state was locking up an ageing, one-dimensional replica rather than a flesh-and-blood menace, forcing him to share the fate of men who had all been tried and found guilty of aggravated assault, manslaughter, murder or rape.[27] A self-fulfilling prophecy shorn of all context and meaning had taken hold of the life of a man on the run.

In the sense that McLoughlin's ideas about courage, loyalty and manliness remained firm, prison life may have suited him. He was a man among men in a male-only world. His reputation as a dangerous criminal stood him in good stead. It meant that there was little or no need, judging from the silences of his record, to protect his dignity or space by resorting to physical violence even though, when roused, he was still capable of displaying real anger. The *shaughraun* was not to be trifled with; all those who crossed him risked the tinker's curse.

He adjusted well to confinement – he could do the time 'standing on his head'. He was more measured and there were long periods of quiet thoughtfulness as he reflected on his past. Inmates respected him but knew almost nothing about his deep background. Indeed, judging by reports on his behaviour over the months that followed he was more introspective, always thinking about his past, and probably depressed.

Part of this accommodating behaviour could be attributed to a maturity that came with age and a diminution of his physical strength. It may, however, also have owed something to the other side of St Helena – its standing as a 'model prison' with a capacity to draw the best out of certain inmates. Throughout the late nineteenth and into the twentieth century the Queensland government insisted on the prison being as financially self-sufficient as possible. The island-prison once produced so much sugar cane that it ran its own refinery but, when the fields left prisoners with a site for proscribed activities, the operation was wound up. All other agricultural and pastoral pursuits continued apace, including cattle, sheep, sisal and vegetable farming on a scale and of a standard considered exemplary at the time. For a one-time vegetable-hawker, labour out in the fields was less supervised than in the workshops, and must have come as a relief as it offered more opportunities for solitude.[28]

Life in 'the stockade' – the prison proper at the centre of the island – followed a mindlessly predictable, utterly inflexible pattern. But not even that upset his composure. There was something reassuring about the way that body and mind aligned themselves to the demands of unseen forces, a bit like unthinking sheep returning to their pen at sunset each day. One year faded into the next almost unnoticed.[29] In 1908, George King, the only person to have seen him outside of a prison, was released. Jack took leave of him at the wooden jetty on the south-west of the island, where the steamboat *Otter* called in twice a week as part of a circuit around the bay that included a stop at the asylum at Dunwich on nearby North Stradbroke Island.[30] The only other thing of note that year was the arrival of another man on the island who shared his name. This 'John McLoughlin' was a former crew member on the busy little *Otter*, who, having tired of the life at sea, suddenly enlisted as a warder.

Jack McLoughlin's retreat into an inner world gave the prison officers no cause for alarm and, as before, in early 1909, they suggested that the supposedly 'dangerous prisoner' qualified for a remission of sentence. Across the bay, where the state authorities had monitored his progress in prison more closely than usual in such cases, the remission was agreed to.

When McLoughlin was informed that his date of release had been brought forward by four months he was uncertain as to how to respond. He was again reminded that his life had telescoped into nothing. The past was gone, the present obliterated, the future unimaginable. His identity had shrunk into nothingness and there was no place he considered home. Time had hollowed him out and, with the exception of a brother living on a frontier that held no appeal for him, there was no one to turn to. He needed to speak to somebody, anybody, who *knew* where he came from, someone who understood that he had been a man who once commanded admiration and respect. He wanted his life back.

Instead, he struggled to imagine what he would do when the *Otter* crossed the blue water of the bay to collect him and he disembarked at the jetty at Wynnum, near where the Brisbane River entered the bay. There was something unfair about it. Like Houdini, he was being asked to wriggle free of three sets of constraints – the prison, the island and the continent beyond it. He had been trapped in them for close on a decade and had grown accustomed to them. It was only the external constraints that lent form and shape to body and mind; inside there was nothing. What would happen if they were removed – would he fall apart?

Two weeks before his release, inmates and staff, including the new warder who shared his name, began to rib him about his imminent departure. Another with access to the *Otter's* schedule teased him, saying that, since he would be leaving on a Friday afternoon, he could bank on a weekend's celebration in Brisbane. The fog of introspection that had been clouding his mind for months lifted slowly and the reality of the situation gradually came home to him. The worst of his fears dissipated and, on hot days, he began to imagine what a cold beer might taste like.

Autumn is poorly defined in the subtropics but it was noticeable that the days were becoming shorter. In Auckland it would have been terrifying, heralding a winter during which cold and damp would fight a long and bitter battle in an attempt to determine a winner. On 12 April, he took up his Monday morning duties knowing that it would be the last time he would have to engage with weekly routine. Tuesday and Wednesday, defying the season's logic, seemed to go on forever and he was beginning to wonder whether it was all part of an illusion when, after lunch on Thursday, he was told to report to the prison administration. He was handed the few personal possessions that had been found on him in Mackay, years before, and shipped along with him to Stewart's Creek.

The next morning a mate or two, anticipating their own release, shouted parting 'good luck' wishes as they walked past his cell where the door, as if to mark his special day, stood ajar. He put on his own clothing and, given that he had not lost weight and still matched his prison description as 'stout', was surprised at how well they fitted and felt. He screwed the cork hand onto his prosthesis and looked himself over to check on his overall appearance. His hair and beard were quite grey but, other than that, he looked quite acceptable when he made his way down to the jetty. He was early. There were two prison officials standing around chatting, waiting for the *Otter* to chug into view from Dunwich. Captain Junner brought her alongside. He was reminded how much he loved the sea, and he prepared himself for the short ride across the bay to Wynnum.

Almost all the prison supplies had been unloaded on the morning's inward run. There was nothing to detain the vessel. A few formalities were attended to and he was told that he could board. He shook hands with one of the warders and was reminded of that day, in Pretoria, in 1892, when he had been released by Matthew de Beer who had said to him: 'until we next see one another'. That had been 14 years ago and much had happened since. He wondered where De Beer might be. It was unlikely that a member of the State Artillery had survived the war.

The *Otter* cleared the jetty and headed south-west. In order to avoid the glare off the water a man would have to turn around, put his back to the sun and take a last look at the island. He watched approvingly as Junner went about his work. Although his own time on the *Albatross* had never been easy, he retained his respect for ship captains – they, more than most men, embodied courage, skill and leadership. The boat made good time in easy conditions and he heard the engine ease back as Junner brought the vessel alongside the Wynnum jetty. As always, there were men standing about on the dockside, waiting to grab the rope, take the strain and secure the vessel. Most of them were workers clad in everyday working clothes; only one, dressed in a suit, stood out. Unlike that day in Lyttelton, back in 1900, there was no one to meet him.

He waited for the passengers from Dunwich, folk who had somewhere to go and seemed to be in a hurry to disembark. He then made his way slowly onto the gangway and took a pace or two, but his way was then barred by the suited man. The man stepped forward and introduced him-self as Sergeant Kenny from the Criminal Justice Branch, Brisbane. Kenny produced a provisional warrant for his arrest, for the murder of George Stevenson and Hadji Joseph Mustaffa, in Johannesburg, on 26 January, 1895. Half-surprised, half-resigned, he stood rooted and said nothing. Kenny, sensing that he was not going to resist arrest, ushered him back aboard the *Otter,* onto the deck leading to the cabin, so that his greying prisoner would not have to suffer the indignity of having to be handcuffed in full view of any passers-by or the workers moving about the dock.

Kenny told him that they were on their way to the Boggo Road Gaol, and he watched as the wrist of his left arm was joined to the officer's right. It was going to be an uncomfortable ride into Brisbane. He suddenly felt the need to question what Kenny had put to him. What could, what did, some little plain-clothes man from nowhere know about his past life, about Johannesburg, about his relationship with Stevo? He blurted out:

> That man's name was not Stevenson, so far as I can remember it was Steve Davidson. He shelved me and two of my pals for a job in Pretoria, one of them got five years and I got away to Kimberley. Sometime after somebody handed Stevo a bit of lead, and a Malay man, who was there, got a bit, too. I happened to be in Johannesburg that Saturday night and they blamed me for it. I was told that whoever shot Stevo went to his room and pushed his door open and shot him through the stomach, in the bed. [31]

Fourteen years after he had shot his collaborator-betrayer, friend-lover and alter-ego nemesis, he still could not help referring to his victim in anything other than the affectionate, diminutive form of 'Stevo' rather than 'Davidson', 'Stevenson', or even 'the victim'. Stevo was long since dead, but his affection for him was undying.

At Boggo Road, it was the same old thing. Every detail about his person meticulously recorded in the 'Prisoner Description Book'.[32] He was, he said, 'English' and a 'Roman Catholic'; all the rest was as recorded in two other Queensland prisons, one in New South Wales, and in several trans-Tasman versions of the *Police Gazette*. It was tedious rather than frightening and he was interested to see what the police had by way of real evidence. The following morning he was hauled before the Central Police Court and, as the *Brisbane Courier* informed its readers the following Monday morning: 'An elderly man named J McLoughlin was remanded on a charge of murder…'[33]

That account and the fact that it was later reported that the suspect had been arrested on board the *Otter* caused some confusion. A few eyebrows were raised in the city and several readers drew the mistaken conclusion that the prisoner in question was the former crew member on the *Otter* turned warder. It required an intervention by Captain Junner and a letter to the Editor to clear the unfortunate warder's name.[34]

McLoughlin was content for the case in the Central Police Court to be put on hold but concerned when Sub-Inspector Short explained that the state needed more time to prepare for the extradition. 'All the necessary papers had been received through his Excellency,' Short said, 'but they were awaiting the arrival of an officer from the Transvaal.' So, the Eye had not slept through his sojourn on St Helena! It had been open all the time, using its new-found telegraphic nerves to pass information back and forth across the width of the continent and the Indian Ocean.

The Eye had granted him three years in an island-prison reserved for the most violent of men, but only on the understanding that it would then have its day in court so as to get the chance to take what was left of his life. It made sense legally, as the law did, but for an uneducated man it was a travesty. The law and justice often did things together but they were hardly a Siamese twin, and the two could get badly out of step. The case was re-manded until 24 April 1909, and thereafter, every week for six weeks. He sat it out in Boggo Road for close on two months waiting for the bureaucrats to get together something they had had three years to prepare for. Where did *that* sentence come from? And what was it for? He was not to appear before a full court until early June 1909. A curse on all of them.

୧୧✿✿ଚ୨ଚ

The Tinker's Curse

BRISBANE TO DURBAN

— 1909 —

Ships that pass in the night, and speak each other in passing;
Only a signal shown and a distant voice in the darkness;
So on the ocean of life we pass and speak one another,
Only a look and a voice; then the darkness again and a silence.

LONGFELLOW

A mongst the first documents that General Louis Botha, the new Prime Minister of the Transvaal and South African War hero, discovered on his desk upon taking office, in February 1909, were papers relating to the extradition of Jack McLoughlin dating back to 1906. Recent changes to the constitution of the colony had slowed the momentum but Botha knew that McLoughlin was due to be released in April 1909, and was determined to hurry the process along. Using Section 29 of the Imperial Fugitive Offenders Act of 1881, he requested the Governor, Lord Selborne, to resume earlier efforts to have McLoughlin extradited through the offices of the Governor of Queensland, Lord Chelmsford.[1]

A burst of telegraphic fire between Johannesburg and Brisbane followed. But not even electric pulses directed across the ocean could help to align due process with the speed demanded by commonsense compassion and justice. Chelmsford was a former Fellow of All Souls, a notable who would go on to become the Viceroy of India as well as First Lord of the Admiralty. A cautious man, he was not about to be nudged into a false step, even though he trusted Selborne, another Oxford man.

On the same afternoon that a one-armed hopeful had anticipated the *Otter* carrying him to freedom, 16 April 1909, Selborne felt the need for a little more insistent probing. 'Will extradition McLoughlin be granted on documents already submitted?' he telegraphed Chelmsford. 'Upon affirmative reply,' he continued, 'officer will be sent to produce original documents and identify McLoughlin.'[2] In Pretoria, both Botha and Selborne were becoming concerned. In 1906, the Australian courts had taken months to extradite McKelvey, a Durban insolvent, back to Natal.[3]

But telegrams can settle in a Governor's in-tray almost as gently as snowflakes on fox fur. Five days later, on 21 April, Chelmsford, correct right down to the flourish beneath his expansive signature, replied: 'All now required is identification of prisoner and of signatures to documents by officer from Transvaal. McLoughlin remanded until 24th April.'[4] Selborne was so pleased to get a response that he telephoned the Prime Minister to let him know that the Eye had winked in agreement to a request first initiated by the Kruger government 11 years earlier. The club was always more comfortable doing business with members. And as the wheels of justice ground round and round, the subject of the enquiries sat it out in the Boggo Road Gaol on remand, week after week.

Granted provisional approval, the Botha administration, cautious to the point of suspicion, yet revelling in being a newly admitted member of the imperial family, responded with alacrity and professionalism. Mindful of diplomatic niceties and the need to be able to supplicate in English, it was decided that two men rather than one should be sent to escort the fugitive back to South Africa. Given McLoughlin's fearsome reputation it might also need two officers to subdue him should he decide to play up. The policemen, one English- and the other Afrikaans-speaking, could also play 'good cop/bad cop' roles. The state's choices were inspired.

The roots of the Mynotts lay in the fenlands of East Anglia and, more particularly, Cambridgeshire. Charles Albert Mynott, drawn into the country by the South African War, was an educated, well-spoken detective.

Difficult to intimidate and a keen observer, Mynott would be comfortable providing testimony in a Queensland Magistrate's Court and dealing with the paper-work. But, since Mynott was unacquainted with the fugitive, he would be accompanied and relieved, when necessary, by someone from the Transvaal Town Police – a man familiar with the old Irish Brigade, who knew McLoughlin from time spent in the old Visagie Street gaol in the early 1890s. It was indeed Constable Matthew John de Beer, the same man who, as a former member of Kruger's State Artillery, had in 1892 taken leave of McLoughlin by saying 'tot siens'.[5]

Mynott and De Beer were given only hours to prepare for two voyages across the Indian Ocean before heading to Park Station. They scrambled aboard the night train across the Orange Free State and pushed south, across the Karoo. They would be gone for three months. The outward passage, at £15 for a shared berth, was one of the few perks of their working lives – a cruise aboard one of the truly great ocean liners of the day. They boarded the White Star's SS *Persic* in Cape Town on 28 April. Selborne promptly sent Chelmsford a telegram confirming their departure.[6] The ship on its regular run from Liverpool to Brisbane via the Cape and Sydney was greatly admired by the passengers. But the *Persic*'s officers, keen to promote the line's rivalry with Cunard, spoke only about the hull of a larger vessel that had just been laid in the yards of Harland & Wolff, in Belfast – the *Titanic*.

After a month in southern seas it took a few hours before Brisbane's streets steadied themselves beneath Mynott and De Beer's feet. After a while they found their bearings but the unfamiliar surroundings lent an air of unreality to proceedings. It was as if they were locked into time, suspended. The closing days of May were spent shuffling from pillar to post, dealing with unknown officials and strange places, lodging papers, preparing for McLoughlin's final appearance in the Central Police Court.

Like Hermes, herald of the Olympian gods and patron of boundaries, they sought to smooth the way back home by making reservations for the inbound passage from Brisbane to Sydney and then on to Durban. Once their choice of dates and vessels became apparent, however, Hermes, who knew how all lives ended, may have smiled. Poseidon had made him party to a truth that would take weeks to manifest itself. And, down the Boggo Road, where his hatred of the Australians was becoming as pronounced as his dislike of New Zealand authorities, a one-time Irish 'tinker' sat and fumed as he waited. Could it be that Hermes, Robber and Trickster had been moved by a thief's plight and decided to grant him a last chance before deciding what to do with him?

If he had, there was no sign of it on 2 June, when proceedings in the Central Police Court got under way before Magistrate RA Ranking. Far from being comforted by the idea that after so many years the Johannesburg police were unlikely to come up with any surprises, McLoughlin was astounded to be confronted by a man whose words had haunted him ever since he had taken leave of him in 1892. It could not be – and yet there he was – Matthew de Beer. He was as amazed as he was when Kenny had arrested him on the *Otter,* but this time he would give away nothing. But what would he say if De Beer confirmed his identity?

Angry questions ripped through his mind as due process – like an old dog following its master to the village shop – padded along behind the law. Chelmsford, away on official duties, had not missed a trick. No less than a barrister of the Queensland Supreme Court, LW Marsland, had been retained to argue that the Imperial Eye was within its rights in seeking extradition. McLoughlin failed to understand the intricacies of the argument and was in no position to offer a counter-argument. For all that, he felt that somewhere within proceedings that had dragged on in two countries for eight years, lengthy sentences with hard labour, and seemingly endless remands, lay an injustice of sorts. As a reporter noted: 'On one occasion, in court, he declared that there were no grounds whatever for the charge against him. He likewise declared, somewhat bitterly, that an Englishman had no chance in the colonies.'[7]

The hearing ground on and on and Mynott took forever to lodge a slew of affidavits along with a description and a photograph of the fugitive. When the Magistrate asked McLoughlin whether he wanted to put any questions to Mynott, he smiled and replied: 'I do not know the gentleman, and I am sure he does not know me.' It was true. But De Beer was then called and he confirmed the prisoner's identity. When Ranking asked

McLoughlin if he had any questions to put to De Beer, he stepped forward and told the big lie: 'I do not know the man.'[8]

McLoughlin hoped to say no more and leave it at that. But, when the Magistrate indicated that he would be recommending that the extradition order be granted, subject to the approval of Sir Arthur Morgan, who was acting Lieutenant Governor during Chelmsford's absence, the prisoner asked permission to address the court. He again stated that 'he did not know the man De Beer, and that Constable de Beer had never seen him before'. 'He does not know me from a cod-fish; but, of course, he has been put up to it,' he said, positing the well-worn old conspiracy theory.[9]

He was escorted back to Boggo Road under guard and in low spirits to wait on Morgan's word. He waited. He seemed always to be waiting, waiting for somebody or for something to happen. When and how would this business be concluded? The gaol, as forbidding as any he had been in, seemed gloomier than ever. The inmates were subdued, waiting on news more awful than any he could receive, yet somehow only too pertinent. A 21-year-old, Arthur Ross, was awaiting execution for having shot a bank clerk while hoping to empty a safe at the Gayndah Branch of a Sydney bank.[10] He, too, was just waiting.

Ranking was nothing if not efficient. He conveyed his decision to support the request for extradition to Morgan that same Wednesday afternoon.[11] The rest of the week limped along, with no news forthcoming by the time that the inmates settled down for the long period of uninterrupted isolation that characterised Saturdays and Sundays. Then, early on the Monday morning of 7 June, well before the normal prison routine could be activated, Ross was hanged. McLoughlin and the other inmates were mired in resentment.

Two days after the execution, on 9 June, Sir Arthur Morgan telegraphed Selborne to let him know that, three years after the matter was first mooted, the extradition had been approved.[12] After a decent interval the information was allowed to filter down through the ranks of the bureaucracy. In keeping with protocol, Mynott and De Beer were told that they could call in at Boggo Road and inform their prisoner of the arrangements they had made for a journey from which there would be no return. They found

McLoughlin so low in spirits that they agreed that he might be considering taking his own life. It had the makings of a logistical nightmare, and for some long and painful watches aboard ship.

He remained locked up on the Boggo Road during the second week of June. It was hard to know which was worse – being confined in a cell of his own, or being out in the yard where the whisperings of the inmates still centred on the execution of Ross. Then on the morning of the 19th, Mynott and De Beer appeared to collect him for the first leg of the journey to a place which, for all the difference it made, even he considered to be 'home'.

Once clear of the gaol he sensed his mood improving. It was good to be out and heading for the docks. He enjoyed being out, on the open sea, and it was not as if he was on a train to Johannesburg. Yet. It would, he convinced himself, be a short but pleasant run down the coast. The dismal, far longer, haul to South Africa would, in truth, only commence once they embarked at Sydney.

As he had learnt when seeing the *Mount Sirion* for the first time, there was one thing agreeable about travelling at government expense. The state had no interest in lining the pockets of owners of inferior ships. They would not be sailing on some sea-stained old tub with seagull-shit dripping down the wheel-house and rusted chains cluttering the deck. All treasuries liked doing business with established shipping lines, helping to reinforce the circles of influence, power and wealth that kept the rich ruling with the rest of humanity following at a respectful distance.

The six-ton SS *Wyreema* did not disappoint. All bold brass and smoothed paint, she was not yet a year out of a Clydeside yard and built to provide passengers along the Pacific fringes with all the comforts of modern steamship travel. Mynott was shown to the two cabins that had been reserved for the three of them. The policemen took turns to unpack their belongings and they all settled in as the ship nosed slowly out into Moreton Bay and then, at a brisker pace, on past St Helena Island. It felt good to be leaving the bay and even better after he had been served lunch in his cabin-cell. It was no hotel, but he was in an expansive mood.

Mynott recalled well one of the few animated conversations the officers had with Jack McLoughlin on a voyage that lasted a month:

> Shortly after lunch the accused was very talkative. From the time I took him over he was very talkative about Australia [and] the old days of the Transvaal. He was asking De Beer many things about people who had done time and speaking about the prisoners escaping from Pretoria Gaol and it led to him telling me about the Pretoria safe robbery. It was quite voluntary. I asked him no questions whatever.[13]

It was a seminal moment and helped determine McLoughlin's attitude towards both men for the rest of their time aboard ship. He enjoyed chatting to the anglicised Afrikaner, De Beer, because they had things in common. They shared experiences including tales about the Visagie Street prison. De Beer knew most of the burglars, coach-robbers, gold-thieves, highwaymen and safe-robbers who had operated on the Witwatersrand frontier long before the railways had sidelined horses. He knew most of the members of the old Irish Brigade, including the legendary bank robber turned social bandit who had escaped to Australia, Jack McKeone.

Most important of all, however, Constable de Beer understood who *he* – 'One-Armed Jack' McLoughlin – was. He respected his status and standing in prison and in the Johannesburg underworld; he appreciated his reputation for courage and daring, and he knew about his unparalleled success as a safe-cracker. In short, De Beer brought him round briefly from a prolonged state of social death – he saw him as a living, functioning, person with both a past and a present, if not a future. By contrast, McLoughlin was wholly contemptuous of Mynott, a Johnny-come-lately, an officer and gentleman who got on with the higher-ups, a man who bore no knowledge of him or the exploits of the Irish Brigade on the frontier. It was Mynott and his type who had made his life hell ever since that night at the Red Lion. And it was Charles Mynott who now had to sanction his every waking moment. A curse on Mynott too![14]

The tension between a rough-hewn son of an Irishman raised in the mills of Manchester and Mynott, a scion of rural East Anglia, was palpable. It eased only briefly when they reached Sydney, where, in line with arrangements, they boarded the vessel that would take them on to Durban almost immediately upon disembarking. McLoughlin's musings about the quality of a berth when travelling at government expense were again vindicated. The *Wyreema* had been comfortable, but the new liner was simply magnificent, modern and luxurious in almost every respect.

Barely eight months out of Clydeside, the 16 000 tonner was on only its second voyage between Australia and the United Kingdom. It was the flagship of the Lund brothers' Blue Anchor Line and under the command of Captain JE Ilbury, a 69-year-old Lancastrian.[15] Ilbury, the very experienced Commodore of the Fleet, was an easy choice as captain of a new vessel propelled by twin screws and state-of-the-art marine engineering. Although pre-eminently a passenger liner with an impressively stacked superstructure that housed 100 first-class cabins and 300 more second-class berths, there was a cleverly designed duality to what undoubtedly was the pride of the line.[16]

On the outward leg, from Liverpool, the vessel's convertible holds were turned into dormitories catering for the lucrative emigrant trade as Britain continued to feed its colonies with settlers. A crew of 150 served over 1 000 passengers in eight state rooms, a music lounge with a 'minstrels' gallery', a saloon and promenade decks. But on the inward leg, to England, the dormitories disappeared and refrigerated holds were stuffed with the colonial foodstuffs, fresh produce and raw materials needed back 'home'. The name of this new floating wonder was derived from New South Wales's most striking flower – the Waratah.[17]

★ ★ ★

As representatives of the Blue Anchor Line and Mynott both appreciated, Jack McLoughlin's presence on board was a source of potential embarrassment for some of the ship's well-heeled passengers. A one-armed convict from St Helena being extradited to face a charge of murder was about as welcome on board a liner as a rag-and-bone man at the Lord Mayor's banquet. The fact that it was midwinter and there were therefore fewer bookings to the United Kingdom than expected helped, but did not solve the problem. There were questions of safety and standards to consider and so the names of the small party joining from Brisbane did not appear on the list of passengers who had boarded the ship at Sydney.[18] Common courtesy demanded that the prisoner be kept out of sight. Mynott decided that any meals in the lounge would be at the end of sittings with the prisoner handcuffed.

For McLoughlin, sensitive about his missing hand, the arrangement combined hardship and humiliation. Already subject to Mynott's authority for permission to be freed of the cuffs in order to clean himself, shave, or use the toilet, he now had to be seen in public with his 'good' left hand shackled to a detective. So he promptly stopped shaving. Not only did it save him from having to supplicate, but it would make it more difficult for witnesses at any identity parade to recognise him. At the time of Stevenson's shooting he was clean-shaven but for a large, military-style moustache. But shaving was the least of his problems and he found the restrictions and dependency alike deeply distressing.[19]

In Sydney, he watched gloomily as a paltry score of passengers boarded the *Waratah*, including one or two from New Zealand. Among the latter was Claude Sawyer, a well-travelled engineer of extremely nervous disposition who was keeping his options open as to whether he would disembark in South Africa or carry on directly to the United Kingdom.[20] The ship's hold swallowed hundreds of bales of wool as well as oats, skins and tallow before they eventually set sail in a southerly direction on 26 June.

Confined to cabin and in low spirits, he found it difficult to come to terms with the fact that he was leaving Australia permanently, that he was bound for Natal and, beyond that, the Witwatersrand and the unknown. It reminded him of earlier, life-defining moments in his career. He had said nothing to Mynott or De Beer about his earlier visits to Sydney or Melbourne in the mid-1880s, or of that in 1900 while on his way to Fremantle. In Melbourne the *Waratah* slumped into an all-too-familiar routine; for all the difference it made to him he might as well have been back on St Helena. The Blue Anchor Line man was disappointed by how few joining passengers there were. Only 20 boarded the vessel, but it did take on 1 000 boxes of butter destined for South Africa.

When the ship left Melbourne and first encountered open water, on

1 July, Sawyer noted that the *Waratah* listed to port for a while before right-ing itself. Later, in more unsettled seas, it appeared to list to starboard. He may not have been the only one to think that there could be a problem. The ship's movements became the subject of small talk around the dining table. Sawyer was left with the impression that there were others who felt that the ship rolled more than was usual for a vessel of its size. But with largely fine weather after leaving Melbourne and across the Bight, the problem faded and he said little more about it.

Given the cost of berths and freight charges, it was predictable that Port Adelaide – the last Australian port before crossing the Indian and Atlantic oceans – would see more activity than in the east-coast ports. Captain Ilbury, aware of the challenge ahead, took on seven new crew members and looked on with satisfaction as no fewer than 82 new passengers boarded his ship. The *Waratah* also took on additional consignments of butter, frozen meat and grain and 300 tons of lead concentrate.[21] Given all the additional cargo, weighing 6 000 tons, and some folks' misgivings about the vessel's al-leged propensity to list, it may be noteworthy that some passengers claimed later that, while in port, Ilbury had insisted on personally overseeing the loading of the ship.

For Mynott, De Beer and McLoughlin, the stop-over in Port Adelaide promised a change of routine and the chance for some respite from inter-personal tensions. The ever-efficient Mynott got the Adelaide police to agree to keep his prisoner confined in the local gaol for the duration of the *Waratah*'s stay. For McLoughlin, it was another bittersweet moment. On being handed over he said to one of the warders in Adelaide: 'I know this place. I spent a month here once.'[22] Indeed he had, and he had then gone on to acquire sufficient funds to re-cross the Tasman Sea and engage his passion for gambling and the horses in distant Auckland.

Mynott and the Blue Anchor people were relieved to have the one-armed man away from the ship and out of sight of any new passengers for a couple of days. Their efforts were successful but they had a narrow escape. On the afternoon that the ship sailed, 8 July, an enterprising reporter on the *Adelaide Advertiser* who had been following the McLoughlin story ever since his arrest on board the *Otter*, got wind of the fact that he was being held in the local gaol. The following morning, shortly after the vessel had sailed, readers in the city awoke to get their first account of McLoughlin's recent exploits. While passengers aboard the *Waratah* remained ignorant about their shipmate, McLoughlin's name, already well known in many parts, was being spread further around the shores of the antipodean world.[23]

Had McLoughlin got to see it, the report in the *Advertiser* would have cheered him up. It was affirmation of a sort. Instead, he grew more despondent as the ship put distance between itself and Adelaide. Midwinter meant there were more storms and less sunlight around than he had been accustomed to on the Queensland coast. Mynott and De Beer took no chances. 'We were handcuffed to him six hours a day and he was prevented from making away with himself.'[24] Elsewhere on the ship, Sawyer was wrestling his old demons. He grew even more concerned when, one day, he noted that the water in his bath was inclined at an angle of 45 degrees.[25] Hurrying up on deck to see what was happening he noted that whenever confronting the swell head-on the ship's bow seemed more inclined to plough through a wave than rise up on the incoming surge. Despite all the additional cargo the vessel had taken on, the *Waratah* still appeared to be slightly top-heavy.

In the second-class cell that doubled as a cabin, tensions between McLoughlin and Mynott were approaching boiling point. Unfortunately, it is only Mynott's account that survived:

> I told [McLoughlin] on board ship I would make it hot for him if he did not behave himself. He called me a bloody mongrel and said he would pull my wind-pipe out. He wanted to see the captain and would not come out of the cabin and I told him to come out and stand outside to let the steward scrub the cabin out. He used a lot of bad language and would not come out and called me everything that he could lay his tongue to. After the captain had seen him he refused to have the handcuffs on whilst we went to lunch. He jumped up and attempted to strike me and used bad language and I thought he was going to strike me when I put the handcuffs on and I shoved him over.[26]

It is difficult to know what to make of this version but two things do stand

out. First, an old sea dog, McLoughlin knew where the ultimate authority on board ship lay. He won a significant battle by getting Ilbury to in-
tervene. The captain was not unsympathetic to McLoughlin's complaints
about being handcuffed at lunch. The fact that they were both Lancastrians
and older than Mynott might have helped.[27] Secondly, regardless of the
outcome, Mynott only got his way on other issues by overpowering the
prisoner, and thereafter had to 'put up with a lot of inconvenience'. The
handcuffs bound two men, not just one.

Once clear of the depression-driven winter weather off south-western
Australia the *Waratah* made better than expected progress, even if its pitch-
ing and rolling continued to trouble some passengers. Sawyer's suspicions
about a possible structural problem in the ship's design deepened when a
female passenger lost her footing during a minor tempest and had to be
kept in a wheelchair for the remainder of the voyage.[28] It is also possible
that Sawyer had by then talked himself into a position where he might have
lost face among some of his shipmates if he was not seen to act upon his
misgivings about the ship's stability.

The *Waratah* steamed into Durban a day earlier than expected, docking
on 19 July. Most of the onward passengers, refreshed after 10 uninterrupted
nights at sea, were pleased to learn that they would be in port for a week
and set about exploring the city. But the two policemen and their prisoner
had seen enough of the cabin to last a lifetime. Mynott was in a hurry to
get back to the Witwatersrand and to rid himself of his prisoner. It had been
four long weeks since they had set sail from Brisbane and the detective lost
no time at all in getting reservations on the night train to Johannesburg.
Local journalists were either unaware of the three men's presence, or not
particularly interested in their arrival.[29]

For different reasons, Sawyer was as relieved to get off the *Waratah* as the
Mynott party. He decided not to continue his journey and scurried off to
the post office to send a telegram to his wife, waiting in London. 'Thought
Waratah top-heavy,' he informed her, so 'landed Durban'. Sawyer may have
been a bit unstable, because he later claimed to have had bad dreams about
the ship's fate.[30] That said, he may have been correct in his assessment of the
Waratah's alleged propensity to list. The condition of his mental or physical

health was not necessarily at variance with his professional judgement. It is impossible to know.

Mynott and De Beer were home and Jack McLoughlin in The Fort, in Johannesburg, by the time that the *Waratah* put to sea on 26 July. The ship had over 200 passengers and crew for the three-day voyage down the coast to Cape Town. It was midwinter and the weather turned foul, with gale-force gusts of wind and huge swells. On the evening of 27 July, amidst stormy weather that showed no sign of abating, two passing ships made partial contact with a vessel they believed to be the *Waratah*.[31] But the ship never reached Cape Town. No more was heard or seen of the vessel. Her disappearance remains the great unsolved mystery of the southern ocean.

Within days of the vessel being reported overdue three of the Royal Navy's Simonstown-based cruisers – *Forte*, *Pandora* and *Hermes* – were sent to search for the ship or wreckage, but nothing conclusive was found.[32] The lack of news about the *Waratah's* fate occasioned great distress all around Australasian shores, and nowhere more so than in Adelaide, where the ship had taken on its largest contingent of passengers and additional crew. Incomplete or misleadingly optimistic reports compounded mounting tension. On 10 August, a telegram from South Africa claimed that the ship had been sighted slowly making her way to Durban. The Speaker of the House in the Australian Parliament interrupted proceedings to convey what turned out to be a false report. In Adelaide, church bells rang out for hope raised and lost.

The failed Royal Navy search was followed by another, paid for by the Blue Anchor Line. Yet others, privately funded or partially financed through public subscription, followed. Days turned into weeks and weeks into months before it was conceded that the ship had been lost at sea for reasons unknown.[33] Early on, amidst the on-going anguish, newspapers around the Pacific learnt that Jack McLoughlin had been aboard when the ship left Adelaide. There was speculation as to whether or not a man well known in Australia and New Zealand had gone down with the SS *Waratah*.[34] In South Africa nobody bothered to make the connection.

By then a silent synchronicity, ordained by a Greek god or flowing from a tinker's curse, had set in across the southern world. Between July and

December 1909, men and women around Australasia were in purgatory, waiting, month upon month, to see whether members of their families, friends or loved ones aboard the *Waratah* had been doomed or saved. And as they waited on Tasman shores, somewhere in a cell in Johannesburg, another man sat and waited to hear the date of the trial that would determine whether he would live or die. For four months the counsel of priests was freely sought. The souls of the living waited for news of those damned to a watery grave, and one of the living dead waited to hear about his own fate. For a time, the hand of fate and the Eye of Empire were perfectly coordinated in their unspeakable cruelty.

But a tinker's curse could often be more personal than Poseidon's indiscriminate wrath. Once officers and men in Johannesburg's central police station accepted that the *Waratah* had been lost, they took to referring to Mynott as 'Lucky Mynott' – as part of a joking tribute to his fortunate escape. The sobriquet, however, held for barely forty-eight months. In July 1914, Mynott was fatally wounded while attempting to arrest members of the 'Foster Gang' hiding in a house in the city's southern suburbs. Robert Foster, who shot Mynott, was another South African gangster of Irish extraction who, like Jack McKeone, had been raised in the foothills of the Drakensberg before moving on to Kimberley.

In Johannesburg, McLoughlin relapsed into a *Waratah*-like trance. By December 1909, that sunny afternoon in Moreton Bay, back in April, seemed not only half a world, but half a lifetime away. The seven intervening months had been spent waiting to find out when the Johannesburg court that would decide whether he was to live or die might sit. But, under almost every judicial system, outside the church, living in the Valley of the Shadow of Death counted for precisely nothing. It was something just added to a death sentence if it were to be passed.

He often thought about things that he could, or might, say in court about the shooting of Stevo. But it was impossible to come up with anything that would easily be understood by anybody who had not been there at the time. So much had changed since that night that it would be impossible to conjure up place, time or motive in ways that seemed meaningful or relevant. It now all seemed so trivial, so meaningless that it was difficult to believe that he had done it, or that he had shot the unfortunate Hadji Mustaffa. Try as he might, he could not come up with anything that sounded remotely like a convincing defence or a motive that a jury might understand. It was depressing. But then, as men are wont to do under adverse circumstances, he attempted to wring hope out of the hopeless. If he could not conjure up the past in a way that evoked sympathy, then surely the prosecution would find it equally difficult to conjure up the events at the Red Lion after so many years?

ᘉᕄᕄᘒ

Courts and Contexts: Men and Mindsets

JOHANNESBURG
— 1909 —

You cannot judge a man until you know his whole story.
THOMAS FULLER

Must a government, of necessity, be too strong for the liberties of its own people,
or too weak to maintain its own existence?
ABRAHAM LINCOLN

A ll trials, regardless of how well they are focused on the alleged crime and the letter of the law, are set within historical contexts. The pursuit of justice, even when manifestly free of fear or favour, takes place in courts which are themselves part of the theatre of everyday life. Legal processes play themselves out before judges and juries who, no matter how impartial by way of ethical disposition or professional training, are themselves the partial products of the past and the issues of the day. These invisible links between the pursuit of justice, time elapsed and the present are as problematic as they are enduring. Although such deep-seated difficulties never render the exercise of justice futile, they complicate legal processes in countless subtle ways.

In Jack McLoughlin's case, 14 years separated the shooting at the Red Lion Beer Hall, in 1895, and his trial, in Johannesburg, in 1909. The way in which an intervening decade-and-a-half was to be reconciled with the administration of justice was an issue that could not be avoided. The judge at his trial was aware of the importance of the issue and attempted to ensure that the jury, too, understood what was at stake:

> The lapse of time placed both parties at the greatest disadvantage – the Crown in collecting evidence for the prosecution, and the accused in collecting the evidence necessary for himself. The disadvantages told more heavily against the accused, as the Crown could search far and wide for evidence, and the accused had no one to help him. After the lapse of all those years, it was very difficult for him, assuming he had a defence, to collect evidence. The jury should therefore carefully examine every bit of evidence and be satisfied with it before they accepted it or allowed it to influence their minds.[1]

'Reasonable doubt', he cautioned, had to be founded on circumstances and evidence and could not be 'merely a sentimental doubt or pity for the man who was brought back for trial after all those years'. The judge's instruction may, however, not have gone far enough. It was a case where the complexities arising from the interval separating the alleged crime and trial were without precedent – and, even today, probably remain without meaningful parallel. There were other, hidden, considerations about context, time and place that the judge was perhaps not at liberty to raise directly but that nevertheless flowed directly from the pivotal issue that he had identified. McLoughlin's counsel, too, would have been well advised to explore these questions more thoroughly during the course of the trial itself. In order to appreciate what these veiled issues might have been, it is necessary to examine the face of the rapidly mutating state that the defendant faced.

By the time of McLoughlin's trial in 1909, the area beyond the Vaal River, centred on the economic heartland of the Witwatersrand, had seen four different political dispensations in 10 years and was destined for a fifth. The shootings had occurred in the South African Republic, which had tried to have McLoughlin extradited so that he might stand trial in 1895. In 1900 the Boer republic was conquered by imperial forces and, for a time, administered under martial law. In 1902, as the newly conquered state

moved towards civilian rule, a few more desultory enquiries were made as
to McLoughlin's whereabouts in New Zealand.

Military rule was followed by an authoritarian British administration.
It was part-appointed, part-elected under the centralising and modernis-
ing leadership of Sir (then Lord) Alfred Milner. His highly regulated reconstruction regime lasted five years, from 1900 to 1905. Then, as Britain
prepared to hand power back to an elected 'responsible government' under
General Botha's *Het Volk,* in 1906, another unsuccessful attempt was made
to extradite McLoughlin. His extradition was eventually only effected in
1909. By that time, the Transvaal Colony was being prepared to be folded into a fifth constitutional dispensation. In 1910, the Transvaal became a
province in the newly constituted Union of South Africa. Seen against that
backdrop it is easier to appreciate why a colony that was about to become a
province, in an extended state with a new jurisdiction, was so keen to have
the longstanding matter of Rex vs McLoughlin disposed of expeditiously.

From 1902 to 1910 the Transvaal and more especially the Witwatersrand
were in a state of political, economic and social turbulence. A series of
internally sanctioned or externally imposed white authorities sought to
transform a formerly independent, newly conquered Boer republic with
an un-enfranchised black majority into a colony. An industrialising self-
governing colony, producing most of the gold needed to underwrite global
trade, then had to be incorporated into a larger dominion. That dominion in turn lay within a British Empire controlled by men and women of
European descent. Questions about authority, legitimacy and loyalty were
the order of the day. Rulers had to wrestle with the problem once posed
by Jean-Jacques Rousseau – how to transform strength into right and obedience into duty. Rapid change and ongoing political contestation were
exacerbated by underlying economic uncertainties.

When the Rand gold mines re-opened after the South African War, the
industry was at once confronted by a challenge from black mineworkers. Africans refused to provide un- or semi-skilled labour at newly reduced wage rates in anything like the numbers considered necessary for
continued economic expansion. The resulting impasse was resolved in
1904, when, amidst some opposition, imperial authorities used their global

reach to sanction the importation of indentured miners from the Far East. Thousands of Chinese labourers worked at low wages to underwrite the reconstruction of the mining industry. The last of the contracted workers were sent back to China in 1910. But, even so, the depression lasting from 1906 to 1908 exacerbated the anxieties of a white 'labour aristocracy' of un-ionised English miners who feared their replacement by the cheaper labour of urbanising Afrikaners or African migrant workers.[2]

On 1 May 1907, white miners on the east Rand struck when the man-agement demanded that they supervise the work of three rather than two semi-skilled drillers on each shift. The Transvaal Miners' Association ap-proved the stoppage and, within days, a 'general strike' spread across the length of the Witwatersrand. It was the first in a series of increasingly vio-lent confrontations that took place between mineworkers and the state in 1907, 1913, 1922 and 1946. The government supported the mine owners and on each occasion – led by General JC Smuts, acting in differing capacities – used either departing imperial troops or the new Union Defence Force to defeat the workers.

The 1907 strike pre-dated McLoughlin's trial, at which he was said to be 'a miner' and his principal victim, Stevenson, a 'riveter', by less than 36 months. It was not the best of circumstances in which to be cast as a mine-worker. The strike had, on more than one occasion, seen white workers use dynamite to advance their cause and the government was forced to call on the imperial garrison to secure the property and lives of non-strikers. A house occupied by three English miners who refused to support the strike was demolished and one man killed when an explosion tore apart premises belonging to a shift boss on 14 June. Two weeks later, on 2 July, an unexploded charge was discovered at the house of an Afrikaner 'scab' in Johannesburg, and two weeks after that an explosion at Kilfoil's Hotel in Boksburg killed two men under circumstances that again pointed directly to white miners.[3]

White working-class radicalism did not abate readily. On the contrary, several leaders within the labour movement openly advocated the merits of socialism and the need for a more focused parliamentary programme in an expanded state. The constitution and name of the consolidated labour movement – the South African Labour Party – was formally adopted, in November 1909, just three weeks before McLoughlin's trial.[4]

Wanted for the murder of a police informer and known for his use of dynamite, McLoughlin found himself back at a juncture where the distinction between the actions of criminals and those of white working-class activists was once more being conflated. Indeed, the political climate was not entirely dissimilar to that which had prevailed between 1888 and 1892. Back then, diggers were being transformed into white workers and antagonism towards the mine owners was sufficiently pronounced for them to utilise dynamite in their struggle. A deteriorating political environment then had assisted him to operate as something akin to a 'social bandit'. Structural change in the mining industry always blurred criminal and political actions. As a member of the 'dangerous classes' posing a radical threat to those who governed the society and owned its gold mines, McLoughlin embodied some of the same problematic proletarian values that capitalists and the state abhorred.

In a volatile political climate which, although still far from revolutionary, was nevertheless tense and unstable, the state's prosecutors would have been hard-pressed to frame a lesser charge than murder for the Red Lion shootings. In McLoughlin's lifetime Johannesburg had passed through several moments of political uncertainty. In 1895, Joseph Chamberlain, various regional imperialists, and certain mine owners used the Jameson Raid as a top-down capitalist initiative to *encourage* criminal and white working-class unrest against a republican government. By 1909, having captured the state, essentially the same constellation of forces was deeply *opposed* to a challenge from below by white working-class radicals informed by socialist ideals and willing to engage in criminal acts. Change itself was not at issue, it was a constant. What mattered was the nature of the state and who controlled and directed the processes of change in the emerging country. Many citizens, including most of those on jury duty at McLoughlin's trial, sensed that the rules of the game had somehow changed and that a double standard was being applied. Accelerated economic change complicated the way in which crime and punishment were reconciled and the jurymen in the McLoughlin trial found it impossible to articulate their misgivings with any accuracy.

If the laymen in the jury found it difficult to give clear expression to reservations predicated on changed contexts, the learned judge would have had less trouble and could perhaps have aspired to greater precision. He would certainly have appreciated the altered circumstances and advent of a new order. Indeed, as we will see shortly, his appointment to the Transvaal bench had been predicated, in large part, on his having just such an understanding. But, that said, there may have been other considerations in the case that he might have been unaware of without the aid of skilful counsel for the defence.

The judge may not have appreciated fully how the shooting of Stevenson had been informed by 'Irish' notions of opposition to British or imperial rule as played out in nineteenth-century Lancashire's criminal, immigrant and working-class cultures. Nor may he have understood exactly how those ideas had been imported and incorporated into working-class culture on the Witwatersrand after 1886.[5] Throughout the trial the judge, like counsel for the defence, remained strangely unconcerned about questions of culture, ethnic identity and how they might inform the premeditated decision to shoot Stevenson. Likewise, without suitably led evidence, the judge would have found it difficult to appreciate the ways in which a code of masculinity manifested itself in criminal and working-class cultures in what was, in 1895, still in many ways a frontier-like setting.

Alfred Milner, who took over from the military in 1900, was aware that a centralised, imposed British administration would eventually have to make way for more inclusive, elected and representative government. Milner constructed the Transvaal's new courts and 'Law Department' – the ministry of justice – with an eye to the future. He raided the nearest English-speaking enclave for its finest administrative, legal and political talent. As he explained to Prime Minister WP Schreiner of the Cape Colony, in a letter in early 1901:

> ... if I could I would plunder the Cape even further ... I don't know of anything which can help soften the rigour of the *necessary period of autocratic government* so much as to get men of unquestioned ability and integrity and South African experience and sympathies into important administrative and judicial posts.[6]

The written and unwritten rules governing politics and society had changed considerably by 1909, but they were still being implemented by judges acknowledged to be without peer in pre-Union South Africa, by men whose views fell within the parameters set for constructing a society more in keeping with an industrialising capitalist economy and the larger imperial project. Milner's insistence on a taut administration, however, extended beyond a careful construction of the new bench.

Knowing that the Transvaal towns and countryside required different degrees and types of control, Milner established a bifurcated police force. The South African Constabulary (1900–1908) patrolled the rural areas while the new Transvaal Town Police was given responsibility for serving the Crown prosecution and maintaining law and order along the Witwatersrand.[7] Both forces, however, had to be constituted from a standing start. The result was that they lacked sufficient experienced or professionally trained personnel and struggled to operate consistently at the highest levels of proficiency. By 1909, the reputation of the slightly longer-lived Transvaal Town Police force was at an all-time low and the hard-pushed state sorely in need of a few high-profile successes.[8]

McLoughlin's trial came onto the roll at a moment when the government, judiciary and police were interacting more closely than at any other time in the recent history of the former Boer republics. After 14 years the accused, who faced charges that would have been difficult to defend himself against in 1895, found himself in the wrong place and at the wrong time. History, most certainly, was not on his side.

★   ★   ★

Delays occasioned by the imperial authorities had denied McLoughlin the opportunity of defending himself within the same cultural, legal or political environment in which the shootings had taken place. The jurors at his trial – supposedly drawn from his peers – were not drawn from a cohort that would have easily understood the compelling code of honour and masculinity that had informed his behaviour back in 1895. And the judge at his trial was the product of a colonial border town. He was a man who may have been familiar with the background to military conflict between blacks and whites, but he bore little knowledge of the patterns of underworld or working-class behaviour in a frontier mining settlement.

The challenges facing Jack McLoughlin were therefore not confined to the administrative and legal complexities arising from the need to collect and present evidence after the lapse of so many years. They extended into the underlying mindsets and differing worldviews of the judge and the members of the jury. And, even if judge and jury were more *au fait* with the original settings in which the shootings had taken place than might reasonably be expected of them, the state was asking much more of them. The state was in search not only of a punishment that fitted the original crime committed 14 years earlier, in 1895. That state, the former republican state, was long since gone. What the new state, increasingly locked into the realities of empire, was also looking for was an outcome that somehow also addressed the turbulent contemporary environment on the Witwatersrand. In 1909, that included an economic climate in which certain members of the white working class were manifesting radical opposition that did not always eschew the use of violence.

It is impossible to know to what extent these subliminal factors had a role to play in the thinking of those who determined McLoughlin's fate, but it is unlikely that they could have been avoided entirely. The pursuit of justice, through the law, seeks not only to control contemporary behaviour, but to help construct a future – better – society. The past, the present and the future are linked along a seamless spectrum. All trials are set in the history of the period in which they take place, but those where a great lapse in time separates the crime from the hearing obviously demand more attention to 'historical moment' than do others.

Moreover, in the case of Jack McLoughlin, neither judge nor jury ever explicitly addressed the fact that the principal responsibility for the delay between the time that the crimes took place and the trial did not lie solely with the defendant, a fugitive from justice. His whereabouts were known within months of the shootings. It was the imperial authorities who at first declined to have him extradited, and who, at a later date, agreed not only to his extradition, but wished to have his trial concluded before the advent of the Union. It is within this troubling context, then, that McLoughlin's re-entry to the unsettled Witwatersrand has to be considered.

★ ★ ★

Mynott and De Beer were relieved to unshackle their prisoner for the last time and see him safely behind bars in Johannesburg. But there was no rest for them; the state's legal machinery was re-activated the following morning. An identity parade, on 27 July, was the first of five. The last was held on 30 November, hours before the trial commenced.[9]

Greying and rotund, Jack McLoughlin knew what was at stake in the parades at a time when personal identification trumped any forensic evidence. He defended his interests as best he could. Between 18 and 20 men were lined up in the police courtyard, including several resembling him in age and height, at the prisoner's insistence. Those assembled stood close together, hands behind backs, so that there was no easy, tell-tale, way of picking him out. Witnesses who had been separated so as to avoid any possibility of collusion either before, or even after the parade, were asked to identify the accused.

Over nine weeks close on two score men and women were called upon, in different combinations, and at varying times, to help identify the man behind the death and mayhem in and around the Red Lion that night in 1895. With the exception of two or three who remained terrified out of their wits by the suspect – including Max/'Murch' Goldberg, who had just missed taking a bullet to the head outside the Princess Bar – the majority of witnesses had little difficulty identifying the one-armed man.[10]

If the unending identity parades did not persuade McLoughlin about the gravity of the situation he was facing, they should have. The seriousness of the state's intention had been underscored earlier when the Crown – at its own expense – had appointed a criminal attorney, Lewis Levy, to arrange for the defence of the accused on a *pro Deo* basis. Levy found and instructed a bright young advocate to lead the case for the defence.

Within hours of the first identity parade, news that 'One-armed Mac' was back in town started filtering back into criminal networks – where, despite the best efforts of first the military and then the Milner administrations, underworld continuities were as much in evidence as was change. By the time the Preliminary Examination was conducted, in late August, before the same Police Magistrate as had presided in Kruger's day, NJ van den Bergh, many in the underworld were impatient to catch a glimpse of the man who, in his time, had been a frontier legend. As one local journalist cited in a far-off New Zealand newspaper reported:

> The usual unsavoury crowd of Police Court frequenters was augmented to such an extent that it was a difficult matter for even officials to get into 'A' Court but a noticeable feature was the presence of many disreputable grey-haired persons – people who probably knew Johannesburg in its earlier and less reputable days, and were, in fact, residents during the period when the tragedy occurred.[11]

The presence in court of familiar faces in search of free entertainment at a moment that fell between the decline of the music halls and the rise of the cinema, may have been another warning sign for the accused. The city's past was clearly not buried, perhaps not even past. Even more worrying was the strength of the case laid out by the Crown at the Preliminary Examination. The Magistrate, easily convinced, referred the case to the High Court. The trial, set for the first day of December 1909, would be followed no less avidly than the earlier proceedings. As Lewis Levy studied the trial documents he became increasingly concerned about the fate of a stubborn and untutored client who failed to appreciate how carefully the case for the Crown had been constructed or just how damning the evidence for the prosecution was.

With the exception of just one witness who had since died, the Crown Prosecutor, EW Douglass, assisted by Advocate JW Tindall, had assembled virtually every witness of substance who in one way or another had witnessed the events in and around the shootings. Among the witnesses the Crown would call were a fair number of cab drivers, tailors and prostitutes from the

Cape Malay community who knew the one-armed man personally, or those who had been friends or family of the unfortunate Hadji Mustaffa.

Principal among the Crown witnesses and crucial to the state's case was Stevenson's former lover and Jack McLoughlin's *bête noire*, Sarah Fredericks. She was by then using her new married name of Sarah McNeil. But unwilling to rely too heavily on coloured witnesses in a state where race was gaining in importance and the jury was white, the Crown had also tracked down an impressive number of Europeans who either knew the accused or were familiar with the events that had played themselves out at the Red Lion that night. Among the latter were Johannesburg's corrupt and disgraced former Chief Detective, Robert Ferguson, who had arrested the accused in the Pretoria Station robbery, and his successor, Andrew Trimble, who had been forced to take over the investigation into the shootings at the Red Lion at short notice. Others included Harry Lobb, Stevenson's one-time public rival for Sarah Fredericks's favours, Veld Kornet Frederick Kretzmar, who had taken a statement from the dying man that identified McLoughlin as his assassin, and Zarps who could testify to the accused man's earlier close friendship with the murdered boxer-gangster-informer. Medical evidence was to be provided by Dr John van Niekerk, who had not only treated Stevenson on site before he expired, but had performed the amputation on McLoughlin's arm in 1890, and Dr C Schultz, who had conducted the post mortems on the victims.

It was clear, from the outset, that Douglass was going to present a formidable, probably incontrovertible, case for the prosecution. Under the circumstances, there was not much point in McLoughlin denying that he had deliberately sought out and shot Stevenson and then, under different circumstances, killed Mustaffa while attempting to make good his escape. Public sensitivities would not allow McLoughlin to reveal the full extent or exact nature of his relationship with Stevenson. He may therefore have been better served by pleading guilty. By underscoring the context and motive for the killing of an erstwhile criminal collaborator and intimate friend who betrayed him by becoming a police informer, he might avoid incurring the ultimate penalty for the shootings.

In order for that to have happened, however, McLoughlin would have had to have had access to excellent legal counsel from the moment he was arrested in Brisbane and even more so once he was back on the Rand. His attorney, Levy, was suitably argumentative and pugnacious but not particularly effective in court; by the time the Preliminary Examination was concluded most of the damage was already done.

McLoughlin may have sensed the weakness of his position, but he was a prisoner of his personality and had, long since, settled on what he thought his best line of defence might be. He was accustomed to brazening things out, taking pride in having shown 'confidence in myself' and confronting things head-on, a tactic that left nuance and subtlety at a premium. He denied any involvement in, or personal knowledge of the shootings. He questioned any description that pointed to his having a moustache rather than a beard at the time of the shootings. He also suggested that he may have been confused with some other, unknown, man who had also lost a right arm. It was a line of defence that was as implausible as it was weak. It left Levy with little to work with as the worried attorney looked around for senior counsel to represent his client.

The man best qualified for the job, FAW Lucas, probably presented himself. Lucas was the son of an architect with Irish Catholic roots, a man originally from Melbourne, where he had married into a family famous for its politically progressive feminist daughters.[12] Lucas had done his schooling at Marist Brothers College, Johannesburg, before going on to read law at the South African College in Cape Town. Academically gifted, he won a scholarship to Oxford and completed his training with a studentship at the prestigious Middle Temple where he won a gold medal for the 'law of evidence' and 'criminal procedure' before eventually returning to the Transvaal and being admitted to the Bar in Johannesburg in 1906. Strongly influenced by the political values of those on the maternal side of the family, Lucas was a radical with a well-developed interest in socialism in the southern hemisphere colonies and closely concerned about the fate of the working classes of all colours. In 1915, as a member of the Transvaal Provincial Council, he oversaw the granting of the vote to white women in municipal elections.[13]

Lucas's ethnic roots, legal training, sympathy for the underdog and understanding of Catholicism all appeared to make him ideally suited to championing McLoughlin's cause. Well-handled counsel for the defence may have been able to stave off the death sentence, even if he could not save the accused from a lengthy prison sentence. Alas, Lucas fell hopelessly short of the asking price. For various reasons, many of which lay beyond his control, the recently married young advocate was badly out of his depth before, during and after the trial. Lucas simply lacked the experience and temperament necessary to mount the type of imaginative and spirited defence that the McLoughlin case demanded.

Like many who shared his political convictions, Lucas was so taken with the purely economic dimensions of the concept of class that he failed to appreciate fully how it helped shape culture and social structures. Not once during the trial did he challenge the description in court documents of his client as being 'English'. By allowing McLoughlin to be cast as 'English' and failing to present him as 'Irish' or, at very least, as having been strongly shaped by an Anglo-Irish upbringing in Ancoats, Lucas cut himself off from a line of explanation and questioning that even the newspapers at the time of the shootings had pointed to.[14]

Lucas's unwillingness to point to the protruding ethnic edges of his client's identity was not without cost. It meant his having to abandon any reference to McLoughlin's romantic albeit warped notions of honour or duelling and his propensity for oath-taking. It also meant that he had to forego exposing the deeper historical roots of Irish oppositional culture to British rule as manifested by the execution of the informer, James Carey, by Patrick O'Donnell in southern African waters, in 1882. Lucas's silence about his client's ethnicity effectively denied the possibility of there being a quasi-political element to McLoughlin's shooting of an informer. It also made it impossible to set the accused man's behaviour within the context of his former standing within the old 'Irish Brigade' where primitive 'social banditry' bore testimony of its own as to how closely the 'criminal' and 'political' sub-cultures had been intertwined.[15]

If Lucas was reluctant or unable to explore the wider ethno-political dimensions to the execution of a close friend who had turned police informer, he was even less willing to probe the emotional depth and nature of McLoughlin and Stevenson's relationship prior to the shootings. A decade and a half after Oscar Wilde's trial, in 1895, it was still not acceptable to explore publicly how codes of Victorian masculinity could – simultaneously – encourage brotherly love and male emotional intimacy, yet forbid any thought that it might entail physical expression.

Counsel for the defence, the prosecutor and judge all proved to be extraordinarily hard of hearing when a policeman, Andries Smorenberg, described McLoughlin and Stevenson's friendship as 'intimate'. Nor did they take cognisance of the underlying and transparently emotional content of some of Jack McLoughlin's testimony when he took the stand. McLoughlin stated openly that he knew that 'Stevo' 'did not care [for him]' when he turned state's evidence and that 'I could not say that I was in love with him after that'. Nor, more pertinently and revealingly still, did they take note when the accused said that he had once received a message from Stevenson to the effect that 'if only I would make friends again he would not care for anybody else in Johannesburg'.[16] The fact that the two men were 'close' was permissible and could be publicly stated. But anything that went on to describe their relationship other than as one of close friendship, as caring, probably even loving, was plainly unthinkable.

The advocate's failure to raise questions about McLoughlin's ethnic identity or the code of masculinity that governed his client's affection for and behaviour towards Stevenson was partly understandable. Lucas was young and inexperienced – and appearing before a judge, already revered, who would go on and assume the highest legal office in the expanding South African state. Lucas's head and heart were not in the proceedings. By late 1909, his real interest lay elsewhere – in constitutional issues – and, above all else, in the coming order. A few months earlier he had won an essay competition on 'Closer Union' and he had been chosen as one of just eight legal advisers to guide the deliberations for a new constitution. Lucas's reluctance to underscore the ethnic, social and emotional elements in the decision to execute the police informer increased the risk of his client getting the death sentence. By failing to establish the fuller context of the shootings, he left the way open for the informer's execution to be seen only as a criminal act – one motivated solely by revenge, a cold and murderous deed.

★ ★ ★

With the Crown Prosecutor, EW Douglass, set to make the running and the expertise of Lucas restricted largely to procedural issues or technical questions about the law of evidence, it would be left to the presiding judge to bring some balance to what might otherwise degenerate into a hopelessly lopsided procedure. In particular, an enormous responsibility would devolve upon the judge when it came to instructing the jury in a case of murder where the life of the accused was at stake. Members of the bench and staff in the Law Department were only too aware of the gravity of the charges facing the accused and of the need to avoid any slip-up in a trial taking place just six months before the advent of Union.

With one important exception, cases heard in the Witwatersrand High Court were usually allocated to the bench on a strictly rotational basis. But, with so much local, inter-colonial and imperial reputational capital at stake at a time of profound constitutional change the Law Department needed to be guaranteed a swift and legally persuasive conclusion in the matter of Rex vs McLoughlin. The matter could not be left to chance and the case was allocated only after careful deliberation. The state appointed its pre-eminent jurist, the man Milner had chosen as the first Chief Justice of the Transvaal Colony, a senior judge already spoken of as a possible future Chief Justice in the Union of South Africa, Sir James Rose Innes.

Innes was born into and had also married into the English-speaking elite of the Eastern Cape and qualified as a lawyer before going on to establish a highly successful legal practice in Cape Town in the 1880s. His considerable personal qualities – a capacity for hard work, easy-going manner and inherent sense of fair play, along with his integrity and ability as an analyst and debater – all encouraged him to think about standing for political office. Elected to parliament, he twice served as Attorney General in the cabinet of the Cape Colony where his on-going loyalty to crown and empire were duly recognised with a knighthood.

By inclination Innes was, however, better suited to a life in law than in politics.[17] Milner's offer of the post of Chief Justice in the Transvaal thus presented him with a fine outlet for his talents as a jurist although it also posed the severest challenge to his admirably liberal values and belief in a non-racial future. Industrial Johannesburg was not commercial Cape Town. As a judge, his legal experience and personality may have made him more suited to hearing the administrative and constitutional issues that he had a preference for than to tackling criminal cases in a mining centre with a well-developed and turbulent underworld. Innes had virtually no personal knowledge of industrialising society and, for all his reputation as an endearing and eminently reasonable man, he was singularly unsuited to understanding behaviour that was both overtly criminal in intent and yet informed by low levels of political consciousness.

Innes was, notes one scholar, 'perceptive if not unusually imaginative', a man with 'an extremely high, almost inflexible, code of personal behaviour', and was almost always 'reluctant to compromise on political issues even when he perceived that such a compromise might actually further the pursuit of his high-minded goals'.[18] A Chief Justice with those traits, well known and rewarded for his service to empire, would find it difficult to think his way into the mental universe of an Irish social bandit or a man with a complex sexual identity.

James Rose Innes's experience and understanding of radical – criminal-political – Irish opposition to imperialism was indirect and limited. He happened to have been in London at the time of Dublin's Phoenix Park murders, in 1882. But, like many others, he could find no moral justification for them. Nor could he bring himself to acknowledge the passion that the struggle for independence evoked among Irishmen. Ever the formalist, the feature of the Phoenix Park murders that endured longest in his mind was the 'most impressive' scenes in the House of Commons that followed. Likewise, when the sequel played itself out aboard the *Melrose Castle* in Cape waters and O'Donnell shot Carey, Innes could see it only as a 'political crime' carried out in 'cold blood'. It was a strange juxtaposition. For a liberal constitutionalist serving the empire it was difficult to concede that nationalism might inflame the emotions to the point where they might motivate either planned or spontaneous violence. For Innes, like McLoughlin, self-control was a cardinal virtue.[19]

Closer to home and more pertinently, the Chief Justice had only recently been reminded of the insidious role that informers played in the policing of the Witwatersrand underworld, the contempt they aroused in those with Irish connections, and the murderous instincts they could unleash.

In May 1908, barely a year before the trial of Jack McLoughlin, Innes had presided in the case of Rex vs JW Barry *alias* 'Ginger London'. London, raised in 'Little Ireland' in Clerkenwell, had been accused of murdering Meyer Hasenfus, the sidekick of a notorious police informer, Leon Rosenblatt. But given the circumstances of a stabbing that proved fatal, London had been convicted only of manslaughter. In his summing up the Chief Justice was unsparing of the police and the role of informers, claiming that police spies endangered 'the administration of justice and the good order of society'. Innes was, however, admiring of the Irish-Australian Neil 'Paddy' McMahon for conducting his own defence competently in a linked case, though he remained wholly unimpressed by the fact that McMahon had refused to betray his underworld associates. Innes was largely tone deaf to the many and complex links between ethnicity and politics and the ways in which they might help shape criminal acts.[20]

If Lucas entertained doubts about the wisdom of unpacking the reasons behind the slaying of Stevenson before the trial, so as to prevent the shooting from being seen only as a criminal act that had more to do with 'honour among thieves' than with ethnicity or masculinity, they could only have been compounded when he learnt that the case was to be heard by Rose Innes. It was all the more reason for Lucas to confine his main interventions to narrower questions of criminal procedure and the law of evidence. And, if the accused man's counsel for the defence and the Chief Justice offered Jack McLoughlin little hope of avoiding the death penalty, then the composition of the jury seemed to hold out even less.

In practice, on the Witwatersrand, the legendary 'twelve men good and true' consisted of just nine white males. The surviving documents reveal nothing about their status as regards age, class, marital status, occupation or religious belief. From the archival record it is impossible to know how many, if any of them, might have been drawn from a cohort that bore some knowledge of McLoughlin, the Irish Brigade or Johannesburg at a time when it was a frontier-like town and carrying a revolver was almost *de rigueur*. For the most part they appear to have been uniformly 'English' and robustly heterosexual in a gold mining centre long known for its ethnic diversity and masculinity. In keeping with the recently enforced new imperial order nervously making way for another, not one of the jurors bore a name that could be considered as being self-evidently 'Afrikaner', 'Irish' or 'Jewish'. Taken on its own – as a list of citizens in good standing and without a criminal record – the jurors may well have felt more at home in Birmingham than in Boksburg. This may, of course, have been a small blessing in disguise since throughout the proceedings it was assumed that McLoughlin was an 'English' national and a bachelor.[21]

McLoughlin went to his trial knowing that justice was an ideal but that its pursuit was driven by men, not God. The real trial, he began to think, perhaps lay in some other place.

ᗏᏋᏊᏋᏊ

The Trial

JOHANNESBURG
— 1909 —

Nothing dies harder than the desire to think well of oneself.
TS ELIOT

When the Criminal Sessions commenced in the High Court, on Wednesday, 1 December 1909, the room filled to hear an indictment on two charges of murder – of George Stevenson and Hadji Mustaffa. The charges were read out on behalf of the Acting Attorney-General of the Transvaal, 'Jan Christiaan Smuts'. If convicted, the Acting Attorney-General 'prayed for judgment against the accused' – whose name was given only as 'Jack McLoughlin' – to proceed 'according to law'. Did it matter that his name at baptism was John, not Jack? Perhaps not. Enquiring too closely into the life of an accused distances the law and humanises the pursuit of justice beyond limits that many states are comfortable with.

Throughout the trial there was always something on display to remind one of the bravado of the leader of the 'Irish Brigade', the terror of every publican along the mining frontier and of the Johannesburg underworld. But there were also telltale signs of a man who was never fully at ease with his body image and who had failed to recapture fully his manly posture after losing a limb.[1] It did not help that, after Mynott and De Beer had handed him over to men at Marshall Square, the besieged Chief Detective, Major

TE Mavrogordato, had seen fit to confiscate his 'false hand' and immediately place it on display in the police museum.[2] The state had its trophy even before the outcome of the hunt was clear.

As ever, Jack McLoughlin insisted on presenting himself as self-confident and well-kempt. He steadfastly refused to cast himself as anyone's victim, including that of the young man whose betrayal had shattered his barely cohering self-image in 1894. According to a not entirely unsympathetic court reporter:

> McLoughlin appeared to be in the best of health and spirits, although whenever a particularly damaging statement was made his facial muscles quivered for a second or so. But in every instance the quivering ended in a smile. He was neatly clad and well groomed; and he seemed to take particular care to conceal his right arm, the hand of which had been amputated. From time to time he scanned the faces of the morbid-minded crowd which filled the public section of the Sessions room as though he was looking for somebody.[3]

The first and most damaging day of the trial belonged entirely to the prosecution. Douglass's preparation had been meticulous and he examined a string of witnesses as to the events in the rooms behind the Red Lion Beer Hall to devastating effect. Most of the Crown's witnesses were either working-class coloured men and women, or former prostitutes. The principal exception was Harry Lobb, the mason and one-time boxer who, along with Jack McCann, had been present at the infamous dinner McLoughlin presided over in Rosenthal's Café on the night of the shootings. The star witness of the first day, however, was undoubtedly George Stevenson's in-amorata and McLoughlin's long-time rival for the young man's affections – Sarah Fredericks/McNeil.[4]

Determined and feisty, Fredericks made an excellent impression. She was an unwavering witness for the prosecution, recalling details around the shooting of her lover with graphic precision. She was full and frank about her comparatively long and loving relationship with Stevenson as well as the fatal consequence of his decision to provide evidence for the state in the Pretoria Station robbery case. Fredericks was careful to avoid disclosing the sources of her own income or the nature of her earlier acquaintance or relationships with either Jack McLoughlin or Harry Lobb, her former lover. Her complicated past remained largely secret.

Sensing that it would be difficult, if not impossible, to shake Fredericks's testimony about a shooting that she had witnessed at point-blank range, Lucas's cross examination of her took a different tack. He questioned her insistently about her prior relationship with Lobb and how it had led to a street-fight with Stevenson that had to be settled by way of a boxing match in order to determine who would be the recipient of her favours. The defence hoped to portray her as a common prostitute with questionable credibility and to suggest that she had surrounded herself with men of a violent disposition – some of whom, presumably, might have had their own reasons for wanting to settle scores with her former lover.

Fredericks, however, was as intelligent as she was persuasive. It was difficult to cast her as a mere hawker of sex. Her complex relationships with a string of men could not easily be portrayed as casual, on-going whoring. Not beyond telling the odd lie, she denied any knowledge of the boxing match or the press report that it had evoked. Her single-minded, monogamous devotion to Stevenson had endured until his death and occasioned sufficient sacrifice for it be credibly presented as something close to a common law marriage. When that line of questioning proved unpromising, Lucas prepared the way for an arcane point he was to raise later. He attempted to establish Stevenson's religious beliefs. She told the court that, as far as she could tell, her lover had not had any.[5]

The rest of the day was spent interrogating various men and women who had been in the rooms off the passage, or elsewhere in the Red Lion at the time of the shooting. It was brought to a conclusion with a brief examination of Lobb about the celebratory dinner at Rosenthal's. Lobb, still wary of McLoughlin, was as elusive and vague as possible. 'I could not say I knew him well,' he suggested. Sarah and I 'did not exactly live together,' he claimed, and so on. But Lobb could not deny that by the time of the dinner he knew that Stevenson had been shot, and that he was aware that his one-armed friend was the only suspect.[6]

On Thursday, the second day of the trial, Douglass and Tindall bolstered an already devastating case for the prosecution by calling 20 more witnesses. Almost all offered testimony about the shooting of Stevenson or the tragic street-slaying of young Hadji Mustaffa that was as focused as it was clear. A notable exception was Johannesburg's venal Chief Detective of the mid-1890s, one of about a half-dozen policemen who had known the accused. Robert Ferguson was a shell of a man, an officer of the law whom McLoughlin, at the height of his powers, had cowed and humiliated to a point where he lost all respect and was then forced to resign from his position by the press.

Taking comfort from the fact that many years separated him from the shootings, and hoping that nobody would contradict or question him by referring to reports at the time, Ferguson dissembled and equivocated so as to place even more distance between him and the events that had proved to be his undoing. He claimed to have resigned days *before* the shootings. 'I am not certain whether I was in town that evening or not,' he lied. 'I came into town the following night or two nights afterwards from Heidelberg if I was not in that evening.' He also denied having subsequently seen the accused in Delagoa Bay. Ferguson epitomised everything that McLoughlin despised, the man he feared he would have become had he not shot Stevenson. In his own testimony he again hinted at the detective's cowardice.[7]

Ferguson aside, the Crown Prosecutor and most of the policemen did exceptionally well. When the trial concluded the Chief Justice, mindful of the fact that the police had got a drubbing from the press for their shoddy public performance over the past few months, was fulsome in his praise. Sir James was struck by 'the vigilance, capacity and industry of those concerned in investigating the case'.[8] Of all the witnesses for the prosecution on the second day, however, few carried more weight than did Ferguson's successor as Chief Detective, Andrew Trimble, and the Veld Kornet at the time, FE Kretzmar. Between them, they had taken an affidavit from George Stevenson, as he lay dying, and in which he had clearly identified his assassin as his one-time partner, McLoughlin.[9]

But neither Trimble nor Kretzmar's testimony was beyond question, and it was at this point that Lucas saw his best chance to put to use his reputed skill as an expert on the law of evidence. He drew attention to the fact that, despite an extensive search in the police archives, the prosecution had been unable to come up with Stevenson's original, sworn and signed statement, implying that this relegated the officials' evidence to something approximating to hearsay. In addition, Lucas averred that his questioning of Sarah Fredericks had revealed clearly that Stevenson was a non-believer and that, as such, any supposedly 'sworn' statement should count for nothing in a court of law.

The Chief Justice halted proceedings in order to hear these objections, the validity of which were immediately contested by Douglass. Sir James listened carefully but was singularly unimpressed by what he heard from counsel for the defence. In commonsense, no-nonsense, mode he dismissed Lucas's argument, suggesting that the rule was that 'the best evidence must be produced if possible, but if not, the secondary evidence should be taken' and that, 'the fact of a man having no religious belief did not in the opinion of the Court make any difference'.[10]

Lucas's moment had come and gone. He had little to show for his efforts. Much of the rest of the day saw McLoughlin himself in the witness stand. The accused man's evidence was, for the main part, disingenuous – a crude mixture of dissembling, strategic silences and outright lies. But, as had happened while chatting to Mynott aboard the *Wyreema* on leaving Brisbane, just recalling the early days on the Rand breathed new life into him. A reporter noted that there was a 'twinkle' in his eye while recalling events on the day of the shooting. Unable to render explicitly or fully the code of masculinity and oath-taking that had informed his behaviour in frontier Johannesburg 14 years earlier, he nevertheless made it clear that he considered his own conduct to have been above reproach – manly – and quite unlike that of Stevenson.

His testimony was punctuated by short sentences. Like a pit-bull straining at the leash, the anger and hubris was barely contained. 'I knew all the town but I did not know the Red Lion,' he said. 'I had confidence in myself,' but 'I did not use a revolver that day' – even though many other white men carried concealed weapons. 'I could shoot with a revolver the same as any other man but I was not an expert shot,' but then, with poorly disguised pride: 'I could use it as well as if I had a right hand,' because, back then, Johannesburg was a 'rough place'.[11]

He made much of the confusion as to whether or not he had sported a beard on the day of the shootings, tried to do some misleading about a supposed one-armed look-alike, and generally played down the dinner at Rosenthal's and his brazen movements around town later that day. He had seen the one-armed man 'continually for two or three months' – yet, despite sharing an affliction, 'did not know his occupation or anything about him'. He had dinner with friends that night but had not lingered in town. 'Is it feasible,' he asked, that 'I should go moping about Commissioner Street between the Central Hotel and the Height's Hotel if I had murdered this man? It is one of the most dangerous places in Johannesburg.'[12] But he was rowing against wave upon wave of contradictory evidence. And amidst all the self-generated turbulence, the only thing that the unfortunate Lucas could do was to hang on grimly.

Predictably, the weakest part of McLoughlin's testimony related to the emotions that had engulfed him, Stevenson and Sarah Fredericks in the weeks leading up to the Pretoria Station robbery. With breathtaking understatement he conceded only that 'Stevo was a friend of mine at one time or another', but then went on to underscore how, after the robbery, '[Stevo] was despised by everybody in town' – presumably himself included. He never once referred to the dying man's deposition identifying him as the assassin. He claimed never to have had problems with Fredericks, whom he had got to know well before she met Stevenson. But then, in an unguarded moment, he hinted at an underlying problem of jealousy, rejecting her testimony by suggesting that: '… I do not know why she should tell lies except that she was living with Stevo'.[13]

Although often revealing his own complex and vulnerable make-up, McLoughlin's testimony failed to diffuse the prosecution's unrelenting focus on the events leading up to and after the shootings. McLoughlin insisted that he knew nothing about the shootings at the Red Lion Beer Hall, other than through hearsay, which he had dismissed as 'a joke'.

The court proceedings on Friday, the third and final day of the trial, followed a painfully well-worn path. The case for the Crown had been assembled with such diligence that Douglass had little to do in addressing the jury other than point out the obvious. Nobody, he said, had disputed the fact that the first victim had been shot by a man with 'only one arm and that he had held the revolver in his left hand', or that Stevenson had been 'in the best position to know who shot him'. The shooting of Mustaffa had been so well established by many witnesses that there was no need to dwell upon it. The accused was clearly guilty.[14]

In his closing address Lucas attempted to deal with Sarah Fredericks's first-hand account of the shooting. He tried to sow small seeds of doubt in a field of stones by pointing to Stevenson's allegedly 'cowardly' behaviour after the station robbery. He underscored Stevenson and Fredericks's alleged lack of composure at the moment of the shooting:

> They were afraid of their shadows and in a state of mind that they had the fear of some particular persons [Lobb and McLoughlin?] continually before them. They were afraid of McLoughlin and thought they saw him every time they saw anybody. When the knock came to the door and the man entered they naturally thought of McLoughlin. It was dark. Sarah McNeil, who stood behind Stevenson – who was a big man – could not see, and yet said it was McLoughlin. She shouted out 'McLoughlin has shot Stevo', and that fathered the whole testimony in the case. As time passed the impression on the people's mind was confirmed.[15]

According to Lucas, the whole episode was no more than history viewed through the collective imagination – an eerily post-modern suggestion. But his closing address had long since been reduced to an exercise in shadow-boxing. Douglass had punched out a compelling argument. It was a hopeless mismatch. So gross was the disparity that both counsel for the defence and the Crown Prosecutor had failed to engage with some of the more arcane and intriguing elements that had arisen during the hearing. There were a few loose ends, seemingly contradictory evidence, that might yet come to trouble the jury during its deliberations.

★   ★   ★

Sir James Rose Innes had picked up on the loose ends and knew that he would have to deal with them when instructing the jury. For one, he had taken note of the accused man's seemingly inexplicable behaviour before and after the shootings. But, try as he might, the judge was at a loss to situate such a daring and self-controlled manner in its appropriate, wider, context. Rose Innes simply could not see a once-charismatic gang leader attempting to regain caste in an underworld that operated within the prescriptions of the Victorian cult of masculinity. He used his summing up to sew up the troubling loose ends around Stevenson's shooting, taking that of the Hadji as having been proved beyond doubt.

The Chief Justice prefaced his comments to the jury by noting how well various law-enforcement agencies had done to ferret out an 'alleged perpetrator of the murder – a cold-blooded murder – committed fifteen years ago'.[16] Rose Innes could detect no signs of passion. He went on to remind jury members, without offering any detail that might inform their deliberations, how a lengthy interval between the commission of the crime and the trial might bedevil the administration of justice. It was an anaemic formulation designed to discourage questions as to whether there may have been an ethnic, emotional, ideological or singularly personal motive – as opposed to a merely criminal one – behind the shooting. It was a pared-down view of the complicated events that had led up to the execution of a police informer. Only someone with a tin ear, or someone intent on extracting a clear-cut verdict, could have ignored the deep feelings that linked Fredericks, Stevenson and McLoughlin.

By reducing the reasons behind the shooting to just one – revenge, pure and simple – the learned judge brought the motive and the act into alignment. The intention of the one-armed assassin, which had never been fully probed, was assumed to have been demonstrated beyond all reasonable doubt. But if the assassin, a man comfortable with a revolver and known to be a good shot, was intent only on slaying his victim, why had he fired but a single bullet at Stevenson and then left, perhaps knowing that the victim had probably only been seriously wounded? *Had* his intent been all that clearly demonstrated? Could it not have been that he had left knowing only that he had inflicted serious harm, of indeterminate consequence, on his victim? The accused had not panicked or fled helter-skelter; witnesses recalled that, upon leaving Fredericks's room, the one-armed man had deliberately walked away and said to the two men he passed in the passage: 'All right boys, I won't harm you.'[17]

More pertinently, if the shooting was simply an act of revenge of the sort occasionally encountered among the under-classes, one where the intention was to kill by way of clinical execution with a single shot, why had the alleged murderer sent his victim a message telling him that he would be a dead man by nightfall? It was surely unusual for a murderer to give his victim advance notice of his impending death and, as in this case, allow him the time to find and load his own revolver and prepare for a possible shootout? The truth was that there had been a primitive, underlying, duel-like dimension to the shooting which, had Stevenson been slightly more alert and vigilant, might have given rise to a different and wholly unpredictable outcome. These were awkward, potentially messy, considerations – but here too, Sir James was having none of it:

> His Lordship dealt with the evidence of the witnesses, and on continuing, referred to the warning alleged to have been given by the accused. Would he have given that warning before committing murder? It might be unlikely but it was possible. Men often warned their intended victims from various motives – from a rough sense of fair play or perhaps anxious to make it as miserable as possible for the victim. The fact that a warning was given was not greatly in favour of the accused when examined as they would be prepared to regard it at first blush [sic]. If the story of Sarah McNeil [Fredericks] was true, it was a cold-blooded deliberate murder.[18]

So much for a 'rough sense of fair play'. It was, yet again, a parsimonious albeit logical reading of the events leading up to the shootings, one that rested largely on Fredericks's account, in which she, like McLoughlin – for reasons of his own – was at pains to play down the emotional cross-currents in a triangle of deep affection, if not love.

The dinner at Rosenthal's, McLoughlin's week-long stay in the inner city and his night-time sortie past the police station where he had learnt that, like any 'outlaw', he was 'wanted dead or alive' and had heard the police interrogating 'his girl', constituted further potential distractions for the jury. They were bold acts which, in truth, were probably calculated not only to flaunt McLoughlin's newly recovered status in the underworld, but to consciously produce a dissembling pattern of behaviour that would be difficult to reconcile with the conduct of someone who had just shot two men.

The Chief Justice, however, having already downplayed the importance of a duel-like element to the confrontation between the men – a formulation that denied the assailant having even a modicum of courage – was equally unwilling to cast events in a light that might credit the accused with the semblance of real bravery. Sir James's view of the events was clear:

> If [McLoughlin] was the guilty man it was a most foolhardy and daring
> [act] that having shot a man, and being followed by a crowd of people
> who must have recognised him on account of his deformity, a man
> known in Johannesburg for a long time, and then to have gone with
> Lobb to the café when he must have known that a hue and cry was
> already raised. He might be a very desperate and daring man but it was
> a foolhardy thing to do.[19]

In the eyes of the Chief Justice, after the shootings McLoughlin had been, in that order, 'foolhardy and daring' or 'desperate and daring'. On Sir James's reading, the accused had only been reckless or mindlessly provocative in an otherwise hopeless situation. His behaviour was ill-considered, his deeds probably best construed as either rash or resigned. It was a view, conveyed to the jury, that allowed for no *controlled* acts of courage on the part of a man with a physical handicap, a 'deformity'; a man who was attempting to regain respect, including self-respect, in a sub-culture obsessed with notions of masculinity. Rose Innes's view was part of a perception that also made no allowance for the possibility of an 'outlaw' intent on staging a successful, well-planned exit from the city and country he had spent the better part of a decade in. It was a 'cold blooded murder' by a man more foolish than he was brave. In short, there was nothing to commend the man or his deeds.

After the summing-up, the court adjourned, allowing everyone to have lunch before the jury retired. In a nearby holding cell McLoughlin resolved that, whatever the outcome, he would again attempt to conduct himself with the necessary dignity and refuse to supplicate before the court. Lucas had offered him no grounds for optimism on the way out. The nine men could do as they thought fit, he would surely say no more.

The jury members wrestled with the problems as best they could and experienced little difficulty in moving to a consensus position. The Crown Prosecutor had effectively put the question beyond doubt by the end of the first day. Counsel for the defence had done nothing to dent the testimony of a score or more witnesses. The charge on the second count, the murder of the Hadji, required almost no debate at all, it had been proved conclusively. It was the murder of Stevenson that was difficult to deal with; *that* was the horse that would have to pull the cart through the swamps of muddied logic.

The problem for the members of the jury was that Rose Innes had left them with almost no room in which to manoeuvre when it came to the murder of Stevenson. It was their verdict in that matter that would do most to shape the attitude of the skittish white working classes to the outcome of the trial. Everybody knew that they were living in difficult times, attitudes were hardening and class conflict was becoming ever sharper. Miners, in particular, would expect the jury to show more signs of compassion than might be expected from a judge or a prosecutor.

The jury sensed that there were underlying issues in the case that had not been properly explored but, in his summing up, Sir James Rose Innes had all but sealed them off too. The only straw the Chief Justice had left for them to clutch at was his acknowledgement that the enormous lapse in time between the shootings and the accused coming to trial had constituted a serious problem for all the parties – and more especially so for the accused. With one exception, members of the jury agreed that it probably *was* a mitigating factor and that they should attempt to seek unanimity and somehow build it into their findings. But the lone dissenter among them could not be persuaded to abandon his hard line. It was Friday afternoon, and after a while they agreed to bring in a unanimous verdict with a majority recommendation.

Shortly after the customary hour devoted to lunch ended it was announced that the court would reconvene in 30 minutes. When the doors to the courtroom opened, at 2.15 pm sharp:

> there was a general rush on the part of the public for admission They came along in such a large body that one youth was pushed through the glass panel of the inside door. Within two minutes the space allotted to the public outside the barriers was completely crowded. [20]

Judge, jury and the accused all entered the courtroom promptly at 2.30 pm. The Registrar of the Court, Charles Rorke, addressed the foreman:

> Gentlemen, have you agreed upon your verdict?
> The Foreman: We have.
> Do you find the prisoner at the bar guilty or not guilty on the first count?
> The Foreman: Guilty, my Lord.
> The Registrar: And on the second count?
> The Foreman: Guilty. We wish, my Lord, to add the recommendation to mercy, by eight to one, owing to the time which has elapsed since the commission of the crime and the trial.
> The Registrar then asked [the convicted man] whether he had anything to say why the sentence of death should not be pronounced upon him. McLoughlin replied in a firm voice: 'No, sir'. [21]

True to his promise to himself, Jack McLoughin 'remained unmoved', tapping his fingers on the front of the dock. Like Ned Kelly and other outlaw heroes of the age, he, too, wanted 'to die game', to show that he was a man. As the Chief Justice prepared to hand down the sentence he knew what was coming:

> Well McLoughlin, the jury had found you guilty after a very fair and very careful trial and personally I do not think any other verdict was possible from the evidence. I do not wish by any words of mine to add

to the pain of your position. The jury has recommended you to mercy, and I shall have much pleasure in forwarding that recommendation to the proper quarters, but in view of the evidence, I do not want to give you an exaggerated hope as a result of that recommendation so as to interfere with the making of your peace with God. I have only one sentence to pass.[22]

The convicted man 'looked straight at the Judge while the sentence was being passed' and, at the conclusion, 'walked firmly and quickly out of the dock in charge of the Court Orderly'.[23] He left the courtroom with the clearest understanding possible of what would happen next. Sir James Rose Innes, Chief Justice, constitutionalist, imperialist and liberal, had told him, in polite language, that it was to be a case of no hope rather than one of 'exaggerated hope'. While standing about, waiting for 'the Black Maria to convey him on his last journey to the Fort', he turned and remarked to the warders: 'Well Boys' – his long-favoured mode of fraternal address – 'I shan't see the Seven Stars Inn at Manchester or the Mersey again.'[24] The need to be constantly on the move had ended; there was only one short, or very long, journey left.

CHAPTER TWENTY-SIX

༼ఴఴ༽

Death

PRETORIA
— 1910 —

The worst evil of all is to leave the ranks of the living before one dies.
SENECA

The courage we desire and prize is not the courage to die decently, but to live manfully.
THOMAS CARLYLE

Back in the Fort that weekend there was little room for careful reflection. Thoughts and impressions of the trial were stacked and re-stacked in his mind in varying combinations until they threatened his sanity. It was strange because it was all meaningless, like packing up so many unused socks and shirts into a box for a trip done years earlier. And frustrating, too, because soon enough case and content alike would be redundant.

It was only in the train, on the way from Johannesburg and back to prison in the capital for the last time, that he could pore over a few things that really mattered for the journey that lay beyond. In a way it was a relief to be returning to the cells. This time it would not be to the old Visagie Street gaol where he had spent 18 months in 1891, drying out after taking a potshot at Henry Higgins. The Transvaal had an imposing new prison more in keeping with a modern industrialising state – Pretoria Central.

He could, at last, stop running. It was not so much the shootings at the Red Lion that had prompted his long retreat. He had been trying to get away from alcohol, cotton-mills, domesticity, routine, family, parents, poverty, wage-labour and those who sought most to enslave one psychologically – women – for most of his life. Any spirited lad who aspired to confidence, freedom and self-respect, everything the urban industrialising world was intent on denying humanity other than on its own parsimonious terms, had to try to get as much distance between himself and those hazards as possible. The gateway to a meaningful life lay far away, in that most transient arena of space and time, out on the frontier.

It was only at the edges of empire that the chrysalis of hope did not instantly mutate into the insect of death. There, codes of honour and masculinity, bound tightly into fraternal solidarity, paved the way for action and adventure demanding courage. Frontiers challenged men living in a world that was closing in on them through trains, steamships and undersea cables that spewed out telegrams. He and a few displaced Irishmen, bandits on horseback, mere criminals in the eyes of Boers and British alike, had fought a brave and romantic, albeit an ultimately losing battle, against a rapidly encroaching modern world.[1]

It was his father, William who, when in his cups, had first awakened his curiosity and stirred his imagination with tales of bandits, highwaymen, horses, duels, hedge-schools, priests, illicit stills, excise men, smugglers, soldiers, sailors, spies and secret societies back in Inishowen, on the banks of Loch Swilly. That was long before the famine had driven the Irish west, across the Atlantic to America, or east, to Lancashire, in droves. But he had grown up to hate his father, his mother, Manchester, and almost all that the bustling, self-consciously modern north stood for. He had never wanted to return there. It was the great under-explored south and the Indian Ocean that appealed to him most. He had criss-crossed them often and, measured in miles, he had been around the world two-and-a-half times in just under three decades.

Personally, he cared not a fig for 'the empire' that had proved to be his undoing, but, along with some of the other social discards of the Industrial Revolution, had turned those parts of it where gold was to be found into a playground for the imagination. The factories, furnaces, mills and warehouses of Birmingham, Liverpool and Manchester failed to obliterate the dreams of boys they hoped to turn into machine-men in a smokestack world. Raised on tales about Dick Turpin and other English heroes of the eighteenth century, the new proletariat's sons allowed their flights of fancy to take them to the far ends of an expanding, but still English, world. The chase after profits provided an outward thrust and the Union Jack followed. And it was all within almost anyone's reach. The army or navy gave a man a billet, subsidised travel on a grand scale, and provided a training for life on any of the mining frontiers of the south.

Of course there were no guarantees; some of the turns he had taken had led nowhere and ended in failure. He had misread India entirely. It was not a colony of settlement and the Mysore goldfields had a secretive underworld so socially and economically complex that it had proved impenetrable to him as a European outsider. In New Zealand, where the only significant gold rushes had petered out decades before his arrival, he had stumbled into an agricultural economy and a hopelessly introverted society which, even in urban Auckland, held deep within it an almost hysterical fear of 'vagrants'. He had been forced to spend years in prison there without even getting close to cracking a safe.

The time spent in Australia – all in all, about 13 years – had seen mixed fortunes. During the first stay, at a time when Ned Kelly's name was still on everyone's lips, he too had learned how to cope with life in the bush and colonial towns. The knowledge and craft skills acquired back then had later enabled him to negotiate the countryside during the six years that he was on the run before being sent to prison in Moreton Bay. His second visit to Australia had seen many hidden successes.

But it was on the frontier of gold in nineteenth-century southern Africa – then still largely in its constituent parts, neither wholly in nor wholly out of the encroaching empire – where, despite the loss of an arm and his painful misadventures with Stevenson, he had seen the best years of his life. Army deserter turned Irish Brigade member, he had gone on to become a burglar, footpad, highwayman, mercenary, miner, railway navvy and an extraordinarily successful safe-cracker who had acquired near legendary status on the early Witwatersrand. He had covered the subcontinent from Natal and Mozambique in the east to Bechuanaland in the west, and from

Rhodesia and Vendaland in the north to the Transvaal in the south, plying his trade in town and countryside with equal facility.

They were crossing Visagie Street on the way to the new prison when, out of the Black Maria, he caught a glimpse of the Loreto Convent. He remembered how it was from the grounds of the adjacent convent that an unsuccessful attempt had been launched to spring a significant number of Irish Brigade members, including himself, in October 1891. Principal among their number at the time were the highwaymen Hugh McKeone, brother of the Krugersdorp bank robber, and wild William Cooper, who had been sentenced to death by public hanging. Back then, Catholics throughout southern Africa and some notables from abroad, including the King of Portugal, had been rallied and placed the State President and government of the old South African Republic under sufficient pressure to win the condemned men a last-minute reprieve.

But he was no longer in a Boer republic seeking an outlet to the sea via Portuguese East Africa; he was in a self-governing colony locked into the wider politics of empire. This time there would be no organised solidarity coming from co-religionists, no republicans to buckle beneath international diplomatic pressure. Like many other Englishmen, he had hated the Kruger government; he had even trained black men to engage it militarily, but as an 'Irishman' he may have been better off under the old republicans. Only the naïve believed that culture, ethnicity, race or politics had no bearing whatsoever on hangings for criminal offences. Innes – whose famous liberalism was locked into constitutionalism and unwavering imperial loyalties, had warned him not to hold out too much hope. But, despite himself, he could not abandon it entirely either.

Starting on 6 December 1909, every week and for some weeks thereafter his inner-self pulsed to a pattern agonisingly predictable. Sunday nights were worst – and not only because they marked the end of another of those meaningless units that men chose to measure time in. He remembered all too clearly how, in both Adelaide and at the Boggo Road gaol, Monday was invariably the day designated for executions. Who determined such things? And why did it always have to be the same day everywhere? Was it another of those workings of empire?

But if the seventh day passed without word from the prison Governor then Mondays and Tuesdays – sometimes even Wednesdays – were tolerably calm as the forces of hope and resignation wrestled each other to a stand-still and he tried to savour what passed for life. By mid-week, however, the ministers of state and their small army of suited clerks may have had time enough to dispose of their most pressing tasks, and a final notice might land on the Governor's desk. Thursday and Friday, the last full working days of the week, were spent in a constant state of alert, waiting for a call from the chief warder or an unexpected visit from the Governor. Saturday brought some relief but, on Sunday night, the mind again started rehearsing what the week that followed might hold in store.

The coming celebrations, a new year and the fact that on 23 January he would turn 51 only added to the torment of waiting on a response to the jury's recommendation of mercy. Not knowing seemed to be an integral part of a death sentence, one wholly unlegislated for. There was no telling on what date the Chief Justice had forwarded the jury's recommendation to the Transvaal authorities, or what enthusiasm he had evinced in so doing. On the one hand, time passed, like that followed by a tug on the fisherman's line, unleashed only anticipation. But, on the other, markers passed only increased fear of what lay ahead.

During his first stay at Visagie Street, the prison authorities were still staging hangings in the open which, on occasion, were well attended. He recalled that visitors from Johannesburg were already assembling in the town to witness another such gory spectacle when McKeone and Cooper were granted a reprieve at the eleventh hour. After that Kruger had put a stop to public hangings. In the empire, where the carrot of a 'civilising mission' and justice was always backed by the stick of crowd control, there would be no harking back to Tyburn of old. But, if he were to be hanged, he would try to go in a way that befitted a man.

Not being able to witness an execution dampened, but failed to extinguish entirely the curiosity of many of the colony's citizens. As the press noted at the time of the trial, there were still enough men familiar with frontier times on the Rand for him not to have been forgotten. Although much diminished in stature, he could still breathe a little life into urban myth and rumour. In mid-December a macabre story began to do the rounds that he was to be hanged around Christmas Day. On 26 December, the *Sunday Times* reported that, 'metaphorically speaking', the public had 'feasted on the rumour' but noted that there was no factual basis to the tale and that he would live to see out Boxing Day.[2]

But how many days after that? Well, almost certainly all those in December, for it was the holiday season. At that time of year even those who operated the machinery that ground out the decisions as to when and where a man was to lose his life paused to catch their breath for the year ahead. They wished to remember the birth of their saviour. On New Year's Day, it was a month since his trial had commenced. It was supposed to be a day of anticipation and celebration rather than reflection. He had little to look forward to with confidence, so he could engage in yet more introspection – was he really just another 'cold blooded' murderer?

A few late adolescent and bar-room disturbances aside, he had always prized self-control and sought to avoid violence as far as possible. The safe-cracking exploits of the Irish Brigade had, for the most part, taken place at night so as to avoid physical confrontations. At the Red Lion he had shot Stevenson once, sought to minimise his interaction with Sarah Fredericks and staged an orderly retreat, shooting only when it seemed as if Goldberg or the Hadji might want to apprehend him. After that he had never again carried a revolver or assaulted anyone, resisted arrest, or attempted to escape from prisons where his behaviour had invariably been considered 'good'. Even his drinking had become measured – and, throughout it all, and whenever questioned, he had never once denied his faith. His beliefs might have been flawed but they had been constant. To the extent that a man's *behaviour*, rather than his *utterances*, testified to regret, he had long experienced a measure of remorse.

It was while he was still in that receptive frame of mind that Tom Ryan first called in on him. Father Ryan was a friend of Jan Smuts and it may have been at the latter's suggestion that the Oblate first sought him out. Smuts, cold and steely-eyed as the position of Acting Attorney-General demanded, was familiar with the problem that Ireland and Irish nationalists posed to empire, but had never been comfortable with the imposition of capital punishment. Whatever prompted the priest's visit, McLoughlin welcomed the chance to share his thoughts with the Irishman, who began to visit him regularly. Just talking to Ryan calmed his spirits and when Monday, 3 January, came and went without notice there was another, small, upwelling of hope. No news, they said, was good news?

But the new year was fully upon the world and the state's functionaries were well advanced in their planning on how to take a man's life legally. There was, everyone knew, a world of difference between 'the administration of justice' and murder. The papers of empire took precedence over preparation of the rope. It was a case of no less than 'The King against Jack McLoughlin', and consenting to the execution was the Governor of the Transvaal, Lord Selborne, intent on ushering in a new order free of lingering republican complications. The Governor's approval was passed on to the Registrar to the Supreme Court and Sheriff of the Transvaal, Charles Rorke, who had handed it to Sir William Smith, a Judge of the Supreme Court. Sir William signed the black-edged instruction to the 'Sheriff of the Transvaal or his Lawful Deputy' to organise the execution.[3] The condemned man was 'to be hanged by the neck until he be dead' on Monday, 10 January 1909, 'between the hours of six and ten forenoon'. It was left to Rorke to pass on the details to AJ Wilson, Governor of the Gaol, to arrange for the executioner, a Mr Simpson, and take care of any outstanding business. Once all was ready, the Sheriff could inform the condemned man. It was 'The King', it was claimed, who wanted a man's life, but, at the end of the day, a lowly contracted worker would have to do the deed for him.

The first days of the new week, the third and fourth of January, followed what had become a familiar pattern for Mondays and Tuesdays. Little of consequence transpired. Like those responsible for the turkey's well-being shortly before Christmas, the dedicated prison staff continued to do their best for the condemned man. McLoughlin 'relied a great deal on the jury's recommendation to mercy', they noted, and observed that he 'maintained a perfectly calm demeanour. He ate heartily and his weight increased.'[4] Ryan visited more often, and stayed longer; the men, who shared much by way of belief, ethnicity, travel and even personality, appeared to be growing significantly closer to one another.

By Wednesday, a man might have been forgiven for thinking that McLoughlin would live to see out another of those sets of the seven days by which human beings ordered their affairs, but that afternoon the Sheriff appeared. He told him – just as McLoughlin himself had once told Stevo – that by Monday night next, he would be a dead man. McLoughlin remained composed but Rorke clearly had no stomach for the proceedings and thereafter left things in the hands of his deputy, Joseph Dyer. Even Tom Ryan, used to seeing men into and out of the world, was struggling to cope and asked a fellow Oblate, Father Urquhart, to join him for the final preparations. Executions shave the souls of all who are called upon to facilitate them.

Father Tom spent as much time as possible with McLoughlin over the next three days and then, on Sunday evening, he and Urquhart moved into the cell with him, quietly counselling him throughout the night. 'As a result of their ministrations he was quite reconciled to his fate,' it was claimed. Daylight came too quickly, and hopelessly too slowly. Just before 7.00 am, the hour set for the execution, Dyer suddenly appeared and a man who in a way had never left the Church, 'told the Deputy Sheriff that he had nothing to say to anyone on earth; he had made his peace with God.'[5]

Neither God nor the King could be kept waiting; punctuality and precision remained the order of the day. Minutes later 'the executioner and his assistant entered the condemned cell and, having placed the black cap over the murderer's head pinioned him and led him to the scaffold'. It was said later that McLoughlin left the cell clutching a small crucifix in his hand. 'As the noose was being adjusted he said: "Jesus have mercy on my soul",' and 30 seconds later he was dead. The body was taken down and examined before being speedily removed.[6]

The five commanded to be present at the *articulo mortis*, the point of death, Dyer, the prison Governor, two medical officers and the executioner, appended their signatures to a document certifying that they had examined 'the body of Jack McLoughlin upon whom the sentence of death has been executed and that life is extinct'.[7] The King's will had been done and the body was taken to Pretoria's Rebecca Street cemetery and placed in the unmarked grave where the bones lie still.

In Manchester, where the bodies of tens of thousands born into the Industrial Revolution lay forgotten and neglected, not a soul noted the passing of yet another of Ancoats' many sons. In an epoch remembered largely for its economic progress, one in which the use of the bodies of the marginalised took precedence over the cultivation of the human spirit and its imagination, few rose above the banalities of a quotidian existence. Yet, every now and then, in between the barges, canals and rivers that pointed the way to the sea, a restless and rebellious soul was born with an unquenchable thirst for life, adventure and independence. Monday, 10 January 1909, was just another cold wet day in Lancashire, but the following morning, in cities right across the southern hemisphere, people from many walks of life noted that one such restless Irishman had passed their way and moved on. It was 'One-armed Jack' McLoughlin.[8]

Notes

Introduction: Dystopia's Militants

1 See C van Onselen, *Masked Raiders; Irish Banditry in Southern Africa, 1880–1899* (Cape Town 2010), p 13 [hereafter van Onselen, *Masked Raiders*].

2 See J Bourke, 'Irish Masculinity and the Home, 1880–1914', in M Cohen and MJ Curtin (eds), *Reclaiming Gender: Transgressive Identities in Modern Ireland* (New York 1999), pp 93–106.

3 'Prison Work in Barberton', *All the World*, Vol 7, No 1, January 1891, p 197 [hereafter, 'Prison Work in Barberton'].

4 A Davies, *The Gangs of Manchester* (Preston 2008), p 17. Also WH Davies, *The Autobiography of a Super-Tramp* (London 1908).

5 GA Sala, *The Strange Adventures of Captain Dangerous: Who was a Soldier, a Sailor, a Merchant, a Spy, a Slave among the Moors, a Bashaw in the Service of the Grand Turk* (London 1863), Vol 2, p 53.

6 See Davies, *The Gangs of Manchester*.

7 See J Belich, *Replenishing the Earth: The Settler Revolution and the Rise of the Anglo World, 1783–1939* (Oxford 2009), pp 107–108 [hereafter Belich, *Replenishing the Earth*].

8 On the expansion of the British Army, navy and Merchant Navy see J Darwin, *The Empire Project: The Rise and Fall of the British World System, 1830–1970* (Cambridge 2009), pp 25, 33–35, 39, 77 and 104 [hereafter, Darwin, *The Empire Project*].

9 'Prison Work in Barberton', 1891, p 199. Note, too, how closely some of this behaviour mirrors features in the early gangs of 'scuttlers' in Manchester – see, for example, Davies, *The Gangs of Manchester*, pp 16–17. In imperial Britain, the army helped to give shape to youth culture in the cities just as surely as urban youth culture, in turn, fed into the class culture of regiments drawn from the industrial north.

10 See especially J Hyslop, 'The Imperial Working Class Makes itself "White": White Labourism in Britain, Australia and South Africa before the First World War', *Journal of Historical Sociology* (1999), Vol 12, No 3, pp 398–421.

11 See P Laidlaw, 'A Passing Occupation: An Exploration of the History and Heritage of Itinerant Workers in Rural New South Wales, 1850–1914', DPhil thesis, Charles Sturt University, 2009. It is within this broad context that the idea of 'crew culture' was

developed – Belich, *Replenishing the Earth*, pp 319–24.

12 See 'The Eighteenth Brumaire of Louis Napoleon', *Selected Works of Marx and Engels* (London 1968), p 138.

13 See Darwin, *The Empire Project*, pp 43 and 59.

14 See AH Davies, *The Autobiography of a Super-Tramp* (London 1908), p 7; AH Roskell, *Six Years of a Tramp's Life in South Africa* (Cape Town 1887); and AA Horn, *Waters of Africa* (London 1929) p 148. The long-neglected work by Roskell is the subject of new scholarly interest by Paul la Hausse who kindly drew it to my attention.

15 See LM Friedman, 'Crimes of Mobility', *Stanford Law Review*, Vol 43, No 3, February

1991, pp 637–58.

16 See A McLeod, 'On the Origins of Consorting Laws', *Melbourne University Law Review*, Vol 37, No 1, August 2013.

17 S De, *Marginal Europeans in Colonial India: 1860–1920* (Kolkota 2008), p 145.

18 Davies, *Super-Tramp*, pp xiii and 103.

19 On the Masons see, for example, GB Magee and AS Thompson, *Empire and Globalisation: Networks of People, Goods and Capital in the British World c 1850–1914* (Cambridge 2010), p 136.

20 Roskell, *Six Years of a Tramp's Life in South Africa*, p 102.

21 Van Onselen, *Masked Raiders*, pp 50–51 and 80–85.

Chapter One: Deep Code

1 The date of birth of William McLoughlin is best verified via the United Kingdom (UK), Censuses of 1851 and 1861. See UK *Census 1851*, RG 9/2935, Folio 5, p 4, Manchester, Sub Region, Ancoats, Municipal Ward New Cross, entry 20 for 72 Union St, which lists his age as 38, and UK *Census 1861*, RG 10/4033, Manchester, Sub Region, Ancoats, Municipal Ward New Cross, Entry No 151, for 6 Willoughby's Court. This accords with the date and place of his birth, given as Fahan, Donegal, on 21 May 1823 in the *International Genealogical Index*, Vol 5, British Isles, which also records his parents' names as George McLoughlin and Hester Caldwell.

2 For the history of the McLoughlin clan see chapters 3, 5 and 15 of TH and JE Mullin, *The Clans of Ulster* (Limavady, Northern Ireland 1989).

3 The history of Ireland before and after 1800 is summarised in J Coohill, *Ireland: A Short History* (Oxford 2005), pp 7–38 [hereafter Coohill, *Ireland*]. Much of the background to Irish history as relayed here is taken from the same source.

4 See, among others, Coohill, *Ireland*, pp 20–21.

5 This paragraph is a distillation of views derived from several sources, including: J

Bourke, 'Irish Masculinity and the Home, 1880–1914' in M Cohen and MJ Curtin (eds), *Reclaiming Gender: Transgressive Identities in Modern Ireland* (New York 1999), pp 93–106; A Court, *Puck of the Droms: The Lives and Literature of the Irish Tinkers* (Los Angeles 1985); T Fennel, *The Royal Irish Constabulary* (Dublin 2003); LM Geary, 'The Whole Country was in Motion": Mendicancy and Vagrancy in Pre-famine Ireland' in J Hill and C Lennon, *Luxury and Austerity*, Historical Studies XXl (Dublin 1999), pp 121–36; TW Guinnane, *The Vanishing Irish: Households, Migration and the Rural Economy in Ireland, 1850–1914* (Princeton 1997); G Jones and E Malcolm (eds) *Medicine, Disease and the State in Ireland, 1650–1940* (Cork 1990); and F Sweeney, *The Murder of Conell Boyle, County Donegal, 1898* (Dublin 2001).

6 See TD Williams (ed), *Secret Societies in Ireland* (Dublin 1973) [hereafter Williams (ed), *Secret Societies*].

7 See, for example, S Clark, *Social Origins of the Irish Land War* (Princeton 1979), pp 82–83; and, more especially the Introduction to Williams (ed), *Secret Societies*, pp 1–12.

8 See 'Maghtochair', *Inishowen: Its History, Traditions, and Antiquities* (Dublin 1985),

pp 74–75 [hereafter, Maghtochair, Inishowen]. Carefully researched and written by Michael Harkin and first published in 1867, this work offers a splendid base of historical information about the social history of the peninsula. It was reprinted, in 1985, by Three Candles Press of Dublin with a foreword by D Dickson and it is this latter edition that informs most of what is relayed in this chapter about early Buncrana and Upper and Lower Fahan.

9 See WJ Doherty, 'The Abbey of Fahan', Paper read at the Royal Irish Academy, 28 February 1881. More importantly, however, see Maghtochair, Inishowen, pp 71, 74, 83, 120, 195, 206–7 and 213–16.

10 See, for example, CK Byrne, 'Hedge Schools of Inishowen', Inish Times, 17 August 2005.

11 See especially entry on 'Fahan' and 'Fahan (Lower)' in S Lewis, A Topographical Dictionary of Ireland (1837) and Maghtochair, Inishowen, p 61.

12 For some of the continuities in this sceptical attitude, see J MacLaughlin, 'The Politics of Nation-Building in Post-Famine Donegal' in W Nolan, L Ronayne and M Dunlevy (eds), Donegal, History & Society: Interdisciplinary Essays on the History of an Irish County (Dublin 1995), pp 583–623, but more especially the section on 'Priestly Politics and Nationalist Hegemony in Donegal', pp 611–19.

13 See, for example, S Clark, Social Origins of the Irish Land War (Princeton 1979), pp 60 and 79 [hereafter, Clark, Origins of the Land War].

14 See Coohill, Ireland, p 32.

15 This is based on Coohil, Ireland, pp 39–51, but on McGhee, see also Maghtochair, Inishowen, p 169.

16 See Clark, The Irish Land War, pp 25 and 159; Coohill, Ireland, pp 59–79; and, more especially, Maghtochair, Inishowen, pp 60 and 67.

17 See especially Coohill, Ireland, pp 81–83; Maghtochair, Inishowen, pp 49–58; and Clark, Origins of the Land War, p 28.

18 See entry on 'Fahan (Lower)', Lewis, A Topographical Dictionary of Ireland. See also, 'Social Class Impact of the Famine in Donegal' in J MacLaughlin, The Making of a Northern County (Dublin 2007).

19 See Maghtochair, Inishowen, p 69.

20 Ibid, p 127.

21 See E Malcolm, 'Ireland Sober, Ireland Free': Drink and Temperance in Nineteenth-Century Ireland (Syracuse 1986), pp 22 and 34 [hereafter, Malcolm, 'Ireland Sober, Ireland Free'].

22 This and most of what follows derives from Malcolm's 'Ireland Sober, Ireland Free', especially, pp 21–55. See also, however, the useful section on 'Illicit Distillation in Inishowen' in B Bonner, Our Inis Eoghain Heritage (Coleraine 2010), first published in 1972 [hereafter Bonner, Our Inis]. Significantly, Michael Harkin, too, devoted a full chapter of his 1867 survey of the peninsula to 'Illicit Distillation' – see Maghtochair, Inishowen, pp 127–36.

23 See Malcolm, 'Ireland Free, Ireland Sober', p 34.

24 As quoted in K Marx and F Engels, On Ireland (London 1972), p 86.

25 See Maghtochair, Inishowen, pp 127–28 and 158–67. It may have been significant that the murderers – paid for their services by subscription – were former members of an agrarian secret society. See also Bonner, Our Inis.

26 See Bonner, Our Inis.

27 See, for example, Maghtochair, Inishowen, pp 80, 117, and 160–62. Local linen production dated back to mills founded in 1745 by Colonel Vaughan. In 1784, these were supplemented by cotton mills that fed the Manchester market and which survived until a fire destroyed them in 1830. See 'Buncrana' in Lewis, A Topographical Dictionary of Ireland.

28 Malcolm, 'Ireland Free, Ireland Sober', pp 29–34; and Maghtochair, Inishowen, pp 160–62.

29 See Maghtochair, Inishowen, pp 81–82 and 165.

30 See, amongst others, Clark, Origins of the Land War, pp 79–83; C Conley, 'The Agreeable Recreation of Fighting', Journal of Social History, Vol 33, No 1 (Autumn 1999), pp 57–72; and M Johnson, 'Violence Transported: Aspects of Irish Peasant Society' in O MacDonagh and WF Mandle (eds), Ireland and Irish-Australia: Studies in Cultural and Political History (Kent and Surrey Hills,

1986), p 141 [hereafter, Johnson, 'Violence Transported'].

31 In some cases, as with the Ribbonmen of the north, this cyclical dimension, along with some seasonal periodicity, was particularly noticeable during the period 1814–34. See, for example, J Lee, 'Ribbonmen' in Williams (ed), *Secret Societies*, pp 27–31.

32 See, for example, B Mac Suibhne, 'Agrarian Improvement and Social Unrest: Lord George Hill and the Gaoth Dobhair Sheep War' in W Nolan, L Ronayne and M Dunlevy (eds), *Donegal, History & Society: Interdisciplinary Essays on the History of an Irish County* (Dublin 1995), pp 547–82; and P O'Donnell, *The Irish Faction Fighters of the 19th Century* (Dublin, 1975), pp 1778–79.

33 See Johnson, 'Violence Transported', p 140.

34 For the broader background to such ritualised or other 'spontaneous' conflicts see J Kelly, *That Damn'd Thing Called Honour: Duelling in Ireland* (Cork 1996); and the introduction to S Carroll (ed), *Cultures of Violence: Interpersonal Violence in Historical Perspective* (Basingstoke 2007), especially pp 20–24.

35 See Coohill, *Ireland*, pp 59–78

36 Ibid. See also, amongst others, DH Akenson, *The Irish Diaspora* (Toronto 1993); and D Fitzpatrick, *Irish Emigration* (Dundalk 1985), pp 1–13.

37 See Maghtochair, *Inishowen*, p 181.

Chapter Two: The Codes Adapted

1 This and much that follows draws heavily on A Kidd's excellent *Manchester: A History* (Lancaster 2006). See especially pp 1–7 [hereafter, Kidd, *Manchester*].

2 Ibid, p 17.

3 A list of notables would include the names of, amongst several others at least as important – Edwin Chadwick, Alex de Tocqueville, Benjamin Disraeli, Friedrich Engels, Elizabeth Gaskell, Dr James Kay and Hippolyte Taine. Set this against Kidd's helpful contextualising comments in *Manchester*, p 19. See also GS Messinger, *Manchester in the Victorian Age: The Half-Known City* (Manchester 1985), especially 'Social Reform' and 'Legendary Manchester', pp 33–64 and 89–114 [hereafter, Messinger, *The Half-Known City*]; and T Thomas, 'Representations of the Manchester Working Class in Fiction, 1850–1990' in AJ Kidd and KW Roberts (eds), *City, Class and Culture: Studies of Social Policy and Cultural Production in Victorian Manchester* (Manchester 1985), pp 193–217.

4 Data taken from Messinger, *The Half-Known City*, p 21; and Kidd, *Manchester*, pp 16 and 20.

5 See M Williams, 'The Mills of Ancoats', *Manchester Region History Review*, Vol 7, 1993, p 32 [hereafter, Williams, 'Mills of Ancoats'].

6 See, for example, Kidd, *Manchester*, pp 24–29 and 101–2. In many ways the Manchester Ship Canal (constructed 1887–94), was the culmination of this extensive supplementary system. Also see Messinger, 'National Resurrection: The Manchester Ship Canal' in *The Half-Known City*, pp 160–72.

7 Kidd, *Manchester*, pp 22–24.

8 See A Davies, 'Saturday Night Markets in Manchester and Salford, 1840–1939', *Manchester Region History Review*, 1987, pp 3–12 [hereafter Davies, 'Saturday Night Markets']; and R Scola, 'Food Markets and Shops in Manchester, 1770–1870', *Journal of Historical Geography*, Vol 1, No 2, 1975, pp 153–68.

9 Kidd, *Manchester*, p 17.

10 Ibid, especially pp 102, 109, 116 and 120. Also RL Greenall, *The Making of Victorian Salford* (Lancaster 2000), p 231 [hereafter, Greenall, *Victorian Salford*].

11 See, for example, Kidd, *Manchester*, pp 34 and 77.

12 The classic formulation of these changes and the challenges they engendered is to be found in EP Thompson, 'Time, Work-Discipline and Industrial Capitalism', *Past &*

Present, Vol 38, No 1, 1967, pp 56–97.

13 See, for example, the comments of Canon
Richard Parkinson of Manchester as quoted
in Messinger, *The Half-Known City,* pp 22–23.

14 As quoted in M Burleigh, *Earthly Powers:
Religion and Politics in Europe from the
Enlightenment to the Great War* (London 2006),
pp 366–68.

15 See S Brady, *Masculinity and Male
Homosexuality in Britain, 1861–1913* (London
2005), pp 25–30.

16 See Davies, 'Saturday Night Markets', pp 4–6;
and, on Smithfield, Kidd, *Manchester,* p 122.
Within the context of this study, however,
see also the important observations about the
markets in J O'Neill, *Crime City: Manchester's
Victorian Underworld* (Preston 2008), pp 24,
36–37 and 58–59 [hereafter, O'Neill, *Crime
City*]. Despite an absence of footnotes
indicating primary or secondary sources,
O'Neill's work remains a fine read and an
invaluable point of reference for anyone with
an interest in nineteenth-century crime in
Manchester.

17 See J Roberts, '"A densely populated
and unlovely tract": The Residential
Development of Ancoats', *Manchester
Region History Review,* Vol 7, 1993,
pp 15–26 [hereafter, Roberts, 'Residential
Development of Ancoats'].

18 R Lloyd-Jones and M Lewis, 'Housing
Factory Workers: Ancoats in the Early
Nineteenth Century', *Manchester Region
History Review,* Vol 7, 1993, p 33 [hereafter
Lloyd-Jones and Lewis, 'Housing Factory
Workers'].

19 Paragraph based on material drawn from
Kidd, *Manchester,* pp 33–36 and 39–41; and
Messinger, *The Half-Known City,* p 24. See
also, WJ Lowe, *The Irish in Mid-Victorian
Lancashire: The Shaping of a Working-Class
Community* (New York 1989), p 15 [hereafter,
Lowe, *Mid-Victorian Lancashire*].

20 On Irish cellar dwellers in Ancoats see
O'Neil, *Crime City,* pp 21–24.

21 Kidd, *Manchester,* pp 34–35.

22 These include John Kay, 'The Moral and
Physical Conditions of the Working Classes'
(1832); Edwin Chadwick, 'Report on the
Sanitary Conditions of the Labouring Population'

(1842), and, of course, Friedrich Engels, *The
Condition of the Working Class in England*
(1845), which, first published in German,
only appeared in English three decades
later. See also Roberts, 'The Residential
Development of Ancoats', pp 18–21.

23 For a brief chronology and outline of the
Factory Acts and the changing conditions
of labour in the mills and elsewhere, see
Messinger, *The Half-Known City,* pp 24–26.

24 See especially Kidd, *Manchester,* pp 39–44;
also O'Neill, *Crime City,* p 21.

25 See Lowe, *Mid-Victorian Manchester,* pp 34
and 147; Messinger, *The Half-Known City,*
p 177; and R Roberts, *The Classic Slum:
Salford Life in the First Quarter of the Century*
(Harmondsworth 1973), pp 22 and 110.

26 On the immediate manifestations of the
Great Famine in Manchester in 1847, see
for example, Lowe, *Mid-Victorian Manchester,*
p 34. More generally, see F Neal, *Black '47;
Britain and the Famine Irish* (London 1988)
and the chapter on Liverpool, pp 123–56.

27 See especially MA Busteed and RI Hodgson,
'Irish Migrant Responses to Urban Life in
Early Nineteenth-Century Manchester', *The
Geographical Journal,* Vol 162, Part 2, July 1996,
pp 145–49 [hereafter, Busteed and Hodgson,
'Irish Migrant responses to Manchester'];
and S Fielding, 'A Separate Culture? Irish
Catholics in Working-Class Manchester
and Salford, c 1890–1939' in A Davies and
S Fielding (eds), *Workers' Worlds: Cultures
and Communities in Manchester and Salford,
1880–1939* (Manchester 1992), pp 23–29
[hereafter, Davies and Fielding, *Workers'
Worlds*]; also, Kidd, *Manchester,* p 122 and
Lowe, *Mid-Victorian Manchester,* p 70.

28 This paragraph is based on Busteed and
Hodgson, 'Irish Migrant responses to
Manchester', pp 141 and 144–45.

29 See, for example, O'Neill, *Crime City,*
pp 29–30.

30 Lowe, *Mid-Victorian Manchester,* pp 111–24.

31 A Davies, *The Gangs of Manchester: The Story of
the Scuttlers, Britain's First Youth Cult* (Preston
2008), pp 45–46 [hereafter, Davies, *The Gangs
of Manchester*].

32 Busteed and Hodgson, 'Irish Migrant
responses to Manchester', p 151.

33 See, for example, the case of Athens in the late nineteenth century as commented on in the introduction to S Carroll (ed), *Cultures of Violence: Interpersonal Violence in Cultural Perspective* (London 2005), p 19 [hereafter Carroll, *Cultures of Violence*].

34 On shared English and Irish values regarding 'hardness', interpersonal violence and manliness, see, for example, O'Neill, *Crime City*, pp 42–43 and p 46. For specifically English attitudes to fisticuffs, honour and self-restraint, see C Emsley *The English and Violence since 1750* (Basingstoke 2007) especially pp 12–13, 40–44 [hereafter, Emsley, *The English and Violence*]. On self-restraint as a by-product of modernity, see also the introduction to S Carroll (ed), *Cultures of Violence*, p 4.

35 For some examples see Busteed and Hodgson, 'Irish Migrant responses to Manchester', pp 149–50.

36 A tone of bewilderment as to possible underlying causes of Irish faction fights besets the work of many recent analysts of Manchester's nineteenth-century social history; see especially Busteed and Hodgson, 'Irish Migrant Responses to Manchester', p 149, but also Davies, *The Gangs of Manchester*, p 47.

37 On 'scuttling' see Davies, *The Gangs of Manchester*, pp 9–22.

38 Ibid, p 28; Kidd, *Manchester*, p 45; and Lowe, *Mid-Victorian Manchester*, p 37.

39 Busteed and Hodgson, 'Irish Migrant responses to Manchester', p 150. For some of the deeper roots of Irish mental instability, see J Bourke, 'Irish Masculinity and the Home, 1880–1914' in M Cohen and MJ Curtin (eds), *Reclaiming Gender: Transgressive Identities in Modern Ireland* (New York 1999),

pp 101–2.

40 Busteed and Hodgson, 'Irish Migrant responses to Manchester', p 151.

41 Paragraph based on Lowe, *Mid-Victorian Manchester*, p 150; O'Neill, *Crime City*, pp 64 and 251; and TD Williams, 'The Irish Republican Brotherhood' in TD Williams (ed), *Secret Societies in Ireland* (Dublin 1973), p 139.

42 O'Neill, *Crime City*, p 248.

43 See Busteed and Hodgson, 'Irish Migrant responses to Manchester', pp 148 and 151.

44 See, for example, Davies, *The Gangs of Manchester*, p 282, and, for the tradition 'exported' to the colonies, C van Onselen, *Masked Raiders: Irish Banditry in Southern Africa* (Cape Town 2010), p 152 [hereafter, van Onselen, *Masked Raiders*].

45 Emsley, *The English and Violence*, pp. 60–66.

46 Ibid, p 60; and, more especially, Davies, *The Gangs of Manchester*, pp 241–56.

47 See, for example, Busteed and Hodgson, 'Irish Migrant responses to Manchester', pp 148–49.

48 For manifestations of anti-clericalism in Ireland, see, for example, S Clark, *Social Origins of the Irish Land War* (Princeton 1979), p 79; and, more pertinently, A McLaren, *The Trials of Masculinity; Policing Sexual Boundaries, 1870–1930* (Chicago 1997), especially pp 150–51. For an example of the problems arising from the sexuality of priests in a neighbouring local context see Greenall, *Victorian Salford*, p 225.

49 Lowe, *Mid-Victorian Manchester*, p 103.

50 For a brief introduction to post-famine attitudes towards religion and marriage among Irish males in the late nineteenth century see van Onselen, *Masked Raiders*, pp 16–18.

Chapter Three: The Family

1 See P Rushton, 'Family Survival Strategies in Mid-Victorian Ancoats', *Manchester Region History Review*, Vol 7, 1993, p 38.

2 United Kingdom (UK), Manchester, Central Library, St Peter's Square, Archives and Local Studies, Greater Manchester County Records, Records of West Gorton Gaol, Belle Vue, Entry No 89438, 21 August

1873, William McLoughlin [hereafter UK, Manchester Archives].

3 UK, Manchester Archives, Records of West Gorton Gaol, Belle Vue, Entry No 89438, 21 August 1873, William McLoughlin.

4 See R Lloyd-Jones and M Lewis, 'Housing Factory Workers: Ancoats in the Early Nineteenth Century'; and J Roberts, '"A Densely Populated and Unlovely Tract": The Residential Development of Ancoats', in *Manchester Region History Review*, Vol 7, 1993, pp 33–36 and 15–26.

5 See especially M Williams, 'The Mills of Ancoats', *Manchester Region History Review*, Vol 7, 1993, pp 27–32 [hereafter, Williams, 'The Mills of Ancoats'].

6 See United Kingdom (UK) *Census 1851*, Manchester, Piece 107/2225, Folio 136, p 7, 30 March, which records 14 people ranging in age from 1 to 55 living at 1 German Street.

7 The International Genealogical Index (IGI) of the Church of the Latter Day Saints records the birth of Elizabeth Sloan to James Sloan and Mary Beck as being at Donegore, Antrim, Ireland, on 8 September 1831.

8 On the three Sloan women, see UK *Census 1851*: Manchester, Piece 226, Folio 129, p 28, which records the presence of Mary Sloan ('housekeeper') and Ann at no 4 Back Potts Street; for the sister, Elizabeth ('Eliza'), who on the night of the census – perhaps significantly – was not at home and spent the night as a visitor at the home of an Irish musician and his wife who provided various female textile workers with lodgings at 40 Back Woodward Street, see Manchester, Piece 2226, Folio 268, p 24. See UK, London, Family Record Centre, for the record of the marriage of John Scott ('labourer') to Bridget-Ann Sloan ('spindler'), both illiterate, on 17 September 1871.

9 UK, General Register Office, Manchester, record of the birth of Ellen Sloan at 2 Back Potts Street, on 20 March 1853; and for baptism, Manchester, Records of the Catholic Family History Society (CFHS), 1848–1874, Register of Baptisms, St Anne's, Junction Street, Manchester [hereafter CFHS].

10 UK, General Register Office, Manchester,

record of the marriage of John Saxon (age 21), a 'spinner', to Ellen McLoughlin (aged 22), a spinster at St Peter's, Oldham Road, Manchester on 25 December 1876.

11 UK, Manchester, Records of the CFHS, 1848–1874, Register of Baptisms, Joseph Scott on 11 April 1870 at St Anne's, Junction Street, Manchester.

12 For the context of this see M Ford, '"My Ancestors include Criminals and Wealthy Mill-Owners"' (Interview with J Desoldato) in *Who Do You Think You Are?* (BBC Magazines, Bristol), Issue 48, June 2011, pp 38–41.

13 On Sarah Ann McLoughlin, see UK, *Census 1861 and 1871*, Manchester, Piece No 2935, Folio 5, p 4, Entry for 72 Union Street, Ancoats, and Piece No 4033, Folio 37, p 29, Entry for 6 Willoughby's Court, Ancoats. See also, Preston, Lancashire Records Office, RCMW/1/5, Baptisms at St Wilfred's, Hulme, Diocese of Salford, for her nomination as godmother to John Saxon Jnr on 13 July 1877.

14 See, among others, J Bourke, 'Irish Masculinity and the Home, 1880–1914' in M Cohen and MJ Curtin (eds), *Reclaiming Gender: Transgressive Identities in Modern Ireland* (New York 1999), pp 93–106; C Nash, 'Men Again: Irish Masculinity, Nature and Nationhood in the Early Twentieth Century', *Ecumene*, 1996, Vol 3, No 4, pp 427–53; J Richards, '"Passing the Love of Women": Manly love in Victorian Society' in JA Mangan and J Walvin (eds), *Manliness and Morality: Middle Class Masculinity in Britain and America, 1800–1940* (Manchester 1987); and especially J Tosh, 'What should Historians do with Masculinity? Reflections on Nineteenth-century Britain', *History Workshop Journal*, Issue 38, 1994.

15 On Father Peter Liptrott and his brother Richard's links to St Anne's parish, see CA Bolton, *Salford Diocese and its Catholic Past* (Manchester 1950).

16 See UK, Manchester, CFHS, Record of Baptisms, St Anne's, Junction Street, 23 January 1859. On the godmother, Catherine Crilley, see UK *Census 1861*, Piece 2927, Folio 69, p 1, entry for 77 Primrose

Street, New Cross. For the background to
the emergence of St Anne's parish, see CA
Bolton, *Salford Diocese and its Catholic Past*
(Salford 1950); and, on Father Peter Liptrott,
J Gillow, *A Literary and Biographical History
or Biographical Dictionary of English Catholics,
From the Breach with Rome, in 1534, to the
Present Time, Vol 4, 1885–1902* (London, Burns
& Oates, no date), pp 278–80.

17 For a family snapshot on the eve of William
junior's birth, see UK *Census 1861*, Piece
2935, Folio 5, p 4, entry for 72 Union Street.
On Murray's mills, see Williams, 'The Mills
of Ancoats', pp 28–29.

18 See J O'Neill, *Crime City: Manchester's
Victorian Underworld* (Preston 2008), pp 57
and 69 [hereafter, O'Neill, *Crime City*].

19 N Richardson, *The Old Pubs of Ancoats*
(Manchester 1987), p 12.

20 On crime in Ancoats in the 1830s, see GS
Messinger, *Manchester in the Victorian Age, the
Half-Known City* (Manchester 1986), p 42,
and Union Street in mid-century, O'Neill,
Crime City, p 242. On the Irish in weekend
turmoil, see, for example, WJ Lowe, *The Irish
in Mid-Victorian Lancashire: The Shaping of a
Working Class Community* (New York 1989),
pp 127–28 [hereafter, *The Irish in Mid-
Victorian Lancashire*] .

21 For Thomas McLoughlin, see UK *Census
1871*, Piece No 4033, Folio 37, p 29, entry for
6 Willoughby's Court; and for his younger
sister, Manchester, CFHS, Register of
Baptisms, 1848–1874, St Anne's, Junction
Street, Mary McLoughlin, 15 November
1866 – the family address at that time
recorded as 6 Back Love Lane.

22 See Manchester, CFHS, Register of
Baptisms, 1848–1874, St Anne's, Junction
Street, Elizabeth McLoughlin, baptised,
11 September 1879. It is noteworthy,
however, that the child had been born on
16 April 1870 and that it took the mother
nearly six months to get around to having
her baptised. It may have been yet another
sign of the increasing strain under which
Eliza McLoughlin was attempting to operate.

23 'In the 1870s, for instance, a man working
in a cotton mill in the Manchester area
might expect to earn between sixteen and

twenty-eight shillings a week. A woman, girl
or boy would earn between seven and twelve
"bob". The poverty line of a man with a
wife and two children was around thirty
bob a week. In good times, these people
just about made ends meet without falling
into debt' – O'Neill, *Crime City*, p 56, also
pp 208–209. For other accounts of wages,
including those of spinners during this era
see A Kidd, *Manchester, A History* (Lancaster
2006), p 34 [hereafter, Kidd, *Manchester*]. On
schools and child labour, see Lowe, *The Irish
in Mid-Victorian Lancashire*, p 124.

24 This assumption derives from her
involvement in the receipt of goods stolen
during the family break-in at a pawnshop in
1878 – see below, Chapter Four. On the Irish
and hawking around Smithfield Market at
the time, see A Kidd, *Manchester*, p 122; and
O'Neill, *Crime City*, pp 36–37 and, more
especially, pp 88–89.

25 UK, Manchester Archives, Greater
Manchester County Records, City Gaol
General Register No 24851, 24 June 1887,
records the arrest and discharge, on 30 July,
of Elizabeth McLoughlin along with
distinguishing marks. On 1874 as a high-
point in the local wife-beating calendar, see
O'Neill, *Crime City*, p 179.

26 See, for example, A Davies, *The Gangs of
Manchester; The Story of the Scuttlers, Britain's
First Youth Cult* (Preston 2008), pp 30–31.

27 See UK, National Archives, Kew, England
and Wales, Criminal Registers, 1791–1892,
Manchester Sessions, 5 July 1875, General
Quarter Sessions of the Peace held at
Lancaster, 28 June 1875, Entry No 99,
Thomas McLoughlin. The boy would not
have wanted for company. Between 1870 and
1891, at least 5 000 'neglected' Manchester
and Salford children were sent to industrial
schools – see O'Neill, *Crime City*, p 73. See
also S Jolly, 'The Origins of the Manchester
and Salford Reformatory for Juvenile
Criminals 1853–1860', *Manchester Region
History Review*, No 15, 2001, pp 2–8.

28 See UK Manchester Archives, Court
Register, County of Lancaster, General
Quarter Sessions of the Peace, 25 June 1875,
entry No 9, Thomas McLoughlin. Also S

Jolly, 'The Origin of the Manchester and Salford Reformatory for Juvenile Criminals, 1853–1860', *Manchester Region History Review*, No 15, 2001, pp 2–8; and O'Neill, *Crime City*, p 73.

29 Manchester Archives, Records of Greater Manchester County, Manchester City Gaol Register No 32501 – 39000, June 1878–2 April 1879, Entry 36521, Eliza McLoughlin.

30 The hard-pressed Scott family occupied the lowest ranks of the employed in Ancoats. For 10 years or more, John Scott was employed as a 'scavenger', an occupation which was later also followed by at least one of his sons. See UK *Census 1861*, Piece No 2928, Folio 124, p 35, entry for 7 Elizabeth Street; and UK *Census 1871,* Piece No 4029, Folio 44, p 11, entry for 68 Loom Court. Acute poverty as well as being in some awe of the McLoughlin family and his cousins may have paved the way for young Dennis Scott's involvement in the 1878 pawnshop break.

31 On the 1877–79 recession, central to the fate of the McLoughlin family, and the winter of 1878, which was particularly bleak, see Kidd, *Manchester,* pp 102 and 120.

32 See UK, Manchester Archives, Records of Great Manchester County, Manchester City Gaol, General Registers, M600/1/1/18, 19 June – 2 April 1878, Reg No 36521, entry for Eliza McLoughlin, discharged 10 June 1879.

33 See, among others, JL Sanders, 'Were our Forebears Aware of Prenatal Alcohol Exposure and its Effects? A History

of Fetal Alcohol Spectrum Disorder', *Canadian Journal of Clinical Pharmacology and Therapeutics,* Vol 16, No 2, Summer 2009, pp 288–95; PW Kodituwakku, 'Defining the Behavioural Phenotype in Children with Fetal Alcohol Spectrum Disorders: A Review', *Neuroscience and Biobehavioral Reviews,* Vol 31, 2007, pp 192–201; and A Niccols, 'Fetal Alcohol Syndrome and the Developing Socio-Emotional Brain', *Brain and Cognition,* Vol 65, 2007, pp 135–42. I am indebted to Prof Robert Kaplan for these and all other references to published medical research in this work. For Mary McLoughlin's criminal record, which involved a change of identity and dated back to a conviction for theft at Bradford in June 1879, but continued into 1886 with several further convictions for theft, abusive behaviour and prostitution, see UK, National Archives, Kew; Calendar of Prisoners, HO 140/81 – 1885, entry No 63 for Mary McLoughlin, 'factory operative'; and Calendar of Prisoners, HO 140/89 – 1886, entry No 3, Mary McLoughlin, 'factory operative'.

34 UK, Manchester Archives, Records of Greater Manchester County, Creed Registers 1880–1882, M327/2/2/4, entry for Elizabeth McLoughlin, dated 17 February 1880 (admitted 16 February 1880); and Withington Workhouse Hospital, Death Registers 1857–1892, entry for Elizabeth McLoughlin, dated 22 August 1881.

Chapter Four: The Makings of the Man

1 See MA Busteed and RL Hodgson, 'Irish Migrant Responses to Urban Life in Early Nineteenth-Century Manchester', *The Geographical Journal,* Vol 162, Part 2, July 1996, pp 150–51; A Kidd, *Manchester: A History* (Lancaster 2006), p 45 [hereafter, Kidd, *Manchester*]; and N Richardson, *The Old Pubs of Ancoats* (Manchester 1987), for the choices available. For a neighbouring

community during a later period and the general attitude towards drinking among working men see also R Roberts, *The Classic Slum: Salford Life in the First Quarter of the Century* (Harmondsworth 1973), p 121 [hereafter Roberts, *The Classic Slum*].

2 In later life this bifurcation could be seen in the American and English coats of arms tattooed on Jack McLoughlin's arms. See

below, Chapter Seven.

3 See above, Chapter Two.

4 Some idea of what such an education might have involved can be gleaned from S Fleming, 'A Separate Culture? Irish Catholics in Working-class Manchester, c 1890–1939', pp 33–35 in A Davies and S Fielding (eds), *Workers' Worlds: Cultures and Communities in Manchester and Salford, 1880–1939* (Manchester 1992) [hereafter, Fleming in *Workers' Worlds*]. See also WJ Lowe, *The Irish in Mid-Victorian Lancashire: The Shaping of a Working Class Community* (New York 1989), pp 124, 147 and 163 [hereafter Lowe, *The Irish in Mid-Victorian Lancashire*].

5 See Fleming in *Workers' Worlds*, p 40; EER Green, 'The Fenians Abroad' in TD Williams (ed), *Secret Societies in Ireland* (Dublin 1973), pp 86–87; Lowe, *The Irish in Mid-Victorian Lancashire*, pp 195–96; and J O'Neill, *Crime City: Manchester's Victorian Underworld* (Preston 2008), pp 34 and 233 [hereafter, O'Neill, *Crime City*]. On O'Brien and his unlikely claim about the Manchester Martyrs, see C van Onselen, *Masked Raiders: Irish Banditry in Southern Africa* (Cape Town 2010), pp 103–4 [hereafter, van Onselen, *Masked Raiders*].

6 See Lowe, *The Irish in Mid-Victorian Lancashire*, pp 150 and 163; and O'Neill, *Crime City*, p 39. For a fuller appreciation of the context of these conflicts see DM Macraild, *Faith, Fraternity and Fighting: The Orange Order and Irish Migrants in Northern England, c 1850–1920* (Liverpool 2005), especially pp 46, 56 and 188.

7 See below, Chapter Ten.

8 On broader patterns of boys' reading in the mid-nineteenth century, see, for example, A Davies, *The Gangs of Manchester: The Story of the Scuttlers, Britain's First Youth Cult* (Preston 2008), p 17 [hereafter Davies, *The Gangs of Manchester*]; and O'Neill, *Crime City*, p 74. But see especially TJ Couzens, *Tramp Royal: The True Story of Trader Horn* (Johannesburg 1992), pp 48 and 81.

9 See T Wyke, '"More than an Example": Ancoats in Historical Perspective', *Manchester Region History Review*, Vol 7, 1993, pp 11–12.

10 Davies, *The Gangs of Manchester*, pp 38–45.

11 See Davies, *The Gangs of Manchester*, pp 47, 73–75 and 137; and O'Neill, *Crime City*, pp 202–3. But, for the full historical and sociological context as well as the many gender-specific elements in and around the scuttling phenomenon, see also A Davies, '"These Viragoes Are No Less Cruel Than the Lads": Young Women Gangs and Violence in Late Victorian Manchester and Salford', *British Journal of Criminology*, Vol 39, No 1, Special Issue, 1999, pp 72 –89; and J Burchill, '"The Carnival Revels of Manchester's Vagabonds": Young Working-Class Women and Monkey Parades in the 1870s', *Women's History Review*, Vol 15, No 2, 2006, pp 229–52 [hereafter Burchill, 'Carnival Revels'].

12 See Davies, *The Gangs of Manchester*, p 75; and van Onselen, *Masked Raiders*, pp 11–43.

13 Burchill, 'Carnival Revels', pp 237–43.

14 See the comment of Mabel Sharman as reported in C Emsley, *Hard Men: The English and Violence Since 1750* (London 2005), p 60 [hereafter, Emsley, *Hard Men*]. For instances of physical abuse – 'bonneting' – of young women in Manchester and music hall derision of the institution of marriage, see Davies, *The Gangs of Manchester*, pp 30 and 260–61. Also, O'Neill, on 'An Epidemic of Wife-beating' in *Crime City*, pp 168–69.

15 According to S Brady, *Masculinity and Male Homosexuality in Britain, 1861–1913* (London 2005), at p 218, 'In the matter of sex and sexuality between men, Britain was one of the most hostile and intolerant cultures in the Western world.'

16 See J Tosh's seminal article, 'What Should Historians do with Masculinity? Reflections on Nineteenth-Century Britain', *History Workshop Journal*, Vol 38, No 1, 1994, p 187.

17 See, for example, AN Gilbert, 'Buggery in the British Navy', *Journal of Social History*, Vol 10, No 1 (Autumn 1976), pp 72–98. Scuttlers, like young males in certain African societies (with whom they were on occasion compared at the time as 'savages') occupied a liminal position in a society filled with possibilities. See especially VW Turner, *The Forest of Symbols: Aspects of Ndembu Ritual* (Ithaca 1967) and *Dramas, Fields and Metaphors: Symbolic Action in Human*

Society (Ithaca 1974).

18 See, for example, N Rees, *A Word in Your Shell* (Glasgow 2004), pp 299–300, who portrays it as largely a late-twentieth-century salutation.

19 See O'Neill, *Crime City*, p 202.

20 See Davies, *The Gangs of Manchester*, pp 257–58.

21 Ibid, p 57 and WR Gray, '"For Whom the Bell Tolled": The Decline of British Prize Fighting in the Victorian Era', *Journal of Popular Culture*, Vol 21, No 2, 1987, pp 53–64 [hereafter Gray, 'The Decline of British Prize Fighting']. For the wider, Irish, background to this, see C Conley, 'The Agreeable Recreation of Fighting', *Journal of Social History*, Vol 33, No 1 (Autumn 1999), pp 57–72; Davies, *The Gangs of Manchester*, p 47; and Lowe, *The Irish in Mid-Victorian Lancashire*, p 40. On the English, see, for example, Emsley, *Hard Men*, pp 40–44 and O'Neill, *Crime City*, p 46.

22 Davies, *The Gangs of Manchester*, pp 47–49; and O'Neill, *Crime City*, pp 113–14.

23 Emsley, *Hard Men*, p 56.

24 See S Carroll (ed), *Cultures of Violence: Interpersonal Violence in Historical Perspective* (Basingstoke 2007), 'Introduction', pp 15–25, and, in the same collection, SC Hughes, '"Swords and Daggers": Class Conceptions of Interpersonal Violence in Liberal Italy', especially pp 212–15.

25 For further examples of the use of guns among scuttlers, see Davies, *The Gangs of Manchester*, pp 72 and 179.

26 See especially the chapter on 'Green: Fenian Dynamiters' in M Burleigh, *Blood and Rage: A Cultural History of Terrorism* (London 2008).

27 Davies, *The Gangs of Manchester*, p 30; and for the wider context, A Davies, 'Saturday Night Markets in Manchester and Salford, 1840–1939', *Manchester Region History Review*, 1987, p 4 [hereafter, Davies, 'Saturday Night Markets'].

28 Davies, *The Gangs of Manchester*, pp 27, 49 and 58; and O'Neill, *Crime City*, pp 114–120.

29 See Gray, 'The Decline of British Prize Fighting', p 61, and Lowe, *The Irish in Mid-Victorian Lancashire*, p 126.

30 See Emsley, *Hard Men*, p 46, and Davies, *The Gangs of Manchester*, pp 289–312.

31 See Davies, *The Gangs of Manchester*, pp 261–62 and, more generally, A Kidd, *Manchester; A History* (Lancaster 2006), p 128.

32 A Court, *Puck of the Droms: The Lives and Literature of the Irish Tinkers* (Los Angeles 1985), p 5.

33 See M Clapson, *A Bit of a Flutter: Popular Gambling and English Society, c 1823–1961* (Manchester 1992), p 4 [hereafter Clapson, *Popular Gambling*]; and R McKibbin, 'Working Class Gambling in Britain, 1880–1939', *Past and Present*, No 82, February 1979, pp 147–48 [hereafter, McKibbin, 'Working Class Gambling'].

34 Clapson, *Popular Gambling*, p 18.

35 Ibid, pp 22–24 and 44–45; and McKibbin, 'Working Class Gambling', p 147.

36 Clapson, *Popular Gambling*, pp 24–29. For horse racing as an indirect spur to literacy, even during the later Edwardian period, see Roberts, *The Classic Slum*, p 163.

37 See P Rushton, 'Family Survival Strategies in Mid-Victorian Ancoats', *Manchester Region History Review*, Vol 7, 1993, p 43; and Davies, 'Saturday Night Markets', p 4.

38 See Clapson, *Popular Gambling*, p 115; Kidd, *Manchester*, pp 41 and 131; and Roberts, *The Classic Slum*, p 37.

39 O'Neill, *Crime City*, p 258.

40 For an outline of Peace's career, see O'Neill, *Crime City*, pp 212–21; but, more importantly, D Ward, *King of the Lags; The Story of Charles Peace* (London 1963).

41 O'Neill, *Crime City*, pp 82–86.

Chapter Five: Criminal Cousins

1 United Kingdom (UK), Manchester, Central Library, St Peter's Square, Archives and Local Studies, Police Court Records, Petty Sessions, Summary Convictions, John McLoughlin, 18 February 1878 [hereafter, Manchester Archives].

2 Irish tinkers, unlike other groupings to be found around much of the world, never constituted a nomadic criminal fraternity though some English local authorities were no doubt inclined to view them as such, and not always without reason. As a group of independent hawkers, itinerant craftsmen and seasonal labourers who pre- and post-dated industrial society, however, they were predictably well represented in Lancashire around Liverpool and Manchester: see A Court, *Puck of the Droms; The Lives and Literature of the Irish Tinkers* (Los Angeles 1988), p 27. In Ireland itself, see T Fennell, *The Royal Irish Constabulary* (Dublin 2003), pp 136–37. Elements of tinker culture can readily be identified in the lifestyles of 'Irish' hoboes, tramps, swaggerers, sundowners, vagrants and wayfarers who became such a feature of colonial Australia, Canada, India, South Africa and New Zealand in the closing decades of the nineteenth century; see, for example, S De, *Marginal Europeans in Colonial India; 1860–1920* (Kolkota 2008).

3 See S Cordery, *British Friendly Societies, 1750–1914* (Basingstoke 2003), pp 21, 30 and 69; and, on societies in Manchester and Salford, RL Greenall, *The Making of Victorian Salford* (Lancaster 2000), pp 7–8, 79 and 231–34.

4 See especially 'Introduction' in J Caplan (ed), *Written on the Body: The Tattoo in European and American History* (London 2000), pp i–xxii [hereafter, Caplan, *Written on the Body*].

5 See J Bradley, 'Body Commodification? Class and Tattoos in Victorian Britain' in Caplan, *Written on the Body*, p 138.

6 The core members of this group were John W Brown, John McLoughlin, Charles Beswick and Joseph Wild. For the markings on their bodies, see UK Manchester Archives, Manchester City Gaol, General Registers, 3000–3251, M 600/1, Belle Vue Prison, 1878–79, entries for JW Brown and J McLoughlin, Registration Numbers 36518 and 36519; blue dots on left forearms. For the other two, see UK Manchester Archives, Strangeways Gaol Register, 29 November 1876 – 12 September 1877, entry for C Beswick, blue dot between thumb and first finger of left hand; and Strangeways Gaol Register No 15402, 25 March 1876 – 29 Nov 1876, Entry for Joseph Wild, two blue dots on left eyelid.

7 'The young men of whom I speak admire rather than abjure criminality. I first noticed this twenty years ago when young men came to me as patients who had tattooed on their cheek the blue spot that former inmates of borstals used as a sign of graduation, without their ever having been to borstal themselves.' T Dalrymple, 'Appetite for Destruction', *The Spectator*, 13 August 2011.

8 JW Brown was born on 5 December 1858. See UK, Manchester, Records of the Catholic Family History Society (CFHS), 1848–1874, Register of Baptisms, St Anne's, Junction Street, Manchester.

9 The outlines of John James Brown's changing family can be traced via UK, *Census*, in chronological order, *1861*, Piece No 2935, Folio 111, p 13; *1871*, Piece 4034, Folio 45, p 1; *1881*, Piece 3983, Folio 77, pp 10–11, and *1891*, Piece No 3233, Folio 40, p 12.

10 See UK, *Index of Births, Deaths and Marriages*, April–June 1862, Vol 8d, p 101; Ann Brown.

11 For some months in the early 1890s and for some time thereafter, for whatever reason, JW Brown took to telling the police that his nickname was 'Jack the Ripper' – see, for example, 'Burglarious Implements', *The Star* (Johannesburg), 24 December 1892.

12 See UK, *Census 1891*, Piece No 3233, Folio 40, p 12.

13 UK, Manchester Archives, Police Court Records, Petty Sessions, 23 Sept 1872. On errands boys as targets for criminals, see O'Neill, *Crime City*, pp 70–71.

14 UK, Manchester, Police Court Registers, entries for JW Brown and various others dated 12–13 June 1876, 14 April 1877, 4 January 1878 and 12 June 1878.

15 UK, Manchester Archives, Police Court, Summary Convictions 1877, C Beswick, 29 March 1876.

16 See UK, Manchester Archives, Police Court Register, 26 June 1876; Strangeways' Gaol Registers, 25 March 1876 – 20 November 1876 No 15402; Register No 15402, entry for J Wild; and Police Court Register, 25 July 1855. On pickpockets see also O'Neill, *Crime City*, p 67.

17 The Harding family can be traced in *UK Census 1851, 1861* and *1871*, at HO2226, Folio 715, p 12; RG9/2869, Folio 86, p 9; and RG10/3976, Folio 107, p 10 – as they moved from Great Ancoats Street to Stockport Road and their oldest son Charles Harding progressed from 'scholar' to clerk in the yarn trade.

18 See UK, Manchester Archives, *England and Wales Criminal Registers, 1791–1892* (1872 edition), HO27, Piece 162, p 30, entry, 8 April 1872, 'Thomas Whelan, Larceny, before convicted Felony, sentence – 1 month and on its expiration, to be sent to a reformatory school for five years'; and HO27, Piece 177, p 14, Entry, 19 February 1877, Thomas Whelan, the elder and Thomas Whelan, the younger, assault on a constable. Sentence, elder 4 months and younger, 3 months.

19 On Fisher see UK *Census 1861*, Piece 2948, Folio 65, p 33 entry for 6 Pigeon Street.

20 O'Neill, *Crime City*, p 50.

21 Ibid, pp 237–256.

22 See UK, Manchester Archives, 'Thursday; The Violent Assault with a Poker' in *Manchester Weekly Post*, January – December 1878, 23 February 1870.

23 UK, Manchester Archives, Police Court Records, 26 May 1879, and Prison Register, M600/1/1/19, Entry No 40168 for Thomas Loughlin (*sic*).

24. On the 1878 recession see Kidd, *Manchester*, pp 102 and 120.

25 This paragraph draws extensively on M Tebbutt, *Making Ends Meet; Pawnbroking and Working-Class Credit* (Leicester 1983),

pp 1–10. For a more personalised picture of the social dynamics surrounding pawnbrokers, albeit at a later date, see R Roberts, *The Classic Slum; Salford Life in the First Quarter of the Century* (Harmondsworth 1973), pp 25–27.

26 O'Neill, *Crime City*, pp 88–89 and especially pp 97–100.

27 See UK *Census 1871*, Piece RG10/4033, Folio 47, p 75, entry for 175 Great Ancoats, New Cross.

28 UK, Manchester Archives, City Sessions, 6 June 1877, case of JW Brown and J Mackey who stole books from JH Wells.

29 On William Chorlton, his Ancoats-born wife, Elizabeth, and their children who continued to run the business into the early twentieth century see, for example, UK *Census 1871*, RG10/40444, Folio No 126, p 5, and UK *Census 1891*, RG13/3755, Folio 74, p 31.

30 UK Manchester Archives, Records of Manchester City Quarter Sessions 1878, 12 December 1878, Felony Nos 87–91.

31 O'Neill, *Crime City*, p 251.

32 See, for example, K Chesney, *The Victorian Underworld* (Harmondsworth 1974), pp 218–20.

33 UK Manchester Archives, *Manchester Evening News*, 13 December 1878. See also items in MFMC 83, October – December 1878, *Manchester Courier*, 13 December 1878; and the *Manchester Weekly Post*, January – December 1878.

34 UK, Manchester Archives, Records of Manchester City Quarter Sessions 1878, 12 December 1878, Felony Nos 87–91.

35 UK Manchester Archives, M327/1/2/6, Death Registers 1857–1892, Entry for Elizabeth McLoughlin, 22 August 1881.

36 See below, Chapter 26; and N Richardson, *The Pubs of Old Ancoats* (Manchester 1987), p 19.

37 For blue dot markings on the 'groom' Thomas McLoughlin, see Australia, *Victoria, Police Gazette,* list of prisoners released in the second week of February 1883.

38 See UK Manchester Archives, 'Robberies with Violence', *Manchester Guardian,* and *Manchester Courier,* 24 January 1880.

39 See UK, Manchester Archives, County of

Lancaster, Assizes Court, 22 January 1880; and UK, National Archives, Kew, England and Wales Criminal Registers, 1791–1892.

40 Taken from C Lloyd, *The British Seaman* (Bungay 1970), p 209. For the wider,

theoretical context see E Goffman, 'On the Characteristics of Total Institutions – The Inmate World' in DR Cressey (ed), *The Prison: Studies in Institutional Organisation and Change* (New York 1961).

Chapter Six: Escape into Empire

1 This and much of the section that follows is based largely on J Darwin's fine overview, *The Empire Project: The Rise and Fall of the British World-System, 1830–1970* (Cambridge 2009). [Hereafter, Darwin, *The Empire*.]

2 See, for example, J Belich, *Replenishing the Earth: The Settler Revolution and the Rise of the Anglo-World, 1873–1939* (Oxford 2009), p 122 [hereafter, Belich, *The Settler Revolution*].

3 See especially Darwin's 'Introduction' to *The Empire*, pp 1–20 and, for themes highlighted in this paragraph pp 24–27, 35–37, 57–58 and 68–69; and Belich, *The Settler Revolution*, p 126.

4 GB Magee and AS Thompson, *Empire and Globalisation; Networks of People, Goods and Capital in the British World, c. 1850–1914* (Cambridge 2010), p 172, [hereafter, Magee and Thompson, *Empire and Globalisation*]; and Darwin, *The Empire*, as cited in footnote 5 below.

5 Darwin, *The Empire*, especially pp 5, 37, 69, 98, 100, 110, 160–163, and 170–171.

6 Belich, *The Settler Revolution*, pp 107–114.

7 Darwin, *The Empire*, pp 39–40, 98, 115 and 161. See also Magee and Thompson, *Empire and Globalisation*, pp 64–116. For a case study of how an internationally integrated transport system could shape mass migration as well as create new social problems see C van Onselen, 'Jewish Marginality in the Atlantic World: Organised Crime in the Era of the Great Migrations, 1880–1914', *South African Historical Journal*, Vol 43, November 2000, pp 96–137.

8 See Belich, *The Settler Revolution*, pp 122–23.

9 Darwin, *The Empire*, especially pp 5, 25, 39, 48, 100 and 112–22 and, in greater detail, T Standige, *The Victorian Internet: The Remarkable*

Story of the Telegraph and the Nineteenth Century's On-line Pioneers (New York City 1998). See also Belich, *The Settler Revolution*, pp 106–33 but more particularly, pp 120–23.

10 For examples of men seeking to elude the law and being undone by newspaper reports see D Blackburn and WW Caddell, *Secret Service in South Africa* (London 1911), pp 61–63. More generally, see Magee and Thompson, *Empire and Globalisation*, pp 17–18 and 28–31, and Chapters 19–22 below.

11 See also Belich, *The Settler Revolution*, Chapter 4 and, more especially, pp 122–23. Within this system sensational news via cables, as provided by Reuters, had a central role – see Magee and Thompson, *Empire and Globalisation*, pp 189–90.

12 EJ Grove, *The Royal Navy since 1815* (Basingstoke 2005), 'The Ironclad Age', pp 39–68 [hereafter, Grove, *The Royal Navy*].

13 Darwin, *The Empire*, pp 33, 39 and 77.

14 See Grove, *The Royal Navy*, pp 55–58 and 65.

15 For the immediate context of the voyage of the *Albatross* see Darwin, *The Empire*, pp 70–71 and 130–31. See also, N Stone, *Turkey; A Short History* (London 2010), pp 112–20.

16 Grove, *The Royal Navy*, p 56 – although not mentioned by name, the *Albatross* was one of the six 940-tonners laid down in 1873–74.

17 United Kingdom (UK), National Archives, Kew, ADM 53/11743, Records and Log of the HMS *Albatross* [hereafter, ADM 53/11743].

18 See *The Cork Examiner*, 9 May 1864.

19 UK, National Archives, Kew, ADM 53/11743, Log, HMS *Albatross*.

20 See UK, National Archives, Kew, ADM 53/11743, Log HMS *Albatross*, and P Knepper, 'A Few Detectives would be Very Useful:

Crime, Immorality and Policing in Valetta, 1881–1914', *Journal of Social History*, Vol 43, 2009, pp 385–406.

21 For the immediate context see Darwin, *The Empire*, pp 4, 56, 70–71 and 130–31.

22 UK, National Archives, Kew, ADM 53/11743, Log, HMS *Albatross.*

23 UK, National Archives, Kew, ADM 53/11743, Log, HMS *Albatross*; but more especially N Sherry's excellent *Conrad's Eastern World* (Cambridge 1880), pp 55–64. These tales circulated not only around the Arabian Sea but as far east and south as New Zealand. See, for example, 'SS Jeddah', *Wanganui Herald*, Vol 14, Issue 3994, 10 November 1882.

24 See Darwin, *The Empire*, pp 25 and 87–88.

25 UK, National Archives, Kew, ADM 53/11743, Log, HMS *Albatross.* On Bombay see A Seal, *The Emergence of Indian Nationalism: Competition and Collaboration in the Later Nineteenth Century* (Cambridge 1971), p 66.

26 UK, National Archives, Kew, ADM 53/11743, Log, HMS *Albatross.*

27 UK, National Archives, Kew, ADM 53/11743, Log, HMS *Albatross*; and UK *Census 1881*, Vessel '*Albatross*', Royal Navy, at sea or in a foreign port, RH 11/5633, Folio 62, p 6, J McLouglin [sic].

28 See also Belich, *Replenishing the Earth*, pp 306–30.

29 See Darwin, *The Empire*, p 25. On changing British perceptions, see V. Kiernan, *The Lords of Human Kind; European Attitudes to other Cultures in the Imperial Age* (London 1969), pp 85–91 [hereafter, Kiernan, *The Lords of Human Kind*].

30 Kiernan, *The Lords of Human Kind*, p 85.

31 UK, National Archives, Kew, ADM 53/11743,

Log, HMS *Albatross.*

32 This and the two paragraphs that follow should be read against the broader contexts as laid out in A McLaren, 'Introduction' to *The Trials of Masculinity; Policing Sexual Boundaries, 1870–1930* (Chicago 1997), pp 1–10; and J Tosh 'What should Historians do with Masculinity? Reflections on Nineteenth-century Britain', *History Workshop Journal*, Vol 38, No 1, pp 179–202.

33 This, despite the fact that excessive discipline was increasingly frowned upon after mid-century after the Naval Discipline Act of 1866, which did much to bring naval justice into line with English Criminal law. See MJ Wiener, 'Race, Class and Maritime Authority in Late Victorian England: The Surprising Cases of Charles Arthur (1888) and Bagwahn Jassiswara (1891) in S Carroll (ed), *Cultures of Violence: Interpersonal Violence in Historical Perspective* (Basingstoke 2007); introductory comment on p 29 but, more especially, Wiener's observation at p 239.

34 See Kiernan's observations about perceptions of Arabs and Indians and, more especially the Chinese in *The Lords of Human Kind*, pp 79–80, 85–91 and 152–78.

35 Belich, too, has noted what he terms the importance of 'crew culture' during settler expansionism and stretches the category to include several other occupational groupings; see Belich, *Replenishing the Earth*, pp 319–24. For the immediate context and its relevance to patterns of male sexuality, see PN Stevens, 'Buggery and the British Navy, 1700–1861', *Journal of Social History*, Vol 10, No 1, Autumn 1976, p 87.

Chapter Seven: Among Legends and Myths of the Bush

1 The nineteenth-century revolution in international postal communication can be traced in, among others, J Belich, *Replenishing the Earth: The Settler Revolution and the Rise of the Anglo World, 1783–1939* (Oxford 2009), p 122 [hereafter, Belich, *The*

Settler Revolution]; J Darwin, *The Empire Project: The Rise and Fall of the British World System* (Cambridge 2009), pp 5, 100 and 112 [hereafter, Darwin, *The Empire*]; and GB Magee and A Thompson, *Empire and Globalisation: Networks of People, Goods and*

Capital in the British World (Cambridge 2010),
p 83 [hereafter, Magee and Thompson,
Empire and Globalisation].

2 See P Laidlaw, 'A Passing Occupation: An
Exploration of the History and Heritage of
Itinerant Workers in Rural New South Wales,
1850–1914', unpublished PhD thesis, Charles
Sturt University, March 2009 [hereafter,
Laidlaw, 'Itinerant Workers in Rural New
South Wales, 1850–1914'].

3 Belich, *The Settler Revolution,* pp 357–58; and
Darwin, *The Empire*, pp 160–62.

4 The classic, founding, text for this is Russel
Ward's *The Australian Legend* (Melbourne
1958), which has been moderated and refined
by work such as that of Richard Waterhouse,
*The Vision Splendid: A Social and Cultural
History of Rural Australia* (Fremantle 2005)
[hereafter, Waterhouse, *The Vision Splendid*].

5 In this regard see especially G Seal, *Tell
'Em I Died Game; The Legend of Ned Kelly*
(Flemington 2002), pp 2–3 and p 30
[hereafter Seal, *The Legend of Ned Kelly*];
and G Seal, *The Outlaw Legend: A Cultural
Tradition in Britain, America and Australia*
(Cambridge 1996), pp 148–80 [hereafter Seal,
The Outlaw Legend].

6 On this paradox within the Australian
context see Seal, *The Legend of Ned Kelly,* p 2
and, more generally, EJ Hobsbawm, *Bandits*
(Harmondsworth 1969), p 131.

7 Much of this is based on a reading of Ward,
The Australian Legend – see especially pp 1–12,
86–93, 168 and 208; but also Waterhouse's
persuasive rider as outlined in *The Vision
Splendid* on pp 111–12. On homosexuality
see, for example, the same works by Ward and
Waterhouse at pp 93 and 124 respectively.

8 This paragraph is based largely on J Jupp
(ed), *The Australian People, An Encyclopedia
of the Nation, its People and their Origins*
(Cambridge 2001), pp 443–486. But see also
'Celts and Currency' in Ward, *The Australian
Legend*, pp 43–64; and DH Akenson, *The Irish
Diaspora: A Primer* (Belfast 1993), pp 91–123,
who, while uncomfortable with elevated
crime rates attributed to the influence of the
Irish in early Australia, admits, at p 119, that
'there was probably something real here and
not just in Australia'.

9 The person most likely to have first penned
this description and almost certainly the
best-placed to make the observation was
Louis Cohen, who took a close interest in
criminals on both the gold and diamond
fields. See United States of America, Yale
University Library, New Haven, AC 565,
Box 7, Folder 75, Louis Cohen Scrapbooks,
Manuscript for his work on Johannesburg
and Kimberley (no date), p 17. Cohen or his
manuscript may also have been the source
for Douglas Blackburn, an agent in Kruger's
intelligence agency in the mid-1890s who
later met McLoughlin when he was a
fugitive living in the northern Transvaal bush
in 1894. See D Blackburn and WW Caddell,
Secret Service in South Africa (London 1911),
p 105. Blackburn, in turn, may have been
a part source for TV Bulpin's sometimes
unreliable account in his *Storm over the
Transvaal* (Cape Town 1955), p 218. It should
be noted, however, that all three of these
sources fail to disclose their primary sources
and are all guilty to differing degrees of
embroidering aspects of McLoughlin's life
in ways that cannot be reconciled with
contemporary newspaper sources.

10 See J McQuilton, *The Kelly Outbreak: The
Geographical Dimension of Social Banditry*
(Melbourne 1979), pp 8–68 [hereafter
McQuilton, *The Kelly Outbreak*].

11 See especially Belich, *The Settler Revolution*,
pp 356–58.

12 On inmate life in Pentridge Prison in the
1870s, see I Jones, *Ned Kelly: A Short Life*
(Melbourne 1996), pp 72–73 [hereafter,
Jones, *Ned Kelly*]. On Tommy McLoughlin
in Pentridge, see 'Released from Prison',
Police Gazette, Victoria, 1884. I have been
unable to trace details relating to either the
original offence as might be reported in
local newspapers, or the court and prison
records relating to Tommy McLoughlin's
incarceration in 1883. It should also be
noted that the note in the *Gazette,* which is
otherwise accurate in all respects, including
details about his age and physical description,
renders his name as 'McLaughlin' rather than
McLoughlin.

13 On Kelly and Power see Jones, *Ned Kelly,*

especially pp 32–67.

14 For Jack McLoughlin's recalling of his
and Tommy's last meeting in Australia in
1884 and his first criminal conviction in
Australia, see Republic of South Africa,
National Archives of South Africa, Pretoria,
Witwatersrand Local Division (WLD),
377/1909, Rex vs Jack McLoughlin, p 63
[hereafter, RSA, Rex vs McLoughlin, 1909].

15 See Laidlaw, 'Itinerant Workers in Rural New
South Wales, 1850–1914', pp 361–67.

16 On Scott and supposed interactions with the
Kelly gang in Victoria as 'Captain Moonlite'
see, for example, Jones, *Ned Kelly*, pp 215–16.

17 On John Hutchings as 'Captain Moonlite' at
work in southern Africa, see C van Onselen,
*Masked Raiders: Irish Banditry in Southern
Africa* (Cape Town 2010), pp 33–35.

18 *The Maitland Mercury & Hunter River General
Advertiser*, 19 July 1884. I am indebted to Dr
Sue Summers for drawing this and the item

that follows about Tommy McLoughlin to
my attention. It should be noted, however,
that here – as in the record in Pentridge
Prison – the name is incorrectly rendered as
'McLaughlin' rather than 'McLoughlin'.

19 See *Clarence and Richmond Examiner & New
England Advertiser,* 3 January 1885.

20 See below, Chapter Twenty-One.

21 See 'By One of His Pals', *Standard and Diggers'
News,* 2 February 1895; and 'Where are the
Police?', *The Star*, 2 February 1895.

22 Ibid. See 'By One of His Pals', *Standard and
Diggers' News,* 2 February 1895; and 'Where
are the Police?', *The Star*, 2 February 1895.

23 See especially McQuilton, *The Kelly
Outbreak*, pp 8–47.

24 Jones, *Ned Kelly*, pp 222–32.

25 Ibid, pp 230–31.

26 Ibid, pp 240–57.

27 See McQuilton, *The Kelly Outbreak,* p 144;
and Seal, *The Legend of Ned Kelly,* p 116.

Chapter Eight: The Southern African Mineral Revolution and the College of Banditry

1 Delagoa Bay, as a liminal zone in southern
Africa, is the subject of ongoing research by
the author.

2 See 'Sketches at Delagoa Bay', *Illustrated
London News*, 1 February 1890, p 146. See
also C van Onselen, 'Randlords and Rotgut:
1886–1903; The Role of Alcohol in the
Development of European Imperialism and
Southern African Capitalism with Special
Reference to Black Mineworkers in the
Transvaal Republic' in C van Onselen, *New
Babylon, New Nineveh: Everyday Life on the
Witwatersrand, 1886–1914* (Cape Town 2001),
pp 47–108.

3 See, for example, 'Wanted – Extradition
Treaties', *The Star,* 14 February 1895.

4 See C van Onselen, *Masked Raiders: Irish
Banditry in Southern Africa, 1880–1899* (Cape
Town 2010), pp 11–26 [hereafter, van
Onselen, *Masked Raiders*].

5 DH Akenson, *The Irish Diaspora: A Primer*
(Belfast 1993), p 143.

6 This paragraph and much of the evidence
that follows about the quotidian dynamics
of Fort Napier relies on G Dominy, 'The
Imperial Garrison in Natal with Special
Reference to Fort Napier, 1843–1914',
unpublished D Phil thesis, University of
London, 1995 [hereafter, Dominy, 'The
Imperial Garrison']. See also the footnotes in
van Onselen, *Masked Raiders*, pp 11–25.

7 See G Dominy, 'More than just a "Drunken
Brawl": The Mystery of the Mutiny of the
Inniskilling Fusiliers at Fort Napier, 1887',
in DP McCracken (ed), *Southern African –
Irish Studies, Vol 1* (Durban 1991), pp 56–72
[hereafter, Dominy, 'The Mutiny of the
Inniskillings'].

8 See 'One-Armed Mac', *Sunday Times*
(Johannesburg), 5 December 1909. The
report, however, suggests, incorrectly, that
McLoughlin had enlisted in the 'South
Staffordshire Regiment'. The South
Staffordshire Regiment was not based at

Fort Napier at the time but the North
Staffordshire Regiment was. See Dominy,
'The Imperial Garrison', Appendix 1, p 431.
9 See van Onselen, *Masked Raiders*, p 23.
10 Ibid, pp 22–23.
11 For Hutching's career in the army and
attendant problems see United Kingdom
(UK), National Archives (NA), Kew, WO
16/1716, Book 3 and WO 16/1717; and, in
South Africa, van Onselen, *Masked Raiders*,
pp 27–28, 32–35 and 93.
12 Van Onselen, *Masked Raiders*, p 93.
13 UK, NA, Kew, WO 16/1716 and 1717. For
O' Brien's career in South Africa see van
Onselen, *Masked Raiders*, pp 28–30 and
103–4.
14 For the early criminal careers of the
Williams brothers see, for example, 'Police
Intelligence', *The Mercury and Weekly Courier*,
9 February 1884. On 'WJ Kelly's' Australian
background and his evolution into a bank
robber moving about southern Africa see,
'The Circuit Court', in *The Star* of 25 and
26 June, 1894 and 23 July 1894. Also, van
Onselen, *Masked Raiders*, pp 95–97.
15 John McCann's career in the British Army
can be traced in UK, NA, Kew, WO 97/3337
and WO 16/1607 and WO 16/1608, Musters
Book of the Royal Inniskilling Fusiliers,
1884–86 and 1886–88.
16 On McLoughlin and McCann's criminal

co-operation in South Africa see, for
example, van Onselen, *Masked Raiders*,
pp 132–34 and 172–73.
17 See Dominy, 'The Mutiny of the
Inniskillings', pp 56–72; and van Onselen,
Masked Raiders, p 23.
18 See van Onselen, *Masked Raiders*, p 27.
19 See F Metrowich's – often anecdotal – *Scotty
Smith: South Africa's Robin Hood* (Cape Town
1970).
20 On McCann in Kimberley see Republic
of South Africa (RSA), National Archives
(NA), Pretoria, Witwatersrand Local Division
(WLD), 377/1909, Rex vs Jack McLoughlin,
p 72; and van Onselen, *Masked Raiders*, p 27.
21 UK, NA, Kew, WO 16/1718, South
Lancashire, List of 'Men became Ineffective',
covering the year 1886. See also, WO
Vol 16/1211, 6th Dragoons , Deserters as
recorded on Form 32.
22 See, for example, HA Chilvers, *Out of the
Crucible* (London 1929), p 65.
23 On the coach service from the Rand to
Natal see, for example, *The Standard and
Transvaal Mining Chronicle*, 29 February
1888. There is an excellent account of the
perils of the coach journey from Natal to
Johannesburg by the Manchester-Irish actor
and impressionist, Charles du Val, in *The
Standard and Transvaal Mining Chronicle* of 5
and 9 May 1888.

Chapter Nine: The Frontiers of Gold and Beyond

1 *Barberton Herald*, 2 December 1887.
2 'A Chequered Career', *Potchefstroom Budget*,
6 August 1890.
3 The careers of these three members of
the 'Irish Brigade' can be traced in C van
Onselen, *Masked Raiders: Irish Banditry in
Southern Africa* (Cape Town 2010) [hereafter
van Onselen, *Masked Raiders*], and relevant
chapters below.
4 On 'Cockney Liz' see, for example, H
Borman, *Barberton, Photo Album* (Barberton
2007), p 22. On the change in numbers in
the town over weekends – when as many as

8 000 people could be strolling the streets –
see, for example, 'The Vagabond', 'Notes on
Gold Seeking' in *The Age*, 19 May 1888.
5 P Meiring, *Dynamite and Daisies: The Story
of Barberton* (Cape Town, 1976), pp 80–84
[hereafter, Meiring, *Dynamite and Daisies*].
6 M Leveson (ed), *South African Odyssey:
The Autobiography of Bertha Goudvis*
(Johannesburg, 2011), pp 22–23, captures
some of frontier-entrepreneurial spirit
around Eureka City at the time [hereafter,
Goudvis, *South African Odyssey*].
7 See 'The Vagabond', 'Notes on Gold

Seeking', *The Age*, 19 May 1888.

8 'Eureka City', *Gold Fields Times*, 15 April 1887.

9 'Eureka City', *Gold Fields Times*, 6 May 1887.

10 There is a popularised account of this lynching which can be largely substantiated from other, contemporary historical sources in TV Bulpin, *Lost Trails of the Transvaal* (Cape Town, 2002), pp 93–94 [hereafter, Bulpin, *Lost Trails*]. See also van Onselen, *Masked Raiders*, pp 38 and 96.

11 Hobsbawm suggests that deserters and ex-soldiers are among those who, given a measure of choice, are likely to choose antisocial pathways to banditry. See EJ Hobsbawm, *Bandits* (Harmondsworth, 1972), p 40.

12 See van Onselen, *Masked Raiders*, pp 19 and 29.

13 Ibid, pp 140–46.

14 Ibid, p 30.

15 G Dawson, *Soldier Heroes: British Adventure, Empire and the Imagining of Masculinities* (London 1994), p 1.

16 I Jones, *Ned Kelly: A Short Life* (Melbourne, 1995), pp 85 and 217 [hereafter Jones, *Ned Kelly*].

17 WD Curor (revised and enlarged by J Bornman), *Golden Memories of Barberton* (Barberton, 2002), p 67; and Meiring, *Dynamite and Daisies*, p 84. For earlier coach robberies in the De Kaap Valley, pre-dating the arrival of the Irish Brigade, see Bulpin, *Lost Trails*, pp 352–53.

18 See Jones, *Ned Kelly*; and J McQuilton, *The Kelly Outbreak: The Geographical Dimension of Social Banditry* (Melbourne 1979).

19 'Eureka City', *Barberton Herald*, 1 March 1887. See also Meiring, *Dynamite and Daisies*, p 84. Note, however, that the date suggested for the invasion of Eureka City in the latter source is almost certainly incorrect.

20 'Eureka City', *Barberton Herald*, 1 March 1887.

21 The chances are that this 'William Smith' is the same as that who later appeared with WJ Kelly in court in Johannesburg – see 'Attempted Gaol Breaking', *The Star*, 23 January 1893.

22 'The Irish Brigade', *Barberton Herald*, 1 March 1887. For Dwyer's courtroom behaviour in

comparative perspective see A Davies, *The Gangs of Manchester: The Story of the Scuttlers, Britain's First Youth Cult* (Preston 2008), pp 240 and 282.

23 Meiring, *Dynamite and Daisies*, p 123.

24 For a fine illustration of the career pathway of one such dystopian militant – 'JJ' – see 'Prison Work in Barberton', *All the World*, Vol VII, No 1, January 1891, pp 197–200. I am indebted to Joel Cabrita for drawing this source to my attention.

25 On Kruger's early concessions policy see, for example, C van Onselen, *New Babylon, New Nineveh: Everyday Life on the Witwatersrand, 1886–1914* (Cape Town, 2001), pp 47–51.

26 Among others see L van Onselen, *Head of Steel* (Cape Town, 1962), pp 92–93 [hereafter, van Onselen, *Head of Steel*].

27 See T Coleman, *The Railway Navvies* (Harmondsworth 1982).

28 See TV Bulpin, *Storm over the Transvaal* (Cape Town 1955), p 42; B Roonan, *Forty South African Years: Journalistic, Political, Social, Theatrical and Pioneering* (London, 1919), pp 107–13 [hereafter Roonan, *Forty South African Years*], and van Onselen, *Head of Steel*, p 93.

29 See TV Bulpin, *Storm over the Transvaal* (Cape Town, 1955), p 42; Roonan, *Forty South African Years*, pp 107–13; and van Onselen, *Head of Steel*, p 93.

30 For such tensions, albeit at a slightly later date, see, for example, Goudvis, *South African Odyssey*, p 96; and, in the specific context of the railway problems that followed, 'The Delagoa Bay Railway Story', *Illustrated London News*, 25 January 1890, p 102. See also MJ Jessett, *The Key to South Africa: Delagoa Bay* (London, 1899); and P Henshaw, 'The "Key to South Africa" in the 1890s: Delagoa Bay and the Origins of the South African War', *Journal of Southern African Studies*, Vol 24, No 3, September 1998, pp 527–35.

31 Roonan, *Forty South African Years*, p 116.

32 Ibid, p 119, and Bulpin, *Storm over the Transvaal*, p 45.

33 Roonan, *Forty South African Years*, pp 119–20.

34 Ibid, pp 112–14, and Bulpin, *Storm over the Transvaal*, p 45. For a sanitised version of the proceedings, which excludes any mention

of the Irish navvies, see 'The Delagoa Bay
Railway', *Illustrated London News*, 25 February
1888, p 189.

35 Roonan, *Forty South African Years*, pp 104–5,
110 and 120.

Chapter Ten: Organised Crime in a Frontier Town

1 Jack McLoughlin later claimed to have been
in Johannesburg in 1887, but 1888 seems the
more likely date – see Republic of South
Africa (RSA), Pretoria, National Archives
of South Africa (NASA), Witwatersrand
Local Division (WLD), 3777/1909, Rex vs
McLoughlin, 1909, p 68 [hereafter, Rex vs
McLoughlin, 1909].

2 On 'first' and 'second-class' boarding houses,
see *Standard & Diggers' News*, 18 December
1889.

3 *Diamond Fields Advertiser*, 22 February 1888.

4 'Crime in Johannesburg', *The Standard and
Transvaal Mining Chronicle*, 18 February 1888.

5 See C van Onselen, *Masked Raiders: Irish
Banditry in Southern Africa, 1880–1899* (Cape
Town 2010), pp 36–37 [hereafter, van
Onselen, *Masked Raiders*].

6 'Shocking Tragedy in Johannesburg', *The
Standard and Transvaal Mining Chronicle*,
18 February 1888. On contemporary notions
about cowardice and knife-crimes, see, for
example, C Emsley, *Hard Men: The English and
Violence since 1750* (London 2005), pp 56 and
87; and SC Hughes, '"Swords and Daggers",
Class Conceptions of Interpersonal Violence
in Liberal Italy' in S Carroll (ed), *Cultures
of Violence: Interpersonal Violence in Historical
Perspective* (Basingstoke 2007), pp 214–22.

7 'Shocking Tragedy in Johannesburg', *The
Standard and Transvaal Mining Chronicle*,
18 February 1888.

8 Van Onselen, *Masked Raiders*, p 37.

9 'Shocking Tragedy in Johannesburg', and
'The Recent Murder Case', *The Standard
and Transvaal Mining Chronicle*, 18 and
22 February 1888.

10 *The Standard and Transvaal Mining Chronicle*, 21
and 28 March 1888.

11 See H Sauer, *Ex Africa* (Bulawayo 1973),
p 136; and van Onselen, *Masked Raiders*,

pp 227–28.

12 See van Onselen, *Masked Raiders*, pp 226–28.
For links between criminal syndicates,
big business and the mining industry, see
'Randlords and Rotgut' in C van Onselen,
*New Babylon, New Nineveh: Everyday Life on
the Witwatersrand, 1886–1914* (Johannesburg
2010), pp 47–108 [hereafter, van Onselen,
New Babylon, New Nineveh].

13 For JW Brown's criminal history in Ancoats,
see above, Chapter Five. As a highwayman
in South Africa, see *The Diamond Fields
Advertiser*, 16 March 1888; and, in criminal
projects gone wrong with McLoughlin and
as 'Jack the Ripper', *The Star*, 24 December
1892 and 19 and 23 January 1893; also van
Onselen, *Masked Raiders*, pp 79–80.

14 United Kingdom (UK) *Census 1871*,
RG10/4052, Folio 97, p 11. For Hart as jewel
thief involved in cross-border operations, see
Diamond Fields Advertiser, 8 December 1887;
and as dog lover, *The Star*, 7 June 1893. On
organised dog fights see *The Star*, 17 June
1893. For Hart's exploits, including one
with Jack McLoughlin, see van Onselen,
Masked Raiders, p 111. On Hart's friendship
with Ferguson, see L Cohen, *Reminiscences of
Johannesburg and London* (Johannesburg, 1976),
p 102.

15 For these men's backgrounds see Chapter
Five above. Also, United Kingdom (UK)
Census 1851, HO/2226, Folio 715, p 12;
Census 1861, RG9/2869, Folio 86, p 9; and
Census 1871, RG10/3976, Folio 107, p 10.
On Harding in the Orange Free State and
the Transvaal in the early 1890s as well as
his later exploits with McLoughlin, see,
for example, RSA, NASA, TAB (Transvaal
Archive Bureau), SS (State Secretary), File R
15508/93 and van Onselen, *Masked Raiders*,
pp 82, 87 and 116–18.

16 See 'Lancashire Lads', *The Star*, 19 March
1893. On the Oddfellows and Rechabites,
see *The Star*, 7 August 1893 and van Onselen,
Masked Raiders, p 174.

17 On the Cornish, see, for example, *The Star*,
6 April 1891; 9 January 1892 and 14 April
1892. On the Irish at Langlaagte, see RSA,
Archives of the Witwatersrand Chamber
of Mines, Johannesburg, Letter Book No 5
(1890–1892). For McLoughlin at Langlaagte,
see RSA, NASA, Pretoria, WLD, 377/1909,
Rex vs McLoughlin, Affidavit by Sarah
McNeil (nee Fredericks), 24 November 1906.

18 On Irish criminality and Krugersdorp, see
van Onselen, *Masked Raiders*, especially pp 4,
47–49, 51–58 and 171–72.

19 'Pyrites and Cheap Treatment of Ore',
Standard & Diggers' News, 31 December 1889.

20 See 'The World the Mine Owners Made'
in van Onselen, *New Babylon, New Nineveh*,
pp 4–5.

21 See 'An Old Digger' to the Editor of *The
Standard and Transvaal Mining Chronicle*,
10 March 1888.

22 'Last Year's Finances', *Standard & Diggers'
News*, 30 January 1891.

23 'Local and General', *Standard & Diggers' News*,
16 April 1891.

24 Van Onselen, 'The World the Mineowners'
Made', *New Babylon, New Nineveh*, pp 1–5.

25 *Third Annual Report of the Witwatersrand
Chamber of Mines, 1891*, p 14.

26 'Rand Central Ore Reduction Company',
The Star, 30 August 1893; and on the Mine
Employees' Union, J and RE Simons,
Class and Colour in South Africa, 1850–1950
(Harmondsworth 1969) p 53 [hereafter,
Simons, *Class and Colour*].

27 Simons, *Class and Colour*, p 53.

28 See EB Rose, *The Truth about the Transvaal:
A Record of Facts based upon Twelve Years'
Residence in the Country* (London, 1902),
p 27 [hereafter, Rose, *The Truth about the
Transvaal*]; also, Simons, *Class and Colour*,
p 53.

29 See C van Onselen, *The Small Matter of a
Horse: The Life of 'Nongoloza' Mathebula,
1867–1948* (Pretoria 2008); and J Steinberg,
The Number (Cape Town 2004). On African
burglars, see, for example, *Standard & Diggers'
News*, 30 January 1890.

30 See reports in *Standard & Diggers' News*, 5 and
10 December 1889, and for a later, post-rail
link period, *Standard & Diggers' News*, 11 and
19 February 1895.

31 See *Fourth Annual Report of the Witwatersrand
Chamber of Mines, 1892*, p 66.

32 The earliest pawnbrokers operated without
licences – see *Standard & Diggers' News* and
The Star of 11 February 1891 and 8 July 1893.
At some point in the post-Jameson Raid this
changed and the 'Pawnbrokers Act' on the
Rand was proudly said to be more advanced
and progressive than that in England; see EB
Rose, *The Truth about the Transvaal*, p 43.

33 See M Pearson, *The Indian Ocean* (Abingdon
2003), pp 62–112; and 'Police News', *Standard
& Diggers' News*, 31 December 1889.

34 For pawnbroking problems see the cases of
Goldberg or Belcher, *Standard & Diggers'
News*, 8 July 1893 and 13 March 1895.
On second-hand clothes, see 'Life in
Johannesburg', *Diamond Fields Advertiser*,
14 March 1890. For attempts to expel
Chinese and Indian traders, see *Standard &
Diggers' News*, 13 and 17 February, 14 April
and 5 May 1890. On Jews 'fronting' for
Chinese traders see, for example, *The Star*,
15 March 1895.

35 On crime statistics for 1890 and the
progressive decline in the number of arrests,
see *Standard & Diggers' News*, 10 January 1891.
These can be compared with the figures for
1892 and the first quarter of 1893 as reported
in the same newspaper on 7 January and
29 July 1893 to provide trend lines for aspects
of white crime.

36 The papers of the day carried regular reports
on the value of gold shipped by various
banks – see, for example, 'Natal – Gold
Shipments', *Standard & Diggers' News*,
23 January 1892; also van Onselen, *Masked
Raiders*, pp 95–96. See also, R Ally, *Gold and
Empire: The Bank of England and South Africa's
Gold Producers, 1886–1926* (Johannesburg
1994), p 15.

37 See *The Star*, 27 January 1890 and
27 September 1890. For the wider context
see KSO Beavon, *Johannesburg: The Making
and Shaping of a City* (Pretoria 2004), p 28.

38 McLoughlin's career illustrates what happened in Rustenburg and Potchefstroom, while those of the highwaymen Hugh McKeone and William Cooper took in the western circuits of Klerksdorp, Vryburg and Mafeking; see van Onselen, *Masked Raiders,* Chapters 4 and 5, and below.

39 See van Onselen, *Masked Raiders,* pp 45–70.

40 See J McQuilton, *The Kelly Outbreak, 1878–1880: The Geographical Dimension of Social Banditry* (Melbourne 1979), p 172; and van Onselen, *Masked Raiders,* p 56.

41 See *Standard & Diggers' News,* 18 June 1890 and, for earlier public sympathy, 18 April 1890.

42 See DE Schutte to the Editor, *Standard & Diggers' News,* 11 October 1894; and van Onselen, *New Babylon, New Nineveh,* pp 66–67.

43 On brands, gun-dealers and revolvers, see items in *The Star,* 5 and 14 March 1895. This contradicts the view offered in AP Cartwright, *The Gold Miners* (Johannesburg 1983), p 111.

44 'The Lady and the Landlord', *The Star,* 2 September 1893. For more depression-era use of revolvers see *Standard & Diggers' News,* 14 December 1889; *The Star,* 12 February 1890; *Transvaal Observer,* 7 and 11 January 1891; *Standard & Diggers' News,* 23 and 27 June 1891; and *The Star,* 15 August 1891 and 9 and 13 January 1892.

45 'The Masks Law', *Standard & Diggers' News,* 29 May 1891. See also the complaints of a Kimberley judge as reported in the *Diamond Fields Advertiser,* 10 May 1890.

46 *Standard & Diggers' News,* 29 May 1891.

47 See, for example, the case of Marthinus Lotter, 'Robbery of Specie from the Mail Coach', *Standard & Diggers' News,* 16 July 1889. For more examples see *Standard & Diggers' News,* 23 January and 31 May 1892.

48 See 'Johannesburg and Pretoria Gaols', *The Star,* 15 March 1890.

49 See Letter to the Editor from 'Just Out' under the headline 'The Prison System' in *The Star,* 20 May 1895.

50 For a selection of attempts at escape see any of the following in *The Star:* 'Attempted Gaol-Breaking', 7 December 1891; 'Escape of a Convict', 22 March 1892; 'Escape of Prisoners', 10 February 1892; 'Affairs at the Gaol', 31 May 1892; 'More Gaol-Breaking', 4 June 1892; 'Escaping from Gaol', 11 June 1892; 'Attempted Escape', 20 August 1892, or the following, drawn from the *Standard & Diggers' News:* 'Another Escape of a Prisoner at Pretoria', 21 May 1890; 'A Daring Attempt', 22 June 1891; 'Attempted Gaol-Breaking', 23 January 1892; 'Escape of White Prisoners', 30 May 1892; or 'Attempted Gaol-Breaking', 17 April 1893.

51 See 'Johannesburg and Pretoria Gaols', *The Star,* 15 March 1890.

52 See, 'Barberton Notes', *Diamond Fields Advertiser,* 17 June 1890.

53 Such as the notorious Joseph Silver; see *Standard & Diggers' News,* 27 September 1899.

54 Menton's career can be traced in van Onselen, *Masked Raiders,* pp 43, 167 and 237; but see also 'Trouble in the Jail', 19 January 1895; and 'The Prison System', *The Star,* 20 May 1895; and for another Irish guard, 'Allowing Convicts to Escape', *The Star,* 17 August 1892.

55 See RSA, NASA, Pretoria, SS Vol 2479, Ref R111066A/90 for accusations and counter-accusations among the white prison staff.

56 'Unruly Convicts', *The Star,* 12 August 1893. On use of detonators and dynamite in Johannesburg, see items in *The Star,* 3 June 1890 and 30 March 1893.

57 'Gaol Inspection', *Standard & Diggers' News,* 14 July 1893.

58 Van Onselen, *Masked Raiders,* p 55. On the use of stocks, see 'Affairs at the Gaol', *The Star,* 31 May 1892. In Britain, the pillory was abolished in 1837 and stocks in 1872.

59 On the use of chains, see, for example, 'McKeone the Bank Robber', 21 September 1889, *Standard & Diggers' News;* 'To be Kept in Irons', 30 March 1892, and 'A Violent Convict', *The Star,* 31 May 1892.

60 See, for example, 'Annoying Prisoners', *The Star,* 21 May 1892.

61 'The Flogging of Whites', *The Star,* 16 May 1892.

62 'To Cat or Not to Cat', *Standard & Diggers' News,* 29 June 1891.

63 'The Cat', *Standard & Diggers' News,*

27 June 1891. These were the words of a
Mr Labuschagne, rather than those in the
memorial. On highwaymen at Heidelberg,
see, for example, 'Highway Robbery',
Standard & Diggers' News, 3 February 1891.
64 'Highway Robbery', *The Star*, 7 November
1893.
65 'Lashing a White Convict', *The Star*, 8 August
1892.
66 Kelly's career can be traced in RSA, Pretoria,

NASA, File SPR 5163/95 and in *The Star*,
23 January 1892; *Standard & Diggers' News*,
27 January 1892 and 30 May 1892; and then
again in *The Star*, 9 August 1893, 10 August
1893, 12 August 1893 and 24 September
1894. See also van Onselen, *Masked Raiders*,
pp 95–97.
67 'The Sentence and Lashing', *The Star*,
19 August 1892.
68 See van Onselen, *Masked Raiders*, pp 224–26.

Chapter Eleven: Metamorphosis

1 See 'Circuit Court', *The Star*, 18 July 1889.
2 See Republic of South Africa (RSA),
Pietermaritzburg, KwaZulu-Natal (KZN)
Archive Depot (KAD), Colonial Secretary's
Office (CSO), Vol 1213, File R 1391/1889 and
File R 1689/1889, which contains the records
of the preliminary examination [hereafter,
RSA, Pietermaritzburg, KAD, CSO, Vol 1213,
R 1689/1889, Prelim Exam].
3 On Mignonette's early career see RSA,
Pietermaritzburg, KAD, R 1689/1889 and,
in mid-career, 'Is it Amalgam' and 'The
Amalgam Case', *The Star*, 9 and 12 August
1893. See also agent J Treu's report to
JC Smuts of 2 August 1898 in the State
Attorney's 'Secret Minutes' in RSA, Pretoria,
SP Vol 193, GR 12/98 which suggests that
Ferguson and Mignonette were involved in
illicit gold dealings.
4 RSA, Pretoria, NASA, SP Vol 193, File GR
12/98, J Treu to JC Smuts, 2 August 1898.
5 For the context see C van Onselen, *Masked
Raiders: Irish Banditry in Southern Africa,
1880–1899* (Cape Town 2010), p 119 [hereafter,
van Onselen, *Masked Raiders*].
6 'Circuit Court', *Standard & Diggers' News*,
18 July 1889.
7 RSA, Pietermaritzburg, KAD, CSO, Vol 1213,
R 1689/1889, Prelim Exam.
8 On Burns and McCann in Steynsdorp and
Mozambique, see RSA, Pretoria, SP Vol 16,
File SPR 1131/89. On McCann in Natal see
RSA, Pietermaritzburg, KAD, CSO, Vol 1213,
File 1391/89 and 779/1889. McCann's

recapture, in Natal, is noted in *The Star*,
3 April 1889.
9 'Circuit Court', *The Star*, 18 July 1889.
10 On McCann's appeal see RSA, Pretoria,
NASA, SS Vol 2576, File 1469/90.
11 On Wolff's dealings with the police see
RSA, Pretoria, NASA, SP Vol 28, File
2595, Telegram from Public Prosecutor,
Johannesburg to State Attorney, 8 September
1891. On his later problems see RSA,
Pretoria, NASA, ZTPD, R 8/2856, Illiquid
Case, African Banking Corporation Limited
versus Victor Wolff, 1 February 1895. On
Wolff and Ferguson see RSA, Pretoria,
NASA, WLD 377/1909, Rex versus Jack
McLoughlin, 1 December 1909, p 67.
12 See 'Circuit Court – Dynamite Theft',
Standard & Diggers' News, 27 January 1892.
13 See van Onselen, *Masked Raiders*, p 98.
14 Ibid, pp 99–100.
15 *Standard & Diggers' News*, 1 February 1890.
16 *Diamond Fields Advertiser*, 3 May 1890.
17 'The Rustenburg Robbery', *The Star*,
12 August 1890.
18 See van Onselen, *Masked Raiders*, p 120.
19 For a list of Williams's aliases see 'The Great
Bank Robbery', *The Star*, 25 June 1894.
20 With the Rand's criminal sluice-gates
fully open, downstream Kimberley soon
experienced one or two attempts at safe-
cracking and other robberies that may have
been more sophisticated than those to which
it was accustomed. See, for example, *Diamond
Fields Advertiser*, 23 May 1890.

21 'Burglary at Rustenburg', *Standard & Diggers'
News*, 21 May 1890; and 'Robbery at
Rustenburg', *The Star*, 24 May 1890.

22 *Standard & Diggers' News*, 21 May 1890.

23 *The Star*, 24 May 1890.

24 See especially AH Roskell, *Six Years of a
Tramp's Life in South Africa* (Cape Town 1886).
I am indebted to Paul la Hausse for having
drawn my attention to this source.

25 'A Chequered Career', *Potchefstroom Budget*,
6 August 1890.

26 'Daring Robbery at the Convent',
Potchefstroom Budget, 28 June 1890.

27 'Potchefstroom News', *Standard & Diggers'
News*, 28 June 1890.

28 'Daring Robbery at the Convent',
Potchefstroom Budget, 28 June 1890.

29 'The Convent Robbery', *Potchefstroom Budget*,
2 July 1890.

30 'The Gaol Outbreak', *Potchefstroom Budget*,
30 July 1890. For the official view see
RSA, Pretoria, NASA, SS Vol 2458, File R
10475/90 and SP Vol 21, File SPR 2182/90.

31 'The Gaol Outbreak', *Potchefstroom Budget*,
30 July 1890.

32 'A Successful Operation' and 'Local and
Other Items – Still Bad', in the *Potchefstroom

Budget*, 6 and 20 August 1890.

33 See RSA, Pretoria, NASA, File SPR 2597/94,
'The State v William James Kelly alias WJ
Read alias LV Waters alias John Williams'; and
'The Great Bank Note Robbery', *The Star*,
25 June 1894.

34 RSA, Pretoria, NASA, WLD 377/1909, Rex
versus McLoughlin, 1 December 1909, p 72.

35 See JH Gear and HM Salmon, 'The
Johannesburg Hospital: A Historical Outline
of the First Fifty Years', *South African Medical
Journal*, October 1965, pp 882–91 [hereafter,
Gear and Salmon, 'The Johannesburg
Hospital'].

36 See RSA, Pretoria, NASA, WLD 377/1909,
Rex versus McLoughlin, 1 December
1909, evidence of John van Niekerk, p 50;
and Gear and Salmon, 'The Johannesburg
Hospital', p 885.

37 Gear and Salmon, 'The Johannesburg
Hospital', p 885.

38 In relation to the nursing sisters at the
Johannesburg Hospital, see also RSA,
Pretoria, NASA, WLD 377/1909, Rex versus
McLoughlin, 1 December 1909, evidence of
J McLoughlin, p 63.

Chapter Twelve: Humiliation and Rage

1 On the limits of biography in this context
see H Lee, *Body Parts: Essays on Life Writing*
(London 2005).

2 See S Jensen, B Krebs, J Nielsen and
P Rasmussen, 'Immediate and Long-Term
Phantom Limb Pain in Amputees: Incidence,
Clinical Characteristics and Relationship to
Pre-Amputation Limb Pain', *Pain* Vol 21, No
3, 1985, pp 267–78; K MacIver, DM Lloyd, S
Kelly, N Roberts and T Nurmikko, 'Phantom
Limb Pain, Cortical Reorganisation and
the Therapeutic Effect of Mental Imagery',
Brain, Vol 131, No 8, 2008, pp 2181–91; and
VS Ramachandran and W Hirstein, 'The
Perception of Phantom Limbs', *Brain* Vol 11,
No 9, 1998, pp 1603–30. I am indebted
to Prof Robert Kaplan for drawing my

attention to these sources.

3 See, for example, the case of Tom Logan as
reported in the *Bulawayo Chronicle*, 19 July
1892.

4 There is a long-standing, albeit inconclusive,
link adduced between the Irish and alcohol.
See, for example, L Greenslade, M Pearson
and M Madden, 'A Good Man's Fault:
Alcohol and Irish People at Home and
Abroad', *Alcohol and Alcoholism*, Vol 30, No
4, 1994, pp 406–17; or D Walsh, 'Alcoholism
and the Irish', *Alcohol and Alcoholism*, Vol 6,
No 2, 1972, pp 4–47.

5 Republic of South Africa (RSA), Pretoria,
National Archives of South Africa (NASA),
Witwatersrand Local Division (WLD),
377/1909, Rex v Jack McLoughlin, p 68,

evidence of McLoughlin [hereafter, Rex v McLoughlin].

6 The number of licensed canteens on the Witwatersrand rose from 147 in 1888 to 552 by 1892 – see C van Onselen, 'The World the Mine Owners Made', *New Babylon, New Nineveh: Everyday Life on the Witwatersrand, 1886–1914* (Johannesburg 2001), p 7.

7 'Attempted Murder', *Standard & Diggers' News*, 11 May 1891.

8 It was not unheard of for criminal elements drawn from Manchester to mimic elements of working-class culture in this way. John O'Brien, keen to arrange a Christmas Eve reception for a friend about to be released from gaol, 'started a sort of soiree' and collected 13 shillings which he spent on liquor before Williams aka WJ Kelly got out of prison. See 'A Chequered Career', *Potchefstroom Budget*, 6 August 1890.

9 Rex v McLoughlin, evidence of McLoughlin, p 71.

10 'McLoughlin's Friends', *The Star*, 29 January 1895.

11 On Hollander see RSA, Pretoria, NASA, SP Vol 12A, Telegram from Public Prosecutor, Johannesburg, to State Attorney, Pretoria, 9 June 1888 and SP Vol 59, Chief Detective, Johannesburg to State Attorney, 26 December 1894. Also 'Life on the Witwatersrand', *Diamond Fields Advertiser*, 28 December 1887.

12 See United Kingdom (UK), *Census 1861* and *1871*, RG9/2871, Folio 50, p 6 and RG10/1043, Folio 153, p 23.

13 For Higgins's criminal background see 'Gambling Hells' and 'Raid on a Gambling House' in *The Star*, 19 August and 14 December 1891; and, especially, 'Gambling Hells' in the *Transvaal Observer* of 16 November 1891. On his later career see 'The Post Office Case – Dismissed', *The Star*, 25 June 1892.

14 See court proceedings as reported in *The Star* of 3 September 1891.

15 See reports in *Standard & Diggers' News* – 'Attempted Murder – Sunday Sport' and 'Attempted Murder' which appeared on 5 and 11 May 1891; and *The Star*, 3 September 1891.

16 'Attempted Murder', *Standard & Diggers' News*, 11 May 1891.

17 On the link between self-restraint and the idea of masculinity see, amongst others, G Mosse, *The Image of Man: The Creation of Modern Masculinity* (Oxford 1996), p 15

18 See S Carroll (ed), *Cultures of Violence: Interpersonal Violence in Historical Perspective* (Basingstoke 2007), pp 4, 20 and 226.

19 On Edna Lyall's novel – not to be confused with Byron's poem 'When We Two Parted' – being discovered in McLoughlin's cell, see 'A Daring Attempt', *Standard & Diggers News'*, 22 June 1891.

20 See C van Onselen, *Masked Raiders: Irish Banditry in Southern Africa, 1880–1899* (Cape Town 2010), pp 45-70 [hereafter, van Onselen, *Masked Raiders*].

21 On prisons at the start of the recession, see 'Johannesburg and Pretoria Gaols' and 'Crime' in *The Star*, 15 March and 3 August 1890.

22 See 'A Slippery Customer', *Standard & Diggers' News*, 25 and 31 March 1892.

23 'A Daring Attempt', *Standard & Diggers' News*, 22 June 1891.

24 'A Daring Escape' and 'The Prison Breakers', *Standard & Diggers' News*, 22 and 24 June 1891.

25 See 'The Circuit Court', *Standard & Diggers' News*, 18 August 1891; and a report from the *Rand Daily Mail* carried in the *Hawera and Normanby Star* (New Zealand), 28 August 1909, in which Van den Bergh recalled the break-in although not the attempted arson. See also RSA, Pretoria, NASA, SS 4039, R 15508/93, Edwards and Harding, plea for remission of sentence, 5 December 1893.

26 'The Circuit Court', *Standard & Diggers' News*, 18 August 1891; and *The Star*, 3 September 1891.

27 Sir JG Kotzé, *Memoirs and Reminiscences,* Vol 2 (Cape Town nd), pp 143–55; and for the wider context, van Onselen, *Masked Raiders*, pp 80–92.

28 See van Onselen, *Masked Raiders*, pp 83–87.

29 Ibid, pp 156–59.

30 'Visitors to the Capital' and 'They May Flit', *The Star*, 31 October 1891. On Harding, who appears to have been reasonably well

educated, as might be expected of one who started his career as a clerk, see RSA, Pretoria, NASA, SP Vol 4039, Ref 15508/93, C Harding to State Attorney, 21 November 1893.

31 Van Onselen, *Masked Raiders*, pp 102–3.

32 'They May Flit', *The Star*, 31 October 1891.

33 Van Onselen, *Masked Raiders*, pp 88–89.

34 Ibid, p 89.

35 Ibid, pp 156–59.

36 Ibid, pp 90–91.

37 'Mutiny in Pretoria Gaol' and 'Lash for Mutinous Gaolbirds', *Cape Argus*, 10 and 11 November 1891. The legislation was forthcoming six months later, in mid-1892.

38 On MJ de Beer, see Rex vs McLoughlin 1909, pp 3 and 51.

Chapter Thirteen: Regaining Caste

1 See Chapters 11–27 of F Vane, *Back to the Mines; Tailings from the Randt* (London 1902) which provides an excellent overview of the 1889–92 recession [hereafter, Vane, *Back to the Mines*].

2 See C van Onselen, 'The World the Mine Owners Made', in *New Babylon, New Nineveh: Everyday Life on the Witwatersrand, 1886–1914* (Cape Town 2001), pp 12–16 [hereafter, van Onselen, *New Babylon, New Nineveh*].

3 See, for example, 'As in a Looking Glass – Some Johannesburg Jottings', *Standard & Diggers' News,* 1 April 1893.

4 See C van Onselen, 'The Witches of Suburbia: Domestic Service on the Witwatersrand, 1890–1914', in *New Babylon, New Nineveh*, pp 207–212.

5 See 'Mr Searelle's Chorus Girls' and, among many others, 'The Fracas at the Music Hall', in *The Star*, 12 June 1890 and 23 August 1893.

6 See C van Onselen , 'Prostitutes and Proletarians, 1886–1914', *New Babylon, New Nineveh*, pp 109–15.

7 See, for example, 'Johannesburg by Night', *Standard & Diggers' News*, 24 July 1893.

8 On barmaid indiscretions, see, for example, 'Matrimonial Troubles', *Standard & Diggers' News*, 7 January 1890, and 'She Indignantly Refused' and 'The Green-Eyed Monster' in *The Star*, 5 March 1892 and 2 April 1892. On Mr JM Frost, 'a mechanic' and his wife, 'Miss Martin', the barmaid at the 'Welsh Harp' and the Hon AJ Bethell MP, see 'Serious Assault, *The Star*, 2 July 1892 and 'Serious Assault',

Standard & Diggers' News , 15 November 1892.

9 See van Onselen, 'Prostitutes and Proletarians', *New Babylon, New Nineveh*, p 113.

10 On the 1886–94 era see ibid, pp 112–15; and, on the post-1895 era, C van Onselen, *The Fox and the Flies: The Criminal Empire of the Whitechapel Murderer* (London 2007), pp 160–80.

11 'The Dance at the Garrick', *Standard & Diggers' News*, 18 June 1890, and 'Fight the Crowd', *The Star*, 17 February 1893. On the link between alcohol and prostitution see reports on the Liquor Licensing Board sittings in *Standard & Diggers' News*, 20 March 1895. On brothels see, for example, 'Sunday Night Scandal', *The Star*, 30 October 1893.

12 See Chapter 22 in Vane, *Back to the Mines*.

13 See M Clapson, *A Bit of a Flutter: Popular Gambling and English Society, c 1823–1961* (Manchester 1992), p 4; and R McKibbin, 'Working Class Gambling in Britain, 1880–1939', *Past and Present*, No 82 (February 1979), pp 147–48.

14 See the *Diggers' News and Witwatersrand Advertiser* of 21 May, 20 June and 20 July 1889. During the gambling craze of 1893, the tattersalls were crowded from 'morn to night' and a leading bookmakers, WA Phillips, organised a sweepstake with 10 000 subscribers and a first prize of £5 000. See 'Tailings' and 'The Turf' in *The Star* of 22 August and 14 November 1893.

15 See 'Sundays, Horses, Bets', *Standard & Diggers' News*, 8 August 1891.

16 'The Gambling Raid', *The Star*, 11 February 1893. For earlier examples of organised criminal acts see 'Gambling Hells' in the *Transvaal Observer*, 13 and 16 November 1891; or *The Star*, 19 August and 14 December 1891.

17 See 'Rats and Mice', *Standard & Diggers' News*, 5 December 1889, and, on 'ratting' itself, items in *The Star*, 1, 15 and 24 May or 16 August 1893.

18 See, for example, 'Dog-Fighting' in *The Star*, 19 and 26 September 1891; and on other organised dog-fighting, 'The Kennel', *The Star*, 17 June 1893. Once the recession lifted, 'respectable' dog-lovers attempted to increase the social distance between themselves and the riff-raff by taking the 'sport' out of the pubs and founding new, outdoor-based institutions. See, for example, 'The Kennel' and 'Coursing' in *The Star*, 22 April and 29 July 1893.

19 'The Prize Ring', *The Star*, 26 July 1893.

20 'Sequel to the Fight', *The Star*, 7 July 1893.

21 On choices between London Prize Ring and Queensberry Rules and JR Couper putting on an exhibition to illustrate the difference between the two, see 'Prize Ring' in *The Star*, 2 May and 21 August 1893.

22 See, among others, items about the Newcastle Bar in *Standard & Diggers' News* of 16 November 1889 and 31 December 1889. For the police and a prize fight in 'private rooms', see, for example, 'A Prize Fight', *Standard & Diggers News'*, 6 April 1891.

23 'A Knock Out – Fifty Pounds a Side', *Standard & Diggers' News*, 9 June 1890. For the 'Malone – Holloway Fight', on a farm beside the Klip River, see *The Star*, 4 July 1893. It was this fight that outraged the authorities and resulted in the prosecution of several local notables – see 'Sequel to the Fight', *The Star*, 7 July 1893.

24 See any of the following: 'Prize Fight' in *The Star*, 23 April and 1 May 1889; 'Prize Fight', *Standard & Diggers' News*, 9 June 1890; 'Fight', *Transvaal Observer*, 16 February 1891; 'Fisticuffs', *The Star*, 18 June 1891; or 'The Ring – Midnight Pugilists', *The Star*, 19 September 1891.

25 'What No Duel After All'? and 'A Tame Ending', *The Star*, 13 and 14 January 1894; and 'Plaatselijk en Algemeen', *De Volksstem*, 17 January 1893.

26 *Standard & Diggers' News,* 21 May 1895.

27 On Irish 'boxing' amidst a faction-fighting tradition, see C Conley, 'The Agreeable Recreation of Fighting', *Journal of Social History*, Vol 33, No 1, Autumn 1999, p 62.

28 See J Belich, *Replenishing the Earth: The Settler Revolution and the Rise of the Anglo World* (Oxford 2009).

29 On Australian immigration to the Witwatersrand, see, for example, *The Star*, 22 August 1893; and increase in postal deliveries between the countries as reported in the *Standard & Diggers' News*, 18 May 1895.

30 See *Standard & Diggers' News*, 9 September 1893.

31 For bookmakers, see 'The Turf', *The Star*, 10 April 1893. By January 1893, there were sufficient Australians in town for WA Phillips to announce that he would run a sweepstake on the Melbourne Cup later that year, *The Star*, 14 January 1893. On billiard players, see items in *The Star*, 18 May, 26 June and 5 August 1893. On Irish-Australian boxers, including Jimmy Murphy and Owen Sullivan, see items in *The Star*, 17 April and 2 September 1893.

32 See also D Blackburn and WW Caddell, *Secret Service in South Africa* (London 1911), p 160 [hereafter, Blackburn and Caddell, *Secret Service*].

33 See C van Onselen, *Masked Raiders: Irish Banditry in Southern Africa, 1880–1899* (Cape Town 2010), pp 79–80 [hereafter, van Onselen, *Masked Raiders*].

34 'Burglarious Implements', *The Star*, 24 December 1892.

35 See especially van Onselen, 'The Parameters of Popular Support' in *Masked Raiders*, pp 139–42.

36 See 'Burglary at Boksburg' and 'The Florida Robbery', *Standard & Diggers' News*, 17 June and 24 August 1892.

37 See van Onselen, *Masked Raiders*, p 142.

38 See especially L Herschbach, 'Prosthetic Reconstruction: Making the Industry, Re-Making the Body, Modelling the Nation', *History Workshop Journal*, No 44, 1997,

pp 23–57.

39 See Republic of South Africa (RSA), Pretoria, National Archives of South Africa (NASA), Witwatersrand Local Division (WLD), Vol 377/09, Rex versus Jack McLoughlin, pp 4 and 64 [hereafter Rex vs McLoughlin].

40 See, for example, 'A Sensational Saturday Night', *The Star*, 28 January 1895. The author, Louis Cohen, an author of non-fiction, was not beyond exploiting this myth – see United States of America, New Haven, Yale University Library, AC 565, Box 7, Folder 75, Scrapbook and manuscript for his work on Johannesburg and Kimberley, pp 12–13.

41 See P Haining, *The Legend and Bizarre Crimes of Spring Heeled Jack* (London 1977).

42 The terror-inducing myth or reality evoked by the artificial hand can also be traced in Blackburn and Caddell, *Secret Service*, pp 163–67.

43 See Rex vs McLoughlin, pp 64 and 72.

44 See 'By One of His Pals', *Standard & Diggers' News*, 2 February 1895.

45 'Burglarious Instruments – Curious Defence', *The Star*, 24 December 1892. I have been unable to find any sequel to the appeal.

46 'Audacious Burglary', *The Star*, 3 January 1893.

47 'The Arrests', *The Star*, 3 January 1893.

48 'Police Returns', *The Star*, 7 January 1893. By late 1892, the Chamber of Mines had already appointed Captain George J Couper, brother of the more famous boxer, JR Couper, to try and combat gold thefts on the Rand – see, for example 'Amalgam Theft on the Rand', *Standard & Diggers' News*, 22 October 1892. The panic around the issue culminated in the aborted Gold Theft Bill of 1893 – see HJ and RE Simons, *Class and Colour in South Africa, 1850–1950* (Harmondsworth 1969), pp 54–55. By 1894, with the bill defeated, the situation was said to be out of control – see Blackburn and Caddell, *Secret Service*, pp 127–28. Ferguson was later dismissed for illegal dealings in gold – see WK Hancock, *Smuts, 1: The Sanguine Years, 1870–1919* (Cambridge 1962), p 80, although there is other evidence which suggests that this might be incorrect.

49 These proceedings can be traced in *The Star*, in items on 3, 5, 14, 16, 19, 21 and 22 January 1893.

Chapter Fourteen: The Lures of Domesticity

1 See C van Onselen, 'The Main Reef Road into the Working Class' in *New Babylon, New Nineveh: Everyday Life on the Witwatersrand, 1886–1914* (Johannesburg 2001), pp 309–67.

2 See 'Raid on a Gambling Den', *The Star*, 31 July 1893; and, for the wider context, 'Free Chinese in the Transvaal' in KL Harris, 'A History of the Chinese in South Africa to 1912', D Phil thesis, University of South Africa, 1998.

3 'The Mohammedan New Year', *The Star*, 20 July 1893.

4 See Republic of South Africa (RSA), Pretoria, National Archives of South Africa (NASA), Witwatersrand Local Division (WLD), File 377/1909, Rex vs J McLoughlin, 1909, pp 69 and 71 [hereafter Rex vs McLoughlin]. For criminal violence on Commissioner Street, see, for example, C van Onselen, *The Fox and the Flies* (London 2008), p 154.

5 'Pickpockets in Trouble', *The Star*, 22 September 1893. The report mentions the 'Red Lamp' pub but this is almost certainly an incorrect reference to the Red Lion Beer Hall.

6 'Attempted Gaol-Breaking', *The Star*, 17 April 1893.

7 This composite picture of Sarah Fredericks/ McNeil is constructed from two principal archival sources – RSA, Pretoria, NASA, Gov Vol 1025, File 75/15/06, Affidavit 'B', sworn by Sarah McNeil (née Fredericks) at Johannesburg, 24 November 1906; and evidence of Sarah McNeil, Rex vs McLoughlin, 1909, pp 8–19. See also, in the

Standard & Diggers' News, 'Serious Charges
against Women', 'A Maiden Tribute', 'A
Maiden Tribute' [again] and 'The Fairy Four'
– on 29 August, 30 August, 2 September and
6 September 1893.

8 Rex vs McLoughlin, 1909, evidence of Rosie
Petersen, p 6.

9 United Kingdom (UK), Stafford,
Staffordshire Record Office (SRO), File
CES/3/2/8/2, Werrington Industrial School,
Licence on Discharge Register, entry for
George Stevenson, discharged 1885.

10 UK, *Census 1871,* RG10/2820, Folio 57, p 1,
entry for hamlet of Hixon, Parish of Stowe
and Colwich.

11 UK, Stafford, SRO, CES/3/2/8/2,
Werrington, Discharge Register, Letter from
Joseph Stevenson, 12 November 1886, noting
the enlistment of his son in the army.

12 On Parker, see 'A Little Mill – Ingleton-
Parker', *The Star,* 5 August 1893.

13 See items on a 'A Slippery Customer',
Standard & Diggers' News, 25 and 31 March
1892.

14 RSA, Pretoria, NASA, SP Vol 34, File
SPR 312/92 and R143/93, Appeals to the
State President from J Davidson dated
14 November 1892 and 2 January 1893.

15 For a selection of private 'feuds' informing
arranged fights manifesting the 'delayed
gratification' considered central to 'civilised
life' in the nineteenth century, see, for
example, 'Prize Fight', *Standard & Diggers'
News,* 6 April and reports on the 'Prize Ring'
in *The Star,* 19 June and 22 August 1893.

16 The two biggest fights that winter season
were Barney Malone v James Holloway (see
'Malone-Holloway Fight', *The Star,* 4 July
1893) and 'Darkey' Parker v Ingleton ('A
Little Mill', *The Star,* 5 August 1893).

17 See Rex vs McLoughlin, 1909, evidence of
Harry Lobb, p 35.

18 See 'Prize Ring', *The Star,* 24 May, 1893.

19 'Prize Ring – Steele vs Lobb', *The Star,*
25 May 1893.

20 Stevenson was seconded by Glanville and
another who did not wish to be named,
and Lobb by Garcial and Glendenning,
see 'Prize Ring – Steele v Lobb', *The Star,*
25 May 1893. For boxers in trouble with the

law, including Garcial, see, for example, 'The
Commissioner St Row' and 'Pugilists and the
Police', *The Star,* 24 and 26 September 1893.

21 Rex vs McLoughlin, 1909, evidence of
McLoughlin, p 68.

22 Rex vs McLoughlin, 1909, evidence of Nasa
Dien Burgess (cab driver) and Abdol Gesont
(tailor), pp 27-30 and pp 37–38.

23 C van Onselen, *Masked Raiders: Irish Banditry
in Southern Africa, 1880–1899* (Cape Town
2010), pp 115 [hereafter, van Onselen, *Masked
Raiders*].

24 P Maguire and CM Parkes, 'Coping with
Loss: Surgery and Loss of Body Parts', *British
Medical Journal,* 1998, 316, p 1086.

25 Rex vs McLoughlin, 1909, p 52, evidence of
Smorenberg.

26 Rex vs McLoughlin, 1909, evidence of
McLoughlin, pp 63–70 (emphasis added).

27 RSA, Pretoria, NASA, Gov Vol 1025, File
75/15/06, Affidavit by Sarah McNeil, signed
at Johannesburg, 24 November 1906.

28 On Langlaagte's attractions for a safecracker,
see 'Another Five-Figure Return', *The Star,*
7 November 1893. It may be significant that,
when a barman was murdered at Langlaagte
a year later, it was rumoured that he may
have fallen foul of the McLoughlin gang. See
'Another Ghastly Murder' and 'The Murder
of Casey – The Champ D'Or Deep Gang' in
The Star, 4 and 5 March 1893.

29 This unusual drop off in underworld
activity may have been a by-product of
McLoughlin and Stevenson's stressful
relationship. See also van Onselen, *Masked
Raiders,* p 116.

30 'Serious Charges against Women', 'A Maiden
Tribute', another – 'A Maiden Tribute' – and
'The Fairy Four', in the *Standard & Diggers'
News* of 29 August, 30 August, 2 September
and 6 September 1893.

31 'Boxing – Sullivan's Entertainment', *The Star,*
9 October 1893.

32 See RSA, Pretoria, NASA, Gov Vol 1025, File
75/15/06, Affidavit by Sarah McNeil, signed
at Johannesburg, 24 November 1906.

33 Rex vs McLoughlin, 1909, Evidence of
McLoughlin, p 68.

34 Ibid.

35 See RSA, Pretoria, NASA, SP Vol 4039, File

SPR 15508/93, Remission of Sentence, W
Edwards and C Harding, 4 December 1893.
36 Rex vs McLoughlin, 1909, p 68, evidence
of McLoughlin.

37 RSA, Pretoria, NASA, Gov Vol 1025, File
75/15/06, Affidavit by Sarah McNeil, signed
at Johannesburg, 24 November 1906.

Chapter Fifteen: Retreat to the New Frontiers

1 'The Pretoria Railway Robbery', *The Star*,
18 April 1894.
2 Ibid.
3 Ibid.
4 Ibid.
5 Ibid. The words attributed here to
McLoughlin are as told to Detective
Charles Mynott some years later. See
Republic of South Africa (RSA), Pretoria,
National Archives of South Africa (NASA),
Witwatersrand Local Division (WLD),
Vol 377/1909, Rex vs McLoughlin,
1909, evidence of Mynott, pp 3–4, and
McLoughlin, p 69 [hereafter, Rex vs
McLoughlin, 1909].
6 Rex vs McLoughlin, 1909, evidence of
Mynott, p 4.
7 'The Pretoria Railway Robbery', *The Star*,
18 April 1894.
8 Rex vs McLoughlin, 1909, evidence of
Mynott, p 4.
9 See Rex vs McLoughlin, 1909, evidence of
Mynott, p 4; and 'Double Murder', *The Star*,
28 January 1895.
10 Rex vs McLoughlin, 1909, evidence of
Mynott, p 4.
11 On Peace, see J O'Neill, *Crime City:
Manchester's Victorian Underworld* (Manchester
2008), pp 212–21; and HB Irving, *A Book
of Remarkable Criminals* (London 1918). On
McLoughlin being seen locally as a latter-day
Charles Peace, see 'Where are the Police',
The Star, 28 January 1895.
12 See 'Double Murder', *The Star*, 28 January
1895; and an item in *Land en Volk*, 31 January
1895; also, Rex vs McLoughlin, 1909, p 4,
evidence of Mynott.
13 Rex vs McLoughlin, 1909, p 4, evidence
of Mynott; and 'Double Murder', *The Star*,
28 January 1895.

14 See Rex vs McLoughlin, 1909, p 4, evidence
of Mynott.
15 See especially F Vane, *Back to the Mines or
Tailings from the Randt* (London 1902).
16 See RSA, Pretoria, NASA, Gov Vol 1025,
File 75/15/a Affidavit 'B', by Sarah McNeil
(Fredericks), sworn before WS Cohn, Justice
of the Peace, Johannesburg, 16 November
1906; and Rex vs McLoughlin, 1909, p 4,
evidence of Mynott.
17 Rex vs McLoughlin, 1909, p 53, evidence of
Ferguson.
18 RSA, Pretoria, NASA, Gov Vol 1025, File
75/15/a Affidavit 'B', by Sarah McNeil,
16 November 1906.
19 Ibid.
20 Ibid. See also, 'The Pretoria Railway
Robbery', *The Star*, 18 April 1894 – 'In
cross-examination witness [Stevenson] gave
as his reasons for turning State Evidence, that
he was wrongly dealt with, and that Howard
endeavoured to fix another crime on him, of
which he was innocent'.
21 On criminal elements in the 'Pioneer
Column' see C van Onselen, *Masked Raiders:
Irish Banditry in Southern Africa, 1880–1889*
(Cape Town 2010), p 229.
22 See *Standard & Diggers' News* – 'Burglars
Abroad', 10 February 1891, 'Burglary at
Simpson's', 11 February 1891, 'Jewellery
Robbery', 27 February 1891 and 'Caught at
Last', 10 April 1891. The internationalisation
of South African crimes and its place in the
wider world awaits its historian. No one
should hold their breath.
23 Rex vs McLoughlin, 1909, p 69, evidence of
McLoughlin.
24 Ibid.
25 United States of America (USA), New
Haven, Yale University Library, Ac 565, Box 7,

Folder 75, Louis Cohen Scrapbooks.

26 See Rex vs McLoughlin, 1909, p 63; and S Glass, *The Matabele War* (London 1968).

27 See Rex vs McLoughlin, 1909, p 72, evidence of McLoughlin.

28 USA, New Haven, Yale University Library, Ac 565, Box 7, Folder 75, Louis Cohen Scrapbooks. See also 'Daring Double Murder', *Cape Argus*, 31 January 1895 and items in *The Star*, 28 January 1895.

29 See, 'Local and General' in the *Rhodesian Herald*, 1 and 8 June 1894, and 24 August 1894.

30 'The Pretoria Railway Robbery', *The Star*, 18 April 1894.

31 See Rex vs McLoughlin, 1909, pp 69–71, evidence of McLoughlin.

32 'Double Murder', *The Star*, 2 February 1895.

33 RSA, Pretoria, NASA, Gov Vol 1025, File 75/15/a Affidavit 'B', by Sarah McNeil, 16 November 1906.

34 Ibid.

35 Rex vs McLoughlin, 1909, p 67, evidence of McLoughlin.

36 USA, New Haven, Yale University Library, Ac 565, Box 7, Folder 75, Louis Cohen Scrapbooks.

37 J Tempelhoff and H Nemudzivadi, 'Riding the Storm of Change: Makhado, Venda and the South African Republic, 1864–1895', *New Contree*, No 45, September 1999, pp 101–14 [hereafter, Tempelhoff and Nemudzivida, 'Riding the Storm of Change].

38 See A Kirkaldy, *Capturing the Soul: The Vhavenda and the Missionaries* (Pretoria 2005), pp 129–40 [hereafter Kirkaldy, *Capturing the Soul*] and 'General Joubert's Ultimatum', *The Star*, 1 February 1895.

39 Tempelhoff and Nemudzivadi, 'Riding the Storm of Change', pp 104–5; and Kirkaldy, *Capturing the Soul*, pp 127–28. On Makhado and the Maxim gun, see D Blackburn and WW Caddell, *Secret Service in South Africa* (London 1911), p 94 [hereafter, Blackburn and Caddell, *Secret Service*].

40 Tempelhoff and Nemudzivadi, 'Riding the Storm of Change', pp 105–6; and Kirkaldy, *Capturing the Soul*, pp 21–22.

41 See JWN Tempelhoff, *Die Okkupasiestelsel in die Distrik Soutpansberg* (Pretoria 1997),

pp 71–131.

42 Kirkaldy, *Capturing the Soul*, p 30.

43 See JT Hyslop, *The Notorious Syndicalist JT Bain: A Scottish Rebel in Colonial South Africa* (Johannesburg 2004).

44 Blackburn and Caddell, *Secret Service*, p 91.

45 Ibid, p 94.

46 Hickey's career prior to his involvement with Makhado in 1894 is unknown, but see RSA, Pretoria, NASA, KG Vol 141, Ref CR 5425/95 and CR 5426/95. In early 1899 Hickey was selling alcohol and dynamite to the Swazis – see SS Vol 7733, Ref RA 2992/99 – and later that year was accused of high treason by the Boers – see SP Vol 220, Ref 9823/99.

47 Blackburn and Caddell, *Secret Service*, p 105. It should be noted, however, that Blackburn, who was referring to McLoughlin, has his chronology wrong in claiming that, in 1894, McLoughlin was 'wanted for murder' – something that was only true after late January 1895.

48 Tempelhoff and Nemudzivadi, 'Riding the Storm of Change', p 114.

49 TV Bulpin, *Storm over the Transvaal* (Cape Town 1955), p 244 [hereafter Bulpin, *Storm over the Transvaal*]. As with Louis Cohen, however, Bulpin gets the dart on the board but, because he does not reveal his sources, often seems to miss the bull's-eye. In this case, however, the outlines of the tale can be traced in Blackburn and Caddell, *Secret Service* – an account not without problems of its own.

50 See Blackburn and Caddell, *Secret Service*, pp 163–64; and Bulpin, *Storm over the Transvaal*, p 244.

51 Blackburn and Caddell, *Secret Service*, pp 163–67.

52 Ibid, p 163.

53 See 'General Joubert's Ultimatum', *The Star*, 1 February 1895.

54 Blackburn and Caddell, *Secret Service*, p 90; Tempelhoff and Nemudzivadi, 'Riding the Storm of Change', p 112; and 'General Joubert's Ultimatum', *The Star*, 1 February 1895.

55 Tempelhoff and Nemudzivadi, 'Riding the Storm of Change', p 112.

56 See 'Dr Krause's Dismissal', 'The Two State Attorneys', and 'A Strange Appointment', all in *The Star,* 6 January 1894. Also, in the same newspaper, 'The New Police Commissioner', 11 February 1895.
57 Evidence of LB Donovan to 'The Detective Enquiry', *The Star,* 15 May 1895.
58 Evidence of A Trimble to 'The Detective Enquiry', *The Star,* 17 May 1895.

59 'Where are the Police', *The Star,* 2 February 1895.
60 See RSA, Pretoria, NASA, SPR Vol 1364/95, Telegram, Landdrost, Pietersburg to State Attorney, Pretoria, 21 February 1895; and a hand-written note, a few days later, from Public Prosecutor, Pietersburg, to State Attorney, Criminal Division, 25 February 1895.

Chapter Sixteen: The Grammar of Justice

1 See 'Champ Deep Safe Robbery – McLoughlin, Harding & Co', *The Star,* 9 March 1895.
2 The detective department's shortcomings in the capital, including in relation to McLoughlin, can be traced through the evidence presented to a commission of enquiry that met in mid-1895 then closed *sine die.* See the evidence as reported in *The Star* between 7 and 18 May 1895. On the Australian-Irish connection in Pretoria, see 'Detective Inquiry' in *The Star,* 7 and 17 May 1895.
3 'By one of his Pals', *Standard & Diggers' News,* 2 February 1895.
4 Republic of South Africa (RSA), Pretoria. National Archives of South Africa (NASA), Witwatersrand Local Division (WLD), WLD 377/1909, Rex vs Jack McLoughlin, 1909, evidence of Sarah McNeil, pp 10 and 16–17 [hereafter, Rex vs McLoughlin, 1909].
5 Ibid, p 11.
6 Ibid, p 19.
7 Ibid, pp 16 and 18.
8 This accords with McLoughlin's claim in Rex vs McLoughlin, 1909, at p 63. A close study of the trial record would indicate that he spent most of the time at Ahmed's but, as he suggests, may later have moved briefly to the German beer hall in President Street.
9 See Rex vs McLoughlin, 1909, p 66.
10 Ibid, p 66, evidence of McLoughlin; and pp 48–49, evidence of Dr J van Niekerk.
11 Ibid, p 10, evidence of Sarah McNeil.
12 This picture and the detail is all taken from

Rex vs McLoughlin, 1909.
13 On Gill see 'Daring Double Murder', *Cape Argus,* 31 January 1895.
14 As Emsley argues, for the English it was 'dishonourable to take an unfair advantage'. See C Emsley, *Hard Men: The English and Violence since 1750* (London 2005), pp 13 and 41. Despite having long since passed their heyday, duels and duelling remained a subject of enduring interest in English and colonial societies. In late 1897 and early 1898, for example, the London-based *Cornhill Magazine* ran a series on 'Duels of all Nations', which were reproduced, in parts, in Australia and New Zealand. See, for example, *Australian Town and Country Journal,* 22 January 1898 or the *Otago Witness* of 29 December 1897.
15 Later a rumour got afoot that, at about that time, McLoughlin had attended a dance at the Height's Hotel in the town centre where 'nearly the whole of the detective department' was present. See 'Double Murder', *The Star,* 2 February 1895.
16 McLoughlin's weapon is identified as a Colt in 'A Sensational Saturday Night', *The Star,* 28 January 1895.
17 Rex vs McLoughlin, 1909, p 11, evidence of Sarah McNeil.
18 Ibid, p 34, evidence of Harry Lobb.
19 Ibid, p 68, evidence of McLoughlin. Ibid, p 34, evidence of Lobb.
20 Ibid, p 34, evidence of Lobb, and 'The Double Murder' *The Star,* 2 February 1895.
21 Rex vs McLoughlin, 1909, p 7, evidence of Petersen.

22 Ibid.

23 Ibid, p 13, evidence of Sarah McNeil.

24 Ibid, pp 12–13.

25 'Commissioner Street Murder', *The Star*, 28 January 1895.

26 Rex vs McLoughlin, 1909, pp 37 and 40, evidence of Gesont and Salie.

27 Ibid, p 27, evidence of Burgess.

28 This account of the shooting is drawn exclusively from primary sources. The most important of these are two affidavits made by Sarah Fredericks. The emphasis is mine and I have chosen to give more weight to Fredericks's earlier statement, the one made in 1895, when her memory of events was likely to have been sharper than a second, made 11 years later, in 1906. RSA, Pretoria, NASA, SP, Vol 61, File SPR 1251/95, Affidavit by Sarah Slotenkamp [Fredericks – indeed the name Slotenkamp may have been her true maiden name] before Andrew Trimble at Johannesburg, 8 February 1895; and Affidavit 'B' by Sarah McNeil [Fredericks] before WS Cohn JP at Johannesburg, 24 November 1906. See also, RSA, Pretoria, NASA, SP Vol 61, File SPR 1251/95, statement made by Johanna Yessman [aka 'Jane Absolum' and 'Mrs Dopes'] before Andrew Trimble at Johannesburg, 8 February 1895. See also WLD 377/1909, Rex vs McLoughlin, 1909, evidence of McNeil/Fredericks, Jane Absolum/Dokes, Mahomed Arends/Ou Vader, EG Isaacs and Nasa Din Burgess at

pp 1214, 20–21, 22–23, 24–26 and 27–28.

29 Rex vs McLoughlin, 1909, p 26, evidence of Isaacs.

30 McLoughlin, who often caused mayhem in Johannesburg pubs, terrified Max Goldberg to the point where, 14 years later, he remained a reluctant witness for the prosecution – see Rex vs McLoughlin, 1909, p 37, evidence of Goldberg. Like many bystanders, Goldberg's tale moderated with the passage of time. Compare and contrast 'Sensational Saturday Night', *Standard & Diggers' News*, 28 January 1895, with his evidence as presented in court where the bullet 'whizzed past, over my head'.

31 Most witnesses were insistent that throughout his retreat McLoughlin was walking rather than running – which points to his determination to remain calm. See Rex vs McLoughlin, 1909, pp 37 and 43, evidence of Goldberg and Ben.

32 Rex vs McLoughlin, 1909, pp 44 and 47, evidence of Mrs Jack and Mrs du Plooy.

33 Ibid, especially pp 40, 41 and 42, evidence of Salie, Wilmot and Carr.

34 Ibid, p 42, evidence of Ben.

35 RSA, Pretoria, NASA, WLD 377/09, Affidavit 'B', sworn by Sarah McNeil, at Johannesburg on 16 November 1906, at p 3.

36 Rex vs McLoughlin, 1909, p 54.

37 Ibid, pp 48–49, evidence of Van Niekerk.

38 Ibid, pp 15–16, evidence of Fredericks.

Chapter Seventeen: The Spectres of Success

1 See Republic of South Africa (RSA). Pretoria, National Archives of South Africa (NASA), Witwatersrand Local Division (WLD), Vol 377/1909, Rex vs Jack McLoughlin, 1909, p 34, evidence of Lobb [hereafter, Rex vs McLoughlin, 1909].

2 'A Menace to the Town', *Standard & Diggers' News*, 30 January 1895.

3 See 'Mr Ferguson's Denial', *The Star*, 2 February 1895. The Chief Detective's denial was written on 31 January 1895, five

days after the shootings, but the damage had already been done. As one part-time journalist noted later, 'As to Ferguson he never recovered his kudos'; see United States of America (USA), New Haven, Yale University Library, Ac 565, Box 7, Folder 75, Louis Cohen Scrapbooks [hereafter, USA, Yale University Library, 'Cohen Scrapbooks'].

4 'A Menace to the Town', *Standard & Diggers' News*, 30 January 1895.

5 See Rex vs McLoughlin, 1909, p 70.

6 'Commissioner Street Murder', *Standard & Diggers' News,* 28 January 1895.

7 See 'Double Murder' and 'Where are the Police', *The Star,* 28 January 1895, as carried on 2 February 1895.

8 See Philip Carr to the Editor, *The Star,* 2 February 1895.

9 See *The Star,* 28 January 1895, the *Standard & Diggers' News* of 5 February and 19 July 1895, and TV Bulpin, *Storm over the Transvaal* (Cape Town 1955), p 219. Also 'McLachlan the Murderer', *Standard & Diggers' News,* 5 and 7 February 1895.

10 'A Sensational Saturday Night', *The Star,* 28 January 1895. See also C van Onselen, *Masked Raiders: Irish Banditry in Southern Africa, 1880–1899* (Cape Town 1910), p 145; and P Haining, *The Legend and Bizarre Crimes of Spring Heeled Jack* (London 1977).

11 See USA, Yale University Library, Cohen's Scrapbook, pp 12–13; and TV Bulpin, *Storm over the Transvaal* (Cape Town 1955), p 219. McLoughlin did indeed have a hook many years later, but even then it was not made of 'polished steel'.

12 *Rex vs McLoughlin,* 1909, p 70, evidence of McLoughlin.

13 See *Standard & Diggers' News,* 1 and 2 February 1895.

14 See 'Daring Double Murder' and 'McLoughlin's Friends' in the *Cape Argus* and *The Star,* 31 January and 2 February 1895.

15 'The Detective and the Murderer', *The Star,* 29 January 1895.

16 'A Menace to the Town', *Standard & Diggers' News,* 30 January 1895.

17 The saga surrounding the absence of a description of the wanted man can be traced in a report carried on 'The McLoughlin Murder' in the *Diamond Fields Advertiser* reproduced in *Standard & Diggers' News* of 7 February 1895. For the official police notice, see, 'The Double Murder – Description of McLoughlin', *The Star,* 30 January 1895.

18 See 'Mr Ferguson's Denial' and the Editor's response in *The Star,* 31 January 1895; and 'A Pretty State of Things', *Cape Argus,* 31 January 1895.

19 'Chief Detective Ferguson', *Standard & Diggers' News,* 8 February 1895.

20 For Irish nationalists following in the path of Lancashire-Irish criminals, see van Onselen, *Masked Raiders,* pp 179-218.

21 'Detecting Detectives', *The Star,* 29 January 1895.

22 'The Detective Enquiry', *The Star,* 18 May 1895.

23 See *Rex vs McLoughlin,* 1909, p 55, evidence of Trimble.

24 See 'Daring Double Murder' and 'At Large in Johannesburg', *Cape Argus,* 31 January 1895.

25 *Rex vs McLoughlin,* 1909, evidence of Mynott, p 5.

26 'Double Murder', *The Star,* 2 February 1895.

27 *Rex vs McLoughlin,* 1909, p 4, evidence of Mynott.

28 See South African Republic, *Government Gazette,* 20 February 1895.

29 See F Jeppe and JA Kotzé (eds), *De Lokale Wetten der Zuid-Afrikaansche Republiek, 1849–1885* (Pretoria 1887), Artikel 9 and M Josson, *Schets van het Recht van de Zuid Afrikaansche Republiek* (Pretoria 1897), which refers to Article 33 of the resolution of the Volksraad, 12 May 1864. (I am indebted to Prof AJ van der Walt, Ms M Heese, P van der Merwe and E Marais for uncovering these sources for me.)

30 For Trimble's experiences with Colonel Warren see 'The Detective Enquiry', *The Star,* 17 May, 1895. On Hamilton see RSA, Pretoria, NASA, SPR 1444/95; two telegrams – one from the Landdrost, Pietersburg, to State Attorney, Pretoria, 20 February 1895, and the other, from Trimble, who became disillusioned with Hamilton's performance which he saw as being more reward-driven than professional – to the State Attorney, 28 February 1895.

31 RSA, Pretoria, NASA, SPR 1364/95, Telegram, Landdrost, Pietersburg to State Attorney, 20 February 1895.

32 See *Rex vs McLoughlin,* 1909, p 70, evidence of McLoughlin.

33 In addition to the usual core gang members at least four other men and a woman were involved in the robbery that followed – Alfred Lear, Fred Wray, T Wells, DFC Barr and Lillian Pitt – see 'Champ Deep Safe

Robbery', *The Star*, 9 May 1895.

34 'Cranmer', whose real name was Creamer – sometimes also rendered as Cramer – was raised in Bengal Street, Ancoats, Manchester, by his stepmother, Julia Smith, who ran a boarding house after his father had died. See United Kingdom (UK), *Census 1871*, RG10/3976 Folio 103, p 1 and RG10/4029, Folio 79, p 25. For Creamer's earliest criminal record see UK, Manchester, Central Records, M600/1/1/11, Police Court Register, 26 June 1872, entry No 80023 which lists four other offences before the age of 16. For his prior trouble with the law in the South African Republic see, for example, RSA, Pretoria, NASA, SP Vol 54A, SPR, 125 1259/94. Pitt's problems are recounted in 'The Circuit Court – Criminal Session', *Standard & Diggers' News*, 20 June 1895.

35 'The Circuit Court', *Standard & Diggers' News*, 20 June 1895.

36 'Circuit Court', *Standard & Diggers' News*, 22 June 1895.

37 See RSA, Pretoria, NASA, UR 9907, Thomas Whelan to His Excellency, the State President, 10 October 1895.

38 This account is based on the evidence presented at the Preliminary Enquiry as reported in, *The Star*, 9 May 1895.

39 'Champ Deep Safe Robbery', *The Star*, 9 May 1895.

40 See 'Another Mine Safe Robbery', *Standard & Diggers' News*, 4 February 1895 and, 'Circuit Court', *Standard & Diggers' News*, 20 June 1895.

41 His experience in trying to run down McLoughlin left the detective disillusioned and out of pocket. See evidence of WH Ueckermann before the Commission of Enquiry into the Detective Department as reported in *The Star*, 7 May 1895.

42 'An Alleged Accomplice – Arrest at Pretoria', *Standard & Diggers' News*, 5 February 1895.

43 'Champ Deep Safe Robbery', *The Star*, 9 May 1895; and 'The Circuit Court Criminal Session", *Standard & Diggers' News*, 20 June 1895.

44 'The Champ Deep Safe Robbery', *The Star*, 9 May 1895.

45 'Champ Deep Safe Robbery', *The Star*,

9 May 1895; and 'The Circuit Court – Criminal Session', *Standard & Diggers' News*, 20 June 1895.

46 See 'The Champ d'Or Deep Burglary', *The Star*, 18 June 1895; and 'The Circuit Court – Criminal Session', *Standard & Digger's News*, 20 June 1895.

47 Four months later 'military adventurers', including 'Captain Hickey' were still based at Makhado's, much to the annoyance of the government – see RSA, Pretoria, NASA, TAB KG Vol 122, File CR 3001/95.

48 RSA, Pretoria, NASA, File 1364/95, letter from an unknown informant, and telegram from Hamilton to the State Attorney, Pretoria, dated 11 and 19 February 1895 respectively. This was good news for the beleaguered police and almost instantly leaked to the press – see 'McLoughlin the Murderer', *Cape Argus*, 16 February 1895.

49 McCann's extradition is noted in the *Bulawayo Chronicle*, 2 August 1895. See also the following items in RSA, NASA, Pretoria, SP, SPR 6239/95, SPR 307/96 and SPR 9453/95.

50 RSA, Pretoria, NASA, Vol 61, SPR 1251/95, WH Ueckermann to State Attorney, 13 February 1895.

51 See DL Wheeler, 'Gungunyane the Negotiator: A Study in African Diplomacy', *Journal of African History*, Vol 9, No 4, 1968, p 596. These events were, of course, closely followed on the Witwatersrand – see, for example, 'Latest from Lourenço', *Standard & Diggers' News*, 30 January and 5 February 1895; and 'The Situation at Delagoa', *The Star*, 6 February 1895.

52 RSA, Pretoria, NASA, TAB SP Vol 81, Ref GR 17/95, Telegram State Secretary, Pretoria to Colonial Secretary, Natal, 20 March 1895.

53 Rex vs McLoughlin, 1909, pp 67 and 72, evidence of McLoughlin.

54 Ibid, p 67.

55 'McLoughlin the Murderer', *The Star*, 9 March 1895.

56 'Opinion in Pretoria', *The Star*, 6 March 1895.

57 See, amongst others, 'The New Police Commissioner', *Standard & Diggers' News*, 11 February 1895; 'The Police Force – Hundred Men Applied For', *The Star*,

11 March 1895; and 'The Detective Inquiry', *The Star*, 7 May 1895. For mention of McLoughlin during the commission of enquiry into the Detective Department, see 'The Detective Enquiry', *The Star*, 7 and 15 May 1895.

58 'Wanted – Extradition Treaties', *The Star*, 14 February 1895.

59 See items in *The Star*, 5 and 14 March 1895.

60 *The Star*, 5 March 1895.

61 'The Epidemic of Murder', *The Star*, 6 March 1895.

62 See C van Onselen, 'Cowboy Capitalists and Capitalist Cowboys: The Jameson Raid of 1895 and the Wild West' [forthcoming].

Chapter Eighteen: The Reality of Failure

1 See Republic of South Africa (RSA), National Archives of South Africa (NASA), Pretoria, Witwatersrand Local Division (WLD), Vol 377/1909, Rex vs Jack McLoughlin, 1 December 1909, evidence of Detective Charles Mynott, p 5, and J McLoughlin, p 72 [hereafter, Rex vs McLoughlin, 1909].

2 J Nair, *Miners and Millhands: Work, Culture and Politics in Princely Mysore* (Delhi 1998), p 15 [hereafter, Nair, *Miners and Millhands*].

3 This short economic history of the Kolar goldfields is derived from CVP Kumar, PG Revathi and KT Rammohan, 'Kolar Gold Mines: An Unfinished Biography of Colonialism', *Economic and Political Weekly*, 13 June 1998, pp 1467–71 [hereafter Kumar *et al*, 'Kolar Gold Mines']; J Nair, 'Representing Labour in Old Mysore: Kolar Gold Fields Strike of 1930', *Economic and Political Weekly*, 28 July 1990 [hereafter Nair, 'Representing Labour']; and an unpublished paper by S Mollan of the University of Durham, 'The Business Network of John Taylor & Son: 1890, 1900 and 1910' [hereafter, Mollan, 'The Business Network of John Taylor & Son'], 13 pp.

4 See Kumar *et al*, 'Kolar Gold Mines', pp 1468–70; and Nair, 'Representing Labour', pp 74–75.

5 Nair, 'Representing Labour', p 74; and Kumar *et al*, 'Kolar Gold Mines', pp 1469–70.

6 Nair, 'Representing Labour', p 75 and Kumar *et al*, 'Kolar Gold Fields', p 1471.

7 See especially Nair, *Miners and Millhands*, pp 95–110.

8 On theft from the Kolar mines, see Nair, *Miners and Millhands*, p 45; and, more extensively, J Nair, 'Dangerous Labour: Crime and Punishment in the Kolar Gold Fields, 1890–1946', *Studies in History*, Vol 13, No 1, 1997, pp 24–34 [hereafter, Nair, 'Dangerous Labour'].

9 India, Kolkota, State Archives of West Bengal, Government of Bengal, Marine Department, Proceedings 1–5, File Formula No 3 R/14.1 (1 July 1895), Dispatch No 4 Public/522, 28 March 1895.

10 See 'Alleged Possession of House-breaking Tools', *New Zealand Herald*, 11 March 1897.

11 Kumar *et al*, 'Kolar Gold Fields', p 1469.

12 See Nair, 'Dangerous Labour', p 26.

13 For the deeper and wider context see H Fischer-Tiné, '"The Drinking Habits of our Countrymen": European Alcohol Consumption and Colonial Power in British India', *The Journal of Imperial and Commonwealth History*, Vol 40, No 3, September 2012, pp 383–408 [hereafter, Fischer-Tiné, '"The Drinking Habits of our Countrymen"'].

14 What follows draws extensively on Sarmistha De's *Marginal Europeans in Colonial India: 1860–1920* (Kolkota 2008) [hereafter De, *Marginal Europeans*]. See also H Fisher-Tiné, *Low and Licentious Europeans: Race, Class and White Subalternity in Colonial India* (New Delhi, 2009).

15 From a southern African perspective, see, for example, B le Cordeur, 'Natal, the Cape and the Indian Ocean, 1846–1880', *Journal of African History*, Vol VII, No 2, 1966,

pp 247–62.

16 On skills, see De, *Marginal Europeans*, pp 113, and on the amendment to the act, p 145.

17 See C Anderson, 'Multiple Border Crossings: "Convicts and other Persons escaped from Botany Bay and residing in Calcutta"', *Journal of Australian Colonial History*, Vol 3, No 2, pp 1–22 [hereafter Anderson, 'Multiple Border Crossings'].

18 See especially the comments of the report of the Vagrancy Amendment Sub-committee of 1892 as recorded in De, *Marginal Europeans*, p 135.

19 For the existence of precisely such networks of information about travel in the Indian Ocean region, long before the opening of the Suez Canal, see also Anderson, 'Multiple Border Crossings', pp 1–22.

20 De, *Marginal Europeans*, pp 23 and 147.

21 Ibid, pp 144 and 151.

22 Ibid, p 99.

23 For some idea of how this journey would have been accomplished see, for example, H Fischer-Tiné, 'The Drinking Habits of our Countrymen', p 395.

24 For the broader historical context see, H Fischer-Tiné, 'Flotsam and Jetsam of the Empire? European Seamen and Spaces of Disease and Disorder in mid-Nineteenth Century Calcutta' in A Tambe and H Fischer-Tiné (eds), *The Limits of British Colonial Control in South Asia: Spaces of Disorder in the Indian Ocean Region* (London 2008), pp 116–49.

25 India, Kolkata, West Bengal State Archives, Government of Bengal, Judicial Proceedings, Number of Proceedings; B, 183–184, File Formula, J 1, V/14, 29 July 1895, deportation of Thomas Kenny.

26 Details of the ship's voyage are recorded in 'Mount Sirion', *New Zealand Herald*, 31 August 1895.

Chapter Nineteen: The Imperial Eye Averted

1 See 'The Mount Sirion', *New Zealand Herald*, 31 August 1895; and 'Charter of New Steamer', *Evening Post*, Vol XLIX, Issue 118, 20 May 1895. More technical details about the vessel are to be found in 'The SS Mount Sirion', *The Press*, Vol LII, Issue 9213, 17 September 1895.

2 'For New Zealand Ports', *The Singapore Free Press and Mercantile Advertiser*, 2 August 1895.

3 'SS Mount Sirion', *Evening Post*, Vol L, Issue 58, 5 September 1895.

4 'McCann on his Way', *The Star* (Johannesburg), 10 August 1895.

5 See 'The Mount Sirion', *New Zealand Herald*, 31 August 1895.

6 Ibid.

7 On the *Rathdown*, see items in the shipping columns of the *Auckland Star*, 17 and 18 October 1895, and the *New Zealand Herald*, 19 October 1895.

8 See 'Shipping – Arrivals', *New Zealand Herald*, 31 August 1895.

9 See J Darwin, *The Empire Project: The Rise and Fall of the British World-System, 1830–1970* (Cambridge 2009), pp 170–71 [hereafter, Darwin, *The Empire Project*].

10 This and much of what follows has been shaped by J Pratt, 'The Dark Side of Paradise: Explaining New Zealand's History of High Imprisonment', *British Journal of Criminology*, 46, 2006, pp 541–60 [hereafter 'The Dark Side of Paradise']. In this context see also part three of M Fairburn, *The Ideal Society and its Enemies: The Foundations of Modern New Zealand Society, 1850–1900* (Auckland 1989).

11 Darwin, *The Empire Project*, pp 173–76. See also J Belich, *Replenishing the Earth: The Settler Revolution and the Rise of the Anglo World, 1783–1939* (Oxford 2009), p 71.

12 In certain limited respects, this bore a similarity to anti-witchcraft movements in other societies. See, for example, M Fairburn, 'Vagrants, "Folk Devils" and Nineteenth-Century New Zealand as a Bondless Society', *Historical Studies*, Vol 21, No 85, October 1985, pp 502–3 [hereafter Fairburn, 'Vagrants']. The nineteenth-century use of vagrancy laws in this way extended across the Tasman – see S Davies, '"Ragged, Dirty … Infamous and Obscene": The "Vagrant" in Late Nineteenth-Century Melbourne' in D Phillips and S Davies

(eds), *A Nation of Rogues; Crime, Law and Punishment in Colonial Australia* (Melbourne 1994), especially p 8 and then pp 141–65 [hereafter Davies, 'Ragged, Dirty']. See also A McLeod, 'Origins of Consorting Laws', *Melbourne University Law Review*, Vol 37, No 1, Dec 2013, pp 103–42.

13 See Pratt, 'The Dark Side of Paradise', p 545 and G Curry, 'A Bundle of Vague Diverse Offences: The Vagrancy Laws with Special Reference to the New Zealand Experience', *Anglo-American Law Review*, 1972.

14 Pratt, 'The Dark Side of Paradise', p 545.

15 See Darwin, *The Empire Project*, pp 174–75.

16 See especially, Fairburn, 'Vagrants', pp 507 and 512.

17 'A Burglar's Kit', *Auckland Star*, 13 November 1895.

18 On Wilkinson's back-pay, see 'Alleged Possession of Housebreaking Tools', *New Zealand Herald*, 20 November 1895 [hereafter, 'Alleged Possession', *New Zealand Herald*, 20 November 1895.]

19 'A Burglar's Kit', *Auckland Star*, 13 November 1895; and 'Alleged Possession', *New Zealand Herald*, 20 November 1895.

20 Contrast this with Melbourne in 1895, when the police consciously used the vagrancy laws to apprehend one of the country's leading safe-crackers, Christopher Jackson – see Davies, 'Ragged, Dirty', p 154. Indeed, New Zealand police continued to complain about the lack of appropriate legislation governing the acquisition of explosives for many years – see 'A Paradise for Safe-Blowers', *Truth*, 6 February 1930. (I am indebted to Graeme Dunstall for drawing this item to my attention.)

21 On the difficulties of distinguishing 'vagrants' from ordinary swaggers, see, for example, Fairburn, 'Vagrants', p 507.

22 'A Burglar's Kit', *Auckland Star*, 13 November 1895; and 'Alleged Possession', *New Zealand Herald*, 20 November 1895.

23 See GB Magee and AS Thompson, *Empire and Globalisation: Networks of People, Capital and Goods in the British World, 1850–1914* (Cambridge 2010), p 83.

24 Republic of South Africa (RSA), National Archives of South Africa (NASA), Pretoria,

SSA (1896) Vol 338, File RA 849/96 (Part 1), MB Robinson, Commissioner of Police to The Secretary, Law Department, Cape Town, 16 January 1896 [hereafter, RSA, NASA, Pretoria, RA 849/96 (Part 1)].

25 RSA, NASA, Pretoria, RA 849/96 (Part 1), Commissioner of Police to Secretary, Law Department, Cape Town, 16 January 1896.

26 'Alleged Possession', *New Zealand Herald*, 20 November and, in the same edition, 'The Albert Park "Find"'.

27 'The Alleged Burglars', *New Zealand Herald*, 21 November 1895.

28 This profile of Wilkinson is based on entries for him in *New Zealand Police Gazette* of 11 December 1895, p 196, and 19 February 1896, p 33. On his reported departure for Melbourne, see RSA, NASA, Pretoria, RA 849/96 (Part 1), State Secretary, Pretoria to British Agent, Pretoria, 4 September 1896.

29 New Zealand (NZ), National Archives (NA), Wellington, Ref: BBAE, Auckland Crown Book (Supreme Court), 1894–1898, pp 172 and 188 [hereafter, NZNA].

30 See Republic of South Africa, Pretoria, National Archives of South Africa, Witwatersrand Local Division, WLD Vol 377/1909, Rex vs Jack McLoughlin, 1 December 1909, p 72, evidence of J McLoughlin.

31 RSA, NASA, Pretoria, RA 849/96 (Part 1), Attorney-General, Cape Town to State Attorney, Pretoria, 29 January 1896.

32 RSA, NASA, Pretoria, RA 849/96 (Part 1), SPR 4324/96, Attorney-General, Cape Town to State Attorney, Pretoria, 22 May 1896.

33 See C van Onselen, *Masked Raiders: Irish Banditry in Southern Africa, 1880–1899* (Cape Town 2010), pp 219–38.

34 See various documents in RSA, NASA, Pretoria, RA 849/96 (Part 1) and, more particularly, State Secretary to British Agent, Pretoria, 4 September 1896 and the draft letter that preceded it.

35 See RSA, NASA, Pretoria, RA 849/96 (Part 1), SPR 4324/96, Attorney-General, Cape Town to State Attorney, Pretoria, 22 May 1896.

36 RSA, NASA, Pretoria, RA 849/96 (Part 1), SPR 4324/96, Memo, Under-State Secretary,

15 July 1896.

37 Republic of South Africa, Cape Town, Cape Archives Depot, GH 1896, 1/462, Glasgow to Joseph Chamberlain, 12 August 1896, and Selborne (on behalf of Joseph Chamberlain) to Glasgow, 1 October 1896.

38 See *New Zealand Police Gazette 1896*, p 210.

39 RSA, NASA, Pretoria, RA 849/96 (Part 1), SPR 4324/96, Copy, Letter from the Governor of New Zealand to the High Commissioner, Cape Town, 20 November 1896, and appended, undated copy of legal opinion headed 'Application for the Extradition of one Kenny alias McLoughlin'. The registers to the Governor of New Zealand's correspondence, in the National Archives at Wellington, show that there were once four items of correspondence relating

to McLoughlin that can no longer be traced – one in 1896, two in 1897 and one more in 1898. The numbers attached to the missing items are DM 237/96, DM 32.204/97 and P104/97 and 257/98 (the latter being a letter to the Cape Colony).

40 RSA, NASA, Pretoria, RA 849/96 (Part 1), SPR 4324/96, Copy, Letter from the Governor of New Zealand to the High Commissioner, Cape Town, 20 November, 1896, and appended, undated copy of legal opinion headed 'Application for the Extradition of one Kenny alias McLoughlin'. See also, 'Return of Prisoners reported as discharged from gaols during the fortnight ended 28 November, 1896', *New Zealand Police Gazette 1896*, p 210.

Chapter Twenty: Courting Solitude

1 The problem of a acquiring a 'mate' outside of prison, let alone mobilising 'gangs' for criminal purposes, is explored in M Fairburn, 'Vagrants, "Folk Devils" and Nineteenth-Century New Zealand as a Bondless Society', *Historical Studies*, Vol 21, No 85, Oct 1985, pp 499–500 [hereafter Fairburn, 'Vagrants'].

2 See 'Supreme Court', *New Zealand Herald*, 10 March 1897.

3 Ibid.

4 On Connolly's background see R Cooke (ed), *Portrait of a Profession: The Centennial Book of the New Zealand Law Society* (Wellington 1969), p 311. (I am indebted to Graeme Dunstall for drawing this and other sources in this chapter to my attention.)

5 See, for example, the case of Herbert Allandale before Judge Edwards, as reported in *Evening Post*, 11 March 1897, and 'True Bills', *Auckland Star*, 6 March 1899.

6 'Supreme Court', *New Zealand Herald*, 10 March 1897.

7 Ibid.

8 For details of on-going official interest in McLoughlin during 1897 and 1898, see

Chapter 19 above.

9 'Return of Prisoners as discharged from Gaols during the fortnight ending 2 September, 1899', *New Zealand Police Gazette*, 13 September 1899, p 203.

10 For the relevant social context, see, for example, Fairburn, 'Vagrants', pp 505–8.

11 On the difficulty that ordinary swaggers experienced in distinguishing themselves from 'vagrants', see Fairburn, 'Vagrants', pp 507–8.

12 See A Court, *Puck of the Droms: The Lives and Literature of the Irish Tinkers* (Los Angeles 1985), p 27 [hereafter, Court, *Puck of the Droms*].

13 See 'Special Enquiry', *New Zealand Police Gazette*, 28 August 1901, p 203.

14 See Darwin, *The Empire Project: The Rise and Fall of the British World System* (Oxford 2009), pp 173–74; and JE Martin's excellent *The Forgotten Worker: The Rural Wage Earners in Nineteenth-Century New Zealand* (Wellington 1990), pp 3, 24 and 30 [hereafter, Martin, *The Forgotten Worker*].

15 On McLoughlin as cook, see 'Special Enquiry', *New Zealand Police Gazette*,

28 August 1901, p 203; and more generally, Martin, *The Forgotten Worker*, p 137. On the rudimentary diet of swaggers see, for example, Fairburn, 'Vagrants', p 507.

16 Court, *Puck of the Droms,* p 29.

17 Ibid, pp 39–40.

18 Ibid, p 50.

19 Ibid, pp xi, 6 and 40; and Martin, *The Forgotten Worker*, pp 2, 30, 146 and 158.

20 Court, *Puck of the Droms,* p 12; and S O'Suilleabhain, *Irish Folk Custom and Belief* (Kildare 1977), p 30.

21 See GW Rice, *Lyttelton: Port and Town, An Illustrated History* (Christchurch 2005).

22 See 'The Lyttelton Celebrations', *The Press*, Vol LVII, Issue 10841, 17 December 1900; and Martin, *The Forgotten Worker*, p 184.

23 See DH Akenson, *Half the World from Home:*

Perspectives on the Irish in New Zealand, 1860– 1950 (Wellington 1990), p 67 and pp 81–82.

24 'Return of Prisoners Reported as Discharged from Gaols during the fortnight ending 18 August, 1900', *New Zealand Police Gazette 1900,* p 199.

25 'Magisterial – Lyttelton', *Lyttelton Times*, 25 July 1900.

26 Martin, *The Forgotten Worker*, pp 49–50 and 137–42.

27 Ibid, pp 35, 47–48 and 158.

28 Ibid, p 158.

29 McLoughlin's presence in Christchurch, in November 1900, is recorded in 'Special Enquiry', *New Zealand Police Gazette 1901,* p 203.

30 *New Zealand Police Gazette 1901,* August 1901, p 203.

Chapter Twenty-one: The Great Walkabout

1 JE Martin, *The Forgotten Worker: The Rural Wage Earner in Nineteenth-Century New Zealand* (Wellington 1990), pp 17 and 48. The trans-hemispheric criminal circuits of the late nineteenth century await their historian.

2 See 'Special Enquiry', *New Zealand Police Gazette*, 28 August 1901, p 203.

3 'John Bourke' may have been the identity that Jack McLoughlin adopted when first he entered Australia, as a runaway sailor, in late 1882–83.

4 See J Belich, *Replenishing the Earth: The Settler Revolution and the Rise of the Anglo World, 1783–1934* (Oxford 2009), pp 356–60; and J Darwin, *The Empire Project: The Rise and Fall of the British World-System, 1830–1970* (Cambridge 2009), pp 160–68.

5 His second visit may have been facilitated by the fact that there had been a significant decrease in the number of police in the city. See S Davies, 'Ragged, Dirty … Infamous and Obscene': The "Vagrant" in Nineteenth-Century Melbourne' in D Phillips and S Davies (eds), *A Nation of Rogues: Crime, Law and Punishment in Colonial Australia* (Melbourne 1994), p 164.

6 'Burglaries at East Moree', *The Moree News*, 26 August 1902.

7 See also Republic of South Africa (RSA), Pretoria, National Archives of South Africa (NASA), Witwatersrand Local Division (WLD), Vol 377/1909, Rex vs Jack McLoughlin, 1 December 1909, p 72 [hereafter, Rex vs McLoughlin, 1909].

8 On the relatively late cable connections between Australia and South Africa, see SJ Potter, *News and the British World, The Emergence of an Imperial Press System* (Oxford 2003), pp 44–45.

9 Rex vs McLoughlin, 1909, p 72; and R Waterhouse, *The Vision Splendid: A Social and Cultural History of Rural Australia* (Fremantle 2005), p 147 [hereafter Waterhouse, *The Vision Splendid*].

10 On Thomas McLoughlin (name rendered as 'McLaughlin' in police correspondence – as was that of his brother on more than one occasion in several countries) and his Queensland connections, see *Police Gazette, Western Australia for the Year 1901*, p 388.

11 See Patrick Durack (1834–1898), *Australian Dictionary of Biography*, Vol 4

(Manchester 1972).

12 Michael Patrick Durack (1865–1950), *Australian Dictionary of Biography,* Vol 4 (Manchester 1972).

13 See 'Commercial News', *The West Australian,* 29 September 1899; and entry for Michael Patrick Durack (1865–1950), *Australian Dictionary of Biography,* Vol 4 (Manchester 1972).

14 Such as Jesse James. See, for example, G Seal, *Outlaw Heroes in Myth and History* (London 2011), p 88.

15 On Tommy McLoughlin's use of a Mauser, see C Owen, '"The police appear to be a useless lot up there": Law and Order in the East Kimberley, 1884–1895', *Aboriginal History,* No 27, 2003, p 126.

16 The murder of 'Friday' and 'Jimmy' by Tommy McLoughlin can be traced in the archives as well as several secondary sources. See State Records Office of Western Australia (SRO), Perth, for court record and police correspondence – AN 5/2, Acc 430, File No 1382 of 1905, 'Alleged Murder of Two Natives by Thomas McLaughlin' (1905) [hereafter, File 1382/1905] but also 1906/8545, 'Pastoral Leases operated by T McLaughlin' and A Gregor', Kimberley Division 1, January 1906–31 December 1908. The first press report appears to be 'Alleged Murder in the Nor'-West' in *The West Australian,* 18 November 1891. The wider context of the murder is laid out in C Clement, 'Monotony, Manhunts and Malice: East Kimberley Law-Enforcement, 1896–1908', *Early Days; Journal and Proceedings of the Royal Western Australian Historical Society,* Vol 10, Part 1, 1989, pp 85–96 [hereafter, Clement 'East Kimberley Law-Enforcement'].

17 See Clement, 'East Kimberley Law-Enforcement', p 93; 'Alleged Murder', *The West Australian,* 18 November 1901; and *Police Gazette, South Australia,* 20 November 1901, p 200.

18 Much the same ethos can be traced in B Bridge, *Travels and Adventures of Ben Bridge, Throughout Western Australia and Northern Territory* (Carlisle 1950), pp 49–55 [hereafter Bridge, *Travels and Adventures of Ben Bridge*].

19 Clement, 'East Kimberley

Law-Enforcement', p 94.

20 It will be recalled that – as in the case of Tommy McLoughlin – Jack McLoughlin was the beneficiary of the proceeds of the Champ D'Or safe robbery, undertaken by criminals, part-time mine employees, who wanted to provide him with a 'good send-off' after the Stevenson murder – see Chapter 17 above.

21 See SRO, Perth, File 1382/1905; and *Police Gazette, South Australia,* 20 November 1901, p 200. See also, more generally, Bridge, *Travels and Adventures of Ben Bridge.*

22 SRO, Perth, File 1382.1905.

23 Ibid.

24 See 'Burglaries at East Moree', *The Moree News,* 26 August 1902.

25 This paragraph draws extensively on Waterhouse, *The Vision Splendid* – especially pp 31 and 103–9.

26 Ibid, pp 118 and 124.

27 On the development of Broken Hill in the 1890s, see P Laidlaw, 'A Passing Occupation: An Exploration of the History and Heritage of Itinerant Workers in Rural New South Wales, 1850–1914', unpublished D Phil thesis, Charles Sturt University, Australia, 2009, p 199 [hereafter, Laidlaw, 'A Passing Occupation'].

28 On Hogan see Australia (Aus), New South Wales Archives (NSWA), Sydney Record Centre, The Rocks, NRS 1998, Item 35966, Reel 5087, p 73, Bathurst Gaol, Photo 2362, date 6 November 1917; and, on Day, NRS Series 2138, Item 3/6085, Reel 5117, Darlinghurst Prison, 16 April 1914.

29 See, for example, reports on local drought and disaster and prayers for rain in the towns of Bourke and Narrabri carried in *The Narrabri Age* of 11 and 25 February 1902.

30 On the town of Bourke as a launching pad providing the requisite social cover on the road for a journey east, see, for example, Laidlaw, 'A Passing Occupation', p 43.

31 In view of what followed and with the benefit of hindsight, the editorial in *The Narrabri Age* of 5 November 1901 seems particularly pertinent, as does that on 'Law and Order' in *The Moree Examiner,* 26 July 1902.

32 See 'Stowaways on Trains', *The Moree Examiner*, 16 August 1902; and Laidlaw, 'A Passing Occupation', p 72.

33 See especially 'A Gang of Burglars', 'Burglaries at East Moree' in *The Narrabri Age*, 7 March 1902 and *The Moree News*, 26 August 1902.

34 See RWB Lewis's 'Afterword' to Herman Melville, *The Confidence Man* (New York 1964), p 269, but more especially Lewis Hyde's brilliant *Trickster Makes this World: Mischief, Myth and Art* (New York 1998), pp 7 and 121 [hereafter, Hyde, *Trickster Makes this World*].

35 Hyde, *Trickster Makes this World*, pp 10 and 13.

36 For train connections and times in and out of Narrabri, see *The Narrabri Age*, 3 January 1902; and for the wider rail system see Laidlaw, 'A Passing Occupation', p 362.

37 'A Gang of Burglars', *The Narrabri Age*, 7 March 1902.

38 'A Daring Burglary – Safe Blown Up', *The Narrabri Herald*, 7 March 1902.

39 Ibid.

40 'Petty Thieving', *Bourke Banner and Darling River Representative*, 19 March 1902.

41 Paragraph based on 'The Railway Robbery' and 'Burglaries at East Moree' in *The Moree News* of 8 April and 26 August 1902.

42 *The Moree News*, 8 April 1902.

43 See 'The Railway Robbery' in the *Moree Examiner*, 12 and 15 April, 1902; and the *Narrabri Age* and *Moree News* of 18 and 29 April, 1902.

44 The fate of the three can be traced in *The Moree Examiner* of 19 April and 14 June, 1902, and in *The Moree News*, 26 August 1902.

45 See *The Moree News*, 1 August 1902.

46 'Burglaries at East Moree', *The Moree News*, 26 August 1902.

47 'Barry & Stafford's Store Entered' and 'Two Charges Preferred', *The Moree News*, 26 August 1902.

48 'Another Burglary at the Railway Station', *The Moree News*, 26 August 1902.

49 Ibid.

50 'Bourke's subsequent career was, however, eventually added to his prison record at Tamworth under his authentic name, McLoughlin. See Aus State Records, New South Wales, Sydney, Container 3/5997, Item Photo No 87, Tamworth Gaol Photo Description Book, 1824–1929, 'John Bourke alias Jack McLoughlin', 16 November 1902; and 2/3084–86, Reel 2762, Frame 332, Clerk of the Peace: Register of Criminal Dispositions Received, December 1902–October 1908, Entry No 417, John Bourke.

51 'The Police Court', *Moree Examiner*, 30 August 1902.

52 Ibid.

53 'Apprehensions', *Police Gazette, New South Wales*, No 37, 10 September 1902, p 359. See also, 'Barry & Stafford's Store Entered' and 'Two Charges Preferred', *The Moree News*, 26 August 1902.

54 'Quarter Sessions', *The Moree Examiner*, 18 October 1902.

55 See 'Return of Prisoners Tried at the Different Circuit Courts and Courts of Quarter Sessions', *Police Gazette, New South Wales*, Vol 44, 29 October 1902, p 423; and 'Return of Prisoners Discharged to Freedom', *Police Gazette, New South Wales*, Vol 45, 3 February 1903, p 51.

Chapter Twenty-two: The Fatal Cicuit

1 Notably the Irish playwright Dion Boucicault's popular *The Shaughraun* (1874), and, before that, an untitled poem by William Wordsworth written in 1815, at the end of the Napoleonic Wars.

2 See, for example, 'Burglary at Manna Hill' and 'Burglary in Rundle', *The Advertiser* (Adelaide), 22 February and 27 April 1905.

3 *The Advertiser*, 12 January 1905.

4 See 'Wanted in the Transvaal', *The Advertiser*, 9 July 1909.

5 See, for example, 'Hanged for Murder',

Barrier Miner (Broken Hill), 6 January 1905.

6 It is worth remembering that when McLoughlin's world first collapsed, when his hand was amputated in 1891, his choice of an alternative profession was selling vegetables – something that spoke of a familiarity with nature and the outdoors. Likewise, it is noteworthy how, when keen to convey a sense of relaxed engagement he used words such as 'rambling' and 'strolling' or 'walking leisurely' – formulations that are all more easily reconciled with the countryside than with towns. See Republic of South Africa (RSA), Pretoria, National Archives of South Africa (NASA), Witwatersrand Local Division (WLD), Rex vs Jack McLoughlin, December 1909, especially pp 70–71, evidence of J McLoughlin.

7 *New Zealand Police Gazette,* Wellington, Wednesday, 15 March 1905, p 1.

8 The parameters and problems of Aboriginals obtaining justice in these circumstances can be inferred from G Highland, 'A Tangle of Paradoxes: Race, Justice and Criminal Law in North Queensland, 1882–1894', pp 123–40 in D Phillips and S Davies (eds), *A Nation of Rogues? Crime, Law and Punishment in Colonial Australia* (Melbourne 1994).

9 State Records Office of Western Australia (SRO), Perth, AN 5/2, Acc 430, File 1906/8545, Pastoral Leases operated by T McLaughlin and A Gregor, Kimberley Division 1, January 1906–31 December 1908.

10 See CA Wallace, *A Visit to Queensland and her Goldfields* (London 1870); L Ford, *'Below these Mountains; The Adventures of John Henry Mills, Pioneer, Photographer and Gold Miner* (Cairns 2001); and L Wallace, *Nomads of the 19ᵗʰ Century Queensland Goldfields* (Rockhampton 2000) [hereafter, Wallace, *Nomads*].

11 See Australia (Aus), Brisbane, Queensland State Archives (QSA), PRI/1/15 A, 2930, Stewart's Creek Gaol Description Book, 1906, Entry No 975, King George [hereafter, Aus, Brisbane, QSA, PRI/1/15 A, SCGDB].

12 Wallace, *Nomads*, p 123.

13 See 'Stealing – Thursday October 11', *The Mackay Standard*, 19 October, 1906.

14 Ibid.

15 Ibid.

16 Ibid.

17 Ibid.

18 Ibid.

19 See Aus, Brisbane, QSA, PRI/1/15 A, 2930, Entry 973, Mackay General Prisoner Description Book, 1906; and A/45975, Stewart's Creek Prison Register, 1906, Entry No 217/4856, 17 October 1906.

20 'Charge of Murder – Extradition Order', *The Telegraph* (Brisbane), 3 June 1909.

21 Ibid. This press report should be read with care since there are some dates and sequences that are at odds with the far more reliable official records of the time.

22 Aus, Brisbane, QSA, PRE/G53, unsigned letter from a civil servant to The Hon, The Prime Minister of the Commonwealth, Melbourne, date 21 December 1906.

23 Republic of South Africa (RSA), Pretoria, National Archives of South Africa (NASA), various items in LD Vol 678, including – Unsigned affidavit by Murch Goldberg, dated 24 November 1906; H Tennant, Sec to the Law Dept to the Commissioner of Police, Johannesburg, 6 December 1906, and Selborne, Governor of the Transvaal to His Excellency, The Governor of Queensland, Brisbane, 22 December 1906.

24 Aus, Brisbane, QSA, PRI G26, Comptroller of Prisons to the Under-Secretary, Home Department and The Superintendent, HM Penal Establishment, Stewart's Creek, dated respectively 10 and 11 December 1906.

25 See R Evans, *A History of Queensland* (Brisbane 2007), p 29.

26 See J Finger, *The St Helena Story: An Illustrated History of Colonial Queensland's Island Prison* (Brisbane 2010), pp 143–62.

27 Ibid, pp 105–22.

28 Ibid, pp 53–68.

29 Ibid, pp 43–52.

30 Ibid, p 231.

31 'Alleged Murder', *The Brisbane Telegraph*, 17 April 1909.

32 Aus, Brisbane, QSA, PRI 1/15B, Item No 2931, Boggo Road Gaol, Prisoner Description Book, 1909, Entry 407, 17 April, 1909.

33 'To-Day', *The Brisbane Courier*, 19 April 1909.

34 See 'The South African Case' and 'A Similarity in Names', *The Brisbane Courier*, 4 and 8 June 1909.

Chapter Twenty-three: The Tinker's Curse

1 Republic of South Africa (RSA), Pretoria, National Archives of South Africa (NASA), Gov Vol 1216, 75/02/1909, Minute No 78, Prime Minister Louis Botha to Jacob de Villiers Roos.

2 RSA, Pretoria, NASA, Gov Vol 1216, 75/02/09, Governor, Johannesburg to Governor, Queensland, 16 April 1909.

3 See, for example, 'The McKelvery Case', *The Advertiser* (Adelaide), 20 April 1906, or 'Case of William McKelvery', *Kalgoorlie Western Argus,* 13 March 1906.

4 RSA, Pretoria, NASA, Gov 1216, 75/02/09, Governor, Brisbane to Governor, Johannesburg, 21 April 1909.

5 See RSA, Pretoria, NASA, Witwatersrand Local Division (WLD), Vol 377/1909, Rex vs Jack McLoughlin, 30 August 1909, evidence of Charles Albert Mynott and Matthew John de Beer, at pp 3–6 and 51 [hereafter Rex vs McLoughlin]. On De Beer's familiarity with McLoughlin, dating back to 1892, see also 'The Finger of Fate', *New Zealand Truth,* 26 June 1909.

6 RSA, Pretoria, NASA, Gov Vol 1216, 75/02/09, Governor, Transvaal to Governor, Queensland, 28 April 1909.

7 'Charge of Murder', *The Telegraph*, 6 June, 1909 [Brisbane, evening paper].

8 'South African Case', *Brisbane Courier*, 3 June 1909.

9 Ibid.

10 See the *Hawera and Normanby Star*, 1 May 1909 and *Wanganui Herald*, 8 June 1909 [New Zealand].

11 RSA, Pretoria, NASA, LD Vol 678, RA Ranking, Police Magistrate to His Excellency, Sir Arthur Morgan, Lieutenant Governor of Queensland, 2 June 1909.

12 RSA, Pretoria, NASA, Gov Vol 1216, Lieutenant Governor, Queensland, Sir Arthur Morgan to The Governor of the Transvaal, Lord Selborne, 9 June 1909.

13 RSA, Pretoria, NASA, Rex vs McLoughlin, evidence of Mynott, p 3.

14 For Mynott's troubles with the prisoner see, for example, RSA, Pretoria, NASA, Rex vs McLoughlin, 1909, evidence of Mynott,

pp 5–6.

15 PJ Smith, *The Lost Ship SS Waratah: Searching for the Titanic of the South* (Stroud 2009), p 18, puts the ship's displacement at about 10 000 tons but I have chosen to follow other sources on this [hereafter, Smith, *The Lost Ship*].

16 Ibid, p 20, however, suggests that the ship had no second-class passengers – only first and third class.

17 Ibid, p 18.

18 Ibid. Smith appears to be unaware of the presence of the two policemen and their prisoner.

19 See RSA, Pretoria, NASA, Rex vs McLoughlin, 1909, evidence of Mynott, pp 5–6.

20 See Smith, *The Lost Ship,* pp 31–32.

21 Ibid. On p 24 Smith points to lead concentrates as well as lead being taken on board.

22 'Wanted in the Transvaal', *The Advertiser,* 9 July 1909 (Adelaide).

23 See 'Double Murder in the Transvaal' and 'Wanted in the Transvaal', *The Advertiser,* 19 April and 9 July 1909 (Adelaide).

24 RSA, Pretoria, NASA, Rex vs McLoughlin, evidence of Mynott, p 3.

25 Smith, *The Lost Ship,* pp 31–32.

26 RSA, Pretoria, NASA, Rex vs McLoughlin, evidence of Mynott, pp 5–6.

27 Ibury's background can be traced in Smith, *The Lost Ship,* pp 37–38.

28 Ibid, p 31.

29 It may be significant that the London-based *South Africa Magazine* of 21 August 1909, under its 'Domestic Announcements', did note McLoughlin's arrival aboard the *Waratah* and the fact that he was then escorted to Johannesburg.

30 Smith, *The Lost Ship,* pp 47–48.

31 Ibid, p 24.

32 On the various official and private searches for the *Waratah,* see ibid, pp 71–155.

33 See, for example, 'Search for the Waratah', *Auckland Star,* 13 August 1909; 'The Waratah', *Advertiser* (Adelaide), 18 August 1909; 'The Waratah', *New Zealand Tablet,* 30 September

1909; and 'The Waratah – Experts
without Hope', *Sydney Morning Herald*,
31 December 1909.

34 See, for example, 'Prisoner and Escort',
The Advertiser (Adelaide), 18 August
1909; 'A Dangerous Criminal', *Evening
Post* (Auckland), 26 August 1909 [this

item appeared in at least five other New
Zealand newspapers at the time]; 'One of
the Waratah's Passengers', *Otago Witness*,
1 September 1909; and, 'A South African
Crime – McLoughlin the One-Armed Man',
Hawera and Normanby Star, 28 August 1909.

Chapter Twenty-four: Courts and Contexts

1 Sir James Rose Innes, summing up, as
reported in 'A Crime of Long Ago – The
Trial of "One-Armed Mac"', *Rand Daily
Mail*, 11 December 1909.

2 For a comprehensive, detailed account of
white labour during the period leading up
to the general strike of 1913, see EN Katz,
A Trade Union Aristocracy (Johannesburg
1976); and, more especially, J Hyslop, *The
Notorious Syndicalist. JT Bain: A Scottish Rebel
in Colonial South Africa* (Johannesburg 2004),
pp 158–98.

3 For the immediate context see C van
Onselen, *New Babylon, New Nineveh:
Everyday Life on the Witwatersrand, 1886–1914*
(Johannesburg 2011), pp 347–49.

4 See EN Katz, *A Trade Union Aristocracy*
(Johannesburg 1976), pp 190 and 263.

5 The Chief Justice presiding at McLoughlin's
trial, Sir James Rose Innes, was certainly
aware not only of how Irish 'political
crimes' could play themselves out – as in the
Phoenix Park murders, in 1882 – but also
of how such emotions could extend into
murders committed in southern Africa. See
*James Rose Innes, Chief Justice of South Africa,
1914–1927, Autobiography* (London 1949),
pp 49–50 [hereafter, *James Rose Innes*]. In
the absence of any suggestion from defence
counsel that McLoughlin's shooting of a
police informer may, in some measure, have
been motivated by the type of low-level
political sentiments expected of someone
raised 'Irish', Rose Innes was either unable
or unwilling to consider the shooting of
Stevenson as anything other than a purely
criminal act.

6 As quoted in D Denoon, *A Grand Illusion:
The Failure of Imperial Policy in the Transvaal
Colony during the Period of Reconstruction,
1900–05* (London 1973), p 48 [emphasis
added].

7 This, too, was not without problems. On
policing the countryside see A Grundlingh,
'"Protectors and Friends of the People"? The
South African Constabulary in the Transvaal
and Orange River Colony, 1900–1908' in
DM Anderson and D Killingray (eds), *Policing
the Empire: Government, Authority and Control,
1830–1940* (Manchester 1994), pp 168–82;
and, on the Town Police, C van Onselen,
'Who Killed Meyer Hasenfus? Organised
Crime, Policing and Informing on the
Witwatersrand, 1902–1908', *History Workshop
Journal*, Issue 67, 2009, pp 1–22 [hereafter, van
Onselen, 'Who Killed Meyer Hasenfus?'].

8 See especially 'Police and Prisons' and the
cartoon on 'Bobby Sykes' in the *Sunday Times*
of 22 and 29 August 1909.

9 See especially, 'A Crime of Long Ago', *Rand
Daily Mail*, 2 and 4 December 1909.

10 See Republic of South Africa (RSA),
Pretoria, National Archives of South Africa
(NASA), Witwatersrand Local Division
(WLD), WLD Vol 377/1909, Rex vs Jack
McLoughlin, 1–3 December 1909, evidence
of Richard Metcalf, p 61–62 [hereafter Rex
vs McLoughlin, 1909].

11 A *Rand Daily Mail* report as carried in *The
Hawera and Normanby Star* (New Zealand),
28 August 1905.

12 See especially L Rushen, 'Margaret McLean
– The First Signatory on the 1891 Women's
Suffrage Petition', unpublished talk presented

to the East Melbourne Historical Society,
18 June 2008.

13 See entry for FAW Lucas in CJ Beyers,
Dictionary of South African Biography, Human
Sciences Research Council, 1968, Vol IV.

14 As when referring to 'An Informers Fate' and
'The Carey Tragedy Repeated', *Standard &
Diggers' News,* 28 January 1895.

15 See C van Onselen, *Masked Raiders: Irish
Banditry in Southern Africa, 1880–1899* (Cape
Town 2010).

16 Republic of South Africa (RSA), Pretoria,
National Archives of South Africa (NASA),
Witwatersrand Local Division (WLD),
Vol 377/1909, Rex vs McLoughlin, 1909,
evidence of A Smorenberg at p 52 and
J McLoughlin at pp 64–65, 66 and 70
[hereafter, Rex vs McLoughlin, 1909].

17 In this I am following the line of analysis
offered by HM Wright in his introduction
to *Sir James Rose Innes Selected Correspondence
(1884–1902),* (Cape Town 1973, Van Riebeeck
Society, Second Series, No 3).

18 Ibid, pp 1–2.

19 See BA Tindall (ed), *James Rose Innes, Chief
Justice of South Africa, 1914–27, Autobiography*
(Cape Town 1949), pp 49–50. Note also
Innes's criticism of his contemporary at the
bar, the brilliant JW Leonard, for his lack of
self-control, at pp 33–34.

20 See C van Onselen, 'Who Killed Meyer
Hasenfus?', pp 1–22.

21 See 'Jury empanelled, sworn and charged
with the trial of the prisoner', Rex vs
McLoughlin, 1909.

Chapter Twenty-five: The Trial

1 To the point where he foolishly denied
that he had lost his arm after attempting
unsuccessfully to break out of the prison
at Potchefstroom – a puzzling denial given
the circumstances, but one that spoke to
his shame of having robbed a priest. See
Republic of South Africa (RSA), Pretoria,
National Archives of South Africa (NASA),
Witwatersrand Local Division (WLD),
Vol 377/1909, Rex vs J McLoughlin, 1909,
evidence of McLoughlin, p 72 [hereafter Rex
vs McLoughlin, 1909].

2 On Mavrorgordato's background and
troubles securing promotion see C van
Onselen, 'Who Killed Meyer Hasenfus?
Organised Crime, Policing and Informing
on the Witwatersrand, 1902–1908', *History
Workshop Journal,* Issue 67, 2009, pp 6–7; and
on the confiscation of the 'false hand', 'One
Armed Mac', *Sunday Times* (Johannesburg),
5 December 1909.

3 'A Crime of Long Ago', *Rand Daily Mail,*
2 December 1909.

4 See Rex vs McLoughlin, 1909, pp 1–35 and,
for popular accounts, 'A Crime of Long Ago',
Rand Daily Mail, 2 December 1909, and

'McLoughlin's Trial', *Star,* 1 December 1909.

5 Rex vs McLoughlin, 1909, pp 8–19, evidence
of Sarah McNeil.

6 Ibid, pp 33–35.

7 Ibid, pp 52–53, evidence of Robert Ferguson,
and pp 67–73, evidence of J McLoughlin.

8 'The Murder Trial', *Star,* 3 December 1909.

9 Rex vs McLoughlin, 1909, pp 53–58,
evidence of Andrew Trimble and Frederick
Kretzmar.

10 See 'The Murder Trial' in the *Star,* 2 and
3 December 1909.

11 Rex vs McLoughlin, 1909, pp 63–72,
evidence of J McLoughlin.

12 Ibid, p 63–72, evidence of J McLoughlin.

13 Ibid, p 68, evidence of J McLoughlin.

14 'A Crime of Long Ago', *Rand Daily Mail,*
4 December 1909. Rex vs McLoughlin,
1909, at p 73 records only that Mr Douglass
addressed the jury.

15 A Crime of Long Ago', *Rand Daily Mail,* 1909,
4 December 1909. Rex vs McLoughlin, 1909,
at p 73 records only that Mr Lucas addressed
the jury.

16 See 'The Murder Trial', *Star,* 3 December
1909. Rex vs McLoughlin, 1909, at p 73

notes only that the Chief Justice summed up [emphasis added].

17 Rex vs McLoughlin, 1909, p 26, evidence of EG Isaacs.

18 See 'The Murder Trial', *Star*, 3 December 1909. Rex vs McLoughlin, 1909, at p 73 notes only that the Chief Justice summed up.

19 See 'The Murder Trial', *Star*, 3 December 1909; Rex vs McLoughlin, 1909, at p 73.

20 'The Murder Trial', *Star*, 3 December 1909.

21 Ibid.

22 Ibid.

23 'A Crime of Long Ago', *Rand Daily Mail*, 4 December 1909.

24 'One Armed Mac', *Sunday Times,* 5 December 1909. In the original press report McLoughlin was said to have referred to the 'Seven Sisters Inn' but there was no such public house in inner Manchester during his childhood or early manhood. There was, however, a Seven Stars public house in Withy Grove, near the Smithfield Market on Shude Hill, close by the pawnbrokers' shops that he had broken into as a teenager. The other – even more likely – possibility was the Seven Stars in Dickson Street, Ancoats – see N Richardson, *The Old Pubs of Ancoats* (Manchester 1987), pp 19 and 47.

Chapter Twenty-six: Death

1 In this context see the insightful comments on bandits as reactionaries and traditionalists in EJ Hobsbawm, *Bandits* (Harmondsworth 1969), pp 26–27.

2 'One-Armed Mac – No Execution Today', *Sunday Times*, 26 December 1909.

3 Republic of South Africa (RSA), Pretoria, National Archives of South Africa (NASA), Witwatersrand Local Division (WLD), WLD 377/09, WJ Smith, undated to The Sheriff of the Transvaal or his Lawful Deputy.

4 'One-Armed Mac Hanged', *Rand Daily Mail*, 11 January 1910.

5 Ibid.

6 Ibid; and *Volkstem*, 11 January 1910.

7 RSA, Pretoria, NASA, WLD Vol 377/09, Certificate signed by C Rorke, 10 January 1910.

8 See untitled item in *Poverty Bay Herald* (New Zealand), 19 January 1910; 'Execution at Pretoria', *The Brisbane Courier*, 14 February 1910 , or 'After Fifteen Years – Murderer Hanged', *The Kalgoorlie Miner*, 17 March 1910.

A Note on Sources

This biography is constructed, in large part, around the recorded, type-written proceedings of the case of Rex vs Jack McLoughlin, as heard in the Johannesburg High Court in 1909 and preserved in the South African National Archives. Despite various alternative spellings in some of the official documents I have chosen to render the name in its authentic, correct, form as McLoughlin rather than any of its variants such as McLaughlin or MacLachlan. Along with supplementary documentation relating to the court appearances, deportation, extradition and imprisonment of McLoughlin – in Australia, India, New Zealand and southern Africa, as found in the national archives of the states concerned – it forms the primary research backbone of the study. The background and development of the McLoughlin family and their associates, in Manchester, have been determined through a search of the United Kingdom census records for the period 1851–91. This, in turn, has been supplemented through the use of other primary sources relating to the courts and prisons as held in the Archives and Local Studies section of Manchester's Central Library. The precise details relating to individual sources can be traced in the endnotes of each chapter to be found in the main work.

Phantom outlines spirited up from archival vaults, however, have insufficient flesh-and-blood for them to appear on the stage of social history unadorned. For historical ghosts to come to life and move persuasively in and out of relevant historical backgrounds, the accents, attitudes,

486

complexion, language, mannerisms and poise of characters have to be retrieved from everyday, unofficial sources. The voices of authority, control and destiny – all with their own ideological and political inflexions – have to be offset against the everyday beliefs, perceptions and values of ordinary folk and members of the underworld. The deep, bass tones coming from the archives have to be offset by the animating, lighter voices of the choir with the conductor taking great care to hear, explain and understand those which may be discordant or off-key. In the case of Jack McLoughlin, that choir is composed largely from the voices of local – at best provincial – newspapers.

The Victorian era was notable for not only for the number but the quality of its small town newspapers. The morning or evening newspapers, sometimes both, often provided excellent accounts of court proceedings as well as the actions of the local police or regional prison authorities. Read carefully and with critical intelligence, news reports provide a first-class foil to the official voice and provide essential, meaningful detail that is seldom recorded in the archives. Local, small-town newspapers in Australia and New Zealand have, in my experience, been excellently managed and preserved and are readily accessible, in electronic format, to all researchers. In South Africa, however, decay, mismanagement and neglect are the order of the day. Not even the daily or weekly newspapers of the Witwatersrand – the economic engine of South Africa – are being dealt with professionally or preserved in ways that might encourage historians of the future whose intellectual interests transcend hagiography or the achievements of nationalist political parties. Countries get the archives and the historiographies they deserve. Mine will be the last generation of South African historians who can meaningfully offset the archival record (itself in serious disarray) against the everyday experiences of the majority of the population as recorded in the newspapers of the day. The greater the edifice of 'heritage' in a country, the greater the rot in its real sources of history.

Of course, all primary and secondary evidence has to be set within the wider context of secondary literature, then and now. This study has benefited from a range of new and exciting new histories not only of individual colonies, but of 'globalisation' (a familiar old fellow now sporting a new coat) and the systematic expansion of the British empire. The web of older texts as well the most influential of the new that inform this biography are to be found in the Select Bibliography.

Select Bibliography

The archival, manuscript and other primary sources underpinning this study are as listed in each chapter's endnotes.

Articles

Anderson C, 'Multiple Border Crossings: Convicts and other Persons escaped from Botany Bay and residing in Calcutta', *Journal of Australian Colonial History,* Vol 3, No 2, 2001, pp 1–22.

Busteed MA and Hodgson RI, 'Irish Migrant Responses to Urban Life in early Nineteenth-Century Manchester', *The Geographical Journal,* Vol 162, Part 2, July 1996, pp 139–54.

Clement C, 'Monotony, Manhunts and Malice: East Kimberley Law-Enforcement, 1896-1908', *Early Days: Journal and Proceedings of the Royal Western Australian Historical Society,* Vol 10, Part 1, 1989, pp 85–96.

Conley C, 'The Agreeable Recreation of Fighting', *Journal of Social History,* Vol 33, No 1, Autumn 1999, pp 57–72.

Davies A, 'Saturday Night Markets in Manchester and Salford, 1840–1939', *Manchester Region History Review,* 1987, pp 3–12.

Fairburn M, 'Vagrants, "Folk Devils" and Nineteenth-Century New Zealand as a Bondless Society', *Australian Historical Studies,* Vol 21, No 85, October 1985, pp 495–514.

Fischer-Tiné H, '"The Drinking Habits of our Countrymen": European Alcohol Consumption and Colonial Power in British India', *The Journal of Imperial and Commonwealth History*, Vol 40, No 3, September 2012, pp 383–408.

Ford M, '"My Ancestors include Criminals and Wealthy Mill-Owners"' (Interview with J Desoldato) in *Who Do You Think You Are* (BBC Magazines, Bristol), Issue 48, June 2011, pp 38–41.

Gilbert A, 'Buggery and the British Navy, 1700–1861', *Journal of Social History*, Vol 10, No 1 (Autumn 1976), pp 72–98.

Greenslade L, Pearson M and Madden M, 'A Good Man's Fault: Alcohol and Irish People at Home and Abroad', *Alcohol and Alcoholism,* Vol 30, No 4, 1994, pp 406–17.

Herschbach L, 'Prosthetic Reconstruction: Making the Industry, Re-Making the Body, Modelling the Nation', *History Workshop Journal*, No 44, Autumn 1997, pp 22–57.

Jensen TS, Krebs B, Nielsen J and Rasmussen P, 'Immediate and Long-Term Phantom Limb Pain in Amputees: Incidence, Clinical Characteristics and Relationship to Pre-Amputation Limb Pain', *Pain,* Vol 21, No 3, 1985, pp 267–78.

Jolly S, 'The Origins of the Manchester and Salford Reformatory for Juvenile Criminals 1853–1860', *Manchester Region History Review,* No 15, 2001, pp 2–8.

Knepper P, '"A Few Detectives would be Very Useful": Crime, Immorality and Policing in Valletta, 1881–1914', *Journal of Social History*, Vol 43, Issue 2, Winter 2009, pp 385–406.

Kumar CVP, Revathi PG and Rammohan KT, 'Kolar Gold Mines: An Unfinished Biography of Colonialism', *Economic and Political Weekly,* 13 June 1998, pp 1467–71.

Le Cordeur B, 'Natal, the Cape and the Indian Ocean, 1846–1880', *Journal of African History*, Vol 7, No 2, 1966, pp 247–62.

Lloyd-Jones R and Lewis M, 'Housing Factory Workers: Ancoats in the Early Nineteenth Century', in *Manchester Region History Review*, Vol 7, 1993, pp 33–36 and 15–26.

MacIver K, Lloyd DM, Kelly S, Roberts N and Nurmikko T, 'Phantom

Limb Pain, Cortical Reorganistation and the Therapeutic Effect of Mental Imagery', *Brain*, Vol 131, No 8, 2008, pp 2181–91.

Maguire P and Parkes CM, 'Coping with Loss: Surgery and Loss of Body Parts', *British Medical Journal*, 1998, 316: 7137, 1086–88.

McKibbin R, 'Working Class Gambling in Britain, 1880–1939', *Past and Present*, No 82, February 1979, pp 147–78.

Nair J, 'Representing Labour in Old Mysore: Kolar Gold Fields Strike of 1930', *Economic and Political Weekly*, Vol 25, No 30, 28 July 1990, PE73-PE79 + PE84-PE86.

Nash C, 'Men again: Irish Masculinity, Nature and Nationhood in the Early Twentieth Century', *Ecumene*, Vol 3, No 4, 1996, pp. 427–53.

Niccols A, 'Fetal Alcohol Syndrome and the Developing Socio-Emotional Brain', *Brain and Cognition*, Vol 65, Issue 1, 2007, pp 135–42.

Pratt J, 'The Dark Side of Paradise: Explaining New Zealand's History of High Imprisonment', *British Journal of Criminology*, Vol 46, 2006, pp 541–60.

Ramachandran VS and Hirstein W, 'The Perception of Phantom Limbs', The DO Hebb Lecture, *Brain*, Vol 11, No 9, 1998, pp 1603–30.

Roberts J, '"A Densely populated and unlovely tract": The Residential Development of Ancoats', in *Manchester Region History Review*, Vol 7, 1993, pp 15–26.

Rushton P, 'Family Survival Strategies in Mid-Victorian Ancoats', *Manchester Region History Review*, Vol 7, 1993, pp 37–44.

Sanders JL, 'Were our Forebears Aware of Prenatal Alcohol Exposure and its Effects? A History of Fetal Alcohol Spectrum Disorder', *Canadian Journal of Clinical Pharmacology and Therapeutics*, Vol 16, No 2, Summer 2009, pp 288–95.

Scola R, 'Food Markets and Shops in Manchester, 1770–1870', *Journal of Historical Geography*, Vol 1, No 2, 1975, pp 153–68.

Tempelhoff J and Nemudzivadi H, 'Riding the Storm of Change: Makhado, Venda and the South African Republic, 1864–1895', *New Contree*, No 45, September 1999, pp 101–14.

Thompson EP, 'Time, Work-Discipline and Industrial Capitalism', *Past & Present*, Vol 38, No 1, 1967, pp 56–97.

Tosh J, 'What should Historians do with Masculinity? Reflections on Nineteenth-century Britain', *History Workshop Journal*, Issue 38, 1994, pp 179–202.

Van Onselen C, 'Jewish Marginality in the Atlantic World: Organised Crime in the Era of the Great Migrations, 1880–1914', *South African Historical Journal*, Vol 43, November 2000, pp 96–137.

Van Onselen C, 'Who Killed Meyer Hasenfus? Organised Crime, Policing and Informing on the Witwatersrand, 1902–1908', *History Workshop Journal*, Issue 67, 2009, pp 1–22.

Walsh D, 'Alcoholism and the Irish', *Alcohol and Alcoholism,* Vol 6, No 2, 1972, pp 4–47.

Wheeler DL, 'Gungunyane the Negotiator: A Study in African Diplomacy, *Journal of African History*, Vol 9, No 4, October 1968, pp 585–602.

Williams M, 'The Mills of Ancoats', *Manchester Region History Review*, Vol 7, 1993, pp 27–32.

Unpublished works

Doherty WJ, 'The Abbey of Fahan', Paper read at the Royal Irish Academy, 28 February 1881.

Dominy G, 'The Imperial Garrison in Natal with Special Reference to Fort Napier, 1843–1914', unpublished D Phil thesis, University of London, 1995.

Mollan S, 'The Business Network of John Taylor & Son: 1890, 1900 and 1910, unpublished paper. University of Durham, 2003.

Rushen L, 'Margaret McLean – The First Signatory on the 1891 Women's Suffrage Petition', unpublished talk presented to the East Melbourne Historical Society, 18 June 2008.

Chapters in books

Bourke J, 'Irish Masculinity and the Home, 1880–1914' in Cohen M and Curtin MJ (eds), *Reclaiming Gender: Transgressive Identities in Modern Ireland* (New York, 1999).

Bradley J, 'Body Commodification? Class and Tattoos in Victorian Britain' in Caplan J (ed), *Written on the Body: The Tattoo in European and American History* (London 2000).

Davies S, '"Ragged, Dirty … Infamous and Obscene": The "Vagrant" in Late Nineteenth-Century Melbourne', in Phillips D and Davies S (eds), *A Nation of Rogues; Crime, Law and Punishment in Colonial Australia* (Melbourne 1994).

Dominy G, '"More than just a "Drunken Brawl": The Mystery of the Mutiny of the Inniskilling Fusiliers at Fort Napier, 1887', in McCracken DP (ed), *Southern African–Irish Studies, Vol 1* (Durban 1991).

Fielding S, 'A Separate Culture? Irish Catholics in Working-Class Manchester and Salford, c 1890–1939' in Davies A and Fielding S (eds), *Workers' Worlds: Cultures and Communities in Manchester and Salford, 1880–1939* (Manchester 1992).

Geary LM, '"The Whole Country was in Motion": Mendicancy and Vagrancy in pre-famine Ireland' in Hill J and Lennon C (eds), *Luxury and Austerity*, Historical Studies XXI (Dublin 1999).

Johnson M, 'Violence Transported: Aspects of Irish Peasant Society' in MacDonagh O and Mandle WF (eds), *Ireland and Irish-Australia: Studies in Cultural and Political History* (Kent and Surrey Hills, 1986).

Lee J, 'Ribbonmen' in Williams TD (ed), *Secret Societies in Dublin* (Dublin 1973).

Richards J, '"Passing the love of women": Manly love in Victorian Society' in Mangan JA and Walvin J (eds), *Manliness and Morality: Middle Class Masculinity in Britain and America, 1800–1940* (Manchester 1987).

Shaw GB, Preface to Davies WH, *The Autobiography of a Super-Tramp* (London 1908).

Thomas T, 'Representations of the Manchester Working Class in Fiction, 1850–1990' in Kidd AJ and Roberts KW (eds), *City, Class and Culture:*

Studies of Social Policy and Cultural Production in Victorian Manchester (Manchester 1985).

Wiener MJ, 'Race, Class and Maritime Authority in Late Victorian England: The Surprising Cases of Charles Arthur (1888)' in Carroll S (ed), *Cultures of Violence: Interpersonal Violence in Historical Perspective* (Basingstoke 2007).

Books

Akenson DH, *Half the World from Home: Perspectives on the Irish in New Zealand, 1860–1950* (Wellington 1990).

Akenson DH, *The Irish Diaspora* (Toronto 1993).

Akenson DH, *The Irish Diaspora: A Primer* (Belfast 1993).

Anderson D and Killingray D, *Policing the Empire: Government, Authority and Control, 1830–1940* (Manchester 1991).

Beavon KSO, *Johannesburg: The Making and Shaping of a City* (Pretoria 2004).

Belich J, *Replenishing the Earth: The Settler Revolution and the Rise of the Anglo World, 1783–1939* (Oxford 2009).

Blackburn D and Caddell WW, *Secret Service in South Africa* (London 1911).

Bonner B, *Our Inisoghain Heritage* (Coleraine 2010).

Brady S, *Masculinity and Male Homosexuality in Britain, 1861–1913* (London 2005).

Bulpin TV, *Storm over the Transvaal* (Cape Town 1955).

Burleigh M, *Earthly Powers: Religion and Politics in Europe from the Enlightenment to the Great War* (London 2006).

Caplan J (ed), *Written on the Body: The Tattoo in European and American History* (London 2000).

Carroll S (ed), *Cultures of Violence: Interpersonal Violence in Historical Perspective* (Basingstoke 2007).

Clapson M, *A Bit of a Flutter: Popular Gambling and English Society, c 1823–1961* (Manchester 1992).

Clark S, *Social Origins of the Irish Land War* (Princeton 1979).

Cohen L, *Reminiscences of Johannesburg and London* (Johannesburg 1976).

Coleman T, *The Railway Navvies* (Harmondsworth 1982).

Coohill J, *Ireland: A Short History* (Oxford 2005)

Cordery S, *British Friendly Societies, 1750–1914* (Basingstoke 2003).

Court A, *Puck of the Droms: The Lives and Literature of the Irish Tinkers* (Los Angeles 1985).

Curor WD (revised and enlarged by J Bornman), *Golden Memories of Barberton* (Barberton, 2002).

Darwin J, *The Empire Project: The Rise and Fall of the British World-System, 1830–1970* (Cambridge 2009).

Davies A, *The Gangs of Manchester: The Story of the Scuttlers, Britain's First Youth Cult* (Preston 2008).

De S, *Marginal Europeans in Colonial India: 1860–1920* (Kolkota 2008).

Denoon D, *A Grand Illusion: The Failure of Imperial Policy in the Transvaal Colony during the Period of Reconstruction, 1900–05* (London 1973).

Emsley C, *Hard Men: The English and Violence since 1750* (London 2005).

Emsley C, *The English and Violence since 1750* (Basingstoke 2007).

Engels F, *The Condition of the Working Class in England* (1845).

Evans R, *A History of Queensland* (Brisbane 2007).

Fairburn M, *The Ideal Society and its Enemies: The Foundations of Modern New Zealand Society, 1850–1900* (Auckland 1989).

Fennel T, *The Royal Irish Constabulary* (Dublin 2003).

Finger J, *The St Helena Story: An Illustrated History of Colonial Queensland's Island Prison* (Brisbane 2010).

Fisher-Tiné H, *Low and Licentious Europeans: Race, Class and White Subalternity in Colonial India* (New Delhi 2009).

Fitzpatrick D, *Irish Emigration* (Dundalk 1985).

Ford L, *Below these Mountains: The Adventures of John Henry Mills, Pioneer, Photographer and Gold Miner* (Cairns 2001).

Greenall RL, *The Making of Victorian Salford* (Lancaster 2000).

Guinnane TW, *The Vanishing Irish: Households, Migration and the Rural Economy in Ireland, 1850–1914* (Princeton 1997).

Haining P, *The Legend and Bizarre Crimes of Spring Heeled Jack* (London 1977).

Hancock WK, *Smuts, 1: The Sanguine Years, 1870–1919* (Cambridge 1962).

Harkin M, 'Maghtochair', *Inishowen: Its History, Traditions, and Antiquities*, (1867), reprinted (Three Candles Press, 1985).

Hobsbawm EJ, *Bandits* (Harmondsworth 1969).

Hyslop JT, *The Notorious Syndicalist JT Bain: A Scottish Rebel in Colonial South Africa* (Johannesburg 2004).

Irving HB, *A Book of Remarkable Criminals* (London 1918).

Jeppe F and Kotzé JG (eds), *De Lokale Wetten der Zuid-Afrikaansche Republiek, 1849–1885* (Pretoria 1887).

Jessett MJ, *The Key to South Africa: Delagoa Bay* (London, 1899).

Jones G and Malcolm E (eds), *Medicine, Disease and the State in Ireland, 1650–1940* (Cork 1990).

Jones I, *Ned Kelly: A Short Life* (Melbourne 1996).

Josson M, *Schets van het Recht van de Zuid Afrikaansche Republiek* (Pretoria 1897).

Jupp J (ed), *The Australian People, An Encyclopedia of the Nation, its People and their Origins* (Cambridge 2001).

Kay J, 'The Moral and Physical Conditions of the Working Classes' (1832).

Kelly J, *That Damn'd Thing Called Honour: Duelling in Ireland* (Cork 1996).

Kidd A, *Manchester: A History* (Lancaster 2006).

Kiernan V, *The Lords of Human Kind: European Attitudes to other Cultures in the Imperial Age* (London 1969).

Kirkaldy A, *Capturing the Soul: The Vhavenda and the Missionaries* (Pretoria 2005).

Kotzé Sir JG, *Memoirs and Reminiscences, Vol 2* (Cape Town nd).

Lawson G, *Soldiers Heroes: British Adventure, Empire and the Imaging of Masculinities* (London 1994).

Lee H, *Body Parts: Essays on Life Writing* (London 2005).

Lewis S, *A Topographical Dictionary of Ireland* (1837).

Lowe WJ, *The Irish in Mid-Victorian Lancashire: The Shaping of a Working-Class Community* (New York 1989).

MacLaughlin J, *The Politics of Nation-Building in Post-Famine Donegal* (1993).

MacLaughlin J, *The Making of a Northern County* (Dublin 2007).

Magee GB and Thompson A, *Empire and Globalisation: Networks of People, Goods and Capital in the British World* (Cambridge 2010).

Malcolm E, *'Ireland Sober, Ireland Free': Drink and Temperance in Nineteenth-Century Ireland* (Syracuse 1986).

Martin JE, *The Forgotten Worker: The Rural Wage Earners in Nineteenth-Century New Zealand* (Wellington 1990).

Marx K and Engels F, *On Ireland* (London 1972).

McLaren A, *The Trials of Masculinity: Policing Sexual Boundaries, 1870–1930* (Chicago 1997).

McQuilton J, *The Kelly Outbreak: The Geographical Dimension of Social Banditry* (Melbourne 1979).

Meiring P, *Dynamite and Daisies; The Story of Barberton* (Cape Town 1976).

Messinger GS, *Manchester in the Victorian Age: The Half-Known City* (Manchester 1985).

Metrowich F, *Scotty Smith: South Africa's Robin Hood* (Cape Town 1970).

Mosse G, *The Image of Man: The Creation of Modern Masculinity* (Oxford 1996).

Nair J, *Miners and Millhands: Work, Culture and Politics in Princely Mysore* (Delhi 1998).

Neal F, *Black '47; Britain and the Famine Irish* (London 1988).

Nolan W, Ronayne L and Dunlevy M (eds), *Donegal, History & Society: Interdisciplinary Essays on the History of an Irish County* (Dublin 1995).

O' Donnell P, *The Irish Faction Fighters of the 19th Century* (Dublin 1975).

O' Neill J, *Crime City: Manchester's Victorian Underworld* (Preston 2008).

O' Suilleabhain S, *Irish Folk Custom and Belief* (Kildare 1977).

Phillips D and Davies S (eds), *A Nation of Rogues? Crime, Law and Punishment in Colonial Australia* (Melbourne 1994).

Potter SJ, *News and the British World. The Emergence of an Imperial Press System* (Oxford 2003).

Rice GW, *Lyttleton: Port and Town, An Illustrated History* (Christchurch 2005).

Richardson N, *The Old Pubs of Ancoats* (Manchester 1987).

Roberts R, *The Classic Slum: Salford Life in the First Quarter of the Century* (Harmondsworth 1973).

Roonan B, *Forty South African Years: Journalistic, Political, Social, Theatrical and Pioneering* (London 1919).

Rose EB, *The Truth about the Transvaal: A Record of Facts based upon Twelve Years' Residence in the Country* (London 1902).

Rose Innes J. *Autobiography: James Rose Innes, Chief Justice of South Africa, 1914–1927* (London 1949).

Sauer H, *Ex Africa* (Bulawayo 1973).

Seal A, *The Emergence of Indian Nationalism: Competition and Collaboration in the Later Nineteenth Century* (Cambridge 1971).

Seal G, *Outlaw Heroes in Myth and History* (London 2011).

Seal G, *Tell 'Em I Died Game: The Legend of Ned Kelly* (Flemington 2002).

Seal G, *The Outlaw Legend: A Cultural Tradition in Britain, America and Australia* (Cambridge 1996).

Simons J and RE, *Class and Colour in South Africa, 1850–1950* (Harmondsworth 1969).

Smith PJ, *The Lost Ship SS Waratah: Searching for the Titanic of the South* (Stroud 2009).

Standige T, *The Victorian Internet: The Remarkable Story of the Telegraph and the Nineteenth Century's On-line Pioneers* (New York City 1998).

Sweeney F, *The Murder of Conell Boyle, County Donegal, 1898* (Dublin 2001).

Tambe A and Fischer-Tiné H (eds), *The Limits of British Colonial Control in South Asia: Spaces of Disorder in the Indian Ocean Region* (London 2008).

Tebbutt M, *Making Ends Meet: Pawnbroking and Working-Cass Credit* (Leicester 1983).

Tempelhoff JWN, *Die Okkupasiestelsel in die Distrik Soutpansberg* (Pretoria 1997).

Tindall BA (ed), *James Rose Innes, Chief Justice of South Africa, 1914–27, Autobiography* (Cape Town 1949).

Van Onselen C, *Masked Raiders, Irish Banditry in Southern Africa* (Cape Town 2010).

Van Onselen C, *New Babylon, New Nineveh: Everyday Life on the Witwatersrand, 1886–1914* (Cape Town 2001).

Van Onselen C, *The Small Matter of a Horse: The Life of 'Nongoloza' Mathebula, 1867–1948* (Pretoria 2008).

Van Onselen L, *Head of Steel* (Cape Town 1962).

Vane F, *Back to the Mines: Tailings from the Randt* (London 1902).

Wallace CA, *A Visit to Queensland and her Goldfields* (London 1870).

Wallace L, *Nomads of the 19th Century Queensland Goldfields* (Rockhampton 2000).

Ward R, *The Australian Legend* (Melbourne 1958).

Waterhouse R, *The Vision Splendid: A Social and Cultural History of Rural Australia* (Fremantle 2005).

Williams TD (ed), *Secret Societies in Ireland* (Dublin 1973).

Acknowledgements

Since my liberation, in 1999, I have been the beneficiary of the scholarly largesse of the University of Pretoria and, more recently, of the Institute for the Advancement of Scholarship. I have been provided with a uniquely congenial and supportive environment in which to conduct research and writing. In 2012, I was the recipient of the Inaugural Oppenheimer Fellowship at the WEB Du Bois Institute at Harvard University where I enjoyed a spell of unparalleled productivity. Professors Robin Crewe, in Pretoria, and Henry Gates, in Cambridge, Massachusetts, have overseen my personal and professional well-being in exemplary ways, for which I thank them most sincerely. Generous funding from the National Research Foundation (NRF) has enabled me to undertake the research for this and a previous work. I am happy to acknowledge the support of the NRF for historical research at a time when few institutions in this country offer meaningful support for such unfashionable enquiries.

The personal vicissitudes of the curmudgeonly are less easily catered for. I assume that my closest friends and family, including my sister and wife, do not need to be identified by name. They know who they are and have all at one point or another been seared by the fires of frustration and impatience that light up the darkness of authorial retreat. But they should also know that my greatest debt, by far, is to all of them. Without their confidence, generosity, love and reassurance this book would not have been completed. It is the collective 'you' who allow and enable me to write history. It is a special privilege that sets aside those who write from those otherwise locked into quotidian time and space. I am happiest when allowed to roam and many have encouraged me.

Eugene Ashton, Keith Beavon, Tim Couzens, Karen Harris, John Higginson, Bruce Murray, Ian Phimister, Paul la Hausse, Bill Johnson, Robert Kaplan and June Sinclair have all helped me in countless personal and professional ways over many years. They and many other friends and associates defy easy categorisation. Each one of them possesses attributes and skills which have either enriched my understanding of the material that I try to shape into something approaching an integrated narrative or have provided me with wise counsel, sometimes both. Thank you all.

Crafting the biographies of great men and women is often facilitated by substantial collections of official or personal documents housed in easily accessible, well-known public or private repositories. The documentary footprints of the famous are usually well preserved. Writing the biography of the obscure forces one to travel lesser-known paths in search of often faint traces. In the country of the well-hidden, knowledgeable insiders are indispensable. Only they will know where the secret lairs and trails of the quarry are to be found. No hunter of tales should embark on such an expedition without the help of experienced locals and this work would not have been possible without the unflagging assistance of the finest of such guides. I would be failing in a pleasant duty if I failed to identify them, so let them step forward.

Deborah Green knows how to find and mine every archival pit of history opened during the Industrial Revolution. I have benefited from the advice of Alan Kidd whose knowledge of the history of early Manchester is exemplary. Graham Seal, Sue Summers and Shane White helped me negotiate the Australian outback and, in New Zealand, Graeme Dunstall not only assisted me but enriched my understanding of the island country's rich but lesser known histories by directing me to specialist studies. India and Kolkota are entirely unknown to me. Without the assistance of Priyanker Dey, Harald Fischer-Tiné, Bodishsattva Kar and Radhika Singha, I would never have traced Jack McLoughlin's passage through Kolkota. He was as lost as was I and, without the assistance of Janaki Nair, I would be even more ignorant than I am about the labour history of the Kolar goldfields.

I would also like to thank Jon Hyslop – who knows more about much of the historical terrain covered in this book than do I – for helpful commentary on an early version of the manuscript. I am indebted to him for his encouragement and support over many years. His scholarship is exemplary. Philip Stickler, as always, has provided me with a wonderful set of maps for which I thank him. My thanks to Jeremy Boraine and his hard-working production team; also to Angela Buckley and Robin Smith for filling two gaps in the photo section.

The only biography that really interests me is that which is cemented in detail. It is when the beam of history is refracted through the prisms of process and structure and the emerging spectrum highlights personal attributes that historical behaviour, such as that at the Red Lion, becomes more comprehensible. And, if the author is intent on searching out minutiae, he or she will be dependent on the help of scores of others. All the people listed below have assisted me in this quest to find the specific. I list them here in the way that the alphabet renders anodyne, if not offensive. For that, my apologies. Every one of them has contributed directly to the joy of writing a close-as-possible biography. If the whole exceeds the sum of the parts then my sincere thanks is due to each of you.

S Ally, C Anderson, Y Ashworth, P Atwell, P Badassy, C Bailie, C Beasley, E Bell, JH Bergh, DW Boardman, H Bornman, JP Brain, M Brown, RN Buckley, K Burns, C Burns, JL Cartwright, L Changuioun, N Clay, A Cobley, P Comensoli, LM Connell, I Cornelius, EM Crooke, A Daimon, J Dasgupta, A Davies, P Dawson, J Desoldato, G Dominy, J Duckworth, S du Plooy, U Fecteau, R Foster, R Grantham, A Graves, J Grenham, J Grobler, T Groom, A Hampton, A Harper, J Harrison, G Hendrich, L Hiorns, D Hughes, D Hume, M Hurst, J Irwin, B Jeffery, K Kalopulu, A Kanduza, M Karabus, V Kasi, PJ Kenney, E Knight, G Krozewski, BC Lategan, M Law, P le Roux, M Lewis, T Lodge, A Mahlangu, J Martens, JH Martin, S Mathieson, P Maylam, H Maxwell-Stewart, A McCallum, U McGarrigle, D McCracken, P McCracken, T McCarthy, J McGuire, J McQuilton, A Mentz, A Mlambo, J Mujere, C Muller, ME Mubai, S Ojha, J Pieterse, R Pilossof, J Phillipson, K Priestley, S Raath, JG Rechner, N Roos, D Schafer,

ACKNOWLEDGEMENTS

D Seagrave, R Snowden, D Somerville, F Soysal, B Strydom, E Talbot Rice, A Tambe, J Tempelhoff, AS Thompson, T Tomlinson, WT Turner, R Tombs, C Townsend, S Turner, J Twist, H Unwin, AJ van der Walt, N Valman, S van Gaalen, M Ward, R Williams, G Williams and M Whittle.

Finally, my apologies to all of those who have also contributed in countless other small but valuable ways whose names I may, unintentionally, have failed to record and thank.

Charles van Onselen
Johannesburg, January 2015

Index